MASTER THE GRE® CAT

THE

Thomas H. Martinson

2 0 0 2

TEACHER-TESTED STRATEGIES AND

TECHNIQUES FOR SCORING HIGH

ARCO
THOMSON LEARNING

Australia • Canada • Mexico • Singapore • Spain • United Kingdom • United States

ARCO
™
THOMSON LEARNING

An ARCO Book

ARCO is a registered trademark of Thomson Learning, Inc., and is used herein under license by Peterson's.

About Peterson's

Founded in 1966, Peterson's, a division of Thomson Learning, is the nation's largest and most respected provider of lifelong learning online resources, software, reference guides, and books. The Education Supersite℠ at petersons.com—the Web's most heavily traveled education resource—has searchable databases and interactive tools for contacting U.S.-accredited institutions and programs. CollegeQuest® (CollegeQuest.com) offers a complete solution for every step of the college decision-making process. GradAdvantage™ (GradAdvantage.org), developed with Educational Testing Service, is the only electronic admissions service capable of sending official graduate test score reports with a candidate's online application. Peterson's serves more than 55 million education consumers annually.

Thomson Learning is among the world's leading providers of lifelong learning, serving the needs of individuals, learning institutions, and corporations with products and services for both traditional classrooms and for online learning. For more information about the products and services offered by Thomson Learning, please visit www.thomsonlearning.com. Headquartered in Stamford, Connecticut, with offices worldwide, Thomson Learning is part of The Thomson Corporation (www.thomson.com), a leading e-information and solutions company in the business, professional, and education marketplaces. The Corporation's common shares are listed on the Toronto and London stock exchanges.

For more information, contact Peterson's, 2000 Lenox Drive, Lawrenceville, NJ 08648; 800-338-3282; or find us on the World Wide Web at: www.petersons.com/about

ISSN: International Standard Serial Number information available upon request.
ISBN (book only): 0-7689-0641-5
ISBN (book with CD-ROM): 0-7689-0642-3

Printed in the United States of America

10 9 8 7 6 5 4 3 2 1   03 02

THIS BOOK IS THE BEST PREPARATION FOR THE GRE CAT!

Although the GRE is now completely computer based, a book is still the best method of preparing for the exam. The CAT makes it easier to take the test (no more broken pencil lead or eraser marks to worry about); but you still need a study plan for preparing for the exam, and you now have to know a few things about computers to boot. For preparing for the GRE, you just can't beat the systematic approach that is unique to this book, along with the convenience and ease of reference to important points and explanatory material.

This book offers you a general look at the GRE and the kinds of questions you'll see. It also includes a Diagnostic Exam you can take to find out your strengths and weaknesses. In addition, you'll find a separate chapter devoted to each of the question types used on the GRE, complete with in-depth analysis, strategies, examples, and review. You'll do practice exercises dedicated to the skills taught specifically in each chapter. After you've laid a solid foundation, then you'll want to use the practice exams to refine the skills you've learned.

If you have the CAT CD edition, you have purchased the gateway to our online CAT examination. This is an actual practice CAT exam, designed to help you become familiar with the GRE CAT before you have to take the actual test. It will have the look and feel of the real thing, and you will be able to take this practice test up to three times in order to become comfortable with the format. Remember that the CAT exam adapts to your answers, and each time you take this test, you will receive new questions.

The first thing you must do is write down the 10-digit number that is printed on the CD itself. Once you have done that, you can then insert the CD into your computer. On most machines the program will launch itself and take you right to our Web site, www.petersons.com. You will be asked to enter that 10-digit number, so keep it handy. You will then be assigned a user name and password that enable you to take the test over again or stop at any point and come back at another time. Just make sure you keep a record of your user name and password.

We suggest that you begin by taking the test on line as a diagnostic exam. Once you have an idea of how you did and where to focus your studying, come back to the book. You can take the tests in the book, review the material throughout the book, and then go back and take the other two tests on line. Very little has been left to chance here, and you have been given a wide range of preparatory materials, both on line and in this book. Try to review as much as possible.

Good Luck!

THE TOP 10 WAYS TO RAISE YOUR SCORE

When it comes to taking the computer-adaptive GRE, some test-taking skills will do you more good than others. There are concepts you can learn, techniques you can follow, and tricks you can use that will give you the biggest "bang for your buck." Here's our pick for the top 10:

1. **Make a study plan and follow it.** The right GRE study plan will help you get the most out of this book in whatever time you have. *See chapter 1.*

2. **Learn the directions in advance.** If you already know the directions, you won't have to waste your precious test time reading them. You'll be able to jump right in and start answering questions as soon as the test clock starts. *See chapter 2.*

3. **Don't get bogged down on any one question.** Since you have to answer questions in order to keep moving, you can't afford to get stuck on any one problem. *See chapter 2.*

4. **In sentence completions, look for clue words.** These words will reveal the meaning of the sentence and point you in the right direction. *See chapter 5.*

5. **In analogy questions, a sentence can make the connection.** Analogies are about word relationships. The best way to figure out the relationship is to summarize it in a sentence. *See chapter 6.*

6. **In reading comprehension, read for structure, not details.** When you read GRE passages, don't let the details bog you down. Most of the questions will ask about the structure of the passage rather than specific facts. If you need the facts, they're always there in the passage. This is particularly important because you'll probably have to scroll to read the entire passage. *See chapter 7.*

7. **If a problem-solving math question stumps you, work backwards from the answers.** The right answer has to be one of the five choices. Since the choices are arranged in size order, starting with (C) results in the fewest calculations. *See chapter 9.*

8. **In quantitative comparisons, consider all possibilities.** Think what would happen if you plugged in 1, 0, a fraction, or a negative number for x in the expressions you're comparing. *See chapter 10.*

9. **In the analytical reasoning questions, set up a "bookkeeping" system using the scratch paper given to you during the test to summarize the information.** Use your own notational devices or adapt the ones shown in this book. *See chapter 12.*

10. **In logical reasoning questions, start by finding the conclusion.** Since the conclusion is the main point of the argument, it's the key to answering every question of this type. *See chapter 13.*

TRACK YOUR PROGRESS

For each exam:

1. Enter the number of questions that you answered *correctly* in each part (Verbal, Math, Analytical) in the appropriate rows. (Ignore wrong responses.)

2. To keep track of your progress in each of the content areas, enter the number of items of each type that you answered correctly into the appropriate row.

   Enter your overall (3-digit) score for each part (Verbal, Math, Analytical) using the table provided on page 5.

Note: Exercise caution in interpreting the data. Because a book-based exam cannot simulate in every respect a computer-based exam, results tend to be volatile. Do not place much emphasis on small differences in performance.

GRE SCORE TRACKER

Diagnostic Exam	Practice Test 1	Practice Test 2	Practice Test 3	Practice Test 4	Practice Test 5
Verbal Total					
Antonyms					
Sentence Completions					
Reading Comp.					
Verbal Score					
Math Total					
Problem Solving					
Quantitative Comparison					
Graphs					
Math Score					
Analytical Total					
Analytical Reasoning					
Logical Reasoning					
Analytical Score					

HOW WILL THIS BOOK HELP YOU?

Taking the GRE is a skill; and as such, it shares some things in common with other skills such as playing basketball or singing opera. These are skills that can be improved by coaching, but ultimately improvement also requires practice. This book gives you both.

- Part One provides essential general information about the GRE CAT.

- Part Two is a full-length Diagnostic Examination. It can show you where your skills are strong—and where they need some shoring up.

- Parts Three through Five are the coaching program. They analyze each question type and give you powerful strategies for taking on the test on its own terms.

- Part Six contains five full-length sample GREs followed by a detailed analysis of each question. The detailed analysis is very important because it is there that you can learn from your mistakes.

- Part Seven is a full-scale review of GRE mathematics. If your math skills are rusty and need refreshing, this section is for you.

- Part Eight contains two appendices—one will prepare you for the Writing Assessment portion of the GRE (if you're required to take it), and the other offers some helpful information on financing your way through graduate school.

ABOUT THE AUTHOR

Professor Thomas H. Martinson is widely acknowledged to be America's leading authority on test preparation. Educated at Harvard University with an advanced degree and 12 years of postgraduate research, Professor Martinson has published over three dozen books and computer programs on test preparation. He is routinely invited to lecture on test preparation and related topics at top colleges and universities throughout the United States and abroad. Visit the author's Web site, www.cyberprep.com, where you'll find additional study materials and drills to help you score even higher.

Contents

PART FOUR: GRE Math Questions

PART FIVE: GRE Analytical Questions

PART SIX: Practice Examinations

PART SEVEN: GRE Math Review

PART EIGHT: Appendices

PART

ONE

EVERYTHING YOU NEED!

GRE Basics

PREVIEW

CHAPTER 1

Getting Started

You'll Find Answers to These Questions

Can you prepare for the GRE?
What is a GRE study plan?
What's the best study plan for you?
How can you tell if your work is paying off?
Can you predict your GRE score?

CAN YOU PREPARE FOR THE GRE?

This is the question of the day. Can you indeed prepare for an exam that purports to test your aptitude for success in grad school rather than your mastery of any particular subject? Of course you can. The GRE is long, and some of its questions are tough, but it's not unconquerable.

There are many ways to prepare and many tricks and tips to learn. One of the most important things to learn is to think like the test-makers so you can find the answers they have designated as best. Once you learn "GRE thinking," you'll be more likely to pick the best answer—and up will go your scores.

TOP **10** TIP

WHAT IS A GRE STUDY PLAN?

As you can tell, this book contains a lot of information about the GRE, and you'll need a plan for getting through it. The right study plan will help you manage your time so that you get the most out of this book whether you have three months, three weeks, or only a few days to prepare. It will help you work efficiently and keep you from getting stressed out.

WHAT'S THE BEST STUDY PLAN FOR YOU?

To decide on your study plan, answer these two questions: (1) How long do you have until the test? (2) How much time can you devote to GRE study?

TIME MANAGER STUDY PLANS

PLAN A: ACCELERATED

This plan is your best bet if you have at least 30 days to prepare. You'll probably have to sacrifice a bit on the practice, but you'll cover all of the chapters, learn about each question type, work plenty of sample questions, and take some sample exams. You'll find directions for Plan A at the beginning of each chapter.

PLAN B: TOP SPEED

You'll need to shift into Plan B, the Top Speed Course, if the GRE is coming up in two weeks or less. This superconcentrated study plan includes only the Diagnostic Examination and the critical parts of each chapter. You'll find directions for following Plan B at the beginning of each chapter.

3

HERE'S
THE ANSWER

Is there a secret to preparing for the GRE?

There's no secret, but you have to have a plan. You can follow one of the plans listed here or create your own. Either way, a plan will keep you on track.

TESTSMARTS

Start with the tough stuff. To make the most of your study time, study the difficult sections first. If you run out of time later, you can just skim the sections that are easy for you.

Here are some suggestions to make your job easier. If you are starting early and the GRE is two or three months away, go for broke. Complete the book from beginning to end. If the GRE is a month or less away and you need a more concentrated course, go for one of the Time Manager plans (see sidebar).

One more thing: Depending on your time frame and how many sections you want to cover, you can customize the plans to work best for you.

HOW CAN YOU TELL IF YOUR WORK IS PAYING OFF?

No matter what plan you choose, you should start by taking the Diagnostic Examination found in Part Two. After you score it, you'll be able to see where you need to concentrate your efforts.

The next step is to see how you do with the exercises at the end of each chapter in Part Three (Verbal), Part Four (Math), and Part Five (Analytical). Compare your scores to your results on the Diagnostic Exam. Have you improved? Where do you still need work?

When you're ready, take the Practice Examinations found in Part Six. These are like the tests you'll take in terms of content, number of questions, and time limit. You should try to simulate test conditions as nearly as you can. After you score a Practice Examination, make another comparison to the chapter exercises and to the Diagnostic Exam. This will show you how your work is paying off.

CAN YOU PREDICT YOUR GRE SCORE?

The use of computer adaptive testing technology makes it difficult to predict your actual GRE score based on your performance on a paper and pencil practice test. We have tried, however, to develop a scoring table that provides a general idea of your performance at this point in your preparation. To predict your score on the practice tests in this book, count the correct answers in each section and find that number in the left column of the charts below. The corresponding number in the right column represents an approximation of your GRE test score.

Analytical Subscore (C = Correct, S = Score)

C	S	C	S	C	S	C	S	C	S
35	800	27	650	19	450	11	250	4	200
34	800	26	620	18	420	10	220	3	200
33	800	25	600	17	400	9	200	2	200
32	770	24	570	16	370	8	200	1	200
31	750	23	550	15	350	7	200	0	200
30	720	22	520	14	320	6	200		
29	700	21	500	13	300	5	200		
28	670	20	470	12	270				

Math Subscore (C = Correct, S = Score)

C	S	C	S	C	S	C	S	C	S
28	800	22	650	16	500	10	350	4	200
27	780	21	630	15	480	9	330	3	200
26	750	20	600	14	450	8	300	2	200
25	730	19	580	13	430	7	280	1	200
24	700	18	550	12	400	6	250	0	200
23	680	17	530	11	380	5	230		

Verbal Subscore (C = Correct, S = Score)

C	S	C	S	C	S	C	S	C	S
30	800	23	620	16	450	9	270	3	200
29	770	22	600	15	420	8	250	2	200
28	750	21	570	14	400	7	220	1	200
27	720	20	550	13	370	6	200	0	200
26	700	19	520	12	350	5	200		
25	670	18	500	11	320	4	200		
24	650	17	470	10	300				

CHAPTER 2

All About the GRE

TIME MANAGER
STUDY PLANS

You'll Find Answers to These Questions

What is the GRE?
What is the CAT?
How do you register for the GRE?
What kinds of questions are on the test?
How is the test structured?
How is the test scored?
What do smart test-takers know?

PLAN A: ACCELERATED

- *Read* "What Kinds of Questions Are on the Test?"
- *Read* "How Is the Test Structured?"
- *Read* "How Is the Test Scored?"
- *Read* "What Smart Test-takers Know"

PLAN B: TOP SPEED

- *Read* "What Kinds of Questions Are on the Test?"
- *Read* "How Is the Test Structured?"
- *Read* "What Smart Test-takers Know"

WHAT IS THE GRE?

The letters GRE stand for Graduate Record Examination—a standardized exam given at various locations in the United States and around the world. You'll be taking what is called the GRE CAT (which stands for Computer Adaptive Test). It's a computer-based exam given year-round at universities and learning centers. You'll need to register for the test and make an appointment for your testing session. (See "How Do You Register for the GRE?" below.)

The GRE testing program includes a General Test as well as Subject Tests in disciplines such as Biology, Mathematics, and Psychology. This book is devoted to the GRE General Test, the most widely used of the GREs. For the purpose of simplicity, from here on in this book the term *GRE* will be used to refer to the General Test.

WHAT IS THE CAT?

CAT exams are the wave of the future for all types of exams, and the GRE is no exception. In previous years, the GRE was a paper-based exam, but as of now, the GRE is totally computerized.

The GRE CAT differs from a paper-based exam in that a computer program chooses problems based on a candidate's responses to previous questions. Thus, the CAT is "adaptive" or "interactive." Whereas candidates taking a paper-based test are presented with a range of questions (including easy, moderately difficult, and difficult items), a CAT selects questions according to each candidate's ability.

During a CAT, the computer controls the order in which test items appear, basing its selection on the candidate's responses to earlier items. Because the CAT is interactive, it uses fewer items and takes less time to administer than the paper-based version.

At the risk of oversimplifying, the testing procedure can be described as follows. The computer has access to a large number of test items classified according to question type (graphs, antonyms, reading comprehension, and so on) and arranged in order of difficulty. At the outset, the computer presents you with a couple of "seed" questions, items of average level of difficulty. If you answer those successfully, the program selects for the next question an item of greater difficulty; if you do not answer the "seed" questions correctly, the program lowers the level of difficulty. This process is repeated, with the program continuing to adjust the level of difficulty of questions, until you have provided all the answers that the computer needs to calculate your score.

TESTSMARTS

Get the latest GRE information on the Web. You can get up-to-the-minute GRE information on the World Wide Web. The address is http://www.gre.org.

HOW DO YOU REGISTER FOR THE GRE?

One way you can register to take the exam is through the *GRE Bulletin*, which includes registration forms. You can obtain the *GRE Bulletin* from your Career Placement Office or by writing to:

Graduate Record Examinations Program
P.O. Box 6000
Princeton, NJ 08541 6000

The CAT is given at hundreds of Sylvan Technology Centers, ETS Field Service offices, or other designated test sites nationwide. To schedule an appointment to take the CAT, call the test center or (800) GRE-CALL during regular business hours. If you are paying for the test by credit card, you can make the appointment and arrange for payment over the telephone. Otherwise, you will need to submit the registration form by mail and wait two to four weeks for authorization to schedule a test appointment.

You can also get information on-line at www.gre.org.

WHAT KINDS OF QUESTIONS ARE ON THE TEST?

The GRE includes verbal, mathematics, and analytical questions. Each question type includes a variety of testing styles. Here's an overview of questions:

Verbal Questions

- **Sentence Completions.** Sentence completion questions ask you to choose a word or words that fill in the blanks in a given sentence.

- **Analogies.** Analogy questions present a pair of words that have some logical relationship. Then the choices present other pairs of words. You have to choose the pair that has the same kind of relationship as the first pair.

- **Reading Comprehension.** Reading comprehension questions relate to a passage that is provided for you to read. The passage can be about almost anything, and the questions about it test how well you understood the passage and the information in it.

- **Antonyms.** Antonym questions present a single vocabulary word. You must pick the answer choice that is most nearly opposite in meaning to the given word.

Mathematics Questions

- **Quantitative Comparisons.** Quantitative comparison questions test your skills in comparing information and in estimating. You'll see two quantities, one in Column A and one in Column B. The task is to compare the two quantities and decide if one is greater than the other, if they are equal, or if no comparison is possible.

- **Problem Solving.** Problem-solving questions present multiple-choice problems in arithmetic, basic algebra, and elementary geometry. The task is to solve the problems and choose the correct answer from among five answer choices.

- **Graphs.** Graph questions present mathematical information in pictorial form. Each graph is followed by questions about it.

Analytical Questions

- **Analytical Reasoning.** Analytical reasoning questions present a situation and some conditions. Based on this information, you must draw logical conclusions.

- **Logical Reasoning.** Logical reasoning questions present an argument that you are asked to analyze. Questions may require you to draw a conclusion, to identify assumptions, or to recognize strengths or weaknesses in the argument.

TESTSMARTS

In every section, the first few questions count more than the last few. Take a little extra time at the beginning to make sure you get those all-important questions right.

HOW IS THE TEST STRUCTURED?

The test itself is over 2½ hours long and begins with a Warm Up period that doesn't count towards your time or score. Instead, the Warm Up allows candidates to become familiar with the computer (the mouse in particular) and with the functioning of the CAT program.

Beyond the Warm Up period, the GRE is divided into three sections. Each section is separately timed. The test includes one verbal section, one math section, and one analytical section. Your test may also include a "research" section. The "research" section may be verbal, or math, or analytical, but it will not count toward your score. The "research" section contains questions being tried out for future GREs. Also, within each section are embedded experimental questions, which also will not affect your score. You will not, however, know which ones they are because they have been embedded in the sequence of scored items.

Anatomy of a Typical GRE CAT

Section	Number of Questions	Time Limit
Warm Up	—	Untimed
Verbal	30	30 min.
Math	28	45 min.
Analytical	35	60 min.
Research Section	—	0 min.

The "research" section could have any configuration. The order of the three other sections is subject to change.

HOW IS THE TEST SCORED?

Your score is based on a combination of the number of questions you answered correctly and the difficulty level of the questions answered. You get more credit for answering a harder question than you get for answering an easier one. There is no deduction for wrong answers; in fact, you will be penalized for any question left unanswered when time runs out. The scoring scale runs from 200 (the minimum) to 800 (the maximum). Your score report will include three different scores: a verbal score, a quantitative or math score, and an analytical score. It will also include a percentile ranking for each section.

WHAT SMART TEST-TAKERS KNOW

YOU HAVE TO BEAT THE CLOCK.

Many years ago, there was a program on television called *Beat the Clock*. Contestants were given silly things to do within a certain time limit. For example, a contestant might be asked to stack 100 paper cups on top of each other in 30 seconds—while blindfolded! On the television studio wall was a large clock with a single hand so contestants could keep track of the passing time. The GRE is a lot like this, but without the blindfold.

Your computer screen keeps track of the time and the number of questions you've answered on the exam. Use the information to stay on track. (If you find the timer function distracting, then you can suppress it; but it will reappear automatically at the five minute mark and won't go away.)

THE GRE TAKES CONCENTRATION.

The GRE is an arduous task. There is no way that you can maintain your concentration throughout all three of the sections. There will be times when your attention begins to flag. Learn to recognize this. For example, if you find that you are reading and rereading the same line without understanding, sit back in your chair, close your eyes, take a deep breath or two (or rub your eyes or whatever), and then get back to work.

THE ANSWERS ARE ALL THERE IN FRONT OF YOU.

Because of the multiple-choice format, you have a real advantage over the GRE. The correct answer is always right there on the monitor screen. To be sure, it's surrounded by wrong choices, but it may be possible to eliminate one or more of those other choices as non-answers. Look at the following reading comprehension question:

> The author argues that the evidence supporting
> the new theory is
>
> (A) hypothetical
>
> (B) biased
>
> (C) empirical
>
> (D) speculative
>
> (E) fragmentary

You might think that it is impossible to make any progress on a reading comprehension question without the reading selection, but you can eliminate three of the five answers in this question as non-answers. Study the question stem. We can infer that the author of the selection has at least implicitly passed judgment on the evidence supporting the new theory. What kind of judgment might someone make about the evidence adduced to

TOP **10** TIP

T E S T S M A R T S

On the real GRE CAT, the answer choices will *not* be lettered. However, we will letter them throughout this book for ease of reference.

support a theory? (A), (C), and (D) all seem extremely unlikely. As for (A), while the theory is itself a hypothesis, the evidence supporting the theory would not be hypothetical. As for (C), evidence is empirical by definition. So it is unlikely that anyone would argue "This evidence is empirical." And (D) can be eliminated for the same reason as (A). Admittedly, this leaves you with a choice of (B) or (E), a choice that depends on the content of the reading selection; but at least you have a 50-50 chance of getting the question correct—even without reading the selection.

BIORHYTHMS COUNT.

We all have biorhythms. Some of us are morning people, some afternoon. Schedule your appointment for the GRE for a time when you are likely to be at your peak.

IF YOU ARE A "COMPUTER DUMMY," YOU SHOULD BUY, BEG, BORROW, OR RENT ONE.

Now, first of all, you are not a "complete dummy" even if you have never used a computer. You've certainly seen them in a bank, or a grocery store, or at a friend's home, so you have some idea of what one looks like and what it is supposed to do. But there is a big difference between knowing what a car looks like and knowing how to drive one. If you have to, go down to your local office service or computer store and buy an hour or two of time on a computer. Play with the machine. If you purchased the book/disk version of this guide, take your disk with you. A technical support rep will help you load it onto the computer so you can practice taking a CAT.

IT'S WORTH SPENDING TIME ON THE TUTORIALS.

The computerized version of the GRE begins with these tutorials:

- How to Use a Mouse
- How to Select an Answer
- How to Use the Testing Tools
- How to Scroll

The program forces you to work through these tutorials, and you should pay careful attention to the directions. If you have never before worked with a mouse and a scroll bar, stay in the appropriate tutorials until you are comfortable with the mechanics of the computer. Time spent on the tutorials is not taken away from your time on the testing sections. And even if you are already "computer literate" and don't need to practice those techniques, you should nonetheless pay careful attention to the idiosyncrasies of the CAT program, e.g., how to indicate an answer, how to change an answer, how to move forward and backward, and what the various screen icons mean.

SCROLLING IS THE ONLY WAY TO SEE ALL OF SOME QUESTIONS.

In many computer programs, when a body of text is too long to be displayed in its entirety on the screen, you have the option of "scrolling" through the text. You can scroll up or down. The scroll function removes the top (or bottom) line and moves the other lines of text up (or down) one line on the screen, adding the next (or preceding) line of text. Your first experience with the scroll function may be a bit frustrating because it can be very sensitive. If you have the opportunity to play with a computer in advance of the test, you should also test a program that manipulates text, e.g., a word processing program. Pay particular attention to the scrolling feature.

YOU HAVE TO DISMISS THE DIRECTIONS.

When you begin a new section or question type, the directions for that part will appear. But they don't time out. So your first order of business is to get rid of them from the screen: Point and click on the "Dismiss Directions" box.

YOU HAVE TO CONFIRM YOUR ANSWER CHOICES.

You select your choice by directing the pointer to an oval and clicking. This illuminates the oval, indicating that you have selected the associated answer choice. Then you click on the "Arrow" button. But that's not the last step. You still have to confirm your choice using the "Confirm" button on the toolbar.

This is both a good and a bad feature of the program. On the one hand, it reduces the risk that you'll make a silly mistake because you have to confirm your choice. On the other hand, you could wind up wasting a lot of time if you forget to confirm your choice. If you don't confirm, the machine acts as though you're still working and sits there patiently waiting for additional input.

YOU SHOULD ANSWER EVERY QUESTION.

Because on the CAT you'll be penalized for any questions left unanswered when time runs out, the best strategy is to answer every question in a section. The screen display will tell you how many questions you have yet to answer, so you can pace yourself to make sure you complete the section.

YOU MUST ANSWER QUESTIONS IN THE ORDER PRESENTED.

While the "adaptive" aspect of the CAT should have no effect on your preparation, it has a great effect on your approach to the exam itself. On a CAT exam, you MUST ANSWER THE QUESTIONS IN THE ORDER PRESENTED. Since the exam adapts itself in response to your answers, you cannot skip and later return to any questions. And, you cannot rethink and change your answer at a later time. You cannot seek out and answer the easier question styles first. In other words, you must do the best you can to answer each question. Choose the answer that you have determined is best, or guess if necessary, confirm your choice, and move on to the next question.

TESTSMARTS

"Dismiss" the directions. The on-screen directions do not disappear automatically. Instead, you have to "dismiss" them by clicking on the "Dismiss Directions" box. Do this immediately so you can get started on the test.

AVOID THE TRAPS!

Don't spin your wheels. Don't spend too much time on any one question. Give it some thought, take your best shot, and move along.

THE FIRST HALF OF A SECTION IS WHERE THE POINTS ARE.

On the CAT, how well you do on the first half of each section plays a very big part in determining your final score. That's because the first half of each section is where the computer program that moves you up and down the ladder of difficulty does the major part of its work. If you do well early in the test, the computer will give you harder questions—and those questions are worth more points. So work carefully through the first half of each section. If you find that time is running out, you can always pick up the pace in the second half.

GUESSING IS PART OF THE GAME.

On the CAT there will be two times when you'll have to guess. First, any time you have no idea of how to solve a problem, you'll have to choose an answer just to move on to the next question. Second, if time is running out, it will be worth your while to guess at the answers to any remaining questions—there's always the chance that you'll guess right, and you'll be penalized if you leave questions unanswered.

CHAPTER 3

GRE Questions: A First Look

TIME MANAGER STUDY PLANS

PLAN A: ACCELERATED
- *Read* the chapter
- *Study* the answer explanations

PLAN B: TOP SPEED
- *Read* the chapter
- *Skim* the answer explanations

You'll Find Answers to These Questions

What can you expect on the test?
How does the GRE test verbal reasoning?
How does the GRE test mathematical reasoning?
How does the GRE test analytical reasoning?

WHAT CAN YOU EXPECT ON THE TEST?

The GRE uses nine different types of questions to test your verbal, mathematical, and analytical reasoning abilities. This chapter will describe each question type in turn and show you samples. Learning the question types in advance is the best way to prepare for the GRE. That way, you'll know what to expect, and you won't have any unpleasant surprises on test day.

HOW DOES THE GRE TEST VERBAL REASONING?

The GRE tests your verbal reasoning ability with these four question types:

- sentence completions
- analogies
- reading comprehension
- antonyms

The verbal section includes 5 to 7 sentence completions, 6 to 8 analogies, 7 to 9 antonyms, and 9 or so reading comprehension questions.

HERE'S
THE ANSWER

What other kinds of questions will there be on the GRE?

What you see is what you get. The questions on these pages show you what you'll find.

Sentence Completions

Sentence completion questions consist of a sentence, a part or parts of which have been omitted, followed by five letter choices that are possible substitutions for the omitted parts. The idea is to select the choice that best completes the sentence.

Here are the directions for sentence completion questions and a sample question:

> **Directions:** The sentence that follows contains one or more blank spaces indicating that something has been omitted. It is followed by five (5) lettered words or sets of words. Read and determine the general sense of the sentence. Then choose the word or set of words which, when inserted in the sentence, best fits the meaning of the sentence.

1. Her desire for —— soon became apparent when she adamantly refused to answer questions about her identity or mission.

    (A) assistance

    (B) anonymity

    (C) success

    (D) publicity

    (E) recognition

The best completion is offered by (B). The logic of the sentence requires that the missing element indicate a desire for something that can be achieved only by refusing to give information. If you don't give any information about your identity or your activities, you hope to ensure that you remain anonymous.

Analogy Questions

A GRE analogy consists of one capitalized word pair followed by five answer choices (also word pairs). The idea is to select from among the choices a word pair that expresses a relationship similar to that expressed by the capitalized word pair.

Here are the directions for analogy questions and a sample question:

> **Directions:** The following question consists of a related pair of words or phrases in capital letters followed by five (5) lettered pairs of words or phrases. Choose the lettered pair which best expresses a relationship similar to that expressed by the original pair.

2. MINISTER : PULPIT : :

    (A) doctor : patient

    (B) student : teacher

    (C) mechanic : engine

    (D) programmer : logic

    (E) judge : bench

The best choice is (E). The PULPIT is the place where the MINISTER does his or her job, and the bench is the place where the judge does her or his job.

Reading Comprehension

Reading comprehension questions, as the name implies, test your ability to understand the substance and logical structure of a written selection. The GRE uses reading passages of various lengths, ranging from 200 to 550 words. A long passage will be the basis for as many as seven or eight questions while a shorter passage might support only three or four questions. The questions ask about the main point of the passage, about what the author specifically states, about what can be logically inferred from the passage, and about the author's attitude or tone. Here are the directions for reading comprehension questions and an example of a shorter reading passage. (The passage is followed by only two questions, rather than the usual three or four.)

Directions: Below is a reading selection followed by a number of questions. Read the selection. Then based on your understanding of the selection, select the best answer to each question.

The international software market represents a significant business opportunity for U.S. micro-computer software companies, but illegal copying of programs is limiting the growth of sales abroad.
(5) If not dealt with quickly, international piracy of software could become one of the most serious trade problems faced by the United States.

Software piracy is already the biggest barrier to U.S. software companies entering foreign markets.
(10) One reason is that software is extremely easy and inexpensive to duplicate compared to the cost of developing and marketing the software. The actual cost of duplicating a software program, which may have a retail value of $400 or more, can be as little
(15) as a dollar or two—the main component being the cost of the diskette. The cost of counterfeiting software is substantially less than the cost of dupli-cating watches, books, or blue jeans. Given that the

difference between the true value of the original and
(20) the cost of the counterfeit is so great for software,
international piracy has become big business. Unfortunately, many foreign governments view software piracy as an industry in and of itself and look the
other way.
(25)   U.S. firms stand to lose millions of dollars in
new business, and diminished U.S. sales not only
harm individual firms but also adversely affect the
entire U.S. economy.

3. In this passage, the author's primary purpose is
   to

   (A) criticize foreign governments for stealing
       U.S. computer secrets

   (B) describe the economic hazards software
       piracy poses to the United States

   (C) demand that software pirates immediately
       cease their illegal operations

   (D) present a comprehensive proposal to coun-
       teract the effects of international software
       piracy

   (E) disparage the attempts of the U.S. govern-
       ment to control software piracy

The best answer to question 3 is (B). This question, typical of the GRE, asks
about the main point of the selection. (A) is incorrect. Though the author
implies criticism of foreign governments, their mistake, so far as we are told,
is not stealing secrets but tacitly allowing the operation of a software black
market. (C) is incorrect since this is not the main point of the selection. You
can infer that the author would approve of such a demand, but issuing the
demand is not the main point of the selection you just read. (D) can be
eliminated for a similar reason. Though the author might elsewhere offer a
specific proposal, there is no such proposal in the selection you just read. (E)
also is wrong since no such attempts are ever discussed. Finally, notice how
well (B) does describe the main issue. The author's concern is to identify a
problem and to discuss its causes.

4. The author's attitude toward international software piracy can best be described as

   (A) concern

   (B) rage

   (C) disinterest

   (D) pride

   (E) condescension

The best answer to question 4 is (A). This question asks about the tone of the passage, and concern very neatly captures that tone. You can eliminate (B) as an overstatement. Though the author condemns the piracy, the tone is not so violent as to qualify as rage. (C) must surely be incorrect since the author does express concern and, therefore, cannot be disinterested.

Antonym Questions

An antonym item consists of a single, capitalized word followed by five answer choices. The basic idea is to pick the answer that has the meaning which is most nearly opposite that of the capitalized word.

Here are the directions for antonym questions and a sample question:

> **Directions:** The following question consists of a word printed in capital letters, followed by five (5) lettered words or phrases. Select the word or phrase which is most nearly opposite to the capitalized word in meaning.

5. WAIVE :
   (A) repeat
   (B) conclude
   (C) insist upon
   (D) improve on
   (E) peruse

The best answer is (C). To WAIVE means to forgo or to relinquish. A fairly precise opposite is "to insist upon."

HOW DOES THE GRE TEST MATHEMATICAL REASONING?

The GRE tests mathematical reasoning ability with these three question types:

- problem solving
- quantitative comparisons
- graph questions

The math sections test your knowledge of arithmetic, basic algebra, elementary geometry, and common charts and graphs.

The math section includes 9 to 11 problem-solving items, 13 to 15 data sufficiency items, and 4 or so graph items.

WHAT'S THE ANSWER?

Do you need to know college-level math to do well on the GRE?

No, you do not need to know college-level math. The GRE math sections test only the basic math concepts you learned in high school.

Problem Solving

If you have taken any other standardized exams that included math questions (such as the SAT), then you have probably already seen examples of problem-solving questions. These are your typical word problem questions. Here are the directions for problem-solving questions and three sample questions:

> **Directions:** For each of the following questions, select the best of the answer choices.
>
> *Numbers:* All numbers used are real numbers.
>
> *Figures:* The diagrams and figures that accompany these questions are for the purpose of providing information useful in answering the questions. Unless it is stated that a specific figure is not drawn to scale, the diagrams and figures are drawn as accurately as possible. All figures are in a plane unless otherwise indicated.

6. Betty left home with $60 in her wallet. She spent $\frac{1}{3}$ of that amount at the supermarket, and she spent $\frac{1}{2}$ of what remained at the drugstore. If Betty made no other expenditures, how much money did she have when she returned home?

    (A) $10

    (B) $15

    (C) $20

    (D) $40

    (E) $50

A quick calculation will show that the correct answer is (C). Betty spent $\frac{1}{3}$ of $60, or $20, at the supermarket, leaving her with $40. Of the $40, she spent $\frac{1}{2}$, or $20, at the drugstore, leaving her with $20 when she returned home.

7. If $2x + 3y = 8$ and $y = 2x$, then what is the value of x?

    (A) –6

    (B) –4

    (C) 0

    (D) 1

    (E) 4

The best answer is (D). To answer the question, you need to solve for x. Since $y = 2x$, you can substitute $2x$ for y in the first equation:

$$2x + 3(2x) = 8$$

Multiply: $2x + 6x = 8$

Add: $8x = 8$

Divide: $x = 1$

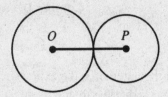

8. In the figure above, circle *O* and circle *P* are tangent to each other. If the circle with center *O* has a diameter of 8 and the circle with center *P* has a diameter 6, what is the length of segment *OP*?

  (A) 7

  (B) 10

  (C) 14

  (D) 20

  (E) 28

The correct answer is (A). The segment *OP* is made up of the radius of circle *O* and the radius of circle *P*. To find the length of *OP*, you need to know the lengths of the two radii. Since the length of the radius is one half that of the diameter, the radius of circle *O* is $\frac{1}{2}(8)$ or 4, and the radius of circle *P* is $\frac{1}{2}(6)$ or 3. So the length of *OP* is $3 + 4 = 7$.

Quantitative Comparisons

Quantitative comparisons are presented in an unusual format with special instructions. Without trying to understand all of the subtleties of the type, you can get the general idea of quantitative comparisons by reading the directions and studying the sample questions that follow.

> **Directions:** For each of the following questions two quantities are given, one in Column A and one in Column B. Compare the two quantities and choose:
>
>   (A) if the quantity in Column A is the greater
>
>   (B) if the quantity in Column B is the greater
>
>   (C) if the two quantities are equal
>
>   (D) if the relationship cannot be determined from the information given.

AVOID THE TRAPS!

Don't pick (E). Quantitative comparisons have only answer choices (A) through (D). Marking (E) won't get you any credit.

Column A	Column B
9. $6 - \dfrac{4}{2}$	$5 - \dfrac{4}{4}$

The correct answer is (C). Column A is just $6 - 2 = 4$, and Column B is $5 - 1 = 4$. Both columns have the value of 4, so they are equal.

Column A	**Column B**
10. $x + 1$	$x - 1$

The correct answer is (A). Whatever the value of x, the expression $x + 1$ is one more than x, and the expression $x - 1$ is one less than x. So no matter what the value of x, Column A is 2 larger than Column B.

Column A	**Column B**

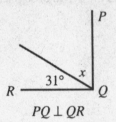

$$PQ \perp QR$$

Column A	**Column B**
11. x	60

The correct answer is (B). PQ is perpendicular to QR, so PQR is a 90-degree angle. Since one of the two angles making up the right angle is 31 degrees, the other must be 59 degrees. So $x = 59$, and Column B (which is 60) is larger.

Column A	**Column B**
12. The price of a sweater that is marked 25% off	The price of a coat that is marked 20% off

The correct answer is (D). You are asked to compare the prices of the two articles. Although you know the percent discount taken on each, you have no way of knowing the actual cost of the item. Since the comparison cannot be made on the basis of what is given, the correct choice is (D).

Graphs

Graph questions are like problem-solving items except that the information to be used in solving the problem is presented in pictorial form. Here are some sample graph questions:

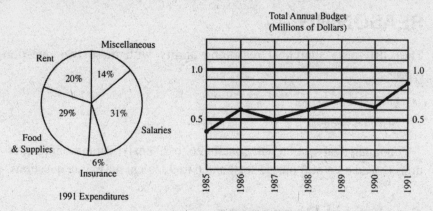

HILLTOP DAY SCHOOL
FINANCIAL INFORMATION

13. The total annual budget for Hilltop Day School
    increased by what percent from 1985 to 1991?

    (A) 4%

    (B) 8%

    (C) 50%

    (D) 125%

    (E) 200%

The correct answer is (D). The operating budget increased from $0.4 million
in 1985 to $0.9 million in 1991—an increase of $0.5 million. Expressed as
a percentage increase: $\frac{0.5}{0.4} \times 100 = 1.25 \times 100 = 125\%$

14. How much money did Hilltop Day School spend
    for rent in 1991?

    (A) $180,000

    (B) $225,000

    (C) $240,000

    (D) $800,000

    (E) $2,000,000

The correct answer is (A). From the graph on the right, we learn that the total
budget for 1991 was $0.9 million. The graph on the left breaks down the
budget for 1991. It shows that 20% of the 1991 budget went for rent: 20%
of $0.9 million = $180,000.

HOW DOES THE GRE TEST ANALYTICAL REASONING?

The GRE tests analytical reasoning ability with these two question types:

- analytical reasoning
- logical reasoning

Your analytical section will contain 26 to 29 analytical reasoning questions (based on 4 or 5 puzzle sets) and 6 to 9 logical reasoning questions.

Analytical Reasoning

Analytical reasoning questions involve a situation such as people standing in a row, or choosing items from a menu, or scheduling vacations. Based on the conditions described, you are asked to draw logical conclusions about the situation. Here are the directions for this question type and two sample questions:

> **Directions:** Each of the following questions or groups of questions is based on a short passage or a set of propositions. In answering these questions, it may sometimes be helpful to draw a simple picture or chart. For each question, select the best answer.

AVOID THE TRAPS!

Make the best of it. Note that these directions ask you to choose the best answer. That's why you should always read all the answer choices before you make your final selection.

Questions 15–16

Five people, P, Q, R, S, and T, are standing single file in a ticket line. All are facing the ticket window.

Q is the second person behind P.

P is not the second person in the line.

R is somewhere ahead of S.

15. T could occupy all of the following positions in the line EXCEPT:

(A) 1

(B) 2

(C) 3

(D) 4

(E) 5

The correct answer to question 15 is (C), as shown by the following reasoning. The initial conditions establish that Q is behind P separated by one person, an arrangement that can be shown as Q ? P. And since P cannot be the second person in line, only two arrangements are possible for Q and P:

```
        1     2     3     4     5
        P           Q
or                  P           Q
```

Since these are the only two possibilities, either Q or P must be third in line, which means no one else can be third. Therefore, T cannot stand in the third position.

16. If R is the fourth person in line, which of the
    following must be true?

    (A) T is the second person in line.

    (B) Q is the second person in line.

    (C) P is the third person in line.

    (D) S is the third person in line.

    (E) Q is the fifth person in line.

The correct answer to question 15 is (A). Here we are given additional information to use in answering this item. Given that R is the fourth in line, since R is ahead of S, S must be fifth in line.

```
        1     2     3     4     5
                          R     S
```

This forces P and Q into positions 1 and 3:

```
        1     2     3     4     5
        P           Q     R     S
```

Finally, T must be second in line:

```
        1     2     3     4     5
        P     T     Q     R     S
```

Logical Reasoning

A typical logical reasoning question presents an argument or an explanation which you are asked to analyze. You may be asked to describe the argument, draw further conclusions from it, attack or defend it, or just find the assumptions of the argument. Here are the directions for this question type and a sample question:

17. Wilfred commented, "Of all the musical instruments I have studied, the trombone is the most difficult instrument to play."

    Which of the following statements, if true, would most seriously weaken Wilfred's conclusion?

    (A) The trombone is relatively easy for trumpet players to learn to play.

    (B) Wilfred has not studied trombone as seriously as he has studied other instruments.

    (C) Wilfred finds he can play the violin and the cello with equal facility.

    (D) The trombone is easier to learn as a second instrument than as a first instrument.

    (E) There are several instruments which Wilfred has not studied and which are very difficult to play.

The best choice is (B). The question asks you to identify a possible weakness in the argument. The conclusion of the argument is that the trombone is intrinsically more difficult to play than other instruments. The question asks you to find another explanation for Wilfred's impression. Choice (B) suggests the fault is not in the trombone but in Wilfred. The seeming difficulty of the trombone stems from the fact that Wilfred did not study it as diligently as he has studied other instruments.

What You Must Know About the GRE

- The GRE is a test of verbal, mathematical, and analytical reasoning skills.
- If you know the directions in advance, you won't have to waste time reading them.
- On the GRE, the answers are all there in front of you. One of the choices has to be right.
- You must answer every question before the time expires. If you don't know the answer, eliminate obviously wrong choices and make an educated guess.
- The computer chooses problems based on your answers to previous questions.

SUMMING IT UP

TWO

EVERYTHING YOU NEED!

Diagnosing Strengths and Weaknesses

CHAPTER 4

Diagnostic Examination

PREVIEW →

TIME MANAGER
STUDY PLANS

PLAN A: ACCELERATED

- *Take* the Diagnostic Exam
- *Check* your answers

PLAN B: TOP SPEED

- *Take* the Diagnostic Exam
- *Check* your answers

Diagnostic Examination
Answer Sheet

Answer each question in the test and indicate your response by filling in the oval of your choice. In order to simulate the testing experience of the CAT, you should answer the questions in the order presented, entering a choice for each one before going on to the next. Once you have entered your choice, you may NOT return to that problem or to any problems presented earlier. When time has expired or you have entered your choice for the last item in a section, you are finished with that section. You may not return to problems earlier in the section nor to earlier sections.

TEAR HERE

VERBAL SECTION

1. Ⓐ Ⓑ Ⓒ Ⓓ Ⓔ   7. Ⓐ Ⓑ Ⓒ Ⓓ Ⓔ   13. Ⓐ Ⓑ Ⓒ Ⓓ Ⓔ   19. Ⓐ Ⓑ Ⓒ Ⓓ Ⓔ   25. Ⓐ Ⓑ Ⓒ Ⓓ Ⓔ
2. Ⓐ Ⓑ Ⓒ Ⓓ Ⓔ   8. Ⓐ Ⓑ Ⓒ Ⓓ Ⓔ   14. Ⓐ Ⓑ Ⓒ Ⓓ Ⓔ   20. Ⓐ Ⓑ Ⓒ Ⓓ Ⓔ   26. Ⓐ Ⓑ Ⓒ Ⓓ Ⓔ
3. Ⓐ Ⓑ Ⓒ Ⓓ Ⓔ   9. Ⓐ Ⓑ Ⓒ Ⓓ Ⓔ   15. Ⓐ Ⓑ Ⓒ Ⓓ Ⓔ   21. Ⓐ Ⓑ Ⓒ Ⓓ Ⓔ   27. Ⓐ Ⓑ Ⓒ Ⓓ Ⓔ
4. Ⓐ Ⓑ Ⓒ Ⓓ Ⓔ   10. Ⓐ Ⓑ Ⓒ Ⓓ Ⓔ   16. Ⓐ Ⓑ Ⓒ Ⓓ Ⓔ   22. Ⓐ Ⓑ Ⓒ Ⓓ Ⓔ   28. Ⓐ Ⓑ Ⓒ Ⓓ Ⓔ
5. Ⓐ Ⓑ Ⓒ Ⓓ Ⓔ   11. Ⓐ Ⓑ Ⓒ Ⓓ Ⓔ   17. Ⓐ Ⓑ Ⓒ Ⓓ Ⓔ   23. Ⓐ Ⓑ Ⓒ Ⓓ Ⓔ   29. Ⓐ Ⓑ Ⓒ Ⓓ Ⓔ
6. Ⓐ Ⓑ Ⓒ Ⓓ Ⓔ   12. Ⓐ Ⓑ Ⓒ Ⓓ Ⓔ   18. Ⓐ Ⓑ Ⓒ Ⓓ Ⓔ   24. Ⓐ Ⓑ Ⓒ Ⓓ Ⓔ   30. Ⓐ Ⓑ Ⓒ Ⓓ Ⓔ

MATH SECTION

1. Ⓐ Ⓑ Ⓒ Ⓓ Ⓔ   7. Ⓐ Ⓑ Ⓒ Ⓓ Ⓔ   13. Ⓐ Ⓑ Ⓒ Ⓓ Ⓔ   19. Ⓐ Ⓑ Ⓒ Ⓓ Ⓔ   25. Ⓐ Ⓑ Ⓒ Ⓓ Ⓔ
2. Ⓐ Ⓑ Ⓒ Ⓓ Ⓔ   8. Ⓐ Ⓑ Ⓒ Ⓓ Ⓔ   14. Ⓐ Ⓑ Ⓒ Ⓓ Ⓔ   20. Ⓐ Ⓑ Ⓒ Ⓓ Ⓔ   26. Ⓐ Ⓑ Ⓒ Ⓓ Ⓔ
3. Ⓐ Ⓑ Ⓒ Ⓓ Ⓔ   9. Ⓐ Ⓑ Ⓒ Ⓓ Ⓔ   15. Ⓐ Ⓑ Ⓒ Ⓓ Ⓔ   21. Ⓐ Ⓑ Ⓒ Ⓓ Ⓔ   27. Ⓐ Ⓑ Ⓒ Ⓓ Ⓔ
4. Ⓐ Ⓑ Ⓒ Ⓓ Ⓔ   10. Ⓐ Ⓑ Ⓒ Ⓓ Ⓔ   16. Ⓐ Ⓑ Ⓒ Ⓓ Ⓔ   22. Ⓐ Ⓑ Ⓒ Ⓓ Ⓔ   28. Ⓐ Ⓑ Ⓒ Ⓓ Ⓔ
5. Ⓐ Ⓑ Ⓒ Ⓓ Ⓔ   11. Ⓐ Ⓑ Ⓒ Ⓓ Ⓔ   17. Ⓐ Ⓑ Ⓒ Ⓓ Ⓔ   23. Ⓐ Ⓑ Ⓒ Ⓓ Ⓔ
6. Ⓐ Ⓑ Ⓒ Ⓓ Ⓔ   12. Ⓐ Ⓑ Ⓒ Ⓓ Ⓔ   18. Ⓐ Ⓑ Ⓒ Ⓓ Ⓔ   24. Ⓐ Ⓑ Ⓒ Ⓓ Ⓔ

ANALYTICAL SECTION

1. Ⓐ Ⓑ Ⓒ Ⓓ Ⓔ   8. Ⓐ Ⓑ Ⓒ Ⓓ Ⓔ   15. Ⓐ Ⓑ Ⓒ Ⓓ Ⓔ   22. Ⓐ Ⓑ Ⓒ Ⓓ Ⓔ   29. Ⓐ Ⓑ Ⓒ Ⓓ Ⓔ
2. Ⓐ Ⓑ Ⓒ Ⓓ Ⓔ   9. Ⓐ Ⓑ Ⓒ Ⓓ Ⓔ   16. Ⓐ Ⓑ Ⓒ Ⓓ Ⓔ   23. Ⓐ Ⓑ Ⓒ Ⓓ Ⓔ   30. Ⓐ Ⓑ Ⓒ Ⓓ Ⓔ
3. Ⓐ Ⓑ Ⓒ Ⓓ Ⓔ   10. Ⓐ Ⓑ Ⓒ Ⓓ Ⓔ   17. Ⓐ Ⓑ Ⓒ Ⓓ Ⓔ   24. Ⓐ Ⓑ Ⓒ Ⓓ Ⓔ   31. Ⓐ Ⓑ Ⓒ Ⓓ Ⓔ
4. Ⓐ Ⓑ Ⓒ Ⓓ Ⓔ   11. Ⓐ Ⓑ Ⓒ Ⓓ Ⓔ   18. Ⓐ Ⓑ Ⓒ Ⓓ Ⓔ   25. Ⓐ Ⓑ Ⓒ Ⓓ Ⓔ   32. Ⓐ Ⓑ Ⓒ Ⓓ Ⓔ
5. Ⓐ Ⓑ Ⓒ Ⓓ Ⓔ   12. Ⓐ Ⓑ Ⓒ Ⓓ Ⓔ   19. Ⓐ Ⓑ Ⓒ Ⓓ Ⓔ   26. Ⓐ Ⓑ Ⓒ Ⓓ Ⓔ   33. Ⓐ Ⓑ Ⓒ Ⓓ Ⓔ
6. Ⓐ Ⓑ Ⓒ Ⓓ Ⓔ   13. Ⓐ Ⓑ Ⓒ Ⓓ Ⓔ   20. Ⓐ Ⓑ Ⓒ Ⓓ Ⓔ   27. Ⓐ Ⓑ Ⓒ Ⓓ Ⓔ   34. Ⓐ Ⓑ Ⓒ Ⓓ Ⓔ
7. Ⓐ Ⓑ Ⓒ Ⓓ Ⓔ   14. Ⓐ Ⓑ Ⓒ Ⓓ Ⓔ   21. Ⓐ Ⓑ Ⓒ Ⓓ Ⓔ   28. Ⓐ Ⓑ Ⓒ Ⓓ Ⓔ   35. Ⓐ Ⓑ Ⓒ Ⓓ Ⓔ

31

Diagnostic Examination

Verbal Section

30 QUESTIONS • TIME — 30 MINUTES

Directions: Each of the questions below contains one or more blank spaces, each blank indicating an omitted word. Each sentence is followed by five (5) words or sets of words. Read and determine the general sense of each sentence. Then choose the word, or set of words, that, when inserted in the sentence, best fits the meaning of the sentence.

1. —— and piety seem to have been two qualities almost universally shared by the original settlers of the Northeast who faced the almost —— problems of the weather and disease.

   (A) Candor . . insignificant
   (B) Veracity . . understandable
   (C) Cowardice . . enduring
   (D) Avarice . . threatening
   (E) Fortitude . . insurmountable

2. A —— review of the recent performance of *La Bohème* called the production grotesque and the conducting of the orchestra ——.

   (A) glowing . . benign
   (B) scathing . . pedestrian
   (C) laudatory . . heretical
   (D) premeditated . . prejudicial
   (E) concentrated . . munificent

3. The young soloist broke a string in the middle of the performance of the Tchaikovsky Violin Concerto and motioned to the concertmaster to hand over his own violin so that she might —— her performance, demonstrating —— rare in one so young.

   (A) interrupt . . confidence
   (B) continue . . aplomb
   (C) rehearse . . stage presence
   (D) illuminate . . perseverity
   (E) renew . . elegance

Directions: In each of the following questions, you are given a related pair of words or phrases in capital letters. Each capitalized pair is followed by five (5) pairs of words or phrases. Choose the pair that best expresses a relationship similar to that expressed by the original pair.

4. TRAP : GAME ::

   (A) novel : author
   (B) net : fish
   (C) leash : dog
   (D) wall : house
   (E) curtain : window

5. MANSARD : ROOF ::

   (A) ice : igloo
   (B) spine : book
   (C) closet : hallway
   (D) dormer : window
   (E) tent : military

6. PASTOR : CONGREGATION ::

   (A) shepherd : flock
   (B) teacher : faculty
   (C) chef : restaurant
   (D) clerk : market
   (E) painter : canvas

33

GO ON TO THE NEXT PAGE

War has escaped the battlefield and now can, with modern guidance systems on missiles, touch virtually every square yard of the earth's surface. War has also lost most of its utility in achieving the traditional goals
(5) of conflict. Control of territory carries with it the obligation to provide subject peoples certain administrative, health, education, and other social services; such obligations far outweigh the benefits of control. If the ruled population is ethnically or racially different from
(10) the rulers, tensions and chronic unrest often exist, which further reduce the benefits and increase the costs of domination. Large populations no longer necessarily enhance state power and, in the absence of high levels of economic development, can impose severe burdens
(15) on food supply, jobs, and the broad range of services expected of modern governments. The noneconomic security reasons for the control of territory have been progressively undermined by the advances of modern technology. The benefits of forcing another nation to
(20) surrender its wealth are vastly outweighed by the benefits of persuading that nation to produce and exchange goods and services. In brief, imperialism no longer pays.

Making war has been one of the most persistent of
(25) human activities in the 80 centuries since men and women settled in cities and thereby became "civilized," but the modernization of the past 80 years has fundamentally changed the role and function of war. In premodernized societies, successful warfare brought
(30) significant material rewards, the most obvious of which were the stored wealth of the defeated. Equally important was human labor—control over people as slaves or levies for the victor's army, and there was the productive capacity—agricultural lands and mines. Successful
(35) warfare also produced psychic benefits. The removal or destruction of a threat brought a sense of security, and power gained over others created pride and national self-esteem.

War was accepted in the premodernized society as a
(40) part of the human condition, a mechanism of change, and an unavoidable, even noble, aspect of life. The excitement and drama of war made it a vital part of literature and legends.

7. According to the passage, leaders of premodernized society considered war to be
(A) a valid tool of national policy
(B) an immoral act of aggression
(C) economically wasteful and socially unfeasible
(D) restricted in scope to military participants
(E) necessary to spur development of unoccupied lands

8. The author most likely places the word "civilized" in quotation marks (lines 26–27) in order to
(A) show dissatisfaction at not having found a better word
(B) acknowledge that the word was borrowed from another source
(C) express irony that war should be a part of civilization
(D) impress upon the reader the tragedy of war
(E) raise a question about the value of war in modernized society

9. The author mentions all of the following as possible reasons for going to war in a premodernized society EXCEPT
(A) possibility of material gain
(B) total annihilation of the enemy and destruction of enemy territory
(C) potential for increasing the security of the nation
(D) desire to capture productive farming lands
(E) need for workers to fill certain jobs

10. RESIDENT:
(A) factual
(B) constrained
(C) transitory
(D) lofty
(E) merciful

11. PROLIFIC:

(A) worthless

(B) barren

(C) practical

(D) baleful

(E) youthful

12. LAMBAST:

(A) deny

(B) understand

(C) praise

(D) imagine

(E) flatten

13. COURT:

(A) reject

(B) uncover

(C) infect

(D) subject

(E) elect

Directions: The passage below is followed by questions based on its content. Choose the best answer to each question.

There is extraordinary exposure in the United States to the risks of injury and death from motor vehicle accidents. More than 80 percent of all households own passenger cars or light trucks and each of these is driven (5) an average of more than 11,000 miles each year. Almost one-half of fatally injured drivers have a blood alcohol concentration (BAC) of 0.1 percent or higher. For the average adult, over five ounces of 80 proof spirits would have to be consumed over a short period of time to attain (10) these levels. A third of drivers who have been drinking, but fewer than 4 percent of all drivers, demonstrate these levels. Although less than 1 percent of drivers with BACs of 0.1 percent or more are involved in fatal crashes, the probability of their involvement is 27 times (15) higher than for those without alcohol in their blood.

There are a number of different approaches to reducing injuries in which intoxication plays a role. Based on the observation that excessive consumption correlates with the total alcohol consumption of a country's popu- (20) lation, it has been suggested that higher taxes on alcohol would reduce both. While the heaviest drinkers would be taxed the most, anyone who drinks at all would be penalized by this approach.

To make drinking and driving a criminal offense is (25) an approach directed only at intoxicated drivers. In some states, the law empowers police to request breath tests of drivers cited for any traffic offense and elevated BAC can be the basis for arrest. The National Highway Traffic Safety Administration estimates, however, that (30) even with increased arrests, there are about 700 violations for every arrest. At this level there is little evidence that laws serve as deterrents to driving while intoxicated. In Britain, motor vehicle fatalities fell 25 percent immediately following implementation of the Road (35) Safety Act in 1967. As the British increasingly recognized that they could drink and not be stopped, the effectiveness declined, although in the ensuing three years the fatality rate seldom reached that observed in the seven years prior to the Act.

(40) Whether penalties for driving with a high BAC or excessive taxation on consumption of alcoholic beverages will deter the excessive drinker responsible for most fatalities is unclear. In part, the answer depends on the extent to which those with high BACs involved in (45) crashes are capable of controlling their intake in response to economic or penal threat. Therapeutic programs which range from individual and group counseling and psychotherapy to chemotherapy constitute another approach, but they have not diminished the pro- (50) portion of accidents in which alcohol was a factor. In the few controlled trials that have been reported, there is little evidence that rehabilitation programs for those repeatedly arrested for drunken behavior have reduced either the recidivism or crash rates. Thus far, there is no (55) firm evidence that Alcohol Safety Action Project supported programs, in which rehabilitation measures are requested by the court, have decreased recidivism or crash involvement for clients exposed to them, although knowledge and attitudes have improved. One thing is (60) clear, however; unless we deal with automobile and highway safety and reduce accidents in which alcoholic intoxication plays a role, many will continue to die.

GO ON TO THE NEXT PAGE

14. The author is primarily concerned with

    (A) interpreting the results of surveys on traffic fatalities

    (B) reviewing the effectiveness of attempts to curb drunk driving

    (C) suggesting reasons for the prevalence of drunk driving in the United States

    (D) analyzing the causes of the large number of annual traffic fatalities

    (E) making an international comparison of the U.S. and Britain

15. It can be inferred that the 1967 Road Safety Act in Britain

    (A) changed an existing law to lower the BAC level which defined driving while intoxicated

    (B) made it illegal to drive while intoxicated

    (C) increased the number of drunk driving arrests

    (D) placed a tax on the sale of alcoholic drinks

    (E) required drivers convicted under the law to undergo rehabilitation therapy

16. The author implies that a BAC of 0.1 percent

    (A) is unreasonably high as a definition of intoxication for purposes of driving

    (B) penalizes the moderate drinker while allowing the heavy drinker to consume without limit

    (C) will operate as an effective deterrent to over 90 percent of the people who might drink and drive

    (D) is well below the BAC of most drivers who are involved in fatal collisions

    (E) proves that a driver has consumed five ounces of 80 proof spirits over a short time

17. With which of the following statements about making driving while intoxicated a criminal offense versus increasing taxes on alcohol consumption would the author most likely agree?

    (A) Making driving while intoxicated a criminal offense is preferable to increased taxes on alcohol because the former is aimed only at those who abuse alcohol by driving while intoxicated.

    (B) Increased taxation on alcohol consumption is likely to be more effective in reducing traffic fatalities because taxation covers all consumers and not just those who drive.

    (C) Increased taxation on alcohol will constitute less of an interference with personal liberty because of the necessity of blood alcohol tests to determine BACs in drivers suspected of intoxication.

    (D) Since neither increased taxation nor enforcement of criminal laws against drunk drivers is likely to have any significant impact, neither measure is warranted.

    (E) Because arrests of intoxicated drivers have proved to be expensive and administratively cumbersome, increased taxation on alcohol is the most promising means of reducing traffic fatalities.

18. The author cites the British example in order to

    (A) show that the problem of drunk driving is worse in Britain than in the U.S.

    (B) prove that stricter enforcement of laws against intoxicated drivers would reduce traffic deaths

    (C) prove that a slight increase in the number of arrests of intoxicated drivers will not deter drunk driving

    (D) suggest that taxation of alcohol consumption may be more effective than criminal laws

    (E) demonstrate the need to lower BAC levels in states that have laws against drunk driving

19. Which of the following, if true, most weakens the author's statement that the effectiveness of proposals to stop the intoxicated driver depends, in part, on the extent to which the high BAC driver can control his or her intake?

(A) Even if the heavy drinker cannot control intake, criminal laws against driving while intoxicated can deter him or her from driving while intoxicated.

(B) Rehabilitation programs aimed at drivers convicted of driving while intoxicated have not significantly reduced traffic fatalities.

(C) Many traffic fatalities are caused by factors unrelated to the excessive consumption of alcohol by the driver involved.

(D) Even though severe penalties may not deter the intoxicated driver, these laws will punish him or her for the harm caused by driving while intoxicated.

(E) Some sort of therapy may be effective in helping the problem drinker to control the intake of alcohol, thereby keeping him or her off the road.

Directions: In each of the following questions, you are given a related pair of words or phrases in capital letters. Each capitalized pair is followed by five (5) pairs of words or phrases. Choose the pair that best expresses a relationship similar to that expressed by the original pair.

20. ODE : POEM ::

(A) character : novel

(B) brick : building

(C) ballad : song

(D) street : intersection

(E) museum : painting

21. TENACITY : WEAK ::

(A) apathy : caring

(B) pity : strong

(C) immorality : wrong

(D) frequency : known

(E) control : expensive

22. CURATOR : PAINTING ::

(A) jailer : sheriff

(B) treasurer : secretary

(C) archivist : manuscript

(D) general : army

(E) machinist : metal

23. CREPESCULE : TWILIGHT ::

(A) week : calendar

(B) temperature : climate

(C) dawn : daybreak

(D) radiation : sun

(E) commutation : voyage

Directions: Each of the questions below contains one or more blank spaces, each blank indicating an omitted word. Each sentence is followed by five (5) words or sets of words. Read and determine the general sense of each sentence. Then choose the word, or set of words that, when inserted in the sentence, best fits the meaning of the sentence.

24. The Supreme Court, in striking down the state law, ruled the statute had been enacted in an atmosphere charged with religious convictions that had —— the lawmaking process, a —— of the Constitutional provision requiring the separation of church and state.

(A) written..bastion

(B) influenced..harbinger

(C) infected..violation

(D) repealed..fulfillment

(E) sanctified..union

25. Because customers believe that there is a direct correlation between price and value, software manufacturers continue to —— their prices at —— rate.

(A) raise..an astonishing

(B) inflate..a moderate

(C) advertise..a rapid

(D) control..an acceptable

(E) determine..a shared

GO ON TO THE NEXT PAGE

26. The —— performance of the Rachmaninoff Piano Concerto in D Minor, one of the most difficult modern compositions for the piano, —— the audience and earned the pianist a standing ovation.

    (A) virtuoso..thrilled

    (B) excellent..offended

    (C) miserable..excited

    (D) mediocre..incited

    (E) masterful..disappointed

Directions: Each of the following questions consists of a word printed in capital letters, followed by five words or phrases. Choose the word or phrase that is most nearly opposite in meaning to the word in capital letters. Be sure to consider all the choices before deciding which one is best.

27. FORGE :

    (A) continue

    (B) dissolve

    (C) quiet

    (D) invite

    (E) prevent

28. MOTILE :

    (A) confused

    (B) frightened

    (C) immobile

    (D) willing

    (E) nervous

29. LACHRYMOSE :

    (A) sacred

    (B) unknowable

    (C) miraculous

    (D) humble

    (E) joyful

30. QUIESCENCE :

    (A) calamity

    (B) timidity

    (C) persistence

    (D) frenzy

    (E) eternity

WARNING

IF YOU FINISHED THIS SECTION BEFORE TIME EXPIRED, GO IMMEDIATELY TO THE NEXT SECTION. YOU MAY NOT CONTINUE TO WORK ON THIS SECTION AFTER TIME HAS EXPIRED.

Math Section

28 QUESTIONS • TIME—45 MINUTES

Directions: For each of the following questions two quantities are given, one in Column A and one in Column B. Compare the two quantities and choose

A: if the quantity in Column A is the greater

B: if the quantity in Column B is the greater

C: if the two quantities are equal

D: if the relationship cannot be determined from the information given.

Common Information: In any question, information applying to both columns is centered between the columns and above the quantities in columns A and B. Any symbol that appears in both columns represents the same idea or quantity in both columns.

Numbers: All numbers used are real numbers.

Figures: Assume that the position of points, angles, regions, and so forth are in the order shown. Figures are assumed to lie in a plane unless otherwise indicated. Figures accompanying questions are intended to provide information you can use in answering the questions. However, unless a note states that a figure is drawn to scale, you should solve the problems by using your knowledge of mathematics and not by estimating sizes by sight or measurement.

Lines: Assume that lines shown as straight are indeed straight.

	Column A	Column B
1.	$5 - \frac{6}{6}$	$5 - \frac{4}{4}$

x is 4 more than *y*

	Column A	Column B
2.	x	y

	Column A	Column B

The price of a book increased from $7.95 to $8.95.

3.	The percent increase in the price of the book	12%

$M + 2$ is the average (arithmetic mean) of x and y.

4.	$\dfrac{x+y}{2}$	M

5.	$(x+y)(x-y)$	$x^2 - y^2$

Directions: For each of these questions, select the best of the answer choices given.

6. $5^2 + 12^2 =$

(A) 13^2

(B) 17^2

(C) 20^2

(D) 144^2

(E) 169^2

7. A salesperson works 50 weeks each year and makes an average (arithmetic mean) of 100 sales per week. If each sale is worth an average (arithmetic mean) of $1,000, then what is the total value of sales made by the salesperson in a year?

(A) $50,000

(B) $100,000

(C) $500,000

(D) $1,000,000

(E) $5,000,000

GO ON TO THE NEXT PAGE

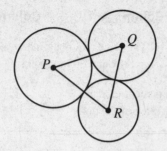

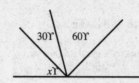 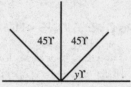

8. In the figure above, the three circles are tangent to each other at the points shown. If circle *P* has a diameter of 10, circle *Q* has a diameter of 8, and circle *R* has a diameter of 6, then what is the perimeter of triangle *PQR*?

(A) 24

(B) 18

(C) 12

(D) 9

(E) 6

9. If $x = 1$ and $y = -2$, then $\dfrac{x^2 - xy}{y} =$

(A) −3

(B) −2

(C) $-\dfrac{3}{2}$

(D) 2

(E) 3

10. Which of the following numbers does NOT satisfy the inequality $5x - 2 < 3x - 1$?

(A) 1

(B) 0

(C) −1

(D) −2

(E) −3

11.   *x*   *y*

The population of City X decreased by 5 percent while the population of City Y decreased by 7.5 percent

12.   The loss of population   The loss of population
      by City X   by City Y

The perimeter of square *PQRS* is $12\sqrt{3}$.

13.   side *PQ* $3\sqrt{3}$

14. $\left(\dfrac{3}{7} \times \dfrac{101}{104}\right) + \left(\dfrac{3}{7} \times \dfrac{4}{104}\right)$ $\dfrac{3}{7}$

Point *P* has coordinates (−2,2); point *Q* has coordinates (2,0).

15.   4   The distance from *P* to *Q*

16. If *x* is an even integer and *y* is an odd integer, then which of the following is an even integer?

(A) $x^2 + y$

(B) $x^2 - y$

(C) $(x^2)(y)$

(D) $x + y$

(E) $x - y$

17. If $pq \neq 0$ and $p = \frac{1}{3}q$, then the ratio of p to $3q$ is

    (A) 9

    (B) 3

    (C) 1

    (D) $\frac{1}{3}$

    (E) $\frac{1}{9}$

18. If a certain chemical costs $50 for 30 gallons, then how many gallons of the chemical can be purchased for $625?

    (A) 12.5

    (B) 24

    (C) 325

    (D) 375

    (E) 425

19. Which of the following can be expressed as the sum of three consecutive integers?

    (A) 17

    (B) 23

    (C) 25

    (D) 30

    (E) 40

20. If the areas of the three different sized faces of a rectangular solid are 6, 8, and 12, then what is the volume of the solid?

    (A) 576

    (B) 288

    (C) 144

    (D) 48

    (E) 24

Questions 21–24 are based on the graphs below:

Directions: For each of these questions, select the best of the answer choices given.

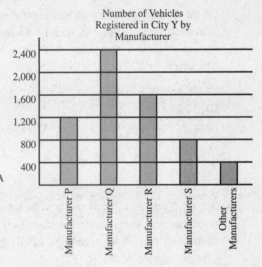

Number of Vehicles Registered in City Y by Manufacturer

SELECTED MOTOR VEHICLE REGISTRATION DATA
FOR TWO CITIES (BY MANUFACTURER)

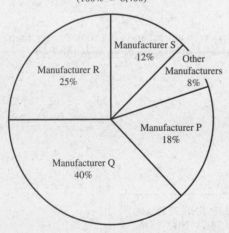

Distribution of Motor Vehicles Registered in City X According to Manufacturer
(100% = 8,400)

Number of Vehicles Registered in City X Manufactured by Other Manufacturers

Manufacturer T	212
Manufacturer U	210
Manufacturer V	250

GO ON TO THE NEXT PAGE

21. In City X, how many of the registered motor vehicles were manufactured by Manufacturer Q?

 (A) 1,512

 (B) 1,600

 (C) 2,400

 (D) 3,360

 (E) 6,000

22. How many more of the motor vehicles registered in City Y were manufactured by Manufacturer R than were manufactured by Manufacturer P?

 (A) 400

 (B) 688

 (C) 800

 (D) 1,200

 (E) 1,688

23. Of the following, which is the closest approximation to the percentage of motor vehicles registered in City X that were manufactured by Manufacturer V?

 (A) 45%

 (B) 37%

 (C) 8%

 (D) 3%

 (E) 1%

24. In City Y, the number of motor vehicles registered that were manufactured by Manufacturer R accounted for what percentage of all motor vehicles registered in City Y?

 (A) 4%

 (B) 8%

 (C) 12.5%

 (D) 16%

 (E) 25%

Directions: For each of the following questions two quantities are given, one in Column A and one in Column B. Compare the two quantities and choose

 A: if the quantity in Column A is the greater

 B: if the quantity in Column B is the greater

 C: if the two quantities are equal

 D: if the relationship cannot be determined from the information given.

Column A	Column B
25. The least positive integer that is divisible by both 18 and 24	The least positive integer that is divisible by both 18 and 28

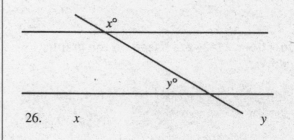

26. x	y

For all real numbers P and Q,
$$P * Q = P + Q - PQ.$$

27. $4 * 1$	$4 * 2$

$j > 0, k > 0, m < 0$

28. $(3j)(3k)(3m)$	$3(j)(k)(m)$

WARNING

IF YOU FINISHED THIS SECTION BEFORE TIME EXPIRED, GO IMMEDIATELY TO THE NEXT SECTION. YOU MAY NOT CONTINUE TO WORK ON THIS SECTION AFTER TIME HAS EXPIRED.

Analytical Section

35 QUESTIONS • TIME—60 MINUTES

Directions: Each of the following questions or groups of questions is based on a short passage or a set of propositions. In answering these questions it may sometimes be helpful to draw a simple picture or chart. When you have selected the best answer to each question, darken the corresponding circle on your answer sheet.

Questions 1–6

A railway system consists of six stations, G, H, I, J, K, and L. Trains run only according to the following conditions:

From G to H

From H to G and from H to I

From I to J

From J to H and from J to K

From L to G, from L to K, and from L to I

From K to J

It is possible to transfer at a station for another train.

1. How is it possible to get from H to J?
   (A) A direct train from H to J
   (B) A train to G and transfer for a train to J
   (C) A train to L and transfer for a train to J
   (D) A train to I and transfer for a train to J
   (E) It is impossible to reach J from H.

2. Which of the following stations CANNOT be reached by a train from any of the other stations?
   (A) G
   (B) H
   (C) I
   (D) K
   (E) L

3. Which of the following is a complete and accurate listing of the stations from which it is possible to reach I with exactly one transfer?
   (A) G and H
   (B) G and J
   (C) J and K
   (D) J and L
   (E) J, G, and L

4. What is the greatest number of stations that can be visited without visiting any station more than once?
   (A) 2
   (B) 3
   (C) 4
   (D) 5
   (E) 6

5. Which of the following trips requires the greatest number of transfers?
   (A) G to I
   (B) H to K
   (C) L to H
   (D) L to I
   (E) L to K

6. If station I is closed, which of the following trips is impossible?
   (A) G to J
   (B) J to K
   (C) L to K
   (D) L to J
   (E) L to G

GO ON TO THE NEXT PAGE

7. Since all swans I have encountered have been white, it follows that the swans I will see when I visit the Bronx Zoo will also be white.

Which of the following most closely parallels the reasoning of the preceding argument?

(A) Some birds are incapable of flight; therefore, swans are probably incapable of flight.

(B) Every ballet I have attended has failed to interest me; so a theatrical production which fails to interest me must be a ballet.

(C) Since all cases of severe depression I have encountered were susceptible to treatment by chlorpromazine, there must be something in the chlorpromazine which adjusts the patient's brain chemistry.

(D) Because every society has a word for justice, the concept of fair play must be inherent in the biological makeup of the human species.

(E) Since no medicine I have tried for my allergy has ever helped, this new product probably will not work either.

8.   ERIKA: Participation in intramural competitive sports teaches students the importance of teamwork, for no one wants to let his or her teammates down.

   NICHOL: That is not correct. The real reason students play hard is that such programs place a premium on winning and no one wants to be a member of a losing team.

Which of the following comments can most reasonably be made about the exchange between Erika and Nichol?

(A) If fewer and fewer schools are sponsoring intramural sports programs now than a decade ago, Erika's position is undermined.

(B) If high schools and universities provide financial assistance for the purchase of sports equipment, Nichol's assertion about the importance of winning is weakened.

(C) If teamwork is essential to success in intramural competitive sports, Erika's position and Nichol's position are not necessarily incompatible.

(D) Since the argument is one about motivation, it should be possible to resolve the issue by taking a survey of deans at schools that have intramural sports programs.

(E) Since the question raised is about hidden psychological states, it is impossible to answer it.

9. A cryptographer has intercepted an enemy message that is in code. He knows that the code is a simple substitution of numbers for letters. Which of the following would be the LEAST helpful in breaking the code?

(A) Knowing the frequency with which the vowels of the language are used

(B) Knowing the frequency with which two vowels appear together in the language

(C) Knowing the frequency with which odd numbers appear relative to even numbers in the message

(D) Knowing the conjugation of the verb to be in the language on which the code is based

(E) Knowing every word in the language that begins with the letter R

10. One way of reducing commuting time for those who work in the cities is to increase the speed at which traffic moves in the heart of the city. This can be accomplished by raising the tolls on the tunnels and bridges connecting the city with other communities. This will discourage auto traffic into the city and will encourage people to use public transportation instead.

Which of the following, if true, would LEAST weaken the argument above?

(A) Nearly all of the traffic in the center of the city is commercial traffic, which will continue despite toll increases.

(B) Some people now driving alone into the city would choose to carpool with each other rather than use public transportation.

(C) Any temporary improvement in traffic flow would be lost because the improvement itself would attract more cars.

(D) The numbers of commuters who would be deterred by the toll increases would be insignificant.

(E) The public transportation system is not able to handle any significant increase in the number of commuters using the system.

Questions 11–16

A travel agent is arranging tours that visit various cities: L, M, N, O, P, Q, R, S, and T. Each tour must be arranged in accordance with the following restrictions:

If M is included in a tour, both Q and R must also be included.

P can be included in a tour only if O is also included.

If Q is included in a tour, M must be included along with N or T or both.

P and Q cannot both be included in a tour.

A tour cannot include O, R, and T.

A tour cannot include N, S, and R.

A tour cannot include L and R.

11. If M is included in a tour, what is the minimum number of other cities that must be included in the tour?

(A) 2

(B) 3

(C) 4

(D) 5

(E) 6

12. Which of the following cities cannot be included in a tour that includes P?

(A) M

(B) N

(C) O

(D) S

(E) R

13. Which of the following is an acceptable group of cities for a tour?

(A) M, N, O, P

(B) M, N, Q, R

(C) M, N, Q, S

(D) L, M, Q, R

(E) N, S, R, T

14. Which one city would have to be deleted from the group M, Q, O, R, T to form an acceptable tour?

(A) M

(B) Q

(C) O

(D) R

(E) T

15. Which of the following could be made into an acceptable tour by adding exactly one more city?

(A) L, O, R

(B) M, P, Q

(C) M, Q, R

(D) N, S, R

(E) R, T, P

16. Exactly how many of the cities could be used for a tour consisting of only one city?

(A) 2

(B) 3

(C) 4

(D) 5

(E) 6

GO ON TO THE NEXT PAGE

Questions 17–22

A child is stringing 11 different colored beads on a string.

Of the 11, four are yellow, three are red, two are blue, and two are green.

The red beads are adjacent to one another.

The blue beads are adjacent to one another.

The green beads are not adjacent to one another.

A red bead is at one end of the string and a green bead is at the other end.

17. If the sixth and seventh beads are blue and the tenth bead is red, which of the following must be true?

    (A) The second bead is green.

    (B) The fifth bead is yellow.

    (C) The eighth bead is green.

    (D) A green bead is next to a yellow bead.

    (E) A blue bead is next to a green bead.

18. If the four yellow beads are next to each other, and if the tenth bead is yellow, which of the following beads must be blue?

    (A) The fourth

    (B) The fifth

    (C) The sixth

    (D) The seventh

    (E) The eighth

19. If each blue bead is next to a green bead, and if the four yellow beads are next to each other, then which of the following is a complete and accurate listing of the beads that must be yellow?

    (A) fourth and fifth

    (B) fifth and sixth

    (C) sixth and seventh

    (D) fourth, fifth, and sixth

    (E) fifth, sixth, and seventh

20. If the fifth and sixth beads are blue and the ninth bead is red, which of the following must be true?

    (A) One of the green beads is next to a blue bead.

    (B) One of the red beads is next to a green bead.

    (C) Each yellow bead is next to at least one other yellow bead.

    (D) The second bead is yellow.

    (E) The eighth bead is yellow.

21. If the fifth, eighth, ninth, and tenth beads are yellow, then all of the following must be true EXCEPT:

    (A) The fourth bead is green.

    (B) The sixth bead is blue.

    (C) Exactly one red bead is next to a green bead.

    (D) Both blue beads are next to yellow beads.

    (E) The second bead is yellow.

22. If one green bead is next to a red bead and the other green bead is next to a blue bead, which of the following must be true?

    (A) The second bead is blue.

    (B) The fourth bead is green.

    (C) The fourth bead is yellow.

    (D) The seventh bead is yellow.

    (E) The eighth bead is green.

23. Some philosophers have argued that there exist certain human or natural rights that belong to all human beings by virtue of their humanity. But a review of the laws of different societies shows that the rights accorded a person vary from society to society and even within a society over time. Since there is no right that is universally protected, there are no natural rights.

    A defender of the theory that natural rights do exist might respond to this objection by arguing that

    (A) some human beings do not have any natural rights

    (B) some human rights are natural while others derive from a source such as a constitution

(C) people in one society may have natural rights that people in another society lack

(D) all societies have some institution that protects the rights of an individual in that society

(E) natural rights may exist even though they are not protected by some societies

Questions 24 and 25

The single greatest weakness of American parties is their inability to achieve cohesion in the legislature. Although there is some measure of party unity, it is not uncommon for the majority party to be unable to implement important legislation. The unity is strongest during election campaigns; after the primary elections, the losing candidates all promise their support to the party nominee. By the time the Congress convenes, the unity has dissipated. This phenomenon is attributable to the fragmented nature of party politics. The national committees are no more than feudal lords who receive nominal fealty from their vassals. A congressman builds his own power upon a local base. Consequently, a congressman is likely to be responsive to local special interest groups. Evidence of this is seen in the differences in voting patterns between the upper and lower houses. In the Senate, where terms are longer, there is more party unity.

24. Which of the following, if true, would most strengthen the author's argument?

(A) On 30 key issues, 18 of the 67 majority party members in the Senate voted against the party leaders.

(B) On 30 key issues, 70 of the 305 majority party members in the House voted against the party leaders.

(C) On 30 key issues, over half the members of the minority party in both houses voted with the majority party against the leaders of the minority party.

(D) Of 30 key legislative proposals introduced by the president, only eight passed both houses.

(E) Of 30 key legislative proposals introduced by a president whose party controlled a majority in both houses, only four passed both houses.

25. Which of the following, if true, would most weaken the author's argument?

(A) Congressmen receive funds from the national party committee.

(B) Senators vote against the party leaders only two-thirds as often as members of the House.

(C) The primary duty of an officeholder is to be responsive to his local constituency rather than to party leaders.

(D) There is more unity among minority party members than among majority party members.

(E) Much legislation is passed each session despite party disunity.

26. JOCKEY: Horses are the most noble of all animals. They are both loyal and brave. I knew of a farm horse that died of a broken heart shortly after its owner died.

VETERINARIAN: You're wrong. Dogs can be just as loyal and brave. I had a dog who would wait every day on the front steps for me to come home, and if I did not arrive until midnight, he would still be there.

All of the following are true of the claims of the jockey and the veterinarian EXCEPT:

(A) Both claims assume that loyalty and bravery are characteristics that are desirable in animals.

(B) Both claims are, in principle, untestable, so neither can be empirically confirmed or denied.

(C) Both claims assume that human qualities can be attributed to animals.

(D) Both claims are supported by only a single example of animal behavior.

(E) Neither claim is supported by evidence other than the opinions and observations of the speakers.

GO ON TO THE NEXT PAGE ▶

27. If George graduated from the University after 1974, he was required to take Introductory World History.

    The statement above can be logically deduced from which of the following?

    (A) Before 1974, Introductory World History was not a required course in the University.

    (B) Every student who took Introductory World History at the University graduated after 1974.

    (C) No student who graduated from the University before 1974 took Introductory World History.

    (D) All students graduating from the University after 1974 were required to take Introductory World History.

    (E) Before 1974, no student was not permitted to graduate from the University without having taken Introductory World History.

28. Many people ask, "How effective is Painaway?" So, to find out we have been checking the medicine cabinets of the apartments in this typical building. As it turns out, eight out of ten contain a bottle of Painaway. Doesn't it stand to reason that you, too, should have the most effective pain-reliever on the market?

    The appeal of this advertisement would be most weakened by which of the following pieces of evidence?

    (A) Painaway distributed complimentary bottles of medicine to most apartments in the building two days before the advertisement was made.

    (B) The actor who made the advertisement takes a pain-reliever manufactured by a competitor of Painaway.

    (C) Most people want a fast, effective pain-reliever.

    (D) Many people take the advice of their neighborhood druggists about pain-relievers.

    (E) A government survey shows that many people take a pain-reliever before it is really needed.

Questions 29–35

A winery is conducting a tasting of seven wines: J, K, L, M, N, O, and P. Each wine will be tasted in succession according to the following conditions:

J must be tasted either third or seventh.

If J is tasted seventh, then N must be tasted fourth; otherwise N is not tasted fourth.

If J is tasted seventh, then L is tasted sixth.

If J is tasted third, then O is tasted sixth.

N must be the third wine tasted after K.

29. If L is tasted fourth, which wine must be tasted third?

    (A) J
    (B) K
    (C) M
    (D) N
    (E) O

30. If M is tasted immediately following L, which of the following must be true?

    (A) K is tasted first.
    (B) L is tasted second.
    (C) M is tasted third.
    (D) P is tasted fourth.
    (E) P is tasted fifth.

31. If K is tasted first, then which of the following must be true?

    (A) L is tasted sixth.
    (B) O is tasted fifth.
    (C) M is tasted fourth.
    (D) N is tasted third.
    (E) P is tasted third.

32. M CANNOT be which wine in the tasting sequence?

    (A) Second
    (B) Third
    (C) Fourth
    (D) Fifth
    (E) Sixth

33. Which of the following must be true?

    (A) J is tasted earlier than K.

    (B) J is tasted earlier than L.

    (C) K is tasted earlier than L.

    (D) K is tasted earlier than O.

    (E) M is tasted earlier than O.

34. If P is tasted earlier than N but later than O, which of the following must be true?

    (A) O is tasted first.

    (B) L is tasted third.

    (C) O is tasted third.

    (D) M is tasted fifth.

    (E) P is tasted fifth.

35. If M is the second wine tasted after P, in how many different orders can the wines be tasted?

    (A) 1

    (B) 2

    (C) 3

    (D) 4

    (E) 5

WARNING

IF YOU FINISHED THIS SECTION BEFORE TIME EXPIRED, GO IMMEDIATELY TO THE NEXT SECTION. YOU MAY NOT CONTINUE TO WORK ON THIS SECTION AFTER TIME HAS EXPIRED.

Diagnostic Examination

Answer Key

VERBAL SECTION

1. E	7. A	13. A	19. A	25. A
2. B	8. C	14. B	20. C	26. A
3. B	9. B	15. B	21. A	27. B
4. B	10. C	16. A	22. C	28. C
5. D	11. B	17. A	23. C	29. E
6. A	12. C	18. C	24. C	30. D

MATH SECTION

1. C	7. E	13. C	19. D	25. B
2. A	8. A	14. A	20. E	26. D
3. A	9. C	15. B	21. D	27. A
4. A	10. A	16. C	22. A	28. B
5. C	11. D	17. E	23. D	
6. A	12. D	18. D	24. E	

ANALYTICAL SECTION

1. D	8. C	15. C	22. D	29. A
2. E	9. C	16. E	23. E	30. E
3. B	10. B	17. D	24. E	31. A
4. E	11. B	18. B	25. C	32. E
5. B	12. A	19. E	26. B	33. D
6. A	13. B	20. D	27. D	34. D
7. E	14. C	21. E	28. A	35. A

Diagnostic Examination

Explanatory Answers

VERBAL SECTION

1. **(E)** The keys here are the parallelisms or continuations required by each blank. For the first substitution you need something that is parallel to piety, another virtue. On this ground you can eliminate both (C) and (D). Then, in the second blank you will need an adjective describing serious problems such as weather and disease, and only (E) does this.

2. **(B)** The key to this question is the parallel or continuation set up by the structure of the entire sentence. It is possible that the sentence can be completed in one of two ways. Either the review was good, in which case the adjective completing the second blank must suggest something positive, or the review was bad, and the second element must also suggest something negative. If the review labeled the production "grotesque," it must have been a negative review as suggested by answer choice (B).

3. **(B)** There are two ways of attacking this question. First, the initial substitution must make sense in terms of the situation described. It is possible to eliminate (A), (C), and (D) on this basis. For example, since the violinist is already performing, it makes no sense to say that she is rehearsing her performance. You might make an argument for "renew" in choice (E), but you can eliminate (E) on the ground that it fails to carry through the continuation indicated by the action.

4. **(B)** The part of speech of the word "trap" is ambiguous. It might be either a verb or a noun. The issue is settled, however, by consulting choice (A). There the first element is "novel," a word that cannot be a verb. So we formulate the relationship as a TRAP is used to catch GAME. So, too, a *net* is used to catch *fish*. Notice also the "echo" relationship. Both activities are very similar—hunting and fishing.

5. **(D)** The relationship is that of example to category. A MANSARD is a type of ROOF, and a *dormer* is a type of *window*. Further, there is a confirming "echo": Both are architectural features.

6. **(A)** The PASTOR is charged with the care of the CONGREGATION just as the *shepherd* is charged with the care of the *flock*. And there is the interesting and very powerful "echo" between pastor and shepherd and congregation and flock.

7. **(A)** The passage describes the attitude of premodernized society toward war as accepted, even noble, and certainly necessary. Coupled with the goals of war in premodernized societies, we can infer that leaders of premodernized society regarded war as a valid policy tool. On this ground we select (A), eliminating (B) and (C). As for (D), although this can be inferred to have been a feature of war in premodernized society, (D) does not respond to the question: What did the leaders think of war, that is, what was their attitude? (E) can be eliminated on the same ground and also because that "necessity" for war was not that described in (E).

8. **(C)** The author is discussing war, a seemingly uncivilized activity. Yet the author argues that war, at least in premodernized times, was the necessary result of certain economic and social forces. The use of the term "civilized" is ironic. Under other circumstances, the explanations offered by (A) and (B) might be plausible, but there is nothing in this text to support either of them. (D), too, might under other circumstances be a reason for placing the word in quotation marks, but it does not appear that this author is attempting to affect the reader's emotions; the passage is too detached and scientific for that. Finally, (E) does articulate one of the author's objectives, but this is not the reason for putting the one word in quotations. The explanation for that is something more specific than an overall idea of the passage.

9. **(B)** This is an explicit idea question, and (A), (C), (D), and (E) are all mentioned at various points in the passage as reasons for going to war; (B), however, is not explicitly mentioned. Indeed, the author states that control and exploitation, not annihilation and destruction, were goals.

51

10. **(C)** The part of speech of the stem word is ambiguous, but that issue is settled by choice (A), which is an adjective. Something that is *resident* lives in a particular area or, more figuratively, belongs to a particular institution in a permanent fashion. So a good opposite would be *transitory.*

11. **(B)** *Prolific* means "producing in great quantity," as a prolific writer, so a good opposite would be *barren,* which means "unable to produce at all."

12. **(C)** To *lambast* is to heap criticism upon, to scold, or to denounce severely. So a good opposite would be to *praise.*

13. **(A)** The part of speech of the stem word is ambiguous. It might be a verb or it might be a noun. The issue is settled by choice (A). Here *court* is a verb. As a verb, to court means to solicit or to try to get. So a possible opposite is to *reject.*

14. **(B)** This is a main idea question. The author first states that a large number of auto traffic fatalities can be attributed to drivers who are intoxicated and then reviews two approaches to controlling this problem, taxation and drunk driving laws. Neither is very successful. The author finally notes that therapy may be useful, though the extent of its value has not yet been proved. (B) describes this development fairly well. (A) can be eliminated since any conclusions drawn by the author from studies on drunk driving are used for the larger objective described in (B). (C) is incorrect since, aside from suggesting possible ways to reduce the extent of the problem, the author never treats the causes of drunk driving. (D) is incorrect for the same reason. Finally, (E) is incorrect, because the comparison between the U.S. and Britain is only a small part of the passage.

15. **(B)** This is an inference question. In the third paragraph, the author discusses the effect of drunk driving laws and states that after the implementation of the Road Safety Act in Britain, motor vehicle fatalities fell considerably. On this basis, we infer that the RSA was a law aimed at drunk driving. We can eliminate (D) and (E) on this ground. (C) can be eliminated as not warranted on the basis of this information. It is not clear whether the number of arrests increased. Equally consistent with the passage is the conclusion that the number of arrests dropped because people were no longer

driving while intoxicated. (C) is incorrect for a further reason, the justification for (B). (B) and (A) are fairly close since both describe the RSA as a law aimed at drunk driving. But the last sentence of the third paragraph calls for (B) over (A). As people learned that they would not get caught for drunk driving, the law became less effective. This suggests that the RSA made drunk driving illegal, not that it lowered the BAC required for conviction. This makes sense of the sentence ". . . they could drink and not be stopped." If (A) were correct, this sentence would have to read ". . . they could drink the same amount and not be convicted."

16. **(A)** This is an inference question. In the first paragraph, the author states that for a person to attain a BAC of 0.1 percent, he or she would need to drink over five ounces of 80 proof spirits over a *short period of time.* The author is trying to impress on us that that is a considerable quantity of alcohol for most people to drink. (A) explains why the author makes this comment. (B) is incorrect and confuses the first paragraph with the second paragraph. (C) is incorrect since the point of the example is that the BAC is so high most people will not exceed it. This is not to say, however, that people will not drink and drive because of laws establishing maximum BAC levels. Rather, they can continue to drink and drive because the law allows them a considerable margin in the level of BAC. (D) is a misreading of that first paragraph. Of all the very drunk drivers (BAC in excess of 0.1), only 1 percent are involved in accidents. But this does not say that most drivers involved in fatal collisions have BAC levels in excess of 0.1 percent, and that is what (D) says. As for (E), the author never states that the only way to attain a BAC of 0.1 percent is to drink five ounces of 80 proof spirits in a short time; there may be other ways of becoming intoxicated.

17. **(A)** This is an application question. In the second paragraph, the author states that increased taxation on alcohol would tax the heaviest drinkers most, but notes that this would also penalize the moderate and light drinker. In other words, the remedy is not sufficiently focused on the problem. Then, in the third paragraph, the author notes that drunk driving laws are aimed at the specific problem drivers. We can infer from this discussion that the author would

likely advocate drunk driving laws over taxation for the reasons just given. This reasoning is presented in answer (A). (B) is incorrect for the reasons just given and for the further reason that the passage never suggests that taxation is likely to be more effective in solving the problem. The author never really evaluates the effectiveness of taxation in reducing drunk driving. (C) is incorrect for the reason given in support of (A) and for the further reason that the author never raises the issue of personal liberty in conjunction with the BAC test. (D) can be eliminated because the author does not discount the effectiveness of anti-drunk driving measures entirely. Even the British example gives some support to the conclusion that such laws have an effect. (E) is incorrect, for the author never mentions the expense or administrative feasibility of BAC tests.

18. **(C)** This is a question about the logical structure of the passage. In paragraph 3, the author notes that stricter enforcement of laws against drunk driving may result in a few more arrests; but a few more arrests is not likely to have much impact on the problem because the number of arrests is small compared to those who do not get caught. As a consequence, people will continue to drink and drive. The author supports this with the British experience. Once people realize that the chances of being caught are relatively small, they will drink and drive. This is the conclusion of answer (C). (A) is incorrect since the passage does not support the conclusion that the problem is any worse or any better in one country or the other. (B) is incorrect since this is the conclusion the author is arguing against. (D) is wrong because the author is not discussing the effectiveness of taxation in paragraph 3. (E) is a statement the author would likely accept, but that is not the reason for introducing the British example. So answer (E) is true but nonresponsive.

19. **(A)** This is an application question that asks us to examine the logical structure of the argument. In the fourth paragraph, the author argues that the effectiveness of deterrents to drunk driving will depend upon the ability of the drinker to control consumption. But drunk driving has two aspects: being drunk and driving. The author assumes that drunk driving is a function of drinking only. Other-wise, the author would not suggest that control on consumption is necessary as opposed to *helpful*. (A) attacks this assumption by pointing out that it is possible to drink to excess without driving. It is possible that stiff penalties could be effective deterrents to drunk driving if not to drinking to excess. (B) is incorrect because the author makes this point, so this choice does not weaken the argument. (C) is incorrect since the author is concerned only with the problem of fatalities caused by drunk driving. (D) can be eliminated since the author is concerned with eliminating fatalities caused by drunk driving, not with whether the drunk driver ought to be punished. (E) is not a strong attack on the argument since the author does leave open the question of the value of therapy in combating drunk driving.

20. **(C)** The relationship is that of example to general type. An ODE is a kind of POEM, and a *ballad* is a kind of *song*. And again there is an "echo," for there is a kinship between poem and song.

21. **(A)** The relationship here is one of opposition. Someone who displays TENACITY is not WEAK, just as one who displays *apathy* is not *caring*.

22. **(C)** The CURATOR is in charge of caring for PAINTINGS, and the *archivist* has the same relationship to *manuscripts*. And there is an "echo" of kinship between the curator and the archivist and between paintings and manuscripts.

23. **(C)** CREPESCULE means TWILIGHT, so the stem words are synonyms, just as dawn and daybreak are synonyms. And you will notice the "echo" between twilight and daybreak.

24. **(C)** There are two points of attack here. First, you need a word to parallel the idea of a charged atmosphere. What happened to the law? It was infected with religious overtones. Second, you need a parallel to this. As a consequence, what did the law do to the required separation of state and church? It violated it—and this was the reason the law was struck down.

25. **(A)** You should almost be able to complete the sentence even without looking at the choices. Since there is a perceived correlation between price and value, you would expect that sellers would raise prices. This suggests either (A) or (B) as the correct choice. (B), however, fails to carry through the

parallel. Given the correlation, the price increase would not be moderate but very great.

26. **(A)** Parallelism or continuation is the key here. Notice that we must use adjectives with positive overtones—the audience gave the performance a standing ovation. So we can eliminate (C) on the basis of the first element. And we eliminate (B) and (E) on the basis of the second substitution. (A) is the only choice to carry through the positive notion.

27. **(B)** To *forge* has the literal meaning of shaping metal. The more figurative meaning is to create or to shape anything. For example, to forge a union means to create that unity. So a good opposite would be to "un-create" or *dissolve*.

28. **(C)** *Motile* means "having the power of motion or able to move," so a good opposite is *immobile*.

29. **(E)** *Lachrymose* means "tearful" or "sad," so a good opposite is found in (E), *joyful*.

30. **(D)** *Quiescence* refers to a state of quiet or rest. A good opposite would be one referring to a state of motion, even violent motion, such as *frenzy*.

MATH SECTION

1. **(C)** With a problem that indicates a very simple manipulation, as this one does, the easiest way to arrive at a comparison is often just to do the operation. In this case, Column A is $5 - 1 = 4$, and Column B is $5 - 1 = 4$.

2. **(A)** A question like this just tests your understanding of the centered statement. If x is 4 more than y, then x must be larger than y. So Column A is larger than Column B.

3. **(A)** Contrast this question with question 1. Notice that the manipulation here would be more difficult, for to find the percent increase you would create a fraction with the change as the numerator and the original amount as the denominator:

$$\frac{\text{change}}{\text{original amount}} = \frac{\$1.00}{\$7.95}$$

But converting this fraction to a decimal and then to a percent is tiresome. Instead of actually performing the calculation, you should look for an alternative way of making the comparison. In this case, you are asked to compare $\frac{1}{7.95}$ to 12%. $\frac{1}{7.95}$ is very close to $\frac{1}{8}$ (slightly more, since 7.95 is less than 8, and the smaller the denominator the larger the value of the fraction). And $\frac{1}{8}$ is exactly $12\frac{1}{2}$%. So $\frac{1}{7.95}$ must be more than $12\frac{1}{2}$%, and that is enough to justify the conclusion that Column A is larger than Column B.

4. **(A)** Since $M + 2$ is the average of x and y, $\frac{(x+y)}{2} = M + 2$. This means that Column A could be rewritten as $M + 2$. Since Column B is M and Column A is 2 larger than M, Column A must be larger.

5. **(C)** With a question of this type, a good strategy is to do the indicated algebraic manipulation. If we do the multiplication indicated in Column A, we have $(x + y)(x - y) = x^2 + xy - xy - y^2 = x^2 - y^2$. The two expressions are equivalent, so the two columns are equal.

6. **(A)** One way of attacking a question like this with easily performed operations is to do the arithmetic: $5^2 = 25$, $12^2 = 144$, and $25 + 144 = 169$. Then look for an equivalent answer choice: $13^2 = 169$. Alternatively, you might have remembered that one set of "magic" Pythagorean numbers is 5, 12, 13, that is, a triangle with sides of 5, 12, 13 is a right triangle, so $5^2 + 12^2 = 13^2$.

7. **(E)** This is essentially a bookkeeping problem, and all you need to do is multiply the numbers to find the total value of sales: 50 weeks × 100 sales per week = 5,000 sales; 5,000 sales × $1,000 per sale = $5,000,000.

8. **(A)** Given the diameter of a circle, we know the radius, since the radius is just half the diameter:

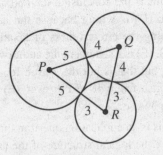

So the perimeter of the triangle formed by the radii of the circles is 24.

9. **(C)** With a question of this type, the best approach is to substitute the values provided into the expression:

$$\frac{x^2 - xy}{y} = \frac{1^2 - (1)(-2)}{-2} = \frac{1 - (-2)}{-2} = \frac{3}{-2}$$

10. **(A)** Here we suggest that you manipulate the inequality until you have a single x on one side:

$$5x - 2 < 3x - 1$$

Subtract $3x$ from both sides: $\quad 2x - 2 < -1$

Add 2 to both sides: $\qquad\qquad\quad 2x < 1$

Divide both sides by 2: $\qquad\qquad x < \frac{1}{2}$

So x is less than $\frac{1}{2}$, which means that 1 is not a possible value of x.

11. **(D)** Remember that figures in this section are not necessarily drawn to scale. Because of that, we cannot make a comparison based upon measuring. Moreover, since the size of the unlabeled angles is unknown, we cannot deduce any conclusion about the size of angles x and y.

12. **(D)** Remember that "percent" means "per 100," and it is just a convenient ratio to work with. But because it is only a ratio, percent itself gives you no information about the actual numbers involved. Although City Y experienced a greater *percentage* decrease than City X, we cannot reach any conclusion about the actual number of persons involved.

13. **(C)** A square has four equal sides, so its perimeter is just 4 times the length of one side. Conversely, the perimeter divided by 4 gives you the length of each side. In this case, the perimeter is $12\sqrt{3}$, so the length of each of the four sides is $12\sqrt{3} \div 4 = 3\sqrt{3}$.

14. **(A)** Here is another question with a difficult manipulation, so we look for another way to make the comparison. Here it is possible to factor out $\frac{3}{7}$ from both terms of the left-hand expression, yielding $\frac{3}{7}\left(\frac{101}{104} + \frac{4}{104}\right)$ which is equal to $\left(\frac{3}{7}\right)\left(\frac{105}{104}\right)$. At this point a comparison is possible. Since $\frac{105}{104}$ is larger than 1, $\frac{3}{7} \times \frac{105}{104}$ must be slightly larger than $\frac{3}{7}$, so Column A must be larger than Column B.

15. **(B)** Since no drawing is provided, you might find it easiest to reach a comparison by sketching the coordinate system:

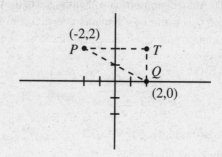

You could now find the distance from P to Q by using the Pythagorean Theorem: $PT^2 + TQ^2 = PQ^2$. There is no need to work out the actual length, however, because you can make your comparison with an approximation. Notice that the length of PT is 4. This means that PQ, which is the hypotenuse of the right triangle, is longer than 4, so Column B must be larger.

16. **(C)** To answer this question, you might try substituting values for x and y, or you might just think generally about the properties of the numbers they describe. As for (A), if x is even, then x^2, which is x times x, must also be even; but since y is an odd number, the entire expression is odd. As for (B), x^2 is even, and since y, an odd number, is subtracted from x, the result must also be an odd number. As for (D) and (E), an even number plus (or minus) an odd number is odd. (C) is the correct choice, for x^2 is even, and an even number multiplied by an odd number generates an even result.

17. **(E)** Here we might manipulate the equation that is given. Since $p = \frac{1}{3}q$, you can set up a direct proportion:

$$\frac{p}{q} = \frac{1}{3}$$

$$\left(\frac{1}{3}\right)\frac{p}{q} = \frac{1}{3}\left(\frac{1}{3}\right)$$

$$\frac{p}{3q} = \frac{1}{9}$$

18. **(D)** A direct proportion will easily solve the problem. Since the cost remains constant, the more chemical purchased the greater the cost, and vice versa:

$$\frac{\$50}{30} = \frac{\$625}{x}$$

Cross-multiply: $50x = 18,750$

Divide by 50: $x = 375$

19. **(D)** The best way to the solution here might be just to try various combinations. For example, for 17 you might try $4 + 5 + 6$, which is 15, and then $5 + 6 + 7$, which is 18. So there is no set of three consecutive integers that will do the trick. When you get to (D), you will find that $9 + 10 + 11 = 30$.

For the mathematically inclined, you can express the sum of three consecutive integers as follows: Let x be the first of the three integers; the second integer is one more, or $x + 1$; and the third is one more than that, or $x + 2$. So the sum of any three consecutive integers is $x + x + 1 + x + 2 = 3x + 3$. For a number to be the sum of three consecutive integers, it must be 3 more than some other number that is divisible by 3. Or, in different words, for a number to be the sum of three consecutive integers, if you subtract 3 from it, what is left will be divisible by 3. Of the available choices, only the number 30 fits this description.

20. **(E)** The information given can be rendered in equation form. Let x, y, and z represent the three sides, x being the shortest and z being the longest. Given the information about the area of the faces: $xy = 6$, $xz = 8$, and $yz = 12$. Now treat these as simultaneous equations. Since $xy = 6$, $x = \frac{6}{y}$. Substitute this value for x in the second equation, and you have $z\left(\frac{6}{y}\right) = 8$, so $z = 8\left(\frac{6}{y}\right) = \left(\frac{4y}{3}\right)$. Now put this value for z in the third equation: $y\left(\frac{4y}{3}\right)$, so $4y^2 = 36$, $y^2 = 9$, and $y = +3$ or -3. Since we are dealing with distances, y cannot be negative, so $y = +3$. From here on in, the solution is easy. If $y = 3$, then $x = 2$; and if $x = 2$, then $z = 4$. So the three sides are 2, 3, and 4, and the volume of the solid is $2 \times 3 \times 4 = 24$.

21. **(D)** The pie chart shows the distribution of motor vehicles in City X according to their manufacturer: 40% were manufactured by Q. Since the total number of motor vehicles registered is 8,400, the number registered that were manufactured by Q is 40% of $8,400 = 3,360$.

22. **(A)** This question is based on the information for City Y, which is given in the bar graph. Consulting that portion of the chart, we find that there were 1,600 motor vehicles registered in City Y manufactured by R and 1,200 manufactured by P: $1,600 - 1,200 = 400$. So there were 400 more vehicles manufactured by R registered in City Y.

23. **(D)** Notice that this question specifically asks for an approximation. If you look at the small table that summarizes the information for City X and manufacturers T, U, and V, you will see that each of those manufacturers accounted for approximately the same number of registrations. The three together accounted for 8% of all City X registrations, as shown in the pie chart. This means that Manufacturer V accounted for about $\frac{1}{3}$ of the 8%, or about 3%, so (D) is the best approximation.

24. **(E)** To answer this question, you will first need the total number of registrations in City Y. Adding the various values we have $1,200 + 2,400 + 1,600 + 800 + 400 = 6,400$, of which 1,600 were from Manufacturer R. And $\frac{1,600}{6,400} = \frac{1}{4} = 25\%$.

25. **(B)** One way to make the comparison is to find the largest common factor for each of the pairs. 18 and 24 have a common factor of 6: $6 \times 3 = 18$ and $6 \times 4 = 24$. Since the smallest number evenly divisible by both 3 and 4 is $3 \times 4 = 12$, the smallest number divisible by 18 and 24 is $6 \times 12 = 72$. On the other side, 18 and 28 have a common factor of 2: $2 \times 9 = 18$ and $2 \times 14 = 28$, the smallest number divisible by both 9 and 14 is $9 \times 14 = 126$, so the smallest number evenly divisible by both 18 and 28 is $2 \times 126 = 252$. Thus, Column B is larger. Alternatively, you might have realized that since 18 is not a factor of either 24 or 28, it's "easier" to find a number divisible by 18 and 24 than by 18 and 28. By easier we mean that if you kept trying number after number, you would get to the one divisible by 18 and 24 before you got to the one divisible by 18 and 28.

26. **(D)** Remember that figures are not necessarily drawn to scale. You cannot conclude, without further information, that the two lines in the figure are parallel to each other. Without that information, you should not attempt to arrive at any conclusion regarding the relative sizes of x and y.

27. **(A)** This question defines a certain operation "*". All you need to do is substitute the numbers provided in the two columns into the definition. Since $P * Q = P + Q - PQ$, to find $4 * 1$, you substitute 4 for P and 1 for Q: $4 + 1 - (4)(1) = 1$. To find $4 * 2$, substitute 4 for P and 2 for Q: $4 + 2 - (4)(2) = -2$. You can see that Column A is larger.

28. **(B)** You might find it useful to perform the algebraic operations indicated: $(3j)(3k)(3m) = 9jkm$ and $3(j)(k)(m) = 3jkm$. But that alone does not answer the question. You need to consider the centered information. Notice that j and k are positive while m is negative. This means that both columns are negative numbers (positive × positive × negative yields a negative number). Consequently, Column A is even smaller than Column B since it is 9 times that negative number rather than 3 times that negative number.

ANALYTICAL SECTION

Questions 1–6

Arranging the Information

This is a fairly simple "connective" set. A "connective" set is a problem set in which one event is somehow connected with another event, e.g., X causes Y, or Y leads to Z. The connection can be expressed by an arrow. We begin with the first condition:

$$G \longleftrightarrow H$$

Adding the second condition:

$$G \longleftrightarrow H \longrightarrow I$$

And the third:

$$G \longleftrightarrow H \longrightarrow I \longrightarrow J$$

And the fourth:

$$G \longleftrightarrow H \longrightarrow I \longrightarrow J \longrightarrow K$$

And the fifth:

$$L \longrightarrow G \longleftrightarrow H \longrightarrow I \longrightarrow J \longrightarrow K$$

And the sixth:

$$L \longrightarrow G \longleftrightarrow H \longrightarrow I \longrightarrow J \rightleftarrows K$$

Of course, there is no necessity that the stations be oriented exactly this way on the page, so long as the relative connections are specified. An equivalent diagram is:

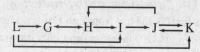

Once the diagram is drawn, answering the questions is merely a matter of using the picture.

Answering the Questions

1. **(D)** The diagram shows that it is possible to get from H to J only via I. (A) is incorrect since the direct connection between J and H runs only from J to H, not vice versa. As for (B), while it is possible to get from H to G, there is no connecting train between G and J. (C) is incorrect because there is no train from H to L. Finally, (E) is incorrect for there is a route from H to J, via I.

2. **(E)** Notice that there are no arrows in the diagram that point toward L. This means that it is possible only to leave L. It is not possible to arrive at L. As for (A), one can arrive at G from L or H. (B) is incorrect since one can arrive at H from either G or J. (C) is incorrect since there is a connection between H and I and between L and I. Finally, (D) is incorrect since K can be reached from either L or J.

3. **(B)** Consulting the diagram, we see that I can be reached from either H or L. H, however, can be reached from either G or J. Thus, one can go from G and J via H and reach I with only one transfer.

4. **(E)** All six stations can be visited, without revisiting any station, if we begin at L. The trip then proceeds: L to G to H to I to J to K.

5. **(B)** To get to K from H, we must go via I and J, and that is a total of two transfers. As for (A), the trip from G to I is accomplished by transferring only at H. As for (C), the trip from L to H is accomplished by going via G, again requiring only one transfer. As for (D), though the trip from L to I would require two transfers if the L-G-H-I route is selected, note that the trip can be made directly from L to I without any transfers. (E) is incorrect because a direct route is available from L to K.

6. **(A)** If I is closed, the only transfer point from H to J is closed, and that means that it is not possible to get from G to J. (B) is incorrect since there is a direct link between J and K. (C) is incorrect since there is a direct link between L and K. (D) is incorrect since the L to K to J route remains unimpaired. (E) is incorrect since there is a direct link from L to G.

7. **(E)** The sample argument is a straightforward generalization: All observed S are P. X is an S. Therefore, X is P. Only (E) replicates this form. The reasoning in (A) is: "Some S are P. All M are S." (All swans are birds, which is a suppressed assumption.) Therefore, all M are P. That is like saying: "Some children are not well behaved. All little girls are children. Therefore, all little girls are not well behaved." (B), too, contains a suppressed premise. Its structure is: "All S are P. All S are M. (All ballets are theatrical productions, which is suppressed.) Therefore, all M are P." That is like saying "All little girls are children. All little girls are human. Therefore, all humans are little girls." (C) is not a generalization at all. It takes a generalization and attempts to explain it by uncovering a causal linkage. (D) is simply a non sequitur. It moves from the universality of the concept of justice to the conclusion that justice is a physical trait of man.

8. **(C)** The dispute here is over the motivation to compete seriously in intramural sports. Erika claims it is a sense of responsibility to one's fellows; Nichol argues it is a desire to win. But the two may actually support one another. In what way could one possibly let one's fellow players down? If the sport was not competitive, it would seem there would be no opportunity to disappoint them. So the desire to win contributes to the desire to be an effective member of the team. Nothing in the exchange presupposes anything about the structure of such programs beyond the fact that they are competitive, that is, that they have winners and losers. How many such programs exist, how they are funded, and similar questions are irrelevant, so both (A) and (B) are incorrect. (D) is close to being correct, but it calls for a survey of deans. The dean is probably not in a position to describe the motivation of the participants. Had (D) specified participants, it too would have been a correct answer. Of course, only one answer can be correct on the GRE. Finally, (E) must be wrong for the reason cited in explaining (D); it should be possible to find out about the motivation.

9. **(C)** To break the code, the cryptographer needs information about the language the code conceals. (A), (B), (D), and (E) all provide such information. (C), however, says nothing about the underlying language. The code could even use all even or all odd numbers for the symbol substitutions without affecting the information to be encoded.

10. **(B)** The question is one that tests the validity or strength of a causal inference. Often such arguments can be attacked by finding intervening causal linkages, that is, variables that might interfere with the predicted result. (A) cites such a variable. If the traffic problem is created by commercial traffic that will not be reduced by toll increases, then the proposed increases will not solve the problem. (C), too, is such a variable. It suggests that the proposal is essentially self-defeating. (D) undermines the claim by arguing that the deterrent effect of a price increase is simply not significant, so the proposal will have little, if any, effect. (E) attacks the argument on a different ground. The ultimate objective of the plan is to reduce commuting time. Even assuming a drop in auto traffic because some commuters use public transportation, no advantage is gained if the public transportation system cannot handle the increase in traffic. (B), however, does very little to the argument. In fact, it could be argued that (B) is one of the predicted results of the plan: a drop in the number of autos because commuters begin to carpool.

Questions 11–16

Arranging the Information

This is a "selection" set; that is, we must select cities for the tours according to the restrictions set forth in the problem set. There are many different ways of summarizing the information, and we each have our own idiosyncratic system of notational devices. There are, however, some fairly standard symbols used by logicians, and we will employ them here. We summarize the information in the following way:

1. $M \rightarrow (Q \& R)$
2. $P \rightarrow O$
3. $Q \rightarrow (M \& N) \vee (M \& T) \vee (M \& N \& T)$
4. $P \neq Q$
5. $\sim (O \& R \& T)$
6. $\sim (N \& S \& R)$
7. $L \neq R$

Some clarifying remarks about this system are in order. We are using the capital-letter designation of each city to make the statement that the city will be included on the tour, e.g., "M" means "M will be included on the tour." The $\rightarrow$ stands for "if . . . , then . . ."; the "&" stands for "and"; the "v" stands for "or"; the "~" stands for "not." We use parentheses as punctuation devices to avoid possible confusion. So the first condition is to be read, "If M, then both Q and R," that is, "If M is included on the trip, then both Q and R must be included on the trip." Notice that the parentheses were necessary, for the statement

$$M \rightarrow Q \& R$$

might be misinterpreted to mean "If M is included on the tour, then Q must also be included. In addition, R must be included on the trip." That would be punctuated with parentheses as:

$$(M \rightarrow Q) \& R$$

As for the second condition, we note simply that if P is included, O must also be included.

As for the third condition, some students will find it easier to write this condition out rather than to use the notational system. That is fine.

Statement 3 is to be read, "If Q, then M and N, or M and T, or all three," which is, of course, equivalent to the statement included in the initial conditions of the problem.

The fourth condition is similar to the second in that we use a nonstandard symbol, "$\neq$". The same information could be written as:
$\sim (P \& Q)$ or $P \rightarrow \sim Q$. This last notation is equivalent to $Q \rightarrow \sim P$, for logically $P \rightarrow \sim Q$ is the same as $Q \rightarrow \sim P$.

The fifth and sixth conditions are to be read, respectively, "It is not the case that O and R and T are included" and "It is not the case that N and S and R are included." And finally, condition seven is summarized using the "$\neq$", which we have already discussed.

We now have the information ready for easy reference, and we turn to the individual questions.

Answering the Questions

11. **(B)** If M is included on the trip, we know that we must also include Q and R. And if Q is included on the trip, we must include N or T (or both, but we are looking for the *minimum* number of other cities). No other cities need be included. So, including M requires both Q and R plus one of the pair N and T. So a total of three *additional* cities are needed.

12. **(A)** By condition 4, Q cannot be included with P. Unfortunately, that is not an available answer choice, so we will have to dig a little deeper. If Q cannot be included on the tour, then we conclude that M cannot be included, for condition 1 requires that Q be included on any tour on which M is a stop.

13. **(B)** This question requires only that we check each of the choices against the summary of conditions. (A) is not acceptable because we have M without Q. (C) is not acceptable because we have M without R. (D) is not acceptable because we have L with R (in violation of condition 7) and because we have Q without either N or T. (E) is not acceptable because we have N, S, and R together, in violation of condition 6. The group in (B), however, meets all of the requirements for an acceptable tour.

14. **(C)** By deleting O, we have the tour M, Q, R, and T. This satisfies condition 1, since Q and R are included with M. And this satisfies condition 3 since we have M and T. No other condition is violated, so the group M, Q, R, T is acceptable. (A) is incorrect, for eliminating M leaves Q in the group (without M), in violation of condition 3. Similarly, eliminating Q leaves M on the tour without Q,

violating condition 1. (D) is incorrect because it also violates condition 1. (E) is incorrect for this would leave Q on the tour without the (M & N) or (M & T) combination required by condition 3.

15. **(C)** To make the group M, Q, R into an acceptable tour, we need only to add N or T. This will finally satisfy both conditions 1 and 3 without violating any other requirement. (A) is incorrect, for adding another city will not remedy the violation of condition 7 (L ≠ R). (B) is incorrect, because satisfying the conditions requires the addition of O (condition 2), R (condition 1), and either N or T (condition 3). (D) is incorrect since the addition of another city will not correct the violation of condition 6. Finally, (E) is incorrect because the addition of O to satisfy condition 2 would then violate condition 5 (O, R, and T on the same tour).

16. **(E)** Here we must test each lettered city. M cannot constitute a tour in and of itself, for condition 1 requires that Q and R be included on any tour that includes M. P, by condition 2, cannot constitute a tour of a single city. Finally, by condition 3, Q's inclusion requires more cities. The remaining cities, L, N, O, R, S and T, however, can be used as single-city tours.

Questions 17–22

Arranging the Information

This set is a linear ordering set. At first glance, the set appears to be very complex, involving as it does the positioning of 11 items. But a closer examination shows the questions are not that difficult, since the particular restrictions considerably simplify the problem. For example, we know that a red bead is on one end, and we also know that all three red beads are together. So there are only two possible arrangements for the red beads:

```
1   2   3   4   5   6   7   8   9   10  11

    R   R   R

                    or

                            R   R   R
```

In fact, each additional condition on the placement of the beads tends to simplify matters for us because it eliminates possible arrangements.

With a linear ordering set, we begin by summarizing the information:

Color	Number	
Blue	2	B = B
Red	3	G ≠ G
Green	2	R = R = R
Yellow	4	G or R = ends
	11	

We have made a note of the number of beads of each color and we have summarized the particular conditions: Blue is next to blue (B = B); green is not next to green (G ≠ G); red is always next to red (R = R = R); the ends are red or green (G or R = ends).

Answering the Questions

17. **(D)** From the given information and our own deductions based on the restrictions that all red beads be together and that one end be red and the other green, we set up the following diagram:

```
1  2  3  4  5  6  7  8  9  10  11
                  B  B        R
G                 B  B     R  R  R
```

This leaves the four yellow beads and the one remaining green bead to be positioned. The only restriction on the placement of these five beads is that the green bead may not be next to the other green bead; that is, the remaining green bead cannot be in position 2. This eliminates (C), since the green bead might be in position 8, though it could also be in positions 3, 4, and 5. This also eliminates (B), since position 5 might be filled by a green bead. (A) is clearly incorrect since that is the one remaining position that cannot be occupied by the other green bead. (E) is incorrect since the green bead could be placed in position 3 or 4, separated from the blue beads by one or more yellow beads. We do know, however, that at least one green bead, the one in position 1, will be next to a yellow bead, for a yellow bead is needed to separate the green beads. Of course, the other green bead may also be next to a yellow bead, but that is not necessary. In any event, the fact that the green bead must be separated from the other green bead is sufficient to show the correctness of (D).

18. **(B)** The question stem stipulates

Y = Y = Y = Y

```
1  2  3  4  5  6  7  8  9  10 11
                              Y
```

Since the last position cannot be yellow, we can deduce

```
1  2  3  4  5  6  7  8  9  10 11
                  Y  Y  Y     Y  G
```

Since the three red beads are together and one of them must be on the end of the string, and since the two blue beads must be together, we know that only two different arrangements are possible:

```
    1  2  3  4  5  6  7  8  9  10 11
    R  R  R  G  B  B  Y  Y  Y  Y  G
or: R  R  R  B  B  G  Y  Y  Y  Y  G
```

Under either arrangement, the fifth bead must be blue.

19. **(E)** The question stem stipulates that each blue bead be next to a green bead. Because the blue beads are next to each other, this means the blue and green beads are arranged as a block: GBBG. According to the stipulation in the question stem, the four yellow beads are also arranged as a block: YYYY. And we know from the initial presentation of restrictions that the three red beads are a block: RRR. The only open question is which end of the string is green and which is red. So there are only two possible arrangements:

```
    1  2  3  4  5  6  7  8  9 10 11
    G  B  B  G  Y  Y  Y  Y  R  R  R
or: R  R  R  Y  Y  Y  Y  G  B  B  G
```

Under either arrangement, positions 5, 6, and 7 are occupied by yellow beads.

20. **(D)** The question stem stipulates

```
1  2  3  4  5  6  7  8  9  10 11
      B  B        R
```

and, given the restriction on the reds and the further restriction on the end beads, we can deduce

```
1  2  3  4  5  6  7  8  9  10 11
G        B  B        R  R  R
```

The only restriction which remains to be observed is the separation of the green beads. This means that the remaining green bead may be next to a yellow or a blue bead, but not next to a green bead. What is established, therefore, is that position 2 must be yellow, not green.

21. **(E)** The question stem stipulates

```
1  2  3  4  5  6  7  8  9  10 11
      Y        Y  Y  Y
```

and we deduce

```
1  2  3  4  5  6  7  8  9  10 11
R  R  R  Y        Y  Y  Y     G
```

on the basis of the restrictions regarding the placement of the red beads and the colors of the end beads. Further, there is only one open pair left for the blue beads, 6 and 7, which means bead 4 will be green:

```
1  2  3  4  5  6  7  8  9  10 11
R  R  R  G  Y  B  B  Y  Y  Y     G
```

22. **(D)** Since we do not know on which end to place the red beads (nor the green bead), we have the possibility

```
1  2  3  4  5  6  7  8  9  10 11
R  R  R  G              B     G
```

and its mirror image

```
1  2  3  4  5  6  7  8  9  10 11
G  B              G  R  R     R
```

We know also that the two blue beads are together, and this means the yellow beads must form a block:

```
    1  2  3  4  5  6  7  8  9  10 11
    R  R  R  G  Y  Y  Y  Y  B  B  G
or: G  B  B  Y  Y  Y  Y  G  R  R  R
```

In either case, the seventh bead must be yellow.

23. **(E)** The argument assumes that a right cannot exist unless it is recognized by the positive law of a society. Against this assumption, it can be argued that a right may exist even though there is no mechanism for protecting or enforcing it. That this is at least plausible has been illustrated by our own history, e.g., minority groups have often been denied rights. These rights, however, existed all the while—they were just not protected by the government. (A) is incorrect, for the proponent of the theory of natural rights cannot deny that some human beings do not have them. That would contradict the very definition of natural right on which the claim is based. (B) is incorrect because it is not responsive to the argument. Even if (B) is true, the attacker of natural rights still has the argument that there are no universally recognized rights, so there are no universal (natural) rights at all. (C), like (A), is inconsistent with the very idea of a "natural" right. (D) is incorrect because it does not respond to the attacker's claim that no one right is protected universally. Consistency or universality within one society does not amount to consistency or universality across all societies.

24. **(E)** The author is arguing that political parties in America are weak because there is no party unity. Because of this lack of unity, the party is unable to pass legislation. (E) would strengthen this contention. (E) provides an example of a government dominated by a single party (control of the presidency and both houses), yet the party is unable to pass its own legislation. (A) provides little, if any, support for the argument. If there are only 18 defectors out of a total of 67 party members, that does not show tremendous fragmentation. (B) is even weaker by the same analysis: 70 defectors out of a total of 305 party members. (C) is weak because it focuses on the minority party. (D) strengthens the argument less clearly than (E) because there are many possible explanations for the failure, e.g., a different party controlled the legislature.

25. **(C)** Here we are looking for the argument that will undermine the position taken by the paragraph. Remember that the ultimate conclusion of the paragraph is that this disunity is a weakness and that this prevents legislation from being passed. One very good way of attacking this argument is to attack the

value judgment upon which the conclusion is based: Is it good to pass the legislation? The author assumes that it would be better to pass the legislation. We could argue, as in (C), that members of the Congress should not pass legislation simply because it is proposed by the party leadership. Rather, the members should represent the views of their constituents. Then, if the legislation fails, it must be the people who did not want it. In that case, it is better not to pass the legislation. (A) does not undermine the argument. That members receive funding proves nothing about unity after elections. As for (B), this seems to strengthen rather than weaken the argument. The author's thesis argues that there is greater unity in the Senate than in the House. (D) would undermine the argument only if we had some additional information to make it relevant. Finally, (E) does not weaken the argument greatly. That some legislation is passed is not a denial of the argument that more should be passed.

26. **(B)** Notice that there is much common ground between the jockey and the veterinarian. The question stem asks you to uncover the areas on which they are in agreement by asking which of the answer choices is NOT a shared assumption. Note that the exception can be an area neither has as well as an area only one has. Examine the dialogue. Both apparently assume that human emotions can be attributed to animals since they talk about them being loyal and brave (C), and both take those characteristics as being noble, that is, admirable (A). Neither speaker offers scientific evidence but rests content with an anecdote (E) and (D). As for (B), it would seem that some kind of study of animal behavior might resolve the issue. We could find out how horses and dogs would react in emergency circumstances—do they show concern for human beings, or do they watch out for themselves? Importantly, it may be wrong to attribute such emotions to animals, but whatever behavior is taken by the speakers to be evidence of those emotions can be tested. So their claims—animals behave in such a way—are, in principle, testable.

27. **(D)** Note the question stem very carefully: We are to find the answer choice *from which* we can deduce the sample argument. You must pay very

careful attention to the question stem in every problem. (D) works very nicely as it gives us the argument structure: "All post-1974 students are required . . . George is a post-1974 student. Therefore, George is required . . . " Actually, the middle premise is phrased in the conditional (with an "if"), but our explanation is close enough, even if it is a bit oversimplified. (A) will not suffice, for while it describes the situation before 1974, it just does not address itself to the post-1974 situation. And George is a post-1974 student. (B) also fails. We cannot conclude from the fact that all of those who took the course graduated after 1974 that George was one of them (any more than we can conclude from the proposition that all airline flight attendants lived after 1900 and that Richard Nixon, who lived after 1900, was therefore one of them). (C) fails for the same reason that (A) fails. (E) is a bit tricky because of the double negative. It makes the sentence awkward. The easiest way to handle such a sentence is to treat the double negative as an affirmative. The negative cancels the negative, just as in arithmetic a negative number times a negative number yields a positive number. So (E) actually says that before 1974 the course was not required. That is equivalent to (A) and must be wrong for the same reason.

28. **(A)** The author reasons from the premise: "there are bottles of this product in the apartments," to the conclusion: "therefore, these people believe the product is effective." The ad obviously wants the hearer to infer that the residents of the apartments decided to purchase the product because they believed it to be effective. (A) directly attacks this linkage. If it were true that the company gave away bottles of the product, this would sever that link. (B) does weaken the ad, but only marginally. To be sure, we might say to ourselves. "Well, a person who touts a product and does not use it himself is not fully to be trusted." But (B) does not aim at the very structure of the argument as does (A). (C) can hardly weaken the argument since it appears to be a premise on which the argument itself is built. (C) therefore actually strengthens the appeal of the advertisement. It also does not link to Painaway's effectiveness. (D) seems to be irrelevant to the appeal of the ad. The ad is designed to change the hearer's mind, so the fact that the hearer does not now accept the conclusion of the ad is not an

argument against the ability of the ad to accomplish its stated objective. Finally, (E) is irrelevant to the purpose of the ad for reasons very similar to those cited for (D).

Questions 29–35

Arranging the Information

This set is an ordering set with a twist: There are two main orders, depending on whether J is tasted third or seventh. We begin then with the following:

$$1 \quad 2 \quad 3 \quad 4 \quad 5 \quad 6 \quad 7$$
$$J$$

or:
$$\qquad\qquad\qquad\qquad\qquad\qquad J$$

Then we enter the second condition:

$$1 \quad 2 \quad 3 \quad 4 \quad 5 \quad 6 \quad 7$$
$$J \quad (\sim N)$$

or:
$$\qquad\qquad N \qquad\qquad\qquad J$$

Then comes the third condition:

$$1 \quad 2 \quad 3 \quad 4 \quad 5 \quad 6 \quad 7$$
$$J \quad (\sim N)$$

or:
$$\qquad\qquad N \quad L \quad J$$

And the fourth condition:

$$1 \quad 2 \quad 3 \quad 4 \quad 5 \quad 6 \quad 7$$
$$J \quad (\sim N)$$
$$\qquad\qquad\qquad\qquad O$$

or:
$$\qquad\qquad N \quad L \quad J$$

and finally:

$$1 \quad 2 \quad 3 \quad 4 \quad 5 \quad 6 \quad 7$$
$$(\sim K) \qquad J(\sim N) \quad O$$

or:
$$K \qquad N \quad L \quad J$$

Answering the Questions

29. **(A)** L can be tasted fourth only if we use the upper order. In that case, it will be J that is tasted third.

30. **(E)** For M to follow L, we cannot use the lower arrangement, for there L is already scheduled as the sixth wine followed immediately by J. We must therefore use the upper arrangement. The key to the solution is to see that there is a further conclusion to be drawn about the scheduling of K and N. Our original diagram shows positions 1 and 4, 2 and 5,

and 4 and 7 as open and available for the K ? ? ? N schedule. A closer look shows that we can eliminate the 1–4 arrangement, because N cannot be the fourth wine tasted in that sequence. So K and N are either 2 and 5, or 4 and 7, respectively. If, however, M must be tasted immediately following the tasting of L, then K cannot be in position 2. Only if K and N are in positions 4 and 7 can we put L and M together in sequence. So the entire sequence is:

1	2	3	4	5	6	7
L	M	J	K	P	O	N

The only position left for P is fifth, and (E) is necessarily true. The other choices are necessarily false.

31. **(A)** See the overview above.

32. **(E)** M is under no particular restriction with regard to another wine, so M can be inserted in any open position. Positions 1, 2, and 4 are open under the first order. Positions 2, 3, and 5 are open under the second order. So depending on when J is tasted, M could be tasted second, third, fourth, or fifth. M cannot be tasted sixth, however, since either O or L is tasted sixth (depending on when J is tasted).

33. **(D)** This question must be answered on the basis of the information provided in the initial set of conditions. In spite of the fact that these conditions leave considerable flexibility in the scheduling of wines, it is necessarily true that K will be tasted earlier than O. In the second possible order, K is tasted first and necessarily ahead of every other wine. In the first order, K must be tasted either second or fourth (so that N can follow as the third wine after K). So (D) is the correct answer. (A) is incorrect because K could be tasted second under the first arrangement. (B) is incorrect since the second arrangement places L before J. (C) is incorrect since K could follow L under the first arrangement. Finally, (E) is incorrect since M is under no restriction and could be tasted in every position except sixth (see explanation for question 32).

34. **(D)** In order for P to be tasted earlier than N and yet later than O, we must use the second possible sequence, placing O in the second tasting position and P in the third. This means that M will be tasted fifth:

1	2	3	4	5	6	7
K	O	P	N	M	L	J

(D) is proved by the diagram to be true, while the other choices are shown by the diagram to be false.

35. **(A)** If M is to be the second wine after P, the first arrangement cannot be used. Under the first arrangement, M and P would have to be tasted second and fourth or fifth and seventh, but K must be second or fourth and N fifth or seventh. Under the second arrangement one sequence is possible: K, O, P, N, M, L, J.

PART

THREE

EVERYTHING YOU NEED!

GRE Verbal Questions

PREVIEW →

CHAPTER 5

Sentence Completions

You'll Find Answers to These Questions

What is sentence completion?
How do you answer sentence completion questions?
What do smart test-takers know about sentence completions?

WHAT IS SENTENCE COMPLETION?

The basic idea of a sentence completion is "fill in the blank." The question type is a sort of hybrid, testing reading comprehension, word usage, and vocabulary. The question type is designed on the premise that it is possible to understand the gist of something even without hearing (or reading) every single word.

A little experiment will show you that this is true. Imagine that you are sitting in a lecture hall, listening to a professor, and someone sitting near you keeps rattling papers so you miss some words:

> Tensions between the United States and Great Britain ---- even after the end of the War of 1812. One important ---- in Anglo-American relations during the nineteenth century was their ---- for one another, rather stronger on the side of the United States. "Twisting the lion's tail" was a favorite American political pastime, vestiges of which were still ---- even in the early part of the twentieth ----.

Even though you are missing some words, you should still be able to make sense of the lecture. In essence, based on the logic of the sentences, you are "automatically" filling in the blanks. There are several words which might be used to fill each blank such as:

> Tensions between the United States and Great Britain continued even after the end of the War of 1812. One important factor in Anglo-American relations during the nineteenth century was their antipathy for one another, rather stronger on the side of the United States. "Twisting the lion's tail" was a

**TIME MANAGER
STUDY PLANS**

PLAN A: ACCELERATED
- *Read* the chapter
- *Study* "What Smart Test-takers Know"
- *Complete* Exercise 1
- *Check* your answers

PLAN B: TOP SPEED
- *Read* "How Do You Answer Sentence Completion Questions?"
- *Study* "What Smart Test-takers Know"
- *Complete* Exercise 2
- *Check* your answers

favorite American political pastime, vestiges of which were still evident even in the early part of the twentieth century.

Of course, these words are not the only possible substitutions, but they will serve to show the general idea of a sentence completion. This technique is the basic strategy for attacking sentence completions. The Verbal portion of the exam will contain 5 to 7 sentence completions.

TESTSMARTS

Don't let sentence completions hold you up. You can't afford to spend more than a minute on one.

GRE Sentence Completion Questions

Here are the directions for GRE sentence completion questions, together with a sample question and its explanation.

Anatomy of a Sentence Completion

Directions: Each of the questions below contains one or more blank spaces, each blank indicating an omitted word or phrase. Each sentence is followed by five words or phrases. Choose the word or set of words which, when inserted in the sentence, best fits the meaning of the sentence.

Familiarize yourself with the directions now. That way, on your test, you'll be able to dismiss them immediately with a click of the mouse and get right to work. The idea is to find an answer choice that makes sense when substituted in the sentence.

1. When Great Britain declared war on Germany in 1914, many people expected Lloyd George to resign because his ---- tendencies made him an unsuitable leader during a time of conflict.

This sentence completion item has only one blank. Some sentence completion items have two blanks.

    (A) conservative

    (B) ambitious

    (C) pacifist

    (D) unfazed

    (E) precocious

The correct answer is (C). The word "unsuitable" sets up a contrast between "conflict" and an opposite. Word clues are very important in sentence completions, so pay careful attention to words that amplify a thought or reverse a thought.

HOW DO YOU ANSWER SENTENCE COMPLETION QUESTIONS?

Here's a simple five-step plan that can help you fill in all the blanks.

Sentence Completions: Getting It Right

1. Read the sentence through for meaning.
2. Try to anticipate the missing word or words.
3. Scan the choices to find one that matches your guess. If it's there, click it, confirm it, and go on.
4. If your guess was not there, test choices to find the one that works best.
5. Test your selection by plugging it into the blank to see if it "sounds right."

Now let's try out these steps on three GRE-type sentence completions.

1. There is no ---- for the United States to sign the treaty since there is every reason to believe no other nation intends to honor its provisions.

   (A) arrangement
   (B) continuation
   (C) incentive
   (D) procedure
   (E) importance

1. Read the sentence.
2. You should be able to anticipate that an appropriate completion would be something like *reason*.
3. Scan the choices. Choice (C), *incentive*, is close to *reason* and makes sense in the sentence, so choose it and move on.

2. Even though he is a leading authority on the French Revolution, the chairperson of the department is a ---- speaker whose lectures on even the most exciting aspect of that historical period cause students to yawn and fidget.

   (A) sublime
   (B) confident
   (C) lackluster
   (D) honest
   (E) meritorious

HERE'S THE ANSWER

What if more than one answer seems to make sense?

Remember that there is only one correct answer. Make your best guess based on the full meaning of the sentence.

1. Read the sentence.

2. You should be able to anticipate that the answer might be a word like *dull* or *boring*.

3. *Dull* and *boring* are not in the answer choices, so look for the closest match. *Lackluster*, choice (C), is a good synonym and is the correct answer.

3. The chairperson, who is a specialist in French history, is a ---- speaker whose lectures on the French Revolution completely ---- students.

   (A) lackluster..entertain
   (B) moving..alienate
   (C) dull..absorb
   (D) forceful..require
   (E) scintillating..enthrall

1. Read the sentence.

2. In this case, you can't anticipate a likely answer without checking the answer choices, since a variety of completions could be correct.

3. Since you can't anticipate an answer, you must go on to step 4.

4. Test choices to find one that works:

   Choice (A) is wrong: A *lackluster* speaker is not likely to *entertain* students.

   Choice (B) is wrong: A *moving* speaker is not likely to *alienate* students.

   Choice (C) is wrong: A *dull* speaker is not likely to *absorb* students.

   Choice (D) is wrong: It makes no sense that a *forceful* speaker would *require* students.

   Choice (E) is correct: A *scintillating* speaker is very likely to *enthrall* students.

WHAT SMART TEST-TAKERS KNOW

SOME BLANKS PRACTICALLY FILL IN THEMSELVES.

If you read the sentence carefully, you're likely to come up with the right answer on your own. Even if the word you guess isn't exactly right, you can often spot a synonym among the answer choices. Click it, confirm it, and go on; you've saved precious time that you can use to make sure you answer all of the questions in the section.

CLUE WORDS CAN TELL YOU WHERE THE SENTENCE IS GOING.

If you can't come up with the missing word immediately, look for clue words in the sentence. Clue words can reveal the logical structure of the sentence. Is it continuing along one line of thought? If so, you're looking for a word that supports that thought. Is it changing direction in midstream? Then you're looking for a word that indicates a contrast between the thoughts expressed in the sentence.

TOP **10** TIP

SOME BLANKS CONTINUE OR AMPLIFY A THOUGHT IN THE SENTENCE.

Often the blank must be filled by a word that will make one part of the sentence parallel to another part by continuing a thought or amplifying a thought. Here is an example:

> The conductor's choice of tempo seemed entirely ----, so that each successive movement of the piece seemed to have no necessary connection to what had come before.
>
> (A) musical
> (B) believable
> (C) arbitrary
> (D) subtle
> (E) cautious

The best choice is (C). The logical clue is the parallel that is required. What comes after the comma is intended to clarify or amplify what is contained in the blank. Which of the five choices has a meaning related to "no necessary connection"? Only (C), *arbitrary*, has such a meaning.

> After a period of protracted disuse, a muscle will atrophy, ---- both its strength and the ability to perform its former function.
>
> (A) regaining
> (B) sustaining
> (C) losing
> (D) insuring
> (E) aligning

TEST SMARTS

Some words signal blanks that continue a thought:

and

also

consequently

as a result

thus

hence

so

for example

The best choice is (C). The logical structure requires a continuation of the idea of *atrophy*.

SOME BLANKS REVERSE A THOUGHT IN THE SENTENCE.

Sometimes the substitution must be the reverse of some other thought in the sentence. In such cases, the substitution must create a phrase that contrasts with some other element in the sentence. Look at these examples:

Although the conditions in which she chooses to live suggest that she is miserly, her contributions to charities show that she is ----.

(A) stingy

(B) thrifty

(C) frugal

(D) intolerant

(E) generous

The best choice is (E). The "although" signals a thought-reverser. The idea that comes after the comma must contrast with the idea that comes before the comma. Only (E) sets up the needed contrast: *miserly* vs. *generous*.

There are many dialects of English with radically different pronunciations of the same word, but the spelling of these words is ----.

(A) inconstant

(B) uniform

(C) shortened

(D) contemplated

(E) abbreviated

The best choice is (B). The *but* introduces a thought-reverser. The phrase completed by the substitution must create a contrast with the idea of difference expressed in the first clause. (B) does this nicely, contrasting *uniform* with *different*.

IN SOME SENTENCES, ONE BLANK CONTINUES A THOUGHT AND ANOTHER REVERSES ONE.

The report issued by the committee was completely ----, extolling in great detail the plan's strengths but failing to mention its ----.

(A) comprehensive..proposal

(B) unbiased..weaknesses

(C) one-sided..shortcomings

(D) printed..good points

(E) skewed..defenders

The best choice is (C). The logical structure of this sentence cannot be described as either a thought-reverser or a thought continuer, for there are elements of both. First, the phrase following the comma, taken in isolation, expresses a contrast. The second blank must be filled by a word that is somehow the opposite of *strengths*. Both (B) and (C) will provide the needed contrast. Second, the phrase following the comma, taken as a whole, is a continuer of the thought expressed before the comma. So the first blank must be filled by a word that describes something that covers only the good, not the bad. *One-sided* will do the trick.

> The quarterback's injury was very painful but not ----, and he managed to ---- the game in spite of it.
>
> (A) serious..interrupt
>
> (B) incapacitating..finish
>
> (C) harmful..abandon
>
> (D) conclusive..enter
>
> (E) excruciating..concede

The best answer is (B). The first blank must complete the contrast set up by "but not." Only (A), (B), and (E) are possible choices on this basis. Then, the "in spite of" sets up a contrast between what comes before the comma and what follows. Only (B) provides the needed thought reversal.

THE RIGHT ANSWER ALWAYS CREATES A MEANINGFUL ENGLISH PHRASE.

Eliminate all choices that would not result in an idiomatic construction.

> The plot of the movie was extremely complicated and included many minor characters ---- to the central events.
>
> (A) momentous
>
> (B) tangential
>
> (C) contemporary
>
> (D) essential
>
> (E) impervious

The best choice is (B). Two of the choices can be eliminated because they would not create a meaningful phrase:

> (A) . . . momentous to . . . (WRONG!)
>
> (C) . . . contemporary to . . . (WRONG!)

Then you would use the logic of the sentence to settle on (B). The blank must continue the idea of "minor characters," and (B) does this. The characters were only *tangential* to the main plot.

> The governor's intolerance of ---- among his aides was intensified by his insistence upon total ---- from all.
>
> (A) dissent..loyalty
> (B) dishonesty..imagination
> (C) flattery..communication
> (D) compliance..commitment
> (E) insight..familiarity

You can eliminate (D) and (E) on the basis of their first elements:

> (D) . . . intolerance of compliance . . . (WRONG!)
> (E) . . . intolerance of insight . . . (WRONG!)

It is almost impossible to construct an English sentence using these phrases. (And if you can come up with some bizarre sentence using them, that only proves the point. Such a sentence would not appear on the GRE.) You can eliminate (B) and (C) because the second substitution would not be idiomatic:

> (B) . . . total imagination . . . (WRONG!)
> (C) . . . total communication . . . (WRONG!)

ELIMINATING GIBBERISH ANSWERS IMPROVES YOUR GUESSING ODDS.

Eliminating answer choices that result in gibberish will improve your chances of guessing correctly.

> XXXXX XXXXXX XXXXXXXX XXX X XXXXXXXXXX XX
> XXXXXXX, XXX XXXXXXX XXXX XXX XXXXXXX XXXXX
> ---- our existing resources.
>
> (A) squander
> (B) conserve
> (C) belie
> (D) eliminate
> (E) deny

The sentence above has been concealed from you to put you in the same position you would find yourself in if you were not able to penetrate the logic of a sentence. Still, you can eliminate some choices by tossing out the gibberish. Which of the following phrases are most likely to appear in an English sentence?

> (A) . . . squander our existing resources.
> (B) . . . conserve our existing resources.
> (C) . . . belie our existing resources.

(D) . . . eliminate our existing resources.

(E) . . . deny our existing resources

(A) and (B) are the most likely candidates, and this is a good basis for an educated guess.

TWO BLANKS ARE BETTER THAN ONE.

When there are two blanks in a sentence completion question, you have two ways to eliminate answer choices. You can start with either blank to eliminate choices that don't work. So pick the one that's easier for you. If you can eliminate just one of the words in a two-word answer choice, the whole choice won't work so you can toss it out and go on.

EXERCISES: SENTENCE COMPLETIONS

Exercise 1

10 QUESTIONS • 10 MINUTES

Directions: Each of the questions below contains one or more blank spaces, each blank indicating an omitted word. Each sentence is followed by five (5) words or sets of words. Read and determine the general sense of each sentence. Then choose the word or set of words which, when inserted in the sentence, best fits the meaning of the sentence.

1. Although his work was often ---- and ----, he was promoted anyway, simply because he had been with the company longer than anyone else.

   (A) forceful..extraneous
   (B) negligent..creative
   (C) incomplete..imprecise
   (D) predictable..careful
   (E) expeditious..concise

2. Her acceptance speech was ----, eliciting thunderous applause at several points.

   (A) tedious
   (B) well received
   (C) cowardly
   (D) uninteresting
   (E) poorly written

3. Shopping malls account for 60 percent of the retail business done in the United States because they are controlled environments, which ---- concerns about the weather.

   (A) eliminate
   (B) necessitate
   (C) foster
   (D) justify
   (E) maintain

4. An oppressive ----, and not the festive mood one might have expected, characterized the mood of the gathering.

   (A) senility
   (B) capriciousness
   (C) inanity
   (D) solemnity
   (E) hysteria

5. In order to ---- museums and legitimate investors and to facilitate the ---- of pilfered artifacts,
   art magazines often publish photographs of stolen archaeological treasures.

   (A) perpetuate..return

   (B) protect..recovery

   (C) encourage..excavation

   (D) undermine..discovery

   (E) confuse..repossession

6. Despite some bad reviews, Horowitz' stature
   was not ----, and his fans and critics in Tokyo
   were unanimous in expressing their ---- his
   unique talent.

   (A) distilled..kinship with

   (B) embellished..ignorance of

   (C) criticized..disdain for

   (D) diminished..appreciation of

   (E) convincing..concern for

7. Though the concert had been enjoyable, it was
   overly ---- and the three encores seemed ----.

   (A) extensive..curtailed

   (B) protracted..gratuitous

   (C) inaudible..superfluous

   (D) sublime..fortuitous

   (E) contracted..lengthy

8. Peter, ---- by the repeated rejections of his
   novel, ---- to submit his manuscript to other
   publishers.

   (A) encouraged..declined

   (B) elated..planned

   (C) undaunted..continued

   (D) inspired..complied

   (E) undeterred..refused

9. All ---- artists must struggle with the conflict
   between ---- their own talent and knowledge
   that very few are great enough to succeed.

   (A) great..neglect of

   (B) aspiring..faith in

   (C) ambitious..indifference to

   (D) prophetic..dissolution of

   (E) serious..disregard of

10. The judge, after ruling that the article had
    unjustly ---- the reputation of the architect, or-
    dered the magazine to ---- its libelous statements
    in print.

    (A) praised..communicate

    (B) injured..retract

    (C) sullied..publicize

    (D) damaged..disseminate

    (E) extolled..produce

Exercise 2

5 QUESTIONS • 5 MINUTES

> **Directions:** Each of the questions below contains one or more blank spaces, each blank indicating an omitted word. Each sentence is followed by five (5) words or sets of words. Read and determine the general sense of each sentence. Then choose the word or set of words which, when inserted in the sentence, best fits the meaning of the sentence.

1. Although the language was ---- and considered to be inferior to standard English, Robert Burns wrote his love poetry in the language of the Scots.

   (A) interpreted

   (B) belittled

   (C) distinguished

   (D) appreciated

   (E) elevated

2. Given the Secretary of State's ---- the President's foreign policies, he has no choice but to resign.

   (A) reliance upon

   (B) antipathy toward

   (C) pretense of

   (D) support for

   (E) concurrence with

3. In order to ---- the deadline for submitting the research paper, the student tried to ---- additional time from the professor.

   (A) extend..wheedle

   (B) accelerate..obtain

   (C) postpone..forego

   (D) sustain..imagine

   (E) conceal..procure

4. Joyce's novel *Finnegans' Wake* continues to ---- critics, including those who find it incomprehensible and call it ----.

   (A) appall..genial

   (B) enthrall..nonsensical

   (C) baffle..transparent

   (D) bore..compelling

   (E) entertain..monotonous

5. Jazz is an American art form which is now ---- in Europe through the determined efforts of ---- in France, Scandinavia, and Germany.

   (A) foundering..governments

   (B) diminishing..musicians

   (C) appreciated..opponents

   (D) waning..novices

   (E) flourishing..expatriates

Answer Keys and Explanations

Exercise 1

1. C	3. A	5. B	7. B	9. B
2. B	4. D	6. D	8. C	10. B

1. **(C)** The *although* sets up a contrast between the idea of a promotion and the quality of the person's work. So the work must be bad, even though the person was promoted. Additionally, the two blanks must themselves be parallel, since both describe the poor quality of work.

2. **(B)** The key to this item is a thought-extender; what follows the comma must extend or amplify what comes before it. So your thinking should be "the speech was *something,* and that got applause." You might anticipate several completions with positive overtones such as *brilliant, magnificent,* or *persuasive.* None of these appears as an answer choice, so you should match your anticipated response to the best actual choice available. Only choice (B) has the positive overtones you need to complete the parallel between the quality of the speech and the applause.

3. **(A)** The blank is a thought-extender that explains the result of a controlled environment. What would be the result of a controlled environment? You would not need to worry about the weather.

4. **(D)** The *not,* a thought-reverser, introduces a contrast. The blank must be a word that means the opposite of "a festive mood."

5. **(B)** The logical structure here requires a thought-extender. The information that comes before the comma must explain why art magazines publish photos of stolen property. Additionally, the two blanks must create a parallel. Publishing the photos must do roughly the same thing for museums and legitimate investors that it does for stolen property. In this case, the result must be good. The museums and investors are protected and the stolen property is recovered.

6. **(D)** In this sentence, *despite* introduces a contrast, but notice there is a *not* in the sentence. The blank will actually complete a parallel to bad reviews: Bad reviews but *not* something negative. On this basis, you can eliminate (A), (B), and (E). Then, you should see that the second blank must continue the idea expressed in the first. Only (D) accomplishes this.

7. **(B)** The thought sets up a contrast. The concert was enjoyable, but it suffers from some defect. You can eliminate (D) since to be *sublime* is not a defect. Additionally, the two blanks themselves are parallel, for they complete similar thoughts. (A) and (E) contain words opposite in meaning, so they must be wrong. And the words in (C) are unrelated, so they cannot provide the needed contrast.

8. **(C)** There are several ways to analyze this item. First, you might see that the overall structure is that of a thought-extender. The first blank must complete a phrase set off by commas that explains why Peter does what he does. Also, the word in the first blank must describe an emotional reaction that is an appropriate response to rejection. On this ground you can surely eliminate (A), (B), and (D), since it is not logical for anyone to be *encouraged, elated,* or *inspired* by rejection. (C) and (E) are both possible reactions to rejection, but (E) does not provide the overall logical continuity we need.

9. **(B)** The sentence sets up a contrast between the artists' view of their own talent and the knowledge that few will succeed. You can eliminate (A), (C), and (E) because they fail to provide a contrast. It would not be surprising that an artist who *neglected,* or *was indifferent to,* or *disregarded* his or her talent would not succeed. And you can eliminate (D) on the grounds that the phrase *dissolution of talent* is not meaningful.

10. **(B)** There are several ways of analyzing this item. First, the overall structure is that of a thought-extender. The second blank must explain the results or consequence of the first blank. Additionally, you can rely on key words such as *unjustly* and *libelous* to learn that the action of the magazine was wrong. On this basis you can eliminate (A) and (E) since there is nothing wrong with *praising* or *extolling*. Then, you should eliminate (C) and (D) because they do not explain the natural consequences of the judge's ruling. (B), however, does the job. The judge ruled that the article had wrongly *injured* the architect's reputation, so the magazine was ordered to make amends by *retracting* what it had printed.

Exercise 2

1. B   2. B   3. A   4. B   5. E

1. **(B)** The most obvious logical clue to be found here is the parallel between the blank and the *inferior*. You must find something that has similar negative overtones; and, of the five choices, only (B) will provide the parallel.

2. **(B)** Again, we need a parallel. What is the cause of the Secretary's resignation? It cannot be the fact that the Secretary is in favor of the President's policies, so you can eliminate (D) and (E). Then, you can eliminate (A) and (C) because they do not make meaningful statements. (B), however, does provide the reason you are looking for. Since the Secretary is in disagreement with the President, he will resign.

3. **(A)** We need a thought-extender. The second blank must give the student's reason for doing what is mentioned in the first part of the sentence. Test each choice to see if it does just that. (A) is the only choice that works. The student needs to *extend* the deadline, so he *wheedles* some extra time. (B) and (C) make the opposite statement. (D) and (E) create phrases that are not idiomatic English.

4. **(B)** The key to this item is the parallel setup between *incomprehensible* and the second blank. The second element of the correct choice must be a word like *incomprehensible*.

5. **(E)** You can eliminate (A) by "going to pieces." Although a musical style might be famous, or unknown, or fading out of memory, you would not be likely to say that it is *foundering*. Remember that even eliminating one choice allows you to make an educated guess! Beyond that, the second substitution must extend the idea of the first: The music is doing something thanks to the determined efforts of someone. Given the phrase *determined efforts*, you can eliminate (B) and (D), since diminishing and waning are not things accomplished by determined efforts. And you can eliminate (C) since opponents do not create an appreciation for the things they oppose. Finally, notice how well (E) works. The sentence states that jazz is an American art form flourishing in Europe. How is that possible? Because of the efforts of American expatriates.

CHAPTER 6

Analogies

You'll Find Answers to These Questions

What is an analogy?
How do you answer analogy questions?
What do smart test-takers know about analogy questions?

WHAT IS AN ANALOGY?

GRE analogies are all about relationships. They test your ability to see a relationship between two words and to recognize a similar relationship between two other words. The key to analogy success is being able to express the relationship between the words in a pair.

GRE Analogy Questions

You will have 6 to 8 analogies in the Verbal Part of your GRE. (Out of a total of 30 questions that will also include sentence completions, antonyms, and reading comprehension.)

Question Format

A GRE analogy reads like a mathematical proportion. Colons and double colons are a shorthand way of expressing the relationship. Each analogy starts with a capitalized word pair, which is followed by five other word pairs in lowercase letters. The task is to find the answer choice pair that expresses a relationship similar to that of the capitalized word pair. When you've solved a typical analogy, you can read it like this:

ACTOR		CAST		singer		chorus
ACTOR	:	CAST	: :	singer	:	chorus
ACTOR	is to	CAST	as	singer	is to	chorus

Here are the directions for GRE analogy questions, together with a sample question and its explanation.

PLAN A: ACCELERATED
- *Read* the chapter
- *Study* "What Smart Test-takers Know"
- *Complete* Exercise 1
- *Check* your answers

PLAN B: TOP SPEED
- *Read* "How Do You Answer Analogy Questions?"
- *Study* "What Smart Test-takers Know"
- *Complete* Exercise 2
- *Check* your answers

Anatomy of an Analogy

Directions: In each of the following questions, you are given a related pair of words or phrases in capital letters. Each capitalized pair is followed by five pairs of words or phrases. Choose the pair which best expresses a relationship similar to that expressed by the original pair.

Now that you've read the directions, you won't need to read them again. Instead, you'll recognize analogy items by their format (two capitalized words separated by a colon) and know to look for the similar pair. Click the "DISMISS" directions box immediately.

1. ANALGESIC : PAIN ::

The capitalized words always express a conceptual relationship, and you'll be able to summarize the relationship in a sentence: An analgesic lessens pain.

(A) expenses : audit

(A) is wrong because it doesn't express a relationship. There is no necessary connection between poison and diet.

(B) truss : suspension

(B) expresses a conceptual relationship: the function of a truss is to provide suspension. But this is not the same relationship that connects the capitalized words.

(C) durability : hardware

(C) also expresses a wrong relationship: durability is characteristic of hardware. But analgesic is not characteristic of pain.

(D) improvisation : jazz

(D) too expresses a wrong relationship: improvisation is a characteristic of jazz.

(E) lubricant : friction

(E) is the correct response: a lubricant lessens friction.

HOW DO YOU ANSWER ANALOGY QUESTIONS?

To solve GRE analogies, follow these five steps.

Analogies: Getting It Right

1. Figure out how the capitalized words are related.
2. Create a sentence that expresses that connection.
3. Test the choices with your sentence and eliminate the ones that don't work.

4. If you're left with more than one answer—or no answer at all—go back and refine your sentence.

5. Choose the best answer. If none of the choices fits exactly, choose the one that works best.

Now let's try out these five steps on a typical GRE analogy question.

1. CONDEMNATION : DISAPPROVAL ::

    (A) ignorance : patience

    (B) optimism : insight

    (C) blasphemy : irreverence

    (D) sorrow : intention

    (E) longing : hostility

1. By definition, the relationship is one of "defining characteristic." This is the most common analogy relationship on the GRE.

2. A sentence that expresses this connection is "*Disapproval* is the defining characteristic of *condemnation*."

3. Test the choices with the sentence. Answer (C) works perfectly: "*Irreverence* is the defining characteristic of *blasphemy*." There is no need to go back and refine the sentence, so skip to step 5 and mark your answer.

Other examples of the "defining characteristic" pattern include:

FLUIDITY : LIQUID
HEROISM : EPIC
AGGRESSION : BELLICOSITY
HUMOR : COMEDIAN
RIDICULE : BURLESQUE
FAME : CELEBRITY
POVERTY : MONK
MISCHIEVOUSNESS : IMP

Now use the five-step plan to solve the following examples.

2. LOYALTY : TRAITOR ::

    (A) truthfulness : liar

    (B) hope : optimist

    (C) diligence : worker

    (D) understanding : sage

    (E) longevity : crone

This is the mirror image of the analogy connection just discussed. This time the relationship is "lack of something is the defining characteristic." The best choice is (A).

HERE'S THE ANSWER

What do analogies test?

Analogies are more a test of your verbal reasoning ability than they are of your vocabulary. You'll probably know the meanings of the words in this section, but you'll have to work to figure out how they're related.

Other examples of this pattern are:

>   MATURITY : YOUTHFULNESS
>   WORDS : TACITURN
>   MEMORY : AMNESIA
>   MOVEMENT : PARALYSIS
>   FRICTION : LUBRICATION
>   PREMEDITATION : IMPULSE
>   ENERGY : LETHARGY
>   NOURISHMENT : STARVATION

3. MUMBLE : SPEAK ::

    (A) adorn : denude

    (B) inflame : damage

    (C) delimit : expand

    (D) plagiarize : write

    (E) convert : preach

The best answer is (D). *Mumbling* is a spurious (or defective) form of *speaking*, and *plagiarizing* is a spurious (or defective) form of *writing*.

Here are some more word pairs that fit this analogy pattern:

>   BRAVADO : COURAGE
>   QUACK : PHYSICIAN
>   POACHER : HUNTER
>   MINCE : WALK
>   SIMPER : SMILE
>   ALCHEMY : SCIENCE
>   EMBEZZLE : WITHDRAW
>   MALINGERING : ILLNESS
>   EXTORT : CHARGE

4. TOSS : HURL ::

    (A) speak : shout

    (B) forget : learn

    (C) consider : formulate

    (D) sense : flourish

    (E) prepare : emit

The best choice is (A). The relationship is one of degree. To *hurl* and *toss* are similar actions but one is more violent than the other; similarly, to *shout* and to *speak* are similar, but one is more violent than the other.

Here are some other word pairs that fit this analogy form:

DRIZZLE : POUR

COOL : FRIGID

DISAPPROVED : CONDEMNED

JOG : SPRINT

MERCHANT : MAGNATE

DEFEAT : ROUT

PARTY : ORGY

GIGGLE : LAUGH

TIFF : BATTLE

PROTEST : REVOLUTION

5. NOTE : SCALE ::

    (A) musician : instrument

    (B) conductor : orchestra

    (C) letter : alphabet

    (D) book : cover

    (E) singer : music

The best answer is (C). A *note* is a part of a *scale*, and a *letter* is a part of the *alphabet*.

Here are some other word pairs that fit this pattern:

PAGE : BOOK

CLIMAX : DRAMA

COLOR : SPECTRUM

VOLUME : LIBRARY

VERSE : SONG

LEG : JOURNEY

VERDICT : TRIAL

WICK : CANDLE

NOON : DAY

HERE'S THE ANSWER

What if none of the answer pairs seems exactly right?

Remember: The directions tell you to choose the best answer. The correct answer won't necessarily be a perfect fit, but it will work better than the other choices.

6. BALLAD : SONG ::

    (A) credit : movie

    (B) shutter : darkness

    (C) novel : chapter

    (D) portrait : painting

    (E) melody : rhythm

The best answer is (D). A *ballad* is a type of *song*, and a *portrait* is a type of *painting*.

Here are some more word pairs that fit this pattern:

CARDIOLOGIST : PHYSICIAN
TIGER : CARNIVORE
BEER : BEVERAGE
SOPRANO : VOCALIST
SYNCOPATION : RHYTHM
THYME : SPICE
MONARCHY : GOVERNMENT
MEASLES : DISEASE
PROTESTANTISM : RELIGION
COURAGE : VIRTUE

7. REHEARSAL : PERFORMANCE ::

    (A) entrapment : game

    (B) engagement : marriage

    (C) applause : audience

    (D) antidote : illness

    (E) satisfaction : appetite

The best answer is (B). A *rehearsal* precedes a *performance*, and an *engagement* precedes a *marriage*.

Here are other word pairs that fit this pattern. Notice that some are related as a matter of logical sequence, while others form a causal sequence.

TADPOLE : FROG
TUMBLE : FALL
SWELL : BURST
CONVICT : SENTENCE
INFECTION : ILLNESS
PROSELYTIZE : CONVERT
CROUCH : SPRING
SALUTATION : FAREWELL
CLIMAX : DENOUEMENT

8. RETIREMENT : SERVICE ::

    (A) employment : salary

    (B) arrangement : flowers

    (C) contract : agreement

    (D) graduation : studies

    (E) exchange : communication

The best choice is (D). *Retirement* signifies the end of *service*, and *graduation* signifies the end of *studies*.

Here are some other word pairs that fit this pattern:

RECESS : TRIAL

DISMISSAL : EMPLOYMENT

RELAPSE : RECOVERY

INCARCERATION : RELEASE

LUNCH BREAK : WORKDAY

DIVORCE : MARRIAGE

LAYOVER : JOURNEY

INTERMISSION : PERFORMANCE

DIGRESSION : SPEECH

9. SCALPEL : SURGEON ::

(A) pen : reader

(B) bow : violinist

(C) bed : patient

(D) pistol : angler

(E) auto : soldier

The best answer is (B). The *scalpel* is the tool commonly associated with the *surgeon*, and the *bow* is the tool commonly associated with the *violinist*.

Here are some further examples:

TROWEL : BRICKLAYER

PALLET : PAINTER

FILTER : PURIFICATION

NEEDLE : SEW

PADDLE : CANOE

TACK : JOCKEY

TELESCOPE : ASTRONOMER

KNIFE : WHITTLE

10. UMPIRE : PLAYING FIELD ::

(A) carpenter : cabinet

(B) plumber : wrench

(C) judge : courtroom

(D) player : locker

(E) farmer : city

The best answer is (C). The *umpire* is found on the *playing field,* and the *judge* is found in the *courtroom.*

Here are some further examples:

WATER : RESERVOIR
PROFESSOR : CLASSROOM
COFFEE : MUG
SAILOR : SHIP
ROUSTABOUT : CIRCUS
HORSE : STABLE
PAINTING : MUSEUM
FARMER : FIELD
CHEF : KITCHEN
DOCTOR : HOSPITAL

11.   YAWN : BOREDOM ::

(A) smile : hatred

(B) blink : nausea

(C) sigh : hope

(D) grimace : joy

(E) wince : pain

The best choice is (E). A *yawn* is a sign of *boredom*, and a *wince* is a sign of *pain*.

Here are some further examples:

GRIMACE : PAIN
FIDGET : RESTLESSNESS
SNARL : ANGER
PURR : CONTENTMENT
STRUT : VANITY
GLOAT : SELF SATISFACTION
SIGH : RELIEF
HISS : DISAPPROVAL
APPLAUSE : APPROBATION
SNEER : CONTEMPT

WHAT SMART TEST-TAKERS KNOW

A SENTENCE CAN MAKE THE CONNECTION.

SCRIBBLE : WRITE ::

(A) inform : supply

(B) mutter : listen

(C) nuzzle : feel

(D) ramble : play

(E) stagger : walk

Summarize each analogy relationship with a sentence. In this case, *scribbling is a bad kind of writing*. Use the same sentence to test connections between the words in the answer choices. When you find one that works, you've found your answer.

(A) *Informing* is a bad kind of *supplying*. (No...)

(B) *Muttering* is a bad kind of *listening*. (No...)

(C) *Nuzzling* is a bad kind of *feeling*. (No...)

(D) *Rambling* is a bad kind of *playing*. (No...)

(E) *Staggering* is a bad kind of *walking*. (Yes!)

IT PAYS TO KNOW THE MOST COMMON GRE ANALOGY CATEGORIES.

The vast majority of GRE analogies fall into one of several recognizable categories. Knowing what they are and looking for them as you tackle each problem will make your job much easier. Here are the most common GRE analogy categories:

1. **"Part of the definition of" analogies**

   GENEROSITY : PHILANTHROPIST

   Generosity is part of the definition of a *philanthropist*.

2. **"Lack of something is part of the definition" analogies**

   POVERTY : FUNDS

   Part of the definition of *poverty* is a lack of *funds*.

3. **"This is a spurious form of that" analogies**

   STUMBLE : WALK

   Stumbling is a spurious form of *walking*.

4. **"Degree" analogies**

   BREEZE : GALE

   A *gale* is more powerful than a *breeze*.

5. **"Part to whole" analogies**

   MOVEMENT : SONATA

   A *movement* is a part of a *sonata*.

6. **"Type of" analogies**

   SWORD : WEAPON

   A *sword* is a type of *weapon*.

7. **"Sequence" analogies**

   FOREWORD : APPENDIX

   In books, a *Foreword* precedes the *Appendix*.

8. **"Interruption" analogies**

   LANDING : FLIGHT

   Landing marks an interruption of, or an ending to, a *flight*.

9. **"Tool" analogies**

   PAINTBRUSH : ARTIST

   A *paintbrush* is a tool used by an *artist*.

10. **"A place for" analogies**

    WITNESS : COURTROOM

    A *courtroom* is the place for a *witness*.

11. **"Sign of" analogies**

    GRIMACE : PAIN

    A *grimace* is a sign of *pain*.

THE MORE PRECISE YOUR SENTENCE, THE BETTER.

You cannot expect to solve every GRE analogy by simply plugging in the list of common analogy types. Remember that the analogies get more difficult as you work your way through each group. Use the common categories as a starting point, but be prepared to refine the relationship by making your sentence more precise. Consider this example:

GRAIN : SILO ::

(A) pilot : plane

(B) judge : courtroom

(C) water : reservoir

(D) clock : time

(E) automobile : highway

If you apply the "place where" idea without thinking, here is what happens.

A *silo* is a place where you would find *grain*.

(A) A *plane* is a place where you would find a *pilot*.

(B) A *courtroom* is a place where you would find a *judge*.

(C) A *reservoir* is a place where you would find *water*.

(D) A *clock* is a place where you would find *time*.

(E) A *highway* is a place where you would find *automobiles*.

You can eliminate (D), but that still leaves you with four possible answers. Now is the time to go back and make your original sentence fit better. How can you express the relationship between silo and grain more precisely?

A silo is a place where grain is stored.

(A) A plane is a place where a pilot is stored.

(B) A courtroom is a place where a judge is stored.

(C) A reservoir is a place where water is stored.

(E) A highway is a place where automobiles are stored.

Now it's easy to see that the correct answer is (C).

ANALOGIES WORK ONLY IF THERE'S A CLEAR-CUT CONNECTION.

An analogy depends upon a necessary connection between pairs of words based on the meaning of the words. This clear-cut connection must exist for both the original capitalized word pair and the correct answer choice. That means you can eliminate any answer choice for which you cannot describe a necessary relationship between the words. For example, the pair "career : descriptive" could not possibly be a correct answer choice to a GRE analogy because the words do not exhibit a clear-cut connection. (Check this out by trying to make up a sentence that describes the connection between these words.)

You can use the "clear-cut connection" test to rule out answer choices even when you don't know one of the capitalized words.

XXXXXX : XXXXXXXX

(A) note : scale

(B) ocean : merchandise

(C) expert : automobile

(D) victory : farmland

(E) teacher : classroom

AVOID THE TRAPS!

Non-answers are traps. Two words that have no logical connection can never be the answer to an analogy question. Here are some examples of non-answers:

typewriter : ant

gruesome : pavement

You don't know what the capitalized words are in this analogy, but you can still eliminate choices (B), (C), and (D). There is no clear-cut connection between the words of those choices. (The actual analogy above is LETTER : ALPHABET :: note : scale.)

SOME ANALOGIES WORK BETTER WHEN YOU TURN THEM AROUND.

Sometimes the capitalized words fall easily into a sentence that expresses their relationship—and sometimes they don't. If you're having trouble making up a sentence that relates the two words, be prepared to shift gears. Try reversing the order of the original word pair. Let's see how this technique works on the following analogy.

ICE : GLACIER ::

(A) train : trestle

(B) sand : dune

(C) path : forest

(D) feather : bird

(E) ocean : ship

If you can't come up with a sentence relating ICE to GLACIER, try relating GLACIER to ICE:

A *glacier* is made up of *ice*.

Here's the only catch: If you reverse the order of the capitalized words, you must also reverse the order of the words in each answer choice. So when you apply your sentence to the answer choices, this is how you'll have to do it:

(A) A *trestle* is made up of a *train*.

(B) A *dune* is made up of *sand*.

(C) A *forest* is made up of a *path*.

(D) A *bird* is made up of a *feather*.

(E) A *ship* is made up of an *ocean*.

Clearly (B) exhibits the same relationship as the original pair.

YOU CAN LEARN A LOT FROM THE ANSWER CHOICES.

Many words have different meanings depending upon whether they are used as nouns or verbs or adjectives. If you are not sure how one of the capitalized words is being used, just check the answer choices. In GRE analogies, all the answer choices will have the same grammatical structure as the capitalized word pair. That means if the answer choices are noun : noun, the capitalized pair will be NOUN : NOUN. On the other hand, if the answer choices are adjective : noun, then the capitalized pair will be ADJECTIVE : NOUN.

TESTSMARTS

Order counts! If the sentence you create reverses the order of the capitalized words, remember to reverse the order of the answer choice words as well.

EXERCISES: ANALOGIES

Exercise 1

10 QUESTIONS • 8 MINUTES

Directions: In each of the following questions, you are given a related pair of words or phrases in capital letters. Each capitalized pair is followed by five pairs of words or phrases. Choose the pair which best expresses a relationship similar to that expressed by the original pair.

1. HEAR : INAUDIBLE ::
   (A) touch : intangible
   (B) mumble : praiseworthy
   (C) spend : wealthy
   (D) prepare : ready
   (E) enjoy : illegal

2. GARGOYLE : GROTESQUE ::
   (A) magician : elegant
   (B) boulevard : serene
   (C) government : amicable
   (D) miser : affectionate
   (E) philanthropist : benevolent

3. EXTINGUISHED : RELIT ::
   (A) completed : discouraged
   (B) announced : publicized
   (C) collapsed : rebuilt
   (D) evicted : purchased
   (E) imagined : denied

4. VACUUM : AIR ::
   (A) invitation : host
   (B) vacancy : occupant
   (C) love : passion
   (D) literacy : writing
   (E) bait : trap

5. BLAME : SCAPEGOAT ::
   (A) explain : answer
   (B) convict : punishment
   (C) lionize : hero
   (D) appreciate : art
   (E) relate : secret

6. LIBEL : DEFAMATORY ::
   (A) praise : laudatory
   (B) option : selective
   (C) value : sparse
   (D) insult : apologetic
   (E) struggle : victorious

7. ANNEX : BUILDING ::
   (A) bedroom : apartment
   (B) fountain : park
   (C) epilogue : novel
   (D) dining car : train
   (E) memory : computer

8. BOOK : TOME ::
   (A) page : binding
   (B) plot : character
   (C) omission : diligence
   (D) library : borrower
   (E) story : saga

9. GREGARIOUSNESS : SOCIABILITY ::

   (A) courageousness : fearfulness

   (B) reliability : esteem

   (C) forgetfulness : memorability

   (D) affability : friendliness

   (E) gullibility : believability

10. HARBINGER : BEGINNING ::

   (A) ordain : decree

   (B) herald : advent

   (C) amend : correction

   (D) emancipate : freedom

   (E) commiserate : news

Exercise 2

5 QUESTIONS • 4 MINUTES

Directions: In each of the following questions, you are given a related pair of words or phrases in capital letters. Each capitalized pair is followed by five pairs of words or phrases. Choose the pair which best expresses a relationship similar to that expressed by the original pair.

1. FOREST : TREES

   (A) fleet : ships

   (B) lumber : wood

   (C) rose : thorns

   (D) shelf : books

   (E) camera : film

2. RAMPART : FORTRESS ::

   (A) bicycle : wheel

   (B) river : lake

   (C) cage : animal

   (D) ladder : roof

   (E) fence : house

3. SCYTHE : REAPING ::

   (A) screws : turning

   (B) crops : planting

   (C) lights : reading

   (D) shears : cutting

   (E) saws : gluing

4. MOISTEN : DRENCH ::

   (A) pump : replenish

   (B) chill : freeze

   (C) deny : pretend

   (D) dance : rejoice

   (E) announce : suppress

5. MAVERICK : STRAY ::

   (A) hermit : recluse

   (B) expert : ignorance

   (C) trickster : payment

   (D) miser : money

   (E) rumor : truth

Answer Keys and Explanations

Exercise 1

1. A	3. C	5. C	7. C	9. D
2. E	4. B	6. A	8. E	10. B

1. **(A)** The defining characteristic of something that is INAUDIBLE is that it cannot be HEARD, and the defining characteristic of something that is *intangible* is that it cannot be *touched*. Additionally, you can eliminate (B), (C), and (E) as non-answers.

2. **(E)** GROTESQUENESS is a defining characteristic of a GARGOYLE, and *benevolence* is a defining characteristic of a *philanthropist*.

3. **(C)** RELIGHTING follows EXTINGUISHING, and *rebuilding* follows *collapse*. This is an analogy based on sequence. You can eliminate (A), (D), and (E) as non-answers. (B) is a possible analogy, but it does not fit the sequence pattern.

4. **(B)** Lack of AIR is a defining characteristic of a VACUUM, and lack of an *occupant* is a defining characteristic of a *vacancy*. The other choices are possible analogies, but they do not fit the pattern for lack.

5. **(C)** BLAME is a defining characteristic of a SCAPEGOAT, and *lionize* is a defining characteristic of a *hero*. You can eliminate (A), (D), and (E) as non-answers. Further, (B) does not fit the defining characteristic pattern.

6. **(A)** DEFAMATORY is a defining characteristic of what it is to LIBEL, and *laudatory* is a defining characteristic of what it is to *praise*. In any case, the remaining choices are so weak as to be non-answers.

7. **(C)** This analogy does not fit any of our standard patterns. An ANNEX is not really a part of a BUILDING, but something added to an already existing building. Similarly, an *epilogue* is a section or comment added to a play or a *novel*. Perhaps it best fits as a sequence. An ANNEX comes after the original BUILDING, and an *epilogue* comes after the original *novel*. You can eliminate (A), for a *bedroom* is part of, not added to, an *apartment*. And for the same reason you can eliminate (D) and (E). Finally, (B) qualifies as a non-answer. A *fountain* is not necessarily found in a *park*, and a *park* does not necessarily contain a *fountain*.

8. **(E)** A TOME is a large BOOK, and a *saga* is a lengthy *story*. The analogy is one of degree, but to see this you have to be attentive to the precise meaning of TOME. This is what makes the analogy difficult. A TOME is not merely a BOOK; it is a large BOOK. (C) can be eliminated as a non-answer, and the others must be incorrect since they do not fit the pattern for degree.

9. **(D)** SOCIABILITY is a defining characteristic of GREGARIOUSNESS, and *friendliness* is a defining characteristic of *affability*.

10. **(B)** To HARBINGER is to announce the BEGINNING of something, and to *herald* is to announce the *advent* of something. This is a difficult analogy because of the HARBINGER, and it is made more difficult because HARBINGER is used as a verb. (It is usually used as a noun: "The robin is a harbinger of spring.") But even if you do not know the meaning of the key word in this analogy, you should be able to eliminate (E) as a non-answer.

Exercise 2

1. A   2. E   3. D   4. B   5. A

1. **(A)** A TREE is a part of the FOREST, and a *ship* is part of the *fleet*. Once we change the word order, the fairly common "is part of" pattern becomes evident. You might, however, need to refine your sentence to eliminate some of the other choices. You might try: a FOREST is a group of TREES, and a *fleet* is a group of *ships*.

2. **(E)** This is a fairly odd analogy. It doesn't fit any of the patterns. It is based on a physical similarity. A RAMPART is an embankment encircling a FORTRESS, and a *fence* encircles a *house*. Occasionally, the GRE will have analogies based on physical similarities, e.g., FRAME : PICTURE :: envelope : letter. (The FRAME surrounds the PICTURE, and the *envelope* surrounds the *letter*.) You could have eliminated both (B) and (D) as non-answers.

3. **(D)** SCYTHE is a tool for REAPING, and *shears* are a tool for *cutting*. (A), (C), and (E) are non-answers, and (B) does not fit the tool pattern.

4. **(B)** To DRENCH is to do more than just MOISTEN, and to *freeze* is to do more than just *chill*. This analogy is based upon a relationship of degree. You can eliminate (A), (C), and (D) as non-answers; and (E), though a possible analogy, does not fit the pattern we are looking for.

5. **(A)** A defining characteristic of a MAVERICK is that it is a STRAY, and a defining characteristic of a *hermit* is that he is a *recluse*. You can easily eliminate (C) as a non-answer. And (B) and (E) fail because they are based upon the "is a lack of" pattern. What about (D)? It is the love of *money*, or greed, that is the defining characteristic of a *miser*. Had (D) read *miser : greed*, it would have been better. Since we can improve (D), we know it is not the best choice as it originally stands.

CHAPTER 7

Reading Comprehension

TIME MANAGER STUDY PLANS

PLAN A: ACCELERATED
- *Read* the chapter
- *Study* "What Smart Test-takers Know"
- *Complete* Exercise 1
- *Check* your answers

PLAN B: TOP SPEED
- *Read* "How Do You Answer Reading Comprehension Questions?"
- *Study* "What Smart Test-takers Know"
- *Complete* Exercise 2
- *Check* your answers

You'll Find Answers to These Questions

What is reading comprehension?
How do you answer reading comprehension questions?
What do smart test-takers know about reading comprehension?

WHAT IS READING COMPREHENSION?

GRE reading comprehension is a test of your ability to read and understand unfamiliar materials and to answer questions about them. You will be presented with passages of varying lengths drawn from a variety of subject areas, including both the humanities and the sciences. The questions will ask you to analyze what is stated in the passage and to identify underlying assumptions and implications.

Question Format

Reading comprehension questions follow the standard multiple-choice format with five answer choices each. All of the questions fall into one of the following six categories:

- the main idea of the passage
- specific details mentioned in the passage
- the author's attitude or tone
- the logical structure of the passage
- further inferences that might be drawn from the text
- application of the ideas in the text to new situations.

Here are the directions for GRE reading comprehension, along with some sample questions and explanations.

Anatomy of a Reading Comprehension Passage

Directions: The passage below is followed by questions based upon its content. Choose the best answer to each question.

The directions are deceptively simple: Read the selection; answer the questions. There's a lot more to Reading Comprehension than just "read and answer." Since the directions are not helpful, be sure to dismiss as quickly as possible when they appear.

Instead of casting aside traditional values, the Meiji Restoration of 1868 dismantled feudalism and modernized the country while preserving certain traditions as the foundations for a modern
(5) Japan. The oldest tradition and basis of the entire Japanese value system was respect for and even worship of the Emperor. During the early centuries of Japanese history, the Shinto cult in which the imperial family traced its ancestry to the Sun
(10) Goddess became the people's sustaining faith. Although later subordinated to imported Buddhism and Confucianism, Shintoism was perpetuated in Ise and Izumo until the Meiji modernizers established it as a quasi-state religion.
(15)   Another enduring tradition was the hierarchical system or social relations based on feudalism and reinforced by Neo-Confucianism, which had been the official ideology of the pre-modern world. Confucianism prescribed a pattern of ethical con-
(20) duct between groups of people within a fixed hierarchy. Four of the five Confucian relationships were vertical, requiring loyalty and obedience from the inferior toward the superior. Only the relationship between friend and friend was horizontal, and
(25) even there the emphasis was on reciprocal duties.

Typically, reading passages discuss an unfamiliar topic—such as the Meiji Restoration. The first sentence here summarizes the main point of this selection. This is fairly common. Also typical is a lot of supporting detail, only some of which will be the basis for a question.

Most passages discuss competing theories or different factors that contribute to the events being discussed. Here you have more detail. While it's relevant to the author's argument, it may not be important in so far as your answering questions is concerned.

1. The author is primarily concerned with

The part of the question leading to the choices is called the "stem." The question stem here asks about the central theme of the selection. "Main Idea" questions often appear first.

(A) providing a history of the rise of feudalism in Japan

(B) identifying the influences of Confucianism on Japanese society

(C) speculating on the probable development of Japanese society

(D) developing a history of religion in Japan

(E) describing some important features of the Meiji Restoration

The correct answer is (E). The right answer to a "Main Idea" question has to describe the overall development of the selection.

2. The passage mentions all of the following as being elements of Japanese society EXCEPT:

   (A) obedience to authority
   (B) sense of duty
   (C) respect for the Emperor
   (D) concern for education
   (E) loyalty to one's superior

This question stem asks about details that are explicitly stated in the passage. The "EXCEPT" indicates that four of the five choices are mentioned in the selection. The one that is NOT mentioned is the right choice.

Concern for education is not mentioned, so the correct answer is (D).

3. It can be inferred from the passage that those who led Japan into the modern age were concerned primarily with

   (A) maintaining a stable society
   (B) building a new industrial base
   (C) expanding the nation's territory
   (D) gaining new adherents of Confucianism
   (E) creating a new middle class

This question stem asks about an idea that is not explicitly stated in the selection but can be inferred from what is stated. Inference questions are usually of above-average difficulty.

The correct answer is (A). Preserving the old traditions was a primary concern of the architects of the Meiji Restoration.

HOW DO YOU ANSWER READING COMPREHENSION QUESTIONS?

To answer reading comprehension questions, follow these steps:

Reading Comprehension: Getting It Right

1. Preview key sentences.
2. Read for structure; ignore details.
3. Do a mental wrap-up.

Now let's look at this process in more detail.

1. **Preview key sentences.** The first sentence of a paragraph is often the topic sentence. It will give you an overview of the paragraph. Previewing the first sentence of each paragraph will give you a general sense of the logical structure of the passage. You should also preview the very last sentence of the passage because it often contains the main

conclusion of the passage. On the computer-based test, you can view key sentences by scrolling through the passage as it appears on screen.

2. **Read for structure; ignore details.** This is an open-book test, so you do not have to memorize anything. Additionally, most of the questions ask about the *structure* of the passage rather than specific facts. As you read, consciously ask yourself "What is the main point of the passage?" and "Why is the author introducing this idea?"

   Your academic training has taught you to read for details because you know that you will be tested on them. Do *not* dwell on the particulars. In the first place, there are only three to eight questions, so there are not likely to be many questions about details. And in the second place, this is an open-book test, so you can refer to the passage.

3. **Do a mental wrap-up.** Before moving on to the questions, pause for just a few seconds and review in your mind what you have just read. Try to summarize in your own words the main point of the selection (think up a title for the passage) and to see in your mind's eye an outline of the passage.

Now let's look at a sample reading comprehension passage and questions about it. As you read the explanations, think about how the solution process applies.

Directions: The passage below is followed by questions based upon its content. After reading the passage, choose the best answer to each question. Answer all of the questions on the basis of what is *stated* or *implied* in the passage.

A fundamental principle of pharmacology is that all drugs have multiple actions. Actions that are desirable in the treatment of disease are considered therapeutic, while those that are undesir-
(5) able or pose risks to the patient are called "effects." Adverse drug effects range from the trivial, e.g., nausea or dry mouth, to the serious, e.g., massive gastrointestinal bleeding or thromboembolism; and some drugs can be lethal. Therefore, an
(10) effective system for the detection of adverse drug effects is an important component of the health care system of any advanced nation. Much of the research conducted on new drugs aims at identifying the conditions of use that maximize ben-
(15) eficial effects and minimize the risk of adverse effects. The intent of drug labeling is to reflect this body of knowledge accurately so that physicians can properly prescribe the drug; or, if it is to be sold without prescription, so that con-
(20) sumers can properly use the drug.

The current system of drug investigation in the United States has proved very useful and accurate

(In this passage the author announces a "fundamental principle" of pharmacology. The paragraph then goes on to contrast "desirable" and "adverse" drug effects. The author emphasizes the need for an effective system of making this information available to doctors.)

(In this next paragraph, the author says that the current system of drug investigation is useful and

in identifying the common side effects associated with new prescription drugs. By the time a new drug
(25) is approved by the Food and Drug Administration, its side effects are usually well described in the package insert for physicians. The investigational process, however, cannot be counted on to detect all adverse effects because of the relatively
(30) small number of patients involved in premarketing studies and the relatively short duration of the studies. Animal toxicology studies are, of course, done prior to marketing in an attempt to identify any potential for toxicity, but negative results do not guar-
(35) antee the safety of a drug in humans, as evidenced by such well known examples as the birth deformities due to thalidomide.

This recognition prompted the establishment in many countries of programs to which physi-
(40) cians report adverse drug effects. The United States and other countries also send reports to an international program operated by the World Health Organization. These programs, however, are voluntary reporting programs and are intended
(45) to serve a limited goal: alerting a government or private agency to adverse drug effects detected by physicians in the course of practice. Other approaches must be used to confirm suspected drug reactions and to estimate incidence rates. These
(50) other approaches include conducting retrospective control studies; for example, the studies associating endometrial cancer with estrogen use, and systematic monitoring of hospitalized patients to determine the incidence of acute com-
(55) mon side effects, as typified by the Boston Collaborative Drug Surveillance Program.

Thus, the overall drug surveillance system of the United States is composed of a set of information bases, special studies, and monitoring pro-
(60) grams, each contributing in its own way to our knowledge about marketed drugs. The system is decentralized among a number of governmental units and is not administered as a coordinated function. Still, it would be inappropriate at this
(65) time to attempt to unite all of the disparate elements into a comprehensive surveillance program. Instead, the challenge is to improve each segment of the system and to take advantage of new computer strategies to improve coordination
(70) and communication.

accurate. But then the author goes on to identify some weaknesses in the system.)

(In the next paragraph, the author claims that the system has been improved by establishing programs that keep records of reports by doctors of adverse drug consequences. But, the author notes, these reporting programs are not perfect.)

(In the final paragraph, the author summarizes by saying that the system is a composite one with many different aspects. And the last sentence summarizes the conclusion of the passage.)

1. The author is primarily concerned with discussing
   (A) methods for testing the effects of new drugs on humans
   (B) the importance of having accurate information about the effects of drugs
   (C) procedures for determining the long-term effects of new drugs
   (D) attempts to curb the abuse of prescription drugs
   (E) the difference between the therapeutic and nontherapeutic actions of drugs

This is a main idea question. (B) correctly describes the overall point of the passage. The author starts by stating that all drugs have both good and bad effects, and that correct use of a drug requires balancing the effects. For such a balancing to take place, it is essential to have good information about how the drugs work. Some of this can be obtained prior to approval of the drug, but some information will not become available until after years of use.

(A) is incorrect, for the different methods for testing drugs are mentioned only as a part of the development just described. The author is not concerned with talking about how drugs are tested but about why it is important that they be tested. (C) is incorrect for the same reason. As for (E), this is the starting point for the discussion—not the main point of the discussion. Finally, as for (D), the idea of drug abuse is not part of the passage at all.

2. The author implies that a drug with adverse side effects
   (A) will not be approved for use by consumers without a doctor's prescription
   (B) must wait for approval until lengthy studies prove the effects are not permanent
   (C) should be used only if its therapeutic value outweighs its adverse effects
   (D) should be withdrawn from the marketplace pending a government investigation
   (E) could be used in foreign countries even though it is not approved for use in the United States

This is an inference question, and the correct answer is (C). In the first paragraph, the author states that all drugs have effects and that these effects range from the unimportant to the very important. One purpose of drug labeling is to ensure that physicians (and ultimately consumers) are aware of these effects. We can infer, therefore, that drugs with side effects are used—provided the gain is worth the risks. And this is what (C) says.

(A) seems to be contradicted by the passage. One purpose of labeling, according to the author, is to let consumers of nonprescription drugs know of possible side effects of those drugs. As for (B) and (D), the analysis in the preceding paragraph clearly shows that drugs are approved for use and used even though they have unwanted side effects. Finally, there is nothing in the passage to support the conclusion expressed in (E).

3. Which of the following can be inferred from the passage?

    (A) Drugs with serious side effects are never approved for distribution.

    (B) A centralized drug oversight function would improve public health.

    (C) Most physicians are not aware that prescription drugs have side effects.

    (D) Some rare adverse drug effects are not discovered during the limited testing.

    (E) Consumers are seldom unable to understand directions for proper use of a drug.

This is an inference question, and the correct answer is (D). Although this conclusion is not stated in so many words, the author does say that some effects are not uncovered because of the short duration of the studies. We may therefore infer that some effects do not manifest themselves for a long period.

4. The author introduces the example of thalidomide (lines 37–38) to show that some

    (A) drugs do not have the same actions in humans that they do in animals

    (B) drug testing procedures are ignored by careless laboratory workers

    (C) drugs have no therapeutic value for humans

    (D) drugs have adverse side effects as well as beneficial actions

    (E) drugs are prescribed by physicians who have not read the manufacturer's recommendations

This is a logical structure question, and the correct answer is (A). The example is introduced in lines 32–37 where the author is discussing animal studies. The author says that the fact that a drug shows no dangerous effects in animals does not necessarily mean that it will not adversely affect humans and then gives the example. Thus, the example proves that a drug does not necessarily work in humans the same way it does in animals.

5. The author of the passage regards current drug investigation procedures as

    (A) important but generally ineffectual

    (B) lackadaisical and generally in need of improvement

    (C) necessary and generally effective

    (D) comprehensive but generally unnecessary

    (E) superfluous but generally harmless

This is an author's attitude question, and the correct answer is (C). We have already determined that the author regards drug investigation procedures as necessary, so we can eliminate (D) and (E). And at various points in the passage the author speaks of the current mechanism for gathering information as effective. For example, the author states that unwanted side effects are usually described in detail in the pamphlets distributed to physicians and also mentions that there is an entire discipline devoted to this area, so you can eliminate (A) and (B).

AVOID THE TRAPS!

"So what" answers are traps. Test-writers love to include something actually mentioned in the passage as a wrong answer. People look at the answer and think "Yes, that is in the passage, so it must be right." But it can be in the passage and still not be an answer *to the question asked.*

6. It can be inferred that the estrogen study mentioned in lines 52–53

    (A) uncovered long term side effects of a drug that had already been approved for sale by the Food and Drug Administration

    (B) discovered potential side effects of a drug that was still awaiting approval for sale by the Food and Drug Administration

    (C) revealed possible new applications of a drug that had previously been approved for a different treatment

    (D) is an example of a study that could be more efficiently conducted by a centralized authority than by volunteer reporting

    (E) proved that the use of the drug estrogen was not associated with side effects such as thromboembolism

This is an inference question, and the correct answer is (A). The key to this question is the word "retrospective." This tells you that the control study mentioned was done after the drug was already in use. (B) is incorrect because although the study uncovered harmful side effects, according to the passage, the drug was already in use. (C) is incorrect because the paragraph in which this study is mentioned deals with methods of reporting adverse drug effects, not new applications for drugs. (D) is incorrect first because the author does not mention the efficiency of the study and second because the author is not in favor of a centralized authority. In fact, in the last paragraph the author says that it would be inappropriate at this time to attempt to unite all of the disparate elements into a comprehensive surveillance program. Finally, (E) is incorrect because although thromboembolism is mentioned in the passage as one of the possible harmful side effects of drugs, it is not mentioned in connection with estrogen. The use of estrogen is mentioned in connection with endometrial cancer.

7. The author is most probably leading up to a discussion of some suggestions about how to

   (A) centralize authority for drug surveillance in the United States

   (B) centralize authority for drug surveillance among international agencies

   (C) coordinate better the sharing of information among the drug surveillance agencies

   (D) eliminate the availability and sale of certain drugs now on the market

   (E) improve drug testing procedures to detect dangerous effects before drugs are approved

This is an application question, and the correct answer is (C). In the last paragraph the author suggests that uniting disparate elements into a comprehensive surveillance program is inappropriate at this time. This eliminates choices (A) and (B). The author suggests, however, that improvements are possible in each segment of the system and urges reliance on computers to improve coordination and communication, so (C) is the correct answer. (D) is wrong because although the author might advocate the elimination of the availability of certain drugs, that is not what the passage is leading up to. As for (E), although the author acknowledges that preapproval studies are not infallible, this notion is too narrow in scope to be the next logical topic for discussion.

8. The author relies on which of the following in developing the passage?

(A) statistics

(B) analogy

(C) examples

(D) authority

(E) rhetorical questions

This is a logical structure question, and the correct answer is (C). The author frequently illustrates the argument's points by using examples. In the first paragraph, there are examples of side effects. In the second paragraph, there is an example of side effects not detected by animal studies, and in the third, the Boston Collaborative Drug Surveillance Program is an example. The author does not, however, use statistics (no numbers in this passage), does not use an analogy (no "this is like that"), does not mention an authority (citing an example is not the same as appealing to an authority), and doesn't use rhetorical questions.

WHAT SMART TEST-TAKERS KNOW

READING COMPREHENSION QUESTIONS CALL FOR DIFFERENT LEVELS OF UNDERSTANDING.

According to the test-writers, good reading involves three levels of understanding and evaluation. First, you must be able to grasp the overall idea or main point of the selection along with its general organization. Second, you must be able to subject the specific details to greater scrutiny and explain what something means and why it was introduced. Finally, you should be able to evaluate what the author has written, determining what further conclusions might be drawn and judging whether the argument is good or bad. This sequence dictates the strategy you should follow in reading the selection.

DETAILS CAN BOG YOU DOWN.

If a part of a passage gets too detailed, just skip it. Bracket it mentally. You do not need to have a full understanding of every single detail to appreciate the organization of the passage and to answer some, perhaps even all, of the questions.

THE GRE USES SIX—AND ONLY SIX—READING COMPREHENSION QUESTIONS.

Identify the type of question asked, and you are halfway home to finding the correct answer.

1. Main idea questions ask about the central theme or main point of the passage.

2. Specific detail questions ask about details included by the author to support or to develop the main theme.

3. Inference questions ask about ideas that are not explicitly stated in the selection but are strongly implied.

4. Logical structure questions ask about the organization or the overall development of the passage.

5. Application questions ask you to take what you have learned from the passage and apply it to a new situation.

6. Attitude or tone questions ask you to identify the overall tone of the passage or the author's attitude toward something discussed in the passage.

For each of the six question types, there are special clues in the answer choices that help you tell right ones from wrong ones.

IN MAIN IDEA QUESTIONS, THE "GOLDILOCKS PRINCIPLE" APPLIES.

On a main idea question, choose an answer that refers to all of the important elements of the passage without going beyond the scope of the passage. The correct answer to a main idea question will summarize the main point of the passage. The wrong answers are too broad or too narrow. Some will be too broad and attribute too much to the passage. Others will be too narrow and focus on one small element of the selection, thereby ignoring the overall point.

IN SOME MAIN IDEA QUESTIONS, THE ANSWER LIES IN THE FIRST WORD OF EACH CHOICE.

Some main idea questions are phrased as sentence completions. With a main idea question in sentence completion form, the first word of each choice may be all you need to pick the answer. Here's an example:

> The author's primary purpose is to
>
> (A) argue for . . .
>
> (B) criticize . . .
>
> (C) describe . . .
>
> (D) persuade . . .
>
> (E) denounce . . .

Note that the first word in each choice describes the passage differently. If the selection were neutral in tone, providing nothing more than a description of some phenomenon, you could safely eliminate (A), (B), (D), and (E).

IN SPECIFIC DETAIL QUESTIONS, LOCATOR WORDS POINT THE WAY.

A detail question basically asks "What did the author say?" So, the correct answer to a detail question will be found right there in the passage. And there will be a word or phrase in the question stem to direct you to the appropriate part of the passage. Just find the relevant information and answer the question.

IN SPECIFIC DETAIL QUESTIONS, "SO WHAT" ANSWERS ARE WRONG.

Often wrong answer choices look like right ones because they refer to specific points in the passage. The point is right there in the passage, but it is not an answer to the question asked. So your reaction to such answer choices should be "Yes, this is mentioned, but so what?"

IN SPECIFIC DETAIL QUESTIONS, "WAY OUT" ANSWERS ARE WRONG.

Wrong answers can also refer to things never mentioned in the selection. On a detail question, eliminate answer choices referring to something not mentioned in the passage or anything going beyond the scope of the passage. One way the test writers have of preparing wrong answers is to mention things related to the general topic of the selection but not specifically discussed there. An answer to an explicit question will appear in the selection.

IN SPECIFIC DETAIL QUESTIONS, THOUGHT-REVERSERS TURN A QUESTION INSIDE-OUT.

Sometimes the test writer will use a thought-reverser. For example:

> The author mentions all of the following EXCEPT:

Sometimes a detail question uses a thought-reverser. In that case, it is asking for what is not mentioned in the selection. Out of the five choices, four will actually appear in the selection. The fifth, and wrong, choice will not.

INFERENCE QUESTIONS CALL FOR A FURTHER CONCLUSION.

An inference question should not require a long chain of deductive reasoning. It is usually a one-step inference. For example, the selection might make a statement to the effect that "X only occurs in the presence of Y." The question might ask, "In the absence of Y, what result should be expected?" The correct answer would be: "X does not occur."

LOGICAL STRUCTURE QUESTIONS ARE ALL ABOUT ORGANIZATION.

Some logical structure questions ask about the overall structure of the passage. The correct answer to this kind of question should describe in general terms the overall development of the selection.

Another kind of logical structure question asks about the logical function of specific details. For this kind of question, find the appropriate reference and determine why the author introduced the detail at just that point.

APPLICATION QUESTIONS ARE THE TOUGHEST, AND YOU MAY HAVE TO JUST GUESS.

Application questions are the most abstract and therefore the most difficult kind of question. There is no "silver bullet" for this type of question, and you may find that it is better to make a guess and just move on.

FOR ATTITUDE/TONE QUESTIONS, THE ANSWER CHOICES RUN A GAMUT.

Attitude or tone questions often have answer choices that run a gamut of judgments or emotions, from negative to positive. On this kind of question, try to create a continuum of the answer choices and locate the author's attitude or tone on that continuum. Here's an example:

AVOID THE TRAPS!

Your academic training is hazardous to your test-taking health. In college, you are rewarded for memorizing details. The GRE penalizes for this. This is an open-book test. Do not waste time trying to understand insignificant points.

The tone of the passage is best described as one of

(A) outrage

(B) approval

(C) objectivity

(D) alarm

(E) enthusiasm

Arrange these attitudes in a line, from the most negative to the most positive:

(–) . . outrage . . alarm . . objectivity . . approval . . enthusiasm . . (+)

EXERCISES: READING COMPREHENSION

Exercise 1

14 QUESTIONS • 20 MINUTES

Directions: Each passage below is followed by questions based upon its content. After reading the passage, choose the best answer to each question. Answer all of the questions on the basis of what is *stated* or *implied* in the passage.

The mental health movement in the United States began with a period of considerable enlightenment. Dorothea Dix was shocked to find the mentally ill in jails and almshouses and cru-
(5) saded for the establishment of asylums in which people could receive humane care in hospital-like environments and treatment which might help restore them to sanity. By the mid 1800s, 20 states had established asylums, but during the late 1800s
(10) and early 1900s, in the face of economic depression, legislatures were unable to appropriate sufficient funds for decent care. Asylums became overcrowded and prison-like. Additionally, patients were more resistant to treatment than the
(15) pioneers in the mental health field had anticipated, and security and restraint were needed to protect patients and others. Mental institutions became frightening and depressing places in which the rights of patients were all but forgotten.
(20) These conditions continued until after World War II. At that time, new treatments were discovered for some major mental illnesses theretofore considered untreatable (penicillin for syphilis of the brain and insulin treatment for schizophrenia
(25) and depressions), and a succession of books, motion pictures, and newspaper exposés called attention to the plight of the mentally ill. Improvements were made, and Dr. David Vail's Humane Practices Program is a beacon for today. But
(30) changes were slow in coming until the early 1960s. At that time, the Civil Rights movement led lawyers to investigate America's prisons, which were disproportionately populated by blacks, and

they in turn followed prisoners into the only
(35) institutions that were worse than the prisons—
the hospitals for the criminally insane. The prisons were filled with angry young men who, encouraged by legal support, were quick to demand their rights. The hospitals for the crimi-
(40) nally insane, by contrast, were populated with people who were considered "crazy" and who were often kept obediently in their place through the use of severe bodily restraints and large doses of major tranquilizers. The young cadre of public
(45) interest lawyers liked their role in the mental hospitals. The lawyers found a population that was both passive and easy to champion. These were, after all, people who, unlike criminals, had done nothing wrong. And in many states, they
(50) were being kept in horrendous institutions, an injustice, which once exposed, was bound to shock the public and, particularly, the judicial conscience. Patients' rights groups successfully encouraged reform by lobbying in state
(55) legislatures.

Judicial interventions have had some definite positive effects, but there is growing awareness that courts cannot provide the standards and the review mechanisms that assure good patient care.
(60) The details of providing day-to-day care simply cannot be mandated by a court, so it is time to take from the courts the responsibility for delivery of mental health care and assurance of patient rights and return it to the state mental
(65) health administrators to whom the mandate was originally given. Though it is a difficult task,

administrators must undertake to write rules and standards and to provide the training and surveillance to assure that treatment is given and patient (70) rights are respected.

1. The main purpose of the passage is to

   (A) discuss the influence of Dorothea Dix on the mental health movement

   (B) provide an historical perspective on problems of mental health care

   (C) increase public awareness of the plight of the mentally ill

   (D) shock the reader with vivid descriptions of asylums

   (E) describe the invention of new treatments for mental illness

2. According to the passage, all of the following contributed to the deterioration of the asylum system EXCEPT:

   (A) Scarcity of public funds to maintain the asylums

   (B) Influx of more patients than the system was designed to handle

   (C) Lack of effective treatments for many mental illnesses

   (D) Need to employ restraints to maintain order and ensure safety

   (E) Waning interest in patient rights on the part of lawyers

3. It can be inferred from the passage that which of the following factors contributed to post-war reform of state mental institutions?

   (A) Increased funding provided by state legislatures to rehabilitate asylums

   (B) Availability of drugs to sedate and otherwise render passive mental patients

   (C) Discovery of effective treatments for illnesses previously considered untreatable

   (D) Realization that some criminal behavior is attributable to mental illness

   (E) Advances in penology that de-emphasized the value of incarceration

4. The author's attitude toward people who are patients in state institutions can best be described as

   (A) inflexible and insensitive

   (B) detached and neutral

   (C) understanding and sympathetic

   (D) enthusiastic and supportive

   (E) uncaring and unemotional

5. The passage provides information that would help answer all of the following questions EXCEPT

   (A) Who are some people who have had an important influence on the public health movement in the United States?

   (B) What were some of the mental illnesses that were considered untreatable until the 1950s?

   (C) What were some of the new treatments for mental illness that were adopted in the 1950s?

   (D) What were some of the most important legal cases that contributed to the new concern for patients' rights?

   (E) What effect did the Civil Rights movement have on the rights of prisoners?

6. It can be inferred from the passage that, had the Civil Rights movement not prompted an investigation of prison conditions,

   (A) states would never have established asylums for the mentally ill

   (B) new treatments for major mental illness would have likely remained untested

   (C) the Civil Rights movement in America would have been politically ineffective

   (D) conditions in mental hospitals might have escaped judicial scrutiny

   (E) many mentally ill prisoners would have been transferred from hospitals back to prisons

7. The tone of the final paragraph can best be described as

    (A) stridently contentious

    (B) overly emotional

    (C) cleverly deceptive

    (D) cautiously optimistic

    (E) fiercely independent

     The beginning of what was to become the United States was characterized by inconsistencies in the values and behavior of its population, inconsistencies that were reflected by its spokes-
(5) men, who took conflicting stances in many areas; but on the subject of race, the conflicts were particularly vivid. The idea that the Caucasian race and European civilization were superior was well entrenched in the culture of the colonists at
(10) the very time that the "egalitarian" republic was founded. Voluminous historical evidence indicates that, in the mind of the average colonist, the African was a heathen, he was black, and he was different in crucial philosophical ways. As time
(15) progressed, he was also increasingly captive, adding to the conception of deviance. The African, therefore, could be justifiably (and even philanthropically) treated as property according to the reasoning of slavetraders and slaveholders.
(20)   Although slaves were treated as objects, bountiful evidence suggests that they did not view themselves similarly. There are many published autobiographies of slaves; African-American scholars are beginning to know enough about
(25) West African culture to appreciate the existential climate in which the early captives were raised and which therefore could not be totally destroyed by the enslavement experience. This was a climate that defined individuality in collective
(30) terms. Individuals were members of a tribe, within which they had prescribed roles determined by the history of their family within the tribe. Individuals were inherently a part of the natural elements on which they depended, and they were
(35) actively related to those tribal members who once lived and to those not yet born.
    The colonial plantation system which was established and into which Africans were thrust did virtually eliminate tribal affiliations.
(40) Individuals were separated from kin; interrelationships among kin kept together were often

transient because of sales. A new identification with those slaves working and living together in a given place could satisfy what was undoubtedly
(45) a natural tendency to be a member of a group. New family units became the most important attachments of individual slaves. Thus, as the system of slavery was gradually institutionalized, West African affiliation tendencies adapted to it.
(50)   This exceedingly complex dual influence is still reflected in black community life, and the double consciousness of black Americans is the major characteristic of African-American mentality. DuBois articulated this divided conscious-
(55) ness as follows:
    The history of the American Negro is the history of this strife—this longing to attain self-conscious manhood, to merge his double self into a better and truer self. In this merging, he wishes
(60) neither of the older selves to be best.
    Several black political movements have looked upon this duality as destructively conflictual and have variously urged its reconciliation. Thus, the integrationists and the black
(65) nationalists, to be crudely general, have both been concerned with resolving the conflict, but in opposite directions.

8. Which of the following would be the most appropriate title for the passage?

    (A) The History of Black People in the United States

    (B) West African Tribal Relations

    (C) The Origin of Modern African-American Consciousness

    (D) Slavery: A Democratic Anomaly

    (E) The Legacy of Slavery: A Modern Nation Divided

9. The author makes all of the following points about Africans who were forcibly brought to America EXCEPT:

(A) They did not regard themselves as the objects of someone else's ownership.

(B) They formed new groups to replace the tribal associations that had been destroyed.

(C) The cultural forms brought from Africa were never completely eradicated by the enslavement experience.

(D) New affective relationships evolved to replace those made ineffectual by the practice of slavery.

(E) They brought with them a sense of intertribal unity in which all were regarded as members of the same group.

10. Which of the following can be inferred about the viewpoint expressed in the second paragraph of the passage?

(A) It is a reinterpretation of slave life based on new research done by African-American scholars.

(B) It is based entirely on recently published descriptions of slave life written by slaves themselves.

(C) It is biased and overly sympathetic to the views of white, colonial slaveholders.

(D) It is highly speculative and supported by little actual historical evidence.

(E) It is supported by descriptions of slave life written by early Americans who actually owned slaves.

11. The author puts the word *egalitarian* on line 10 in quotation marks to

(A) emphasize his admiration for the early Americans

(B) ridicule the idea of democracy

(C) remind the reader of the principles of the new nation

(D) underscore the fact that equality did not extend to everyone

(E) express his surprise that slavery could have existed in America

12. The tone of the passage could best be described as

(A) informed and anecdotal

(B) critical and argumentative

(C) impassioned and angry

(D) analytical and objective

(E) caustic and humorous

13. It can be inferred that which of the following pairs are the two elements of the "dual influence" mentioned at line 50?

(A) slavery and West African culture

(B) tribal affiliations in West Africa and family affiliations in West Africa

(C) a sense of individuality and a sense of tribal identification

(D) the history of West Africa and modern black political movements

(E) integrationism and black nationalism

14. The author's argument logically depends upon which of the following assumptions?

(A) The duality that characterizes the consciousness of modern Black Americans is so deeply rooted that it cannot be eliminated by political action.

(B) African captives who were brought to North America had learned a basic orientation toward the world which remained with them.

(C) At the time of the beginning of the United States, white Americans were not aware of the contradiction between the notion of equality and the institution of slavery.

(D) The influence of the slavery experience on the West Africans was more powerful than the memory of West African attitudes.

(E) Black Americans today are knowledgeable about the world view that was dominant in West Africa at the time of the beginning of slavery in America.

Exercise 2

7 QUESTIONS • 10 MINUTES

Directions: The passage below is followed by questions based upon its content. After reading the passage, choose the best answer to each question. Answer all of the questions on the basis of what is *stated* or *implied* in the passage.

In the summer of 999, Leif Erikson voyaged to Norway and spent the following winter with King Olaf Tryggvason. Substantially the same account is given by both the Saga of Eric the Red and the
(5) Flat Island Book. The latter says nothing about Leif's return voyage to Greenland, but according to the former it was during this return voyage that Leif discovered America. The Flat Island Book, however, tells of another and earlier landfall by
(10) Biarni, the son of a prominent man named Heriulf, and makes that the inspiration for the voyage to the new land by Leif. In brief, like Leif, Biarni and his companions sight three countries in succession before reaching Greenland, and to come
(15) upon each new land takes 1 "doegr" more than the last until Biarni comes to land directly in front of his father's house in the last-mentioned country.

This narrative has been rejected by most later writers, and they may be justified. Possibly, Biarni
(20) was a companion of Leif when he voyaged from Norway to Greenland via America, or it may be that the entire tale is but a garbled account of that voyage and Biarni another name for Leif. It should be noted, however, that the stories of Leif's visit
(25) to King Olaf and Biarni's to that king's predecessor are in the same narrative in the Flat Island Book, so there is less likelihood of duplication than if they were from different sources. Also, Biarni landed on none of the lands he passed, but
(30) Leif apparently landed on one, for he brought back specimens of wheat, vines, and timber. Nor is there any good reason to believe that the first land visited by Biarni was Wineland. The first land was "level and covered with woods," and
(35) "there were small hillocks upon it." Of forests, later writers do not emphasize them particularly in connection with Wineland, though they are often noted incidentally; and of hills, the Saga says of Wineland only that "wherever there was
(40) hilly ground, there were vines."

Additionally, if the two narratives were taken from the same source we should expect a closer resemblance of Helluland. The Saga says of it: "They found there hellus (large flat stones)."
(45) According to the Biarni narrative, however, "this land was high and mountainous." The intervals of 1, 2, 3, and 4 "doegr" in both narratives are suggestive, but mythic formulas of this kind may be introduced into narratives without altogether
(50) destroying their historicity. It is also held against the Biarni narrative that its hero is made to come upon the coast of Greenland exactly in front of his father's home. But it should be recalled that Heriulfsness lay below two high mountains which
(55) served as landmarks for navigators.

I would give up Biarni more readily were it not that the story of Leif's voyage contained in the supposedly more reliable Saga is almost as amazing. But Leif's voyage across the entire
(60) width of the North Atlantic is said to be "probable" because it is incorporated into the narrative of a preferred authority, while Biarni's is "improbable" or even "impossible" because the document containing it has been condemned.

1. The author's primary concern is to demonstrate that

    (A) Leif Erikson did not visit America

    (B) Biarni might have visited America before Leif Erikson

    (C) Biarni did not visit Wineland

    (D) Leif Erikson visited Wineland first

    (E) Leif Erikson was the same person as Biarni

2. The author specifically defines which of the following terms?

   (A) Flat Island Book

   (B) Helluland

   (C) Heriulfsness

   (D) doegr

   (E) hellus

3. According to the passage, Wineland was characterized by all of the following EXCEPT:

   (A) forests

   (B) hills

   (C) mountains

   (D) vines

   (E) hilly ground

4. It can be inferred from the passage that scholars who doubt the authenticity of the Biarni narrative make all of the following objections BUT

   (A) Biarni might have accompanied Leif Erikson on the voyage to America, and that is why a separate, erroneous narrative was invented.

   (B) The similarity of the voyages described in the Saga and in the Flat Island Book indicates that there was but one voyage, not two voyages.

   (C) It seems very improbable that a ship, having sailed from America to Greenland, could have found its way to a precise point on the coast of Greenland.

   (D) The historicity of the Saga of Eric the Red is well-documented, while the historicity of the Flat Island Book is very doubtful.

   (E) Both the Saga of Eric the Red and the Flat Island Book make use of mythical formulas, so it is probable that they were written by the same person.

5. The author mentions the two high mountains in order to show that it is

   (A) reasonable for Biarni to land precisely at his father's home

   (B) possible to sail from Norway to Greenland without modern navigational equipment

   (C) likely that Biarni landed on America at least 100 years before Leif Erikson

   (D) probable that Leif Erikson followed the same course as Biarni

   (E) questionable whether Biarni required the same length of time to complete his voyage as Leif Erikson

6. All of the following are mentioned as similarities between Leif Erikson's voyage and Biarni's voyage EXCEPT

   (A) Both visited Norway.

   (B) On the return voyage, both visited three different lands.

   (C) Both returned to Greenland.

   (D) Both visited Wineland.

   (E) Both visited Helluland.

7. It can be inferred that the author regards the historicity of the Biarni narrative as

   (A) conclusively proved

   (B) almost conclusively proved

   (C) possibly true

   (D) highly unlikely

   (E) conclusively disproved

Answer Keys and Explanations

Exercise 1

1. B	4. C	7. D	10. A	13. A
2. E	5. D	8. C	11. D	14. B
3. C	6. D	9. E	12. D	

1. **(B)** This is a main idea question, and by now the drill for answering such questions should be familiar to you. The passage does summarize the history of mental health care in the United States, so (B) is a good choice.

    You can eliminate (D) on the basis of the word "shock." There are no vivid images, and there is nothing in the passage that would shock a reader. You can eliminate (C) for a similar reason. Although a side-effect of the selection may be to make some readers aware of a problem, the primary purpose of the passage is to describe, not to increase awareness.

    Finally, (A) and (E) violate that part of the main idea rule which states that the correct answer cannot be too narrow. Both (A) and (E) refer to interesting points made by the author, but neither is the main theme of the selection.

2. **(E)** This is a specific detail question—with a thought-reverser. Four of the five ideas are mentioned in the selection; one—the correct answer—is not. The information you need is in the first paragraph. There, the author mentions that, due to economic conditions, public funding for the asylums dried up, the asylums became overcrowded, mental illness was less susceptible to treatment than had been hoped, and administrators found it necessary to use restraints and similar measures. The correct answer, (E), is not mentioned in this paragraph. The discussion of lawyers and patients' rights—and this is typical of wrong answers to this type of question—is found in a different part of the selection, here the second paragraph.

3. **(C)** This is an implied idea question: Which of the statements can be logically deduced form the selection? We need to focus on the second paragraph, since the question asks about the causes of postwar reform. There the author mentions in passing that new treatments had been discovered. When coupled with the point made in the first paragraph about the lack of treatment for some conditions, this strongly implies that the new treatments made reform more likely. Now look at the wrong answers. (A) can be eliminated because the asylums were not "rehabilitated." (B) is wrong because powerful drugs were part of the problem. (D) and (E) simply have no support in the text.

4. **(C)** This is a tone question, and the drill for tone questions should be familiar by now. Here it is possible to arrange all five choices to create a spectrum of attitudes ranging from positive to negative:

MOST POSITIVE:	enthusiastic and supportive
	understanding and sympathetic
	detached and neutral
	uncaring and unemotional
MOST NEGATIVE:	inflexible and insensitive

    Start by dividing the range in the middle. Does the passage tend toward the negative or positive direction? The author's attitude inclines more to the positive side. The passage speaks of the "plight" of the patient, a term that would not be used by someone who was detached, or uncaring, or insensitive.

    Now the question is one of degree. How positive is the tone? Although the attitude toward patients might be described as either "sympathetic" or "supportive," "understanding" is a better description than "enthusiastic." The author seems to understand the position of the patient, but he is not a cheerleader for the patient.

5. **(D)** This is a specific detail question. You will find information in the passage that would be useful in answering four of the five questions. As for (A), two names, Dorothea Dix and Dr. David Vail, are mentioned in the passage. As for (B) and (C), help for answering these questions can be found in the second sentence of the second paragraph. And as for (E), an answer to this question is contained later in the second paragraph. (D), however, cannot be answered on the basis of the passage, for no specific case names are included.

6. **(D)** This is an implied idea question. The author states that civil rights lawyers who represented black prisoners were drawn naturally into representing patients in mental hospitals. In other words, x caused y. The question stem asks us to assume that x did not occur, and on that basis we can infer that y might not have occurred. This is (D).

   (A) is incorrect, for the cause of the establishment of the asylum system was Dorothea Dix's crusade. (B) is incorrect, for the passage does not state that judicial activism resulted in the discovery of any new treatments (even though it may have resulted in better treatment). (C) goes far beyond the scope of the passage. We cannot conclude that a failure in the area of prison reform would have meant complete failure of the Civil Rights movements. Finally, as for (E), nothing in the passage suggests that judicial activism resulted in the transfer of prisoners to hospitals, so a lack of judicial activism would not necessarily have this effect.

7. **(D)** This is an author's attitude question that focuses on the final paragraph. There the author makes a specific proposal, which, he acknowledges, will require effort to implement. Since the author made the proposal, he must be optimistic about its chance for success. And since he acknowledges that it will not be easy, we can call the author cautious as well.

   As for (A) and (B), though the author does make an argument in that paragraph, he does so in rather neutral terms. The paragraph is not contentious or strident or emotional. As for (C), there is nothing in the selection to suggest that the author is attempting to mislead the reader. You may or may not agree with the author's suggestion in that last paragraph, but there is no warrant for the conclusion that he is trying to fool you. Finally, as for (E), although the author evidently does his own thinking, the tone of the final paragraph cannot be described in these terms.

8. **(C)** Here we have a main idea question presented in the format "Name that passage." We'll go down the list of choices, eliminating those that are too narrow or too broad.

   We eliminate (A) because it is too broad. Most of the discussion focuses on an early period of this country's history, even though there is the one paragraph which points out the modern implications of this history. This hardly constitutes an entire history of black people in the United States. Next, we eliminate (B) because it is too narrow. Though the discussion of West African tribal relations is an important element of the passage, it is not the main theme. The correct answer must be a title that also includes reference to the implications of these cultural elements.

   (C) gives us what we are looking for. The passage contrasts white attitudes toward slaves with the attitudes the Africans themselves held about themselves and then shows what implications this cultural history has for modern black Americans. You can eliminate (D), since the main theme of the passage is not really the relationship between slavery and democracy. The anomaly of slavery in a supposedly egalitarian society is only a small part of the discussion. Finally, (E) has the merit of using the phrase "legacy of slavery," which is an important element in the discussion. But the division mentioned in the final paragraph is a division of consciousness—not the division of a nation.

9. **(E)** This is a specific detail question. You will find the ideas expressed by (A) through (D) specifically mentioned in the second paragraph. (E), however, is contradicted by the passage. The author states that West Africans felt a *tribal* unity, not an *intertribal* unity.

10. **(A)** This is an implied idea question. It's difficult because you have to pick up on the key phrase "African-American scholars are beginning to know" in the second paragraph; but the question stem doesn't tell you that is the key to the question.

That phrase implies that something new has been learned that has prompted scholars to change their ideas about the experience of slavery. In other words, the scholars have rejected the traditional view of what Africans thought of slavery. So we infer that the position outlined in the last two paragraphs is a new interpretation, and (A) correctly describes this.

(B) is incorrect since the author mentions evidence other than the published autobiographies. And in any case, it is the information about West African culture that has been newly discovered, not the autobiographies. (C) is incorrect since the second paragraph doesn't even deal with the attitudes of the white slaveholders.

Next, given that the author cites two sources in support of his interpretation (autobiographies and new research), we can eliminate (D). Finally, (E) is incorrect since the paragraphs in question do not discuss the attitudes of those who owned slaves.

11. **(D)** This is a logical structure question. Why does the author place the term "egalitarian" in quotation marks? The term appears in the first paragraph, where the author is discussing the contradictions in early American attitudes. They are particularly evident in the area of race. These "egalitarian" thinkers believed that they were superior to the Africans.

The author places the term in quotation marks to indicate that he thinks the early White Americans were not really egalitarian. This surely eliminates (A) and (C). (B), however, overstates the case. The author is not implying that democracy, as a concept, is indefensible—only that the early American thinkers did not do a very good job of implementing the idea. Additionally, you can eliminate (E) because the passage does not express surprise. It treats slavery as an historical fact.

12. **(D)** This is a tone question using answer choices with two words. On the basis of first words, we can eliminate both (C) and (E). Although the topic is obviously of interest to the author, the treatment does not qualify as impassioned. Further, though the author's use of quotation marks to surround the word egalitarian might qualify as irony or even sarcasm, the overall tone of the passage is not caustic.

Next, using the second words, we eliminate (A) and (B). The author does not tell stories, so the tone cannot be anecdotal. Finally, the tone is not argumentative. Though the passage develops logically and has the form of a logical argument, it cannot be described as argumentative. Argumentative means contentious and aggressive.

13. **(A)** This is an implied idea question. In the final paragraph, the author refers to the "dual influence" but does not name those influences. Given the context, however, we may conclude that the two influences are slavery and the elements of West African culture that survived. (B) is, therefore, only partially correct. West African culture is only one of the two influences. (C) is a dichotomy mentioned in the selection but it is not the one to which the author is referring in the final paragraph. (D) is only partially correct. The elements of West African culture constitute one of the two influences, but modern black political movements could not be one of the *origins* mentioned by the author (though it is an outcome of the dual influences). Finally, as for (E), the author does mention these two contrasting movements, but they are a reflection of the duality, not the origin of the duality.

14. **(B)** Although this question uses the word *logically,* it is an implied idea question rather than a logical structure question. The question asks you to identify one of the choices as being a hidden premise of the argument. (B) is essential to the argument. For the argument regarding the West African influences to go through, it must be assumed that the West Africans had learned a world view which survived their being uprooted and transported to America. Without that critical assumption, the argument about the influence of West African culture fails.

(A) is not necessary to the author's argument. The author tries to prove the existence of such a duality, but he does not make any suggestion about how it might be eliminated. (C) is incorrect for the author merely states that there was such a contradiction. Whether white Americans were aware of the inconsistency in their behavior and beliefs is irrelevant. (D) is incorrect because the author merely states that there was the "dual" influence. He does not suggest that one or the other was more important in shaping the structure of modern black American consciousness. Finally, as for (E), though the author must assume that West African culture did survive in some form, he need not assume that black Americans today are still familiar with the elements of West African culture during the time of slavery. The legacy of that culture can survive even without conscious knowledge of its elements.

Exercise 2

1. B	3. C	5. A	7. C
2. E	4. E	6. D	

1. **(B)** This is a main idea question. The author offers several reasons for the conclusion that the Biarni narrative does not describe the same series of events described by the Saga. And if he can pull this off, then he can claim that Biarni visited America before Leif Erikson did. This is summarized by (B).

    (A) misinterprets the author's strategy. The author doesn't need to prove that Leif Erikson did not visit America, only that Biarni did so before him. (C) is too narrow. It is true that the author wants to show that the two voyages are to some extent dissimilar, and that is why he tries to prove that Biarni did not visit Wineland. But this is a small part of the overall development. As for (D), as was just noted, the author only needs to argue that Biarni did not visit the same three lands later visited by Leif Erikson. Finally, (E) would be fatal to the author's argument, so this is a point he wishes to disprove.

2. **(E)** This is a specific detail question. The author explicitly defines hellus as meaning large flat stones. While you may infer meanings for the other terms ("doegr" must be a measure of time and "Heriulfsness" apparently was named for Biarni's father), the author does not specifically define those terms.

3. **(C)** This is a specific detail question. The material you need is contained in the second paragraph. There the author states that Wineland is described as having forests or woods as well as hills and hilly ground and, of course, its vines. The mention of mountains comes in the next paragraph and applies to a different place altogether.

4. **(E)** This is an implied idea question. The author doesn't give us a list of the objections to the historicity of the Biarni narrative, but we can infer what some of those objections must be from the refutations of them offered in the selection. As for (A), in the second paragraph, the author acknowledges that Biarni might have been a companion of Leif Erikson's and that the narrative of Biarni might be a garbled tale of that adventure. We can infer, therefore, that the objectors try to explain away the "other voyage" in this way. As for (B), since the author spends so much effort in attempting to prove that the two voyages did not include exactly the same countries, we can infer that the objectors use the similarity between the two as proof that there was but one voyage. As for (C), in the third paragraph, the author argues that it is not unreasonable to believe that Biarni could sail directly to his father's house since the house was situated by a known navigational landmark. And as for (D), the author specifically attributes this objection to them in the closing sentences.

    (E), however, is not an objection that would undermine the historicity of the narrative of Biarni. An objector would insist that the sequence of "doegr" suggests that the two voyages were the same one. The author of this selection points out, however, that this sequence was probably not historically accurate in the first place but was included as a kind of literary device, like the number three or seven in fairy tales. If the author of our selection is correct, then the similarity of the sequence of "doegr" is not surprising. If it is true that a story like this generally contains such a literary device, then the fact that both stories contain such a device doesn't prove that they are based on the same incidents.

5. **(A)** This is a logical detail question. As noted above, one of the objections to the Biarni narrative is that it would have been difficult for Biarni to navigate so accurately. But the author points out that the location of Heriulf's house was clearly indicated by mountains. So the author mentions the mountains to prove that Biarni could have found the location.

6. **(D)** This is a specific detail question, with a thought-reverser. Four of the five ideas are specifically stated in the selection. (A), (B), and (C) are mentioned in the first paragraph, and (E) is mentioned in the third. But the author is at pains to prove that Biarni did not visit Wineland as the first of his three lands.

7. **(C)** This is an author's attitude question. The answer choices are already neatly arranged for us on a spectrum. The best choice is (C). The author gives several arguments for the historicity of the narrative. So we can eliminate (D) and (E). On the other hand, the author does not claim to have proved his case conclusively. In fact, in the first sentence of the second paragraph, he admits that the objectors "may be justified." And in the final paragraph, the phrasing "I should be willing to give up ..." strongly suggests that the author does not regard the issue as settled.

CHAPTER 8

Antonyms

You'll Find Answers to These Questions

What is an antonym?
How do you answer antonym questions?
What do smart test-takers know about antonyms?

WHAT IS AN ANTONYM?

The basic idea of a GRE antonym question is to find an opposite for a word. Antonym items are first and foremost a test of vocabulary.

This is both good and bad news. First the bad news: If you have no idea of the meaning of the given word, there's not much you can do. That's the bad news; now the good news. When you don't know the meaning of an antonym, don't waste a lot of time trying to figure it out. In other words, once you recognize that you are out of ammunition, just click a random guess, confirm it, and move on to the next item.

GRE Antonym Questions

Each GRE antonym starts with a capitalized word, which is followed by five words or phrases in lowercase letters. The task is to find the word or phrase that is most nearly opposite in meaning to the capitalized word.

**TIME MANAGER
STUDY PLANS**

PLAN A: ACCELERATED

- *Read* the chapter
- *Study* "What Smart Test-takers Know"
- *Complete* Exercise 1
- *Check* your answers

PLAN B: TOP SPEED

- *Read* "How Do You Answer Antonym Questions?
- *Study* "What Smart Test-takers Know"
- *Complete* Exercise 2
- *Check* your answers

Anatomy of Antonym Questions

Directions: Each of the following questions consists of a word printed in capital letters, followed by five words or phrases. Choose the word or phrase that is most nearly *opposite* in meaning to the word in capital letters. Be sure to consider all the choices before deciding which one is best.

The directions just say "pick the opposite," so don't bother with them again. On the test, dismiss them and start answering questions. It's true that some antonyms are fairly subtle, so you do want to read all of the choices before confirming your selection.

1. TRANSIENT:

   (A) urgent

   (B) youthful

   (C) original

   (D) eternal

   (E) unfaithful

The word in caps is the one you have to find the opposite of.

The best answer is (D). Transient means temporary or passing, so a good opposite would be eternal.

2. ACARPOUS:

   (A) assiduous

   (B) poignant

   (C) fecund

   (D) reticent

   (E) prolix

The best answer is (C); but unless you know that acarpous means infertile and that fecund means fertile, there's not much you can do with the question except guess. This way you will free up time for other questions in the section. The bad news is not quite as bad as it sounds. You will recognize most of the words.

HERE'S
THE ANSWER

What do antonyms test?

Primarily vocabulary.

HOW DO YOU ANSWER ANTONYM QUESTIONS?

Here's a simple five-step plan that can help you answer GRE antonym questions.

Antonyms: Getting It Right

1. Define the capitalized word.

2. Think of a meaning that is opposite to this word.

3. Read all the answer choices. Eliminate those that do not relate to the meaning you thought of. If only one choice remains, mark it and go on.

4. If more than one choice remains, go back and refine your thinking about the capitalized word.

5. Pick the answer choice that is most nearly opposite to the capitalized word.

Now let's try out these steps on some typical GRE antonym questions.

SQUANDER:

(A) whisper

(B) conserve

(C) import

(D) deny

(E) quarrel

1. The capitalized word means "to waste."
2. The opposite of "to waste" is "to save."
3. Looking at all the answer choices, the only one that is comes closes to meaning "save" is *conserve*. Mark it and go.

TEDIOUS:

(A) unlimited

(B) confined

(C) enthralling

(D) appetizing

(E) illuminating

1. The capitalized word means "boring" or "tiresome"
2. The opposite of "boring" would be something like *exciting* or *interesting*.
3. Looking at all the answer choices, you can immediately eliminate (A), (B), and (E) as having nothing to do with excitement. But that leaves (C), *enthralling,* and (D), *appetizing.*
4. Of the two remaining choices, *enthralling,* which means "captivating" or "fascinating," is more nearly opposite in meaning to *tedious* than *appetizing*, which means "savory," or "delicious."
5. Mark (C), *enthralling*, as the correct choice.

Here is a list of words that have appeared in antonym questions on past GREs. This list is a good indication of the vocabulary level tested on the GRE.

HERE'S
THE ANSWER

What should you do if you do not know the meaning of a word?

Guess and move on.

GRE WORD LIST

TESTSMARTS

Verb or Noun? If the part of speech of the capitalized word is ambiguous, check the answer choices.

ABEYANCE *(noun)*   Temporary suspension of function or activity.

ABROGATE *(verb)*   To repeal, annul, or abolish an authoritative act, for example, a law or decree.

ABSTEMIOUS *(adj.)*   Refraining from pleasure, and from food or strong drink in particular.

ABSTRUSE *(adj.)*   Difficult to comprehend; obscure.

ALACRITY *(noun)*   Cheerfulness; a readiness or promptness to act or serve.

ALLOY *(verb)*   To reduce the purity of (a metal) by mixing with one less valuable; to debase by mixing with something inferior.

AMALGAMATE *(verb)*   To mix, blend, or unite; to alloy with mercury.

AMELIORATE *(verb)*   To improve; to make better.

ANACHRONISTIC *(adj.)*   Erroneous in date; characterized by being out of its historical time.

ANOMALOUS *(adj.)*   Deviating from the general rule; unexpected.

APOCRYPHAL *(adj.)*   False; spurious; of doubtful authenticity.

APOTHEOSIS *(noun)*   A glorification to the point of godliness.

ARDUOUS *(adj.)*   Steep and therefore difficult of ascent; difficult to do; requiring exertion; laborious.

ASSIDUOUS *(adj.)*   Diligent; industrious.

ATTENUATION *(noun)*   The act of making thin or fine.

AUDACIOUS *(adj.)*   Bold or adventuresome.

AVER *(verb)*   To confirm; to declare to be true.

BANE *(noun)*   Poison; the cause of injury or mischief.

BEATIFY *(verb)*   To make happy, to bless; to ascribe extraordinary virtue to; to regard as saintly or blessed.

BEDIZEN *(verb)*   To adorn, especially in a cheap, showy manner.

BILGE *(noun)*   A variant of bulge; the protuberance of a cask, usually around the middle.

BLANDISHMENT *(noun)*   Flattery; enticement.

BREACH *(noun)*   The act of breaking or state of being broken; a gap, break, or rupture.

BROACH *(verb)*   To open up; to mention a subject.

BURNISH *(verb)*   To polish, especially by friction; to make or become smooth or glossy.

CAJOLE *(verb)*   To coax; to wheedle.

CALCIFY *(verb)*   To change into a hard, stony condition.

CALUMNIATE *(verb)*   To slander; to accuse a person falsely.

CAPITULATE *(verb)*   To surrender; to give up; to stop resisting.

CAPRICIOUS *(adj.)*   Whimsical; fickle; changeable.

CASTIGATE *(verb)*   To chastise; to correct by punishing.

CHASTENED *(adj.)*   Corrected; punished.

CODA *(noun)*   A final passage in music bringing a composition to a formal close.

CODICIL *(noun)*   An appendix or supplement; an addition to a will.

COEVAL *(adj.)*   Of the same period; existing at the same time.

COGNIZANT *(adj.)*   Having knowledge of something; informed.

CONJOIN *(verb)*   To join together; to unite.

CONTEMN *(verb)*   To scorn or despise.

CONTENTIOUS *(adj.)*   Argumentative; quarrelsome.

CONTUMACIOUS *(adj.)*   Insubordinate; rebellious; disobedient.

CONUNDRUM *(noun)*   A perplexing question; a riddle.

COUNTENANCE *(verb)*   To favor; to approve; to give support to.

CRAVEN *(adj.)*   Cowardly; base.

DAUNT *(verb)*   To frighten or intimidate.

DEARTH *(noun)*   Scarcity; lack.

DEBACLE *(noun)*   A breakup; an overthrow; a sudden great disaster.

DEMUR *(verb)*   To hesitate; to take exception; to object.

DENOUEMENT *(noun)*   The outcome; the solution; the unraveling of a plot.

DESICCATE *(verb)*   To dry completely; to preserve by drying.

DESUETUDE *(noun)*   The cessation of use; disuse.

DESULTORY *(adj.)*   Random; passing from one thing to another in a disorganized way.

DETUMESCENCE *(noun)*   Diminution of swelling.

DIAPHANOUS *(adj.)*   Transparent or translucent; gauzy.

DIFFIDENCE *(noun)*   Modesty; humility; self doubt.

DILATORY *(adj.)*   Causing or tending to cause delay; procrastinating.

DISINGENUOUSNESS *(noun)*   Insincerity; cunning; craftiness.

DISPARAGE *(verb)*   To belittle; to show disrespect for.

DISSEMBLE *(verb)*   To hide; to conceal; to disguise.

DISSOLUTE *(adj.)*   Loose in behavior and morals; lewd; debauched.

DIVESTITURE *(noun)*   The deprivation of rank, rights, etc.; the stripping of clothing, arms, etc.

DOGGEREL *(noun)*   Trivial, poorly constructed verse.

DOGMATIC *(adj.)*   Arrogant; dictatorial; authoritative.

DUCTILITY *(noun)*   The quality of being easily molded or easily led.

DULCET *(adj.)*   Melodious; harmonious.

ECLECTIC *(adj.)*   Composed of materials or principles gathered together from several different places or fields.

EFFICACIOUS *(adj.)*   Effective; capable of producing the desired result.

EFFLUVIA *(noun)*   An outflow in the form of a vapor or stream of invisible particles; a noxious odor or vapor.

EFFRONTERY *(noun)*   Boldness; impudence.

EMPIRICAL *(adj.)*   Based solely on experiments or experience.

EMULATE *(verb)*   To strive for equality; to compete with successfully.

ENERVATE *(verb)*   To weaken; to enfeeble.

ENIGMA *(noun)*   A puzzle; a perplexing statement; a riddle.

EPHEMERAL *(adj.)*   Fleeting; short lived; transitory.

EPITOME *(noun)*   A part or thing that is representative of the characteristics of the whole; a brief summary or abstract.

EQUANIMITY *(noun)*   Evenness of mind; calm; composure.

EQUIPOISE *(noun)*   Equal distribution of weight; equilibrium.

EQUIVOCATE *(verb)*   To make vague statements; to mislead intentionally by making an ambiguous remark.

ERUDITE *(adj.)*   Learned; scholarly.

EUPHORIC *(adj.)*   Feeling well; buoyant; vigorous.

EVINCE *(verb)*   To show clearly; to indicate; to manifest.

EXCORIATE *(verb)*   To flay, strip, or scratch; to denounce strongly.

EXCULPATE *(verb)*   To clear from a charge of guilt or fault.

EXPATIATE *(verb)*   To roam; to wander freely; in writing, to elaborate.

EXTRAPOLATE *(verb)*   To estimate or infer on the basis of certain known variables.

EXTRICABLE *(adj.)*   Capable of being released, set free, or disentangled.

FALLACIOUS *(adj.)*   Faulty in logic; producing error or mistake; misleading and disappointing.

FATUOUS *(adj.)*   Complacently stupid or inane.

FELICITOUS *(adj.)*   Suitable to the occasion; apt.

FERVID *(adj.)*   Intense; zealous; impassioned.

FLOUT *(verb)*   To mock; to sneer.

FOMENT *(verb)*   To stir up, arouse, or incite; to instigate.

FRENETIC *(adj.)*   Frantic; frenzied.

FROWARD *(adj.)*   Not willing to yield or comply with what is required.

FRUGAL *(adj.)*   Economical; not spending freely.

FULSOME *(adj.)*   Disgusting or offensive especially because of excess.

GAINSAY *(verb)*   To deny; to contradict.

GARISH *(adj.)*   Gaudy; too showy.

GARNER *(verb)*   To store; to gather up and save.

GARRULOUS *(adj.)*   Talkative; loquacious.

GERMINATE *(verb)*   To sprout; to start developing or growing.

GIST *(noun)*   The main point.

GOSSAMER *(adj.)*   Light; thin; filmy.

GRATUITOUS *(adj.)*   Free; voluntary; not required.

GROUSE *(verb)*   To complain; to grumble.

HALLOW *(verb)*   To consecrate; to make holy.

HAPLESS *(adj.)*   Unlucky; unfortunate.

HEDONISTIC *(adj.)*   Self-indulgent; living a life of pleasure.

HERMETIC *(adj.)*   Completely sealed; magical.

HIRSUTE *(adj.)*   Hairy; shaggy.

HONE *(verb)*   To rub and sharpen.

IGNOMINIOUS *(adj.)*   Shameful; dishonorable; disgraceful.

IMPERVIOUS *(adj.)*   Incapable of being penetrated.

IMPRECATION *(noun)*   An invoking of evil; a curse.

INCARCERATE *(verb)*   To imprison.

INCURSION *(noun)*   A running in; an invasion; a raid.

INDEFATIGABILITY *(noun)*   The quality of not being easily exhausted.

INDOMITABLE *(adj.)*   Not easily discouraged or subdued.

INELUCTABLE *(adj.)*   Not to be avoided; certain; inevitable.

INGENUOUS *(adj.)*   Frank; open; candid.

INSALUBRITY *(noun)*   Unhealthfulness; unwholesomeness.

INSCRUTABLE *(adj.)*   Incapable of being discovered or comprehended.

INSOLVENT *(adj.)*   Unable to pay debts; bankrupt.

INSOUCIANT *(adj.)*   Unconcerned; carefree.

INTEMPERANCE *(noun)*   Lack of moderation or restraint; addiction to excessive amounts of alcoholic beverages.

INTRANSIGENCE *(noun)*   Refusal to come to an agreement or compromise.

INTREPID *(adj.)*   Fearless; brave; undaunted.

INVECTIVE *(noun)*   A violent verbal attack; denunciation.

INVEIGH *(verb)*   To attack verbally; to denounce.

JOCOSE *(adj.)*   Merry; given to jesting.

TESTSMARTS

Make sure to read all the answers. To answer antonym questions you'll sometimes have to distinguish fine shades of meaning. That's why you have to consider every answer choice.

LACHRYMOSE *(adj.)*   Teary eyed; mournful; sad.

LACONIC *(adj.)*   Brief; short; pithy.

LASSITUDE *(noun)*   Weakness; weariness; languor.

LAUDATORY *(adj.)*   Praising.

LETHARGIC *(adj.)*   Drowsy; completely indifferent.

LIONIZE *(verb)*   To treat as a celebrity.

LOQUACIOUS *(adj.)*   Talkative; garrulous.

LUGUBRIOUS *(adj.)*   Mournful; very sad.

MALADROIT *(adj.)*   Clumsy; awkward; bungling.

MALLEABLE *(adj.)*   Yielding; amenable; adapting.

MELLIFLUOUS *(adj.)*   Flowing sweetly (said of words).

MENDICANT *(noun)*   A beggar.

METAMORPHOSE *(verb)*   To change from one form into another.

MISANTHROPY *(noun)*   Hatred or distrust of people.

MITIGATE *(verb)*   To alleviate; to relieve; to soften.

MNEMONIC *(adj.)*   Assisting the memory.

MOROSE *(adj.)*   Gloomy; sullen.

MOTILITY *(noun)*   The quality of having the inherent power of motion.

MULTIFARIOUS *(adj.)*   Characterized by great variety or diversity.

MUNIFICENCE *(noun)*   The quality of being extremely generous.

NADIR *(noun)*   The lowest point; the time of greatest depression.

NEFARIOUS *(adj.)*   Wicked; vile.

NEXUS *(noun)*   A connection, tie, or link.

NOISOME *(adj.)*   Noxious to health; harmful; hurtful.

OBDURATE *(adj.)*   Hardened and unrepenting; stubborn; inflexible.

OBFUSCATE *(verb)*   To darken; to obscure; to muddle.

OBSTREPEROUS *(adj.)*   Noisy; vociferous.

OFFICIOUS *(adj.)*   Unnecessarily accommodating; meddlesome.

OSSIFY *(verb)*   To settle or fix rigidly into a practice; to become bone.

PAEAN *(noun)*   A song of praise or triumph.

PALLIATE *(verb)*   To make something (crime) appear less serious than it is; to alleviate; to ease.

PANEGYRIC *(noun)*   A formal speech of praise; a eulogy.

PARADIGM *(noun)*   A pattern; an example; a model.

PARADOX *(noun)*   A statement that seems contradictory.

PARIAH *(noun)*   An outcast; someone rejected and despised by others.

PAUCITY *(noun)*   Dearth; scarcity; lack.

PEDAGOGY *(noun)*   The profession or function of teaching.

PELLUCID *(adj.)*   Transparent; easy to understand.

PEREGRINATION *(noun)*   Traveling from one country to another; wandering.

PERFIDIOUS *(adj.)*   Violating good faith; proceeding from treachery.

PERFUNCTORY *(adj.)*   Performed without care or interest; automatic.

PERIPHERAL *(adj.)*   Pertaining to the outer region of something as opposed to the center or core.

PETROUS *(adj.)*   Like a rock; hard; stony.

PETULANT *(adj.)*   Impatient or irritable.

PHLEGMATIC *(adj.)*   Sluggish, dull, or apathetic.

PILLORY *(verb)*   To punish; to hold up to public scorn.

PIQUANT *(adj.)*   Agreeably pungent; stimulating.

PIQUE *(noun)*   Resentment at being slighted.

PLACATE *(verb)*   To appease or pacify.

PLETHORA *(noun)*   Overabundance; excess.

PRECIPITOUS *(adj.)*   Literally very steep, so by extension, hasty or rash.

PRECOCIOUS *(adj.)*   Characterized by premature development, as a child who shows special talent earlier than usual.

PREDILECTION *(noun)*   A preconceived liking; a preference.

PROCLIVITY *(noun)*   A natural tendency to do something; an inclination; a leaning toward something.

PROFUSE *(adj.)*   Poured forth; given or produced freely and abundantly.

PROLIFERATE *(verb)*   To reproduce in quick succession.

PROLIX *(adj.)*   Long and wordy.

PROPINQUITY *(noun)*   Nearness in time, place or relationship; affinity of nature.

PROPITIATORY *(adj.)*   Having the power to make atonement.

PROSAIC *(adj.)*   Dull; tedious; commonplace.

PROSELYTIZE *(verb)*   To make converts.

PROTUBERANCE *(noun)*   The part of a thing that protrudes; a bulge.

PUNDIT *(noun)*   A person of great learning; an authority.

QUAFF *(verb)*   To drink or swallow in large quantities.

QUIXOTIC *(adj.)*   Extravagantly chivalrous or romantically idealistic; impractical.

RAFFISH *(adj.)*   Disreputable; tawdry.

RAMIFY *(verb)*   To be divided or subdivided; to branch.

RAMPANT *(adj.)* Flourishing; spreading unchecked; violent and uncontrollable in action.

RAPACIOUS *(adj.)* Given to plunder; voracious; greedy.

RAUCOUS *(adj.)* Harsh; hoarse; rough sounding.

RECIDIVISM *(noun)* A chronic relapse into antisocial behavior patterns.

RECONDITE *(adj.)* Profound; abstruse; concealed.

RECREANCY *(noun)* Cowardice; a cowardly giving up.

REDOUBTABLE *(adj.)* Formidable; to be feared or dreaded.

REFRACTORY *(adj.)* Stubborn; obstinate.

REFUTE *(verb)* To prove a person or argument wrong.

REPROBATE *(noun)* A depraved, vicious person.

RETICENT *(adj.)* Habitually silent; uncommunicative.

RIBALD *(adj.)* Characterized by coarse joking; vulgar.

RUBRIC *(noun)* Heading, title, or category.

SALIENT *(adj.)* Conspicuous; prominent; highly relevant.

SANGUINE *(adj.)* Cheerful; confident; optimistic.

SATURNINE *(adj.)* Gloomy; morose.

SAUCY *(adj.)* Impudent; rude.

SAVANT *(noun)* A knowledgeable or learned person.

SEDULOUS *(adj.)* Assiduous; diligent; persevering.

SEMINAL *(adj.)* Like seed, constituting a source; originative.

SENTENTIOUS *(adj.)* Short and pithy; often full of maxims and proverbs; trite.

SHARD *(noun)* A piece or fragment of an earthen vessel or of any brittle substance.

SINUOUS *(adj.)* Winding; serpentine; undulating.

SLAKE *(verb)* To assuage; to satisfy; to allay.

SLOTH *(noun)* Habitual indolence or laziness.

SOPHOMORIC *(adj.)* Self assured although immature; affected; bombastic.

SOPORIFIC *(adj.)* Tending to cause sleep; characterized by sleepiness.

SPECIOUS *(adj.)* Simulating, resembling, or apparently corresponding with right or truth.

SPLENETIC *(adj.)* Bad tempered; irritable.

SPURIOUS *(adj.)* Counterfeit; fraudulent.

SQUALID *(adj.)* Foul; filthy; extremely dirty.

STENTORIAN *(adj.)* Extremely loud or powerful.

STYMIE *(verb)* To hinder or obstruct; to check or block.

SUNDRY *(adj.)* Various; miscellaneous; separate.

SURREPTITIOUS *(adj.)* Secretive; clandestine.

SYCOPHANT *(noun)* A person who seeks favor through flattery; a parasite.

TACIT *(adj.)* Silent.

TAWDRY *(adj.)* Cheap; gaudy; showy.

TENACITY *(noun)* Persistence; firmness of hold.

TENUOUS *(adj.)* Unsubstantial; slight; flimsy; weak.

TIMOROUS *(adj.)* Fearful; timid.

TORPOR *(noun)* A state of dormancy; dullness; apathy.

TRACTABLE *(adj.)* Easily led, taught, or managed.

TRANSIENT *(adj.)* Temporary; fleeting.

TRENCHANT *(adj.)* Keen; penetrating; incisive.

TREPIDATION *(noun)* Fear; agitation.

TRUCULENCE *(noun)* The quality of being fierce; savage; cruel.

TURBID *(adj.)* Thick; dense; cloudy.

TURGID *(adj.)* Swollen; bloated; inflated.

TURPITUDE *(noun)* Wickedness; shamefulness.

UNTOWARD *(adj.)* Perverse; unruly; unseemly.

VACILLATE *(verb)* To hesitate; to waver.

VACUITY *(noun)* The quality of being empty; lack of intelligence; inanity.

VAPID *(adj.)* Tasteless; flavorless; dull; uninteresting.

VISCID *(adj.)* Thick; sticky; viscous.

VOLUBLE *(adj.)* Speaking glibly; talking with ease.

ZEAL *(noun)* Ardor; eager interest or enthusiasm.

WHAT SMART TEST-TAKERS KNOW

ANTONYM QUESTIONS OFTEN TEST UNUSUAL MEANINGS OF A WORD THAT YOU KNOW.

Sometimes the test writer selects a word you are likely to be familiar with, but sets up the question to test a meaning you do not ordinarily associate with the word. Here is an example:

PRECIPITOUS:

(A) pleasantly sweet

(B) overly ambitious

(C) agreeably situated

(D) publicly known

(E) gently sloping

The best choice is (E). We most often use the word *precipitous* to mean *rash* or *foolhardy,* but its central meaning is related to *precipice*, a sharp drop-off.

AMPLIFY:

(A) announce

(B) entertain

(C) simplify

(D) covet

(E) require

The best answer is (C). One common meaning of the word *amplify* is "to make louder," for example, amplified sound. But the word means generally "to increase," "to enlarge," or "to make fuller." Thus it can be used to mean "to describe something in increased detail." The best available opposite, therefore, is (C), *simplify*.

YOU CAN LEARN A LOT FROM THE ANSWER CHOICES.

Words can have different meanings based upon their part of speech. If you are uncertain about the part of speech of the capitalized word, just check the answer choices. If they're all verbs, for example, so is the capitalized word. Here's an example:

COUNTENANCE:

(A) procure

(B) insist

(C) disapprove

(D) forego

(E) interpret

TESTSMARTS

Eliminate non-answers. One simple way to eliminate answer choices is to toss out any words that don't have opposite meanings.

The best answer is (C). The word *countenance* can be either a noun (meaning "face") or a verb (meaning "to approve of"). Which meaning is intended? The answer choices are unequivocally verbs, which means the capitalized word must also be a verb. So the capitalized word means "approve of," and (C) is the best opposite.

IT IS OKAY TO PLAY AROUND WITH A WORD.

If it helps to solve the problem, you can alter the part of speech of the capitalized word and answer choices in your own mind. Sometimes an antonym will use a word you know but as a part of speech that is unfamiliar to you. Here is an example:

SUBLIMITY:

(A) erosion

(B) baseness

(C) conciseness

(D) insistence

(E) partiality

The best choice is (B). You may know the word *sublimity* better as the adjective *sublime,* meaning "lofty, high, or noble." So you may find it easier to think about the antonym by changing *sublimity* to the more familiar form *sublime*. As you think about each answer choice, you would then change it in your mind to an adjective. *Baseness*, therefore, would become *base*; and *base* is an opposite of *sublime*.

YOU CAN USE WORD CONNOTATIONS TO ELIMINATE ANSWER CHOICES.

Even if you don't know the exact meaning of a word, you may have a vague recollection of the context in which you first encountered it. So you may know whether the word has positive overtones or negative ones. This recollection may be sufficient to get a correct answer. Here's an example:

RAFFISH:

(A) grotesque

(B) delinquent

(C) uncaring

(D) noble

(E) evil

The correct choice is (D). Let's assume that you do not know that *raffish* means "low, vulgar, and base." And let's further assume, however, that you have a vague knowledge of the word. You've seen it used to describe a character who is dishonest and not trustworthy. So even though you don't know the exact meaning of the word, you know that it has negative overtones. Since you are looking for the opposite of a word with negative

TESTSMARTS

Parts of Speech. It is okay to play around with the part of speech of a word if that helps to answer the question.

overtones, you would eliminate every answer choice with negative overtones. As it turns out, this strategy works perfectly with this antonym; only one word is left. *Noble* is the only word with positive overtones.

YOU CAN UNLOCK WORD MEANINGS BY TAKING THE WORD APART.

Even when you encounter a word for the first time, you may be able to ascertain its meaning from its parts. Here's an example:

COGNOSCITIVE:

(A) courageous

(B) expensive

(C) unconscious

(D) redundant

(E) immature

The best answer is (C). This is a very unusual word, but you can probably figure out its meaning by looking at its root *cog-* . This is the same root found in words such as *cognition* and *recognize*, and it has to do with knowledge. So we infer that *cognoscitive* has something to do with awareness, and (C) looks like a good opposite. A word of caution, however: Don't spend too much time trying to decipher the meaning of a word. Remember that each antonym counts for only one point. On a paper and pencil exam, skip the difficult antonym and come back to it if you have time. On a CAT exam, guess and go on.

Antonyms 137

EXERCISES: ANTONYMS

Exercise 1

10 QUESTIONS • 5 MINUTES

Directions: Each of the following questions consists of a word printed in capital letters, followed by five words or phrases. Choose the word or phrase that is most nearly *opposite* in meaning to the word in capital letters. Be sure to consider all the choices before deciding which one is best.

1. LOUTISH:
   (A) boisterous
   (B) provocative
   (C) calamitous
   (D) sophisticated
   (E) insightful

2. ENIGMATIC:
   (A) talkative
   (B) oppressed
   (C) easily understood
   (D) easily avoided
   (E) very common

3. RECALCITRANT:
   (A) polished
   (B) feckless
   (C) yielding
   (D) somber
   (E) miserly

4. MITIGATE:
   (A) intensify
   (B) defend
   (C) mire
   (D) frequent
   (E) coax

5. TREPIDATION:
   (A) contempt
   (B) restlessness
   (C) rancor
   (D) vigilance
   (E) courage

6. PRECIPITOUS:
   (A) well-planned
   (B) gargantuan
   (C) prolific
   (D) short-lived
   (E) extremely hostile

7. PROCLIVITY:
   (A) prodigality
   (B) avoidance
   (C) credence
   (D) calumny
   (E) inception

8. TENUOUS:
   (A) unseemly
   (B) inherited
   (C) substantial
   (D) forlorn
   (E) awkward

9. SALIENT:

   (A) concealed

   (B) inclined

   (C) stagnant

   (D) blameworthy

   (E) omnipotent

10. ENERVATE:

   (A) invigorate

   (B) contemplate

   (C) necessitate

   (D) evaluate

   (E) elucidate

Exercise 2

5 QUESTIONS • 3 MINUTES

Directions: Each of the following questions consists of a word printed in capital letters, followed by five words or phrases. Choose the word or phrase that is most nearly *opposite* in meaning to the word in capital letters. Be sure to consider all the choices before deciding which one is best.

1. SPURIOUS:

   (A) malignant

   (B) authentic

   (C) incumbent

   (D) gracious

   (E) speculative

2. OPAQUE:

   (A) feverish

   (B) monstrous

   (C) inclined

   (D) resolved

   (E) transparent

3. NEFARIOUS:

   (A) virtuous

   (B) pedestrian

   (C) resourceful

   (D) sordid

   (E) potent

4. INDEFATIGABLE:

   (A) redolent

   (B) exhausted

   (C) famished

   (D) regrettable

   (E) ignorant

5. PLETHORA:

   (A) piety

   (B) agility

   (C) paucity

   (D) chagrin

   (E) harmony

Answer Keys

Exercise 1

1. D	3. C	5. E	7. B	9. A
2. C	4. A	6. A	8. C	10. A

Exercise 2

1. B	2. E	3. A	4. B	5. C

What You Must Know About GRE Verbal Questions

Review these pages the night before you take the GRE. They will help you get the answers to GRE verbal questions.

The four verbal types—sentence completions, analogies, reading comprehension questions, and antonyms—are mixed together in a single scored verbal section.

You can expect to see 5 to 7 sentence completions, 6 to 8 analogies, 7 to 9 antonyms, and about 9 reading comprehension questions. The time limit for the verbal section is 30 minutes.

Sentence Completions

- These steps will help you solve sentence completion questions:

    1. Read the sentence through for meaning.
    2. Try to anticipate the missing word or words.
    3. Scan the choices to find one that matches your guess. If it's there, mark it and go on.
    4. If your guess was not there, test choices to find the one that works best.
    5. Test your selection by plugging it into the blank to see if it "sounds right."

- Clue words can tell you where the sentence is going.
- Some blanks continue or amplify a thought in the sentence; others reverse a thought.

Analogies

- These steps will help you solve analogy questions:

    1. Figure out how the capitalized words are related.
    2. Create a sentence that expresses that connection.
    3. Test the choices with your sentence and eliminate the ones that don't work.
    4. If you're left with more than one answer—or no answer at all—go back and refine your sentence.
    5. Choose the best answer. If none of the choices fits exactly, choose the one that works best.

- A sentence can make the connection
- The most common GRE analogy types are:

1. "Part of the definition of"
2. "Lack of something is part of the definition"
3. "This is a spurious form of that"
4. "Degree"
5. "Part to whole"
6. "Type of"
7. "Sequence"
8. "Interruption"
9. "Tool"
10. "A place for"
11. "Sign of"

Reading Comprehension

- These steps will help you solve reading comprehension questions:

  1. Preview key sentences.
  2. Read for structure; ignore details.
  3. Do a mental wrap-up.

- The GRE uses 6 reading comprehension question types:

  1. Main Idea
  2. Specific Detail
  3. Inference
  4. Logical Structure
  5. Application
  6. Author's Attitude or Tone

Antonyms

- These steps will help you solve antonym questions:

  1. Define the capitalized word.
  2. Think of a meaning that is opposite to this word.
  3. Read all the answer choices. Eliminate those that do not relate to the meaning you thought of. If only one choice remains, mark it and go on.
  4. If more than one choice remains, go back and refine your thinking about the capitalized word.
  5. Pick the answer choice that is most nearly opposite to the capitalized word.

PART

FOUR

GRE Math Questions

PREVIEW →

CHAPTER 9

Problem Solving

TIME MANAGER
STUDY PLANS

You'll Find Answers to These Questions

What is problem solving?
How do you answer problem-solving questions?
What do smart test-takers know about problem solving?

PLAN A: ACCELERATED

- *Read* the chapter
- *Study* "What Smart Test-takers Know"
- *Complete* Exercise 1
- *Check* your answers

WHAT IS PROBLEM SOLVING?

Problem-solving questions are your ordinary, garden-variety math questions—the kind you saw on the SAT. The questions test your mastery of basic mathematical skills and your ability to solve problems using arithmetic, elementary algebra, and geometry. Some problems are strictly math questions such as solving for the value of a variable; the rest will be presented as real-life word problems that require a mathematical solution.

If your basic math skills need work, you'll find plenty of practice in Part Eight of this book. That section provides a complete review of arithmetic, algebra, and geometry, along with exercises to build your skills.

PLAN B: TOP SPEED

- *Read* "How Do You Answer Problem-solving Questions?"
- *Study* "What Smart Test-takers Know"
- *Complete* Exercise 2
- *Check* your answers

GRE Problem-solving Questions

Problem-solving questions are interspersed with quantitative comparisons in the scored math section. You'll have 9 to 11 problem-solving questions.

Here are the directions for GRE problem-solving questions and four sample questions together with their explanations.

Anatomy of Problem-Solving Questions

Directions: For each of the following questions, select the best of the answer choices.

You really don't need the directions at all. Problem solving is your official, school-issue multiple-choice math question.

1. $0.2 \times 0.005 =$
   - (A) 0.0001
   - (B) 0.001
   - (C) 0.01
   - (D) 0.1
   - (E) 1.0

This is a simple manipulation problem. Manipulation problems, as the name implies, test your knowledge of arithmetic or algebraic manipulations. The correct answer is (B). The item tests whether or not you remember how to keep track of the decimal point in multiplication.

2. If $x + 5 = 8$, then $2x - 1 =$
   - (A) 25
   - (B) 12
   - (C) 5
   - (D) 4
   - (E) 0

This manipulation problem tests algebra. The correct answer is (C). Since $x + 5 = 8$, $x = 3$. Then substitute 3 for x in the expression $2x - 1$: $2(3) - 1 = 5$.

3. Joe works two part-time jobs. One week Joe worked 8 hours at one job, earning $150, and 4.5 hours at the other job, earning $90. What were his average hourly earnings for the week?
   - (A) $8.00
   - (B) $9.60
   - (C) $16.00
   - (D) $19.20
   - (E) $32.00

This is a practical word problem. Practical word problems go beyond simple manipulations. They require that you use your knowledge of manipulations in practical situations. The correct choice is (D). To find Joe's average hourly earnings, divide the total earnings by the number of hours worked:

$$\frac{150 + 90}{8 + 4.5} = \frac{240}{12.5} = 19.20$$

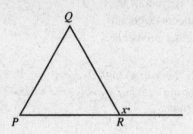

4. In the figure above, $PQ = QR = PR$. What is the value of x?

(A) 30

(B) 45

(C) 60

(D) 90

(E) 120

This is obviously a geometry problem. Equally obvious, geometry problems involve the use of basic principles of geometry. The correct answer is (E). This is an equilateral triangle (one having three equal sides), and equilateral triangles also have three equal angles, each 60 degrees. Then PR, as extended, forms a straight line. So x + 60 = 180, and x = 120.

HOW DO YOU ANSWER PROBLEM-SOLVING QUESTIONS?

Here's a simple, four-step plan that can help you answer GRE problem-solving questions.

Problem-Solving: Getting It Right

1. Read the question carefully.
2. Before solving the problem, check the answers.
3. Eliminate choices that are completely off the radar screen.
4. For complex questions, break down the problem.

Now let's examine each of these steps in more detail.

1. **Read the question carefully.** Some GRE problems are fairly simple, but others are more complex, particularly practical word problems and more difficult geometry problems. The more complex the question, the easier it is to misread and set off down a wrong track. The importance of this point is illustrated by the following very difficult practical word problem.

   The people eating in a certain cafeteria are either faculty members or students, and the number of faculty members is 15 percent of the total number of people in the cafeteria. After some of the students leave, the total number of persons remaining in the cafeteria is 50 percent of the original total. The number of students who left is what fractional part of the original number of students?

(A) $\dfrac{17}{20}$

(B) $\dfrac{10}{17}$

(C) $\dfrac{1}{2}$

(D) $\dfrac{1}{4}$

(E) $\dfrac{7}{20}$

The correct answer is (B). Let T be the total number of people originally in the cafeteria. Faculty account for 15 percent of T, or $.15T$, and students account for the remaining 85 percent of T, or $.85T$. Then some students leave, reducing the total number of people in the cafeteria to half of what it was originally, or $.5T$. The number of faculty, however, does not change. So the difference between $.5T$ and $.15T$ must be students: $.5T - .15T = .35T$. But this is not yet the answer to the question. The question asks "The number of students who left is what fraction of the original number of students?" Originally there were $.85T$ students; now there are only $.35T$ students, so $.50T$ students left. Now, to complete the solution we set up a fraction: $\frac{.50T}{.85}T = \frac{10}{17}$.

By this point, you can appreciate that there are several ways to misread the question. Someone might just put $.35T$ over $.85T$ $\left(\frac{.35}{.85}T = \frac{7}{17}\right)$ and choose (D). But this answers the question "The remaining students are what fraction of the original number of students?" That is not the question asked.

Someone might also put $.35T$ over T $\left(\frac{.35T}{T} = \frac{7}{20}\right)$ and select choice (E). But this too answers a different question: "The number of students who remain is what fractional part of the original number of people in the cafeteria?"

There are probably hundreds of other ways to misread the question, but it would be a shame to know how to answer the question and still miss it just because you did not read the question carefully.

2. **Before solving the problem, check the answers.** As you tackle each problem, start by looking at the answer choices. That way you'll know what form your own solution should take. For example, are the choices all in miles per hour? If so, that's the form your answer must take. Are they all decimals? If so, your solution should be a decimal, not a fraction or a radical.

3. **Eliminate choices that are completely off the radar screen.** The answer choices are generally arranged in a logical order.

X xxx xxxxxxx xxxx xxxxxxxxxxxx xxxxxxx
xxxxxxxxxx xxxx xxxxxxxxxxx xxxx xxxxxxx
xxxxxxxxxxx?

(A) 3200

(B) 4800

(C) 12,000

(D) 16,000

(E) 20,000

Notice that the choices in this dummy question are arranged from least to greatest. Occasionally, choices are arranged from greatest to least. And in algebra questions, the choices are arranged logically according to powers and coefficients of variables.

Additionally, the wrong choices are not just picked at random. They are usually written to correspond to possible mistakes (misreadings, etc.). This actually helps you. To illustrate this, here is an actual question to go with the dummy answers.

In a certain population, 40 percent of all people have biological characteristic X; the others do not. If 8000 people have characteristic X, how many people do not have X?

(A) 3200

(B) 4800

(C) 12,000

(D) 16,000

(E) 20,000

TESTSMARTS

Look for shortcuts. GRE problem-solving questions test your math reasoning, not your ability to make endless calculations. If you find yourself mired in calculations, you probably missed a shortcut that would have made your work easier.

The correct choice is (C). You can arrive at this conclusion by setting up a proportion:

$$\frac{\text{Percent with X}}{\text{Number with X}} = \frac{\text{Percent without X}}{\text{Number without X}}$$

Supplying the appropriate numbers:

$$\frac{40\%}{8000} = \frac{60\%}{x}$$

Cross-multiply: $.40x = .60(8000)$

Solve for x: $x = 12,000$

But you can avoid even this little bit of work. A little common sense, when applied to the answer choices, would have eliminated all but (C). In the first place, 40 percent of the people have X, so more people don't have X. If 8000 people have X, the correct choice has to be greater than 8000. This eliminates both (A) and (B). Next, we reason that if the correct answer were (D), 16,000, then only about $\frac{1}{3}$ of the people would have X. But we know 40 percent have X. This allows us to eliminate (D) and also (E).

4. **For complex questions, break down the problems.** Some practical word problems are fairly complex, and it is easy to get lost. You'll fare better if you break the solution process into separate steps. First, formulate a statement of what is needed; second, find the numbers you need; and third, perform the required calculation.

The enrollments at College X and College Y both grew by 8 percent from 1980 to 1985. If the enrollment at College X grew by 800 and the enrollment at College Y grew by 840, the enrollment at College Y was how much greater than the enrollment at College X in 1985?

(A) 400

(B) 460

(C) 500

(D) 540

(E) 580

The correct choice is (D), but the solution is a good deal more involved than the one needed for the preceding problem, so proceed step by step.

First, isolate the simple question that must be answered:

The enrollments at College X and College Y both grew by 8 percent from 1980 to 1985. If the enrollment at College X grew by 800 and the enrollment at College Y grew by 840, the enrollment at College Y was how much greater than the enrollment at College X in 1985?

This can be summarized as follows:

College Y in 1985 – College X in 1985

So you know you must find the enrollments at both colleges in 1985. How can you do that? The numbers are there in the question; you just have to figure out how to use them. Take College Y first. You know that enrollments grew by 840 and that this represents an increase of 8%. These numbers will allow you to find the enrollment in 1980:

$$8\% \text{ of } 1980 \text{ Total} = 840$$
$$0.08 \times T = 840$$
$$\text{Solve for } T: T = 10,500$$

This was the enrollment at College Y in 1980, but you need to know the enrollment at College Y in 1985. To do that, just add the increase:

$$1980 + \text{Increase} = 1985$$
$$10,500 + 840 = 11,340$$

Now do the same thing for College X:

$$8\% \text{ of } 1980 \text{ Total} = 800$$
$$0.08 \times T = 800$$
$$T = 10,000$$
$$1980 + \text{Increase} = 1985$$
$$10,000 + 800 = 10,800$$

Now you have the numbers you were looking for. Substitute them back into your original solution statement:

College Y in 1985 – College X in 1985 = Final Answer
11,340 – 10,800 = 540

This is not the only way of reaching the correct solution, but it is the one most people would be likely to use. And it is very complex. A problem like this would be one of the last ones in a math section. It does illustrate nicely what you should do when you encounter a complex practical word problem.

Now let's look at some more problem-solving questions and their solutions. As you read the solutions, think about how the four-step process would help you find the answers.

Manipulation Problems

Here are five typical GRE manipulation problems.

1. $0.04 \times 0.25 =$
   (A) 0.0001
   (B) 0.001
   (C) 0.01
   (D) 0.1
   (E) 1.0

Your approach to a manipulation problem like this one depends upon the degree of difficulty of the manipulation.

The correct answer is (C). The manipulation is very simple, so you should just do the indicated multiplication (keeping careful track of the decimal).

2. $\frac{2}{3} \times \frac{3}{4} \times \frac{4}{5} \times \frac{5}{6} \times \frac{6}{7} \times \frac{7}{8} =$
   (A) $\frac{2}{33}$ (D) $\frac{1}{2}$
   (B) $\frac{1}{4}$ (E) $\frac{27}{33}$
   (C) $\frac{3}{8}$

If the problem seems too difficult, look for a way to simplify things. The test-writers have no interest in determining whether you can do "donkey" math. If a manipulation problem looks to be too difficult, then there is a trick to be discovered. The correct choice is (B). Given enough time, you could work the problem out by multiplying all the numerators, multiplying all the denominators, and then reducing. But the very fact that this would be time consuming should prompt you to look for an alternative. Try canceling:

$$\frac{2}{3} \times \frac{3}{4} \times \frac{4}{5} \times \frac{5}{6} \times \frac{6}{7} \times \frac{7}{8}$$

3. $(27 \times 34) - (33 \times 27) =$

    (A) −1
    (B) 1
    (C) 27
    (D) 33
    (E) 918

This time you can simplify matters by factoring:
$(27 \times 34) - (33 \times 27) = 27(34 - 33) = 27(1) = 27$
The correct answer is (C).

4. If $3x - 5 = x + 11$, then $x =$

    (A) 16
    (B) 8
    (C) 3
    (D) 2
    (E) 1

If a problem consists of an equation with just one variable, the solution is almost certainly to solve for the unknown, whether it be x or some other variable. The correct answer is (B), and the appropriate method is to solve for x:

$$3x - 5 = x + 11$$

Combine terms: $2x = 16$
Solve for x: $x = 8$

If a problem presents two equations with two variables, the best strategy is almost certainly to treat them as a system of simultaneous equations.

5. If $x + y = 8$ and $2x - y = 10$, then $x =$

    (A) 16
    (B) 8
    (C) 6
    (D) 4
    (E) 2

The correct answer is (C), and the correct technique is to treat the two equations simultaneously. First, isolate y from the first equation:

$$x + y = 8$$

So: $y = 8 - x$

Next, substitute $8 - x$ into the second equation in place of y:

$$2x - (8 - x) = 10$$

Combine terms: $3x = 18$

Solve for x: $x = 6$

Practical Word Problems

Here is a typical GRE word problem:

> $2000 is deposited into a savings account that earns interest at the rate of 10 percent per year, compounded semiannually. How much money will there be in the account at the end of one year?
>
> (A) $2105
>
> (B) $2200
>
> (C) $2205
>
> (D) $2400
>
> (E) $2600

For complex word problems, break the problem down into smaller parts. First determine what you need to calculate and set up a mathematical expression.

This problem is asking you to calculate the total amount of money in the account at the end of the year. That means you must find the interest earned and add it to the original amount. First, calculate the interest earned during the first six months. To do this, you need to know that the formula for calculating interest is: Principal × Rate × Time = Interest Earned

First Six Months:

Principal	×	Rate	×	Time	=	Interest Earned
$2000	×	10%	×	0.5	=	$100

This $100 is then paid into the account. The new balance is $2100. Now you would calculate the interest earned during the second six months.

Second Six Months:

Principal	×	Rate	×	Time	=	Interest Earned
$2100	×	10%	×	0.5	=	$105

This is then paid into the account. So the final balance is:

$$\$2100 + \$105 = \$2205$$

So the correct answer is (C).

WHAT SMART TEST-TAKERS KNOW

TOP**10**TIP

IT'S SMART TO TEST ANSWER CHOICES.

The GRE is a multiple-choice test, so the correct answer is staring you in the face. Take advantage of this. Solve problems by plugging in the answer choices until you find the one that works.

> $5^3 \times 9 =$
> (A) 5×27
> (B) 15×9
> (C) $15 \times 15 \times 5$
> (D) 25×27
> (E) 125×27

The correct choice is (C), and you learn this by testing each choice to see which one is equivalent to $5^3 \times 9$. The expression $5^3 \times 9 = (5 \times 5 \times 5)$ $(3 \times 3) = 15 \times 15 \times 5$

WHEN TESTING ANSWER CHOICES, IT'S SMART TO START WITH (C).

Remember, the answer is right there in front of you. If you test all the choices, you'll find the right one. However, the smart place to start is with choice (C). Why? Because the quantities in the choices are always arranged in order, either from smallest to largest or the other way around. If you start with (C) and it's too large, you'll only have to concentrate on the two smaller choices. That eliminates three of the five choices right away. Here's how this works.

> A car dealer who gives a customer a 20 percent discount on the list price of a car still realizes a net profit of 25 percent of cost. If the dealer's cost is $4800, what is the usual list price of the car?
> (A) $6000
> (B) $6180
> (C) $7200
> (D) $7500
> (E) $8001

You know that one of these five choices must be correct, so all you have to do is test each one until you find the correct one. Start with (C).

If the usual list price is $7200, what will be the actual selling price after the 20% discount?

Usual List Price – 20% of Usual List Price = Final Selling Price

$7200 – 20% of $7200 = Final Selling Price

$7200 – $1440 = $5760

On that assumption, the dealer's profit would be:

Final Selling Price Cost = Profit

$5760 – $4800 = $960

Is that a profit of 25%?

$960/$4800 is less than $\frac{1}{4}$ and so less than 25%. This proves that (C) is wrong.

Now you need to test another choice, logically either (B) or (D). But which one? Apply a little reasoning to the situation. Assuming a usual cost of $7200, the numbers worked out to a profit that was too small. Therefore, we need a larger price to generate a larger profit. So try (D).

$7500 – (.20)($7500) = $6000

If the final selling price is $6000, that means a profit for the dealer of $1200. And $1200/$4800 = 25%. So (D) must be the correct answer.

Now suppose instead that you had this set of answer choices:

(A) $4000

(B) $6000

(C) $6180

(D) $7200

(E) $7500

In this case, you test (C) first and learn that it is incorrect. Then you go to (D) as above. Again, another wrong choice. Does this mean you have to do a third calculation? No! Since the choices are arranged in order, once you have eliminated (C) and (D), you know that (E) must be correct.

YOU CAN ASSUME NUMBER VALUES FOR UNKNOWNS.

Often it is easier to work with numbers than with unknowns. Therefore, when you are faced with a problem like the one below, in which some numbers are presented as variables, try substituting real numbers for each variable.

At a certain printing plant, each of m machines prints 6 newspapers every s seconds. If all machines work together but independently without interruption, how many minutes will it take to print an entire run of 18,000 newspapers?

(A) $\dfrac{180s}{m}$

(B) $\dfrac{50s}{m}$

(C) $50ms$

(D) $\dfrac{ms}{50}$

(E) $\dfrac{300m}{s}$

Since the information is given algebraically, the letters could stand for any numbers (so long as you don't divide by 0). Pick some values for m and s and see which answer choice works. Start with easy numbers. For purpose of discussion, assume that the plant has 2 machines, so $m = 2$. Also assume that $s = 1$, that is, that each machine produces 6 newspapers each second. On this assumption, each machine prints 360 papers per minute; and with two such machines working, the plant capacity is 720 papers per minute. To find how long it will take the plant to do the work, divide 18,000 by 720.

$$18,000/720 = 25 \text{ minutes}$$

On the assumption that $m = 2$ and $s = 1$, the correct formula should produce the number 25. Test the choices:

(A) $\dfrac{180s}{m} = 180(1)/2$ is not equal to 25 (WRONG!)

(B) $\dfrac{50s}{m} = 50(1)/2$ is equal to 25 (CORRECT!)

(C) $50ms = 50(2)(1)$ is not equal to 25 (WRONG!)

(D) $\dfrac{ms}{50} = (2)(1)/50$ is not equal to 25 (WRONG!)

(E) $\dfrac{300m}{s} = 300(2)/(1)$ is not equal to 25 (WRONG!)

WHEN NO NUMBERS OR VARIABLES ARE SUPPLIED, YOU CAN PICK YOUR OWN.

When no numbers or variables are supplied, you may find it easier to solve the problem if you assign numerical values to the given information. Pick numbers that are easy to work with.

If the value of a piece of property decreases by 10 percent while the tax rate on the property increases by 10 percent, what is the effect on the taxes?

(A) Taxes increase by 10 percent.

(B) Taxes increase by 1 percent.

(C) There is no change in taxes.

(D) Taxes decrease by 1 percent.

(E) Taxes decrease by 10 percent.

The correct answer is (D). Since no numbers are supplied, you are free to supply your own. Assume the piece of property has a value of $1000, and assume further that the original tax rate is 10%. On the basis of those assumptions, the tax bill is originally 10% of $1000 or $100. Now make the specified adjustments. The value of the property drops by 10%, from $1000 to $900, but the tax rate goes up by 10%, from 10% to 11%. The new tax bill is 11% of $900, or $99. The original tax bill was $100; the new tax bill is $99; the net result is a decrease of $1 out of $100, or a 1% decrease.

YOU HAVE TO BE CAREFUL OF YOUR UNITS.

Practical word problems often require you to work with units of measure. Sometimes several different units are involved, so be sure that your answer is expressed in the unit that's asked for.

A certain copy machine produces 13 copies every 10 seconds. If the machine operates without interruption, how many copies will it produce in an hour?

(A) 78

(B) 468

(C) 1800

(D) 2808

(E) 4680

The correct answer is (E). The question stem gives information about copies per 10 seconds, but you must answer in terms of copies per hour. To solve the problem, first convert copies per 10 seconds to copies per minute. This can be done with a proportion:

$$\frac{13 \text{ copies}}{10 \text{ seconds}} = \frac{x \text{ copies}}{60 \text{ seconds}}$$

Solve by cross-multiplication: $13 \times 60 = 10x$

Solve for x: $x = 78$

The correct answer, however, is not 78. A machine that produces 78 copies per minute produces 60 times that in an hour: $60 \times 78 = 4680$.

THOUGHT-REVERSERS CHANGE THE TERMS.

A thought-reverser is any word such as *not, except,* or *but* which turns a question inside-out. It will determine the solution you're looking for, so you'll need to keep it clearly in mind as you make your calculations.

A survey of 100 persons revealed that 72 of them had eaten at restaurant P and that 52 of them had eaten at restaurant Q. Which of the following could not be the number of persons in the surveyed group who had eaten at both P and Q?

(A) 20

(B) 24

(C) 30

(D) 50

(E) 52

The correct answer is (A). Since there are only 100 people in the group, some of them must have eaten at both P and Q. The combined responses for P and Q equal 124, and $124-100=24$. So 24 is the smallest possible number of people who could have eaten at both P and Q. (The largest possible number would be 52, which is possible if all of those who ate at Q had also eaten at P.) Thus far we have been concentrating on the question stem, but the answer choices also deserve special mention.

MOST PROBLEM-SOLVING FIGURES ARE DRAWN TO SCALE.

Most of the problem-solving figures are drawn as accurately as possible. (Note: This is not true of quantitative comparisons.) If a figure is not drawn to scale, it will include the warning: "Note: Figure not drawn to scale."

Unless you are told that a problem-solving figure is not drawn to scale, you may assume that angles and other geometric relationships are as shown. You may also assume that, for example, what looks like a right triangle is a right triangle even if you can't support your assumption with a formal geometric theorem.

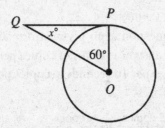

In the figure above, what is the measure of angle x in degrees?

(A) 15

(B) 30

(C) 45

(D) 60

(E) 90

The correct answer is (B). To solve the problem, you need to know that angle P is a right angle. Then you have a triangle whose angles measure 60, 90, and x. Since there are 180 degrees in a triangle, x must be 30.

You probably did realize that angle P must be a right angle and not just by looking at it and seeing that it seems to be 90 degrees. Rather your mind's eye probably told you that for some reason or other, angle P had to be 90 degrees.

In fact, angle *P* must be 90 degrees. *PQ* is a tangent, and *PO* is a radius. A tangent intersects a radius at a 90-degree angle. But you do not need to know the "official" justification to answer correctly. Just trust your spatial intuition.

YOU CAN USE MEASURES OF SIMPLE FIGURES TO FIND MEASURES OF MORE COMPLEX ONES.

Many geometry problems involve complex figures. You can often calculate their measures by breaking them up into simpler figures.

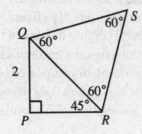

In the figure above, what is the perimeter of triangle *QRS*?

(A) 12

(B) $6\sqrt{2}$

(C) 6

(D) $3\sqrt{2}$

(E) $2\sqrt{2}$

The correct answer is (B). The trick is to see that *QR* is not only a side of triangle *PQR*, but is also a side of triangle *QRS*. Further, *QRS* is an equilateral triangle, so if you can find the length of one side, you know the length of the other sides as well.

How can you find the length of *QR*? *PQR* is a 45-45-90 triangle. Since *QP* is 2, *PR* is also 2. Now you know two legs of the right triangle, and you can use the Pythagorean Theorem to find the hypotenuse:

$$QP^2 + PR^2 = QR^2$$

So:
$$2^2 + 2^2 = QR^2$$
$$4 + 4 = QR^2$$
$$QR^2 = 8$$
$$QR = \sqrt{8}$$
$$QR = 2\sqrt{2}$$

Each of the three sides of *QRS* is equal to $2\sqrt{2}$, so the perimeter of *QRS* $= 3 \times 2\sqrt{2} = 6\sqrt{2}$.

YOU CAN MEASURE IRREGULAR SHADED AREAS BY RELATING THEM TO FIGURES WITH REGULAR SHAPES.

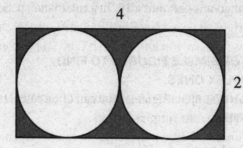

What is the area of the shaded portion of the figure above?

(A) $8 - 8\pi$

(B) $8 - 4\pi$

(C) $8 - 2\pi$

(D) $8 - \pi$

(E) π

The correct answer is (C). The shaded area is what's left over if you take the area of the two circles away from the area of the rectangle:

Rectangle – Two Circles = Shaded Area

First, the area of the rectangle is just $2 \times 4 = 8$. Then, the diameter of the circles is equal to the width of the rectangle. So the diameter of the circles is 2, and the radius is 1. The formula for the area of a circle is πr^2, so each circle has an area of $\pi(1^2) = \pi$. Now we know the area of the shaded part of the diagram:

$$8 - 2(\pi) = 8 - 2\pi$$

BECAUSE A PROBLEM-SOLVING FIGURE IS DRAWN TO SCALE, YOU CAN ESTIMATE MEASURES.

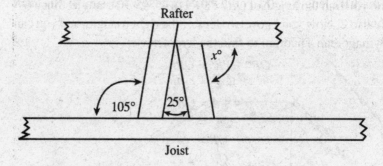

The figure above shows a cross section of a building. If the rafter is parallel to the joist, what is the measure of angle x?

(A) 45

(B) 60

(C) 80

(D) 90

(E) 105

The correct choice is (C), and you can get that without a calculation. Look at the size of *x*. It is not quite a right angle, so you can eliminate both (D) and (E). Is it as small as 60 degrees? No, so you eliminate (B) and (A) as well. This means that (C) must be the correct answer.

BECAUSE A PROBLEM-SOLVING FIGURE IS DRAWN TO SCALE, YOU CAN MEASURE LENGTHS.

Unless it is specified that a figure is not drawn to scale, you can use a pencil or other available straight edge as a ruler to measure lengths.

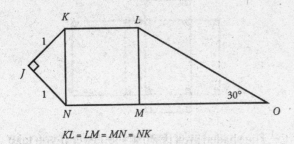

$KL = LM = MN = NK$

In the figure above, what is the length of *LO*?

(A) 2

(B) $2\sqrt{2}$

(C) $2\sqrt{3}$

(D) 4

(E) $4\sqrt{2}$

The correct choice is (B).

Take a piece of scratch paper (you'll be given some at the beginning of the test) and mark the length of *JK*. The distance is 1. Now measure that distance against *LO*.

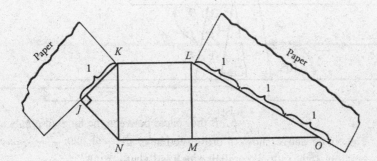

It appears that *LO* is slightly more than 2.5; make it about 2.8. Which answer is closest? The best approximation for $\sqrt{2}$ is 1.4, so (B) is 2(1.4) = 2.8.

EXERCISES: PROBLEM SOLVING

Exercise 1

10 QUESTIONS • 10 MINUTES

Directions: For each of the following questions, select the best of the answer choices.

1. If $\frac{3}{4}x = 1$, then $\frac{2}{3}x =$

   (A) $\frac{1}{3}$

   (B) $\frac{1}{2}$

   (C) $\frac{2}{3}$

   (D) $\frac{8}{9}$

   (E) 2

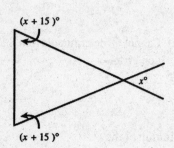

2. In the figure above, $x =$

   (A) 20

   (B) 35

   (C) 50

   (D) 65

   (E) 90

3. If $x = \frac{y}{7}$ and $7x = 12$, then $y =$

   (A) 3

   (B) 5

   (C) 7

   (D) 12

   (E) 72

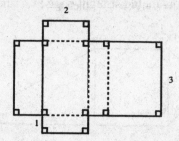

4. A rectangular box with a top is created by folding the figure above along the dotted lines. What is the volume of the box in cubic feet?

   (A) 6

   (B) 9

   (C) 12

   (D) 18

   (E) 24

5. What is the difference of the areas of two squares with sides of 5 and 4, respectively?

   (A) 3

   (B) 4

   (C) 9

   (D) 16

   (E) 41

6. If the spaces between the lettered points in the figure above are all equal, then $\frac{PT}{2} - \frac{QS}{2}$ is equal to which of the following?

   (A) $PS - QR$

   (B) $QR - QS$

   (C) PR

   (D) QT

   (E) ST

7. Exactly three years before the year in which Anna was born, the year was $1980 - x$. In terms of x, on Anna's twentieth birthday, the year will be

   (A) $1977 + x$

   (B) $1997 + x$

   (C) $2003 - x$

   (D) $2003 + x$

   (E) $2006 + x$

8. If $x = k + \frac{1}{2} = \frac{k+3}{2}$, then $x =$

   (A) $\frac{1}{3}$

   (B) $\frac{1}{2}$

   (C) 1

   (D) 2

   (E) $\frac{5}{2}$

9. For how many 3-digit whole numbers is the sum of the digits equal to 3?

   (A) 4

   (B) 5

   (C) 6

   (D) 7

   (E) 8

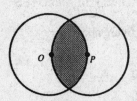

10. In the figure above, if the radius of the circles is 1, then what is the perimeter of the shaded part of the figure?

    (A) $\frac{1}{6}\pi$

    (B) $\frac{2}{3}\pi$

    (C) $\frac{4}{3}\pi$

    (D) $\frac{3}{2}\pi$

    (E) Cannot be determined from the information given.

Exercise 2

5 QUESTIONS • 5 MINUTES

Directions: For each of the following questions, select the best of the answer choices.

1. If $7 - x = 0$, then $10 - x =$

   (A) –3

   (B) 0

   (C) 3

   (D) 7

   (E) 10

2. A triangle with sides of 4, 6, and 8 has the same perimeter as an equilateral triangle with sides of length

   (A) 2

   (B) $\frac{3}{2}$

   (C) 3

   (D) 6

   (E) 8

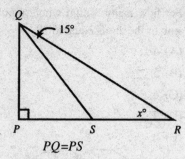

PQ=PS

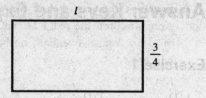

3. In the figure above, $x =$

(A) 15

(B) 30

(C) 40

(D) 60

(E) 75

4. If x and y are negative numbers, which of the following is negative?

(A) xy

(B) $(xy)^2$

(C) $(x-y)^2$

(D) $x + y$

(E) $\dfrac{x}{y}$

5. If the area of the rectangle shown above is equal to 1, then $l =$

(A) $\dfrac{4}{9}$

(B) 1

(C) $\dfrac{4}{3}$

(D) $\dfrac{9}{4}$

(E) Cannot be determined from the information given.

Answer Keys and Explanations

Exercise 1

1. D	3. D	5. C	7. C	9. C
2. C	4. A	6. E	8. E	10. C

1. **(D)** Solve for x. $\frac{3}{4}x = 1$, so $x = \frac{4}{3}$. Then substitute this for x in the expression $\frac{2}{3}x$. $\frac{2}{3}\left(\frac{4}{3}\right) = \frac{8}{9}$.

2. **(C)** Since the unlabeled angle inside the triangle is equal to x:

    $$(x + 15) + (x + 15) + x = 180$$
    $$3x + 30 = 180$$
    $$3x = 150$$
    $$x = 50$$

    You can also estimate the size of the angle. It seems to be slightly less than 60°, so the answer must be (C).

3. **(D)** Treat the two equations as simultaneous equations. You can substitute $\frac{y}{7}$ for x in the second equation. $7\left(\frac{y}{7}\right) = 12$, so $y = 12$.

4. **(A)** The box when assembled looks like this:

    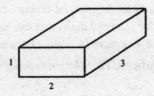

    Its volume is $1 \times 2 \times 3 = 6$.

5. **(C)** The question asks for:

    (Area of square with side 5) minus (area of square with side 4) = $(5 \times 5) - (4 \times 4) = 25 - 16 = 9$.

6. **(E)** $\frac{PT}{2}$ is $\frac{1}{2}$ the length of the entire segment. QS is $\frac{1}{2}$ the length of the segment, and $\frac{QS}{2}$ is $\frac{1}{4}$ of the segment. So $\frac{PT}{2} - \frac{QS}{2}$ is $\frac{1}{2}$ of the segment minus $\frac{1}{4}$ of the segment, which is $\frac{1}{4}$ of the length of the segment. Only (E) is $\frac{1}{4}$ the length of the segment.

    You can also assign numbers to the lengths. Assume that each segment is equal to 1. Then PT is 4, and $\frac{PT}{2} = 2$. And QS is 2, and $\frac{QS}{2} = 1$. Finally, $2 - 1 = 1$. So the correct answer choice should have a length of 1:

    (A) $3 - 1 = 2$ (Wrong.)

    (B) $1 - 2 = -1$ (Wrong.)

    (C) 2 (Wrong.)

    (D) 3 (Wrong.)

    (E) 1 (Correct.)

7. **(C)** Create a formula. Anna was born three years after $1980 - x$, so she was born in $1980 - x + 3$. 20 years later the year will be $1980 - x + 3 + 20 = 2003 - x$.

    You can also substitute numbers. Assume $x = 1$. And then assume Anna was born three years after $1980 - 1 = 1979$, so she was born in 1982. So she will turn 20 in 2002. Substituting 1 for x in each of the answer choices:

(A) $1977 + 1 = 1978$ (Wrong.)

(B) $1997 + 1 = 1998$ (Wrong.)

(C) $2003 - 1 = 2002$ (Correct.)

(D) $2003 + 1 = 2004$ (Wrong.)

(E) $2006 + 1 = 2007$ (Wrong.)

8. **(E)** You really have two equations:

$x = k + \frac{1}{2}$ and $k + \frac{1}{2} = \frac{k+3}{2}$

Solve for k:

$k + \frac{1}{2} = \frac{k+3}{2}$

$2 = \left(k + \frac{1}{2}\right) = k + 3$

$2k + 1 = k + 3$

$k = 2$

Now substitute 2 for k:

$x = k + \frac{1}{2} = 2 + \frac{1}{2} = \frac{5}{2}$

You can also try testing the choices, but the process is tedious. For example, assume that $x = 1$. On that assumption, the first equation gives the value of k as $\frac{1}{2}$, but when $\frac{1}{2}$ is substituted for k into the second equation, the second equation is false. So (C) is incorrect. (E), however, does work. If $x = \frac{5}{2}$, then the value of k in the first equation is 2. And substituting 2 for both ks in the second equation produces a true statement.

9. **(C)** They are 102, 111, 120, 201, 210, and 300. The solution is mostly a matter of mental brute force, just counting the possibilities. But that's not too much to do. The only digits that can be used are 0, 1, 2, and 3. You don't have to worry about numbers using digits of 4 or more (4 is already more than 3).

10. **(C)** This is the last question in the series, and it is very difficult. The solution depends on seeing the following:

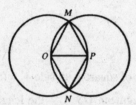

The triangles are equilateral (*OM, ON, PM, PN,* and *OP* are all radii), and angles *MON* and *MPN* are both 120°. So each arc is 120°, or $\frac{1}{3}$ of the circle. Since the radius of the circle is 1, the circumference of each circle is $2\pi(1) = 2\pi$. Therefore, each arc is $\frac{1}{3}$ of 2π, or $\frac{2\pi}{3}$. Together, they total $\frac{2\pi}{3} + \frac{2\pi}{3} = \frac{4\pi}{3}$.

This problem can also be attacked by "guestimation." Each arc looks to be $\frac{1}{3}$ of the circle. Use that assumption and you will select (C).

Exercise 2

1. C   2. D   3. B   4. D   5. C

1. **(C)** Solve for x: $7 - x = 0$, so $7 = x$. Then substitute 7 for x in the expression $10 - x$: $10 - 7 = 3$.

2. **(D)** A triangle with sides of 3, 6, and 9 has a perimeter of $3 + 6 + 9 = 18$. An equilateral triangle with the same perimeter would have a side of $18 \div 3 = 6$.

3. **(B)** Since $PQ = PS$, PQS is a 45-45-90 triangle. Angle PQR is $45° + 15° = 60°$. And $x = 180° - 90° - 60° = 30°$. You should also be able to estimate the angle as $30°$.

4. **(D)** Since x and y are negative, both (A) and (E) must be positive. As for (B) and (C), so long as neither x nor y is zero, those expressions must be positive. (Any number other than zero squared gives a positive result.) (D), however, is negative, since it represents the sum of two negative numbers. And you can also test the choices with numbers.

5. **(C)** Just use the formula for the area of a rectangle: $l \times \frac{3}{4} = 1$, so $l = \frac{4}{3}$. You can also test choices until you find one that works in the area formula, but you should be able to solve a simple equation like this without needing to substitute.

CHAPTER 10

Quantitative Comparison

PLAN A: ACCELERATED

- *Read* the chapter
- *Study* What Smart Test-takers Know"
- *Complete* Exercise 1
- *Check* your answers

PLAN B: TOP SPEED

- *Read* "How Do You Solve Quantitative Comparison Questions?"
- *Study* "What Smart Test-takers Know"
- *Complete* Exercise 2
- *Check* your answers

You'll Find Answers to These Questions

What is quantitative comparison?
How do you solve quantitative comparison questions?
What do smart test-takers know about quantitative comparison?

WHAT IS QUANTITATIVE COMPARISON?

For this type of question, you must compare two quantities, one shown in Column A and one shown in Column B. You must decide if one quantity is greater than the other, if the two quantities are the same, or if the relationship between the quantities cannot be determined from the information given. For each question, you are given four answer choices as follow:

    (A) if the quantity in Column A is the greater

    (B) if the quantity in Column B is the greater

    (C) if the two quantities are equal

    (D) if the relationship cannot be determined from the information given

Note: Since the computer processes your mouse clicks, the answer choices that appear on the monitor screen won't have letters. But for ease of reference in this book, we'll continue to refer to the letters.

GRE Quantitative Comparison Questions

Quantitative comparisons are interspersed with regular problem-solving questions and graphs in the math section. You'll get 13 to 15 quantitative comparison questions.

    Quantitative comparisons cover the same mix of arithmetic, algebra, and geometry that appears in the regular problem-solving questions.

    Here are the directions for GRE quantitative comparison questions, together with some sample questions and explanations.

Anatomy of Quantitative Comparisons

Directions: For each of the following questions two quantities are given, one in Column A and one in Column B. Compare the two quantities and choose the correct conclusion. These are your options:

(A) if the quantity in Column A is the greater

(B) if the quantity in Column B is the greater

(C) if the two quantities are equal

(D) if the relationship cannot be determined from the information given

Common Information: In any question, information applying to both columns is centered between the columns and above the quantities in Columns A and B. Any symbol that appears in both columns represents the same idea or quantity in both columns.

Figures are intended to provide useful information, but unless a note states that a figure is drawn to scale, you should not solve problems by estimating or measuring.

You'll recognize quantitative comparison questions on the test by the Column A/Column B layout. So just dismiss the directions and get right to work.

The answer ovals on your CAT monitor screen won't have letters, so just think:

> *First oval: A is bigger.*
> *Second oval: B is bigger.*
> *Third oval: A and B are equal.*
> *Fourth oval: Cannot be determined.*

Centered information is often an equation, a geometry figure, or a verbal description such as "R is a square room."

You can't trust the figures in quantitative comparisons. You can trust the sequence and relationships, but you can't rely on the apparent magnitudes. An angle that looks to be 90° may not be; a line segment that looks longer than another line segment may not be; and a region that appears to be equal in area to another may not be. So use your knowledge of math instead.

	Column A	**Column B**	
1.	$\dfrac{1}{2} + \dfrac{1}{2}$	$\dfrac{1}{2} \times \dfrac{1}{2}$	*The correct answer is (A). Column A has the value 1 while Column B has the value $\frac{1}{4}$.*
2.	Twice the area of a circle with a radius of 1	Area of a circle with a radius of 2	*The correct answer is (B). The value of Column A is 2π, and the value of Column B is 4π.*
3.	$\dfrac{6x + 6y}{x + y}$	6	*The correct answer is (C). Simplify first by factoring and then by canceling: $6x + 6y = 6(x + y)$. Then you can cancel the $x + y$ in both the numerator and the denominator of Column A, leaving just 6.*
4.	x^2	x^3	*The correct answer is (D). x is a variable and so could be positive, negative, or even zero. Consequently, it cannot be determined which of the two quantities is larger.*

HOW DO YOU SOLVE QUANTITATIVE COMPARISON QUESTIONS?

Here's a simple, five-step plan to help you solve GRE quantitative comparison questions.

Quantitative Comparisons: Getting It Right

1. Memorize the sequence of the answer choices.
2. For each question, read the centered information.
3. Compare the quantity in Column A to the quantity in Column B.
4. Do only as much work as is needed to make the comparison.
5. Choose your answer.

Now let's look at these steps in more detail.

1. **Memorize the sequence of the answer choices, but don't learn the rest of the directions**. This will save you time because you won't need to refer to them for every question.
2. **For each question, read the centered information.** Remember that the centered information governs the entire problem.
3. **Compare the quantity in Column A to the quantity in Column B.** Even though there are two quantities in each question, deal with one at a time. See how each quantity relates to the centered information.
4. **Do only as much work as is needed to make the comparison.** Simplify mathematical expressions. You shouldn't have to do involved calculations to get the answer. If you're calculating endlessly, you've probably missed the mathematical principle the question is asking about. Consider all possibilities for any unknowns. Think what would happen if special numbers such as 0, negative numbers, or fractions were put into play.
5. **Choose the appropriate answer oval by clicking on it with the mouse and then confirm.**

Now let's look at some additional sample quantitative comparison questions. As you read each explanation, think of how the five-step solution process applies.

Column A	Column B
1. $5 \times 6 \times 7 \times 8$	$5 + 6 + 7 + 8$

The correct answer to this quantitative comparison is (A). Column A is 1680 while Column B is 26.

	Column A	Column B
2.	$\dfrac{1}{7} - \dfrac{1}{8}$	$\dfrac{1}{8}$

The correct answer is (B). $\dfrac{1}{7} - \dfrac{1}{8} = \dfrac{1}{56}$. $\dfrac{1}{8}$ is greater than $\dfrac{1}{56}$.

	Column A	Column B
3.	3429	$3(10^3) + 4(10^2)$ $+ 2(10^1) + 9(10^0)$

The correct answer is (C):

$$
\begin{aligned}
3(10^3) = 3(1000) &= 3{,}000 \\
4(10^2) = 4(100) &= 400 \\
2(10^1) = 2(10) &= 20 \\
9(10^0) = 9(1) &= \underline{+\ \ 9} \\
&= 3{,}429
\end{aligned}
$$

So the two quantities are the same.

	Column A	Column B
4.	The product of three numbers between 3 and 4	The product of four numbers between 2 and 3

The correct answer is (D). You don't know the value of any of the numbers. If the three numbers in Column A are almost 4, then Column A could be almost as large as 64. On the other hand, it could be almost as small as 27. As for Column B, if those four numbers are almost as large as 3, then Column B could be almost 81. On the other hand, if they are almost as small as 2, Column B could be almost as small as 16.

	Column A	Column B
	The price of a pound of cheese increased from \$2.00 to \$2.50.	
5.	The percent increase in the price of cheese	25%

The correct answer is (C). Remember that the centered information applies to both columns. The percent increase in the price of cheese is 25%.

	Column A	Column B
6.	$(x)(x)(x)(x)(x)$	x^5

The correct answer is (C). $(x)(x)(x)(x)(x) = x^5$. Remember that according to the directions, any symbol that appears in both columns represents the same idea or quantity in both columns. So the x on the left means the same thing as the x on the right, and the two expressions are the same.

WHAT SMART TEST-TAKERS KNOW

A COMPARISON IS FOREVER.

In quantitative comparisons, the first answer choice (A) is correct only if the quantity is always greater than that in Column B. The reverse is true of the second oval (B); it must always be greater than the information in Column A. If you choose the third oval (C), it means that the two quantities are *always* equal. The condition must hold true regardless of what number you plug in for a variable.

QUANTITATIVE COMPARISONS ARE NOT ABOUT CALCULATING.

If you find yourself calculating up a storm on a quantitative comparison, you've probably missed the boat. There's sure to be a simpler, shorter way to solve the problem. Find a way to reduce the amount of actual math you need to do. Take a look at these examples.

Column A	Column B
$31 \times 32 \times 33$ $\times 34 \times 35$	$32 \times 33 \times 34$ $\times 35 \times 36$

> **AVOID THE TRAPS!**
>
> **Long calculations are a tip-off that something's wrong.** If a quantitative comparison seems to require a calculator, you are not looking at it correctly. Try to find a shortcut such as simplification.

You don't have to do any calculations to get the answer. You would be comparing the product of five consecutive integers, but notice that the integers in Column B are larger. Therefore, the product of those numbers would be greater than Column A. So, the correct answer is (B) and you didn't have to multiply a thing.

Column A	Column B
The formula for the volume of a right circular cylinder is $V = \pi r^2 h$	
The volume of a right circular cylinder with $r = 3$ and $h = 6$	The volume of a right circular cylinder with $r = 6$ and $h = 3$

You might think that for this question you absolutely have to do the complete calculations to find the volume of each cylinder. But you don't! Take a look at how simply this problem can be solved.

Volume $A = \pi(3^2)(6) = (3.14)(3)(3)(6)$
Volume $B = \pi(6^2)(3) = (3.14)(6)(6)(3)$

Since you're doing the same operation for both formulas—multiplying by 3.14—that cancels out. So the problem then shifts to the other factors: Which is larger, $(3^2)(6)$ or $(6^2)(3)$? At this point you should be able to see that the second one is larger. If you still need to take it another step, multiply $(3^2)(6)$ $= (9)(6) = 54$ and then $(6^2)(3) = (36)(3)$. You don't have to finish because you can see that $(36)(3)$ is larger than 54.

IF THE MATH IS NOT DIFFICULT, YOU SHOULD DO IT.

Column A	Column B
$10,000,001 + 0.009$	$10,000,002 - 0.00199$

The correct answer is (B). The indicated addition and subtraction is not that difficult, so you won't lose much time doing it. Instead of trying to find an elegant logical solution to the comparison, use the crude method of adding and subtracting.

Column A	Column B
$(x^3)(x^2)(x^7)$	$(x^3)^4$

The correct answer is (C). Again, you should just do the operations that are indicated. Column A becomes x^{12}; so too does Column B.

WHEN THE CENTERED INFORMATION CONTAINS UNKNOWNS, YOU SHOULD SOLVE FOR THE UNKNOWNS.

Column A	Column B

$$3x = 12$$
$$4y = 20$$

Column A	Column B
x	y

The correct answer is (B). You need values for x and y, so solve for both.

IT PAYS TO SIMPLIFY.

Simplify complex arithmetic or algebraic expressions before trying to make a comparison.

Column A	Column B
$\dfrac{2,000,000}{200,000}$	$\dfrac{1,000}{100}$

The correct answer is (C). Simplify the comparison by canceling, and you wind up comparing $\dfrac{20}{2}$, which is 10, with $\dfrac{10}{1}$, which is also 10.

YOU CAN SIMPLIFY BY ADDING OR SUBTRACTING THE SAME VALUE IN EACH COLUMN.

Column A	Column B
$4x + 5$	$3x + 6$

The correct answer is (D). At first, however, you may not be able to see that the relationship is indeterminate. Start by subtracting 5 from both sides of the comparison. The result is:

Column A	Column B
$4x$	$3x + 1$

Now subtract $3x$ from both sides:

Column A	Column B
x	1

In this form, the comparison is fairly easy. Since you have no information about x, the answer must be (D).

YOU CAN SIMPLIFY BY MULTIPLYING OR DIVIDING EACH COLUMN BY THE SAME POSITIVE NUMBER.

Here's another example, in which the quantities in both columns can be simplified by dividing.

Column A	Column B
$9^{99} - 9^{98}$	9^{98}

The correct answer is (A). Divide both sides by 9^{98}:

Column A	Column B
$\dfrac{9^{99} - 9^{98}}{9^{98}}$	$\dfrac{9^{98}}{9^{98}}$
$9^1 - 9^0$	9^0
$9 - 1$	1
8	1

This proves that Column A is larger. (It doesn't prove how much larger since dividing changed the ratio between the two quantities, but we are only interested in which is larger—not how much larger.)

WARNING!!! DO NOT SIMPLIFY BY MULTIPLICATION OR DIVISION UNLESS YOU KNOW THE QUANTITY YOU ARE USING IS POSITIVE.

Column A	Column B
$3x$	$4x$

The correct answer is (D). But watch what happens if you try to divide both quantities by x:

Column A	Column B
$\dfrac{3x}{x} = 3$	$\dfrac{4x}{x} = 4$

This move is wrong since you do not know for certain that x is positive. As a result, you arrive at the erroneous conclusion that Column B is greater. You can prove this by trying a couple of different values for x. If x is a number like 2 or 5, it is true that Column B is greater. But if x is a negative number,

TESTSMARTS

Use the "good-enough" principle. Do only so much work as you have to to make the comparison. Once you know that one column is larger than the other, enter the answer. You do not have to find out how much larger.

then Column A is greater. Or if x is zero, the columns are equal. This technique only works when you know for certain that the term you are dividing or multiplying by is positive.

YOU HAVE TO CONSIDER ALL THE POSSIBILITIES.

When there are unknowns in the quantities being compared, you have to remember to consider all possibilities for what those unknowns might be. For example, an unknown might be 1, 0, a fraction, or a negative number. In each of these cases, the number has special properties that will affect your calculations.

AN UNKNOWN MIGHT BE ZERO.

Zero has special properties that come into play when you plug it in for an unknown.

Column A	**Column B**

$$x > 0, y > 0, z = 0$$

$3z(2x + 5y)$	$3x(2z + 5y)$

If $z = 0$, then $3z = 0$ and the product of Column A is 0. In Column B, though, $2z = 0$, so it comes out of the comparison. The product will be $(3x)(5y)$, which will be a positive number. This means that (B) is the correct answer choice.

Column A	**Column B**

$$x < 0, y > 0, z = 0$$

$3z(2x + 5y)$	$3x(2z + 5y)$

Again, the product of Column A is 0, because $3z$ still equals 0. The change comes in Column B. Because x is less than 0, $3x$ will be negative and $5y$ will be positive, so the product will be a negative number. This time, (A) is the correct answer.

AN UNKNOWN MIGHT BE A NEGATIVE NUMBER.

Column A	**Column B**

$$3x = 4y$$

x	y

Don't think that (A) is the correct answer, even though if x and y are positive, x is greater than y. What if x and y are negative, as in $3(-4) = 4(-3)$; then y is greater than x. And if x and y are both zero, both columns are equal. Since you have no way of knowing what the values are, the correct answer is (D).

AN UNKNOWN MIGHT BE A FRACTION.

Column A	Column B

$$x > 0 \text{ and } x \neq 1$$

x^2	x

The correct answer to this comparison is (D). If x is larger than 1, then x^2 is larger than x. But if x^2 is between 0 and 1—a fraction—then x^2 is smaller than x.

PROPER FRACTIONS CAN PLAY TRICKS.

Remember that a proper fraction raised to a power is smaller than the fraction itself.

Column A	Column B
$\dfrac{27}{41}$	$\left(\dfrac{27}{41}\right)^{15}$

If you keep the math principle in mind, you don't even have to think about doing these calculations. Since each successive multiplication would result in a smaller fraction, Column A will always be larger than Column B, so your answer is (A).

IN QUANTITATIVE COMPARISONS, FIGURES ARE NOT NECESSARILY DRAWN TO SCALE.

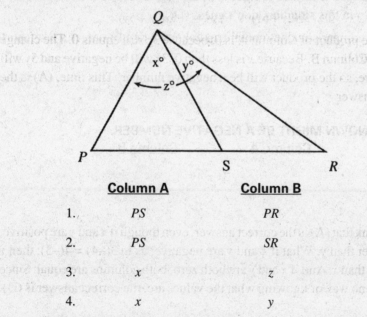

	Column A	Column B
1.	PS	PR
2.	PS	SR
3.	x	z
4.	x	y

Figures in quantitative comparison questions are not necessarily drawn to scale. This is very important. Although you can rely upon the arrangement of points, angles, lines, etc., you cannot trust the apparent magnitude of geometrical quantities.

AVOID THE TRAPS!

Don't trust the drawings. In this part, the figures are *not* necessarily drawn to scale.

The answer to question 1 is (B). Since point *S* lies between *P* and *R*, the entire length of *PR* must be longer than that part which is *PS*.

The answer to question 2 is (D). You are not entitled to assume anything about the location of point *S*—other than that it is on *PR* somewhere between *P* and *R*. Thus, although it looks like *PS* is longer than *SR*, you cannot determine that as a matter of mathematics.

The answer to question 3 is (B). Angle *z* is equal to $x + y$, so the entire angle *z* must be larger than just that part labeled *x*.

The answer to question 4 is (D). The relative size of angles *x* and *y* is determined by the location of point *S*. Again, although *S* lies somewhere between *P* and *R*, its exact location cannot be mathematically determined. So the relative sizes of *x* and *y* remain an unknown.

PLUGGING IN NUMBERS CAN HELP.

If you're stuck on a comparison with unknowns, try substituting numbers. Choose the numbers at random and plug them into the equations. Do this with three different substitutions and see if there is any consistent result. It's not a guarantee, but it's definitely worth a shot.

STRATEGIC GUESSING CAN RAISE YOUR SCORE.

When all else fails, call up your guessing skills. Here's how you can tip the scales in your favor, even if it's only a little bit.

- If a comparison involves only numbers without any unknowns, chances are that you'll be able to figure out the quantities and make a comparison. So in this situation, don't guess (D).

- If the comparison does contain an unknown or a figure, as a last resort guess (D).

EXERCISES: QUANTITATIVE COMPARISON

Exercise 1

15 QUESTIONS • 12 MINUTES

Directions: For each of the following questions two quantities are given, one in Column A and one in Column B. Compare the two quantities and choose

(A) if the quantity in Column A is greater

(B) if the quantity in Column B is greater

(C) if the two quantities are equal

(D) if the relationship cannot be determined from the information given

Common Information: In any question, information applying to both columns is centered between the columns and above the quantities in columns A and B. Any symbol that appears in both columns represents the same idea or quantity in both columns.

	Column A	Column B
1.	$\sqrt{9+16}$	7

$$7n = 7$$

	Column A	Column B
2.	$\dfrac{7}{n}$	$\dfrac{n}{7}$
3.	$\left(\dfrac{1}{2}\right)^{11}$	$\left(-\dfrac{1}{2}\right)^{11}$

The digit 3 in the numeral 123,456 represents $3 \times 10n$

	Column A	Column B
4.	n	5
5.	The greatest prime number less than 29	23

Mary has $5 less than Sam, and Mark has half as much money as Sam.

	Column A	Column B
6.	Amount of money that Mary has	Amount of money that Mark has

	Column A	Column B
7.	x	y
8.	$\dfrac{0.125}{4}$	$\dfrac{0.25}{8}$

$$xy = 25$$

	Column A	Column B
9.	x	y

	Column A	**Column B**

y ———|——— z ———|——— x →

10.	yz	xz

x and y are positive integers

$x < y$

11.	$\dfrac{x}{y}$	$\sqrt{\dfrac{x}{y}}$

$x + y \neq 0$

12.	$\dfrac{5x+5y}{x+y}$	5

	Column A	**Column B**

Questions 13–14

For all non-zero numbers $a, b, c, d,$

$$abcd = ac - bd$$

13.	4321	4
14.	$xyxy$	$(x+y)(x-y)$

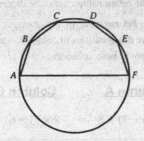

AF is the diameter of the circle.

$AF = 2$

15.	Area of polygon A, B, C, D, E, F	$\dfrac{\pi}{2}$

Exercise 2

8 QUESTIONS • 8 MINUTES

Directions: For each of the following questions two quantities are given, one in Column A and one in Column B. Compare the two quantities and choose

(A) if the quantity in Column A is greater

(B) if the quantity in Column B is greater

(C) if the two quantities are equal

(D) if the relationship cannot be determined from the information given

Common Information: In any question, information applying to both columns is centered between the columns and above the quantities in columns A and B. Any symbol that appears in both columns represents the same idea or quantity in both columns.

Column A	Column B

1. $5 \times (6 \times 7) \times 8$ $8 \times (5 \times 6) \times 7$

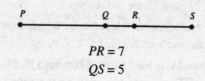

$$PR = 7$$
$$QS = 5$$

2. QR $\qquad$ 2

The weight of package x is more than twice the weights of packages y and z combined.

3. The weight of package z $\qquad$ $\dfrac{1}{3}$ the weight of package x

$$x + y > 3$$

4. $\dfrac{x+y}{3}$ $\qquad$ $\dfrac{3}{x+y}$

$$a + 2b = 3$$
$$a - 2b = 3$$

5. a $\qquad$ b

Column A	Column B

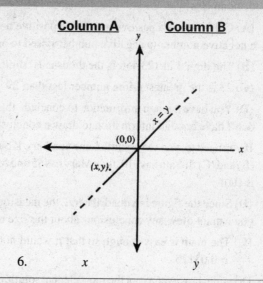

6. x $\qquad$ y

7. Volume of a rectangular solid with sides of lengths $\dfrac{1}{2}$, $\dfrac{1}{3}$, and $\dfrac{1}{6}$ $\qquad$ Volume of a rectangular solid with sides of lengths $\dfrac{1}{6}$, $\dfrac{1}{6}$, and 1

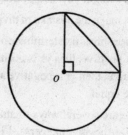

O is the center of the circle.
The area of the triangle is 4.

8. Radius of the circle $\qquad$ 4

Answer Keys and Explanations

Exercise 1

1. B	6. D	11. B
2. A	7. D	12. C
3. A	8. C	13. A
4. B	9. D	14. C
5. C	10. D	15. B

1. **(B)** $\sqrt{9+16} = \sqrt{25} = 5$. So Column B is larger.

2. **(A)** Solve for n in the centered equation: $n = 1$. Then substitute 1 for n in each column. Column A is $\frac{7}{1} = 7$; Column B is $\frac{1}{7}$.

3. **(A)** Column A is a positive number (a positive number raised to a positive power is positive). Column B is a negative number (a negative number raised to an odd power is negative).

4. **(B)** The digit 3 in 123,456 is the thousands' digit. It represents 3,000, which is equal to 3×10^3. So $n = 3$.

5. **(C)** 23 is the greatest prime number less than 29. (24, 25, 26, 27, and 28 are not primes.)

6. **(D)** You have enough information to conclude that both Mary and Mark have less money than Sam, but you don't have enough information to draw a conclusion about how much each has.

    If you need to, you can assume some numbers. If Sam has $20, then Mary has $15 and Mark has $10. Eliminate (B) and (C). If Sam has $10, then Mary has $5 and Mark also has $5. Eliminate (A) as well. So the correct choice is (D).

7. **(D)** Since the figure is a quadrilateral, the measures of the four interior angles total 360°. So, $x + y = 180$, but you cannot draw any conclusions about the size of x or the size of y.

8. **(C)** The math is easy enough so that it would not be a mistake to do the division: $0.125 \div 4 = 0.03125$ and $\frac{0.25}{8} = 0.03125$.

    Division, however, is not the most elegant solution. Since 4 and 8 are positive numbers, you can multiply both sides of the comparison by both 4 and 8. Column A becomes $8(0.125)$ and Column B becomes $4(0.25)$. These operations are easier than division: $8(0.125) = 1$ and $4(0.25) = 1$.

    You can avoid the math altogether by reasoning that the numerator in the fraction in Column A is half the numerator of the fraction in Column B, and the denominator in Column A is half the denominator in Column B. So, the two fractions are equivalent, as are $\frac{1}{2}$ and $\frac{4}{8}$.

9. **(D)** x and y might be 5 and 5. But they might also be 1 and 25 or -1 and -25.

10. **(D)** Don't make the mistake of dividing both sides of the comparison by z. You can't be sure that z is positive.

    The relationship is indeterminate because you don't know the signs of the numbers. If y and z are both negative, while x is positive, then yz is positive and xz is negative (and Column A is larger). If y is negative but x and z are positive, then yz is negative and xz is positive (and Column B is larger). If z happens to be zero, then yz and xz are equal.

11. **(B)** There are several ways to attack this comparison. The most sophisticated is to reason that since $x < y$ (and both are positive integers), $\frac{x}{y}$ is a fraction. Moreover, the square root of a fraction is larger than the fraction itself. (For example, $\sqrt{\frac{1}{4}} = \frac{1}{2}$, and $\frac{1}{2} > \frac{1}{4}$.)

You can also grind out a solution by manipulating both sides of the comparison. Start by squaring both sides. Column A becomes $\frac{x^2}{y^2}$ and Column B becomes $\frac{x}{y}$. Since x and y are both positive, you can then divide both sides by x and multiply both sides by y. Column A becomes $\frac{x}{y}$ and Column B becomes 1. At this point, you should be able to see that $\frac{x}{y}$ is less than 1. If you still are not sure, multiply both sides by y again. Column A becomes simply x and Column B simply y. The centered information states specifically that $x < y$.

Finally, you could substitute some numbers.

12. **(C)** Factor the expression in Column A: $5x + 5y = 5(x + y)$. Then $\frac{x+y}{x+y} = 1$, so Column A is just 5. Of course, if you didn't see the possibility of factoring, you could substitute a few simple numbers. The fact that one or two substitutions show the columns to be equal is not proof that the correct answer is (C), but substitution allows you to eliminate (A) and (B) and strongly guess that the answer is (C) rather than (D).

13. **(A)** Do the indicated operations. $(4)(2) - (3)(1) = 8 - 3 = 5$. So Column A is larger.

14. **(C)** Set up the operation: $(x)(x) - (y)(y) = x^2 - y^2$. By now, you should recognize that this can be factored: $x^2 - y^2 = (x + y)(x - y)$. So the two columns are equal.

15. **(B)** The "good enough" principle is the key to this comparison. First, since the circle has a diameter of 2, it has a radius of 1 and an area of $\pi(1^2) = \pi$. Whatever the area of the polygon really is, it is less than that of the semicircle. So the area of the polygon is less than $\frac{\pi}{2}$.

Exercise 2

1. C	5. A
2. D	6. B
3. D	7. C
4. A	8. B

1. **(C)** There is no need even to do the multiplication. Since the order of multiplication is irrelevant, the two columns are equal.

2. **(D)** Use the technique of distorting the figure:

3. **(D)** No information is supplied about the actual weights of the packages. Assume some numbers. If $x = 100$, $y = 1$, and $z = 1$, then $\frac{1}{3}x > z$. If $x = 100$, $y = 1$, and $z = 48$, then $\frac{1}{3}x < z$.

4. **(A)** You can simplify across the comparison. Multiply both sides by 3 and both sides by $(x + y)$ (you know $x + y$ is positive). Column A becomes $(x + y)^2$ and Column B becomes 3^2. Take the square root of both sides. Column A becomes $x + y$; Column B becomes 3. Since $x + y > 3$, Column A is larger.

   You can reason to the same conclusion. Since $x + y$ is greater than 3, Column A is greater than $\frac{3}{3}$ while Column B is less than $\frac{3}{3}$. In other words, Column A is greater than 1 and Column B is a fraction.

5. **(A)** Solve the centered equations by adding them together. $2a = 6$, so $a = 3$. Thus, b must be zero.

6. **(B)** Since the point (x,y) is above the line $x = y$, the absolute value of x is greater than the absolute value of y. But both coordinates are negative. So x is smaller than y. For example, (x,y) might be $(-3, -2)$.

7. **(C)** The calculations are simple, so do them. $\frac{1}{2} \times \frac{1}{3} \times \frac{1}{6} = \frac{1}{36}$. And $\frac{1}{6} \times \frac{1}{6} \times 1 = \frac{1}{36}$. The volumes are equal.

8. **(B)** The two sides of the triangle that form a right angle can be treated as altitude and base. Since they are both radii of the circle, they are equal. Using r to represent their length:

$$\frac{1}{2}(r)(r) = 4$$
$$r^2 = 8$$
$$r = 2\sqrt{2}$$

CHAPTER 11

Graphs

TIME MANAGER STUDY PLANS

You'll Find Answers to These Questions

What is a graph?
How do you solve graph questions?
What do smart test-takers know about graph questions?

WHAT IS A GRAPH?

A graph is really just a picture of some numbers. Graphs are useful because you can literally see "at a glance" various comparisons and trends.

Learning to read graphs is not that difficult once you understand the fundamental premise underlying all graphs: One Picture Is Worth a Thousand Words.

GRE Graph Questions

Graph questions form a separate set within the mathematics section because the questions are based on the graph. Graph questions are interspersed with problem-solving questions and quantitative comparisons in the scored math section.

The information on which graph questions are based may be presented in several different formats:

- table or chart
- bar graph
- line graph
- pie chart

The directions for GRE graph questions are the same as the directions for regular problem-solving questions. They look like this:

Directions: For each of the following questions select the best answer choices.

Now let's look at some typical GRE graph questions.

PLAN A: ACCELERATED

- *Read* the chapter
- *Study* "What Smart Test-takers Know"
- *Complete* Exercise 1
- *Check* your answers

PLAN B: TOP SPEED

- *Read* "How Do You Solve Graph Questions?"
- *Study* "What Smart Test-takers Know"
- *Complete* Exercise 2
- *Check* your answers

Anatomy of Graph Questions

Directions: For each of the following questions, select the best answer choices.

Questions 1 and 2 refer to the following graph.

This is a simple pie chart. The size of each "slice" corresponds to the numerical value of the sector—in this case, the dollar value of that part of the store's inventory.

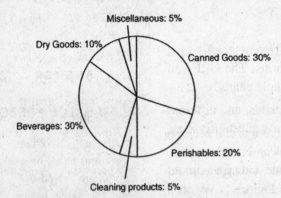

Store Inventory
(Total = $10,000)

Miscellaneous: 5%
Dry Goods: 10%
Canned Goods: 30%
Beverages: 30%
Perishables: 20%
Cleaning products: 5%

1. The dollar value of the Store Inventory of canned goods and perishables combined is:

   (A) $1,000
   (B) $1,500
   (C) $2,500
   (D) $5,000
   (E) $6,000

The correct answer is (D). Together, canned goods and perishables account for 50% of the inventory, and 50% × $10,000 is $5,000.

2. The dollar value of the beverages is how much greater than the dollar value of the dry goods?

   (A) $500
   (B) $750
   (C) $2,000
   (D) $2,500
   (E) $5,000

The correct answer is (C). Beverages account for $3,000 and dry goods for $1,000. So the difference is $2,000.

HOW DO YOU SOLVE GRAPH QUESTIONS?

Here's a simple three-step process to help you solve GRE graph questions.

Graphs: Getting It Right

1. Determine what kind of graph you have.
2. Read all the labels.
3. Answer the questions

Now let's look at these steps in more detail.

1. **Determine what kind of graph you have.** Different graphs give different types of information and in different forms. The GRE can include bar graphs, pie charts, line graphs, and simple charts.

2. **Read all the labels.** Graphs may have a title, legends, and different kinds of accompanying information. Often the key to a question is some clarifying remark contained in an inset or a footnote.

3. **Answer the questions.** Make sure that you estimate and approximate whenever possible.

Now let's look at some additional sample graph questions. As you read the answers, consider how the three-step solution process applies.

HERE'S THE ANSWER

How does "graph math" differ?

It does not. All of the questions based on a graph are solved using the same basic math principles used to answer other problem-solving questions.

Budget of Country X
(In millions of dollars)

	1991	1992	1993	1994	1995
Domestic	$200	$300	$400	$500	$600
Military	$400	$400	$300	$250	$500
Debt	$300	$250	$350	$400	$400

HERE'S THE ANSWER

How important are graphs?

Historically, graphs have accounted for the smallest portion of the math part of the exam.

1. What was the total budget of Country X in 1995?
    (A) $1.5 million
    (B) $15 million
    (C) $1 billion
    (D) $1.5 billion
    (E) $15 billion

The correct answer is (D). The total for 1995 is $600 + $500 + $400 = $1500 million, which is equal to $1.5 billion.

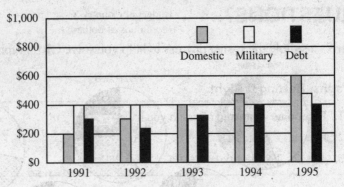

Budget of Country X
(In millions of dollars)

2. For Country X, domestic expenditures in 1995 were how much greater than domestic expenditures in 1993?

   (A) $20 million

   (B) $100 million

   (C) $200 million

   (D) $250 million

   (E) $500 million

The correct answer is (C). For 1995, domestic expenditures were $600 million and in 1993 they were $400 million.

Budget of Country X
(In millions of dollars)

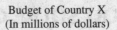

AVOID
THE TRAPS!

Percents can be a trap. Remember that percents are different from absolute quantities. In graph questions, you often have to convert from one to the other.

3. The percent increase in military spending by Country X from 1994 to 1995 was approximately

   (A) 10%

   (B) 50%

   (C) 100%

   (D) 150%

   (E) 200%

The correct answer is (C). In 1994, military spending was approximately $250 million; in 1995 approximately $500 million.

Why does the GRE include graphs?

If you are going to study in a field where math is used, you are probably going to have to work with graphs.

Budget of Country X
(In millions of dollars)

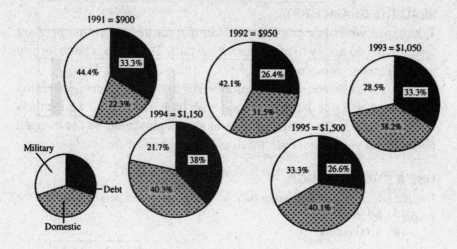

4. In which year did debt account for the greatest percentage of the budget of Country X?

    (A) 1991
    (B) 1992
    (C) 1993
    (D) 1994
    (E) 1995

The correct answer is (D).

WHAT SMART TEST-TAKERS KNOW

READ THE GRAPH FIRST.

Take an overview of the graph to make sure that you understand its important features, but do not try to memorize any details. The graph is there for you to refer to when you need it.

To a certain extent, graph questions are like reading comprehension questions: Some test the most general level of understanding while others test subtle points. Your first reading of the graph should be for its main points. Then you can go back for details if you need them.

USE A STRAIGHT EDGE.

Use the edge of a piece of paper (scratch paper or even a pencil) to make the graph easier to read.

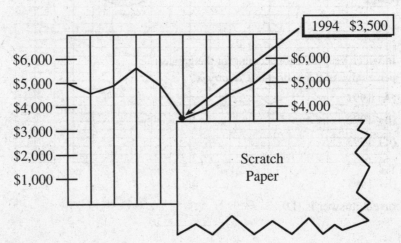

"GUESSTIMATE."

What was the ratio of 1994 to 1995?

(A) $\frac{1}{5}$

(B) $\frac{2}{5}$

(C) $\frac{1}{2}$

(D) $\frac{2}{3}$

(E) $\frac{3}{4}$

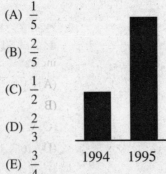

The correct choice is (B). You should be able to "guesstimate" this answer. The length of bar on the left is more than $\frac{1}{5}$ but less than $\frac{1}{2}$ the length of the bar on the right.

EXERCISES: GRAPHS

Exercise 1

5 QUESTIONS • 5 MINUTES

Directions: Each of the following questions has five answer choices. Select the best of the available choices.

Questions 1–5 Refer To The Following Graph.

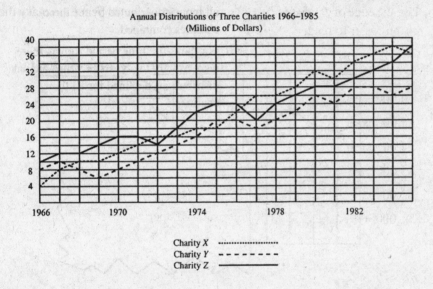

Annual Distributions of Three Charities 1966–1985
(Millions of Dollars)

Charity *X* ·······························
Charity *Y* – – – – – – –
Charity *Z* —————————

1. For how many years was the annual distribution of Charity X greater than those of both Charity Y and Charity Z?

   (A) 4

   (B) 9

   (C) 11

   (D) 14

   (E) 15

2. From 1971 to 1982, by how many millions of dollars did the annual distribution by Charity Z increase?

   (A) 8

   (B) 12

   (C) 14

   (D) 16

   (E) 18

3. From 1970 to 1981, by what percent did the annual distribution by Charity X increase?

   (A) 100%

   (B) 150%

   (C) 200%

   (D) 250%

   (E) 300%

4. In 1977, what were the combined annual distributions of Charity X and Charity Z (in millions of dollars)?

   (A) 38

   (B) 44

   (C) 46

   (D) 52

   (E) 64

5. Which of the following statements can be inferred from the information given?

   (A) For each year after the first year shown, annual distributions by Charity Y failed to increase in exactly four years.

   (B) In 1977, annual distributions for exactly one of the charities fell while those of the other two charities increased.

   (C) For the entire time period shown, total combined annual disbursements for the three charities increase by 900%.

   (D) For the years 1978 and 1979 combined, Charity X accounted for more than $\frac{1}{3}$ of all money distributed by the three charities combined.

   (E) For the entire time period shown, there were exactly two years in which annual distributions declined for all three charities.

Exercise 2

3 QUESTIONS • 3 MINUTES

Directions: Each of the following questions has five answer choices. Select the best of the available choices.

Questions 1–3 Refer to the Following Graph.

Number Visitors to Hotel Convention Center K

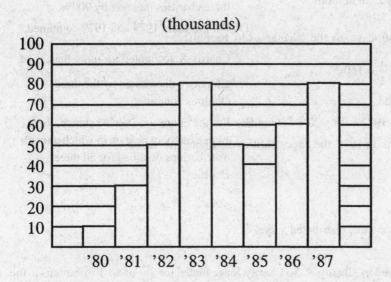

1. For the period shown, what was the amount of the greatest increase in the number of visitors from one year to the next?

   (A) 10,000
   (B) 20,000
   (C) 30,000
   (D) 70,000
   (E) 80,000

2. For the period 1982 to 1986 inclusive, what was the average (arithmetic mean) number of visitors per year?

   (A) 48,000
   (B) 56,000
   (C) 59,250
   (D) 75,000
   (E) 84,000

3. In which of the years from 1981 to 1985 did the number of visitors change by the greatest percent over the previous year?

   (A) 1981
   (B) 1982
   (C) 1983
   (D) 1984
   (E) 1985

Answer Keys and Explanations

Exercise 1

1. B   2. C   3. B   4. C   5. D

1. **(B)** This is purely a graph-reading question. In nine years, the annual distribution of Charity X exceeded the distributions of both Charity Y and Charity Z: 1972, 1977, 1978, 1979, 1980, 1981, 1982, 1983, and 1984.

2. **(C)** In 1971, the distribution by Charity Z was $16 million, and in 1982 it was $30 million. So the difference is:

    30 – 16 = $14 million

3. **(B)** This is a percent change question, so use the "change-over" formula:

    $$\frac{1981 - 1970}{1970} = \frac{30 - 12}{12} = \frac{18}{12} = \frac{3}{2} = 150\%$$

4. **(C)** Find the data you need and add:

    Charity X in 1977 + Charity Z in 1977 = 26 + 20 = $46 million

5. **(D)** This statement can be inferred. In 1978, the three charities distributed a total of:

    26 + 20 + 24 = 70

    And in 1979, a total of:

    28 + 22 + 26 = 76

    So in 1978 and 1979 combined, the three distributed a total of:

    70 + 76 = 146

    Of this, 26 + 28 = 54 was distributed by Charity X. So Charity X accounted for $\frac{54}{146}$ of all distributions in the two years, which is more than one-third.

Exercise 2

1. C   2. B   3. A

1. **(C)** Here, you should rely on the fact that the figure is drawn to scale. Look for the greatest distance between two adjacent bars (provided the bar to the right is longer, since we are looking for the greatest *increase*). The greatest difference is between the bar for 1982 and that for 1983. It's a simple matter to do the subtraction:

    $$80,000 - 50,000 = 30,000$$

    Or you could also use the edge of a sheet of paper. Measure the difference between the two bars and compare that difference against the scale.

2. **(B)** This item asks you to calculate an average. Just make sure you get the right years. Since the scale indicates thousands of visitors, you can work with the units in the scale and later add the "thousands":

    $$\frac{50 + 80 + 50 + 40 + 60}{5} = \frac{280}{5} = 56$$

    This means that the average number of visitors each year for that period was 56,000.

3. **(A)** This item asks about percent change, and for percent change you can use the "change-over" formula. The largest percent increase occurred from 1980 to 1981:

    $$\frac{30 - 10}{10} = \frac{20}{10} = 2 = 200\%$$

    At this point, keep in mind two points about questions that ask you to find the largest percent change. First, the answer to such a question is not likely to be the change that shows the largest difference in absolute terms. Here, for example, the largest increase in the number of visitors occurred between 1982 and 1983, a change of 30,000, but that was a percent increase of only:

    $$\frac{80 - 50}{50} = \frac{30}{50} = 60\%$$

    The point of asking such a question is to determine whether you understand the difference between a change in absolute terms and relative change.

    Second, since percent change is a relative change—relative to the initial quantity—given the same change in absolute terms, the smaller the initial quantity, the larger the relative change. For example, think about what a change of ten units means for various starting points. For a starting point of 1, an increase of 10 units is an increase of 1000 percent. For a starting point of 10, an increase of 10 units is an increase of 100 percent. For a starting point of 100, an increase of 10 units is an increase of 10 percent, and so on.

What You Must Know About GRE Math Questions

Review these pages the night before you take the GRE. They will help you get the answers to GRE math questions.

Problem-solving questions, quantitative comparisons, and graph questions are mixed together in a single scored math section.

You'll have approximately 9 to 11 problem-solving items, 13 to 15 quantitative comparisons, and 4 or so graphs questions.

Problem Solving

- These steps will help you answer problem-solving questions:
    1. Read the question carefully.
    2. Before solving the problem, check the answers.
    3. Eliminate choices that are completely off the radar screen.
    4. For complex questions, break down the problem.
- Solve problems by testing answer choices.
- Solve problems by substituting real numbers for variables.
- In problem-solving questions, most figures are drawn to scale.

Quantitative Comparisons

- These steps will help you solve quantitative comparisons:
    1. Memorize the answer choices.
    2. For each question, read the centered information.
    3. Compare the quantity in Column A to the quantity in Column B.
    4. Do only as much work as is needed to make the comparison.
    5. Choose your answer.
- Quantitative comparisons are not about calculating. If you find yourself doing a long calculation, you've probably missed an important math principle in the problem.
- Consider all the possibilities for unknowns, including 1, 0, a fraction, or a negative number.
- In quantitative comparisons, figures are not necessarily drawn to scale.

Graphs

- These steps will help you solve graph questions:
    1. Determine what kind of graph you have.
    2. Read all the labels.
    3. Answer the questions

PART

FIVE

EVERYTHING YOU NEED!

GRE Analytical Questions

PREVIEW →

CHAPTER 12

Analytical Reasoning

You'll Find Answers to These Questions

What is analytical reasoning?
How do you answer analytical reasoning questions?
What do smart test-takers know about analytical reasoning?

WHAT IS ANALYTICAL REASONING?

Analytical reasoning problems are just logic games. For example:

> Three musicians—J, K, and L—each play exactly
> one instrument: the piano, the bass, or the sax—
> though not necessarily in that order. J, whose sister
> is the sax player, does not play the piano; and L is
> an only child.

You have to use the clues to deduce who plays which instrument.

> L does not play the sax because L is an only child
> (the sax player is J's sister). J cannot be the sax
> player because J's sister plays the sax. Since the sax
> player is not J or L, K plays the sax.

> If J does not play the sax (K plays the sax) or the
> piano (as we are told), then J must play the bass.

> Finally, since J plays the bass and K plays the sax,
> you can deduce that L plays the piano.

So you can figure out which musician plays which instrument: J on bass, K on sax, L on piano.

You have probably seen similar problems in logic books or in the entertainment section of a newspaper or a magazine.

In this book, you will see a variety of logical puzzles, but initial conditions and questions have some very important characteristics in common. The initial conditions establish the structure of the logical game and introduce

PLAN A: ACCELERATED
- *Read* the chapter
- *Study* "What Smart Test-takers Know"
- *Complete* Exercise 1
- *Check* your answers

PLAN B: TOP SPEED
- *Read* "How Do You Answer Analytical Reasoning Questions?"
- *Complete* Exercise 2
- *Check* your answers

you to the individuals involved in the puzzle as well as to the logical connections between and among those individuals.

The individuals involved in an analytical reasoning set are usually designated by letters or names, e.g., eight people, J, K, L, M, N, O, P, and Q, are sitting around a table. Sometimes, the individuals in the problem may be designated by some physical characteristic, e.g., six flags are displayed in a horizontal row, two red, two blue, one yellow, and one green. Further, the initial conditions always give some information about the logical relations that join the individuals to one another, e.g., J is sitting next to K, and M is not sitting next to P, or the red flags are hanging next to each other and the yellow flag is not next to the green flag.

GRE Analytical Reasoning Questions

Your analytical section will have somewhere between 26 and 29 analytical reasoning questions in 4 or 5 puzzles.

Anatomy of an Analytical Reasoning Question Set

Directions: Each group of questions is based on a set of propositions or conditions. Drawing a rough picture or diagram may help in answering some of the questions.

Six runners—J, K, L, M, N, and O—participated in a series of races with the following results:

    J always finished ahead of N but behind O.

    K always finished ahead of L but behind O.

    M always finished ahead of L but behind J.

    There were no ties.

1. Which of the following could be the order of finish of a race from first to last?

    (A) O, J, K, L, M, N

    (B) O, J, K, M, L, N

    (C) O, J, M, N, L, K

    (D) O, M, J, N, K, L

    (E) M, L, J, O, K, N

Linear ordering sets are the most common type of game used on the test. Notice that the order of finish is not completely determined, though it is possible to deduce that O always finished last.

The correct answer is (B). Each of the other choices contradicts one or more of the initial conditions.

2. Which of the following must be true of the order of finish for all of the races?

(A) O finished first.

(B) J finished second.

(C) K finished third.

(D) N finished last.

(E) L finished last.

The correct answer is (A). The first two conditions establish that O finished ahead of J,K, L, and N. Then, since O finished ahead of J, O also finished ahead of M.

3. For any race, which of the following is a complete and accurate listing of the runners who could have finished ahead of M?

(A) J

(B) J, O

(C) J, O, K

(D) J, O, K, N

(E) J, O, K, N, L

The correct answer is (D). The third condition states that M finished ahead of L. So the other four runners could have finished ahead of M.

HOW DO YOU ANSWER ANALYTICAL REASONING QUESTIONS?

Here's a simple, four-step plan that can help you solve analytical reasoning questions.

Analytical Reasoning: Getting It Right

1. Summarize the initial conditions in a "bookkeeping" system.

2. Look for further conclusions.

3. Treat each question separately.

4. Use the answer choices to create a "feedback loop."

Now let's look at these steps in greater detail.

1. **Summarize the initial conditions in a "bookkeeping" system.** This system will include notational devices and diagramming techniques that you invent for yourself or that you adapt from those suggested in this book. You should not regard the "bookkeeping" system used in this book as the only possible system. Rather, you should regard it as a suggested system. Once you understand the system, you can use or adapt whichever parts you wish.

TOP**10**TIP

Use these or other symbols to summarize the initial conditions:

LOGICAL CONNECTIVE	SYMBOL
and	+
or	v
not	~
if, then	⊃
same as, next to	=
not same as, not next to	≠
greater than, older, before	>
if and only if	≡
less than, younger, after	<

Be sure to double-check your summary. A mistake at this stage could be very, very costly. Here is an illustration:

A chef is experimenting with eight ingredients to discover new dishes. The ingredients are J, K, L, M, N, O, P, and Q. The ingredients must be used in accordance with the following conditions:

If M is used in a dish, P and Q must also be used in that dish.

If P is used in a dish, then exactly two of the three ingredients, L, M, and N, must also be used in that dish.

L cannot be used in a dish with P.

N can be used in a dish if and only if J is also used in that dish.

K, L, and M cannot all be used in the same dish.

The information could be summarized as follows:

(1) $M \supset (P \& Q)$

(2) $P \supset (L \& M) \text{ v } (L \& N) \text{ v } (M \& N)$

(3) $L \neq P$

(4) $N \equiv J$

(5) $\sim (K \& L \& M)$

The "horseshoe" is used for the first statement, but the arrow could also be used. Notice also that parentheses are used as punctuation marks. If you do not set P & Q off in parentheses, the statement M ⊃ P & Q could be misinterpreted to read "If M is used, then P must be used; and Q must be used."

The second statement shows the logical structure of the second condition. If P is used, then either L and M must be used or L and N must be used or M and N must be used. Again, you should note the parentheses as punctuation marks.

Statement (3) uses the ≠, which has many other uses, to assert that L and P cannot be used together. Similarly, statement (4) uses the ≡ to assert that N and J, if used, must be used together. Finally, statement (5) can be read to say that it is not the case that K and L and M are used in the same dish. Of course, these are just suggestions; there are many other ways to summarize the information. Later, in the explanations you will find different notational devices that will be explained as they are introduced. Remember, however, only adopt those symbols you find convenient and find substitutes for those that do not work for you.

2. **Look for further conclusions.** The initial conditions may permit you to draw a further conclusion, and a further conclusion is often the key to one or even more questions. Here is an example:

Six students—T, U, V, X, Y, and Z—are being considered for a field trip. The final selection depends on the following restrictions:

If X is selected, then neither Y or Z can be selected.

If T is selected, then U cannot be selected.

If U is selected, then Z must also be selected.

You can deduce that certain pairs are not acceptable. For example, X and Z cannot both be selected.

3. **Treat each question separately.** Some questions provide, by stipulation, information that supplements the initial conditions, e.g., "If the traveler visits Paris on Thursday, then which city will she visit on Friday?"

Additional information provided in a question stem is to be used for that question only. In fact, different questions may ask you to make contradictory assumptions. The second question in a set may ask you to assume that the traveler visits Rome on Thursday while the third question asks you to assume that she visits Rome on Monday.

4. **Use the answer choices to create a "feedback loop."** This is a multiple-choice examination in which one and only one of the options can be correct. And an option in this section will be correct or incorrect as a matter of logic. (In this respect, this section is similar to a math test.) Thus, if your analysis of a question yields one and only one correct answer, this indicates that you have probably done the problem cor-

rectly. If your analysis produces no correct choice, then you have obviously overlooked something. On the other hand, if your analysis produces more than one seemingly correct choice, then you have made an error somewhere.

Now let's look at some sample analytical reasoning puzzles. As you read the explanations, think about how the solution process applies.

Linear Ordering

It's been a couple of decades since analytical reasoning was introduced, and the most commonly used type of problem has been the linear ordering problem. This kind of problem sets up a situation like the following:

Seven people standing in a line.

A dozen students in school in grades 1 through 12.

A musical scale consisting of six notes.

Now let's solve a typical linear ordering puzzle.

Six people, J, K, L, M, N, and O, are sitting in one row of six seats at a concert. The seats all face the stage and are numbered, facing the stage from left to right, 1 through 6, consecutively. Exactly one person is sitting in each seat.

J is not sitting in seat 1 nor in seat 6.

N is not sitting next to L.

N is not sitting next to K.

O is sitting to the immediate left of N.

You would begin your attack by summarizing the initial conditions:

$J \neq (1 \text{ or } 6)$

$N \neq L$

$N \neq K$

$O-N$

Are there any further conclusions to be drawn? Yes and no. Yes, it would be possible to determine every possible seating arrangement given these initial conditions, but that obviously would take a lot of time. Therefore, no, there don't appear to be any further obvious conclusions, so go to the questions.

1. Which of the following seating arrangements, given in order from seat 1 to seat 6, is acceptable?

   (A) L, M, K, O, N, J

   (B) L, J, M, O, N, K

   (C) L, N, O, J, M, K

   (D) K, J, L, O, M, N

   (E) M, K, O, N, J, L

Notice that this question provides no additional information, so it must be answerable just on the basis of the initial conditions. When this is the case, use the initial conditions to eliminate choices.

The first condition states that J is not seated in seat 1 nor in seat 6. Eliminate (A) because that arrangement is inconsistent with the first of the initial conditions. The second condition requires that N not sit next to L, and on that score we can eliminate (C). According to the third condition, N does not sit next to K, and we eliminate (B). Finally, the fourth condition states that O is seated immediately to N's left, and we can eliminate (D). We have eliminated four of the five choices, so (E) must be the only arrangement that respects all of the initial conditions.

2. All of the following seating arrangements, given in order from 1 to 6, are acceptable EXCEPT:

   (A) M, J, L, K, O, N

   (B) K, J, O, N, M, L

   (C) K, O, N, J, M, L

   (D) L, O, N, J, K, M

   (E) K, J, O, N, L, M

This question is the mirror image of the first, but you should use the same strategy. Each choice is consistent with the requirement that J not be seated in position 1 or 6. And (A) through (D) respect the second condition that N not sit next to L. In (E), however, N is seated next to L. (E), therefore, must be the choice we are looking for, as it is NOT an acceptable arrangement.

3. If L is in seat 1 and K is in seat 5, which of the following must be true?

   (A) J is in seat 2.

   (B) M is in seat 3.

   (C) N is in seat 4.

   (D) O is in seat 4.

   (E) M is in seat 6.

This question provides additional information. When this is the case, begin by determining whether further conclusions can be drawn.

A diagram would be helpful. The question stem stipulates that L is in seat 1 and K in seat 5:

1	2	3	4	5	6
L				K	

Now return to the initial conditions. The first doesn't help very much, though you can conclude that J is in seat 2, 3, or 4. The second and third conditions by themselves don't operate to place any person on the diagram, but both together tell you that N must be in seat 3:

1	2	3	4	5	6
L		N		K	

And since O must be seated to N's left:

1	2	3	4	5	6
L	O	N		K	

And since J cannot sit in seat 6, you have a complete order:

1	2	3	4	5	6
L	O	N	J	K	M

So the correct answer is (E).

4. If M and O are in seats 2 and 3, respectively, which of the following must be true?

(A) J is in seat 5.

(B) K is in seat 3

(C) L is in seat 1.

(D) L is in seat 6.

(E) N is in seat 5.

Choice (A) is the correct answer. Begin by processing the initial information:

1	2	3	4	5	6
	M	O			

Since O is seated immediately to N's left:

1	2	3	4	5	6
	M	O	N		

Since neither K nor L can sit next to N, neither can be in seat 5. This means K and L are in seats 1 and 6, though not necessarily respectively:

1	2	3	4	5	6
K/L	M	O	N		K/L

And, of course, J is in seat 5:

1	2	3	4	5	6
K/L	M	O	N	J	K/L

5. If K and L are separated by exactly three seats, what is the maximum number of different arrangements in which the six people could be seated?

(A) 1

(B) 2

(C) 3

(D) 4

(E) 5

This question really asks "What could be true?" What are the possible arrangements given the additional information?

1	2	3	4	5	6
K				L	
L				K	
	K				L
	L				K

And since N cannot be seated next to either L or K, but O and N must be seated together:

1	2	3	4	5	6
K	O	N		L	
L	O	N		K	
	K	O	N		L
	L	O	N		K

And J cannot sit in seats 1 or 6:

1	2	3	4	5	6
K	O	N	J	L	M
L	O	N	J	K	M
M	K	O	N	J	L
M	L	O	N	J	K

So there are only four possible arrangements given the stipulation that K and L are separated by exactly three seats. The correct answer is (D).

6. If K is in seat 2, which of the following is a complete and accurate listing of the seats which O could occupy?

(A) 1
(B) 3
(C) 3 and 4
(D) 1, 3, and 4
(E) 3, 4, and 5

Like the previous question, this question asks about logical possibilities. If K is in seat 2, then there are three possible placements for the O N pair:

1	2	3	4	5	6
	K	O	N		
	K		O	N	
	K			O	N

Are each of these possible? Yes, as you can prove to yourself by completing the three diagrams. O could be seated in seat 3, or 4, or 5, so the correct answer is (E).

Distributed Order

Another common problem type is the distributed order game. In a linear ordering problem, only one individual can occupy a position in the order. In some problem sets, however, a position in the order can accommodate more than one individual.

Six individuals, P, Q, R, S, T, and U, live in a five-story apartment building. Each person lives on one of the floors in the building.

Exactly one of the six lives on the first floor, exactly one of them lives on the fourth floor, and at least two of them live on the second floor.

Of the six people, P lives on the highest floor, and no one lives on the same floor as P.

Q does not live on the first floor or on the second floor.

Neither R nor S lives on the second floor.

When an ordering problem contains distributional restrictions, determine what consequences flow from those restrictions.

The initial conditions establish the following:

5
4   Exactly one
3
2   At least two, not Q, not R, not S
1   Exactly one, not Q

TESTSMARTS

There are four—and only four—analytical reasoning questions.

1. What must be true as a matter of logic?
2. What must be false as a matter of logic?
3. What can be true or false as a matter of logic?
4. What cannot be true or false as a matter of logic?

And, of course, P cannot live on floor two. (P must live on either floor four or floor five.) Since it is a requirement of the distribution that at least two persons live on floor two, we can deduce that T and U (and of the six only T and U) live on floor two:

5

4   Exactly one

3

2   Exactly two: T and U

1   Exactly one, not Q

1. All of the following must be true EXCEPT:

    (A) Exactly two persons live on floor two.

    (B) At most, one person lives on floor five.

    (C) At least one person lives on floor five.

    (D) At least one person lives on floor three.

    (E) P does not live on floor two.

(C) is the correct answer. The diagram shows that (A) is necessarily true. And it has already determined that P must be on floor four or five, so (E) is necessarily true. As for (B), this must be true: either P lives on floor five or P lives on floor four (and none of the other five lives above P). As for (D), either P lives on floor five, in which case the distribution of individuals is 1, 2, 1, 1, and 1 (from first to fifth). Or P lives on floor four, in which case the distribution is 1, 2, 2, 1, 0 (from first to fifth). (C), however, is not necessarily true, for P could live on the fourth floor.

2. Which of the following could be true?

    (A) Either Q or R lives on the third floor.

    (B) T and U do not live on the second floor.

    (C) T and U live on the third floor.

    (D) T lives on the first floor.

    (E) U lives on the fourth floor.

The analysis above shows that (A) could be true. The remaining choices must be false since T and U live on the second floor.

3. If P lives on a floor directly above the floor on which R lives, which of the following must be true?

    (A) R lives on a higher floor than Q.

    (B) R and Q live on the same floor.

    (C) T and U live on different floors.

    (D) Q lives on the third floor.

    (E) S lives on the second floor.

Choice (D) is the correct answer. If R is directly beneath P, then since Q cannot be on the first floor, S must be on the first floor. This means there are two possible arrangements:

5	4	3	2	1
P	R	Q	T,U	S
	P	R,Q	T,U	S

But Q is on the third floor in both arrangements.

Selection Sets

Selection sets are also a common game. Selection sets involve choosing a subset of individuals from a larger collection.

From a group of three faculty members, P, S, and R, four administrators, T, U, V, and W, and three students, X, Y, and Z, the president of a college must choose an ad hoc committee.

The committee will have exactly seven members.

There must be at least as many faculty members on the committee as there are students, though the number of students may be zero.

P and Z cannot both serve on the committee.

If either T or U serves on the committee, the other must also serve on the committee.

If V serves on the committee, then W must serve on the committee.

With a set like this, you begin by summarizing the information using the notational devices suggested above:

Fac. > or = Stu.

$P \neq Z$

$T = U$

$V \rightarrow W$

1. Which of the following must be true of the committee?

   (A) It cannot include more students than administrators.

   (B) It cannot include both T and W.

   (C) It cannot include all three faculty members.

   (D) It must include T and U.

   (E) It must include V and W.

(A) is the correct answer. Since P and Z cannot both be on the committee, and since there must be at least as many faculty members on the committee as students, the maximum number of students who could serve on the committee is two. And the maximum number of faculty who could serve is three. This means a minimum of at least two administrators is required. Thus, (A) correctly notes that it is impossible to have more students than administrators on the committee. As for (B) and (C), the committee of seven could include all three faculty and all four administrators with no students. As for (D) and (E), a committee might consist of three faculty members and two students plus either T and U or V and W. Thus, it is not the case that either T and U or V and W must be included.

2. If the committee is to include exactly two faculty members and exactly two students, which of the following must be true?

   (A) Z is not included on the committee.

   (B) W is included on the committee.

   (C) X is included on the committee.

   (D) Y is included on the committee.

   (E) S is included on the committee.

The correct answer is (B). If four members of the committee are drawn from faculty and the student body, then three must be drawn from the administration. Since T and U cannot be split up, these three must include T and U and either V or W but not both V and W. Since including V requires including W, V cannot be included; therefore W must be included. As for (A), it is possible to include Z by using faculty members S and R (instead of P). As for (C) and (D), either X or Y could serve (with Z) or both X and Y could serve together. Finally, as for (E), any two of the three faculty members could be included on the committee.

3. If both V and Z are chosen for the committee, then which of the following must be true?

   (A) Neither X nor W is chosen.

   (B) Neither X nor Y is chosen.

   (C) Both X and T are chosen.

   (D) Both Y and U are chosen.

   (E) V and either X or Y is chosen.

(B) is the correct answer. If V is chosen, then W must also be chosen. And since Z is chosen, you need at least one faculty member. This gives a total of four people, and you need three more. If you choose another student, this requires another faculty member (for a total of six), but it isn't possible to choose only T or U. Therefore, you cannot include another student. So you must include the other faculty member and T and U. So the committee consists of V, Z, W, S, R, T, and U.

Sleepers

One of the most dangerous things that you can do is to try to guess where the GRE will be going on the very next administration. Like clothes, analytical reasoning puzzles come into fashion and then go out of fashion. There are some that were very popular five years ago but that are not currently the rage. Should you ignore them? Only at your own peril. You never know when they will make a reappearance. The examples that follow fall into this group.

Greater Than, Less Than

Some problem sets rely heavily on the notions of "greater than" and "less than." In the problems you will often be given a list of people, each of whom has more or less of a certain quality, and asked to determine how each one compares to the others in terms of that quality.

The following information is known about a group of five children:

> Alice is taller than Bob and heavier than Charles.
>
> Ed is heavier than both Diane and Alice and is shorter than Bob.
>
> Diane is not taller than Bob and is heavier than Charles.
>
> Charles is taller than Diane and heavier than Bob.

Use relational lines to organize clues for a "greater than/less than" set. In this case, set up two lines, one of which will represent height and the other weight:

Enter each clue on the diagram. First, Alice is taller than Bob and heavier than Charles:

Next, Ed is shorter than Bob and heavier than both Diane and Alice:

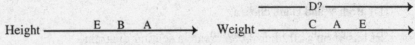

Next, Diane is not taller than Bob and is heavier than Charles:

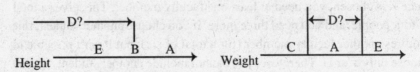

Finally, Charles is taller than Diane and heavier than Bob:

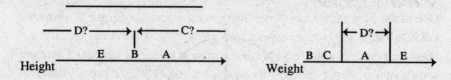

1. Which of the following CANNOT be true?

   (A) Ed is taller than Diane.

   (B) Charles is taller than Alice.

   (C) Bob is taller than Diane.

   (D) Bob weighs more than Diane.

   (E) Ed weighs more than Diane.

Our diagrams show that (C) and (E) are true and that (A) and (B) might be true. Only choice (D) cannot be true.

2. Which of the following could be true?

   (A) The tallest child is also the heaviest child.

   (B) The shortest child is also the heaviest child.

   (C) The lightest child is also the tallest child.

   (D) Charles is both taller and heavier than Alice.

   (E) Bob is both shorter and lighter than Diane.

The correct answer is (B), and you can read the information directly from the completed diagrams.

Seating Arrangements

In some problem sets, individuals are seated around a circular table.

> Eight people, F, G, H, J, K, L, M, and N, are seated in eight equally spaced chairs around a circular table.
>
> K is sitting directly opposite M.
>
> M is sitting immediately to F's left.
>
> G is sitting next to L.
>
> H is sitting opposite J.

For a set based on a circular table, create a seating diagram.

The seats are not distinguishable (that is, there is not a head of the table), so enter the first clue:

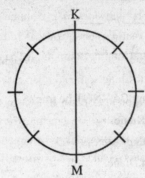

And the second clue:

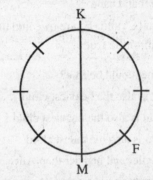

We can't enter the rest of the information without doing a little thinking. H and J are sitting opposite each other, which suggests there are the following possibilities:

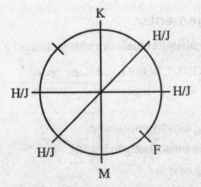

But if either H or J is seated next to F, it isn't possible to place L and G together. Therefore, either H or J is seated next to M:

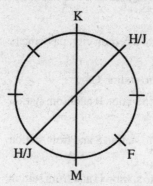

And finally:

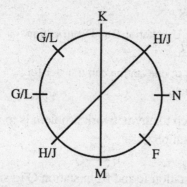

1. Which of the following must be true?

   (A) N is seated next to F.

   (B) N is seated next to H.

   (C) N is seated across from G.

   (D) F is seated across from L.

   (E) G is seated across from F.

As the diagram shows, only (A) makes a necessarily true statement.

2. Only one seating arrangement is possible under which of the following conditions?

   (A) G is seated next to J.

   (B) H is seated next to N.

   (C) G is seated opposite N.

   (D) G is seated opposite F.

   (E) H is seated next to K.

The correct answer is (A). If G is next to J, L is next to K, and H is next to N. So only one order is possible.

Networks

Some problem sets involve spatial or temporal connections between individuals.

> In the subway system of a certain city, passengers can go:
>
> From station P to station Q.
>
> From station Q to station R and from station Q to station S.
>
> From station R to station S and from station R to station T.
>
> From station S to station U and from station S to station P.
>
> From station T to station U and from station T to station R.
>
> From station U to station P and from station U to station S.
>
> A passenger at one station can transfer for another station.

The correct approach to any network problem is to sketch the network. From station P to station Q.

$$P \longrightarrow Q$$

From station Q to station R and from station Q to station S.

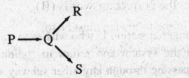

From station R to station S and from station R to station T.

From station S to station U and from station S to station P.

From station T to station U and from station T to station R.

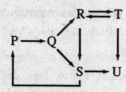

From station U to station P and from station U to station S.

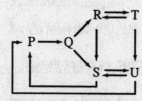

1. A passenger at station T who wishes to travel to station Q must pass through a minimum of how many other stations before finally arriving at Q?

   (A) 1
   (B) 2
   (C) 3
   (D) 4
   (E) 5

Consult the network diagram. The shortest route is U to P and then on to Q. Therefore, the correct answer is (B).

2. A passenger at station U who wishes to travel through the system and return to station U before passing through any other subway station twice can choose from how many different routes?

   (A) 2
   (B) 3
   (C) 4
   (D) 5
   (E) 6

(C) is the correct answer. Simply trace the possibilities with your finger:

   U to P to Q to S to U
   U to P to Q to R to S to U
   U to P to Q to R to T to U
   U to S to P to Q to R to T to U

AVOID THE TRAPS!

Asymmetrical clues. Clues such as "If P, then Q" and "R unless T," can be deadly traps. Avoid the following:

If P, then Q, Q, therefore P. (No!)

R unless T, T, therefore R. (No!)

Matrix Problems

Sometimes a problem will refer to individuals who have or lack certain characteristics, and some questions may ask which characteristics are in turn shared by which individuals.

> Five people, George, Howard, Ingrid, Jean, and Kathy, work in a factory. On any given shift, a person can be assigned to one of five jobs: mechanic, truck driver, packer, weigher, or dispatcher.
>
> > George can function as mechanic, packer, or weigher.
> >
> > Howard can function as either packer or weigher.
> >
> > Ingrid can function as mechanic, truck driver, or dispatcher.
> >
> > Jean can function as truck driver or dispatcher.
> >
> > Kathy can function as truck driver or weigher.
> >
> > The five workers can fill only these jobs, and only these five workers can fill these jobs.

For a problem set in which individuals do or do not share certain characteristics (and those characteristics are or are not shared by the individuals), use a matrix or table.

	M	TD	P	W	D
G					
H					
I					
J					
K					

George can function as mechanic, packer, or weigher.

	M	TD	P	W	D
G	✓		✓	✓	
H					
I					
J					
K					

Howard can function as either packer or weigher.

	M	TD	P	W	D
G	✓		✓	✓	
H			✓	✓	
I					
J					
K					

Ingrid can function as mechanic, truck driver, or dispatcher.

	M	TD	P	W	D
G	✓		✓	✓	
H			✓	✓	
I	✓	✓			✓
J					
K					

Jean can function as truck driver or dispatcher.

	M	TD	P	W	D
G	✓		✓	✓	
H			✓	✓	
I	✓	✓			✓
J		✓			✓
K					

Kathy can function as truck driver or weigher.

	M	TD	P	W	D
G	✓		✓	✓	
H			✓	✓	
I	✓	✓			✓
J		✓			✓
K		✓		✓	

1. If Jean is NOT assigned to function as dispatcher, all of the following must be true EXCEPT:

   (A) George is the mechanic.

   (B) Howard is the dispatcher.

   (C) The truck driver is Jean.

   (D) The packer is Howard.

   (E) The weigher is Kathy.

The correct answer is (B). Ingrid, not Howard, would be the dispatcher. Just enter the new information into the table, and use the grid to draw further conclusions.

2. If George is assigned as mechanic, which of the following must be true?

   (A) Howard is assigned as packer.

   (B) Kathy is assigned as weigher.

   (C) Ingrid is assigned as truck driver.

   (D) Jean is assigned as dispatcher.

   (E) Howard is assigned as weigher.

(A) is the correct answer. If George is assigned as mechanic, then he is not available to be packer or weigher. There is only one other person who can be the packer, and that is Howard.

Family Relationships

> Barbara, an only child, is married, and she and her husband have two children, Ned and Sally.
>
>> Ned is Paula's nephew by blood and Victor's grandson.
>>
>> Victor and his wife had only two children, Frank and his sister, plus four grandchildren, two boys and two girls.
>>
>> Wilma is Sally's grandmother.

Use the information to create a family tree.

Barbara, an only child, is married, and she and her husband have two children, Ned and Sally:

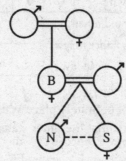

Ned is Paula's nephew by blood and Victor's grandson.

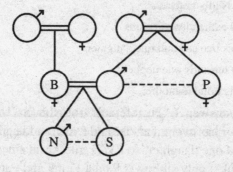

(Since Barbara is an only child, an aunt could be related by blood only by being Ned's father's sister. We don't know, however, whether Victor is Ned's paternal or maternal grandfather.)

Victor and his wife had only two children, Frank and his sister, plus four grandchildren, two boys and two girls.

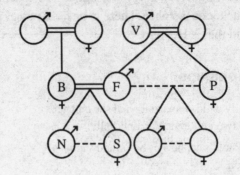

(Since Victor had two children, he could not have been Barbara's father because Barbara is an only child. So in order to be Ned's grandfather, Victor must be Ned's father's father.) It is not possible to enter the last piece of information for it is not clear whether Wilma is Barbara's mother or the mother of Frank and Paula.

1. All of the following must be true EXCEPT:
    (A) Wilma is Victor's wife.
    (B) Victor is Sally's grandfather.
    (C) Victor is Barbara's father in law.
    (D) Paula is Barbara's sister in law.
    (E) Frank is Sally's father.

As we just noted, we cannot definitely place Wilma in the family tree. The diagram, however, confirms that the other statements are true. (A) is the correct answer.

2. Which of the following must be true?
    (A) Sally is Ned's sister.
    (B) Ned has exactly two cousins.
    (C) Paula has one son and one daughter.
    (D) Barbara has only one nephew.
    (E) Wilma is Frank's mother.

(E) is the correct answer. (A) is inferable from the first bit of information. Then, since Victor has two grandsons and two granddaughters, Paula must have one son and one daughter, so (B) is true. And since Barbara has no siblings and Frank's only sibling is Paula, Frank and Paula's children are Ned's only cousins and Barbara's only nieces or nephews. So (C) and (D) are also true. (E), however, is not necessarily true, as noted in our initial discussion of the set.

WHAT SMART TEST-TAKERS KNOW

ACCEPT THE SITUATION AT FACE VALUE.

Most of the situations described by the initial conditions are common ones with which you should be familiar.

> Six people, J, K, L, M, N, and O, are standing in a single-file line at a movie theater.

> Seven corporations, H, I, J, K, L, M, and N, have offices on four floors in the same building.

> Eight office workers, M, N, O, P, Q, R, S, and T, are deciding in which of three restaurants—X, Y, or Z—to eat lunch.

One reason for using familiar situations is that there is less potential for misunderstanding because there is much information implicit in a situation such as a single-file line: Each person is a separate person; each letter designates a different individual; one individual is immediately ahead of or behind another individual; and so on. Since the situations are selected for this feature, you should be careful not to "fight" with the setup. For example, there is no point in arguing that J could be standing on L's shoulders. The test writers will add an explicit clarifying note if there is any danger of a legitimate misunderstanding, e.g., each corporation has its own office.

READ THE CLUES CAREFULLY.

Although you must accept the general situation with a fairly uncritical reading, you must be very careful in reading the particular information given about the individuals. Pay particular attention to words such as:

> *only, exactly, never, always, must be/can be/cannot be, some, all, no, none, entire, each, every, except, but, unless, if, more/less, before/after, immediately (before, after, etc.), possible/impossible, different/same, at least, at most.*

BE CAREFUL OF ASYMMETRICAL CLUES.

You should be especially careful not to misinterpret conditions that are asymmetrical, e.g., if P goes on the trip, Q must also go; or S cannot eat at X restaurant unless T also eats there. In both of these examples, the dependency operates in only one direction. In the first, P depends on Q, but not vice versa (Q can go on the trip without P). Similarly, in the second, S depends on T, but not vice versa (S cannot eat at X restaurant without T, but T can eat there without S).

THE SITUATION WILL BE FLUID.

Often, it will be possible to draw some further inference from the initial conditions, but rarely will it be possible to determine the entire situation using just the information in the initial conditions. For example, a problem set might tell you that X must be standing third in line and that Z is two positions behind X. From this, you can deduce that Z is standing fifth in line. But the initial conditions may not fix the position of any other person in the line.

The open-ended nature of analytical reasoning problems will probably be very annoying. Because you will not be able to deduce a definite sequence or some similar conclusions, you will feel that you have overlooked something in the initial conditions. You haven't. The fluidity of the situation is part of the test design.

IT'S ALL A MATTER OF LOGIC.

Since the problem sets in this section are logical puzzles, the correct answers are determined by logical inference. And the logical status of a statement must fall into one of three categories:

1. The statement is logically deducible from the information given.
2. The statement is logically inconsistent with (contradicts) the information given.
3. The statement is neither logically deducible from the information given nor logically inconsistent with it.

The questions that can be asked fall into one of the following categories:

Which of the following must be true?

All of the following must be true EXCEPT:

Which of the following could be true?

Which of the following CANNOT be true?

The logical status of each choice dictates whether it is correct or incorrect:

*   The correct answer to a question asking "Which must be true?" is a statement that is logically deducible from the information given.
*   The wrong answers to such a question can be statements which are inconsistent with the given information or statements which are not deducible from the information given.
*   The correct answer to a question asking "All must be true except" is either a statement that is logically inconsistent with the information given or a statement that is not deducible from the information given.
*   The wrong answers to this type of question are statements which can be logically deduced from the information given.
*   The correct answer to a question asking "Which can be true?" is a statement that is neither deducible from nor inconsistent with the information given.
*   The correct answer to a question asking "All can be true except" is a statement that is logically inconsistent with the information given.

Although wording may differ from problem set to problem set, every question will fall into one of these four categories. For example, a question that asks:

> If the traveler visits Paris on Wednesday, on which day must she visit Rome?

belongs to the first category. It will be possible to deduce from the information given on which day she must visit Rome. But a question that asks:

> If the traveler visits Paris on Wednesday, then she could visit all of the following cities on Friday EXCEPT:

belongs to the fourth category. The correct answer will generate a logical contradiction with the given information: It will be logically impossible to visit that city on Friday. And a question that asks:

> Which of the following is a complete and accurate listing of the cities that the traveler could visit on Thursday?

belongs to the third category. The correct choice will enumerate all of the logical possibilities.

EXERCISES: ANALYTICAL REASONING

Exercise 1

13 QUESTIONS • 15 MINUTES

Directions: Each group of questions is based on a set of propositions or conditions. Drawing a rough picture or diagram may help in answering some of the questions.

Questions 1–7

A candidate for public office plans to visit each of six cities—J, K, L, M, N, and O—exactly once during her campaign. Her aides are setting up the candidate's schedule according to the following restrictions:

> The candidate can visit M only after she has visited both L and N.
>
> The candidate cannot visit N before J.
>
> The second city visited by the candidate must be K.

1. Which of the following could be the order in which the candidate visits the six cities?

   (A) J, K, N, L, O, M

   (B) K, J, L, N, M, O

   (C) O, K, M, L, J, N

   (D) L, K, O, N, M, J

   (E) M, K, N, J, L, O

2. Which of the following must be true of the candidate's campaign schedule?

(A) She visits J before L.

(B) She visits K before M.

(C) She visits K before J.

(D) She visits M before J.

(E) She visits N before L.

3. If the candidate visits O first, which of the following is a complete and accurate listing of the cities that she could visit third?

(A) J

(B) L

(C) J, L

(D) J, M

(E) M, L

4. If the candidate visits J immediately after O and immediately before N, then she must visit L

(A) first

(B) third

(C) fourth

(D) fifth

(E) sixth

5. Which of the following could be true of the candidate's schedule?

(A) She visits J first.

(B) She visits K first.

(C) She visits L sixth.

(D) She visits M fourth.

(E) She visits N sixth.

6. The candidate could visit any of the following immediately after K EXCEPT

(A) J

(B) L

(C) M

(D) N

(E) O

7. If the candidate visits O last, which of the following could be the first and third cities on her schedule, respectively?

(A) J and L

(B) J and O

(C) L and N

(D) L and O

(E) N and J

Questions 8–13

At a certain restaurant, above the kitchen door there are four small lights, arranged side by side, and numbered consecutively, left to right, from one to four. The lights are used to signal waiters when orders are ready. On a certain shift there are exactly five waiters—David, Ed, Flint, Guy, and Hank.

To signal David, all four lights are illuminated.

To signal Ed, only lights one and two are illuminated.

To signal Flint, only light one is illuminated.

To signal Guy, only lights two, three, and four are illuminated.

To signal Hank, only lights three and four are illuminated.

8. If lights two and three are both off, then the waiter signaled is

(A) David

(B) Ed

(C) Flint

(D) Guy

(E) Hank

9. If lights three and four are illuminated, then which of the following is a complete and accurate listing of the waiters whose signals might be displayed?

(A) David

(B) Guy

(C) David and Guy

(D) Guy and Hank

(E) David, Guy, and Hank

10. If light one is not illuminated, then which of the following is a complete and accurate listing of the waiters whose signals might be displayed?

    (A) Ed

    (B) Guy

    (C) Hank

    (D) Guy, Hank

    (E) Hank, Guy, Ed

11. If light three is on and light two is off, then the waiter signaled is

    (A) David

    (B) Ed

    (C) Flint

    (D) Guy

    (E) Hank

12. If one of the five waiters is being signaled, the lights in which of the following pairs could not both be off?

    (A) one and two

    (B) one and three

    (C) two and three

    (D) two and four

    (E) three and four

13. If light four is on, then which of the following must be true?

    (A) Light one is on.

    (B) Light two is not on.

    (C) If light one is on, David is signaled.

    (D) If light two is not on, Flint is signaled.

    (E) If light three is not on, Ed is signaled.

Exercise 2

7 QUESTIONS • 9 MINUTES

Directions: Each group of questions is based on a set of propositions or conditions. Drawing a rough picture or diagram may help in answering some of the questions.

Questions 1–7

A student planning his curriculum for the upcoming semester must enroll in three courses. The available courses fall into one of five general areas: math, English, social studies, science, and fine arts.

    The student must take courses from at least two different areas.

    If he takes a fine arts course, he cannot take an English course.

    If he takes a science course, he must take a math course; and if he takes a math course, he must take a science course.

    He can take a social studies course only if he takes a fine arts course.

1. Which of the following is an acceptable schedule of courses?

    (A) one science course, one English course, and one fine arts course

    (B) one math course, one science course, and one social studies course

    (C) one math course, one social studies course, and one fine arts course

    (D) one English course, one social studies course, and one fine arts course

    (E) one math course, one science course, and one fine arts course

2. Which of the following is NOT an acceptable schedule?

   (A) two math courses and one science course

   (B) two science courses and one math course

   (C) two fine arts courses and one math course

   (D) two social studies courses and one fine arts course

   (E) one social studies course and two fine arts courses

3. Which of the following courses when taken with one course in social studies is an acceptable schedule?

   (A) one course in math and one in science

   (B) one course in fine arts and one course in English

   (C) two courses in fine arts

   (D) two courses in math

   (E) two courses in English

4. If the student wishes to take a course in math and a course in English, then he must select his third course in the area of

   (A) English

   (B) fine arts

   (C) math

   (D) science

   (E) social studies

5. Which of the following pairs of courses CANNOT be combined in an acceptable schedule?

   (A) a course in math and a course in fine arts

   (B) a course in science and a course in fine arts

   (C) a course in math and a course in English

   (D) a course in social studies and a course in science

   (E) a course in science and a course in English

6. If the student wishes to take a course in science, then which of the following pairs of courses would complete an acceptable schedule?

   (A) two math courses

   (B) two science courses

   (C) two English courses

   (D) one science course and one English course

   (E) one math course and one social studies course

7. An acceptable schedule CANNOT include two courses in

   (A) English

   (B) fine arts

   (C) math

   (D) science

   (E) social studies

Answer Keys and Explanations

Exercise 1

1. A	4. A	7. A	10. D	13. C
2. B	5. A	8. C	11. E	
3. C	6. C	9. E	12. B	

Questions 1–7

Here we have a common ordering set. Begin by summarizing the information:

(L + N) < M

J < N

K = 2

> **Note:** Since the candidate cannot visit two cities simultaneously, the condition "The candidate cannot visit N before J" is equivalent to "She must visit J before N."

1. **(A)** This question supplies no additional information, so just take each condition and apply it to the answer choices, eliminating those that fail to comply with any condition. The first condition requires that L and N come before M. Using this condition, we eliminate (C) and (E). The second condition states that J must come before N, and we eliminate (D). The third condition requires that K be the second city, so we eliminate (B). This leaves us with (A); and (A), which respects all three conditions, is a possible order.

2. **(B)** M must be visited after both L and N, so given that K is visited second, M could not possibly be visited earlier than fourth, which means that K comes before M. So (B) is correct. In fact, given that J comes before N, and N comes before M, M must also come later than J. So M cannot be visited until L, N, J, and K have been visited, which means M is either fifth or sixth. As just noted, J must come before M, so (D) is necessarily false. The other three responses describe possible schedules only:

1	2	3	4	5	6
J	K	N	L	M	O

which shows that (A), (C), and (E) are possible. But:

1	2	3	4	5	6
O	K	L	J	N	M

shows that (A), (C), and (E) are not necessarily true.

3. **(C)** Begin by entering the additional information on a diagram:

1	2	3	4	5	6
O	K				

Next, we reason that J, N, and L must all come before M, which means that M comes last:

1	2	3	4	5	6
O	K				M

The only condition left to take care of is the one that requires J before N, but this still leaves three possibilites:

1	2	3	4	5	6
O	K	J	N	L	M
O	K	J	L	N	M
O	K	L	J	N	M

So either J or L could be third.

4. **(A)** This question stipulates an order for three of the cities: O, J, N. Given that J and N must come before M, this means that the order must be:

1	2	3	4	5	6
	K	O	J	N	M

Which means that L must be visited first:

1	2	3	4	5	6
L	K	O	J	N	M

5. **(A)** This question is a good occasion to talk about test-taking strategy. A question of this form has this peculiarity: a choice like (A) may not contradict any single initial condition and may still be wrong because of the way the initial conditions work together. The only way to exclude this possibility is to devise a complete order, part of which is the segment you want to test—a time-consuming process. What should you do?

   The solution to the dilemma is this: Make a first run through the choices, testing them by each single initial statement. If you can eliminate all but one, then you have your correct answer. If more than one choice remains, then the key to the question is some interaction among the initial conditions, e.g., a further inference that you have overlooked. Then, and only then, try working up an entire order to test the remaining choices.

   Here we are fortunate because we can find the correct choice quickly:

   (A) Doesn't contradict any single condition, so go to the next choice.

   (B) No. (K must be second.)

   (C) No. (L must come before M.)

   (D) No. (M must come after J, L, and N and therefore K as well. So M cannot be visited earlier than fifth.)

   (E) No. (N must come before M, so N cannot be last.)

   Thus, (A) must be the correct choice, so we don't have to try to construct the entire order using (A).

   Just for reasons of completeness of explanation, however, here is a schedule in which J is the first city:

1	2	3	4	5	6
J	K	L	N	M	O

6. **(C)** As just noted, M cannot be earlier than fifth, so M could not immediately follow K. That the others could follow K is shown by the following schedules:

	1	2	3	4	5	6
(A)	O	L	J	J	N	M
(B)	J	K	L	N	M	O
(D)	J	K	N	L	M	O
(E)	J	K	O	N	L	M

7. **(A)** Start by entering the additional information on a diagram:

1	2	3	4	5	6
	K				O

Next, we have already determined that M cannot be earlier than fifth:

1	2	3	4	5	6
J	K	N	L	M	O
J	K	L	N	M	O
L	K	J	N	M	O

(A) describes the second of these possibilities. The other choices do not describe one of the three possible schedules.

Questions 8–13

This is a "characteristics" set; each waiter has a characteristic signal. Summarize the information using a table:

Lights	1	2	3	4
David	ON	ON	ON	ON
Ed	ON	ON		
Flint	ON			
Guy		ON	ON	ON
Hank			ON	ON

Whatever further conclusions you might need are already implicitly contained in the table, so go directly to the questions.

8. **(C)** Flint is the only waiter whose signal lights two and three are both off. For every other waiter, either two or three or both are on.

9. **(E)** As the table shows, if lights three and four are both on, the signal might be for David (all four on), or Guy (two, three, and four on), or Hank (three and four on).

10. **(D)** As the table shows, if light one is off, then the signal might be for either Guy or Hank. It could not be for David, Ed, or Flint, since their signals include an illuminated light one.

11. **(E)** As the table shows, there are three waiters whose signals include light three: David, Guy and Hank. For David and Guy, however, light two must be on; for Guy it must be off. Therefore, if light three is on and light two is off, then Guy is the waiter signaled.

12. **(B)** Consult the table:

    (A)   Lights one and two will be off if Hank is signaled.

    (B)   There is no signal for which both one and three are off.

    (C)   Lights two and three will be off if Flint is signaled.

    (D)   Lights two and four will be off if Flint is signaled.

    (E)   Lights three and four will be off if either Ed or Flint is signaled.

13. **(C)** As the table clearly shows, neither (A) nor (B) is necessarily true. (C), however, is necessarily true, as the table shows. If four is on, then the signal might be for David, Guy, or Hank; but if one is also on, then the signal can only be for David. As for (D), if four is on and two is not, then it is Hank who is signaled— not Flint. As for (E), none of the five signals includes light four on and light three off.

Exercise 2

1. E	3. C	5. D	7. A
2. C	4. D	6. A	

This is a selection set. Begin by summarizing the information:

Two different areas

$(E \supset \sim FA) + (FA \supset \sim E)$

$(S \supset M) + (M \supset S)$

$SS \supset FA$

There are no further obvious conclusions to draw, so go to the questions.

1. **(E)** Just test each choice by the initial conditions. First, the student must select from at least two different areas, and all of the choices pass muster on this score. Next, he cannot take courses in both English and fine arts, and we eliminate (A) and (D). Next, if he takes a science course, he must take a math course, and vice versa, so we eliminate (C). Finally, if he takes a social studies course, he must take a course in fine arts, and we eliminate (B). By the process of elimination, (E) is the correct choice.

   Note: don't misread that last condition. It states only that a course in social studies must be accompanied by a course in fine arts. It is possible to take a fine arts course without taking a social studies course.

2. **(C)** This question is the mirror image of the first. Just test each choice by the initial conditions. All are acceptable on the basis of the first condition (that he take courses in at least two different areas) and the second condition (English and fine arts cannot be taken together). (C), however, runs afoul of the third condition, for there we have a math course without an accompanying science course. (You can check the other choices and see that they do respect the final condition.)

3. **(C)** If the student takes social studies, then he must take a course in fine arts. With a course in fine arts, he cannot take a course in English; and with two courses already scheduled (social studies and fine arts), he cannot take either math or science (for those must go together). His only choice, therefore, is to take another fine arts course (as (C) suggests) or another social studies course.

4. **(D)** If the student takes a course in math, he must also take a course in science, so his third course must be science.

5. **(D)** If you simply screen choices here by the initial conditions, it seems that all of the pairs taken in isolation are acceptable. This means that the trick to the question must be what happens to the third course. As for (A) and (B), math requires science and vice versa, and a schedule of math, science, and fine arts is acceptable. As for (C) and (E), math requires science, and a schedule of math, science, and English is acceptable. (D), however, is not acceptable, social studies requires fine arts, and science requires math, but there is not room on the schedule for both fine arts and science.

6. **(A)** Test each of the choices:

   (A)   science, two math (OK.)

   (B)   three science (No. Must schedule two different areas.)

   (C)   science, two English (No. Math must accompany science.)

   (D)   two science, one English (No. Math must accompany science.)

   (E)   science, math, social studies (No. Fine arts must accompany social studies.)

7. **(A)** Test each choice. As for (A), it is not possible to take two English courses. With two English courses, the student cannot take either math or science (each requires the other), nor social studies (because social studies requires fine arts). It is possible to take two courses in the other areas:

   (B)   two fine arts plus one social studies

   (C)   two math plus one science

   (D)   two science plus one math

   (E)   two social studies plus one fine arts

CHAPTER 13

Logical Reasoning

TIME MANAGER STUDY PLANS

PLAN A: ACCELERATED
- *Read* the chapter
- *Study* "What Smart Test-takers Know"
- *Complete* Exercise 1
- *Check* your answers

PLAN B: TOP SPEED
- *Read* "How Do You Solve Logical Reasoning Questions?"
- *Study* "What Smart Test-takers Know"
- *Complete* Exercise 2
- *Check* your answers

You'll Find Answers to These Questions

What does logical reasoning test?
How do you answer logical reasoning questions?
What do smart test-takers know about logical reasoning?

WHAT DOES LOGICAL REASONING TEST?

As the name implies, logical reasoning tests your ability to think logically, and you will learn a lot about thinking logically in this chapter. The GRE, however, does not test technical points that are taught in the typical "Introduction to Logic" course college. You would not, for example, be asked to define categorical syllogism or *petitio principii,* but you might be asked to recognize that:

> All whales are mammals.
>
> All mammals are warm-blooded creatures.
>
> Therefore, all whales are warm-blooded creatures.

which, technically speaking, is a categorical syllogism, which is a valid argument. And you might be asked to show that you understand that:

> Shakespeare was a better playwright than Shaw. Clearly, Shakespeare's plays are better, so the conclusion that Shakespeare was a better playwright than Shaw is unavoidable.

which, technically speaking, is a *petitio principii*, which is a specious argument because it simply begs the question.

233

GRE Logical Reasoning Questions

Your analytical section will have somewhere between 6 and 9 logical reasoning items, mixed with the logical puzzles.

Logical reasoning questions are constructed from three elements:

Stimulus Material

Stimulus material is the "content" of the item, an initial paragraph or statement that presents an argument or otherwise states a position. The stimulus material can be about almost anything including a medical breakthrough, a moral dilemma, a scientific theory, a philosophical problem, or a marketing phenomenon. But you don't need any special knowledge. Everything you need to know in terms of item content is right there in the stimulus material.

HERE'S
THE ANSWER

What are the three "building blocks" of logical reasoning?

1. Stimulus
2. Question stem
3. Answer choices

And each part is important.

Question Stem

The stem is the "question." It may come in the form of a question, or it may come in the form of an instruction. Either way, the stem tells you what to do with the stimulus material. It may ask you to do any one of the following:

- identify the conclusion of an argument
- point out a premise of an argument
- identify strengths or weaknesses in an argument
- recognize parallel reasoning
- evaluate evidence
- draw conclusions and make inferences

Answer Choices

The answer choices are the possible "responses" to the stem. One of them is the "credited" response or right answer. The wrong answers are known as "distractors" because they are carefully written to distract your attention away from the right answer. In essence, they provide the camouflage in which the test writers hide the right response.

Here are the directions for GRE logical reasoning questions, together with a sample question and its explanation.

Anatomy of a Logical Reasoning Item

Directions: In this section, the questions ask you to analyze and evaluate the reasoning in short paragraphs or passages. For some questions, all of the answer choices may conceivably be answers to the question asked. You should select the best answer to the question, that is, an answer which does not require you to make assumptions which violate commonsense standards by being implausible, redundant, irrelevant, or inconsistent.

The directions are not especially helpful. The idea of logical reasoning is fairly intuitive: Read the paragraph and answer the question. So don't bother with the directions again.

Officials of the State Industrial Safety Board notified the management of A-1 Ironworks that several employees of the plant had complained about discomfort experienced as a result of the high levels of noise of the factory operations. A-1's management responded by pointing out that the complaints came from the newest employee at the plant and that more experienced workers did not find the factory noise to be excessive. Based on this finding, management concluded that the noise was not a problem and declined to take any remedial action.

The initial paragraph is also called the "stimulus material" because it "stimulates" you to think. The reasoning in the stimulus material my be faulty, as it is here: Management has overlooked another possible explanation for why complaints came from new employees and not experienced ones.

1. Which of the following, if true, indicates a flaw in A-1's decision not to take remedial action at the plant?

This is the question stem. It tells you what to do with the stimulus material, e.g., find an assumption, draw a conclusion, describe the logic. In this case, the stem tells you to find the mistake in the reasoning.

(A) Because A-1 is located in an industrial park, no residences are located close enough to the plant to be affected by the noise.

Wrong answers are also called "distractors" because they distract your attention from the right answer. This choice is a distractor because it is irrelevant.

(B) The noise level at the plant varies with activity and is at the highest when the greatest number of employees are on the job.

This is a distractor. This choice does not address the new employee versus experienced employee distinction that is at the heart of management's response.

(C) The experienced employees do not feel discomfort because of significant hearing loss attributable to the high noise level.

The right answer is also called the "credited response" to signal that it may not be the best conceivable choice but is the best of the five. This choice points out the flaw in management's reasoning.

(D) Issuing protective earplugs to all employees would not significantly increase the cost to A-1 of doing business.

This is a distractor. It is a possible reason to correct the problem: but it won't cost you anything. But the question stem asks for a flaw in the reasoning.

(E) The State Industrial Safety Board has no independent authority to enforce a recommendation regarding safety procedures.

A distractor. Whether the Board can or cannot do anything doesn't determine whether there is a logical flaw in management's thinking.

HOW DO YOU ANSWER LOGICAL REASONING QUESTIONS?

Here's a simple, four-step plan that can help you solve logical reasoning questions.

Logical Reasoning: Getting It Right

1. Preview the question stem.
2. Read the stimulus material.
3. Prephrase your answer.
4. Identify the correct answer.

Let's look at these steps in more detail.

1. **Preview the question stem.** There are many things that you could do with the stimulus material. You could attack the conclusion, you could defend the conclusion, you could analyze its structure, you could draw further inferences from it, you could even invent a similar argument, and there are still more things to do. You will be asked to do only one (or, occasionally, two) of these things by the stem. So previewing the stem will help you to focus your thinking.

2. **Read the stimulus material.** This is not as easy at it seems. You are going to have to read more carefully than usual. And this makes sense, since words are the tools of the academic's trade. The following advertisement will help to make the point. Read it carefully, because there will be a test.

ADVERTISEMENT: Lite Cigarettes have 50% less nicotine and tar than regular cigarettes. Seventy-five percent of the doctors surveyed said that they would, if asked by patients, recommend a reduced tar and nicotine cigarette for patients who cannot stop smoking.

Pop Quiz

1. Does the ad say that some doctors are encouraging people to start to smoke?

2. Does the ad say that some doctors recommend Lite Cigarettes for patients who cannot stop smoking?

3. Does the ad say that most doctors would, if asked by a patient, recommend a low tar and nicotine cigarette for patients who cannot stop smoking?

Answers

1. Does the ad say that some doctors are encouraging people to start to smoke?

No. The ad specifically says that the doctors surveyed would recommend a low tar and nicotine cigarette for "for patients who cannot stop smoking." That clearly applies only to people who are already smokers.

2. Does the ad say that some doctors recommend Lite Cigarettes for patients who cannot stop smoking?

   No again. The ad specifically says that the doctors surveyed would recommend "a reduced tar and nicotine cigarette." To be sure, Lite Cigarettes apparently fall into that category, but the ad does not say that the doctors surveyed would recommend Lite Cigarettes as opposed to some other reduced tar and nicotine cigarette.

3. Does the ad say that most doctors, would, if asked by patients, recommend a low tar and nicotine cigarette for patients who cannot stop smoking?

   No once again. The claim is restricted to "doctors surveyed." No information is given about how many doctors were included in the survey—perhaps only four. Nor does the ad disclose how many surveys were done. Even if the market experts had to conduct ten surveys before they found a group of four doctors to back up their claim, the ad would still be true—though, of course, potentially misleading.

The important point is this: Read carefully and pay attention to detail. This does not mean that you need to tie yourself up in paranoid knots. The GRE is not out to get you personally. The GRE is, however, a test that is, in part, designed to separate those who can read carefully and pay attention to detail from those who cannot. So read carefully.

3. **Prephrase your answer.** Many GRE problems have answers that go "click" when you find them. They fit in the same way that a well-made key fits a good lock. After you have previewed the stem and then read carefully the stimulus material, try to anticipate what the correct answer will look like. This is particularly true of questions that ask you to attack or defend an argument. (This technique does not work for questions that ask you to identify a parallel line of thinking.)

4. **Identify the correct answer.** If you have effectively prephrased an answer, then you should be able to identify fairly readily the correct answer. Otherwise, you will have to study the choices carefully. And, again, careful reading means very careful reading. In logical reasoning, each word in the answer choices counts.

Now let's look at some sample GRE logical reasoning questions. As you read the explanations, think about how the solution process applies.

The governor claims that the state faces a drought and has implemented new water-use restrictions; but that's just a move to get some free publicity for his reelection campaign. So far this year we have had 3.5 inches of rain, slightly more than the average amount of rain for the same period over the last three years.

Which of the following, if true, would most weaken the conclusion of the argument above?

(A) The governor did not declare drought emergencies in the previous three years.

(B) City officials who have the authority to mandate water-use restrictions have not done so.

(C) The snowmelt that usually contributes significantly to the state's reservoirs is several inches below normal.

(D) The amount of water the state can draw from rivers that cross state boundaries is limited by federal law,

(E) Water-use restrictions are short-term measures and do little to reduce long-term water consumption.

This question stem asks you to attack the stimulus material. The argument is weak because it depends upon a hidden assumption: Rainfall is the only source of water for the reservoirs. So, your prephrased answer might be "there is another source of water for the reservoirs." (C) fits neatly into this prephrase.

"Channel One" is a 12-minute school news show that includes two minutes of commercials. The show's producers offer high schools $50,000 worth of television equipment to air the program. Many parents and teachers oppose the use of commercial television in schools, arguing that advertisements are tantamount to indoctrination. But students are already familiar with television commercials and know how to distinguish programming from advertising.

The argument assumes that

(A) the effects of an advertisement viewed in a classroom would be similar to those of the same advertisement viewed at home.

(B) many educators would be willing to allow the indoctrination of students in exchange for new equipment for their schools.

(C) television advertising is a more effective way of promoting a product to high school students than print advertising.

(D) high school students are sufficiently interested in world affairs to learn from a television news program.

(E) a television news program produced especially for high school students is an effective teaching tool.

> **AVOID THE TRAPS!**
>
> **Watch out for the common logical fallacies:**
> - Wrong cause
> - False analogy
> - Weak generalization
> - Ambiguous terms
> - Irrelevant evidence
> - Circular argument
> - *Ad hominem* attack

This question stem asks you to identify a hidden assumption of the stimulus material. The argument makes the assumption that television when viewed in the classroom will have a similar effect on children as that when it is viewed at home. This is a questionable assumption since the teacher/pupil relationship is an authoritative one. So your prephrase might be something like "the two situations are similar," and (A) is a hidden assumption of the argument.

> The spate of terrorist acts against airlines and their passengers raises a new question: Should government officials be forced to disclose the fact that they have received warning of an impending terrorist attack? The answer is "yes." The government currently releases information about the health hazards of smoking, the ecological dangers of pesticides, and the health consequences of food.

The argument above relies primarily on

(A) circular reasoning

(B) generalization

(C) authority

(D) analogy

(E) causal analysis

This question stem asks you to describe the reasoning in the stimulus material. The argument draws an analogy between two situations. So your prephrase would almost surely be "analogy." And the correct answer is (D).

When it rains, my car gets wet. Since it hasn't rained recently, my car can't be wet.

Which of the following is logically most similar to the argument above?

(A) Whenever critics give a play a favorable review, people go to see it; Pinter's new play did not receive favorable reviews, so I doubt that anyone will go to see it.

(B) Whenever people go to see a play, critics give it a favorable review; people did go to see Pinter's new play, so it did get a favorable review.

(C) Whenever critics give a play a favorable review, people go to see it; Pinter's new play got favorable reviews, so people will probably go to see it.

(D) Whenever a play is given favorable reviews by the critics, people go to see it; since people are going to see Pinter's new play, it will probably get favorable reviews.

(E) Whenever critics give a play a favorable review, people go to see it; people are not going to see Pinter's new play, so it did not get favorable reviews.

AVOID THE TRAPS!

"Parallel" questions can be tricky. The stimulus for a "parallel" question will probably contain an error. Don't fall into the trap of correcting the error. Just find an answer with a similar mistake.

This question stem asks you to parallel the stimulus material. The fallacy in the argument is confusion over necessary and sufficient causes. A sufficient cause is an event that is sufficient to guarantee some effect; a necessary cause is one that is required for some event. (A) exhibits this same fallacy. (Remember that a prephrase will not be possible with this type of question.)

WHAT SMART TEST-TAKERS KNOW

LOGICAL REASONING STIMULUS MATERIAL HAS A LOGICAL STRUCTURE.

Logical reasoning stimulus material is almost always an argument—even if it is just a single sentence. An argument is one or more statements or assertions, one of which, the conclusion, is supposed to follow from the others, the premises. Some arguments are very short and simple:

Premise: No fish are mammals.

Conclusion: No mammals are fish.

Others are extremely lengthy and complex, taking up entire volumes. Some arguments are good; some are bad. Scientists use arguments to justify a conclusion regarding the cause of some natural phenomenon; politicians use arguments to reach conclusions about the desirability of government policies. But even given this wide variety of structures and uses, arguments fall into one of two general categories—deductive and inductive.

A deductive argument is one in which the inference depends solely on the meanings of the terms used:

Premises: All bats are mammals.

              All mammals are warm blooded.

Conclusion: Therefore, all bats are warm blooded.

You know that this argument has to be correct just by looking at it. No research is necessary to show that the conclusion follows automatically from the premises.

All other arguments are termed inductive or probabilistic:

Premises: My car will not start; and the fuel gauge reads "empty."

Conclusion: Therefore, the car is probably out of gas.

Notice that here, unlike the deductive argument, the conclusion does not follow with certainty; it is not guaranteed. The conclusion does seem to be likely or probable, but there are some gaps in the argument. It is possible, for example, that the fuel gauge is broken, or that there is fuel in the tank and the car will not start because something else is wrong.

LOCATING THE CONCLUSION IS THE FIRST STEP IN EVALUATING AN ARGUMENT.

The conclusion is the main point of an argument, and locating the conclusion is the first step in evaluating the strength of any argument. In fact, some logical reasoning questions simply ask that you identify the conclusion or main point:

Which of the following is the speaker's conclusion?

Which of the following best summarizes the main point of the argument?

The speaker is attempting to prove that . . . .

The speaker is leading to the conclusion that . . . .

So, developing techniques for identifying the conclusion of the argument would be important in any case.

Conclusions, however, are important for yet another reason: You cannot begin to look for fallacies or other weaknesses in a line of reasoning or even find the line of reasoning until you have clearly identified the point the author wishes to prove. Any attempt to skip over this important step can only result in misunderstanding and confusion. You have surely had the experience of discussing a point for some length of time only to say finally, "Oh, now I see what you were saying, and I agree with you."

Locating the main point of an argument sometimes entails a bit of work because the logical structure of an argument is not necessarily dependent on the order in which sentences appear. To be sure, sometimes the main point of an argument is fairly easy to find. It is the last statement in the paragraph:

> Since this watch was manufactured in Switzerland, and all Swiss watches are reliable, this watch must be reliable.

Here the conclusion or the point of the line of reasoning is the part that is underlined. The argument also contains two premises: "this watch was manufactured in Switzerland" and "all Swiss watches are reliable." The same argument could be made, however, with the statements presented in a different order:

> This watch must be reliable since it was manufactured in Switzerland and all Swiss watches are reliable.

or

> This watch must be reliable since all Swiss watches are reliable and this watch was manufactured in Switzerland.

or

> Since this watch was manufactured in Switzerland, it must be reliable because all Swiss watches are reliable.

So you cannot always count on the conclusion of the argument being the last sentence of the paragraph even though sometimes it is. Therefore, it is important to know some techniques for finding the conclusion of an argument.

THE CONCLUSION OF AN ARGUMENT CAN BE THE FIRST SENTENCE.

It is true that speakers often lead up to the conclusion and make it the grand finale. Sometimes, however, speakers announce in advance where they are going and then proceed to develop arguments in support of their position. So the second most common position for the conclusion of an argument is the first sentence of the stimulus material.

KEY WORDS OFTEN SIGNAL A CONCLUSION.

The stimulus material often uses transitional words or phrases to signal a conclusion, for example, "Ms. Slote has a Masters in Education and she has 20 years of teaching experience, <u>therefore</u> she is a good teacher." Other words and phrases to watch include *hence*, *thus*, *so*, *it follows that*, *as a result*, and *consequently*.

KEY WORDS OFTEN SIGNAL AN IMPORTANT PREMISE.

In some arguments the premises rather than the conclusion are signaled. Words that signal premises include *since, because,* and *if.*

> <u>Since</u> Rex has been with the company 20 years and does such a good job, he will probably receive a promotion.

or

> Rex will probably receive a promotion <u>because</u> he has been with the company 20 years and he does such a good job.

or

> <u>If</u> Rex has been with the company 20 years and has done a good job, he will probably receive a promotion.

In each of the three examples just presented, the conclusion is "Rex will probably receive a promotion" and the premise is that "he has been with the company 20 years and does a good job." Of course, many other words can signal premises.

THE CONCLUSION IS THE MAIN POINT OF AN ARGUMENT.

Ask what the author wants to prove. Not all arguments are broken down by the numbers. In such a case, you must use your judgment to answer the question "What is the speaker trying to prove?" For example:

> We must reduce the amount of money we spend on space exploration. Right now, the enemy is launching a massive military buildup, and we need the additional money to purchase military equipment to match the anticipated increase in the enemy's strength.

In this argument there are no key words to announce the conclusion or the premises. Instead, you must ask yourself a series of questions:

> Is the speaker trying to prove that the enemy is beginning a military buildup?

No, because that statement is a premise of the larger argument, so it cannot be the conclusion.

TESTSMARTS

Signal words can help you find a conclusion:

therefore

hence

thus

consequently

accordingly

so

Is the main point that we must match the enemy buildup?

Again the answer is "no," because that, too, is an intermediate step on the way to some other conclusion.

Is the speaker trying to prove that we must cut back on the budget for space exploration?

Now the answer is "yes, and that is the author's point."

Things get more complicated when an argument contains arguments within the main argument. The argument about the need for military expenditures might have included this subargument:

We must reduce the amount of money we spend on space exploration. The enemy is now stockpiling titanium, a metal which is used in building airplanes. And each time the enemy has stockpiled titanium it has launched a massive military buildup. So, right now, the enemy is launching a massive military buildup, and we need the additional money to purchase military equipment to match the anticipated increase in the enemy's strength.

Notice that now one of the premises of the earlier argument is the conclusion of a subargument. The conclusion of the subargument is "the enemy is launching a massive military buildup," which has two explicit premises: "The enemy is now stockpiling titanium" and "a stockpiling of titanium means a military buildup."

No matter how complicated an argument gets, you can always break it down into subarguments. And if it is really complex, those subarguments can be broken down into smaller parts. Of course, the stimulus material on the GRE cannot be overly complicated because the initial argument will not be much more than a hundred or so words in length. So just keep asking yourself "What is the author trying to prove?"

GRE CONCLUSIONS ARE CAREFULLY WORDED.

Defining precisely the main point is also an essential step in evaluating an argument. Once the main point of the argument has been isolated, you must take the second step of exactly defining that point. In particular, you should be looking for three things:

1. Quantifiers
2. Qualifiers
3. The author's intention

GRE CONCLUSIONS ARE CAREFULLY QUANTIFIED.

Quantifiers are words such as *some, none, never, always, everywhere,* and *sometimes*. For example, there is a big difference in the claims:

All mammals live on land.

Most mammals live on land.

The first is false; the second is true. Compare also:

> Women in the United States have always had the right to vote.
>
> Since 1920, women in the United States have had the right to vote.

Again, the first statement is false and the second is true. And compare:

> It is raining and the temperature is predicted to drop below 32 F; therefore, it will surely snow.
>
> It is raining and the temperature is predicted to drop below 32 F; therefore, it will probably snow.

The first is a much less cautious claim than the second, and if it failed to snow the first claim would have been proved false, though not the second. The second statement claims only that it is probable that snow will follow, not that it definitely will. So someone could make the second claim and defend it when the snow failed to materialize by saying, "Well, I allowed for that in my original statement."

GRE CONCLUSIONS ARE CAREFULLY QUALIFIED.

Qualifiers play a role similar to that of quantifiers but they are descriptive rather than numerical. As such, they are more concrete and difficult to enumerate. Just make sure that you stay alert for distinctions like this:

> In nations which have a bicameral legislature, the speed with which legislation is passed is largely a function of the strength of executive leadership.

Notice here that the author makes a claim about "nations," so it would be wrong to apply the author's reasoning to states. Further, you should not conclude that the author believes that bicameral legislatures pass different laws from those passed by unicameral legislatures. The author mentions only the "speed" with which the laws are passed not their content.

> All passenger automobiles manufactured by Detroit auto makers since 1975 have been equipped with seat belts.

You should not conclude from this statement that all trucks have also been equipped with seat belts since the author makes a claim only about "passenger automobiles," nor should you conclude that imported cars have seat belts, for the author mentions Detroit-made cars only.

> No other major department store offers you a low price and a 75-day warranty on parts and labor on this special edition of the XL 30 color television.

The tone of the ad is designed to create a very large impression on the hearer, but the precise claim made is fairly limited. First, the ad's claim is specifically restricted to a comparison of "department" stores, and "major" department stores at that. It is possible that some non-major department store offers a similar warranty and price; also it may be that another type of retail store, say, an electronics store, makes a similar offer. Second, other stores, department or otherwise, may offer a better deal on the product, say, a low price with a three-month warranty, and still the claim would stand so long as no one else offered exactly a "75-day" warranty. Finally, the ad is restricted to a "special edition" of the television, so, depending on what that means, the ad may be even more restrictive in its claim.

ON THE GRE, THE AUTHOR'S INTENTION MAY BE CRUCIAL.

The author's intention may also be important. You must be careful to distinguish between claims of fact and proposals of change. Do not assume that an author's claim to have found a problem means the author knows how to solve it. An author can make a claim about the cause of some event without believing that the event can be prevented or even that it ought to be prevented. For example, from the argument:

> Since the fifth ward vote is crucial to Gordon's campaign, if Gordon fails to win over the ward leaders he will be defeated in the election.

you cannot conclude that the author believes Gordon should or should not be elected. The author gives only a factual analysis without endorsing or condemning either possible outcome. Also, from the argument:

> Each year the rotation of the Earth slows a few tenths of a second. In several million years, it will have stopped altogether, and life as we know it will no longer be able to survive on Earth.

you cannot conclude that the author wants to find a solution for the slowing of Earth's rotation. For all we know, the author thinks the process is inevitable, or even desirable.

PREMISES SUPPORT THE CONCLUSION.

A premise is the logical support for a conclusion. The GRE usually refers to premises as assumptions, but the terminology is not important. It is important not to misunderstand the word *assumption*. Although it is related to the word *assume*, an assumption, as that term is used in logic, does not have the connotation of *surmise* or *guess*. In the argument:

> All humans are mortal.
>
> Socrates is a human.
>
> Therefore, Socrates is mortal.

the first two statements are assumptions—even though they are obviously true. You can use the words *assumption* and *premise* interchangeably.

EXPLICIT PREMISES ARE SPECIFICALLY STATED.

In the detective novel *A Study in Scarlet* by Sir Arthur Conan Doyle, Sherlock Holmes explains to Dr. Watson that it is possible logically to deduce the existence of rivers and oceans from a single drop of water, though such a deduction would require many intermediate steps. While this may be an exaggeration, it is true that arguments can contain several links. For example:

Since there is snow on the ground, it must have snowed last night. If it snowed last night, then the temperature must have dropped below 32° F. The temperature drops below 32° F only in the winter. So, since there is snow on the ground, it must be winter here.

It is easy to imagine a Holmesian chain of reasoning that strings additional links in either direction. Instead of starting with "there is snow on the ground," you could have started with "there is a snowman on the front lawn;" and instead of stopping with "it must be winter here," you could have gone on to "so it is summer in Australia." In other words, you could reason from "there is a snowman on the front lawn" to "it is summer in Australia."

IMPLICIT PREMISES ARE NOT STATED.

In practice, arguments do not extend indefinitely in either direction. We begin reasoning at what seems to be a convenient point and stop with the conclusion we had hoped to prove: It must have snowed last night because there is snow on the ground this morning. Now, it should be obvious to you that the strength of an argument depends in a very important way on the legitimacy of its assumptions. And one of the GRE's favorite tools for building a logical reasoning item is to focus upon an assumption of a special kind: the implicit premise.

Consider some sample arguments:

Premise: My car's fuel tank is full.

Conclusion: Therefore, my car will start.

A very effective attack on this argument can be aimed at the first premise—as anyone who has ever had a car fail to start can attest. The battery might be dead or a hundred other things might be wrong. This shows that the argument is not very strong. In logical terms, the argument depends upon an implicit premise:

Premises: My car's fuel tank is full.

(The only reason my car might not start is lack of fuel.)

Conclusion: Therefore, my car will start.

The statement in parentheses is a necessary part of the argument. Otherwise, the conclusion does not follow.

Implicit premises are also called suppressed premises (or assumptions) or hidden premises (or assumptions). You do not have to worry about terminology; you just have to know one when you see it:

Premise: Edward has less than ten years of experience.

Conclusion: Therefore, Edward is not qualified.

Suppressed Premise: Only people with at least ten years of experience are qualified.

Premise:	This is Tuesday.
Conclusion:	Therefore, the luncheon special is pasta.
Suppressed Premise:	Every Tuesday, the luncheon special is pasta

Premise:	The committee did not announce its choice by 3:00.
Conclusion:	Therefore, Radu did not get the job.
Suppressed Premise:	Radu gets the job only if the announcement is made by 3:00.

Many logical reasoning questions test fallacies.

A fallacy is a mistake in reasoning. Many GRE questions ask you to demonstrate that you know a mistake when you see one. Of course, there are many different ways to make mistakes, so it is not possible to create an exhaustive list of fallacies; but there are certain fallacies that come up on the GRE fairly often. If you know what they look like, then they will be easier to spot.

Each of the following seven tips spotlights a comon GRE logical fallacy.

EXPLANATIONS OFTEN IDENTIFY THE WRONG CAUSE.

The mistake in reasoning that is tested most often by the GRE is the fallacy of the wrong cause. An argument that commits this error attributes a causal relationship between two events where none exists, or at least the relationship is misidentified. For example:

> Every time the doorbell rings I find there is someone at the door. Therefore, it must be the case that the doorbell calls these people to my door.

Obviously, the causal link suggested here is backwards. It is the presence of the person at the door which then leads to the ringing of the bell, not vice versa. A more serious example of the fallacy of the false cause is:

> There were more air traffic fatalities in 1979 than there were in 1969; therefore, the airplanes used in 1979 were more dangerous than those used in 1969.

The difficulty with this argument is that it attributes the increase in fatalities to a lack of safety when, in fact, it is probably attributable to an increase in air travel generally. A typical question stem and correct answer for this type of problem might be:

> Which of the following, if true, most undermines the speaker's argument?
>
> (✓) Total air miles traveled doubled from 1969 to 1979.

ANALOGIES ARE OFTEN FALSE.

A second fallacy that might appear on the GRE is that of false analogy. This error occurs when a conclusion drawn from one situation is applied to another situation—but the two situations are not very similar. For example:

> People should have to be licensed before they are allowed to have children. After all, we require people who operate automobiles to be licensed.

In this case, the two situations—driving and having children—are so dissimilar that we would probably want to say they are not analogous at all. Having children has nothing to do with driving. A GRE problem based upon a faulty analogy is likely to be more subtle. For example:

> The government should pay more to its diplomats who work in countries which are considered potential enemies. This is very similar to paying soldiers combat premiums if they are stationed in a war zone.

The argument here relies on an analogy between diplomats in a potentially dangerous country and soldiers in combat areas. Of course, the analogy is not perfect. No analogy can be more than an analogy. So a typical question stem and right answer for this type of problem might be:

> Which of the following, if true, most weakens the argument above?
>
> (✓) Diplomats are almost always evacuated before hostilities begin.

A GENERALIZATION MAY BE WEAK.

A common weakness in an inductive argument is the hasty generalization, that is, basing a large conclusion on too little data. For example:

> All four times I have visited Chicago it has rained; therefore, Chicago probably gets very little sunshine.

The rather obvious difficulty with the argument is that it moves from a small sample—four visits—to a very broad conclusion: Chicago gets little sunshine. Of course, generalizing on the basis of a sample or limited experience can be legitimate:

> All five of the buses manufactured by Gutmann which we inspected have defective wheel mounts; therefore, some other buses manufactured by Gutmann probably have similar defects.

Admittedly this argument is not airtight. Perhaps the other uninspected buses do not have the same defect, but this second argument is much stronger than the first. So a typical GRE stem and correct answer might be:

> Which of the following, if true, would most weaken the argument above?
>
> (✓) The five inspected buses were prototypes built before design specifications were finalized.

SOME ARGUMENTS USE TERMS AMBIGUOUSLY.

A fourth fallacy which the GRE uses is that of ambiguity. Anytime there is a shifting in the meaning of terms used in an argument, the argument has committed a fallacy of ambiguity. For example:

> The shark has been around for millions of years. The City Aquarium has a shark. Therefore, the City Aquarium has at least one animal that is millions of years old.

The error of the argument is that it uses the word *shark* in two different ways. In the first occurrence, *shark* is used to mean sharks in general. In the second, *shark* refers to one individual animal. Here's another, less playful, example:

> Sin occurs only when a person fails to follow the will of God. But since God is all-powerful, what God wills must actually be. Therefore, it is impossible to deviate from the will of God, so there can be no sin in the world.

The equivocation here is in the word *will*. The first time it is used, the author intends that the will of God is God's wish and implies that it is possible to fail to comply with those wishes. In the second instance, the author uses the word *will* in a way that implies that such deviation is not possible. The argument reaches the conclusion that there is no sin in the world only by playing on these two senses of "will of God." So a representative question stem and correct answer might be:

> The argument above uses which of the following terms in an ambiguous way?
>
> (✓) will

SOME ARGUMENTS USE IRRELEVANT EVIDENCE.

Another fallacy you might encounter in a logical reasoning section is any appeal to irrelevant considerations. For example, an argument that appeals to the popularity of a position to prove the position is fallacious:

> Frederick must be the best choice for chair because most people believe that he is the best person for the job.

That many people hold an opinion obviously does not guarantee its correctness. After all, many people once thought airplanes couldn't fly. A question stem for the argument above plus the correct answer might look like this:

> Which of the following, if true, most weakens the speaker's argument?
>
> (✓) Most people erroneously believe that Frederick holds a Ph.D.

SOME ARGUMENTS ARE CIRCULAR.

A circular argument (begging the question) is an argument in which the conclusion to be proved appears also as a premise. For example:

> Beethoven was the greatest composer of all time, because he wrote the greatest music of any composer, and the one who composes the greatest music must be the greatest composer.

The conclusion of this argument is that Beethoven was the greatest composer of all time, but one of the premises of the argument is that he composed the greatest music, and the other premise states that that is the measure of greatness. The argument is fallacious, for there is really no argument for the conclusion at all, just a restatement of the premise. A typical GRE stem and correct answer are:

> The argument above is weak because
>
> (✓) It assumes what it hopes to prove.

AD HOMINEM ARGUMENTS ATTACK SOMEONE PERSONALLY.

Yes, *ad hominem* is a Latin phrase, and Latin is not tested on the GRE. This phrase is just a useful shorthand for this fallacy. Any argument which is directed against the source of the claim rather than the claim itself is an *ad hominem* attack:

> Professor Peters' analysis of the economic impact of the proposed sports arena for the Blue Birds should be rejected, because Professor Peters is a Red Birds fan—the most fierce rivals of the Blue Birds.

The suggestion is obviously farfetched. And a representative GRE stem plus correct answer might look like this;

> The speaker's argument is weak because it
>
> (✓) confuses a person's loyalty to a sports team with the person's ability to offer an expert economic opinion

EXERCISES: LOGICAL REASONING

Exercise 1

6 QUESTIONS • 8 MINUTES

Directions: Below each of the following passages, you will find questions or incomplete statements about the passage. Each statement or question is followed by words or expressions. Select the word or expression that most satisfactorily completes each statement or answers each question in accordance with the meaning of the passage.

The existence of flying saucers, unidentified flying objects supposedly piloted by extraterrestrial beings, has been shown to be illusory. Skeptical researchers have demonstrated that a number of photographs purportedly showing flying saucers are either crude forgeries or misinterpreted images of such earthly objects as weather balloons or small private planes.

1. If the photographs mentioned above are accurately explained in the passage, which of the following is the best argument AGAINST the conclusion drawn?

   (A) Not all unidentified flying objects can be conclusively shown to be man-made objects.

   (B) The fact that a number of photographs of flying saucers are fake does not generally disprove the phenomenon.

   (C) Some of those who claim to have witnessed flying saucers have no apparent motive for lying.

   (D) Given the size and complexity of the universe, it seems unreasonable to assume that life exists only on the Earth.

   (E) Researchers who are skeptical about flying saucers inevitably bring their own biases and preconceptions to their work.

All the members of the Student Rights Coalition signed the petition calling for a meeting with the university trustees. Philip must be a member of the Student Rights Coalition, since his signature appears on the petition.

2. Which of the following best states the central flaw in the reasoning above?

   (A) Some members of the Student Rights Coalition may not support all of the organization's positions.

   (B) It is possible that Philip's signature on the petition was forged by a member of the Student Rights Coalition.

   (C) Any member of the student body is eligible to sign a petition dealing with university affairs.

   (D) Philip may have resigned from the Student Rights Coalition after signing the petition.

   (E) Some of those who signed the petition may not be members of the Student Rights Coalition.

Questions 3–4

Pollution control can no longer be viewed as a national problem to be addressed by individual countries on the basis of national sovereignty. As the international effects of the Chernobyl nuclear accident made clear, pollutants do not respect political boundaries; thus, every nation has a legitimate stake in the environmental practices and policies of its neighbors.

3. Which of the following would be the most logical continuation of the argument above?

   (A) So, growth of the nuclear power industry should be halted until more rigorous safety procedures have been developed.

   (B) Hence, attempts made by one nation to impose its environmental policies on another should be resisted—if necessary, by force.

   (C) Consequently, issues of pollution should be handled by an international commission with the authority to set policies for all nations.

   (D) Thus, every nation should pledge itself to environmental policies that will minimize the danger to its neighbors.

   (E) As a result, only the ultimate emergence of a sovereign world government will resolve today's most pressing environmental dilemmas.

4. Which of the following, if true, most strongly supports the view expressed in the passage?

   (A) Acid rain from factories in the midwestern United States pollutes lakes in Canada.

   (B) Soviet leaders refused western reporters access to safety records after the Chernobyl accident.

   (C) Neighboring states within the United States are often unable to agree on joint pollution-control efforts.

   (D) Existing international bodies have no authority to impose pollution control regulations on member nations.

   (E) Fishers from Japanese fleets have increasingly depleted fish supplies in United States territorial waters.

The percentage of family income spent on entertainment has remained almost the same over the past twenty years—about twelve percent. When new forms of entertainment become popular, they do not expand this percentage; instead, they take consumer spending away from other forms of entertainment. Therefore, film producers have observed the video boom with concern, knowing that every dollar spent on rental of videos means a dollar less spent on movie theater admissions.

5. Which of the following, if true, most forcefully undermines the argument of the passage above?

   (A) The cost of renting a video is generally substantially less than the price of a movie theater admission.

   (B) Most film producers receive a portion of the income from the sale of video rights to their movies.

   (C) Fears of some film producers that videos would completely supersede movies have not come to pass.

   (D) Since the start of the video boom, money spent on forms of entertainment other than videos and movies has dropped.

   (E) Some movies that were unprofitable when shown in theaters have become successful when released in video form.

The use of petroleum products in the manufacture of plastics should be regulated and limited by law. Our country's need for petroleum for energy production is more vital than our need for plastics, and our growing dependence on foreign sources of petroleum could have serious consequences if, for example, a war cut off our access to those imports. By reducing our use of petroleum products in making plastics, we can take a major step toward national energy independence and so enhance our country's security.

6. Which of the following, if true, would most greatly weaken the argument above?

   (A) Only a small fraction of the petroleum products consumed in this country is used in making plastics.

   (B) New methods of plastics manufacture can somewhat reduce the amount of petroleum needed.

   (C) The development of atomic energy as an alternative to petroleum-based energy has been slowed by legitimate concerns over safety.

   (D) In time of war, combatant nations would be seriously tempted to seize forcibly the territories of petroleum-producing nations.

   (E) Some plastic products, such as aircraft and motor vehicle parts, play vital roles in our nation's defense.

Exercise 2

4 QUESTIONS • 6 MINUTES

Directions: Below each of the following passages, you will find questions or incomplete statements about the passage. Each statement or question is followed by words or expressions. Select the word or expression that most satisfactorily completes each statement or answers each question in accordance with the meaning of the passage.

For the purposes of this study, ten qualities of a livable city were chosen, including a low crime rate, cleanliness, cultural attractions, and other amenities. For each city in the study, scores from 1 (lowest) to 10 (highest) were assigned for each of the ten qualities. The ten scores for each city were then summed, yielding a total livability score for each city. We hope the resulting ratings will help you in choosing your next place of residence.

1. The passage above makes which of the following assumptions?

   (A) Some of the ten qualities of a livable city are more important than other qualities.

   (B) Most people enjoy some degree of personal choice in where they reside.

   (C) Most people who use the survey will reinterpret the statistic in light of their own needs.

   (D) It is possible to assign an accurate numerical score to each of a city's amenities.

   (E) Most people would prefer to live in one of the cities designated as "most livable" by the survey.

Foreign-made electronics products gained popularity in the United States during the 1970s primarily because of their low cost. In recent years, changes in the exchange rates of currencies have increased the prices of imported electronics products relative to those produced in the United States. However, sales of imported electronics products have not declined in recent years.

2. Which of the following, if true, would best explain why sales of imported electronics products remain high?

   (A) Trade ministries in foreign nations have pursued policies that prevented prices of electronics products from rising even faster.

   (B) The cost of manufacturing electronics products abroad is still lower than it is in the United States.

   (C) A coming shortage in consumer credit in the United States is expected to depress sales of imported products during the next two years.

   (D) American consumers now perceive the quality of imports as being high enough to justify the increased prices.

   (E) United States manufacturers have tried to convince Americans to buy United States-made products for patriotic reasons.

Young people who imagine that the life of the writer is one of glamour, riches, or fame soon discover not only the difficulties of the craft but the long odds against achieving any measure of recognition or financial security. Upon being asked, "Aren't most editors failed writers?" T.S. Eliot is said to have remarked, "Yes, but so are most writers."

3. The statement by T.S. Eliot conveys which of the following ideas?

   (A) The profession of editing can be just as creative and challenging as writing.

   (B) Few writers are fortunate enough to attain real success in their profession.

   (C) For a writer, success is measured more by influence exerted than by material gain achieved.

   (D) Many writers find that a stint at editorial work is a beneficial apprenticeship in their craft.

   (E) There are no clear-cut standards of success and failure for writers, but there are such standards for editors.

Superficially, today's problems with the abuse of illegal drugs such as heroin and cocaine resemble the abuse of alcohol during the 1920s, when many people kept drinking in spite of Prohibition. There is, however, a significant difference. The use of drugs such as heroin and cocaine has never been a widespread, socially accepted practice among most middle-class, otherwise law-abiding Americans.

4. An underlying assumption of the passage is that

   (A) during Prohibition, drinking of alcohol was commonly accepted among most Americans

   (B) as long as drugs are available, they will be used despite laws to the contrary

   (C) most Americans consider heroin and cocaine to be in the same category as alcohol

   (D) in a democracy, laws must be based on the fundamental beliefs and values of the majority of citizens

   (E) American popular opinion has always been molded primarily by the values of the middle class

Answer Keys and Explanations

Exercise 1

1. B	2. E	3. C	4. A	5. D	6. A

1. **(B)** The logical structure of this argument is an attempt to conclude from the failure to prove "A" that "Not A" is true. It says in essence, "No one has proven that flying saucers exist, therefore, they do not exist." (B) correctly notes this logical structure.

2. **(E)** This argument has the following logical structure:

    > All S are P.
    > F is a P.
    > Therefore, F is an S.

    The argument is fatally flawed. It's like arguing:

    > All soft drinks are liquids.
    > Water is a liquid.
    > Therefore, water is a soft drink.

    (E) correctly notes this logical flaw.

3. **(C)** This question asks that you draw a further conclusion from the premises given. The argument is leading up to a call for some sort of international agency to control pollution, which, as the author claims, is an international problem. Thus, (C) is the best response. As for (A), the author would consider the Chernobyl incident merely one example of the problem he is addressing; and, in fact, he may or may not oppose nuclear power per se. (B) and (D) contradict the paragraph, for the author is skeptical of the ability of a nation as an individual nation to solve the problems of pollution. Finally, however, (E) overstates the case. The author is concerned with a specific subject area—not world government in general.

4. **(A)** The author cites one example of international pollution, so another example would help strengthen his claim. (A) provides such an example. As for (B), the fact that journalists were not given access to the Chernobyl plant does not show that the incident had international repercussions. As for (C), this is a problem within a nation-state, but the author is addressing the problem of international pollution. As for (D), the fact that there does not yet exist an international agency to control pollution neither strengthens nor weakens the author's claim that there *ought* to be some such authority. Finally, as for (E), this too is a problem that can be handled completely within the jurisdiction of a single nation: Stop the fishers from fishing in the territorial waters.

5. **(D)** This is one of those questions, typical of the GRE, that is answered by finding an alternative causal explanation. The author argues for the following connection: Videos take money away from movies. What choice (D) asserts, in effect, is that the monies spent on videos came from some other source. So the projected cause-effect sequence was incorrect.

6. **(A)** This item asks you to find a hidden assumption of the argument. The speaker claims that in order to ensure that we have sufficient energy, we should quit using petroleum (an energy source) to manufacture plastics. If we do, so he claims, we will have made a significant step toward energy independence. This argument, however, assumes that we use a lot of petroleum in the manufacture of plastic—an assumption questioned by (A).

Exercise 2

1. D   2. D   3. B   4. A

1. **(D)** This item asks you to identify a hidden assumption of the argument. (D) is an assumption of the argument, for the speaker states that he has assigned numerical values for the various aspects—and that presupposes that some sort of quantitative measure is possible. (A) is wrong because the author seems to make the opposite assumption, to wit, that the qualities should all be weighted equally. As for (B) and (C), the speaker doesn't make any logical commitment one way or the other as to what "most" people are able to do or will actually do. And the same reasoning applies to (E): logically, some people may choose to live in a location for reasons altogether unrelated to those offered by the survey.

2. **(D)** This question asks you to examine a causal linkage. Ordinarily, we would expect higher prices to result in less demand for a product. Yet, according to the speaker, in the face of higher prices for imported electronics, demand has not weakened. What alternative causal explanation could account for this? (D) gives a good one. Here (B) is perhaps the second-best answer. If (B) is true, then we would expect some consumers to prefer imports over domestically produced items; but the argument doesn't just claim that there has been less weakening in the demand for imports than might be expected—but no weakening at all.

3. **(B)** The main point of the passage is that most writers don't fare well. This is why the author quotes T.S. Eliot, who, somewhat ironically, points out that even most people who claim to be writers really aren't *successful* writers.

4. **(A)** This item asks for an underlying assumption. The author claims that the situation with heroin and cocaine use is unlike that which existed with respect to alcohol during Prohibition. What is the difference? According to the author, heroin and cocaine are not middle-class drugs of preference. Thus, we can infer (though the author never specifically says so) that alcohol, even during Prohibition, was a middle-class drug of preference.

What You Must Know About GRE Analytical Questions

Review this page the night before you take the GRE. It will help you get the answers to GRE analytical questions.

You can expect to see 26 to 29 analytical reasoning items grouped into 4 or 5 puzzles. And you'll have 6 to 9 logical reasoning items. Although all of the questions based on a single puzzle will be grouped together (presented one after another), the logical reasoning items are interspersed among the different groups. (They do not break up groups.)

Analytical Reasoning

- These steps will help you solve analytical reasoning questions:

    1. Summarize the initial conditions in a "bookkeeping" system.
    2. Look for further conclusions.
    3. Treat each question separately.
    4. Use the answer choices to create a "feedback loop."

- The most common types of analytical reasoning puzzles are linear ordering, distributed order, and selection sets.

Logical Reasoning

- These steps will help you solve logical reasoning problems:

    1. Preview the question stem.
    2. Read the stimulus material.
    3. Prephrase your answer.
    4. Identify the correct answer.

- There are seven common types of logical reasoning questions:

    1. Identify the conclusion
    2. Point out a premise
    3. Identify strengths or weaknesses
    4. Recognize parallel reasoning
    5. Evaluate evidence
    6. Draw a conclusion

- Locating the conclusion is the first step in evaluating an argument.
- Key words often signal the conclusion or an important premise.
- In logical reasoning questions, watch out for the seven most common logical fallacies:

  1. Wrong cause
  2. False analogy
  3. Weak generalization
  4. Ambiguous terms
  5. Irrelevant evidence
  6. Circular argument
  7. *Ad hominem* attack

PART

SIX

EVERYTHING YOU NEED!

Five Practice Examinations

PREVIEW ➔

Practice Examination 1

Practice Examination 2

Practice Examination 3

Practice Examination 4

Practice Examination 5

TIME MANAGER STUDY PLANS

PLAN A: ACCELERATED

- *Complete* all Practice Examinations
- *Study* the Explanatory Answers
- *Evaluate* your results

PLAN B: TOP SPEED

- *Complete* Practice Examination 1 if you have enough study time left
- *Check* your answers with the Answer Key
- If you have more time, do additional Practice Examinations.

Answer Sheet

TEAR HERE

VERBAL SECTION

1. Ⓐ Ⓑ Ⓒ Ⓓ Ⓔ   7. Ⓐ Ⓑ Ⓒ Ⓓ Ⓔ   13. Ⓐ Ⓑ Ⓒ Ⓓ Ⓔ   19. Ⓐ Ⓑ Ⓒ Ⓓ Ⓔ   25. Ⓐ Ⓑ Ⓒ Ⓓ Ⓔ
2. Ⓐ Ⓑ Ⓒ Ⓓ Ⓔ   8. Ⓐ Ⓑ Ⓒ Ⓓ Ⓔ   14. Ⓐ Ⓑ Ⓒ Ⓓ Ⓔ   20. Ⓐ Ⓑ Ⓒ Ⓓ Ⓔ   26. Ⓐ Ⓑ Ⓒ Ⓓ Ⓔ
3. Ⓐ Ⓑ Ⓒ Ⓓ Ⓔ   9. Ⓐ Ⓑ Ⓒ Ⓓ Ⓔ   15. Ⓐ Ⓑ Ⓒ Ⓓ Ⓔ   21. Ⓐ Ⓑ Ⓒ Ⓓ Ⓔ   27. Ⓐ Ⓑ Ⓒ Ⓓ Ⓔ
4. Ⓐ Ⓑ Ⓒ Ⓓ Ⓔ   10. Ⓐ Ⓑ Ⓒ Ⓓ Ⓔ   16. Ⓐ Ⓑ Ⓒ Ⓓ Ⓔ   22. Ⓐ Ⓑ Ⓒ Ⓓ Ⓔ   28. Ⓐ Ⓑ Ⓒ Ⓓ Ⓔ
5. Ⓐ Ⓑ Ⓒ Ⓓ Ⓔ   11. Ⓐ Ⓑ Ⓒ Ⓓ Ⓔ   17. Ⓐ Ⓑ Ⓒ Ⓓ Ⓔ   23. Ⓐ Ⓑ Ⓒ Ⓓ Ⓔ   29. Ⓐ Ⓑ Ⓒ Ⓓ Ⓔ
6. Ⓐ Ⓑ Ⓒ Ⓓ Ⓔ   12. Ⓐ Ⓑ Ⓒ Ⓓ Ⓔ   18. Ⓐ Ⓑ Ⓒ Ⓓ Ⓔ   24. Ⓐ Ⓑ Ⓒ Ⓓ Ⓔ   30. Ⓐ Ⓑ Ⓒ Ⓓ Ⓔ

MATH SECTION

1. Ⓐ Ⓑ Ⓒ Ⓓ Ⓔ   7. Ⓐ Ⓑ Ⓒ Ⓓ Ⓔ   13. Ⓐ Ⓑ Ⓒ Ⓓ Ⓔ   19. Ⓐ Ⓑ Ⓒ Ⓓ Ⓔ   25. Ⓐ Ⓑ Ⓒ Ⓓ Ⓔ
2. Ⓐ Ⓑ Ⓒ Ⓓ Ⓔ   8. Ⓐ Ⓑ Ⓒ Ⓓ Ⓔ   14. Ⓐ Ⓑ Ⓒ Ⓓ Ⓔ   20. Ⓐ Ⓑ Ⓒ Ⓓ Ⓔ   26. Ⓐ Ⓑ Ⓒ Ⓓ Ⓔ
3. Ⓐ Ⓑ Ⓒ Ⓓ Ⓔ   9. Ⓐ Ⓑ Ⓒ Ⓓ Ⓔ   15. Ⓐ Ⓑ Ⓒ Ⓓ Ⓔ   21. Ⓐ Ⓑ Ⓒ Ⓓ Ⓔ   27. Ⓐ Ⓑ Ⓒ Ⓓ Ⓔ
4. Ⓐ Ⓑ Ⓒ Ⓓ Ⓔ   10. Ⓐ Ⓑ Ⓒ Ⓓ Ⓔ   16. Ⓐ Ⓑ Ⓒ Ⓓ Ⓔ   22. Ⓐ Ⓑ Ⓒ Ⓓ Ⓔ   28. Ⓐ Ⓑ Ⓒ Ⓓ Ⓔ
5. Ⓐ Ⓑ Ⓒ Ⓓ Ⓔ   11. Ⓐ Ⓑ Ⓒ Ⓓ Ⓔ   17. Ⓐ Ⓑ Ⓒ Ⓓ Ⓔ   23. Ⓐ Ⓑ Ⓒ Ⓓ Ⓔ
6. Ⓐ Ⓑ Ⓒ Ⓓ Ⓔ   12. Ⓐ Ⓑ Ⓒ Ⓓ Ⓔ   18. Ⓐ Ⓑ Ⓒ Ⓓ Ⓔ   24. Ⓐ Ⓑ Ⓒ Ⓓ Ⓔ

ANALYTICAL SECTION

1. Ⓐ Ⓑ Ⓒ Ⓓ Ⓔ   8. Ⓐ Ⓑ Ⓒ Ⓓ Ⓔ   15. Ⓐ Ⓑ Ⓒ Ⓓ Ⓔ   22. Ⓐ Ⓑ Ⓒ Ⓓ Ⓔ   29. Ⓐ Ⓑ Ⓒ Ⓓ Ⓔ
2. Ⓐ Ⓑ Ⓒ Ⓓ Ⓔ   9. Ⓐ Ⓑ Ⓒ Ⓓ Ⓔ   16. Ⓐ Ⓑ Ⓒ Ⓓ Ⓔ   23. Ⓐ Ⓑ Ⓒ Ⓓ Ⓔ   30. Ⓐ Ⓑ Ⓒ Ⓓ Ⓔ
3. Ⓐ Ⓑ Ⓒ Ⓓ Ⓔ   10. Ⓐ Ⓑ Ⓒ Ⓓ Ⓔ   17. Ⓐ Ⓑ Ⓒ Ⓓ Ⓔ   24. Ⓐ Ⓑ Ⓒ Ⓓ Ⓔ   31. Ⓐ Ⓑ Ⓒ Ⓓ Ⓔ
4. Ⓐ Ⓑ Ⓒ Ⓓ Ⓔ   11. Ⓐ Ⓑ Ⓒ Ⓓ Ⓔ   18. Ⓐ Ⓑ Ⓒ Ⓓ Ⓔ   25. Ⓐ Ⓑ Ⓒ Ⓓ Ⓔ   32. Ⓐ Ⓑ Ⓒ Ⓓ Ⓔ
5. Ⓐ Ⓑ Ⓒ Ⓓ Ⓔ   12. Ⓐ Ⓑ Ⓒ Ⓓ Ⓔ   19. Ⓐ Ⓑ Ⓒ Ⓓ Ⓔ   26. Ⓐ Ⓑ Ⓒ Ⓓ Ⓔ   33. Ⓐ Ⓑ Ⓒ Ⓓ Ⓔ
6. Ⓐ Ⓑ Ⓒ Ⓓ Ⓔ   13. Ⓐ Ⓑ Ⓒ Ⓓ Ⓔ   20. Ⓐ Ⓑ Ⓒ Ⓓ Ⓔ   27. Ⓐ Ⓑ Ⓒ Ⓓ Ⓔ   34. Ⓐ Ⓑ Ⓒ Ⓓ Ⓔ
7. Ⓐ Ⓑ Ⓒ Ⓓ Ⓔ   14. Ⓐ Ⓑ Ⓒ Ⓓ Ⓔ   21. Ⓐ Ⓑ Ⓒ Ⓓ Ⓔ   28. Ⓐ Ⓑ Ⓒ Ⓓ Ⓔ   35. Ⓐ Ⓑ Ⓒ Ⓓ Ⓔ

Verbal Section

30 QUESTIONS • TIME—30 Minutes

Directions: ...

Practice Examination 1

Verbal Section

30 QUESTIONS • TIME—30 MINUTES

Directions: Each of the questions below contains one or more blank spaces, each blank indicating an omitted word. Each sentence is followed by five (5) words or sets of words. Read and determine the general sense of each sentence. Then choose the word, or set of words that, when inserted in the sentence, best fits the meaning of the sentence.

1. It is —— that students do not repay their student loans and thereby make it more —— for future generations of students to obtain them.

    (A) unfortunate..urgent

    (B) regrettable..difficult

    (C) unforgivable..likely

    (D) laudable..practical

    (E) worrisome..imperative

2. Although her initial success was —— by the fact that she was the daughter of a famous actor, the critics later —— her as a star in her own right.

    (A) enhanced..acclaimed

    (B) impeded..criticized

    (C) refuted..summarily acknowledged

    (D) superceded..disavowed

    (E) trivialized..accepted

3. Contrary to popular belief, the Mayans were not peace-loving astronomers but —— warriors who viewed their gods as cruel and ——.

    (A) formidable..vengeful

    (B) skilled..benevolent

    (C) reluctant..omnipotent

    (D) docile..patronizing

    (E) amicable..malevolent

Directions: In each of the following questions, you are given a related pair of words or phrases in capital letters. Each capitalized pair is followed by five (5) pairs of words or phrases. Choose the pair that best expresses a relationship similar to that expressed by the original pair.

4. PROHIBITED : REFRAIN ::

    (A) innocuous : forbid

    (B) deleterious : embark

    (C) required : decide

    (D) compulsory : comply

    (E) ridiculous : laugh

5. OVERTURE : OPERA ::

    (A) epilogue : movie

    (B) preface : book

    (C) concerto : piano

    (D) footnote : paragraph

    (E) singer : aria

6. RESOLVED : DOUBT ::

    (A) confirmed : suspicion

    (B) announced : candidacy

    (C) included : guest

    (D) suggested : idea

    (E) demolished : opponent

GO ON TO THE NEXT PAGE ▶

Desertification in the arid United States is flagrant. Groundwater supplies beneath vast stretches of land are dropping precipitously. Whole river systems have dried up; others are choked with sediment washed from
(5) denuded land. Hundreds of thousands of acres of previously irrigated cropland have been abandoned to wind or weeds. Several million acres of natural grassland are eroding at unnaturally high rates as a result of cultivation or overgrazing. All told, about 225 million acres of
(10) land are undergoing severe desertification.

Federal subsidies encourage the exploitation of arid land resources. Low-interest loans for irrigation and other water delivery systems encourage farmers, industry, and municipalities to mine groundwater. Federal
(15) disaster relief and commodity programs encourage arid-land farmers to plow up natural grassland to plant crops such as wheat and, especially, cotton. Federal grazing fees that are well below the free market price encourage overgrazing of the commons. The market, too, provides
(20) powerful incentives to exploit arid-land resources beyond their carrying capacity. When commodity prices are high relative to the farmer's or rancher's operating costs, the return on a production-enhancing investment is invariably greater than the return on a conservation
(25) investment. And when commodity prices are relatively low, arid-land ranchers and farmers often have to use all their available financial resources to stay solvent.

If the United States is, as it appears, well on its way toward overdrawing the arid-land resources, then the
(30) policy choice is simply to pay now for the appropriate remedies or pay far more later, when productive benefits from arid-land resources have been both realized and largely terminated.

7. The author is primarily concerned with

(A) discussing a solution

(B) describing a problem

(C) replying to a detractor

(D) finding a contradiction

(E) defining a term

8. The passage mentions all of the following as effects of desertification EXCEPT

(A) increased sediment in rivers

(B) erosion of land

(C) overcultivation of land

(D) decreasing groundwater supplies

(E) loss of land to wind or weeds

9. The author's attitude toward desertification can best be described as one of

(A) alarm

(B) optimism

(C) understanding

(D) conciliation

(E) concern

10. COVERT :

(A) protracted

(B) insensitive

(C) reclining

(D) open

(E) taxing

11. SALIENT :

(A) insignificant

(B) climactic

(C) worrisome

(D) awesome

(E) radical

12. MORIBUND :

(A) contentious

(B) malignant

(C) pretentious

(D) detestable

(E) vital

13. PLIANT :

    (A) humble

    (B) rigid

    (C) tactful

    (D) earnest

    (E) solemn

Directions: The passage below is followed by questions based on its content. Choose the best answer to each question.

Reverse discrimination, minority recruitment, racial quotas, and, more generally, affirmative action are phrases that carry powerful emotional charges. But why should affirmative action, of all government policies, be
(5) so controversial? In a sense, affirmative action is like other governmental programs, e.g., defense, conservation, and public schools. Affirmative action programs are designed to achieve legitimate government objectives such as improved economic efficiency, reduced
(10) social tension, and general betterment of the public welfare. While it cannot be denied that there is no guarantee that affirmative action will achieve these results, neither can it be denied that there are plausible, even powerful, sociological and economic arguments
(15) pointing to its likely success.

Government programs, however, entail a cost, that is, the expenditure of social or economic resources. Setting aside cases in which the specific user is charged a fee for service (toll roads and tuition at state institu-
(20) tions), the burdens and benefits of publicly funded or mandated programs are widely shared.

When an individual benefits personally from a government program, it is only because she or he is one member of a larger beneficiary class, e.g., a farmer; and
(25) most government revenue is obtained through a scheme of general taxation to which all are subject.

Affirmative action programs are exceptions to this general rule, though not, as might at first seem, because the beneficiaries of the programs are specific individu-
(30) als. It is still the case that those who ultimately benefit from affirmative action do so only by virtue of their status as members of a larger group, a particular minority. Rather, the difference is the location of the burden. In affirmative action, the burden of "funding" the pro-
(35) gram is not shared universally, and that is inherent in the nature of the case, as can be seen clearly in the case of affirmative action in employment. Often job promotions are allocated along a single dimension, seniority; and when an employer promotes a less senior worker
(40) from a minority group, the person disadvantaged by the move is easily identified: the worker with greatest seniority on a combined minority-nonminority list passed over for promotion.

Now we are confronted with two competing moral
(45) sentiments. On the one hand, there is the idea that those who have been unfairly disadvantaged by past discriminatory practices are entitled to some kind of assistance. On the other, there is the feeling that no person ought to be deprived of what is rightfully his or hers, even for the
(50) worthwhile service of fellow humans. In this respect, disability due to past racial discrimination, at least insofar as there is no connection to the passed-over worker, is like a natural evil. When a villainous man willfully and without provocation strikes and injures
(55) another, there is not only the feeling that the injured person ought to be compensated but there is consensus that the appropriate party to bear the cost is the one who inflicted the injury. Yet, if the same innocent man stumbled and injured himself, it would be surprising to
(60) hear someone argue that the villainous man ought to be taxed for the injury simply because he might have tripped the victim had he been given the opportunity. There may very well be agreement that he should be aided in his recovery with money and personal assis-
(65) tance, and many will give willingly; but there is also agreement that no one individual ought to be singled out and forced to do what must ultimately be considered an act of charity.

14. The passage is primarily concerned with

    (A) comparing affirmative action programs to other government programs

    (B) arguing that affirmative action programs are morally justified

    (C) analyzing the basis for moral judgments about affirmative action programs

    (D) introducing the reader to the importance of affirmative action as a social issue

    (E) describing the benefits that can be obtained through affirmative action programs

GO ON TO THE NEXT PAGE

15. The author mentions toll roads and tuition at state institutions (lines 19–20) in order to

   (A) anticipate a possible objection based on counterexamples

   (B) avoid a contradiction between moral sentiments

   (C) provide illustrations of common government programs

   (D) voice doubts about the social and economic value of affirmative action

   (E) offer examples of government programs that are too costly

16. With which of the following statements would the author most likely agree?

   (A) Affirmative action programs should be discontinued because they place an unfair burden on nonminority persons who bear the cost of the programs.

   (B) Affirmative action programs may be able to achieve legitimate social and economic goals such as improved efficiency.

   (C) Affirmative action programs are justified because they are the only way of correcting injustices created by past discrimination.

   (D) Affirmative action programs must be redesigned so that society as a whole rather than particular individuals bears the cost of the programs.

   (E) Affirmative action programs should be abandoned because they serve no useful social function and place unfair burdens on particular individuals.

17. The author most likely places the word "funding" in quotation marks (line 34) in order to remind the reader that

   (A) affirmative action programs are costly in terms of government revenues

   (B) particular individuals may bear a disproportionate share of the burden of affirmative action

   (C) the cost of most government programs is shared by society at large

   (D) the beneficiaries of affirmative action are members of larger groups

   (E) the cost of affirmative action is not only a monetary expenditure

18. The "villainous man" discussed in lines 53–68 functions primarily as

   (A) an illustration

   (B) a counterexample

   (C) an authority

   (D) an analogy

   (E) a disclaimer

19. According to the passage, affirmative action programs are different from most other government programs in the

   (A) legitimacy of the goals the programs are designed to achieve

   (B) ways in which costs of the programs are distributed

   (C) methods for allocating the benefits of the programs

   (D) legal structures that are enacted to achieve the objectives

   (E) discretion granted to the executive for implementing the programs

Directions: In each of the following questions, you are given a related pair of words or phrases in capital letters. Each capitalized pair is followed by five (5) pairs of words or phrases. Choose the pair that best expresses a relationship similar to that expressed by the original pair.

20. EXEMPLARY : REPROACH ::

   (A) erroneous : correction

   (B) accomplished : praise

   (C) fulfilling : control

   (D) planned : implementation

   (E) unimpeachable : criticism

21. MENDICANT : BEGGING ::
    (A) competitor : joining
    (B) legislator : funding
    (C) miser : donating
    (D) prevaricator : lying
    (E) mechanic : selling

22. RAIN : DELUGE ::
    (A) pond : ocean
    (B) desert : camel
    (C) ore : iron
    (D) street : road
    (E) wheat : crop

23. LUBRICANT : FRICTION ::
    (A) balm : pain
    (B) eraser : correction
    (C) solvent : paint
    (D) reagent : chemical
    (E) merchant : business

Directions: Each of the questions below contains one or more blank spaces, each blank indicating an omitted word. Each sentence is followed by five (5) words or sets of words. Read and determine the general sense of each sentence. Then choose the word, or set of words that, when inserted in the sentence, best fits the meaning of the sentence.

24. Despite the fact that she was much ——, the scientist continued to present her controversial theories to the —— of the Royal Academy, whose members repeatedly denounced her research.
    (A) admired..chagrin
    (B) revered..benefit
    (C) imitated..foreboding
    (D) chastened..temerity
    (E) maligned..consternation

25. Washington Irving, the father of American literature and creator of such delightful characters as Ichabod Crane and Rip Van Winkle, will be remembered more for the —— of his prose than for the originality of his tales, which were —— from popular folklore.
    (A) density..obtained
    (B) vulgarity..stolen
    (C) mediocrity..descended
    (D) charm..borrowed
    (E) pomposity..reduced

26. Although alcoholism has long been regarded as a personality disorder, there is evidence to suggest that alcoholics are often the children of alcoholics and that they are born with a —— the disease.
    (A) respect for
    (B) predisposition to
    (C) liability for
    (D) deterioration of
    (E) misunderstanding of

Directions: Each of the following questions consists of a word printed in capital letters, followed by five words or phrases. Choose the word or phrase that is most nearly opposite in meaning to the word in capital letters. Be sure to consider all the choices before deciding which one is best.

27. DORMANT :
    (A) authoritative
    (B) elastic
    (C) active
    (D) uninteresting
    (E) endearing

28. PLACATE :
    (A) abet
    (B) enrage
    (C) invite
    (D) witness
    (E) repent

GO ON TO THE NEXT PAGE

29. EXTRANEOUS :

(A) outlandish

(B) tumultuous

(C) impetuous

(D) central

(E) guarded

30. RENOWN :

(A) suggestiveness

(B) superficiality

(C) anonymity

(D) deviousness

(E) valor

WARNING

IF YOU FINISHED THIS SECTION BEFORE TIME EXPIRED, GO
IMMEDIATELY TO THE NEXT SECTION. YOU MAY NOT CON-
TINUE TO WORK ON THIS SECTION AFTER TIME HAS EXPIRED.

Math Section

28 QUESTIONS — 45 MINUTES

Directions: For each of these questions, select the best of the answer choices given.

Numbers: All numbers used are real numbers.

Figures: Assume that the position of points, angles, regions and so forth are in the order shown. Figures are assumed to lie in a plane unless otherwise indicated. Figures accompanying questions are intended to provide information you can use in answering the questions. However, unless a note states that a figure is drawn to scale, you should solve the problems by using your knowledge of mathematics and not by estimating sizes by sight or measurement.

Lines: Assume that lines shown as straight are indeed straight.

Directions: For each of the following questions two quantities are given, one in Column A and one in Column B. Compare the two quantities and choose

   A: if the quantity in Column A is the greater

   B: if the quantity in Column B is the greater

   C: if the two quantities are equal

   D: if the relationship cannot be determined from the information given.

Common Information: In any question, information applying to both columns is centered between the columns and above the quantities in columns A and B. Any symbol that appears in both columns represents the same idea or quantity in both columns.

	Column A	Column B
1.	$16 \div 4$	$\frac{4}{11} \times 11$

$$x = \frac{1}{3} \text{ of } 12$$
$$y = \frac{4}{3} \text{ of } 9$$

	Column A	Column B
2.	x	y

When n is divided by 49, the remainder is 0.

	Column A	Column B
3.	The remainder when n is divided by 7	7

	Column A	Column B
4.	$\left(\frac{101}{202}\right)^{11}$	$\left(\frac{-101}{202}\right)^{11}$

An apartment building has 5 floors, one of which has only 2 apartments. Each of the other floors has 4 apartments.

	Column A	Column B
5.	3 times the number of floors in the building	The number of apartments in the building

GO ON TO THE NEXT PAGE

Directions: For each of these questions, select the best of the answer choices given.

6. Which of the following is equal to 0.00127?

    (A) 1.27×10

    (B) 1.27×0.10

    (C) 1.27×0.01

    (D) 1.27×0.001

    (E) 1.27×0.0001

7. A prize of $240 is divided between two persons. If one person receives $180, then what is the difference between the amounts received by the two persons?

    (A) $30

    (B) $60

    (C) $120

    (D) $210

    (E) $420

8. If $3x - 4y = 5$ and $\frac{y}{x} = \frac{1}{3}$, then what is x?

    (A) $-5y$

    (B) $-5x$

    (C) 1

    (D) 3

    (E) 4

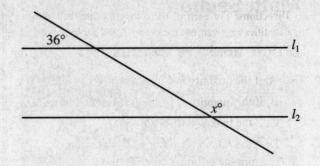

9. In the preceding figure, if $l_1 \parallel l_2$, what is the value of x?

    (A) 36

    (B) 54

    (C) 90

    (D) 144

    (E) 154

10. If $\frac{x-1}{x+1} = \frac{4}{5}$, then $x =$

    (A) 3

    (B) 4

    (C) 5

    (D) 9

    (E) 12

Directions: For each of the following questions two quantities are given, one in Column A and one in Column B. Compare the two quantities and choose

A: if the quantity in Column A is the greater

B: if the quantity in Column B is the greater

C: if the two quantities are equal

D: if the relationship cannot be determined from the information given.

| **Column A** | **Column B** |

$$x^2 - 3x - 4 = (x + m)(x + n)$$

11. m n

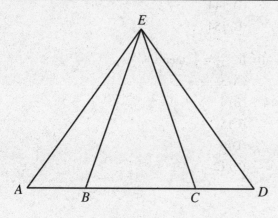

$$AB = CD = \tfrac{1}{2} \times BC$$

12. Area of triangle BEC Sum of the areas of triangles AEB and CED

13. $\sqrt{\dfrac{3}{16}} + \sqrt{\dfrac{3}{16}} + \sqrt{\dfrac{3}{16}}$ $\sqrt{\dfrac{9}{16}}$

14. $5\left(\dfrac{x}{5} + \dfrac{y}{5} + \dfrac{7}{5}\right)$ $x + y - 7$

Point P has coordinates (x, y); point Q has coordinates $(x - 1, y - 1)$.

15. The distance from P to the origin   The distance from Q to the origin

Directions: For each of these questions, select the best of the answer choices given.

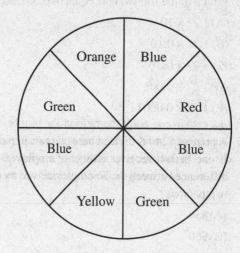

16. The figure above shows a wheel of fortune divided into sections of equal size and painted with the colors indicated. If the wheel has a diameter of 64 centimeters, what is the total area of the wheel that is painted blue (expressed in square centimeters)?

(A) 3π

(B) 24π

(C) 40π

(D) 128π

(E) 384π

17. Right circular cylinder P has a radius of 3 and a height of 4. If the volume of P is equal to the volume of right circular cylinder Q, which has a radius of 2, then what is the height of Q?

(A) 6

(B) 9

(C) 12

(D) 18

(E) 36

GO ON TO THE NEXT PAGE

18. If $\frac{1}{x} - \frac{1}{y} = \frac{1}{z}$, then z is equal to which of the following?

(A) $\frac{y-x}{xy}$

(B) $\frac{x-y}{xy}$

(C) xy

(D) $\frac{xy}{x} - y$

(E) $\frac{xy}{y-x}$

19. In a certain company, the ratio of the number of women employees to the number of men employees is 3 to 2. If the total number of employees is 240, then how many of the employees are men?

(A) 40

(B) 48

(C) 96

(D) 144

(E) 160

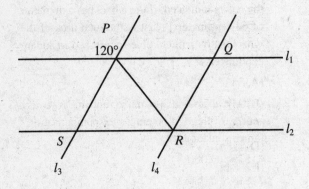

20. In the figure above, $l_1 \parallel l_2$, and $l_3 \parallel l_4$. If $PQ =$ 3 and $QR = 3$, then what is the length of PR?

(A) $6\sqrt{3}$

(B) $3\frac{\sqrt{3}}{2}$

(C) 3

(D) $9\sqrt{5}$

(E) $\frac{\sqrt{3}}{2}$

21. In a certain group of people, $\frac{3}{8}$ of the people are men, and $\frac{2}{3}$ of the men have brown eyes. If $\frac{3}{4}$ of the people have brown eyes, then what fraction of the group are women who do not have brown eyes?

(A) $\frac{1}{8}$

(B) $\frac{3}{16}$

(C) $\frac{1}{4}$

(D) $\frac{5}{16}$

(E) $\frac{3}{8}$

Questions 22–24 are based on the following graphs.

BUDGET INFORMATION FOR COLLEGE M IN YEAR N

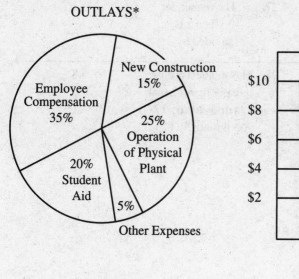

OUTLAYS*

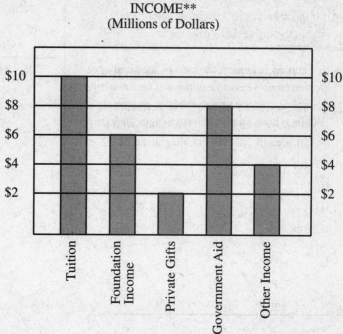

INCOME**
(Millions of Dollars)

* Includes all expenditures

** Includes all sources of income

NOTE: Outlays = Income

22. For the year shown, College M spent how much money on the operation of its physical plant?

(A) $2,500,000

(B) $4,000,000

(C) $7,500,000

(D) $8,000,000

(E) $9,500,000

23. For the year shown, what percentage of College M's income came from foundation income?

(A) 6%

(B) 20%

(C) 25%

(D) 33%

(E) 60%

24. For the year shown, how much more money was spent by College M on employee compensation than on student aid?

(A) $16,500,000

(B) $10,500,000

(C) $6,000,000

(D) $4,500,000

(E) $2,500,000

GO ON TO THE NEXT PAGE

Directions: For each of the following questions two quantities are given, one in Column A and one in Column B. Compare the two quantities and choose

A: if the quantity in Column A is the greater

B: if the quantity in Column B is the greater

C: if the two quantities are equal

D: if the relationship cannot be determined from the information given.

	Column A	Column B
25.	The perimeter of a square with an area of 16	The perimeter of a square with a diagonal of $4\sqrt{2}$
26.	$\dfrac{1}{3} \times \dfrac{2}{3}$	$(.333)(.666)$

When $x + 5$ is divided by 3, the remainder is 2.

	Column A	Column B
27.	The remainder when x is divided by 2	1
28.	The smallest number greater than 12 that is divisible by 12 but not by 8	48

WARNING

IF YOU FINISHED THIS SECTION BEFORE TIME EXPIRED, GO IMMEDIATELY TO THE NEXT SECTION. YOU MAY NOT CONTINUE TO WORK ON THIS SECTION AFTER TIME HAS EXPIRED.

Analytical Section

35 QUESTIONS • TIME—60 MINUTES

Directions: Each of the following questions or groups of questions is based on a short passage or a set of propositions. In answering these questions it may sometimes be helpful to draw a simple picture or chart.

Questions 1–6

A genealogist has determined that M, N, P, Q, R, S, and T are the father, the mother, the aunt, the brother, the sister, the wife, and the daughter of X, but she has been unable to determine which person has which status. She does know:

P and Q are of the same sex.

M and N are not of the same sex.

S was born before M.

Q is not the mother of X.

1. How many of the seven people—M, N, P, Q, R, S, and T—are female?

(A) 3

(B) 4

(C) 5

(D) 6

(E) 7

2. Which of the following must be true?

(A) M is a female.

(B) N is a female.

(C) P is a female.

(D) Q is a male.

(E) S is a male.

3. If T is the daughter of X, which of the following must be true?

(A) M and P are of the same sex.

(B) M and Q are of the same sex.

(C) P is not of the same sex as N.

(D) R is not of the same sex as S.

(E) S is not of the same sex as T.

4. If M and Q are sisters, all of the following must be true EXCEPT

(A) N is a male.

(B) M is X's mother.

(C) Q is X's aunt.

(D) T is X's daughter.

(E) S is not X's brother.

5. If S is N's grandfather, then which of the following must be true?

(A) R is N's aunt.

(B) X is P's son.

(C) M is X's brother.

(D) Q is S's husband.

(E) P is N's aunt.

6. If M is X's wife, all of the following could be true EXCEPT

(A) S is X's daughter.

(B) P is X's sister.

(C) Q is X's sister.

(D) R is X's father.

(E) N is X's brother.

7. AL: If an alien species ever visited Earth, it would surely be because they were looking for other intelligent species with whom they could communicate. Since we have not been contacted by aliens, we may conclude that none have ever visited this planet.

AMY: Or, perhaps, they did not think human beings intelligent.

How is Amy's response related to Al's argument?

(A) She misses Al's point entirely.

(B) She attacks Al personally rather than his reasoning.

(C) She points out that Al made an unwarranted assumption.

(D) She ignores the detailed internal development of Al's logic.

(E) She introduces a false analogy.

GO ON TO THE NEXT PAGE

8. If quarks are the smallest subatomic particles in the universe, then gluons are needed to hold quarks together. Since gluons are needed to hold quarks together, it follows that quarks are the smallest subatomic particles in the universe. The logic of the above argument is most nearly paralleled by which of the following?

(A) If this library has a good French literature collection, it will contain a copy of Les Conquerants by Malraux. The collection does contain a copy of Les Conquerants; therefore, the library has a good French literature collection.

(B) If there is a man-in-the-moon, the moon must be made of green cheese for him to eat. There is a man-in-the-moon, so the moon is made of green cheese.

(C) Either helium or hydrogen is the lightest element of the periodic table. Helium is not the lightest element of the periodic table, so hydrogen must be the lightest element of the periodic table.

(D) If Susan is taller than Bob, and if Bob is taller than Elaine, then if Susan is taller than Bob, Susan is also taller than Elaine.

(E) Whenever it rains, the streets get wet. The streets are not wet. Therefore, it has not rained.

9. In the earliest stages of the common law, a party could have his case heard by a judge only upon the payment of a fee to the court, and then only if his case fit within one of the forms for which there existed a writ. At first the number of such formalized cases of action was very small, but judges invented new forms that brought more cases and greater revenues. Which of the following conclusions is most strongly suggested by the paragraph above?

(A) Early judges often decided cases in an arbitrary and haphazard manner.

(B) In most early cases, the plaintiff rather than the defendant prevailed.

(C) The judiciary at first had greater power than either the legislature or the executive.

(D) One of the motivating forces for the early expansion in judicial power was economic considerations.

(E) The first common law decisions were inconsistent with one another and did not form a coherent body of law.

Questions 10–15

A farmer has three fields, 1, 2, and 3, and is deciding which crops to plant. The crops are F, G, H, I, and J.

F will grow only in fields 1 and 3, but in order for F to grow, it must be fertilized with X.

G will grow in fields 1, 2, and 3, but in order for G to grow, fertilizer X must not be used.

H will grow in fields 1, 2, and 3, but in order for H to grow in field 3, it must be fertilized with Y.

I will grow only in fields 2 and 3, but in order for I to grow in field 2, it must be sprayed with pesticide Z, and in order for I to grow in field 3, it must not be sprayed with Z.

J will grow only in field 2, but in order for J to grow, H must not be planted in the same field.

All crops are planted and harvested at the same time. More than one crop may be planted in a field.

10. It is possible to grow which of the following pairs of crops together in field 1?

(A) F and G

(B) F and J

(C) G and H

(D) J and H

(E) J and G

11. It is possible for which of the following groups of crops to grow together in field 2?

    (A) F, G, and H

    (B) F, H, and I

    (C) G, H, and J

    (D) G, I, and J

    (E) H, I, and J

12. Which of the following is a complete and accurate listing of all crops that will grow alone in field 2 if the only pesticide or fertilizer used is Y?

    (A) F

    (B) F and H

    (C) G and H

    (D) G, H, and J

    (E) G, H, I, and J

13. Which of the following pairs of crops will grow together in field 3 if no other crops are planted in the field and no fertilizers or pesticides are applied?

    (A) F and H

    (B) F and I

    (C) G and H

    (D) G and I

    (E) H and J

14. What is the maximum number of different crops that can be planted together in field 3?

    (A) 1

    (B) 2

    (C) 3

    (D) 4

    (E) 5

15. Which of the following is a complete and accurate list of the crops that will grow alone in field 2 if X is the only pesticide or fertilizer applied?

    (A) H, J

    (B) I, G

    (C) I, H

    (D) I, J

    (E) J, G

Questions 16–21

A group of six players, P, Q, R, S, T, and U, are participating in a challenge tournament. All matches played are challenge matches and are governed by the following rules:

A player may challenge another player if and only if that player is ranked either one or two places above her.

If a player successfully challenges the player ranked immediately above her, the two players exchange ranks.

If a player successfully challenges the player two ranks above her, she moves up two ranks, and both the loser of the match and the player ranked below the loser move down one rank.

If a player is unsuccessful in her challenge, she and the player immediately below her exchange ranks, unless the unsuccessful challenger was already ranked last, in which case the rankings remain unchanged.

The initial rankings from the highest (first) to the lowest (sixth) are P, Q, R, S, T, U.

Only one match is played at a time.

16. Which of the following is possible as the first match of the tournament?

    (A) P challenges Q.

    (B) Q challenges R.

    (C) R challenges P.

    (D) S challenges P.

    (E) T challenges Q.

17. If S reaches first place after the first two matches of the tournament, which of the following must be ranked fourth at that point in play?

    (A) P

    (B) Q

    (C) R

    (D) T

    (E) U

GO ON TO THE NEXT PAGE

18. All of the following are possible rankings, from highest to lowest, after exactly two matches EXCEPT

    (A) P, R, Q, T, S, U

    (B) P, R, Q, S, U, T

    (C) R, P, Q, U, S, T

    (D) Q, P, S, R, T, U

    (E) Q, P, S, R, U, T

19. If exactly two matches have been played, what is the maximum number of players whose initial ranks could have been changed?

    (A) 2

    (B) 3

    (C) 4

    (D) 5

    (E) 6

20. If after a certain number of matches the players are ranked from highest to lowest in the order R, Q, P, U, S, T, what is the minimum number of matches that could have been played?

    (A) 2

    (B) 3

    (C) 4

    (D) 5

    (E) 6

21. If after the initial two matches two players have improved their rankings and four players have each dropped in rank, which of the following could be the third match of the tournament?

    (A) R challenges P.

    (B) R challenges Q.

    (C) Q challenges U.

    (D) U challenges P.

    (E) T challenges Q.

22. A recent survey by the economics department of an Ivy League university revealed that increases in the salaries of preachers are accompanied by increases in the nationwide average of rum consumption. From 1965 to 1970 preachers' salaries increased on the average of 15% and rum sales grew by 14.5%. From 1970 to 1975 average preachers' salaries rose by 17% and rum sales by 17.5%. From 1975 to 1980 rum sales expanded by only 8% and average preachers' salaries also grew by only 8%.

Which of the following is the most likely explanation for the findings cited in the paragraph?

    (A) When preachers have more disposable income, they tend to allocate that extra money to alcohol.

    (B) When preachers are paid more, they preach longer; and longer sermons tend to drive people to drink.

    (C) Since there were more preachers in the country, there were also more people; and a larger population will consume greater quantities of liquor.

    (D) The general standard of living increased from 1965 to 1980, which accounts for both the increase in rum consumption and preachers' average salaries.

    (E) A consortium of rum importers carefully limited the increases in imports of rum during the test period cited.

23. Since all four-door automobiles I have repaired have eight-cylinder engines, all four-door automobiles must have eight-cylinder engines.

The author argues on the basis of

    (A) special training

    (B) generalization

    (C) syllogism

    (D) ambiguity

    (E) deduction

24. Two women, one living in Los Angeles, the other living in New York City, carried on a lengthy correspondence by mail. The subject of the exchange was a dispute over certain personality traits of Winston Churchill. After some two dozen letters, the Los Angeles resident received the following note from her New York City correspondent: "It seems you were right all along. Yesterday I met someone who actually knew Sir Winston, and he confirmed your opinion."

    The two women could have been arguing on the basis of all the following EXCEPT

    (A) published biographical information

    (B) old news film footage

    (C) direct personal acquaintance

    (D) assumption

    (E) third party reports

25. The protection of the right of property by the Constitution is tenuous at best. It is true that the Fifth Amendment states that the government may not take private property for public use without compensation, but it is the government that defines private property.

    Which of the following is most likely the point the author is leading up to?

    (A) Individual rights that are protected by the Supreme Court are secure against government encroachment.

    (B) Private property is neither more nor less than that which the government says is private property.

    (C) The government has no authority to deprive an individual of liberty.

    (D) No government that acts arbitrarily can be justified.

    (E) The keystone of American democracy is the Constitution.

Questions 26–32

A musical scale contains seven notes—J, K, L, M, N, O, and Q—ranked from first (lowest) to seventh (highest), though not necessarily in that order.

The first note of the scale is O and the last note of the scale is Q.

L is lower than M.

N is lower than J.

K is somewhere between J and M on the scale.

26. If N is the fifth note on the scale, which of the following must be true?

    (A) J is the sixth note and M is the fourth note.

    (B) K is the fourth note and L is the third note.

    (C) M is the third note and L is the second note.

    (D) M is the fourth note and L is the third note.

    (E) L is the fourth note and J is the second note.

27. If M is the fifth note, then all of the following must be true EXCEPT:

    (A) L is the sixth note.

    (B) K is the fourth note.

    (C) N is the second note.

    (D) M is immediately above J.

    (E) J is immediately below K.

28. If L is higher than K, then all of the following must be true EXCEPT:

    (A) M is higher than K.

    (B) M is higher than N.

    (C) J is higher than K.

    (D) L is higher than J.

    (E) L is higher than N.

29. If there are exactly two notes on the scale between K and N, which of the following must be true?

    (A) K is the fifth note on the scale.

    (B) L is between J and K on the scale.

    (C) M is the sixth note on the scale.

    (D) M is above J on the scale.

    (E) L and M are separated by exactly one note on the scale.

30. Which of the following CANNOT be true?

    (A) J is the fourth note on the scale.

    (B) J is the third note on the scale.

    (C) K is the third note on the scale.

    (D) K is the fourth note on the scale.

    (E) K is the fifth note on the scale.

31. If N and O are separated by exactly two notes, which of the following must be true?

    (A) J is the sixth note on the scale.

    (B) L is the fifth note on the scale.

    (C) K is below M on the scale.

    (D) K is between N and O on the scale.

    (E) M is above N on the scale.

32. If N is one note above L on the scale, the number of logically possible orderings of all seven notes from the bottom of the scale to the top of the scale is

    (A) 1

    (B) 2

    (C) 3

    (D) 4

    (E) 5

33. CLYDE: You shouldn't drink so much white wine. Alcohol really isn't good for you.

    GERRY: You're wrong about that. I have been drinking the same amount of wine for fifteen years, and I never get drunk.

    Which of the following responses would best strengthen and explain Clyde's argument?

    (A) Many people who drink as much white wine as Gerry does get very drunk.

    (B) Alcohol does not always make a person drunk.

    (C) Getting drunk is not the only reason alcohol is not good for a person.

    (D) If you keep drinking white wine, you may find in the future that you are drinking more and more.

    (E) White wine is not the only drink that contains alcohol.

34. When this proposal to reduce welfare benefits is brought up for debate, we are sure to hear claims by the liberal politicians that the bill will be detrimental to poor people. These politicians fail to understand, however, that budget reductions are accompanied by tax cuts—so everyone will have more money to spend, not less.

    Which of the following, if true, would undermine the author's position?

    (A) Poor people tend to vote for liberal politicians who promise to raise welfare benefits.

    (B) Politicians often make campaign promises that they do not fulfill.

    (C) Poor people pay little or not taxes so a tax cut would be of little advantage to them.

    (D) Any tax advantage enjoyed by the poor will not be offset by cuts in services.

    (E) Budget reductions when accompanied by tax cuts often stimulate economic growth.

35. I maintain that the best way to solve our company's present financial crisis is to bring out a new line of goods. I challenge anyone who disagrees with this proposed course of action to show that it will not work.

A flaw in the preceding argument is that it

(A) employs group classifications without regard to individuals

(B) introduces an analogy that is weak

(C) attempts to shift the burden of proof to those who would object to the plan

(D) fails to provide statistical evidence to show that the plan will actually succeed

(E) relies upon a discredited economic theory

WARNING

Practice Examination 1

Answer Key

VERBAL SECTION

1. B	7. B	13. B	19. B	25. D
2. A	8. C	14. C	20. E	26. B
3. A	9. E	15. A	21. D	27. C
4. D	10. D	16. B	22. A	28. B
5. B	11. A	17. E	23. A	29. D
6. A	12. E	18. D	24. E	30. C

MATH SECTION

1. C	7. C	13. A	19. C	25. C
2. B	8. D	14. C	20. C	26. A
3. B	9. D	15. D	21. A	27. D
4. A	10. D	16. E	22. C	28. B
5. B	11. B	17. B	23. B	
6. D	12. C	18. E	24. D	

ANALYTICAL SECTION

1. C	8. A	15. A	22. D	29. A
2. C	9. D	16. C	23. B	30. C
3. D	10. C	17. C	24. C	31. A
4. D	11. D	18. E	25. B	32. B
5. C	12. D	19. E	26. C	33. C
6. A	13. D	20. B	27. D	34. C
7. C	14. C	21. D	28. C	35. C

Practice Examination 1

Explanatory Answers

VERBAL SECTION

1. **(B)** For the first substitution, we need a choice that passes some judgment about the students who do not repay their loans; on that ground we can eliminate (D). The remaining choices seem acceptable on the basis of the first element. For the second element, we need a choice that will show a logical connection between the failure of some students to repay loans and the later availability of loan money for others. Choice (B) is best since it shows that the failure of some students to pay back what they owe will adversely affect the availability of money for other students desiring loans later.

2. **(A)** The "Although . . . ," structure requires a contrast between the thoughts in the first clause and those in the second clause; (A) nicely provides this contrast. The other choices can be eliminated on various grounds. (B) can be eliminated on the basis of the second element, for it makes no sense to say that the critics criticized her as a star in her own right. (C) can be eliminated on the first element since you would not say that initial success was "refuted." And you can eliminate (D) and (E) for similar reasons.

3. **(A)** There are two keys to this question. First, the "Contrary to . . . ," structure sets up a contrast between peace-loving and something else. Additionally, you will want a pair of words that will apply to both the warriors and the gods, bringing them into a parallel relationship. (A) does this by first contrasting peace-loving astronomers with formidable warriors, then establishing a parallel between the formidable warriors and the vengeful gods.

4. **(D)** A good attack strategy is to formulate a sentence expressing the relationship between the stem words. Remember that you can take some liberties here, changing the parts of speech if you wish or reversing the word order. Here you might have used the sentence "One should REFRAIN from doing that which is PROHIBITED." Similarly, "One should comply with that which is compulsory." Notice also that there is a confirming "echo" between first elements of each pair and the second elements of

each pair. Compulsory is the opposite of prohibited and comply is somewhat opposite to refrain.

5. **(B)** The relationship here is one of order of elements. The OVERTURE is the opening portion of an OPERA and the *preface* is the opening portion of a *book*.

6. **(A)** To RESOLVE a DOUBT is to eliminate it, just as to *confirm* a *suspicion* eliminates it by making it a certainty. There is also an "echo" here, since *resolve* and *confirm* are similar, and *doubt* and *suspicion* are similar.

7. **(B)** This is a main idea question. The author's primary concern is to discuss the problem of desertification. So choice (B) is correct. A natural extension of the discussion would be a proposal to slow the process of desertification, but that is not included in the passage as written, so (A) must be incorrect. (C), (D), and (E) are each incorrect because we find no elements in the passage to support those choices. Even admitting that the author intends to define, implicitly, the term "desertification," that is surely not the main point of the passage. The author also dwells at length on the causes of the problem.

8. **(C)** This is an explicit idea question. In the first paragraph, the author mentions (A), (B), (D), and (E) as features of desertification. (C), however, is one of the causes of desertification.

9. **(E)** This is a tone question. We can surely eliminate (B), (C), and (D) as not expressing the appropriate element of worry. Then, in choosing between (A) and (E), we find that (A) overstates the case. The author says we solve the problem now or we solve it later (at a higher cost). But that is an expression of concern, not alarm.

10. **(D)** *Covert* means "undercover" or "concealed," so a good opposite would be *open*.

11. **(A)** The literal meaning of *salient* is "projecting forward" or "jutting out," and it has come to have the related (and more figurative) meaning of standing out from the rest as obvious or important. A good opposite, then, would be *insignificant*.

285

12. **(E)** *Moribund* means "dying," so a good opposite would be a word referring to life or good health, such as *vital*.

13. **(B)** *Pliant* means "bending," as found in the composite word "compliant." A good opposite, therefore, is *rigid*.

14. **(C)** This is a main idea question. The passage begins by posing the question: Why are affirmative action programs so controversial? It then argues that affirmative action is unlike ordinary government programs in the way the burden of the program is allocated. Because of this, the passage concludes, we are torn between supporting the programs (because they have legitimate goals) and condemning the programs (because of the way the cost is allocated). (C) neatly describes this development. The author analyzes the structure of the moral dilemma. (A) is incorrect since the comparison is but a subpart of the overall development and is used in the service of the larger analysis. (B) is incorrect since the author reaches no such clear-cut decision. Rather, we are left with the question posed by the dilemma. (D) is incorrect since the author presupposes that the reader already understands the importance of the issue. Finally, (E) is incorrect since the advantages of the programs are mentioned only in passing.

15. **(A)** This is a logical structure question. In the second paragraph, the author will describe the general structure of government programs in order to set up the contrast with affirmative action. The discussion begins with "Setting aside . . . ," indicating the author recognizes such cases and does not wish to discuss them in detail. Tolls and tuition are exceptions to the general rule, so the author explicitly sets them aside in order to preempt a possible objection to the analysis based on claimed counterexamples. (B) is incorrect since the overall point of the passage is to discuss this dilemma, but the main point of the passage will not answer the question about the logical substructure of the argument. (C) is incorrect since tolls and tuition are not ordinary government programs. (D) is incorrect since the author never raises such doubts. Finally, (E) misses the point of the examples. The point is not that they are costly but that the cost is borne by the specific user.

16. **(B)** This is an application question. In the first paragraph, the author states that affirmative action is designed to achieve social and economic objectives. Although this claim is qualified, the author seems to believe that those arguments are in favor of affirmative action. So (B) is clearly supported by the text. (A) is not supported by the text since the author leaves us with a question; the issue is not resolved. (C) can be eliminated on the same ground. The author neither embraces nor rejects affirmative action. (D) goes beyond the scope of the argument. While the author might wish that this were possible, nothing in the passage indicates such restructuring is possible. Indeed, in paragraph 3, the author remarks that the "funding" problem seems to be inherent. Finally, (E) can be eliminated on the same ground as (A). The author recognizes the unfairness of affirmative action, but also believes that the programs are valuable.

17. **(E)** In paragraph 2, the author mentions that government programs entail both social and economic costs. Then the cost of the specific example, the passed-over worker, is not a government expenditure in the sense that money is laid out to purchase something. So the author is using the term "funding" in a nonstandard way and wishes to call the reader's attention to this usage. (E) parallels this explanation. (A) is incorrect since it is inconsistent with the reasoning just provided. (B) is incorrect, for though the author may believe that individuals bear a disproportionate share of the burden, this is not a response to the question asked. (C) is incorrect for the same reason: It is a true but nonresponsive statement. Finally, (D) fails for the same reason. Though the author notes that affirmative action programs are similar to other government programs in this respect, this is not an explanation for the author's placing "funding" in quotation marks.

18. **(D)** This is a logical structure question. In the final paragraph, the author analyzes another, similar situation. This technique is called arguing from analogy. The strength of the argument depends on our seeing the similarity and accepting the conclusion of the one argument (the villainous man") as applicable to the other argument (affirmative action). (A) is perhaps the second best response, but

the author is not offering an illustration, e.g., an example of affirmative action. To be sure, the author is attempting to prove a point, but attempting to prove a conclusion is not equivalent to illustrating a contention. (B) is incorrect since the author adduces the situation to support his contention. (C) is incorrect because the author cites no authority. Finally, (E) can be eliminated since the author uses the case of the villainous man to support, not to weaken, the case.

19. **(B)** This is an explicit idea question. In paragraph 1, the author mentions that affirmative action is like other government programs in that it is designed to achieve certain social and economic goals. So (A) cites a similarity rather than a difference. (C) can also be eliminated. In paragraph 3, the author states that the relevant difference is not the method of allocating benefits. The salient difference is set forth in the same paragraph, and it is the difference described by (B). (D) and (E) are simply not mentioned anywhere in the selection.

20. **(E)** This relationship might be expressed as "That which is EXEMPLARY is beyond REPROACH." So, too, that which is *unimpeachable* is not subject to *criticism*.

21. **(D)** Here the relationship is one of defining characteristic. The MENDICANT is a BEGGAR and the *prevaricator* is a *liar*.

22. **(A)** This relationship is simply one of degree: A DELUGE is a big RAIN and an *ocean* is a big *pond*.

23. **(A)** The relationship here is that of agent to effect. The effect of a LUBRICANT is to reduce FRICTION, and the effect of a *balm* is to reduce *pain*. Notice also that there is an "echo" here. *Friction* and *pain* are somewhat similar in that *friction* is something that "afflicts" a machine as *pain* afflicts a body. And a *lubricant* is something like a "medicine" or *balm* that solves the problem.

24. **(E)** You can eliminate (B), (C), and (D) on the basis of their second elements. They really make no sense when substituted into the second blank. And you can probably see that (E) is a good answer because it both provides the needed contrast indicated by the introductory word Despite" and supplies a second element that could be used to describe the feeling of the Academy. (A), perhaps, is an arguably correct choice,

yet if you examine (A) closely, you will see that it fails. Although "admired" is syntactically acceptable for the first blank, it really does not make a meaningful statement. It does not explain the perseverance of the scientist.

25. **(D)** All but one of the choices can be eliminated on the basis of the first substitution. Notice that the question refers to the "delightful" characters of Irving. Only "charm" is consistent with such a judgment. Additionally, only "borrowed, of all the possible second elements, provides the logical contrast required by the second part of the sentence: more for this than for that.

26. **(B)** The "Although" that introduces the sentence requires a contrast in the second portion of the sentence; only (B) provides this. The contrast between personality disorder and physical disease must be established.

27. **(C)** *Dormant* means "sleeping" or "inactive," and a fairly clear opposite is *active*.

28. **(B)** *Placate* is related to *placid*, and to *placate* means to *calm down*. So a good opposite would be a word meaning to stir up—as here to stir up anger is to *enrage*.

29. **(D)** *Extraneous* means "coming from outside, foreign or alien to something else." The word is also used to mean "not pertinent," so a good opposite would be *central:* That which is extraneous to an inquiry is surely not central to it.

30. **(C)** *Renown* means "fame," so a good opposite would be a word describing the complete lack of fame, *anonymity*.

MATH SECTION

1. **(C)** The arithmetic operations indicated here are very simple, so the best approach to the comparison is to perform the indicated operations. For Column A, 16 divided by 4 is 4. For Column B, $\frac{4}{11}$ multiplied by 11 is 4. So the two columns are equal.

2. **(B)** Again, performing the indicated operations may be the best attack strategy. In this case, the operation is to solve for the variables in the equations in the centered information. In the first equation, $x = 4$; in the second, $y = 12$. So Column B is greater.

3. **(B)** This type of question appears with some regularity in various guises. The heart of the question is the centered information that 49 is one of the factors of n. Then the key to the comparison is recognizing that since 7 is a factor of 49, 7 must also be a factor of n. Thus, when n is divided by 7 (just as when it is divided by 49), there is no remainder. So Column A is 0 while Column B is 7. So Column B is larger.

4. **(A)** Since the operations indicated here are much too cumbersome to be performed, you should look for a shortcut. The key is to recognize that since the fraction in Column A is positive, the final result of performing the operation indicated would also be a positive number. Since the fraction in Column B is negative, the final result of raising the fraction to an odd power will be negative. Thus, the positive quantity in Column A must be larger.

5. **(B)** This question is really not so much a matter of mathematics as just common sense. Indeed, you can probably solve it easily just by counting on your fingers (or multiplying and adding). First, Column A must be 15 since $5 \times 3 = 15$. As for Column B, since there is 1 floor with 2 apartments and 4 floors with 4 apartments, the total number of apartments in the building is 18. So Column B is larger.

6. **(D)** This question is nothing more than a test of your ability to move decimal points. All of the answer choices are expressed as variations of 1.27. To change 0.00127 to 1.27 times some number, you must move the decimal point three places to the right. In "official" notation, $0.00127 = 1.27 \times 10^{-3}$. $10^{-3} = 0.001$, so $0.00127 = 1.27 \times 0.001$.

7. **(C)** The key to this question is careful reading. If the $240 prize is divided between two people, and if one person receives $180, then the other person receives $60. The difference in the amounts received is $180 - 60 = 120$.

8. **(D)** One way of solving this problem is to treat the equations as simultaneous equations, isolating a variable in one, substituting it into the other, and then solving for that variable. One way of doing this is to isolate y in the second equation. Since $\frac{y}{x} = \frac{1}{3}$, $y = \frac{x}{3}$. Substitute this value of y into the other equation:

$$3x - \left(\frac{x}{3}\right) = 5$$

$$3x - 4\frac{x}{3} = 5$$

$$\frac{9x - 4x}{3} = 5$$

$$5x = 15$$

$$x = 3$$

9. **(D)** Once it is established that the two lines are parallel, it is possible to calculate the value of all the angles in the figure. The 36° angle and angle x are supplementary angles, that is, they total 180°, so angle x must be 144°.

10. **(D)** With a question of this type, a good strategy is to cross-multiply:

$$5(x - 1) = 4(x + 1)$$

Multiply: $5x - 5 = 4x + 4$

Solve for x: $x = 9$

11. **(B)** When you look at the centered information, you should have the strong suspicion that the solution to the entire comparison will be found by factoring the expression on the left side of the centered equation. This is a correct intuition. If we factor $x^2 - 3x - 4$, we get $(x + 1)(x - 4)$. [You can check this by multiplying $(x + 1)(x - 4)$.] Since one of the factors uses addition $(x + 1)$ and the other uses subtraction $(x - 4)$, we can match them up with m and n in the expression to the right of the equals sign in the centered equation: m must be 1 while n must be 4. So Column B is larger.

12. **(C)** The key to the question is the realization that all three triangles share a common altitude. Drop a line from point E, perpendicular to $ABCD$:

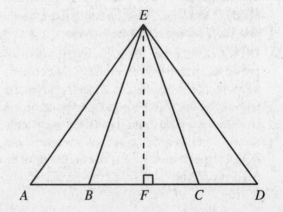

Since the three triangles have a common altitude, whatever difference there might be in their areas must be solely a function of the lengths of their bases. Since AB and CD are half of BC, triangles AEB and CED must have areas equal to half that of BEC. Consequently, the area of triangle BEC is equal to the sum of the areas of triangles AEB and CED.

13. **(A)** Here the key is the proper manipulation of the radicals. Column B is easily manipulated, for you need only to extract the square root, which is $\frac{3}{4}$. In Column A, do not make the mistake of adding the fractions beneath the radicals as you would ordinary fractions. Column A is not equal to Column B; instead, Column A is equal to $3\sqrt{\frac{3}{16}}$. We can extract the square root of $\frac{1}{16}$, which is $\frac{1}{4}$, giving us $\frac{3}{4}\sqrt{3}$ in Column A. Now we can see that Column A is larger, since $\sqrt{3}$ is about 1.7.

14. **(C)** The easiest approach to this question is to do the multiplication indicated in Column A. The fives cancel, so the result is $x + y - 7$ and the two columns are equal.

15. **(D)** This question is a little tricky, but it can be answered using a principle we have used several times earlier: With a variable such as x or y, be alert for possible values such as zero or negative numbers. For example, if $x = 1$ and $y = 1$, then point Q is the origin. But if $x = 0$ and $y = 0$, then point P is the origin (and Q is farther away). Similarly, if $x = \frac{1}{2}$ and $y = \frac{1}{2}$, then Q has coordinates of $\left(-\frac{1}{2}, -\frac{1}{2}\right)$, and P and Q would be at the same distance from the origin.

16. **(E)** The wheel is divided into eight equal sectors, 3 of which are painted blue. So $\frac{3}{8}$ of the wheel's area is blue. What is the area of the wheel? Since it is a circle with a diameter of 64 centimeters, it has a radius of 32 centimeters and an area of $\pi \times 32 \times 32 = 1{,}024\pi$ square centimeters. And $\frac{3}{8}$ of $1{,}024\pi$ is 384π.

17. **(B)** The formula for finding the volume of a right circular cylinder is πr^2 times the height of the cylinder. Here we have cylinders of equal volume so πr^2 times the height of the one must be equal to the other:

$$\pi(3^2) \times 4 = \pi(2^2) \times h$$
$$36\pi = 4\pi \times h$$
$$h = 9$$

18. **(E)** With a question like this, you should perform the indicated operations. First subtract $\frac{1}{y}$ from $\frac{1}{x}$,

using the common denominator of xy. The result is $\frac{y-x}{xy} = \frac{1}{z}$. Now cross-multiply and divide. The result is $z = \frac{xy}{y-x}$.

19. **(C)** Here is a question involving ratio parts. Since the ratio of women to men employed by the company is 3 to 2, there are five $(3 + 2)$ ratio parts; that is, the total number of employees is divisible by 5, of which 3 parts or $\frac{3}{5}$ are women and 2 parts or $\frac{2}{5}$ are men. And $\frac{2}{5}$ of $240 = 96$.

20. **(C)** When you look at this question and see the 120° angle, one of the first things that should come to mind is the possibility that the other angles will be 60° or 30°. If that is correct, then the key to the question will either be an equilateral triangle or the special case of the right triangle, the 30°-60°-90° triangle. As it turns out, the key here is a simple equilateral triangle. The information given is sufficient to establish that all sides are parallel and equal. This means that angles S and Q are 60°. Then the line PR divides angles P and R, which are both 120°, into 60° angles. As a result, PRS turns out to be an equilateral triangle with side 3, so $PR = 3$.

21. **(A)** A table will help us organize the information:

	Brown	Not-Brown	Total
Men			
Women			
Total			

Filling in the information given:

	Brown	Not-Brown	Total
Men	$\frac{1}{4}$		$\frac{3}{8}$
Women			
Total	$\frac{3}{4}$		

Notice that we enter $\frac{1}{4}$ in the square for men with brown eyes. This is because $\frac{2}{3}$ of the $\frac{3}{8}$ of the people who are men have brown eyes. Finally, we complete the table:

	Brown	Not-Brown	Total
Men	$\frac{1}{4}$	$\frac{1}{8}$	$\frac{3}{8}$
Women	$\frac{1}{2}$	$\frac{1}{8}$	$\frac{5}{8}$
Total	$\frac{3}{4}$	$\frac{1}{4}$	1

22. **(C)** To answer this question, you must first determine the total number of dollars in the budget. This can be done by adding together the various sources of income shown in the bar graph: $10 + $6 + $2 + $8 + $4 = $30 (millions of dollars). From the pie chart, we learn that 25%, or $\frac{1}{4}$, of this $30 million was allocated to operation of the physical plant; $\frac{1}{4}$ of $30 million is $7,500,000.

23. **(B)** We already have a start on this question given what we learned in the previous explanation. Income from the foundation accounted for $6 million of the total of $30 million, and $\frac{6}{30} = \frac{1}{5} = 20\%$.

24. **(D)** Given a total budget of $30 million and the distribution shown in the pie chart, the question is answered: 35% of $30 minus 20% of $30 = $4,500,000.

25. **(C)** Whenever you have a question dealing with a square, remember that a number of special relationships exist. First, since a square has four equal sides, you can find the length of each side if you know the perimeter. Also, if you know the length of a side, you know the area. In Column A, a square with an area of 16 has a side of 4 and therefore has a perimeter of 16. In Column B, the diagonal of the square cuts the square into two isosceles right triangles: 45°-45°-90°. In such triangles, the hypotenuse is equal to the length of either of the two shorter sides multiplied by $\sqrt{2}$. Conversely, the shorter sides are each equal to one-half the length of the hypotenuse multiplied by $\sqrt{2}$. So if the diagonal of a square (the hypotenuse of the right triangle) is $4\sqrt{2}$, the side of the triangle (which is also the side of the square) is $\frac{1}{2}\left(4\sqrt{2}\right)\left(\sqrt{2}\right) = 4$. And a side of 4 means a perimeter of 16, so the two squares have the same perimeter.

26. **(A)** You might get away with doing the manipulation indicated here. After all, multiplying .333 by .666 is not too unmanageable; and multiplying $\frac{1}{3}$ by $\frac{2}{3}$ and converting that to a decimal will not take forever. The results will show that Column A is larger. But there is an easier approach: .333 and .666 are approximately, but not exactly, $\frac{1}{3}$ and $\frac{2}{3}$, respectively. But how do they differ from the exact decimal equivalents for $\frac{1}{3}$ and $\frac{2}{3}$? The answer is that the actual decimals obtained by dividing 1 by 3 and 2 by 3 are repeating decimals. In other words, $\frac{1}{3}$ is really .3333… and $\frac{2}{3}$ is really .6666…, which is to say that $\frac{1}{3}$ is really larger than just .333 and $\frac{2}{3}$ is really larger than just .666. So Column A must be larger than Column B.

27. **(D)** Sometimes just substituting numbers is enough to find the pattern needed to answer the question. For example, possible values of x are 6 (6 + 5 ÷ 3 = 3, remainder 2) and 9 (9 + 5 ÷ 3 = 4, remainder of 2). One of these is even and the other odd, which means that when x is divided by 2 you might get a remainder of 0 (in which case Column A is greater) or you might get a remainder of 1 (in which case the columns are equal).

28. **(B)** Here again, trial and error is probably faster than trying to devise an elaborate mathematical proof. What are the first few numbers divisible by 12?: 12, 24, 36, 48, 60, etc. And which is the first one larger than 12 that is not divisible by 8? The answer, as you can see by checking our list, is 36.

ANALYTICAL SECTION

Questions 1–6

Arranging the Information

This set is based upon family relationships. At the outset we note that of the seven people related to X, two are males (father and brother) and five are females (mother, aunt, sister, wife, and daughter). We can summarize the additional information:

   P = Q (same sex)

   M ≠ N (not same sex)

   S > M (born before)

   Q ≠ mother (Q is not X's mother)

There is a further deduction to be drawn. There are only two male relatives. Of the four individuals, P, Q, M, and N there are only two males in the scheme, this means that the three of the same sex are female. So P, Q, and either M or N are females; either M or N is male.

Answering the Questions

1. **(C)** The answer to this question is evident from the analysis above.

2. **(C)** This question is also answerable on the basis of our previous analysis. As for (A) and (B), though we know that of M and N one is male and the other is female, we have no information to justify a

judgment as to who is the female. Nor is there any information to support the conclusions in (D) and (E).

3. **(D)** We have established that P and Q are females, and that either M or N is female. So M or N is male, and of the remaining three relatives, S, R, and T, one is male as well. If T is the daughter of X, this establishes that she is female and, further, that either R or S is the remaining male. (A), (B), and (C) are incorrect since the additional stipulation of this question does not add anything to the analysis of sexual distribution above. (E) is incorrect since it asserts that S is the male, but there is nothing to support that conclusion. (D), however, is necessarily true. Of the pair R and S, one must be male and the other female, so they are not of the same sex.

4. **(D)** In the scheme of relations, there is only one possible pair of sisters: the mother and the aunt. It will not do to argue that X might have married his sister, especially when an ordinary sister relationship is available. In any event, if M and Q represent the mother and the aunt, since Q is not the mother, M must be X's mother, so (B) and (C) are both true. Further, since M must be female, N must be male, and (A) is true. Then, since M is X's mother, and since S was born before M, S could not be X's brother and (E) is true. As for (D), M, Q, and N (a male) are eliminated as daughters, but this still leaves several possibilities.

5. **(C)** There is only one available grandfather-grandchild relationship: S must be X's father and N his daughter. If N is female, then M is male and must be X's brother. So (C) is necessarily true. As for the remaining choices, (A) is possible though not necessary. (B) is also possible since P might be X's mother. (D) is not possible since Q is female. Finally, (E) is possible since P is a female and might be X's sister and so N's aunt.

6. **(A)** Since M was born after S, if M is the mother of X's daughter, S cannot be the daughter. (Again, it will not do to argue about stepdaughters, for that is clearly outside the bounds of the problem.) The remaining choices, however, are possible. As for (B) and (C), no restriction is placed on P and Q. And as for (D), R is not further defined. As for (E), we do know that N is male if M is female, and N could be X's brother.

7. **(C)** Amy points out that Al assumes that any extraterrestrial visitors to Earth, seeking intelligent life, would regard human beings here on Earth as intelligent, and therefore contact us. Amy hints that we might not be intelligent enough to interest them in contacting us. This is why (C) is the best answer. (A) is wrong. Amy does not miss Al's point: She understands it very well and criticizes it. (B) is wrong since Amy is not suggesting that Al is any less intelligent than any other human being, just that the aliens might regard us all as below the level of intelligence they are seeking. (D) is more nearly correct than any other choice save (C). The difficulties with it are threefold: One, there really is not all that much internal development of Al's argument, so (D) does not seem on target; two, in a way Amy does examine what internal structure there is—she notes there is a suppressed assumption that is unsound; finally, even assuming that what (D) says is correct, it really does not describe the point of Amy's remark nearly so well as (C) does. Finally, (E) is incorrect because Amy does not offer an analogy of any sort.

8. **(A)** Let us assign letters to represent the complete clauses of the sentence from which the argument is built. "If quarks ... universe" will be represented by the letter P, the rest of the sentence by Q. The structure of the argument is therefore: "If P then Q. Q. Therefore, P." The argument is obviously not logically valid. If it were, it would work for any substitutions of clauses for the letters, but we can easily think up a case in which the argument will not work: "If this truck is a fire engine, it will be painted red. This truck is painted red; therefore, it is a fire engine." Obviously, many trucks that are not fire engines could also be painted red. The argument's invalidity is not the critical point. Your task was to find the answer choice that paralleled it—and since the argument first presented was incorrect, you should have looked for the argument in the answer choices that makes the same mistake: (A). It has the form: "If P then Q. Q. Therefore, P." (B) has the form: "If P, then Q. P. Therefore, Q," which is both different from our original form and valid to boot. (C) has the form: "P or Q. Not P. Therefore, Q." (D) has the form: "If P, then Q. If Q, then R. Therefore, If P, then R." Finally, (E) has the form: "If P then Q. Not Q. Therefore, not P."

9. **(D)** The author explains that the expansion of judicial power by increasing the number of causes of action had the effect of filling the judicial coffers. A natural conclusion to be drawn from this information is that the desire for economic gain fueled the expansion. (A) is not supported by the text since the judges may have made good decisions—even though they were paid to make them. (E) is incorrect for the same reason. (C) is not supported by the text since no mention is made of the other two bodies (even assuming they existed at the time the author is describing). (B) is also incorrect because there is nothing in the text to support such a conclusion.

Questions 10–15

Arranging the Information

The primary task here is to organize the information. And for that we will use a matrix:

	F	G	H	I	J
1	YES (X)	YES (~X)	YES	NO	NO
2	NO	YES (~X)	YES	YES (Z)	YES (~H)
3	YES (X)	YES (~X)	YES (Y)	YES (~Z)	NO

Once the information has been organized, the questions are readily answerable.

Answering the Questions

10. **(C)** With regard to (A), F and G cannot grow together (because of "X"). (B), (D), and (E) are not possible because J does not grown in Field 1 at all.

11. **(D)** Since F does not grow at all in field 2, (A) and (B) can be eliminated. Then, since J will not grow with H, both (C) and (E) can be eliminated. Combination G, I, and J, however, is consistent with all conditions.

12. **(D)** Notice that this question asks for a list of all crops that could grow alone in field 2. F cannot, since F simply does not grow in field 2. G grows in field 2 so long as X is not applied to the field, so G is part of the correct answer. I will not grow since it requires Z. Finally, J will grow since the question stipulates the crops will grow alone. So the correct answer consists of G, H, and J.

13. **(D)** Neither F nor H will grow in field 3 unless certain fertilizers or pesticides are added, so we can eliminate choices (A), (B), and (C). (E) can be eliminated on the further ground that J simply does not grow in field 3.

14. **(C)** J does not grow in field 3, so that reduces the number of possible crops to four. But F and G cannot grow together, which further reduces the number to three. So the maximum number of crops that can be planted together is three—F, H, and I or G, H, and I.

15. **(A)** Consulting the chart, we see that F does not grow there at all. G will not grow in the presence of X, and I will grow only in the presence of Z. So only H and J will grow under the stipulated conditions.

Questions 16–21

For this set no diagram is needed since the relationships are inherent in the system of arithmetic; that is, five is one more than six, etc. You may find it useful to make a marginal note or two, e.g., "challenge +1 or +2."

16. **(C)** The setup for this group of questions is fairly long, but once the rules of the game are understood, this question is easy. (A) and (B) are incorrect, for a challenge must issue from a player of lower rank. (D) and (E) are incorrect, for a challenge can be issued only to a player at most two ranks superior.

17. **(C)** Since S begins in fourth position, S can reach first in two plays by issuing and winning two challenges. This can be done in two ways. S can first challenge Q and then P, or S can first challenge R and then P. Either way, R must be in fourth position.

18. **(E)** This arrangement could come about only after a minimum of *three* matches: P versus Q, S versus R, and U versus T, with the challenger prevailing in each case. The other rankings are possible after only two matches:

    (A) R versus Q and T versus S

    (B) R versus Q and U versus T

    (C) R versus P and U versus S

    (D) Q versus P and S versus R

19. **(E)** If U challenges and defeats S, the bottom half of the ranking changes from STU to UST; and if R challenges and defeats P, the top half of the ranking changes from PQR to RPQ. So in just two matches, all 6 players could be displaced from their initial rank.

20. **(B)** For P to be moved down to third place, at least two matches must have been played (Q challenging and defeating P and then R challenging and defeating Q, or R challenging and defeating P with Q in turn challenging and defeating P). The UST ordering of the bottom half of the ranking could be obtained in one match, with U challenging and defeating S.

21. **(D)** For one player to improve and two to drop in a single match, a player must have challenged and defeated a player two ranks superior. For such challenges to have the stipulated results, it must have been player 3 challenging and defeating player 1, and player 6 challenging and defeating player 4. So the rankings at the end of two matches will be RPQUST. The third match could pit U against P.

22. **(D)** You must always be careful of naked correlations. Sufficient research would probably turn up some sort of correlation between the length of skirts and the number of potatoes produced by Idaho, but such a correlation is obviously worthless. Here, too, the two numbers are completely unrelated to one another at any concrete cause-and-effect level. What joins them is the very general movement of the economy. The standard of living increases; so, too, does the average salary of a preacher, the number of vacations taken by factory workers, the consumption of beef, the number of color televisions, and the consumption of rum. (D) correctly points out that these two are probably connected only this way. (A) is incorrect for it is inconceivable that preachers, a small portion of the population, could account for so large an increase in rum consumption. (B) is wildly implausible. (C), however, is more likely. It strives for that level of generality of correlation achieved by (D). The difficulty with (C) is that it focuses upon total preachers, not the *average* preacher; and the passage correlates not *total* income for preachers with rum consumption, but *average* income for preachers with consumption of rum. (E) might be arguable if only one period had been used, but the paragraph cites three different times during which this correlation took place.

23. **(B)** This is a relatively easy question. The argument is similar to "All observed instances of S are P; therefore, all S must be P." (All swans I have seen are white; therefore, all swans must be white.)

There is little to suggest the author is a mechanic or a factory worker in an automobile plant; therefore, (A) is incorrect—and would be so even if the author were an expert because he does not argue using that expertise. A syllogism is a formal logical structure such as "All S are M; all M are P; therefore, all S are P," and the argument about automobiles does not fit this structure—so (C) is wrong. By the same token, (E) is wrong since the author generalizes—he does not deduce, as by logic, anything. Finally, (D) is incorrect because the argument is not ambiguous, and one could hardly argue on the basis of ambiguity anyway.

24. **(C)** The key phrase here—and the problem is really just a question of careful reading—is who actually knew." This reveals that neither of the two knew the person whom they were discussing. There are many ways, however, of debating about the character with whom one is not directly acquainted. We often argue about the character of Napoleon or even fictional characters such as David Copperfield. When we do, we are arguing on the basis of indirect information. Perhaps we have read a biography of Napoleon, (A), or maybe we have seen a news film of Churchill, (B). We may have heard from a friend, or a friend of a friend, that so and so does such and such, (E). Finally, sometimes we just make more or less educated guesses, (D). At any event, the two people described in the paragraph could have done all of these things. What they could not have done—since they finally resolved the problem by finding someone who actually knew Churchill—was to have argued on the basis of their own personal knowledge.

25. **(B)** Here we have a question that asks us to draw a conclusion from a set of premises. The author points out that the Constitution provides that the government may not take private property. The irony, according to the author, is that government itself defines what it will classify as private property. We might draw an analogy to a sharing practice among children: You divide the cake and I will choose which piece I want. The idea behind this wisdom is that this ensures fairness to both parties. The author would say that the Constitution is set up so that the government not only divides (defines property), it chooses (takes what and when it wants). (A) is contradicted by this analysis. (C) is wide of the mark

since the author is discussing property rather than liberty. While the two notions are closely connected in the Constitution, this connection is beyond the scope of this argument. (D) is also beyond the scope of the argument. It makes a broad and unqualified claim that is not supported by the text. (E) is really vacuous and, to the extent that we try to give it content, it must fail for the same reason as (A).

Questions 26–32

For this ordering set, the order is so highly undetermined that a single overall diagram is not likely to be of much assistance. Instead, for each problem we will simply sketch the scale using dashes and numbers. To conserve space, we will render the scale horizontally:

1	2	3	4	5	6	7

though a more intuitive approach would use a vertical arrangement:

7
6
5
4
3
2
1

We know:

$$L < M$$
$$N < J$$
$$J < K < M, \text{ or } M < K < J$$

We can effectively ignore O and Q since they are placed in positions 1 and 7 and will not change.

26. **(C)** With N as the fifth note, we know that J, in order to be higher than N, must be the sixth note. Then, to keep M higher than L while keeping K between M and J, we must have the order:

1	2	3	4	5	6	7
O	L	M	K	N	J	Q

which demonstrates that (C) is necessarily true, while each other choice is clearly false.

27. **(D)** If M is the fifth note, then N, J, and K must be below M and in that order, with L in sixth:

1	2	3	4	5	6	7
O	N	J	K	M	L	Q

These are not the only possible arrangements with M as note 6, but this does prove that J and N can be third and second, respectively, and fourth and third, respectively.

28. **(C)** Given the additional information and the initial conditions, the order of the notes must be:

1	2	3	4	5	6	7
O	N	J	K	L	M	Q

29. **(A)** For K and N to be separated by two notes, they must occupy positions 2 and 5 or 3 and 6. Ignoring the other restrictions we would have four possibilities:

1	2	3	4	5	6	7
O	N			K		Q
O		N			K	Q
O	K			N		Q
O		K			N	Q

The second and third possibilities are not permissible because K could not be between J and M. The fourth also can be eliminated since N must be lower than M. Only the first is possible, and this proves that K must be the fifth note on the scale. As for (B), though L might be between J and K:

1	2	3	4	5	6	7
O	N	J	L	K	M	Q

it is not necessarily true that L is between J and K:

1	2	3	4	5	6	7
O	N	L	J	K	M	Q

As for (C), we have just seen it is possible for M to be the sixth note, but that is not necessarily the case:

1	2	3	4	5	6	7
O	N	L	M	K	J	Q

As for (D), our diagrams show this is possibly, though not necessarily, the case. Similarly, (E) is incorrect since the diagrams show that L and M may or may not be separated by exactly one note.

30. **(C)** Since K must be between J and M, either J or M must be lower on the scale than K. Additionally, some other note must be lower than whichever note is lower than K; that is, if J is lower than K, then N is lower than K as well, and if M is lower than K, then L is lower than K as well. This means that K can be no lower than the fourth note. The other choices are possibilities:

(A) and (E)
(B) and (D)

1	2	3	4	5	6	7
1	2	3	4	5	6	7
O	N	L	J	K	M	Q
O	N	J	K	L	M	Q

31. **(A)** If N is separated by two notes from O, then N must be note 4; and we know J must be above N. Since K can be no lower than fourth, this means K must be note 5, and J note 6, leaving L and M as 2 and 3, respectively.

1	2	3	4	5	6	7
O	L	M	N	K	J	Q

The diagram confirms that (A) is necessarily true, while each of the other choices is necessarily false.

32. **(B)** If L and N are together, they must be notes 2 and 3, respectively, for both J and M must be higher than L and N, and K must be between J and M on the scale. This means that J, K, and M are notes 4, 5, and 6, though not necessarily in that order. So we have two possibilities:

	1	2	3	4	5	6	7
	O	L	N	J	K	M	Q
or:	O	L	N	M	K	J	Q

33. **(C)** The weakness in Gerry's argument is that he assumes, incorrectly, that getting drunk is the only harm Clyde has in mind. Clyde could respond very effectively by pointing to some other harms of alcohol. (A) would not be a good response for Clyde since he is concerned with Gerry's welfare. The fact that other people get drunk when Gerry does not is hardly a reason for Gerry to stop drinking. (B) is also incorrect. That other people do or do not get drunk is not going to strengthen Clyde's argument against Gerry. He needs an argu-ment that will impress Clyde, who apparently does not get drunk. (D) is perhaps the second-best answer, but the explicit wording of the paragraph makes it unacceptable. Gerry has been drinking the same quantity for fifteen years. Now, admittedly it is possible he will begin to drink more heavily, but that possibility would not be nearly so strong a point in Clyde's favor as the *present* existence of harm (other than inebriation). Finally, (E) is irrelevant, since it is white wine that Gerry drinks.

34. **(C)** The speaker is arguing that the budget cuts will not ultimately be detrimental to the poor. (C) attacks this conclusion directly by pointing out that they will receive little or no advantage. (A) and (B) are wrong because they are irrelevant: how or why politicians are elected is not a concern of the speaker. And (D) and (E) both seem to strengthen the speaker's position by suggesting ways in which the poor would benefit.

35. **(C)** The problem with this argument is that it contains no argument at all. Nothing is more frustrating than trying to discuss an issue with someone who will not even make an attempt to prove his case, whose only constructive argument is: "Well, that is my position. If I am wrong, you prove I am wrong." This is an illegitimate attempt to shift the burden of proof. The person who advances the argument naturally has the burden of giving some argument for it. (C) points out this problem. (A) is incorrect because the author uses no group classifications. (B) is incorrect because the author does not introduce any analogy. (D) is a weak version of (C). It is true no statistical evidence is provided to prove the author's claim, but neither is any kind of argument at all provided to prove the claim. So if (D) is a legitimate objection to the paragraph (and it is), then (C) must be an even stronger objection. So any argument for answer (D)'s being the correct choice ultimately supports (C) even more strongly. The statement contained in (E) may or may not be correct, but the information in the passage is not sufficient to allow us to isolate the theory upon which the speaker is operating. Therefore, we cannot conclude that it is or is not discredited.

Answer Sheet

TEAR HERE

MATH SECTION

1. Ⓐ Ⓑ Ⓒ Ⓓ Ⓔ   7. Ⓐ Ⓑ Ⓒ Ⓓ Ⓔ   13. Ⓐ Ⓑ Ⓒ Ⓓ Ⓔ   19. Ⓐ Ⓑ Ⓒ Ⓓ Ⓔ   25. Ⓐ Ⓑ Ⓒ Ⓓ Ⓔ
2. Ⓐ Ⓑ Ⓒ Ⓓ Ⓔ   8. Ⓐ Ⓑ Ⓒ Ⓓ Ⓔ   14. Ⓐ Ⓑ Ⓒ Ⓓ Ⓔ   20. Ⓐ Ⓑ Ⓒ Ⓓ Ⓔ   26. Ⓐ Ⓑ Ⓒ Ⓓ Ⓔ
3. Ⓐ Ⓑ Ⓒ Ⓓ Ⓔ   9. Ⓐ Ⓑ Ⓒ Ⓓ Ⓔ   15. Ⓐ Ⓑ Ⓒ Ⓓ Ⓔ   21. Ⓐ Ⓑ Ⓒ Ⓓ Ⓔ   27. Ⓐ Ⓑ Ⓒ Ⓓ Ⓔ
4. Ⓐ Ⓑ Ⓒ Ⓓ Ⓔ   10. Ⓐ Ⓑ Ⓒ Ⓓ Ⓔ   16. Ⓐ Ⓑ Ⓒ Ⓓ Ⓔ   22. Ⓐ Ⓑ Ⓒ Ⓓ Ⓔ   28. Ⓐ Ⓑ Ⓒ Ⓓ Ⓔ
5. Ⓐ Ⓑ Ⓒ Ⓓ Ⓔ   11. Ⓐ Ⓑ Ⓒ Ⓓ Ⓔ   17. Ⓐ Ⓑ Ⓒ Ⓓ Ⓔ   23. Ⓐ Ⓑ Ⓒ Ⓓ Ⓔ
6. Ⓐ Ⓑ Ⓒ Ⓓ Ⓔ   12. Ⓐ Ⓑ Ⓒ Ⓓ Ⓔ   18. Ⓐ Ⓑ Ⓒ Ⓓ Ⓔ   24. Ⓐ Ⓑ Ⓒ Ⓓ Ⓔ

ANALYTICAL SECTION

1. Ⓐ Ⓑ Ⓒ Ⓓ Ⓔ   8. Ⓐ Ⓑ Ⓒ Ⓓ Ⓔ   15. Ⓐ Ⓑ Ⓒ Ⓓ Ⓔ   22. Ⓐ Ⓑ Ⓒ Ⓓ Ⓔ   29. Ⓐ Ⓑ Ⓒ Ⓓ Ⓔ
2. Ⓐ Ⓑ Ⓒ Ⓓ Ⓔ   9. Ⓐ Ⓑ Ⓒ Ⓓ Ⓔ   16. Ⓐ Ⓑ Ⓒ Ⓓ Ⓔ   23. Ⓐ Ⓑ Ⓒ Ⓓ Ⓔ   30. Ⓐ Ⓑ Ⓒ Ⓓ Ⓔ
3. Ⓐ Ⓑ Ⓒ Ⓓ Ⓔ   10. Ⓐ Ⓑ Ⓒ Ⓓ Ⓔ   17. Ⓐ Ⓑ Ⓒ Ⓓ Ⓔ   24. Ⓐ Ⓑ Ⓒ Ⓓ Ⓔ   31. Ⓐ Ⓑ Ⓒ Ⓓ Ⓔ
4. Ⓐ Ⓑ Ⓒ Ⓓ Ⓔ   11. Ⓐ Ⓑ Ⓒ Ⓓ Ⓔ   18. Ⓐ Ⓑ Ⓒ Ⓓ Ⓔ   25. Ⓐ Ⓑ Ⓒ Ⓓ Ⓔ   32. Ⓐ Ⓑ Ⓒ Ⓓ Ⓔ
5. Ⓐ Ⓑ Ⓒ Ⓓ Ⓔ   12. Ⓐ Ⓑ Ⓒ Ⓓ Ⓔ   19. Ⓐ Ⓑ Ⓒ Ⓓ Ⓔ   26. Ⓐ Ⓑ Ⓒ Ⓓ Ⓔ   33. Ⓐ Ⓑ Ⓒ Ⓓ Ⓔ
6. Ⓐ Ⓑ Ⓒ Ⓓ Ⓔ   13. Ⓐ Ⓑ Ⓒ Ⓓ Ⓔ   20. Ⓐ Ⓑ Ⓒ Ⓓ Ⓔ   27. Ⓐ Ⓑ Ⓒ Ⓓ Ⓔ   34. Ⓐ Ⓑ Ⓒ Ⓓ Ⓔ
7. Ⓐ Ⓑ Ⓒ Ⓓ Ⓔ   14. Ⓐ Ⓑ Ⓒ Ⓓ Ⓔ   21. Ⓐ Ⓑ Ⓒ Ⓓ Ⓔ   28. Ⓐ Ⓑ Ⓒ Ⓓ Ⓔ   35. Ⓐ Ⓑ Ⓒ Ⓓ Ⓔ

VERBAL SECTION

1. Ⓐ Ⓑ Ⓒ Ⓓ Ⓔ   7. Ⓐ Ⓑ Ⓒ Ⓓ Ⓔ   13. Ⓐ Ⓑ Ⓒ Ⓓ Ⓔ   19. Ⓐ Ⓑ Ⓒ Ⓓ Ⓔ   25. Ⓐ Ⓑ Ⓒ Ⓓ Ⓔ
2. Ⓐ Ⓑ Ⓒ Ⓓ Ⓔ   8. Ⓐ Ⓑ Ⓒ Ⓓ Ⓔ   14. Ⓐ Ⓑ Ⓒ Ⓓ Ⓔ   20. Ⓐ Ⓑ Ⓒ Ⓓ Ⓔ   26. Ⓐ Ⓑ Ⓒ Ⓓ Ⓔ
3. Ⓐ Ⓑ Ⓒ Ⓓ Ⓔ   9. Ⓐ Ⓑ Ⓒ Ⓓ Ⓔ   15. Ⓐ Ⓑ Ⓒ Ⓓ Ⓔ   21. Ⓐ Ⓑ Ⓒ Ⓓ Ⓔ   27. Ⓐ Ⓑ Ⓒ Ⓓ Ⓔ
4. Ⓐ Ⓑ Ⓒ Ⓓ Ⓔ   10. Ⓐ Ⓑ Ⓒ Ⓓ Ⓔ   16. Ⓐ Ⓑ Ⓒ Ⓓ Ⓔ   22. Ⓐ Ⓑ Ⓒ Ⓓ Ⓔ   28. Ⓐ Ⓑ Ⓒ Ⓓ Ⓔ
5. Ⓐ Ⓑ Ⓒ Ⓓ Ⓔ   11. Ⓐ Ⓑ Ⓒ Ⓓ Ⓔ   17. Ⓐ Ⓑ Ⓒ Ⓓ Ⓔ   23. Ⓐ Ⓑ Ⓒ Ⓓ Ⓔ   29. Ⓐ Ⓑ Ⓒ Ⓓ Ⓔ
6. Ⓐ Ⓑ Ⓒ Ⓓ Ⓔ   12. Ⓐ Ⓑ Ⓒ Ⓓ Ⓔ   18. Ⓐ Ⓑ Ⓒ Ⓓ Ⓔ   24. Ⓐ Ⓑ Ⓒ Ⓓ Ⓔ   30. Ⓐ Ⓑ Ⓒ Ⓓ Ⓔ

Practice Examination 2

Math Section

28 QUESTIONS • TIME—45 MINUTES

Directions: For each of these questions, select the best of the answer choices given.

Numbers: All numbers used are real numbers.

Figures: Assume that the position of points, angles, regions, and so forth are in the order shown. Figures are assumed to lie in a plane unless otherwise indicated. Figures accompanying questions are intended to provide information you can use in answering the questions. However, unless a note states that a figure is drawn to scale, you should solve the problems by using your knowledge of mathematics and not by estimating sizes by sight or measurement.

Lines: Assume that lines shown as straight are indeed straight.

Directions: For each of the following questions two quantities are given, one in Column A and one in Column B. Compare the two quantities and choose

  A: if the quantity in Column A is the greater
  B: if the quantity in Column B is the greater
  C: if the two quantities are equal
  D: if the relationship cannot be determined from the information given.

Common Information: In any question, information applying to both columns is centered between the columns and above the quantities in columns A and B. Any symbol that appears in both columns represents the same idea or quantity in both columns.

	Column A	**Column B**
1.	5% of 36	36% of 5
2.	$\sqrt{15}$	$\sqrt{5}+\sqrt{10}$

$$(346\times23)+p=34{,}731$$
$$(346\times23)+q=35{,}124$$

3.	p	q

$$x° < y°$$
PQRS is a rectangle

4.	PT	TQ

$$x>0$$

5.	x^2	$2x$

GO ON TO THE NEXT PAGE

Directions: For each of these questions, select the best of the answer choices given.

6. From the time 6:15 p.m. to the time 7:45 p.m. of the same day, the minute hand of a standard clock describes an arc of

    (A) 30°

    (B) 90°

    (C) 180°

    (D) 540°

    (E) 910°

7. Which of the following fractions is the LEAST?

    (A) $\dfrac{8}{9}$

    (B) $\dfrac{7}{8}$

    (C) $\dfrac{7}{12}$

    (D) $\dfrac{1}{2}$

    (E) $\dfrac{6}{17}$

8. The length of each side of a square is $\dfrac{3x}{4} + 1$.

    What is the perimeter of the square?

    (A) $x + 1$

    (B) $3x + 1$

    (C) $3x + 4$

    (D) $\dfrac{9x^2}{16} + \dfrac{3x}{2} + 1$

    (E) It cannot be determined from the information given.

9. A truck departed from Newton at 11:53 a.m. and arrived in Far City, 240 miles away, at 4:41 p.m. on the same day. What was the approximate average speed of the truck on this trip?

    (A) $\dfrac{16}{1,200}$ MPH

    (B) $\dfrac{240}{288}$ MPH

    (C) $\dfrac{1,494}{240}$ MPH

    (D) 50 MPH

    (E) $\dfrac{5,640}{5}$ MPH

10. If m, n, o and p are real numbers, each of the following expressions equals $m(nop)$ EXCEPT

    (A) $(op)(mn)$

    (B) $ponm$

    (C) $p(onm)$

    (D) $(mp)(no)$

    (E) $(mn)(mo)(mp)$

Directions: For each of the following questions two quantities are given, one in Column A and one in Column B. Compare the two quantities and choose

    A: if the quantity in Column A is the greater;

    B: if the quantity in Column B is the greater;

    C: if the two quantities are equal;

    D: if the relationship cannot be determined from the information given.

Column A	Column B
11. $\dfrac{4}{5} - \dfrac{3}{4}$	$\dfrac{1}{20}$
12. the ratio 3:13	the ratio 13:51

Let Sn be defined by the equation:

$$Sn = 3n + 2$$

| 13. $S_5 + S_4$ | $S_9 + S_8$ |

Directions: For each of these questions, select the best of the answer choices given.

14. Which of the following fractions expressed in the form $\dfrac{P}{q}$ is most nearly approximated by the decimal $.PQ$, where P is the tenths' digit and Q is the hundredths' digit?

(A) $\dfrac{1}{8}$

(B) $\dfrac{2}{9}$

(C) $\dfrac{3}{4}$

(D) $\dfrac{4}{5}$

(E) $\dfrac{8}{9}$

15. If b books can be purchased for d dollars, how many books can be purchased for m dollars?

(A) $\dfrac{bm}{d}$

(B) bdm

(C) $\dfrac{d}{bm}$

(D) $\dfrac{b+m}{d}$

(E) $\dfrac{b-m}{d}$

Directions: For each of the following questions two quantities are given, one in Column A and one in Column B. Compare the two quantities and choose

A: if the quantity in Column A is the greater;

B: if the quantity in Column B is the greater;

C: if the two quantities are equal;

D: if the relationship cannot be determined from the information given.

Column A	Column B
16. The cost of ten pounds of meat at $2.50 per pound.	The cost of five kilograms of meat at $5.00 per kilogram.
17. $\dfrac{10}{10,000}$	$\dfrac{1,000}{1,000,000}$

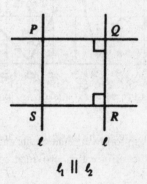

$\ell_1 \parallel \ell_2$

18. Segment $\overline{PQ}$	Segment $\overline{QR}$
19. The number of pears in a cubical box with a side of 24 inches.	The number of potatoes in a cubical box with a side of 36 inches.

$$4x^2 + 3x + 2x^2 + 2x = 3x^2 + 2x + 3x^2 + 2x + 3$$

20. x^2	9

GO ON TO THE NEXT PAGE

Directions: For each of these questions, select the best of the answer choices given.

Questions 21-25 are based on the following graphs:

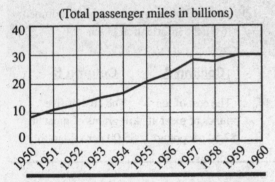

(Total passenger miles in billions)

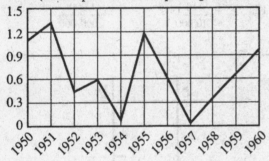

(Deaths per 100 million passenger-miles)

21. All of the following statements can be inferred from the information provided in the graphs EXCEPT:

   (A) The highest rate of passenger deaths per mile traveled during the period covered by the graphs occurred in 1951.

   (B) The largest yearly increase in deaths per mile traveled occurred in the period 1954 to 1955.

   (C) The rate of passenger deaths per mile traveled was approximately the same in both 1954 and 1957.

   (D) Total passenger miles traveled approximately tripled between 1951 and 1959.

   (E) The percentage increase in deaths per 100 million passenger-miles was constant for 1958, 1959, and 1960.

22. In which year did the longest uninterrupted period of increase in the rate of passenger deaths per mile traveled finally end?

   (A) 1951
   (B) 1953
   (C) 1955
   (D) 1957
   (E) 1960

23. How many fatalities were reported in the year 1955?

   (A) 20 billion
   (B) 1.2 million
   (C) 240,000
   (D) 2,000
   (E) 240

24. The greatest number of fatalities were recorded in which year?

   (A) 1960
   (B) 1957
   (C) 1955
   (D) 1953
   (E) 1951

25. In which year did the greatest number of passengers travel by air?

   (A) 1960
   (B) 1955
   (C) 1953
   (D) 1951
   (E) Cannot be determined from the information given.

ABCD is a square.

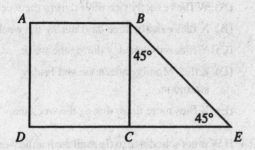

26. If the area of the triangle *BCE* is 8, what is the area of the square *ABCD*?

(A) 4

(B) 8

(C) 16

(D) 22

(E) 82

27. The diagonal of the floor of a rectangular closet is $7\frac{1}{2}$ feet. The shorter side of the closet is $4\frac{1}{2}$ feet. What is the area of the closet in square feet?

(A) 37

(B) 27

(C) $\frac{54}{4}$

(D) $\frac{21}{4}$

(E) 5

28. If the ratio of women to men in a meeting is 4 to 1, what percent of the persons in the meeting are men?

(A) 20%

(B) 25%

(C) $33\frac{1}{3}$%

(D) 80%

(E) 100%

WARNING

IF YOU FINISHED THIS SECTION BEFORE TIME EXPIRED, GO IMMEDIATELY TO THE NEXT SECTION. YOU MAY NOT CONTINUE TO WORK ON THIS SECTION AFTER TIME HAS EXPIRED.

Analytical Section

35 QUESTIONS · TIME—60 MINUTES

> **Directions:** Each of the following questions or groups of questions is based on a short passage or a set of propositions. In answering these questions it may sometimes be helpful to draw a simple picture or chart.

Questions 1-4

The supervisor of a commuter airline is scheduling pilots to fly the round-trip from City X to City Y. The trip takes only two hours, and the airline has one round-trip flight in the morning and one round-trip flight in the afternoon, each day, Monday through Friday. Pilots must be scheduled in accordance with the following rules:

Only W, X, and Y can fly the morning flight.

Only V, X, and Z can fly the afternoon flight.

No pilot may fly twice on the same day.

No pilot may fly on two consecutive days.

X must fly the Wednesday morning flight.

Z must fly the Tuesday afternoon flight.

1. Which of the following must be true?
   (A) W flies the Monday morning flight.
   (B) X flies the Monday afternoon flight.
   (C) Y flies the Tuesday morning flight.
   (D) W flies the Thursday morning flight.
   (E) Z flies the Thursday afternoon flight.

2. If X flies on Friday morning, which of the following must be true?
   (A) X does not fly on Monday afternoon.
   (B) V flies on Friday afternoon.
   (C) W flies Thursday morning.
   (D) Y flies Thursday morning.
   (E) Neither W nor Y flies Thursday morning.

3. If X flies only one morning flight during the week, which of the following must be true?
   (A) W flies exactly two days during the week.
   (B) X flies exactly three days during the week.
   (C) Y flies only one day during the week.
   (D) Z flies Monday afternoon and Friday afternoon.
   (E) X flies more times during the week than V.

4. If W is not scheduled to fly at all during the week, all of the following must be true EXCEPT
   (A) X flies on Monday morning.
   (B) V flies on Monday afternoon.
   (C) Y flies on Thursday morning.
   (D) Z flies on Friday afternoon.
   (E) X flies on Friday morning.

Questions 5-7

SPEAKER 1: Those who oppose abortion upon demand make the foundation of their arguments the sanctity of human life, but this seeming bedrock assumption is actually as weak as shifting sand. And it is not necessary to invoke the red herring that many anti-abortion speakers would allow that human life must sometimes be sacrificed for a greater good, as in the fighting of a just war. There are counter-examples to the principle of the sanctity of life which are even more embarrassing to pro-life advocates. It would be possible to reduce the annual number of traffic fatalities to virtually zero by passing federal legislation mandating a nationwide fifteen-mile-per-hour speed limit on all roads. You see, implicitly we have always been willing to trade off quantity of human life for quality.

SPEAKER 2: The analogy my opponent draws between abortion and traffic fatalities is weak. No one would propose such a speed limit. Imagine people trying to get to and from work under such a law, or imagine them trying to visit a friend or relatives outside their own neighborhoods, or taking in a sports event or a movie. Obviously such a law would be a disaster.

5. Which of the following best characterizes Speaker 2's response to the argument presented by Speaker 1?

(A) Speaker 2's analysis of the traffic fatalities case actually supports the argument of Speaker 1.

(B) Speaker 2's analysis of the traffic fatalities case is an effective rebuttal of the argument of Speaker 1.

(C) Speaker 2's response provides a strong affirmative statement of the anti-abortionist position.

(D) Speaker 2's response is totally irrelevant to the issue raised by Speaker 1.

(E) Speaker 2's counter-argument attacks the character of Speaker 1 instead of the merits of the argument.

6. Which of the following represents the most logical continuation of the reasoning contained in Speaker 1's argument?

(A) Therefore, we should not have any laws on the books to protect human life.

(B) We can only conclude that Speaker 2 is also in favor of strengthening enforcement of existing traffic regulations as a means of reducing the number of traffic fatalities each year.

(C) So the strongest attack on his position is the contradiction posed by Speaker 2's agreement that we should fight a just war even at the risk of considerable loss of human life.

(D) Even the laws against contraception are good examples of this tendency.

(E) The abortion question just makes explicit that which for long has remained hidden from view.

7. Which of the following assumptions are made in the argument of Speaker 1?

(A) The protection of human life is not a justifiable goal of society.

(B) A human fetus should not be considered a "life" for purposes of government protections.

(C) Speed limits and other minor restrictions are an impermissible intrusion by government on human freedom.

(D) An appropriate societal decision is made in the balancing of individual lives and the quality of life.

(E) Government may legitimately protect the interests of individuals but have no authority to act on behalf of families or groups.

Questions 8-12

A restaurant offers three daily specials each day of the week. The daily specials are selected from a list of dishes: P, Q, R, S, T, and U. The daily specials for the menu are selected in accordance with the following restrictions:

On any day that S is on the menu, Q must also be on the menu.

If R is on the menu one day, it cannot be included on the menu the following day.

U can be on the menu only on a day following a day on which T is on the menu.

Only one of the three specials from a given day can be offered the following day.

8. Which of the following could be the list of daily specials offered two days in a row?

(A) S, R, and T; R, P, and Q

(B) Q, S, and R; Q, S, and T

(C) P, Q, and S; S, R, and T

(D) Q, S, and P; T, U, and Q

(E) S, Q, and R; Q, T, and P

GO ON TO THE NEXT PAGE

9. If P and S are on the menu one day, which of the following must be true of the menu the following day?

   (A) U is on the menu.

   (B) S is on the menu.

   (C) T and R are on the menu.

   (D) U and T are on the menu.

   (E) U and R are on the menu.

10. If P, R, and Q are on the menu one day and P, T, and R are on the menu two days later, which daily specials must have appeared on the menu for the intervening day?

    (A) P, R, and T

    (B) P, S, and T

    (C) Q, S, and T

    (D) Q, S, and U

    (E) S, T, and U

11. If on a certain day neither Q nor T is on the menu, how many different combinations of daily specials are possible for that day?

    (A) 1

    (B) 2

    (C) 3

    (D) 4

    (E) 5

12. If Q, R, and S are on the menu one day, which specials must be offered the following day?

    (A) P, Q, and T

    (B) P, R, and T

    (C) P, R, and U

    (D) R, S, and Q

    (E) T, S, and U

Questions 13-17

The personnel director of a company is scheduling interviews for eight people—J, K, L, M, N, O, P, and Q. Each person will have one interview, and all interviews are to be held on Monday through Friday of the same week.

At least one person will be interviewed each day.

More than one interview will be scheduled on exactly two of the days.

O is the only person who will be interviewed on Wednesday.

M and N must be scheduled for interviews exactly three days after Q.

P must be interviewed later in the week than K.

13. Which of the following CANNOT be true?

    (A) O's interview is later in the week than K's interview.

    (B) L's interview is later in the week than J's interview.

    (C) K's interview is later in the week than N's interview.

    (D) L's interview is on the same day as N's interview.

    (E) J's interview is on the same day as K's interview.

14. Which of the following must be true?

    (A) A third interview is scheduled on the same day with M and N.

    (B) Exactly three interviews will be held on one of the days.

    (C) Exactly one person will be interviewed on Monday.

    (D) Exactly two persons will be interviewed on Friday.

    (E) Q will have the only interview on Tuesday.

15. If Q and J are the only persons interviewed on Tuesday, which of the following must be true?

    (A) K's is the only interview on one of the days.

    (B) L's is the only interview on one of the days.

    (C) P's is the only interview on one of the days.

    (D) P's interview is earlier in the week than N's interview.

    (E) L's interview is earlier in the week than O's interview.

16. If M, N, and K are interviewed on the same day, which of the following must be true?

    (A) J is interviewed on Monday.

    (B) Q is interviewed on Monday.

    (C) L is interviewed on Tuesday.

    (D) J and L are interviewed on the same day.

    (E) J and Q are interviewed on the same day.

17. If L is interviewed later in the week than P, which of the following CANNOT be true?

    (A) P is the only person interviewed on one of the days.

    (B) K is the only person interviewed on one of the days.

    (C) L and Q are interviewed on the same day.

    (D) L and J are interviewed on the same day.

    (E) M and P are interviewed on the same day.

Questions 18-21

A university acting class is presenting a series of five skits using six performers, M, N, O, P, Q, and R. Each performer must perform in exactly three of the skits.

Only O and P will perform in the first skit.

R and three others will perform in the second skit.

Only N will perform in the third skit.

More people will perform in the fourth skit than in the fifth skit.

18. Which of the following must be true?

    (A) N and Q perform in the second skit.

    (B) N and R perform in the fifth skit.

    (C) Q does not perform in the fifth skit.

    (D) Exactly four people perform in the fourth skit.

    (E) Exactly five people perform in the fifth skit.

19. For which of the following pairs of performers is it true that if one appears in a skit, the other must also appear?

    (A) M and N

    (B) M and R

    (C) P and O

    (D) P and R

    (E) Q and O

20. Which of the following CANNOT be true?

    (A) Neither O nor P appears in the second skit.

    (B) Neither O nor P appears in the fifth skit.

    (C) N and Q appear in the second skit.

    (D) N appears in the second skit.

    (E) O, P, and Q appear in the fifth skit.

21. If N does not appear in the fifth skit, all of the following must be true EXCEPT:

    (A) P appears in the second skit.

    (B) N appears in the second skit.

    (C) O appears in the fifth skit.

    (D) P appears in the fifth skit.

    (E) Q appears in the fifth skit.

GO ON TO THE NEXT PAGE

22. All high-powered racing engines have stochastic fuel injection. Stochastic fuel injection is not a feature that is normally included in the engines of production-line vehicles.

   Passenger sedans are production-line vehicles. Which of the following conclusions can be drawn from these statements?

   (A) Passenger sedans do not usually have stochastic fuel injection.

   (B) Stochastic fuel injection is found only in high-powered racing cars.

   (C) Car manufacturers do not include stochastic fuel injection in passenger cars because they fear accidents.

   (D) Purchasers of passenger cars do not normally purchase stochastic fuel injection because it is expensive.

   (E) Some passenger sedans are high-powered racing vehicles.

23. CLARENCE: Mary is one of the most important executives at the Trendy Cola Company.

   PETER: How can that be? I know for a fact that Mary drinks only Hobart Cola.

   Peter's statement implies that he believes that

   (A) Hobart Cola is a subsidiary of Trendy Cola

   (B) Mary is an unimportant employee of Hobart Cola

   (C) all cola drinks taste pretty much alike

   (D) an executive uses only that company's products

   (E) Hobart is a better-tasting cola than Trendy

24. Current motion pictures give children a distorted view of the world. Animated features depict animals as loyal friends, compassionate creatures, and tender souls, while "spaghetti Westerns" portray men and women as deceitful and treacherous, cruel and wanton, hard and uncaring. Thus, children are taught to value animals more highly than other human beings.

   Which of the following, if true, would weaken the author's conclusion?

   (A) Children are not allowed to watch "spaghetti Westerns."

   (B) The producers of animated features do not want children to regard animals as higher than human beings.

   (C) Ancient fables, such as Androcles and the Lion, tell stories of the cooperation between humans and animals, and they usually end with a moral about human virtue.

   (D) Children are more likely to choose to watch animated presentations with characters such as animals that those with people as actors.

   (E) Animals often exhibit affection, loyalty, protectiveness, and other traits that are considered desirable characteristics in humans.

25. The Dormitory Canteen Committee decided that the prices of snacks in the Canteen vending machines were already high enough, so they told Vendo Inc., the company holding the vending machine concession for the Canteen, either to maintain prices at the then current levels or to forfeit the concession. Vendo, however, managed to thwart the intent of the Committee's instructions without actually violating the letter of those instructions.

   Which of the following is probably the action taken by Vendo referred to in the above paragraph?

   (A) The president of Vendo met with the University's administration, and they ordered the Committee to rescind its instructions.

   (B) Vendo continued prices at the prescribed levels but reduced the size of the snacks vended in the machines.

   (C) Vendo ignored the Committee's instructions and continued to raise prices.

   (D) Vendo decided it could not make a fair return on its investment if it held the line on prices, so it removed its machines from the Dormitory Canteen.

   (E) Representatives of Vendo met with members of the Dormitory Canteen Committee and offered them free snacks to influence other members to change the Committee's decision.

Questions 26-32

The Executive Officer of a college English department is hiring adjunct-faculty for her evening courses. She must offer exactly eight courses during the academic year, four in the fall semester and four in the spring semester. The candidates are: J, K, L, M, N, and O. Each person, if hired, must teach the following:

J must teach one course on Marlowe and one course on Joyce.

K must teach one course on Shakespeare and one course on Keats.

L must teach one course on Marlowe and one course on Chaucer.

M must teach one course on Shakespeare, one course on Marlowe, and one course on Keats.

N must teach one course on Joyce, one course on Keats, and one course on Chaucer.

O must teach one course on Shakespeare, one course on Marlowe, and one course on Joyce.

Only one course on an author can be offered in a single semester.

26. Which of the following combinations of teachers can be hired?

    (A) J, K, and N
    (B) K, M, and N
    (C) K, M, and O
    (D) L, M, and O
    (E) L, N, and O

27. If L and N are hired, and if N is assigned to teach only in the spring semester, which of the following could be true?

    (A) Neither M nor O will be hired.
    (B) L will teach only in the spring semester.
    (C) L will teach only in the fall semester.
    (D) Courses on Keats and Joyce will be offered in the fall semester.
    (E) Courses on Shakespeare and Marlowe will be offered in the spring semester.

28. If M, N, and a third teacher are hired, which of the following is a complete and accurate listing of the candidates who could be hired as the third teacher?

    (A) J
    (B) K
    (C) L
    (D) J,K
    (E) J,L

29. If M and N are hired, and if M will teach only one of the two semesters and N the other, which of the following must be true?

    (A) J is hired.
    (B) K is hired.
    (C) L is hired.
    (D) A course on Shakespeare will be offered in the fall semester.
    (E) A course on Marlowe will be offered in the spring semester.

30. If K and N are hired, which of the following must be true?

    (A) A course on Joyce is offered in one semester or the other, but not both.
    (B) A course on Keats is offered in one semester or the other, but not both.
    (C) A course on Marlowe is offered both semesters.
    (D) A course on Shakespeare is offered both semesters.
    (E) A course on Chacuer is offered both semesters.

31. If L is hired and will teach both her courses in the fall semester, which of the following must be true?

    (A) M and N are hired.
    (B) M and O are hired.
    (C) N and O are hired.
    (D) A course on Joyce will be offered in the spring semester.
    (E) A course on Chaucer will be offered in the spring semester.

GO ON TO THE NEXT PAGE

32. If K, N, and O are hired, and if N will teach all three of her courses in the fall semester, all of the following must be true EXCEPT:

    (A) A course on Keats will be taught in the spring semester.

    (B) A course on Marlowe will be taught in the spring semester.

    (C) Courses on Keats and Joyce will be taught in both semesters.

    (D) A course on Marlowe and a course on Shakespeare will be taught in the spring semester.

    (E) A course on Shakespeare and a course on Chaucer will be taught in the spring semester.

33. The new car to buy this year is the Goblin. We had 100 randomly selected motorists drive the Goblin and the other two leading sub-compact cars. Seventy-five drivers ranked the Goblin first in handling. Sixty-nine rated the Goblin first in styling. From the responses of these 100 drivers, we can show you that they ranked Goblin first overall in our composite category of style, performance, comfort, and drivability.

    The persuasive appeal of the advertisement's claim is most weakened by its use of the undefined word

    (A) randomly

    (B) handling

    (C) first

    (D) responses

    (E) composite

34. (1) No student who commutes from home to university dates a student who resides at a university.

    (2) Every student who lives at home commutes to his university, and no commuter student ever dates a resident student.

    Which of the following best describes the relationship between the two sentences above?

    (A) If (2) is true, (1) must also be true.

    (B) If (2) is true, (1) must be false.

    (C) If (2) is true, (1) may be either true or false.

    (D) If (1) is true, (2) is unlikely to be false.

    (E) If (2) is false, (1) must also be false.

35. Children in the first three grades who attend private schools spend time each day working with a computerized reading program. Public schools have very few such programs. Tests prove, however, that public-school children are much weaker in reading skills when compared to their private-school counterparts. We conclude, therefore, that public-school children can be good readers only if they participate in a computerized reading program.

    The author's initial statements logically support her conclusion only if which of the following is also true?

    (A) All children can learn to be good readers if they are taught by a computerized reading program.

    (B) All children can learn to read at the same rate if they participate in a computerized reading program.

    (C) Better reading skills produce better students.

    (D) Computerized reading programs are the critical factor in the better reading skills of private-school students.

    (E) Public-school children can be taught better math skills.

WARNING

IF YOU FINISHED THIS SECTION BEFORE TIME EXPIRED, GO IMMEDIATELY TO THE NEXT SECTION. YOU MAY NOT CONTINUE TO WORK ON THIS SECTION AFTER TIME HAS EXPIRED.

Verbal Section

30 QUESTIONS • TIME—30 MINUTES

Directions: Each of the questions below contains one or more blank spaces, each blank indicating an omitted word. Each sentence is followed by five (5) words or sets of words. Read and determine the general sense of each sentence. Then choose the word, or set of words that, when inserted in the sentence, best fits the meaning of the sentence.

1. Despite the millions of dollars spent on improvements, the telephone system in India remains ____ and continues to ____ the citizens who depend on it.

    (A) primitive..inconvenience

    (B) bombastic..upset

    (C) suspicious..connect

    (D) outdated..elate

    (E) impartial..vex

2. Contrary to popular opinion, bats are not generally aggressive and rabid; most are shy and ____.

    (A) turgid

    (B) disfigured

    (C) punctual

    (D) innocuous

    (E) depraved

3. Unlike the images in symbolist poetry which are often vague and ____, the images of surrealist poetry are startlingly ____ and bold.

    (A) extraneous..furtive

    (B) trivial..inadvertent

    (C) obscure..concrete

    (D) spectacular..pallid

    (E) symmetrical..virulent

Directions: In each of the following questions, you are given a related pair of words or phrases in capital letters. Each capitalized pair is followed by five (5) pairs of words or phrases. Choose the pair that best expresses a relationship similar to that expressed by the original pair.

4. CHAPTER : NOVEL ::

    (A) piano : orchestra

    (B) diamond : gem

    (C) scene : drama

    (D) poetry : prose

    (E) fraction : portion

5. IMPLY : AVER ::

    (A) reject : announce

    (B) hint : proclaim

    (C) encourage : absolve

    (D) remind : contradict

    (E) embolden : accept

6. DETENTION : RELEASE ::

    (A) viciousness : attack

    (B) calamity : repair

    (C) qualification : employ

    (D) induction : discharge

    (E) therapy : confuse

7. PONDEROUS : WEIGHT ::

    (A) eternal : temporality

    (B) convincing : decision

    (C) gargantuan : size

    (D) ancient : value

    (E) prototypical : affection

GO ON TO THE NEXT PAGE

8. REVERE :

   (A) collide

   (B) succumb

   (C) threaten

   (D) divide

   (E) despise

9. BOORISH :

   (A) juvenile

   (B) well-mannered

   (C) weak-minded

   (D) unique

   (E) concealed

10. WHIMSICAL :

   (A) chivalrous

   (B) perfect

   (C) predictable

   (D) hidden

   (E) backward

11. NASCENT :

   (A) fully developed

   (B) extremely valuable

   (C) well-regarded

   (D) informative

   (E) measurable

Art, like words, is a form of communication. Words, spoken and written, render accessible to humans of the latest generations all the knowledge discovered by the experience and reflection, both of preceding genera-
(5) tions and of the best and foremost minds of their own times. Art renders accessible to people of the latest generations all the feelings experienced by their prede-cessors, and those already felt by their best and foremost contemporaries. Just as the evolution of knowledge
(10) proceeds by dislodging and replacing that which is mistaken, so too the evolution of feeling proceeds through art. Feelings less kind and less necessary for the well-being of humankind are replaced by others kinder and more essential to that end. This is the purpose of art,
(15) and the more art fulfills that purpose the better the art; the less it fulfills it, the worse the art.

12. The author develops the passage primarily by

   (A) theory and refutation

   (B) example and generalization

   (C) comparison and contrast

   (D) question and answer

   (E) inference and deduction

13. According to the author, knowledge is

   (A) evolutionary and emotional

   (B) cumulative and progressive

   (C) static and unmoving

   (D) dynamic and cyclical

   (E) practical and directionless

14. According to the passage, all of the following are true EXCEPT:

(A) Art is a form of communication.

(B) Art helps to refine sensibilities.

(C) Art is a repository of experience.

(D) Real art can never be bad.

(E) Art is a progressive human endeavor.

Directions: In each of the following questions, you are given a related pair of words or phrases in capital letters. Each capitalized pair is followed by five (5) pairs of words or phrases. Choose the pair that best expresses a relationship similar to that expressed by the original pair.

15. FEBRILE : ILLNESS ::

(A) tenacious : astonishment

(B) juvenile : maturity

(C) classic : cultivation

(D) eccentric : discrimination

(E) delusional : insanity

16. INCOMMUNICADO : CONTACT ::

(A) sequestered : company

(B) pretentious : affectation

(C) submissive : compromise

(D) perpetual : adventure

(E) severed : replacement

17. EQUIVOCATION : MEANING ::

(A) feint : intention

(B) secrecy : stealth

(C) geniality : amiability

(D) travesty : insight

(E) refinement : innovation

Directions: Each passage in this group is followed by questions or incomplete statements about its content. Answer all questions following a passage on the basis of what is stated or implied in that passage.

The most damning thing that can be said about the world's best-endowed and richest country is that it is not only not the leader in health status, but that it is so low in the ranks of the nations. The United States ranks 18th (5) among nations of the world in male life expectancy at birth, 9th in female life expectancy at birth, and 12th in infant mortality. More importantly, huge variations are evident in health status in the United States from one place to the next and from one group to the next.

(10)   The forces that affect health can be aggregated into four groupings that lend themselves to analysis of all health problems. Clearly the largest aggregate of forces resides in the person's environment. His own behavior, in part derived from his experiences with his environ- (15) ment, is the next greatest force affecting his health. Medical care services, treated as separate from other environmental factors because of the special interest we have in them, make a modest contribution to health status. Finally, the contributions of heredity to health (20) are difficult to judge. We are templated at conception as to our basic weaknesses and strengths; but many heredi- tary attributes never become manifest because of envi- ronmental and behavioral forces that act before the genetic forces come to maturity, and other hereditary (25) attributes are increasingly being palliated by medical care.

No other country spends what we do per capita for medical care. The care available is among the best technically, even if used too lavishly and thus danger- (30) ously, but none of the countries that stand above us in health status have such a high proportion of medically disenfranchised persons. Given the evidence that medi- cal care is not that valuable and access to care not that bad, it seems most unlikely that our bad showing is (35) caused by the significant proportion who are poorly served. Other hypotheses have greater explanatory power: excessive poverty, both actual and relative, and excessive affluence.

Excessive poverty is probably more prevalent in the (40) U.S. than in any of the countries that have a better infant mortality rate and female life expectancy at birth. This is

GO ON TO THE NEXT PAGE

probably true also for all but four or five of the countries with a longer male life expectancy. In the notably poor countries that exceed us in male survival, difficult living (45) conditions are a more accepted way of life and in several of them, a good basic diet, basic medical care and basic education, and lifelong employment opportunities are an everyday fact of life. In the U.S. a national unemployment level of 10 percent may be 40 percent in the ghetto (50) while less than 4 percent elsewhere. The countries that have surpassed us in health do not have such severe or entrenched problems. Nor are such a high proportion of their people involved in them.

Excessive affluence is not so obvious a cause of ill (55) health, but, at least until recently, few other nations could afford such unhealthful ways of living. Excessive intake of animal protein and fats, dangerous imbibing of alcohol and use of tobacco and drugs (prescribed and proscribed), and dangerous recreational sports and driv- (60) ing habits are all possible only because of affluence. Our heritage, desires, opportunities, and our machismo, combined with the relatively low cost of bad foods and speedy vehicles, make us particularly vulnerable to our affluence. And those who are not affluent try harder. (65) Our unacceptable health status, then, will not be improved appreciably by expanded medical resources nor by their redistribution so much as by a general attempt to improve the quality of life for all.

18. Which of the following would be the most logical continuation of the passage?

(A) Suggestions for specific proposals to improve the quality of life in America

(B) A listing of the most common causes of death among male and female adults

(C) An explanation of the causes of poverty in America, both absolute and relative

(D) A proposal to ensure that residents of central cities receive more and better medical care

(E) A study of the overcrowding in urban hospitals serving primarily the poor

19. All of the following are mentioned in the passage as factors affecting the health of the population EXCEPT

(A) the availability of medical care services

(B) the genetic endowment of individuals

(C) overall environmental factors

(D) the nation's relative position in health status

(E) an individual's own behavior

20. The author is primarily concerned with

(A) condemning the U.S. for its failure to provide better medical care to the poor

(B) evaluating the relative significance of factors contributing to the poor health status in the U.S.

(C) providing information the reader can use to improve his or her personal health

(D) comparing the general health of the U.S. population with world averages

(E) advocating specific measures designed to improve the health of the U.S. population

21. The passage best supports which of the following conclusions about the relationship between per capita expenditures for medical care and the health of a population?

(A) The per capita expenditure for medical care has relatively little effect on the total amount of medical care available to a population.

(B) The genetic makeup of a population is a more powerful determinant of the health of a population than the per capita expenditure for medical care.

(C) A population may have very high per capita expenditures for medical care and yet have a lower health status than other populations with lower per capita expenditures.

(D) The higher the per capita expenditure on medical care, the more advanced is the medical technology; and the more advanced the technology, the better is the health of the population.

(E) Per capita outlays for medical care devoted to adults are likely to have a greater effect on the status of the population than outlays devoted to infants.

22. The author refers to the excessive intake of alcohol and tobacco and drug use in order to

    (A) show that some health problems cannot be attacked by better medical care

    (B) demonstrate that use of tobacco and intoxicants is detrimental to health

    (C) cite examples of individual behavior that have adverse consequences for health status

    (D) refute the contention that poor health is related to access to medical care

    (E) illustrate ways in which affluence may contribute to poor health status

23. The passage provides information to answer which of the following questions?

    (A) What is the most powerful influence on the health status of a population?

    (B) Which nation in the world leads in health status?

    (C) Is the life expectancy of males in the U.S. longer than that of females?

    (D) What are the most important genetic factors influencing the health of an individual?

    (E) How can the U.S. reduce the incidence of unemployment in the ghetto?

Directions: Each of the following questions consists of a word printed in capital letters, followed by five words or phrases. Choose the word or phrase that is most nearly opposite in meaning to the word in capital letters. Be sure to consider all the choices before deciding which one is best.

24. INURED :

    (A) authoritative

    (B) dissolute

    (C) bereft

    (D) sensitive

    (E) taxing

25. IRASCIBLE :

    (A) even-tempered

    (B) well-informed

    (C) repetitious

    (D) motionless

    (E) synchronous

26. EXONERATE :

    (A) testify

    (B) engender

    (C) accuse

    (D) inundate

    (E) abrogate

27. ALACRITY :

    (A) skullduggery

    (B) reluctance

    (C) interment

    (D) bellicosity

    (E) specificity

Directions: Each of the questions below contains one or more blank spaces, each blank indicating an omitted word. Each sentence is followed by five (5) words or sets of words. Read and determine the general sense of each sentence. Then choose the word, or set of words that, when inserted in the sentence, best fits the meaning of the sentence.

28. A good trial lawyer will argue only what is central to an issue, eliminating ——— information or anything else that might ——— the client.

    (A) seminal..amuse

    (B) extraneous..jeopardize

    (C) erratic..enhance

    (D) prodigious..extol

    (E) reprehensible..initiate

GO ON TO THE NEXT PAGE

29. Psychologists and science fiction writers argue that people persist in believing in extraterrestrial life, even though the Federal government ____ all such beliefs, because people need to feel a personal sense of ____ in a godless universe.

    (A) decries..morbidity

    (B) endorses..despair

    (C) creates..guilt

    (D) discourages..spirituality

    (E) debunks..alienation

30. Pollen grains and spores that are 200 million years old are now being extracted from shale and are ____ the theory that the breakup of the continents occurred in stages; in fact, it seems that the breakups occurred almost ____.

    (A) refining..blatantly

    (B) reshaping..simultaneously

    (C) countermanding..imperceptibly

    (D) forging..vicariously

    (E) supporting..haphazardly

WARNING

IF YOU FINISHED THIS SECTION BEFORE TIME EXPIRED, GO IMMEDIATELY TO THE NEXT SECTION. YOU MAY NOT CONTINUE TO WORK ON THIS SECTION AFTER TIME HAS EXPIRED.

Practice Examination 2
Answer Key

MATH SECTION

1. C	7. E	13. B	19. D	25. E
2. B	8. C	14. E	20. C	26. C
3. B	9. D	15. A	21. E	27. B
4. A	10. E	16. C	22. E	28. A
5. D	11. C	17. C	23. E	
6. D	12. B	18. D	24. A	

ANALYTICAL SECTION

1. E	8. E	15. A	22. A	29. E
2. B	9. C	16. B	23. D	30. D
3. A	10. C	17. C	24. A	31. E
4. D	11. A	18. E	25. B	32. E
5. A	12. A	19. B	26. E	33. E
6. E	13. C	20. B	27. C	34. A
7. D	14. B	21. A	28. E	35. D

VERBAL SECTION

1. A	7. C	13. B	19. D	25. A
2. D	8. E	14. D	20. B	26. C
3. C	9. B	15. E	21. C	27. B
4. C	10. C	16. A	22. E	28. B
5. B	11. A	17. A	23. A	29. D
6. D	12. C	18. A	24. D	30. B

Explanatory Answers

MATH SECTION

1. **(C)** "Of" in this case indicates multiplication. The product of 5 and 36 will be equal to the product of 36 and 5, and .05 and .36 will have the same number of decimal places; therefore, the two quantities must be equal. You do not need to actually do the multiplication in full.

2. **(B)** It is not possible to combine the two radicals of the right column. Although $\sqrt{5} \times \sqrt{10} = \sqrt{50}$, $\sqrt{5} + \sqrt{10} \neq \sqrt{15}$. The operation works only for multiplication. Since $\sqrt{15} < \sqrt{16}$, $\sqrt{15}$ must be less than 4. Since $\sqrt{5} > \sqrt{4}$, $\sqrt{5}$ must be greater than 2; and since $\sqrt{10}$ is greater than $\sqrt{9}$, $\sqrt{10}$ must be greater than 3. The two terms of the right column are slightly greater than 2 and 3 respectively, so their sum must be greater than 5. Column B is slightly greater than 5. Column A is less than 4.

3. **(B)** The (346×23) is only flack. It does not point to any difference between p and q. Since the first term of both equations is the same, we can assign it the constant value k. The given information can now be simplified:

$$k + p = 34,731$$
$$k + q = 35,124$$

Since 35,124 is greater than 34,731, q must be greater than p.

4. **(A)** Remember that the drawings in this subsection are not necessarily drawn to scale. Thus, you should not solve problems on the basis of a visual estimate of size or shape alone. However, manipulating the diagram in your mind—seeing what the possibilities are if some line is lengthened or shortened or some angle varied—can often help you to see the answer to a quantitative comparison problem without computation, or at least will reduce your difficulties.

In this case, exploring what it means to say that $x°$ $< y°$ can start with seeing what it would mean if $x°$ $= y°$. As the first diagram shows, $x° = y°$ means that SRT has two equal legs, ST and TR. T will be in the middle of PQ, hence $PT = QT$. But as $y°$ gets larger, it will result in the line RT hitting the line PQ closer

and closer to Q, thus making TQ smaller and PT larger. Therefore PT is always larger than TQ when $y° > x°$.

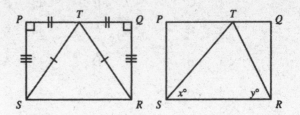

5. **(D)** Since x might be a fraction, it is not possible to determine which of the columns is greater. If x is $\frac{1}{2}$, then Column A is $\frac{1}{4}$ while Column B is 1, making Column B greater in that instance. But if x is 2, Column A is 4 and Column B is 4, making the two columns equal. Finally, if x is greater than 2, say 3, then Column A is 9 and Column B is 6, making A greater.

6. **(D)** The minute hand will make one complete circle of the dial by 7:15. Then it will complete another half circle by 7:45. Since there are 360° in a circle, the arc traveled by the minute hand will be one full 360° plus half of another full 360° yielding $360° + 180° = 540°$.

7. **(E)** One way of solving this problem would be to convert each of the fractions to a decimal or find a common denominator so that a direct comparison can be made. This is too time-consuming. Instead, anytime the GRE asks a question similar to this one, the student can be confident that there is very likely some shortcut available. Here the shortcut is to recognize that every answer choice, except for (E), is either equal to or greater than $\frac{1}{2}$. $\frac{7}{8}$ and $\frac{8}{9}$ are clearly much larger than $\frac{1}{2}$. $\frac{7}{12}$ must be greater than $\frac{1}{2}$ since $\frac{6}{12}$ is equal to $\frac{1}{2}$. But $\frac{6}{17}$ is less than $\frac{1}{2}$

$-\dfrac{6}{12}$ would be $\dfrac{1}{2}$. So (E) is the smallest of the fractions. Even if the shortcut had eliminated only two or three answers, it would have been worthwhile.

8. **(C)** Even though it is not absolutely necessary to draw a figure to solve this problem, anyone finding the solution elusive will likely profit from a "return to basics":

$$\dfrac{3x}{4}+1$$

$\dfrac{3x}{4}+1\ \boxed{}\ \dfrac{3x}{4}+1 \qquad P=4\left(\dfrac{3x}{4}+1\right)$

$$\dfrac{3x}{4}+1$$

Quickly sketching the figure may help you avoid the mistake of multiplying the side of the square by another side, giving the area, answer (D), not the perimeter. The perimeter will be $4s$, not s^2:

$$4\left(\dfrac{3x}{4}+1\right)=\dfrac{12x}{4}+4=3x+4$$

9. **(D)** Average speed is nothing more than miles traveled over the time taken: rate (speed) $=\dfrac{\text{distance}}{\text{time}}$.

The elapsed time here is 4 hours and 48 minutes. 48 minutes is $\dfrac{4}{5}$ hours. Our formula then will be: $\dfrac{240\ \text{miles}}{4\frac{4}{5}\ \text{miles}}$. We attack the problem by converting the denominator to a fraction: $4\frac{4}{5}=\dfrac{24}{5}$, and then we invert and multiply:

$$\dfrac{240}{4\frac{4}{5}}=\dfrac{240}{\frac{24}{5}}=\dfrac{5}{24}\times240=50\ \text{MPH}$$

Notice that setting up the problem in this way avoids a lot of needless arithmetic. This is characteristic of the GRE. Most problems do not require a lengthy calculation. Usually the numbers used in constructing the questions are selected in a way that will allow for canceling, factoring, or other shortcut devices. On the test, fractions are usually easier to work with than decimals.

10. **(E)** Multiplication is both associative and commutative. By associative, we mean that the grouping of the elements is not important—for example, $(5\times6)\times7=5\times(6\times7)$. By commutative we mean

that the order of the elements is unimportant—for example, $5\times6=6\times5$. So (A), (B), (C), and (D) are all alternative forms for $m(nop)$, but (E) is not: $(mn)(mo)(mp)=m^3nop$.

11. **(C)** Since the numbers here are relatively manageable, the easiest solution to this problem is to do the indicated arithmetic operation:

$$\dfrac{4}{5}-\dfrac{3}{4}=\dfrac{16-15}{20}=\dfrac{1}{20}$$

You might also notice that $\dfrac{4}{5}=80\%$ and $\dfrac{3}{4}=75\%$, with their difference being 5%, which is $\dfrac{1}{20}$.

12. **(B)** We can see that the fraction $\dfrac{3}{13}<\dfrac{3}{12}$, thus $\dfrac{3}{13}<\dfrac{1}{4}$; but $\dfrac{13}{51}>\dfrac{13}{52}$, thus $\dfrac{13}{51}>\dfrac{1}{4}$. Therefore, $\dfrac{3}{13}<\dfrac{1}{4}<\dfrac{13}{51}$, answer (B). We look for reference points. For example, the 52 cards in a deck are in four suits of 13 cards each.

13. **(B)** This problem uses the term S_n to indicate that whatever n may be, the S_n value will be found by multiplying n by 3 and adding 2 to the result. One way of solving this problem would be to do the actual work indicated for 5, 4, 9 and 8, finding that S_n for 5 is $S_5=3(5)+2=17$ and $S_4=14$, $S_9=29$, $S_8=26$, with $17+14$ being smaller than $29+26$.

But there is really no reason to do the actual work. Since the QC issue is which column is bigger, we always pay attention to how things get bigger or smaller. S_n will get bigger as n gets bigger because it is just multiplying n by 3. Since Column A has two smaller numbers, the sum is smaller.

14. **(E)** This is an unusual problem, one that requires careful reading rather than some clever mathematical insight. The question asks us to compare the fractions in the form $\dfrac{p}{q}$ with the decimal .PQ. For example, we convert the fraction $\dfrac{1}{8}$ into the decimal .18 for purposes of comparison and ask how closely the second approximates the first. Since $\dfrac{1}{8}$ is .125, we see that the fit is not a very precise one.

Similarly, with $\frac{2}{9}$, the corresponding decimal we are to compare is .29, but the actual decimal equivalent of $\frac{2}{9}$ is .22 $\frac{2}{9}$. The equivalent for $\frac{3}{4}$ is .34, not even close to the actual decimal equivalent of .75.

Similarly, for $\frac{4}{5}$, the artificially derived .45 is not very close to the actual decimal equivalent of .80;

but for $\frac{8}{9}$ we use the decimal .89, and this is fairly close—the closest of all the fractions listed—to the actual decimal equivalent of $\frac{8}{9}$, which is .888 $\frac{8}{9}$.

If you have difficulties in finding the decimals for fractions, try to relate the fractions to percentages, which are in hundredths, or to other, more common decimal-fraction equivalencies. For example, one-third is probably known to you as approximately .33 or 33%. A ninth is one-third of a third; hence a ninth is approximately $\frac{33\%}{3} = 11\%$ or .11. Eight-ninths is thus 8(11%) = 88%.

15. **(A)** If a problem seems a bit too abstract to handle using algebraic notation, a sometimes useful technique is to try to find a similar, more familiar situation. For example, virtually everyone could answer the following question: Books cost $5 each; how many books can be bought for $100? The calculation goes: $\frac{1\ book}{\$5} \times \$100 = 20$ books. So, too, here the number of books that can be purchased per d dollars must be multiplied by the number of dollars to be spent, m: $\frac{b}{d} \times m$, or $\frac{bm}{d}$. Pursuing this line of attack, it might be worthwhile to point out that substitution of real numbers in problems like this is often an effective way of solving the prob-

lem. Since the variables and the formulas are general—that is, they do not depend upon any given number of books or dollars—the correct answer choice must work for all possible values. Suppose we assume, therefore, 2(b) books can be purchased for $5($d$), and that the amount to be spent is $50($m$). Most people can fall back onto common sense to calculate the number of books that can be purchased with $50: 20 books. But of the five formulas offered as answer choices, only (A) gives the number 20 when the values are substituted: For $b = 2$, $d = 5$ and $m = 50$,

(A) $\frac{(2)(50)}{5} = 20$

(B) $(2)(5)(50) = 500$

(C) $\frac{5}{(2)(50)} = \frac{1}{20}$

(D) $\frac{2+50}{5} = \frac{52}{5}$

(E) $\frac{2-50}{5} = \frac{-48}{5}$

Substitution will take longer than a direct algebraic approach, but it is much better than simply guessing, if you have the time and can't get the algebra to work right.

16. **(C)** The problem does *not* presuppose that you're familiar with the metric system. The cost of the meat in Column A is: 10 lbs. × $2.50/lb. = $25.00. The cost of the meat in Column B is: 5 kilos × $5.00/kilo = $25.00.

17. **(C)** The problem is most easily solved by canceling the zeros in each fraction:

$$\frac{1\cancel{0}}{10,00\cancel{0}} = \frac{1}{1,000} \qquad \frac{1,00\cancel{0}}{1,000,0\cancel{00}} = \frac{1}{1,000}$$

So Column A and Column B are both $\frac{1}{1,000}$ and equal.

18. **(D)** Do not try to solve a quantitative comparison by visually estimating lengths of lines. In this case, there is not sufficient information to deduce that *PQRS* is or is not a square—even though it is drawn as one. The following group of drawings will show that no conclusion regarding the relative lengths of *PQ* and *QR* is possible. *PQ* could be equal to *QR*, but it doesn't have to be.

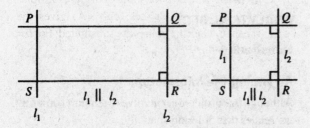

19. **(D)** The information supplied in the two columns is sufficient only to allow us to compute the *capacities* or *volumes* of the boxes described. We have no information regarding the size of pears or the size of potatoes, and we are not even told what part of each box's capacity is being used.

20. **(C)** The problem is most easily solved by grouping like terms and simplifying. We want the *x* terms on one side, pure numbers on the other.

$$4x^2 + 2x^2 + 3x + 2x = 3x^2 + 3x^2 + 2x + 2x + 3$$
$$6x^2 + 5x = 6x^2 + 4x + 3$$
$$x = 3$$

Since $x = 3$, x^2 must be 9 and the two columns are equal.

21. **(E)** Looking at the two charts, we see that the upper one, representing the total passenger miles, shows a smooth increase, generally speaking, while the lower one shows large changes. Since the lower one is deaths per passenger-mile, the sharp changes in the rate must be from sharp changes in the number of deaths.

(A) is inferable since the highest level reached by the line on the lower graph was approximately 1.3, in 1951. (B) is also inferable. The largest jump in the line on the lower graph, for a one-year period, occurred in the period 1954-1955. (C) is also inferable. The two low points on the line of the lower graph occurred in 1954 and 1957; both were approximately .1. (D) is inferable: 10 to 30. But (E) is not inferable. Remember not to confuse absolute numbers and percent increase.

22. **(E)** The question stem asks about the *longest*, not the most severe or greatest increase. Although the *largest* increase ended in 1955, the *longest* increase lasted from 1956 until 1960. The word "finally" is also a clue.

23. **(E)** In 1955, total passenger-miles were 20 billion, and the fatality rate was 1.2 per 100 million miles. To compute the actual number of fatalities, we must multiply the total miles by the rate of fatalities (just as one multiplies 5 gallons by 25 miles per gallon to compute the total miles traveled as 125 miles): $20,000,000,000 \times \dfrac{1.2}{100,000,000} =$ (to make matters easier, we cancel zeros) $20,0\!\!\!/0\!\!\!/0,0\!\!\!/0\!\!\!/0,0\!\!\!/0\!\!\!/0 \dfrac{1.2}{10\!\!\!/0,0\!\!\!/0\!\!\!/0,0\!\!\!/0\!\!\!/0} = 240.$

24. **(A)** Problem 23 shows how the number of fatalities can be found. But it would be counter-productive to spend a lot of time computing the actual number of deaths for each of the five years mentioned. Instead, a rough estimate will suffice. At first glance, it appears that the only reasonable possibilities are 1951, 1955, and 1960, since the fatality rate (lower graph) is at least approximately equal in those years. Now, it is absolutely critical to realize that, though the fatality rate in 1951 was higher than the fatality rate in 1960 (1.3 compared with 1.0), there were three times as many miles traveled in 1960 as in 1951. Similarly, though the fatality rate was higher in 1955 than it was in 1960 (1.2 compared with 1.0), there were 50% more miles traveled in 1960 than in 1955. This reasoning shows that the largest numbers of fatalities occurred in 1960. Even though the fatality rate that year was not as high as those for 1955 and 1951, this was more than offset by the larger number of passenger-miles traveled. Of course, a longer method of attack is to actually do a rough calculation for each:

(A) 1960: $\dfrac{1}{100 \text{ million}} \times 30 \text{ billion} = 300$

(B) 1957: $\dfrac{.1}{100 \text{ million}} \times 25 \text{ billion} = 25$

(C) 1955: $\dfrac{1.2}{100 \text{ million}} \times 20 \text{ billion} = 240$

(D) 1953: $\dfrac{.6}{100 \text{ million}} \times 15 \text{ billion} = 90$

(E) 1951: $\dfrac{1.3}{100 \text{ million}} \times 10 \text{ billion} = 130$

25. **(E)** This problem is at once both easy and difficult. It is easily solved if the key word, "passenger," is not overlooked. The lower graph records passenger miles traveled, but it tells us nothing about the number of different passengers who traveled those miles. The real-world likelihood that more passenger-miles *probably* means more passengers is only a probability and not a basis for a certain calculation.

26. **(C)** There is an easy and a more complicated way to handle this question. The more complex method is to begin with the formula for the area of a triangle: Area $= \frac{1}{2}$ (altitude)(base). Since angle CBE is equal to angle E, BC must be equal to CE, and it is possible to reduce the altitude to the base (or vice versa). So, Area $= \frac{1}{2}$ (side)^2. The area is 8, so $8 = \frac{1}{2} s^2$, and $s = 4$. Of course, s is also the side of the square, so the area of the square *ABCD* is s^2 or 16.

   Now, an easier method of solving the problem is to recognize that *BC* and *CE* are equal to the sides of the square *ABCD*, so the area of *BCE* is simply half that of the square. So the square must be double the triangle, or 16. A 45-45-90 right triangle is half of a square, and its hypotenuse is the diagonal of the square.

27. **(B)** Although some students will be able to solve this problem without the use of a diagram, for most drawing the floor plan of the closet is the logical starting point:

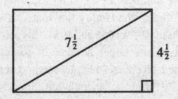

   Now it becomes clear that the Pythagorean Theorem is the key to solving this problem. Once the dimensions are converted to fractions, the problem is simplified further: the triangle is a 3-4-5 right triangle $\left(\frac{9}{12}, \frac{12}{2}, \frac{15}{2}\right)$. The two legs of the right triangle are simultaneously the width and length of the rectangle. So the area of the closet is: $\frac{9}{2} \times 6 = \frac{54}{2} = 27$.

28. **(A)** There are four times as many women as there are men, so if there are x men in the meeting, there are $4x$ women. This means that there is a total of $5x$ persons in the meeting $(x + 4x)$. Since the men are x out of a total of $5x$, the men constitute one-fifth, or 20%. Choices (D) and (E) can be avoided by noting that there are more women than men in the room and men thus come to less than 50%.

ANALYTICAL SECTION

Questions 1-4

Arranging the Information

Although this problem set involves a temporal ordering, we render that ordering spatially:

		M	Tu	Wed	Th	F
W,Y	A.M.			X		
X						
V,Z	P.M.			Z	(V)	(Z)

With X flying on Wednesday morning, X cannot fly Tuesday or Thursday morning, nor on Wednesday or Thursday afternoon. Further, with Z flying on Tuesday, Z is not available for Wednesday afternoon. This means V must fly Wednesday afternoon and Z Thursday afternoon.

Answering the Questions

1. **(E)** We were able to draw only two further conclusions from the initial conditions: V flies Wednesday afternoon and Z flies Thursday afternoon. (A), (B), (C), and (D) are all possibly true; only (E) is necessarily true.

2. **(B)** We begin by processing the additional information. Since X is flying Friday morning, X cannot fly either Thursday morning or Friday afternoon. This means that either W or Y will fly on Thursday morning and that V will fly on Friday afternoon.

	M	Tu	Wed	Th	F
A.M.			X		X
P.M.		Z	V	Z	V

The diagram shows that (A), (C), and (D) are possibly true and that (E) is necessarily false. Only (B) is necessarily true.

3. **(A)** We assume that X flies only one morning flight. This does not allow us to draw any specific conclusion about a particular flight, so we are forced to look to the answer choices; that is, we must test each choice and arrive at the correct answer by the process of elimination. (A) is correct. W and Y must cover Monday, Tuesday, Thursday, and Friday. And since a pilot cannot fly on consecutive days, W must do either Monday or Tuesday and either Thursday or Friday. (B) is incorrect since V could do both Monday and Friday afternoons, and then X would make only the one flight each week. (C) is incorrect as shown by our analysis of (A)—Y also must fly two days each week. (D) is incorrect for Z cannot fly either Monday or Friday. (E) is possibly, though not necessarily, true. We do not know whether Monday and Friday afternoons will go to X or V.

4. **(D)** We begin by processing the additional information:

	M	Tu	Wed	Th	F
A.M.	X	Y	X	Y	X
P.M.	V	Z	V	Z	V

If W does not fly at all during the week, then Y must fly on Tuesday and Thursday. This means that X must fly on Monday morning and Friday morning. Further, we must assign V to Monday and Friday afternoons. The diagram shows that (A), (B), (C), and (E) are all necessarily true and that (D) is necessarily false.

5. **(A)** Speaker 2 unwittingly plays right into the hands of Speaker 1. Speaker 1 tries to show that there are many decisions regarding human life in which we accept the idea that an increase in the quality of life justifies an increase in the danger to human life. All that Speaker 2 does is to help prove this point by stating that the quality of life would suffer if we lowered the speed limit to protect human life. Given this analysis, (B) must be incorrect, for Speaker 2's position is completely ineffective as a rebuttal. Moreover, (C) must be incorrect, for Speaker 2's response is not a strong statement of an anti-abortion position. (D) is incorrect, for while Speaker 2's response is of no value to the anti-abortion position, it cannot be said that it is irrelevant. In fact, as we have just shown, it supports the opposing position. Finally, (E) is not an appropriate characterization of Speaker 2's position.

6. **(E)** Speaker 1 uses the example of traffic fatalities to show that society has always traded the quality of life for the quantity of life. Although we do not always acknowledge that that is what we are doing, if we were honest, we would have to admit that we were making a trade-off. Thus, (E) is the best conclusion of the passage. Speaker 1's defense of abortion amounts to the claim that abortion is just another case in which we trade off one life (the fetus) to make the lives of others (the survivors) better. The only difference is that the life being sacrificed is specifiable and highly visible in the case of abortion, whereas in the case of highway fatalities, no one knows in advance on whom the axe will fall. (A) certainly goes far beyond what the author is advocating. If anything, Speaker 1 probably recognizes that sometimes the trade-off will be drawn in favor of protecting lives, and thus we need some such laws. (B) must be wrong, first because Speaker 2 says so, and second because Speaker 1 would prefer to show that the logical consequence of Speaker 2's response is an argument in favor of abortion. (C) is not an appropriate continuation because Speaker 1 has already said this is a weak counter-example and that there are even stronger points to make. Finally, Speaker 1 might be willing to accept contraception (D) as yet another example of the trade-off, but a stronger conclusion can be made. Speaker 1's conclusion ought to be that abortion is an acceptable practice—not that contraception is an acceptable practice.

7. **(D)** This is a very difficult question. That (D) is an assumption made by Speaker 1 requires careful reading. The attitude about the just war tips us off. Speaker 1 implies that this is an appropriate function of government and, further, that there are even clearer cases. Implicit in the speaker's defense of abortion is that a trade-off must be made and that it is appropriately a collective decision. (A) is not an assumption of the argument. Indeed, the speaker seems to assume, as we have just maintained, that the trade-off is an appropriate goal of society. Speaker 1 does not assume (B); if anything, Speaker 1 accepts that the fetus is a life, but it may be traded off in exchange for an increase in the quality in the lives of others. (C) and (E) use language related to the examples used by Speaker 1 but don't address the logical structure of the argument.

QUESTIONS 8-12

Arranging the Information

This is a selection set, and we begin by summarizing the restrictions on our selections:

(S requires Q)

$R \rightarrow \sim R$ (Not two consecutive days)

(U can only follow T)

Only one carryover

Answering the Questions

8. **(E)** For a question such as this, which does not supply any additional information, we simply check each answer choice against the restrictions we have summarized. (A) is not acceptable because R is used on two consecutive days and, further, because S appears the first day without Q. (B) can be eliminated because two selections carry over from day 1 to day 2 (S and Q). (C) can be eliminated because S appears on day 2 unaccompanied by Q. (D) can be eliminated because U appears on day 2, but T did not appear on day 1. Only (E) is consistent with all of the restrictions.

9. **(C)** If P and S are on the menu, then Q is also on the menu for that day. As for the next day, U cannot be used since T was not offered the day before. Further, S cannot be used since S requires Q and we cannot carry over both S and Q. This leaves us with R and T to be offered along with one dish from the first day (either P or Q).

10. **(C)** We know that neither R nor U can be offered on the intervening day. R cannot be used on two consecutive days, and U must follow T. So we must use S and T. With S offered, we must also offer Q. So the three specials for the intervening day are S, Q, and T.

11. **(A)** If neither Q nor T is on the menu, this leaves us with P, R, S, and U. But S cannot be used without Q, so this leaves only P, R, and U. Hence, there is only one possible combination of specials, given the assumption that Q and T are not offered.

12. **(A)** On the assumption that Q, R, and S are offered on one day, R cannot be offered the following day. Nor can U be offered since T did not appear on the preceding day. This means that both P and T will have to be included since only one of the original three can be carried over. S cannot be carried over because that would also require the carrying over of

Q. Q, however, can appear without S (Q is not "dependent" on S). So the second day, the specials must be P, Q, and T.

QUESTIONS 13-17

Arranging the Information

Here we have an ordering set, but the ordering is not strictly linear. That is, rather than having a single file of items (e.g., books on a shelf), several people here could occupy the same position simultaneously, e.g., three people interviewed on Thursday. We begin by summarizing the information:

M   Tu   Wed   Th   F
              O

(M & N) = Q + 3 (M and N interviewed 3 days after Q)

P later than K

It does not appear possible to draw any definite conclusions about which individual will be interviewed on which day (other than O). But there are some general conclusions available. First, we know that Q must be interviewed on either Monday or Tuesday, with M and N coming on Thursday or Friday, respectively, for those are the only ways of observing the restriction that M and N be interviewed exactly three days after Q. Second, we can also deduce that on one day three persons will be interviewed, on one day two persons will be interviewed, and on the remaining three days only one person will be interviewed. Given that Wednesday is used for only one interview and that only two days have more than one interview, a 1-1-1-2-3 arrangement (though not necessarily in that order) is the only possible distribution.

Answering the Questions

13. **(C)** This problem does not supply us with additional information, so we must find the correct choice using only the initial conditions. You will observe that the answer choices all make relative statements, e.g., O's interview is later in the week than K's interview, and not specific statements, e.g., K is interviewed on Thursday. The incorrect answers can all be shown to be possible by constructing examples:

M   Tu   Wed   Th   F
Q   K   O   M   P
      J   N
                  L

This, of course, is not the only possible schedule, but the diagram shows that (A), (B), (D), and (E) are possible. (C), however, is not possible. At the latest, K could be interviewed on Thursday, since K must be followed by P. At the earliest, M and N could be interviewed on Thursday, since they are interviewed on the third day following Q's interview. So it is impossible to interview K on a day *later* in the week than that set aside for N.

14. **(B)** Again, we have a question that does not supply us with any more information. Our analysis regarding the distribution of interviews proves that (B) is necessarily true. As for the incorrect answers, using our diagram from the preceding explanation, we can prove that they are not necessarily true. As for (A), L can be interviewed on Tuesday with K and J, which proves that the M-N day need not be the day with three interviews. As for (C), we can change the diagram to have K and J on Monday and Q on Tuesday. As for (D) and (E), the diagram already proves these statements are not necessarily true.

15. **(A)** Here we have additional information:

M	Tu	Wed	Th	F
	Q			M
	J			N

We know that M and N must be scheduled for Friday, and we know further that a third person must be scheduled for Friday in order to meet the 1-1-1-2-3 distributional requirement. Beyond that, no further conclusions are evident, and we must turn for guidance to the choices. (A) is the correct answer since P must follow K. This means that K cannot be interviewed on Friday, and we know that K cannot be interviewed on Tuesday. This means that K must be interviewed on either Monday or Thursday, days reserved for only one interview. (B), (C), (D), and (E) are all possible, but not necessarily true.

16. **(B)** Since P must follow K, and since M and N can be interviewed only on Thursday or Friday, the stipulation that K is interviewed with M and N forces us to schedule M and N for Thursday. This requires that we schedule Q for Monday. The remaining statements are all possible, but none of them is necessarily true.

17. **(C)** If L is interviewed later in the week than P, then Thursday is the earliest available date for L (P must follow K). However, the latest date by which Q can be interviewed is Tuesday. So L and Q cannot be scheduled for the same day.

QUESTIONS 18-21

Arranging the Information

For this set we will use an information matrix:

	M	N	O	P	Q	R
1						
2						
3						
4						
5						

This allows us to keep track of which performers are used in which skits. We enter the information:

	M	N	O	P	Q	R
1	NO	NO	YES	YES	NO	NO
2						YES
3	NO	YES	NO	NO	NO	NO
4						
5						

Is there anything more to be learned? Yes. If each of the 6 performers is to appear 3 times, we need a total of 6 x 3, or 18, appearances. Thus far, we have 2 for the first performance, 4 for the second, and 1 for the third, for a total of 7. We need 11 more appearances. Skits 4 and 5 have spaces for 12 performers (6 for each performance), but we are told that fewer people are used in the fifth than in the fourth skit. So skit 5 can use a maximum of 5 people, and 4 can use a maximum of 6 people. But that is exactly the number we need, 11. So all 6 performers must appear in skit 4, and 5 out of 6 in skit 5. Thus, the distribution is 2, 4, 1, 6, and 5, for a total of 18. Now, we can enter further information on our matrix:

	M	N	O	P	Q	R	
1	NO	NO	YES	YES	NO	NO	2
2						YES	4
3	NO	YES	NO	NO	NO	NO	1
4	YES	YES	YES	YES	YES	YES	6
5							5

Total 18

But we also know that each performer must appear three times, so we deduce:

	M	N	O	P	Q	R	
1	NO	NO	YES	YES	NO	NO	2
2	YES				YES	YES	4
3	NO	YES	NO	NO	NO	NO	1
4	YES	YES	YES	YES	YES	YES	6
5	YES				YES	YES	5
	3	3	3	3	3	3	18

Totals

For example, if M does not appear in skits 1 and 3, we know M must appear in 2, 4, and 5.

Answering the Questions

18. **(E)** We were able to deduce this by reflecting on the overall distributional requirements. Our chart shows that (A) and (B) are possibly, though not necessarily, true. (C) and (D) are shown to be false by our chart.

19. **(B)** The chart confirms that (B) is the correct answer, for M and R both appear in skits 2, 4, and 5. (C) is perhaps, though not necessarily, true, as shown by the chart. (A), (D), and (E) are shown by the chart to be false.

20. **(B)** Since we need a total of five performers in the fifth skit (two in addition to M, Q, and R), at least one member of the pair, P and O, must be used. As for (A), it is possible that N will be used and therefore neither P nor O. As for (C) and (D), the same reasoning shows that they are possible. Finally, (E) is possible if N appears in the second skit rather than in the fifth.

21. **(A)** For this question, we add the additional information to our matrix:

	M	N	O	P	Q	R	
1	NO	NO	YES	YES	NO	NO	2
2	YES	(YES)	(NO)	(NO)	YES	YES	4
3	NO	YES	NO	NO	NO	NO	1
4	YES	YES	YES	YES	YES	YES	6
5	YES	(NO)	(YES)	(YES)	YES	YES	5
	3	3	3	3	3	3	18

22. **(A)** (C) and (D) are wrong because they extrapolate without sufficient information. (E) contradicts the last given statement and so cannot be a conclusion of it. That would be like trying to infer "all men are mortal" from the premise that "no men are mortal." (B) commits an error by moving from "all S are P" to "all P are S." Just because all racing engines have SFI does not mean that all SFIs are in racing engines. Some may be found in tractors and heavy-duty machinery.

23. **(D)** Peter's surprise is over the fact that an important executive of a company would use a competitor's product, hence (D). (B) is wrong because Peter's surprise is not due to Mary's being unimportant; rather, he knows Mary is important, and that is the reason for his surprise. (E) is irrelevant to the exchange, for Peter imagines that, regardless of taste, Mary ought to consume the product she is responsible in part for producing. The same reasoning can be applied to (C). Finally, (A) is a distraction.

24. **(A)** The author's point depends upon the assumption that children see both animated features and "spaghetti Westerns." Obviously, if that assumption is untrue, the author cannot claim that the conclusion follows. It may be true that children get a distorted picture of the world from other causes, but the author claims only that the distorted view comes from their seeing animated features and "spaghetti Westerns." Presumably, the two different treatments cause the inversion of values. The intention of the producers in making the films is irrelevant since an action may have an effect not intended by the actor. Hence, (B) would not touch

the author's point. Further, that there are other sources of information that present a proper view of the world does not prove that the problem cited by the author does not produce an inverted view of the world. So (C) would not weaken his point. (D) reminds us of the importance of careful reading. You might want to interpret (D) to say the same thing as (A), but then you'd have to choose (A), because it makes the telling point more forcefully and directly. Finally, (E) is irrelevant to the author's conclusion: children learn to value animals more than people. Of course, as an exercise in debate, you might argue that this is a good thing, but that is not what (E) says.

25. **(B)** One way of "making more money" other than raising the price of a product is to lower the size or quality of the product. This is what Vendo must have done. By doing so, Vendo accomplished the equivalent of a price increase without actually raising the price. (C) contradicts the paragraph that states that Vendo did not violate the letter of the instructions—that is, the literal meaning—though it did violate the intention. (D) also contradicts the paragraph. Had Vendo forfeited the franchise, that would have been within the letter of the "either-or" wording of the instructions. (A) and (E) require much speculation beyond the information given, and you should not indulge in imaginative thinking when there is an obvious answer such as (B) available.

QUESTIONS 26-32

Arranging the Information

The key to this set is organizing the information in such a way that it is usable. We recommend a table:

	Marlowe	Joyce	Shakespeare	Keats	Chaucer
J	YES	YES			
K			YES	YES	
L	YES				YES
M	YES		YES	YES	
N		YES		YES	YES
O	YES	YES	YES		

If you study the table, you will see that only one teacher can be chosen from the group J, K, and L. Two teachers must be chosen from the group M, N, and O. The reason for this is that the only distribution that will give the Executive Officer exactly eight assignments is to have three courses taught by each of two faculty members and two courses by a third, 3 + 3 + 2 = 8. This is an important insight that should have occurred to you.

Further study would also show that there is a limited number of permissible combinations. Theoretically, there are nine possibilities:

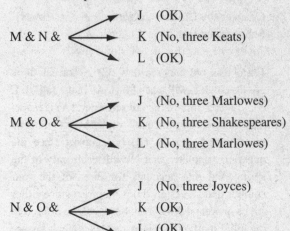

To see this without careful study, however, requires not only powerful insight but considerable luck as well. In any event, it is not necessary to perceive this to answer the questions, for the questions will guide you to the conclusion that some groupings are not permissible.

Having done this preliminary work, we can use our chart of possibilities in explaining the answers to the individual questions.

Answering the Questions

26. **(E)** (A) is incorrect because it generates a total of only seven courses. (B), (C), and (D) are shown to be incorrect by our chart. (E) is the only acceptable combination listed.

27. **(C)** Using the information provided in the question stem, we know:

Spring
Joyce
Keats
Chaucer } (by N)

and that L will teach Marlowe and Chaucer. Then our chart informs us that there are two teachers who can teach with L and N: O or M. Thus, the additional courses will be Marlowe, Joyce, and Shakespeare (by O) or Marlowe, Keats, and Shakespeare (by M). We know, therefore, that both Marlowe and Shakespeare will be offered during the year since both O and M offer those courses. This means Marlowe must be offered in both the fall and the spring, and further that L will teach Chaucer in the fall.

Fall	Spring	
Marlowe (by ?)	Joyce	
Chaucer (by L)	Keats	} (by N)
Shakespeare (by ?)	Chaucer	
Joyce or Keats (by ?)	Marlowe (by ?)	

From this we can see that (C) is correct. It is possible that L will teach Marlowe in the fall, so L could teach only in the fall semester. (A) is incorrect as shown by our chart—either M or O must be hired with L and N. (B) is incorrect since the question stipulates that N will teach only in the spring and that accounts for three of the four courses that semester. (D) is incorrect since either Joyce or Keats, though not both, will be offered in the fall. Finally, (E) is incorrect since Shakespeare can be offered only in the fall.

28. **(E)** See the outline of possibilities in the overview.

29. **(E)** Our chart shows that if M and N are hired, either J or L can be hired. (A) and (C), therefore, are possibly, though not necessarily, true.

Hence, they are both incorrect answers. (B) must also be incorrect as shown by the chart. Hiring M and N, and separating their courses by semester, we have

Semester—M	Semester—N
Marlowe	Joyce
Shakespeare	Keats
Keats	Chaucer

The remaining two courses will be Marlowe and Joyce (by J) or Marlowe and Chaucer (by L). Since both J and L teach Marlowe, that will give a total of two Marlowe courses, so one of them must be offered in the spring. (D) is possibly true, provided that M teaches that course in the fall, but (D) is not necessarily true.

30. **(D)** If K and N are hired, O must also be hired. This gives us a course mix of Shakespeare and Keats (by K); Joyce, Keats, and Chaucer (by N); and Marlowe, Joyce, and Shakespeare (by O). We have two courses on Shakespeare, two on Keats, and two on Joyce. So those three courses must be offered both semesters plus a course on Marlowe one semester and one on Chaucer the other.

31. **(E)** If L is hired to teach only in the fall, this means Marlowe and Chaucer will be offered then. With L, it is possible to hire either M and N or N and O. We must hire N, and this means Joyce, Keats, and Chaucer will be taught. Since both L and N offer Chaucer, N must teach Chaucer in the spring. As for (D), this is possible but is necessarily true only if O, rather than M, is hired. Since that is not a logically necessary choice, (D) is merely possible.

32. **(E)** For this question we are told which teachers will be hired. So the course mix will be

Fall	
Joyce	
Keats	} (by N)
Chaucer	

with courses on Marlowe, Joyce, and Shakespeare (by O) and on Shakespeare and Keats (by K). Observing the restriction that the same courses may not be offered in a single semester, we have

Fall		Spring
Joyce		Joyce (by O)
Keats	} (by N)	Shakespeare (by ?)
Chaucer		Marlowe (by O)
Shakespeare (by ?)		Keats (by K)

We can see that (A), (B), (C), and (D) are all logically necessary. (E) is our exception since Chaucer is taught only in the fall.

33. **(E)** Now, it must be admitted that a liar can abuse just about any word in the English language, and so it is true that each of the five answer choices is *conceivably* correct. But it is important to keep in mind that you are looking for the BEST answer, which will be the one word which, more than all the others, is likely to be abused. As for (A), while there may be different ways of doing a random selection, we should be able to decide whether a sample was, in fact, selected fairly. Although the ad may be lying about the selection of participants in the study, we should be able to determine whether they are lying. In other words, though they may not have selected the sample randomly, they cannot escape by saying, "Oh, by

random we meant anyone who liked the Goblin." The same is true of (C), "first." That is a fairly clear term. You add up the answers you got, and one will be at the top of the list. The same is true of (D)—a "response" is an answer. Now, (B) is open to manipulation. By asking our question correctly, that is, by finagling a bit with what we mean by handling, we can influence the answers we get. For example, compare: "Did you find the Goblin handled well?" "Did you find the Goblin had a nice steering wheel?" "Did you find the wheel was easy to turn?" We could keep it up until we found a question that worked out to give a set of "responses" from "randomly" selected drivers who would rank the Goblin "first." Now, if the one category itself is susceptible to manipulation, imagine how much easier it will be to manipulate a "composite" category. We have only to take those individual categories in which the Goblin scored well, construct from them a "composite" category, and announce the Goblin "first" in the overall category. There is also the question of how the composite was constructed, weighted, added, averaged, etc.

34. **(A)** If (2) is true, then both independent clauses of (2) must be true. This is because a sentence that has the form "P and Q" (Eddie is tall and John is short) can be true only if both subparts are true. If either is false (Eddie is not tall or John is not short) or if both are false, then the entire sentence makes a false claim. If the second clause of (2) is true, then (1) must also be true, for (1) is actually equivalent to the second clause in (2). That is, if "P and Q" is true, then Q must itself be true. On this basis, (B) and (C) can be seen to be incorrect. (D) is wrong, for we can actually define the interrelationship of (1) and (2) as a matter of logic: We do not have to have recourse to a probabilistic statement. (E) is incorrect since a statement of the form "P and Q" might be false and Q could still be true—if P is false, "P and Q" is false even though Q is true.

35. **(D)** The author's recommendation that public schools should have computerized reading programs depends upon the correctness of her explanation of the present deficiency in reading skills in the public schools. Her contrast with private-school students shows that she thinks the deficiency can be attributed to the lack of such a program in the public schools. So one of the author's assumptions, which is what the question stem is asking about, is that the differential in reading skills is a result of the availability of a computerized program in the private-school system and the lack thereof in the public-school system. (E) is, of course, irrelevant to the question of reading skills. (C) tries to force the author to assume a greater burden than she has undertaken. The author claims that the reading skills of public-school children could be improved by a computerized reading program. She is not concerned with arguing the merits of having good reading skills. (A) and (B) are wrong for the same reason. The author's claim must be interpreted to mean "of children who are able to learn, all would benefit from a computerized reading program." When the author claims that "public-school children can be good readers," she is not implying that all children can learn to be good readers nor that all can learn to read equally well.

VERBAL SECTION

1. **(A)** The sentence starts with a thought-reverser, so we know that the correct choice will describe something unexpected given the amount of money invested. The second blank will be a logical continuation of the first blank as the verb *continues* indicates. (B), (C), and (E) can be eliminated immediately because they do not create meaningful phrases when substituted into the first blank. (A) and (D) are possibilities because a phone system can be both primitive and outdated. Next, we eliminate (D) because an outdated phone system would hardly elate those who depend on it. (A) creates a logical sentence. The system is primitive, despite the money spent on it, and it continues to inconvenience those who use it.

2. **(D)** This sentence starts with a thought-reverser, so we know that bats are going to be something that is the opposite of *aggressive* and *rabid*. The item is basically a vocabulary question. We can eliminate (A), (B), and (C) because they are not things one could say about bats and are not opposites of *aggressive* and *rabid*. We can also eliminate (E) because bats would probably not be described as *depraved*. (D), *innocuous*, which means "harmless," is the opposite of *rabid* and goes nicely with *shy*.

3. **(C)** In this sentence a thought-extender and a thought-reverser are the logical keys. The first

blank needs a word that continues the idea of "vagueness"; the second blank is *unlike* the first and must therefore be something close to an opposite. All of the choices make sense since they can all be used to describe images, but only one parallels *vague* and that is *obscure*. The second element, *concrete*, is an opposite of *obscure* and completes the sentence nicely. The second elements of (A), (B), (D), and (E) are not things that could be said of images and make no sense when substituted in the sentence.

4. **(C)** This is clearly a part-to-whole analogy. A CHAPTER is part of a NOVEL and a scene is part of a drama. Don't be deceived by the mention of other literary terms such as *poetry* and *prose* or by other words such as *fraction* and *portion*, which mean "part."

5. **(B)** This analogy is one of degree. To imply is to indicate indirectly; to AVER is to affirm with confidence. To *hint* is to suggest; to *proclaim* is to announce officially.

6. **(D)** This is an analogy based on sequence of events. After DETENTION one may be RELEASED, and after *induction* one may be *discharged*.

7. **(C)** This analogy is based on a defining characteristic. By definition, something that is PONDEROUS has a lot of WEIGHT, and something *gargantuan* is large or *sizable*.

8. **(E)** To *revere* is to regard with deep awe or respect. A straightforward opposite is *despise*.

9. **(B)** *Boorish* means "rude or ill-mannered." A precise opposite, then, is *well-mannered*.

10. **(C)** *Whimsical* means "fanciful or capricious"; therefore, *predictable* is a good antonym.

11. **(A)** *Nascent* means "coming into being" or "beginning to form." A clear opposite, then, is *fully developed*.

12. **(C)** This is a logical structure question that asks about the overall development of the selection. The main organizational principle of the passage is the comparison and contrast of art and knowledge. The author points to both similarities and differences between the two.

    (A) is incorrect. Though the author proposes a theory of the purpose of art, there is no refutation of anything in the passage. As for (B), the author

offers some general conclusions, but makes no generalizations based on examples. As for (D), though the passage can be viewed as an answer to the question "What is art for?" the author does not make question and answer the organizational principle of the selection. Finally, as for (E), the author states bold conclusions, but does not deduce or infer those conclusions from other premises or information.

13. **(B)** This is a specific detail question, so the correct answer will be explicitly stated in the selection. (B) is specifically stated. The author states that the knowledge of prior generations is preserved in speech. So knowledge is cumulative. Later, the author states that knowledge is self-correcting; that is, that errors are, during the passing of time, eliminated. So knowledge is also progressive.

    Since knowledge progresses, you can eliminate (C), (D), and (E). As for (A), though knowledge is evolutionary, it is art, not knowledge, that treats emotions.

14. **(D)** This is a specific detail question. The author specifically says that art is communication (like words), so (A) is mentioned. The author also states that art has the function of producing loftier emotions, so (B) and (E) are mentioned. And the author says that art renders the experience of previous generations accessible to the present, so (C) is mentioned. (D), however, is not said by the author to be true of art. In fact, in the last sentence, the author strongly implies that art can be bad as well as good.

15. **(E)** This analogy is based on the "sign of" relationship. To be FEBRILE is a sign of ILLNESS and to be *delusional* s a sign of *insanity*.

16. **(A)** This analogy is based on the "lack of" relationship. Lack of CONTACT is a defining characteristic of INCOMMUNICADO, and lack of *company* is a defining characteristic of *sequestered*.

17. **(A)** This analogy doesn't belong to any specific category, but you might create diagnostic sentences such as "EQUIVOCATION is ambiguous speech that hides MEANING" and "*Feint* is a deceptive act or sham that serves to hide *intention*." Do not be misled by *secrecy* and *stealth*, which are related to the key words and to each other.

18. **(A)** This is an application question. As we have noted before, application questions tend to be difficult because the correct answer can be understood as correct only in context. With a question such as this, the *most logical continuation* depends upon the choices available. Here the best answer is (A). The author concludes the discussion of the causes of our poor showing on the health status index by asserting that the best way to improve this showing is a general improvement in the quality of life. This is an intriguing suggestion, and an appropriate follow-up would be a list of proposals that might accomplish this. As for (B), this could be part of such a discussion, but a listing of the most common causes of death would not, in and of itself, represent an extension of the development of the argument. (C), too, has some merit. The author might want to talk about the causes of poverty as a way of learning how to improve the quality of life by eliminating the causes of poverty. But this argument actually cuts in favor of (A), for the justification for (C) then depends on (A)—that is, it depends on the assumption that the author should discuss the idea raised in (A). (D) is incorrect because the author specifically states in his closing remarks that redistribution of medical resources is not a high priority. (E) can be eliminated on the same ground.

19. **(D)** This is an explicit idea question, and we find mention of (A), (B), (C), and (E) in the second paragraph. (D), too, is mentioned, but (D) is not a factor "affecting the health of the population." (D) is a measure of, or an effect of, the health of the population, not a factor causing it.

20. **(B)** This is a main idea question. (A) can be eliminated because the author actually minimizes the importance of medical care as a factor affecting the health of a population. (C) can be eliminated because this is not the author's objective. To be sure, an individual may use information supplied in the passage to improve in some way his or her health, but that is not why the author wrote the passage. (D) is incorrect because this is a small part of the argument, a part that is used to advance the major objective outlined in (B). Finally, (E) is incorrect since the author leaves us with a pregnant suggestion but no specific recommendations. (B), however, describes the development of the passage. The author wishes to explain the causes of the poor health status of the

U.S. It is not, he argues, lack of medical care or even poor distribution of medical care, hypotheses that, we can infer from the text, are often proposed. He then goes on to give two alternative explanations: affluence and poverty.

21. **(C)** This is an application question. (C) is strongly supported by the text. In paragraph 3, the author specifically states that we have the highest per capita expenditure for medical care in the world. Yet, as he notes in the first paragraph, we rank rather low in terms of health. (A) is not supported by the arguments given in the passage. Though medical care may not be the most important determinant of health, the author never suggests that expenditure is not correlated with overall availability. (B) is incorrect and specifically contradicted by the second paragraph, where the author states that genetic problems may be covered over by medical care. (D) is incorrect since the author minimizes the importance of technology in improving health. Finally, (E) is simply not supported by any data or argument given in the passage.

22. **(E)** This is a logical detail question. The author refers to excess consumption to illustrate the way in which affluence, one of his two hypotheses, could undermine an individual's health. As for (A), while it is true that such problems may not be susceptible to medical treatment, the author does not introduce them to prove that. He introduces them at the particular point in the argument to prove that affluence can undermine health. (B) is incorrect for a similar reason. The author does not introduce the examples to prove that drinking and smoking are unhealthful activities. He presupposes his readers know that already. Then, on the assumption that the reader already believes that, the author can say, "See, affluence causes smoking and drinking-which we all know to be bad." (C) must fail for the same reason. Finally (D) is incorrect since this is not the reason for introducing the examples. Although the author does argue that medical care and health are not as tightly linked as some people might think, this is not the point he is working on when he introduces smoking and drinking. With a logical detail question of this sort, we must be careful to select an answer that explains why the author makes the move he does at the particular juncture in the argument. Neither general reference to the

overall idea of the passage (e.g., to prove his main point) nor a reference to a collateral argument will turn the trick.

23. **(A)** The answer to the question posed in answer choice (A) is explicitly provided in the second paragraph: environment. As for (B), though some information is given about the health status of the U.S., no other country is mentioned by name. As for (C), though some statistics are given about life expectancies in the U.S., no comparison of male and female life expectancies is given. As for (D), though genetic factors are mentioned generally in paragraph 2, no such factors are ever specified. Finally, the author offers no recommendations, so (E) must be incorrect.

24. **(D)** To be *inured* is to become accustomed to something painful. *Sensitive* is an opposite.

25. **(A)** Since *irascible* means "irritable" or easily provoked to anger," *even-tempered* is a perfect antonym.

26. **(C)** *Exonerate* means "to relieve of blame" or "to clear of guilt." *Accuse* is the best opposite.

27. **(B)** *Alacrity* is a cheerful willingness to act or serve, so *reluctance* is a good opposite.

28. **(B)** This sentence has a thought-reverser and a thought-extender as its logical structure. The sentence says that the lawyer argues only what is central, eliminating something. Logically, what is eliminated is what is not central, so you should look for a word that means not central. (B) is the best answer. A lawyer would seek to eliminate *extraneous* (irrelevant) information or anything that might *jeopardize* (endanger) the client.

29. **(D)** This sentence contains a thought-reverser and a thought-extender. The thought-reverser is signaled by the phrase *even though*. Since people persist, *even though* the government does something, the government must be trying to stop the belief in extraterrestrial life. The second blank requires a thought-extender, something that ex-

tends the idea of personal, and reverses the idea of *godless*. Although (A) might seem correct at first glance, since *decry* means "to condemn," the second word of the pair disqualifies it as the correct choice. To say that people need a personal sense of morbidity makes little sense. (B) is not correct because it fails to reverse the idea that people persist. To say that they persist even though the government endorses their actions is not logical. (C) is not correct for the same reason. If the government creates all such theories, it would not be surprising for people to believe in them. (E) appears to be a possibility since *debunk* has the right negative overtones and it explains why the persistent belief is surprising. The second word of (E), however, does not create a logical thought. People would not need a personal sense of alienation in a godless universe—in fact, that is what this sentence suggests they are trying to avoid.

30. **(B)** This sentence contains a thought-reverser and a thought-extender. The *in fact* in the second part of the sentence is the clue that tells you that the theory of the breakup of the continents is somehow changed. We are therefore looking for the opposite of *occurring in stages* or something close to it. The second blank requires an extension of that idea. (A) is not correct because although *refining* suggests a change in the theory, the second word, *blatantly*, does not reverse the idea of occurring in stages. (C) certainly suggests a strong reversal of the theory, but the second word is practically synonymous with *in stages*. (D) appears plausible, since the idea of forging a theory might suggest something new, but the second word does not make a meaningful sentence. (E) is wrong because it does not reverse the theory, but rather *supports* it; and the idea that the breakup was *haphazard* does not reverse the idea of *gradual*. (B) is correct because the theory is reshaped and the word *simultaneously* reverses the idea that the continents broke up in stages.

Practice Examination 3

Answer Sheet

VERBAL SECTION

1. Ⓐ Ⓑ Ⓒ Ⓓ Ⓔ   7. Ⓐ Ⓑ Ⓒ Ⓓ Ⓔ   13. Ⓐ Ⓑ Ⓒ Ⓓ Ⓔ   19. Ⓐ Ⓑ Ⓒ Ⓓ Ⓔ   25. Ⓐ Ⓑ Ⓒ Ⓓ Ⓔ
2. Ⓐ Ⓑ Ⓒ Ⓓ Ⓔ   8. Ⓐ Ⓑ Ⓒ Ⓓ Ⓔ   14. Ⓐ Ⓑ Ⓒ Ⓓ Ⓔ   20. Ⓐ Ⓑ Ⓒ Ⓓ Ⓔ   26. Ⓐ Ⓑ Ⓒ Ⓓ Ⓔ
3. Ⓐ Ⓑ Ⓒ Ⓓ Ⓔ   9. Ⓐ Ⓑ Ⓒ Ⓓ Ⓔ   15. Ⓐ Ⓑ Ⓒ Ⓓ Ⓔ   21. Ⓐ Ⓑ Ⓒ Ⓓ Ⓔ   27. Ⓐ Ⓑ Ⓒ Ⓓ Ⓔ
4. Ⓐ Ⓑ Ⓒ Ⓓ Ⓔ   10. Ⓐ Ⓑ Ⓒ Ⓓ Ⓔ   16. Ⓐ Ⓑ Ⓒ Ⓓ Ⓔ   22. Ⓐ Ⓑ Ⓒ Ⓓ Ⓔ   28. Ⓐ Ⓑ Ⓒ Ⓓ Ⓔ
5. Ⓐ Ⓑ Ⓒ Ⓓ Ⓔ   11. Ⓐ Ⓑ Ⓒ Ⓓ Ⓔ   17. Ⓐ Ⓑ Ⓒ Ⓓ Ⓔ   23. Ⓐ Ⓑ Ⓒ Ⓓ Ⓔ   29. Ⓐ Ⓑ Ⓒ Ⓓ Ⓔ
6. Ⓐ Ⓑ Ⓒ Ⓓ Ⓔ   12. Ⓐ Ⓑ Ⓒ Ⓓ Ⓔ   18. Ⓐ Ⓑ Ⓒ Ⓓ Ⓔ   24. Ⓐ Ⓑ Ⓒ Ⓓ Ⓔ   30. Ⓐ Ⓑ Ⓒ Ⓓ Ⓔ

MATH SECTION

1. Ⓐ Ⓑ Ⓒ Ⓓ Ⓔ   7. Ⓐ Ⓑ Ⓒ Ⓓ Ⓔ   13. Ⓐ Ⓑ Ⓒ Ⓓ Ⓔ   19. Ⓐ Ⓑ Ⓒ Ⓓ Ⓔ   25. Ⓐ Ⓑ Ⓒ Ⓓ Ⓔ
2. Ⓐ Ⓑ Ⓒ Ⓓ Ⓔ   8. Ⓐ Ⓑ Ⓒ Ⓓ Ⓔ   14. Ⓐ Ⓑ Ⓒ Ⓓ Ⓔ   20. Ⓐ Ⓑ Ⓒ Ⓓ Ⓔ   26. Ⓐ Ⓑ Ⓒ Ⓓ Ⓔ
3. Ⓐ Ⓑ Ⓒ Ⓓ Ⓔ   9. Ⓐ Ⓑ Ⓒ Ⓓ Ⓔ   15. Ⓐ Ⓑ Ⓒ Ⓓ Ⓔ   21. Ⓐ Ⓑ Ⓒ Ⓓ Ⓔ   27. Ⓐ Ⓑ Ⓒ Ⓓ Ⓔ
4. Ⓐ Ⓑ Ⓒ Ⓓ Ⓔ   10. Ⓐ Ⓑ Ⓒ Ⓓ Ⓔ   16. Ⓐ Ⓑ Ⓒ Ⓓ Ⓔ   22. Ⓐ Ⓑ Ⓒ Ⓓ Ⓔ   28. Ⓐ Ⓑ Ⓒ Ⓓ Ⓔ
5. Ⓐ Ⓑ Ⓒ Ⓓ Ⓔ   11. Ⓐ Ⓑ Ⓒ Ⓓ Ⓔ   17. Ⓐ Ⓑ Ⓒ Ⓓ Ⓔ   23. Ⓐ Ⓑ Ⓒ Ⓓ Ⓔ
6. Ⓐ Ⓑ Ⓒ Ⓓ Ⓔ   12. Ⓐ Ⓑ Ⓒ Ⓓ Ⓔ   18. Ⓐ Ⓑ Ⓒ Ⓓ Ⓔ   24. Ⓐ Ⓑ Ⓒ Ⓓ Ⓔ

ANALYTICAL SECTION

1. Ⓐ Ⓑ Ⓒ Ⓓ Ⓔ   8. Ⓐ Ⓑ Ⓒ Ⓓ Ⓔ   15. Ⓐ Ⓑ Ⓒ Ⓓ Ⓔ   22. Ⓐ Ⓑ Ⓒ Ⓓ Ⓔ   29. Ⓐ Ⓑ Ⓒ Ⓓ Ⓔ
2. Ⓐ Ⓑ Ⓒ Ⓓ Ⓔ   9. Ⓐ Ⓑ Ⓒ Ⓓ Ⓔ   16. Ⓐ Ⓑ Ⓒ Ⓓ Ⓔ   23. Ⓐ Ⓑ Ⓒ Ⓓ Ⓔ   30. Ⓐ Ⓑ Ⓒ Ⓓ Ⓔ
3. Ⓐ Ⓑ Ⓒ Ⓓ Ⓔ   10. Ⓐ Ⓑ Ⓒ Ⓓ Ⓔ   17. Ⓐ Ⓑ Ⓒ Ⓓ Ⓔ   24. Ⓐ Ⓑ Ⓒ Ⓓ Ⓔ   31. Ⓐ Ⓑ Ⓒ Ⓓ Ⓔ
4. Ⓐ Ⓑ Ⓒ Ⓓ Ⓔ   11. Ⓐ Ⓑ Ⓒ Ⓓ Ⓔ   18. Ⓐ Ⓑ Ⓒ Ⓓ Ⓔ   25. Ⓐ Ⓑ Ⓒ Ⓓ Ⓔ   32. Ⓐ Ⓑ Ⓒ Ⓓ Ⓔ
5. Ⓐ Ⓑ Ⓒ Ⓓ Ⓔ   12. Ⓐ Ⓑ Ⓒ Ⓓ Ⓔ   19. Ⓐ Ⓑ Ⓒ Ⓓ Ⓔ   26. Ⓐ Ⓑ Ⓒ Ⓓ Ⓔ   33. Ⓐ Ⓑ Ⓒ Ⓓ Ⓔ
6. Ⓐ Ⓑ Ⓒ Ⓓ Ⓔ   13. Ⓐ Ⓑ Ⓒ Ⓓ Ⓔ   20. Ⓐ Ⓑ Ⓒ Ⓓ Ⓔ   27. Ⓐ Ⓑ Ⓒ Ⓓ Ⓔ   34. Ⓐ Ⓑ Ⓒ Ⓓ Ⓔ
7. Ⓐ Ⓑ Ⓒ Ⓓ Ⓔ   14. Ⓐ Ⓑ Ⓒ Ⓓ Ⓔ   21. Ⓐ Ⓑ Ⓒ Ⓓ Ⓔ   28. Ⓐ Ⓑ Ⓒ Ⓓ Ⓔ   35. Ⓐ Ⓑ Ⓒ Ⓓ Ⓔ

Practice Examination 3

Verbal Section

30 QUESTIONS • TIME—30 MINUTES

1. MUTINOUS:
    (A) routine
    (B) clever
    (C) obedient
    (D) helpful
    (E) pitiful

2. TEMERITY:
    (A) fortitude
    (B) capacity
    (C) interest
    (D) caution
    (E) relevance

3. TRACTABLE:
    (A) incoherent
    (B) advisable
    (C) simplistic
    (D) influential
    (E) uncooperative

4. INSOUCIANT:
    (A) amiable
    (B) fretful
    (C) swift
    (D) inferior
    (E) formidable

5. Because he was —— and the life of the party, his friends thought that he was happy; but his wife was —— and shy and was thought to be unhappy.
    (A) melancholy..sympathetic
    (B) philanthrophic..conciliatory
    (C) vitriolic..sophomoric
    (D) garrulous..taciturn
    (E) inimical..gregarious

6. His offhand, rather —— remarks —— a character that was really rather serious and not at all superficial.
    (A) flippant..masked
    (B) pernicious..betrayed
    (C) bellicose..belied
    (D) controversial..revealed
    (E) shallow..enlivened

7. Although the faculty did not always agree with the chairperson of the department, they —— her ideas, mostly in —— her seniority and out of respect for her previous achievements.
    (A) scoffed at..fear of
    (B) harbored..defense of
    (C) implemented..deference to
    (D) marveled at..lieu of
    (E) ignored..honor of

335

GO ON TO THE NEXT PAGE

In the art of the Middle Ages, we never encounter the personality of the artist as an individual; rather, it is diffused through the artistic genius of centuries embodied in the rules of religious art. Art of the Middle Ages
(5) is a sacred script, the symbols and meanings of which were well settled. The circular halo placed vertically behind the head signifies sainthood, while the halo impressed with a cross signifies divinity. By bare feet, we recognize God, the angels, Jesus Christ and the
(10) apostles, but for an artist to have depicted the Virgin Mary with bare feet would have been tantamount to heresy. Several concentric, wavy lines represent the sky, while parallel lines represent water or the sea. A tree, which is to say a single stalk with two or three
(15) stylized leaves, informs us that the scene is laid on earth. A tower with a window indicates a village; and should an angel be watching from the battlements, that city is thereby identified as Jerusalem. Saint Peter is always depicted with curly hair, a short beard and a tonsure,
(20) while Saint Paul always has a bald head and a long beard.

Through this system, even the most mediocre talent was elevated by the genius of the centuries. The artists of the early Renaissance broke with tradition at their
(25) own peril. When they are not outstanding, they are scarcely able to avoid insignificance and banality in their religious works; and even when they are great, they are no more than the equals of the old masters who passively followed the sacred rules.

8. The primary purpose of the passage is to

   (A) theorize about the immediate influences on art of the Middle Ages

   (B) explain why artists of the Middle Ages followed the rules of a sacred script

   (C) discuss some of the important features of art of the Middle Ages

   (D) contrast the art of the Middle Ages with that of the Renaissance

   (E) explain why the Middle Ages had a passion for religious art

9. All of the following are mentioned in the passage as elements of the sacred script EXCEPT

   (A) abstract symbols such as lines to represent physical features

   (B) symbols such as halos and crosses

   (C) clothing used to characterize individuals

   (D) symmetrical juxtaposition of figures

   (E) use of figures to identify locations

10. The passage would most likely be found in a

    (A) sociological analysis of the Middle Ages

    (B) treatise on the influence of the Church in the Middle Ages

    (C) scholarly analysis of art in the Middle Ages

    (D) preface to a biography of a Renaissance artist

    (E) pamphlet discussing religious beliefs

11. By the phrase "diffused through the artistic genius of centuries," the author most likely means

    (A) the individual artists of the Middle Ages did not have serious talent

    (B) great works of art from the Middle Ages have survived until now

    (C) an artist who faithfully followed the rules of religious art was not recognized during his lifetime

    (D) the rules of religious art, developed over time, left little freedom for the artist

    (E) religious art has greater value than the secular art of the Renaissance

12. WEB : ENTANGLE ::

(A) spider : spin

(B) trap : ensnare

(C) treason : betray

(D) ransom : kidnap

(E) grid : delineate

13. LETHARGY : ENERGY ::

(A) appetite : hunger

(B) redemption : sacrament

(C) sorrow : pity

(D) merit : remuneration

(E) apathy : interest

14. THWART : ACHIEVE ::

(A) retain : submit

(B) couch : conceal

(C) silence : speak

(D) pretend : inherit

(E) permeate : infiltrate

15. APOCRYPHAL : GENUINE ::

(A) spurious : authentic

(B) labored : relieved

(C) fragmented : riddled

(D) enigmatic : rambunctious

(E) credulous : flagrant

16. BALEFUL : EVIL ::

(A) fulsome : refinement

(B) disjointed : compatibility

(C) mandatory : requirement

(D) literacy : obstreperousness

(E) dogmatic : hostility

Our current system of unemployment compensation has increased nearly all sources of adult unemployment: seasonal and cyclical variations in the demand for labor, weak labor force attachment, and unnecessarily long
(5) durations of unemployment. First, for those who are already unemployed, the system greatly reduces the cost of extending the period of unemployment. Second, for all types of unsteady work—seasonal, cyclical and casual—it raises the net wage to the employee, relative
(10) to the cost of the employer.

As for the first, consider a worker who earns $500 per month or $6,000 per year if she experiences no unemployment. If she is unemployed for one month, she loses $500 in gross earnings but only $116 in net income.
(15) How does this occur? A reduction of $500 in annual earnings reduces her federal, payroll and state tax liability by $134. Unemployment compensation consists of 50 percent of her wage or $250. Her net income therefore falls from $366 if she is employed, to $250 paid as
(20) unemployment compensation. Moreover, part of the higher income from employment is offset by the cost of transportation to work and other expenses associated with employment; and in some industries, the cost of unemployment is reduced further or even made nega-
(25) tive by the supplementary unemployment benefits paid by employers under collective bargaining agreements. The overall effect is to increase the duration of a typical spell of unemployment and to increase the frequency with which individuals lose jobs and become
(30) unemployed.

The more general effect of unemployment compensation is to increase the seasonal and cyclical fluctuations in the demand for labor and the relative number of short-lived casual jobs. A worker who accepts such
(35) work knows she will be laid off when the season ends. If there were no unemployment compensation, workers could be induced to accept such unstable jobs only if the wage rate were sufficiently higher in those jobs than in the more stable alternative. The higher cost of labor,
(40) then, would induce employers to reduce the instability of employment by smoothing production through increased variation in inventories and delivery lags, by additional development of off-season work and by the

GO ON TO THE NEXT PAGE

introduction of new production techniques, e.g., new
(45) methods of outdoor work in bad weather.

Employers contribute to the state unemployment
compensation fund on the basis of the unemployment
experience of their own previous employees. Within
limits, the more benefits that those former employees
(50) draw, the higher is the employer's tax rate. The theory
of experience rating is clear. If an employer paid the full
cost of the unemployment benefits that his former
employees received, unemployment compensation
would provide no incentive to an excess use of unstable
(55) employment. In practice, however, experience rating is
limited by a maximum rate of employer contribution.
For any firm which pays the maximum rate, there is no
cost for additional unemployment and no gain from a
small reduction in unemployment.

(60) The challenge at this time is to restructure the unemployment system in a way that strengthens its good
features while reducing the harmful disincentive effects. Some gains can be achieved by removing the
ceiling on the employer's rate of contribution and by
(65) lowering the minimum rate to zero. Employers would
then pay the full price of unemployment insurance
benefits and this would encourage employers to stabi-
lize employment and production. Further improvement
could be achieved if unemployment insurance benefits
(70) were taxed in the same way as other earnings. This
would eliminate the anomalous situations in which a
worker's net income is actually reduced when he returns
to work.

17. The author's primary concern is to

(A) defend the system of unemployment
compensation against criticism

(B) advocate expanding the benefits and scope
of coverage of unemployment compensation

(C) point to weaknesses inherent in government programs that subsidize individuals

(D) suggest reforms to eliminate inefficiencies
in unemployment compensation

(E) propose methods of increasing the effectiveness of government programs to reduce
unemployment

18. The author cites the example of a worker earning
$500 per month in order to

(A) show the disincentive created by unemployment compensation for that worker to
return to work

(B) demonstrate that employers do not bear the
full cost of worker compensation

(C) prove that unemployed workers would not
be able to survive without unemployment
compensation

(D) explain why employers prefer to hire
seasonal workers instead of permanent
workers for short-term jobs

(E) condemn workers who prefer to live on
unemployment compensation to taking a
job

19. The author recommends which of the following
changes be made to the unemployment compensation system?

(A) Eliminating taxes on benefits paid to
workers

(B) Shortening the time during which a worker
can draw benefits

(C) Removing any cap on the maximum rate of
employer contribution

(D) Providing workers with job retraining as a
condition of benefits

(E) Requiring unemployed workers to accept
public works positions

20. The author mentions all of the following as ways
by which employers might reduce seasonal and
cyclical unemployment EXCEPT

(A) developing new techniques of production
not affected by weather

(B) slowing delivery schedules to provide
work during slow seasons

(C) adopting a system of supplementary
benefits for workers laid off in slow
periods

(D) manipulating inventory supplies to require year-round rather than short-term employment

(E) finding new jobs to be done by workers during the off-season

21. With which of the following statements about experience rating would the author most likely agree?

(A) Experience rating is theoretically sound but its effectiveness in practice is undermined by maximum contribution ceilings.

(B) Experience rating is an inefficient method of computing employer contribution because an employer has no control over the length of an employee's unemployment.

(C) Experience rating is theoretically invalid and should be replaced by a system in which the employee contributes the full amount of benefits he will later receive.

(D) Experience rating is basically fair, but its performance could be improved by requiring large firms to pay more than small firms.

(E) Experience rating requires an employer to pay a contribution that is completely unrelated to the amount his employees draw in unemployment compensation benefits.

Directions: Each of the following questions consists of a word printed in capital letters, followed by five words or phrases. Choose the word or phrase that is most nearly opposite in meaning to the word in capital letters. Be sure to consider all the choices before deciding which one is best.

22. WATERFALL : CASCADE ::

(A) snow : freeze

(B) missile : launch

(C) tree : exfoliate

(D) wave : undulate

(E) monarch : reign

23. INFLATE : MAGNITUDE ::

(A) measure : weight

(B) extend : duration

(C) magnify : coin

(D) limit : speed

(E) legislate : crime

24. MOCK : DERISION ::

(A) despise : contempt

(B) reject : account

(C) repair : corruption

(D) inspire : muse

(E) observe : refinement

Directions: Each of the questions below contains one or more blank spaces, each blank indicating an omitted word. Each sentence is followed by five (5) words or sets of words. Read and determine the general sense of each sentence. Then choose the word, or set of words that, when inserted in the sentence, best fits the meaning of the sentence.

25. Psychologists agree that human beings have a strong need to —— their time; having too much idle time can be as stressful as having none at all.

(A) threaten

(B) annihilate

(C) structure

(D) punctuate

(E) remand

26. While scientists continue to make advances in the field of ——, some members of the clergy continue to oppose the research, arguing that it is —— for human beings to tamper with life.

(A) psychology..imperative

(B) astronomy..fallacious

(C) genetics..immoral

(D) geology..erroneous

(E) botany..unethical

GO ON TO THE NEXT PAGE

27. Although for centuries literature was considered something that would instruct as well as entertain, the modern reader has little patience with —— works and seeks only to be ——.

    (A) epic..demoralized

    (B) didactic..distracted

    (C) bawdy..absorbed

    (D) superficial..enlightened

    (E) ambiguous..misled

Directions: Each of the following questions consists of a word printed in capital letters, followed by five words or phrases. Choose the word or phrase that is most nearly opposite in meaning to the word in capital letters. Be sure to consider all the choices before deciding which one is best.

28. DIFFIDENCE:

    (A) strong attraction

    (B) violent disagreement

    (C) haughty arrogance

    (D) grievous error

    (E) temporary suspension

29. SEDULOUS:

    (A) tangential

    (B) rampant

    (C) esoteric

    (D) morose

    (E) indolent

30. OBDURATE:

    (A) ambiguous

    (B) demoralized

    (C) vitriolic

    (D) malleable

    (E) inimitable

WARNING

IF YOU FINISHED THIS SECTION BEFORE TIME EXPIRED, GO IMMEDIATELY TO THE NEXT SECTION. YOU MAY NOT CONTINUE TO WORK ON THIS SECTION AFTER TIME HAS EXPIRED.

Math Section

28 QUESTIONS • TIME—45 MINUTES

Directions: For each of these questions, select the best of the answer choices given.

Numbers: All numbers used are real numbers.

Figures: Assume that the position of points, angles, regions, and so forth are in the order shown. Figures are assumed to lie in a plane unless otherwise indicated. Figures accompanying questions are intended to provide information you can use in answering the questions. However, unless a note states that a figure is drawn to scale, you should solve the problems by using your knowledge of mathematics and not by estimating sizes by sight or measurement.

Lines: Assume that lines shown as straight are indeed straight.

Directions: For each of the following questions two quantities are given, one in Column A and one in Column B. Compare the two quantities and choose

    A: if the quantity in Column A is the greater

    B: if the quantity in Column B is the greater

    C: if the two quantities are equal

    D: if the relationship cannot be determined from the information given.

Common Information: In any question, information applying to both columns is centered between the columns and above the quantities in columns A and B. Any symbol that appears in both columns represents the same idea or quantity in both columns.

Column A	Column B
1. The number of hours in 7 days	The number of days in 24 weeks
2. 35% of 60	60% of 35

Column A	Column B
PLAYER	AGE
Juanita	35
Brooke	28
Glenda	40
Marcia	22
Dwight	24
Tom	30

3.   Tom's age   Average (arithmetic mean) age of the six players

$$4 < m < 6$$
$$5 < n < 7$$

4. m n

A square region, P, and a rectangular region, Q, both have areas of 64.

5.   Length of a side of P Length of Q if its width is 4

Directions: For each of these questions, select the best of the answer choices given.

6. If $x = 3$ and $y = 2$, then $2x + 3y =$
(A) 5
(B) 10
(C) 12
(D) 14
(E) 15

7. If the profit on an item is $4 and the sum of the cost and the profit is $20, what is the cost of the item?
(A) $24
(B) $20
(C) $16
(D) $12
(E) Cannot be determined from the information given.

GO ON TO THE NEXT PAGE

8. In 1960, the number of students enrolled at a college was 500. In 1980, the number of students enrolled at the college was $2\frac{1}{2}$ times as great as that in 1960. What was the number of students enrolled at the college in 1980?

(A) 1,750

(B) 1,250

(C) 1,000

(D) 500

(E) 250

Directions: For each of the following questions two quantities are given, one in Column A and one in Column B. Compare the two quantities and choose

A: if the quantity in Column A is the greater

B: if the quantity in Column B is the greater

C: if the two quantities are equal

D: if the relationship cannot be determined from the information given.

Column A	Column B

$x > 0$

9. $3x^3$ $(3x)^3$

$x \cdot y = 1$
$x \neq 0, y \neq 0$

10. x y

---

11. The number of primes of which 11 is an integer multiple   The number of primes of which 13 is an integer multiple

---

x, y, and z are consecutive positive integers, not necessarily in that order, and x and z are odd

12. xy yz

Directions: For each of these questions, select the best of the answer choices given.

13. If n is an integer between 0 and 100, then any of the following could be $3n + 3$ EXCEPT

(A) 300

(B) 297

(C) 208

(D) 63

(E) 6

14. A figure that can be folded over along a straight line so that the result is two equal halves which are then lying on top of one another with no overlap is said to have a line of symmetry. Which of the following figures has only one line of symmetry?

(A) Square

(B) Circle

(C) Equilateral triangle

(D) Isosceles triangle

(E) Rectangle

Directions: For each of the following questions two quantities are given, one in Column A and one in Column B. Compare the two quantities and choose

    A: if the quantity in Column A is the greater

    B: if the quantity in Column B is the greater

    C: if the two quantities are equal

    D: if the relationship cannot be determined from the information given.

Directions: For each of the following questions two quantities are given, one in Column A and one in Column B. Compare the two quantities and choose

    A: if the quantity in Column A is the greater

    B: if the quantity in Column B is the greater

    C: if the two quantities are equal

    D: if the relationship cannot be determined from the information given.

Column A	**Column B**

AD is a transmitter tower held up by support wires AB and AC.

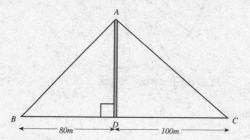

Column A	**Column B**

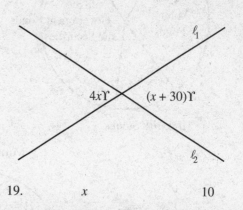

19. x 10

15.   Length of support wire AB Length of support wire AC

A family-size box of cereal contains 10 ounces more and costs 80¢ more than the regular size box of cereal.

16.   2,468 $8 + 6 \cdot 10 + 4 \cdot 10^2 + 2 \times 10^3$

20.   Cost per ounce of the cereal in the family-size box   8¢

$$a^2 = b$$
$$a > 0$$

17. $\dfrac{2a}{b}$ $a \cdot a$

21.   The number of different duos that can be formed from a group of 5 people   The number of different trios that can be formed from a group of 5 people

Directions: For each of these questions, select the best of the answer choices given.

18. A laborer is paid $8 per hour for an 8-hour day and $1\frac{1}{2}$ times that rate for each hour in excess of 8 hours in a single day. If the laborer received $80 for a single day's work, how long did he work on that day?

    (A) 6 hr. 40 min.

    (B) 9 hr. 20 min.

    (C) 9 hr. 30 min.

    (D) 9 hr. 40 min.

    (E) 10 hr.

GO ON TO THE NEXT PAGE

Directions: For each of these questions, select the best of the answer choices given.

Questions 22–25 are based on the following graphs.

INVESTMENT PORTFOLIO

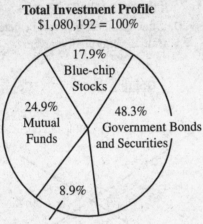

Total Investment Profile
$1,080,192 = 100%

17.9% Blue-chip Stocks
24.9% Mutual Funds
48.3% Government Bonds and Securities
8.9% High-risk Stocks

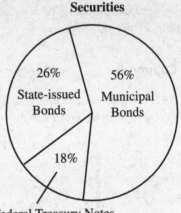

Government Bonds and Securities

26% State-issued Bonds
56% Municipal Bonds
18% Federal Treasury Notes

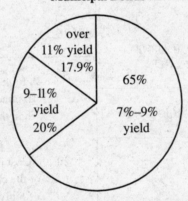

Municipal Bonds

over 11% yield 17.9%
9–11% yield 20%
65% 7%–9% yield

22. According to the graphs, approximately how much money belonging to the investment portfolio was invested in high-risk stocks?

(A) $95,000

(B) $89,000

(C) $50,000

(D) $42,000

(E) $36,000

23. Approximately how much money belonging to the investment portfolio was invested in state-issued bonds?

(A) $260,000

(B) $125,000

(C) $34,000

(D) $26,000

(E) $500

24. Which of the following was the greatest?

    (A) The amount of money invested in municipal bonds that yielded between 7% and 9%

    (B) The amount of money invested in municipal bonds that yielded over 9%

    (C) The amount of money invested in federal treasury notes

    (D) The amount of money invested in state-issued bonds

    (E) The amount of money invested in high-risk stocks

25. Which of the following earned the least amount of money for the investment portfolio?

    (A) Municipal bonds

    (B) State-issued bonds

    (C) Government bonds and securities

    (D) Mutual funds

    (E) Cannot be determined from the information given.

Directions: For each of these questions, select the best of the answer choices given.

26. A vertex of square *MNOP* is located at the center of circle *O*. If arc *NP* is 4 units long, then the perimeter of the square *MNOP* is

    (A) $\frac{32}{\pi}$

    (B) 32π

    (C) 64

    (D) 64π

    (E) Cannot be determined from the information given.

27. How many minutes will it take to completely fill a water tank with a capacity of 3,750 cubic feet if the water is being pumped into the tank at the rate of 800 cubic feet per minute and is being drained out of the tank at the rate of 300 cubic feet per minute?

    (A) 3 min. 36 sec.

    (B) 6 minutes

    (C) 7 min. 30 sec.

    (D) 8 minutes

    (E) 1,875 minutes

28. Paul is standing 180 yards due north of point *P*. Franny is standing 240 yards due west of point *P*. What is the shortest distance between Franny and Paul?

    (A) 60 yards

    (B) 300 yards

    (C) 420 yards

    (D) 900 yards

    (E) 9,000 yards

WARNING

IF YOU FINISHED THIS SECTION BEFORE TIME EXPIRED, GO IMMEDIATELY TO THE NEXT SECTION. YOU MAY NOT CONTINUE TO WORK ON THIS SECTION AFTER TIME HAS EXPIRED.

Analytical Section

35 QUESTIONS • TIME — 40 MINUTES

Directions: Each of the following questions or groups of questions is based on a short passage or a set of propositions. In answering these questions it may sometimes be helpful to draw a simple picture or chart.

Questions 1–6

Six contestants, F, G, H, I, J, and K, are to be ranked first (highest) through sixth (lowest), though not necessarily in that order, at the start of a singles Ping-Pong challenge tournament.

F is ranked above G.

J is ranked above both H and I.

K is ranked two places above H.

F is ranked either third or fourth.

During the tournament, a player may challenge only the player ranked immediately above him or the player ranked two places above him.

1. Which of the following is a possible initial ranking from highest to lowest?

    (A) J, H, K, F, I, G

    (B) K, I, H, J, F, G

    (C) K, G, H, F, J, I

    (D) J, K, F, H, I, G

    (E) J, K, H, F, I, G

2. If K is initially ranked first, which of the following must also be true of the initial ranking?

    (A) J is ranked second.

    (B) H is ranked second.

    (C) F is ranked third.

    (D) G is ranked fifth.

    (E) I is ranked sixth.

3. If F is initially ranked third, which of the following must also be true of the initial ranking?

    (A) J is ranked first.

    (B) K is ranked second.

    (C) G is ranked fourth.

    (D) I is ranked fourth.

    (E) I is ranked sixth.

4. If K is initially ranked third, and if K makes the first challenge, which of the following is a complete and accurate listing of the contestants K could play in the first match?

    (A) I

    (B) J

    (C) J, F

    (D) J, I

    (E) J, F, I

5. If the first challenge of the tournament is made by F against H, all of the following must be true of the initial ranking EXCEPT

    (A) K is ranked first.

    (B) J is ranked second.

    (C) H is ranked third.

    (D) F is ranked fourth.

    (E) I is ranked fifth.

6. If J makes the first challenge of the tournament against K, then which of the following must be true of the initial rankings?

    (A) K is ranked first.

    (B) J is ranked third.

    (C) F is ranked third.

    (D) H is ranked fourth.

    (E) G is ranked fifth.

Questions 7 and 8

A behavioral psychologist interested in animal behavior noticed that dogs who are never physically disciplined (e.g., with a blow from a rolled-up newspaper) never bark at strangers. The psychologist concluded that the best way to keep a dog from barking at strange visitors is to not punish the dog physically.

7. The psychologist's conclusion is based on which of the following assumptions?

(A) Striking a dog with a newspaper or other object is an inappropriate method for conditioning canine behavior.

(B) Dogs that are never physically disciplined grow up better adjusted than dogs that have been subjected to such discipline.

(C) There were no instances of an unpunished dog barking at a stranger that had not been observed.

(D) Dogs normally bark only at strangers who have previously been physically abusive or threatening.

(E) Human children who are physically disciplined are more likely to react negatively to strangers than those who are not.

8. Suppose the psychologist decides to pursue this project further and studies twenty-five dogs that are known to bark at strangers. Which of the following possible findings would undermine the original conclusion?

(A) Some of the owners of the dogs studied did not physically punish the dog when it barked at a stranger.

(B) Some of the dogs studied were never physically punished.

(C) The owners of some of the dogs studied believe that a dog that barks at strangers is a good watchdog.

(D) Some of the dogs barked at people who were not strangers.

(E) None of the dogs was disciplined by the method of a rolled-up newspaper.

9. Only White Bear gives you all-day deodorant protection and the unique White Bear scent.

If this advertising claim is true, which of the following cannot also be true?

(A) Red Flag deodorant gives you all-day deodorant protection.

(B) Open Sea deodorant is a more popular deodorant than White Bear.

(C) White Bear aftershave lotion uses the White Bear scent.

(D) All Day deodorant provides all-day protection and uses a scent with a similar chemical composition to that of White Bear.

(E) Lost Horizons deodorant contains a scent with the same chemical composition as that of White Bear and gives all-day deodorant protection.

Questions 10–15

Seven members of a Town Board—F, G, H, J, K, L, and M—vote on a series of resolutions. On each resolution, every member votes either aye or nay according to the following patterns.

H always votes the same way as G.

If F votes aye, then K votes aye.

Either M or H votes the opposite way from J.

H and M never both vote aye.

L never votes the same way as K.

10. What is the minimum number of aye votes that must be cast for a resolution?

(A) 0

(B) 1

(C) 2

(D) 3

(E) 4

11. Any of the following can be true EXCEPT:

(A) F and L both vote aye.

(B) J and K both vote aye.

(C) G and H both vote aye.

(D) H and M both vote nay.

(E) G and M both vote nay.

GO ON TO THE NEXT PAGE

12. If F votes aye, what is the maximum possible number of nay votes?

   (A) 1
   (B) 2
   (C) 3
   (D) 4
   (E) 5

13. If G and K vote aye, which of the following must be true?

   (A) F votes aye and M votes aye.
   (B) H votes aye and F votes nay.
   (C) H votes aye and J votes nay.
   (D) J votes nay and F votes nay.
   (E) L votes nay and M votes nay.

14. If a resolution passes by a vote of 4-to-3, which of the following is a complete and accurate list of those who could have voted nay?

   (A) F, L, and K
   (B) H, M, and J
   (C) L, M, and H
   (D) L, G, and H
   (E) M, J, and K

15. If a resolution passes by a vote of 5-to-2, then all of the following must be true EXCEPT:

   (A) K votes aye.
   (B) F votes aye.
   (C) H votes aye.
   (D) L votes nay.
   (E) J votes nay.

Questions 16–21

Seven children, J, K, L, M, N, O, and P, are students at a certain grammar school with grades 1 through 7.

One of these children is in each of the seven grades.

N is in the first grade, and P is in the seventh grade.

L is in a higher grade than K.

J is in a higher grade than M.

O is in a grade somewhere between K and M.

16. If there are exactly two grades between J and O, which of the following must be true?

   (A) K is in the second grade.
   (B) J is in the sixth grade.
   (C) M is in a higher grade than K.
   (D) L is in a grade between M and O.
   (E) K and L are separated by exactly one grade.

17. If J is in the third grade, which of the following must be true?

   (A) K is in grade 4 and L is in grade 5.
   (B) K is in grade 5 and L is in grade 6.
   (C) L is in grade 4 and M is in grade 6.
   (D) M is in grade 2 and K is in grade 5.
   (E) O is in grade 4 and L is in grade 5.

18. If K is in the second grade, which of the following is a complete and accurate listing of the students who could be in grade 5?

   (A) J
   (B) J,M
   (C) L,M
   (D) L,M,J
   (E) O,L,M,J

19. If J and N are separated by exactly one grade, which of the following must be true?

    (A) L is in grade 6.

    (B) L is in grade 3.

    (C) K is in a lower grade than J.

    (D) K is in a lower grade than O.

    (E) O is in a grade between J and N.

20. Which of the following CANNOT be true?

    (A) O is in the third grade.

    (B) O is in the fourth grade.

    (C) O is in the fifth grade.

    (D) M is in the fourth grade.

    (E) M is in the fifth grade.

21. If L is in the grade immediately ahead of J, the number of logically possible orderings of all seven children, from the lowest grade to the highest grade, is

    (A) 1

    (B) 2

    (C) 3

    (D) 4

    (E) 5

22. The Supreme Court's recent decision is unfair. It treats non-resident aliens as a special group when it denies them some rights ordinary citizens have. This treatment is discriminatory, and we all know that discrimination is unfair.

    Which of the following arguments is most nearly similar in its reasoning to the above argument?

    (A) Doing good would be our highest duty under the moral law, and that duty would be irrational unless we had the ability to discharge it; but since a finite, sensuous creature could never discharge that duty in his lifetime, we must conclude that if there is moral law, the soul is immortal.

    (B) Required core courses are a good idea because students just entering college do not have as good an idea about what constitutes a good education as do the professional educators; therefore, students should not be left complete freedom to select course work.

    (C) This country is the most free nation on earth largely as a result of the fact that the founding fathers had the foresight to include a Bill of Rights in the Constitution.

    (D) Whiskey and beer do not mix well; every evening that I have drunk both whiskey and beer together, the following morning I have had a hangover.

    (E) I know that this is a beautiful painting because Picasso created only beautiful works of art, and this painting was done by Picasso.

23. During New York City's fiscal crisis of the late 1970s, governmental leaders debated whether to offer federal assistance to New York City. One economist who opposed the suggestion asked, "Are we supposed to help out New York City every time it gets into financial problems?"

    The economist's question can be criticized because it

    (A) uses ambiguous terms

    (B) assumes everyone else agrees New York City should be helped

    (C) appeals to emotions rather than using logic

    (D) relies upon secondhand reports rather than firsthand accounts

    (E) completely ignores the issue at hand

GO ON TO THE NEXT PAGE

24. It is a well-documented fact that for all teenaged couples who marry, the marriages of those who do not have children in the first year of their marriage survive more than twice as long as the marriages of those teenaged couples in which the wife does give birth within the first twelve months of marriage. Therefore, many divorces could be avoided if teenagers who marry were encouraged not to have children during the first year.

The evidence regarding teenaged marriages supports the author's conclusion only if

(A) in those couples in which a child was born within the first twelve months there is not a significant number in which the wife was pregnant at the time of marriage

(B) the children born during the first year of marriage to those divorcing couples lived with the teenaged couple

(C) the child born into such a marriage did not die at birth

(D) society actually has an interest in determining whether or not people should get divorced if there are not children involved

(E) encouraging people to stay married when they do not plan to have any children is a good idea

25. There are no lower bus fares from Washington, D.C., to New York City than those of Flash Bus Line.

Which of the following is logically inconsistent with the above advertising claim?

(A) Long Lines Airways has a Washington, D.C., to New York City fare that is only one-half that charged by Flash.

(B) Rapid Transit Bus Company charges the same fare for a trip from Washington, D.C., to New York City as Flash charges.

(C) Cherokee Bus Corporation has a lower fare from New York City to Boston than does Flash.

(D) Linea Rapida Bus Company has a New York City to Washington, D.C. fare that is less than the corresponding fare of Flash Bus Lines.

(E) Birch Bus Lines offers a late-night fare from Washington, D.C. to New York City that is two-thirds the price of the corresponding fare of Flash Bus Line.

Questions 26–32

Seven persons, J, K, L, M, N, O, and P, participate in a series of swimming races in which the following are always true of the results:

K finishes ahead of L.

N finishes directly behind M.

Either J finishes first and O last, or O finishes first and J last.

There are no ties in any race, and everyone finishes each race.

26. If exactly two swimmers finish between J and L, which of the following must be true?

(A) J finishes first.

(B) O finishes first.

(C) K finishes second.

(D) M finishes fifth.

(E) N finishes fourth.

27. Which of the following CANNOT be true?

(A) K finishes third.

(B) K finishes sixth.

(C) M finishes second.

(D) N finishes fourth.

(E) P finishes third.

28. If N finishes directly ahead of K, then which of the following is a complete and accurate listing of the positions in which M could have finished?

(A) second

(B) third

(C) fourth

(D) second, third

(E) second, third, fourth

29. If O and K finish so that one is directly behind the other, which of the following must be true?

   (A) K finishes sixth.

   (B) O finishes seventh.

   (C) J finishes seventh.

   (D) L finishes third.

   (E) M finishes fourth.

30. If K finishes fourth, which of the following must be true?

   (A) J finishes first.

   (B) N finishes third.

   (C) P finishes third.

   (D) P finishes fifth.

   (E) L finishes fifth.

31. If J finishes first, and if L finishes ahead of N, in how many different orders is it possible for the other swimmers to finish?

   (A) 2

   (B) 3

   (C) 4

   (D) 5

   (E) 6

32. Which of the following additional conditions makes it certain that P finishes sixth?

   (A) J finishes first.

   (B) K finishes second.

   (C) M finishes second.

   (D) N finishes third.

   (E) L finishes fifth.

33. Doctors, in seeking a cure for *aphroditis melancholias*, are guided by their research into the causes of *metaeritocas polymanias* because the symptoms of the two diseases occur in populations of similar ages, manifesting symptoms in both cases of high fever, swollen glands, and lack of appetite. Moreover, the incubation period of both diseases is virtually identical, so these medical researchers are convinced that the virus responsible for *aphroditis melancholias* is very similar to that responsible for *metaeritocas polymanias*.

The conclusion of the author rests on the presupposition that

   (A) *metaeritocas polymanias* is a more serious public health hazard than *aphroditis melancholias*

   (B) for every disease, modern medical science will eventually find a cure

   (C) saving human life is the single most important goal of modern technology

   (D) *aphroditis melancholias* is a disease that occurs only in human beings

   (E) diseases with similar symptoms will have similar causes

34. (1) Everyone who has not read the report either has no opinion in the matter or holds a wrong opinion about it.

   (2) Everyone who holds no opinion in the matter has not read the report.

Which of the following best describes the relationship between the two above propositions?

   (A) If (2) is true, (1) may be either false or true.

   (B) If (2) is true, (1) must also be true.

   (C) If (2) is true, (1) is likely to be true.

   (D) If (1) is true, (2) must also be true.

   (E) If (2) is false, (1) must also be false.

35. ADVERTISEMENT: When you enroll with Future Careers Business Institute (FCBI), you will have access to our placement counseling service. Last year, 92% of our graduates who asked us to help them find jobs found them. So go to FCBI for your future!

The answer to which of the following questions is potentially the LEAST damaging to the claim of the advertising?

(A) How many of your graduates asked FCBI for assistance?

(B) How many people graduated from FCBI last year?

(C) Did those people who asked for jobs find ones in the areas for which they were trained?

(D) Was FCBI responsible for finding the jobs or did graduates find them independently?

(E) Was the person reading the advertisement a paid, professional actor?

WARNING

Practice Examination 3

Answer Key

VERBAL SECTION

1. C	7. C	13. E	19. C	25. C
2. D	8. C	14. C	20. C	26. C
3. E	9. D	15. A	21. A	27. B
4. B	10. C	16. C	22. D	28. C
5. D	11. D	17. D	23. B	29. E
6. A	12. B	18. A	24. A	30. D

MATH SECTION

1. C	7. C	13. C	19. C	25. E
2. C	8. B	14. D	20. D	26. A
3. A	9. B	15. B	21. C	27. C
4. D	10. D	16. C	22. A	28. B
5. B	11. C	17. D	23. B	
6. C	12. D	18. B	24. A	

ANALYTICAL SECTION

1. D	8. B	15. E	22. E	29. C
2. A	9. E	16. B	23. E	30. B
3. A	10. C	17. D	24. A	31. C
4. D	11. A	18. D	25. E	32. E
5. E	12. D	19. A	26. D	33. E
6. A	13. E	20. C	27. B	24. A
7. C	14. D	21. B	28. D	35. E

Practice Examination 3

Explanatory Answers

VERBAL SECTION

1. **(C)** *Mutinous* is "rebellious" or "insubordinate," so *obedient* is a straightforward opposite.

2. **(D)** *Temerity* means "foolish boldness" or "recklessness," so an opposite is *caution*.

3. **(E)** *Tractable* means "easily led" or "docile." *Uncooperative* is a good opposite.

4. **(B)** Since *insouciant* means "gay and careless," *fretful* is the best opposite.

5. **(D)** This question contains a thought-extender and a thought-reverser as its logical elements. The first blank must parallel the idea that someone was the life of the party. We can immediately eliminate (A), because someone who is melancholy is not likely to be the life of a party. (B), (C), and (E) make no logical sense. This is largely a matter of vocabulary since you must know that *garrulous* means "talkative," *inimical* means "hostile," and *vitriolic* means "nasty." Only (D) makes any sense. His wife must be the opposite of fun and talkative. The second element of (D), *taciturn*, which means "silent," works very nicely.

6. **(A)** This sentence begins with a thought-extender and then reverses the idea. The first blank needs an adjective related to "offhand" that could be applied to "remarks." This becomes a vocabulary question because you must know the meanings of all five of the first elements. All five answers make some sense, so it is a matter of substituting each pair to make sure that the logic of the sentence is maintained. If you know the meaning of *flippant*, you don't have to look any further. He was flippant, but this attitude masked a serious nature. This works very well. The logic of "he seemed x but was really y" is maintained.

7. **(C)** This question starts with a thought-reverser, *although*. (A) does not reverse the idea. The same is true of (D) and (E). (B) and (C) remain possibilities, so test the second elements. The faculty might harbor her ideas, but they can't be doing it in defense of her seniority. That makes no sense. (C) works well. The faculty implements her ideas al-

though they do not agree with her. This makes a perfectly logical and idiomatic sentence.

8. **(C)** This is obviously a main idea question. The author discusses the sacred script. The author mentions the Renaissance primarily as a way of praising the art of the Middle Ages. (C) is the best statement of the author's purpose.

9. **(D)** This is an explicit idea question. Each of the incorrect answers is mentioned as an element of the sacred script. As for (A), lines may be used to represent water or the sky. As for (B), these indicate sainthood or divinity. As for (C), shoes are mentioned as an identifying characteristic. And (E) also is mentioned (a tree represents earth). (D), however, is not mentioned as an element of the sacred script.

10. **(C)** This is an application question. Of course, we do not know where the passage actually appeared, and the task is to pick the most likely source. We stress this because it is always possible to make an argument for any of the answer choices to a question of this sort. But the fact that a justification is possible does not make that choice correct; the strongest possible justification makes the choice correct. (C) is the most likely source. The passage focuses on art and is scholarly in tone. (A) can be eliminated, for the passage casts no light on social conditions of the period. (B) can be eliminated for a similar reason. The author treats art in and of itself—not as a social force. And we certainly cannot conclude that by discussing religious art the author wants to discuss the church. (D) is incorrect because the selection focuses on art of the Middle Ages. (E) is incorrect because it is inconsistent with the scholarly and objective tone of the passage.

11. **(D)** This is an inferred idea question, one asking for an interpretation of a phrase. The rules of art in the Middle Ages placed constraints on the artist so that his artistic effort had to be made within certain conventions. As a result, painting was not individualistic. This is most clearly expressed by (D). (A) is incorrect since the author is saying that the artist's talent just did not show as individual talent. (B) is

354

incorrect, for though this is a true statement, it is not a response to the question. (C) is perhaps the second best answer because it at least hints at what (D) says more clearly. But the author does not mean to say the artist was not recognized in his lifetime. Perhaps he was. What the author means to say is that we do not now see the personality of the artist. Finally, (E) is just a confused reading of the last paragraph.

12. **(B)** A WEB may be used to ENTANGLE and a trap is used to *ensnare*. Do not be distracted by (A) because *spider* and *spin* seem related to WEB.

13. **(E)** This analogy is based on a "lack of" relationship. LETHARGY is a lack of ENERGY, and *apathy* is a lack of *interest*.

14. **(C)** This analogy is a twist on the defining characteristic analogy. It is characteristic of THWART that one does not ACHIEVE and of *silence* that one does not *speak*.

15. **(A)** This is a type of "lack of" analogy. Something that is APOCRYPHAL is not GENUINE, and what is *spurious* is not *authentic*.

16. **(C)** This is a defining characteristic analogy. That which is BALEFUL is an EVIL, and that which is *mandatory* is a *requirement*. Note that EVIL in the original pair is a noun and not an adjective.

17. **(D)** This is a main idea question. The main idea of the passage is fairly clear: suggest reforms to correct the problems discussed. Choice (D) is a very good description of this development. (A) is incorrect since the author criticizes the system. (B) is incorrect since no recommendation for expanding benefits and scope is made by the author. (C) overstates the case. The author indicts only unemployment compensation, and indicates a belief that the shortcomings of the system can be remedied. (E) is incorrect because the author is discussing unemployment compensation, not government programs designed to achieve full employment generally. We may infer from the passage that unemployment compensation is not a program designed to achieve full employment, but a program designed to alleviate the hardship of unemployment. On balance, (D) is the most precise description given of the development of the passage.

18. **(A)** This is a logical detail question. In the second paragraph the author introduces the example of a worker who loses surprisingly little by being unemployed. The author does this to show that unemployment insurance encourages people to remain unemployed by reducing the net cost of unemployment. (A) makes this point. (B) is incorrect, for the author does not discuss the problem of employer contribution until the fourth paragraph. (C) is incorrect, for this is not the reason that the author introduces the point. (D) is incorrect because this topic is not taken up until the third paragraph. Finally, (E) is incorrect since the author analyzes the situation in a neutral fashion; there is no hint of condemnation.

19. **(C)** This is an explicit idea, or specific detail, question. (C) is a recommendation made by the author in the final paragraph. (A) is actually inconsistent with statements made in that paragraph, for the author proposes taxing benefits in the same way as wages. (B), (D), and (E) are interesting ideas, but they are mentioned nowhere in the passage—so they cannot possibly be answers to an explicit idea question.

20. **(C)** Here, too, we have an explicit idea question. (A), (B), (D), and (E) are all mentioned in the third paragraph as ways by which an employer might reduce seasonal and cyclical fluctuations in labor needs. (C), however, was not mentioned as a way to minimize unemployment. Indeed, we may infer from other information supplied by the passage that supplementary benefits actually increase unemployment.

21. **(A)** This is an application question. We are asked to apply the author's analysis of the rating system to conclusions given in the answer choices. The author is critical of the rating system because it does not place the full burden of unemployment on the employer. This is because there is a maximum contribution limit, and in the final paragraph the author recommends the ceiling be eliminated. From these remarks, we may infer that the author believes the rating system is, in theory, sound, but that practically it needs to be adjusted. Choice (A) neatly describes this judgment. (B) can be eliminated since the author implies that the system is, in principle, sound. Moreover, the author implies that the employer does have some control over the time his former employees remain out of work. The maximum limit on employer contribution allows

the employer to exploit this control. As for (C), this is contradicted by our analysis thus far and for the further reason that the passage never suggests employee contribution should replace employer contribution. Indeed, the author implies the system serves a useful and necessary social function. (D) can be eliminated because the author never draws a distinction between contributions by large firms and contributions by small firms. Finally, (E) is incorrect since the experience rating system is theoretically tied to the amount drawn by employees. The difficulty is not with the theory of the system, but with its implementation.

22. **(D)** This analogy is a type of defining characteristic. By its nature, a WATERFALL CASCADES and a *wave undulates*. You might be attracted to answer choice (A). But you can eliminate it by trying to improve it. (A) would be more nearly correct if it were *snow: fall*.

23. **(B)** Although this does not fit into any category, the relationship is clear. To INFLATE something means "to increase its MAGNITUDE," and to *extend* something means "to increase its *duration*."

24. **(A)** This analogy is a "defining characteristic." To MOCK is to show DERISION or scorn. Similarly, to *despise* is to show *contempt* or disdain.

25. **(C)** This question contains a type of thought-reversal. Before looking at the choices, you already know that you need a word that prevents time from being "idle." All choices except for (C) can be eliminated because they not only say nothing useful about time, they create meaningless sentences.

26. **(C)** You cannot eliminate any of the choices on the grounds of usage, since each when substituted into the sentence will create phrases. The key to the sentence is the word *life*. The field of study that completes the first blank must be a science that not only studies but directs the course of life, as indicated by the word *tamper*. This eliminates (B), (D), and (E). As for (A), although some members of the clergy might oppose research in psychology, those who do so would not argue that it is *imperative* to tamper with life. By the process of elimination, this leaves only (C).

27. **(B)** The logical key to this question is a double-reversal. *Although* sets up a contrast between the idea in the first clause and the idea in the second

clause. But the second clause contains the word *little,* which functions as a negative. So the blanks will actually extend the thought expressed in the first clause. The first blank is an extender of the concept of literature that instructs as well as entertains, so you should look for an adjective that describes this type of literature. All of the first choices might describe literature, so you must know that *didactic* means "instructive."

28. **(C)** Since *diffidence* means "self-doubt" or "modesty," *haughty arrogance* makes a nice antonym.

29. **(E)** *Sedulous* means "diligent" or "persevering," so *indolent,* which means "lazy," is a good opposite.

30. **(D)** *Obdurate* means "stubborn" or "inflexible," so *malleable* is a fine antonym.

MATH SECTION

1. **(C)** It would be a mistake to start multiplying before setting up the two quantities:

24 hours/day × 7 days

7 days/week × 24 weeks

Both quantities are 24 × 7, and it is not necessary to multiply them out to see that they are equal.

2. **(C)** As in question 1, it is not necessary to actually carry out the indicated multiplication.

   Remembering that a % sign indicates that the number is to be divided by 100, each side becomes $\frac{(35)(60)}{100}$. Thus, (C). Always keep in mind that the % sign or a percentage is just a number like any other number. The % sign is equivalent to the fraction $\frac{1}{100}$.

3. **(A)** Although the most direct way to solve this problem is to add the column of ages and divide by 6 (average = 29.8), you may find it quicker to do a "running average." Assume that the average is 30 (Tom's age). If that is correct, then the sum of ages above 30 must balance exactly the sum of the ages below 30. Juanita makes the balance +5 (above 30). Brooke brings it down by 2, for a total of +3. Glenda adds 10, for +13. Marcia brings it down by 8, for +5. Finally Dwight's age is 6 below 30, which brings the figure down to a −1. This shows that the average will be slightly below 30.

4. **(D)** Since *m* ranges between 4 and 6, and *n* ranges between 5 and 7, it is impossible to determine the relationship between *m* and *n*. For example, *m* and

n might both be 5.5, or *m* might be 4.1 and *n* 6.9, or *m* might be 5.9 and *n* 5.1. Neither *m* nor *n* is restricted to integers.

5. **(B)** The side of the square must be 8, since $s^2 = 64$. The length of the rectangle Q must be 16, since $W \times L = 64$.

6. **(C)** This problem simply requires finding the value of the expression $2x + 3y$, when $x = 3$ and $y = 2$: $2(3) + 3(2) = 12$.

7. **(C)** You do not need a course in business arithmetic to solve this problem, only the common-sense notion that profit is equal to gross revenue less cost. Expressed algebraically, we have $P = GR - C$; then, transposing the C term, we have $C + P = GR$, which is read: cost plus profit (or markup) is equal to gross revenue (or selling price). In this case, $P = \$4$, $GR = \$20$: $C + 4 = 20$, so $C = 16$.

8. **(B)** The information given says that the 1980 student population is $2\frac{1}{2}$ times as great as the 1960 student population. So: '80SP = '60SP $\times 2\frac{1}{2}$, or '80SP $= 500 \times 2\frac{1}{2} = 500 \times \frac{5}{2} = 1,250$.

9. **(B)** The simplest way to solve this problem is first to perform the indicated operation for Column B: $(3x)^3 = 27x^3$. Now, since $x > 0$, x^3 must be positive, and it is permissible to divide both columns by x^3. The result is that Column A becomes 3 while column B becomes 27, so (B) is correct.

10. **(D)** Since it is not specified that x and y are equal to one another, the relationship is indeterminate. You can see this by visualizing x and y varying inversely with one another, e.g., when x is 2, y is $\frac{1}{2}$, when x is 3, y is $\frac{1}{3}$, etc. Also if you use substitution: if $x = 2$, then y must be $\frac{1}{2}$. On the other hand, x might be $\frac{1}{2}$, in which case y is 2.

11. **(C)** Since 11 is itself a prime number, it is factorable only by itself and 1, and that is one instance in which 11 is an integer multiple of a prime number. But it is also the only one. Any other number that is factorable by 11—say, 22—cannot, by definition, be a prime number (it would be factorable by 11 and some other number, as well as by itself and 1). Thirteen is also a prime number, which means that the only prime number of which it is an integer multiple is itself. So both 11 and 13 are each integer factors of only one prime number—themselves.

12. **(D)** Although we know that y is the even integer and that, of x and z, one is the next-largest and the other is the next-smallest integer from y, we do not know which is which. If x is the smaller and z the larger, then Column B may be greater, but if x is the larger and z the smaller, Column A may be greater. Consequently, the correct answer here must be (D).

13. **(C)** We must test each of the answer choices. The question asks for the one choice in which the answer is not equal to $3n + 3$. In (A), for example, does $300 = 3n + 3$? A quick manipulation will show that there is an integer, n, that solves the equation: $297 = 3n$, so $n = 99$. For (C), however, no integral n exists: $3n + 3 = 208$, $3n = 205$, $n = 68\frac{1}{3}$. So (C) is the answer we want. Another approach is to test each of the answer choices for being divisible by 3 since $3n + 3$ is divisible by 3 when n is an integer. If the sum of all the single digits in a number add to a number divisible by 3, the number is itself divisible by 3; if not, the number isn't (208, for example: $2 + 0 + 8 = 10$, is not divisible by 3). Being divisible by 3 does not mean an answer fits the conditions, but not being divisible by 3 means that it doesn't.

14. **(D)** The easiest approach to this problem is to draw the figures.

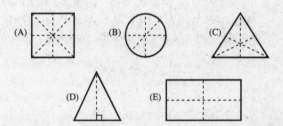

The dotted lines show possible lines of symmetry—that is, these are lines along which a paper cutout of the figure could be folded and the result will be that the two halves exactly match one another. (D) must be our answer, since it is the only figure with but one line of symmetry.

15. **(B)** Of course, the problem is really about right triangles, not about transmitter towers, and the actual height of the tower is not important. The tower forms the common leg of two right triangles, so our triangles will have one leg of, say, length *t*. Then, the triangle on the left has a second leg that is shorter than the second leg of the triangle on the right (80 m vs. 100 m). Consequently, the hypotenuse (the support wire) of the triangle on the left (AB) must be shorter than that of the triangle on the right (AC).

16. **(C)** Notice that the number in Column A can be understood to be the sum of 2 times 1,000 (the 2 is in the thousands position), 4 times 100 (the 4 is in the hundreds position), 6 times 10 (the 6 is in the tens position), and 8 (the eight is in the units position). This is equivalent to the expression in Column B. The only differences are that the ordering of the elements is reversed in Column B and the hundreds and thousands are expressed in powers of ten.

17. **(D)** Since $a^2 = b$, we can substitute a^2 wherever b appears. Thus Column A can be rewritten as: $\frac{2a}{a^2}$, which is equal to $\frac{2}{a}$. Since a is positive, we can multiply both columns by a. Thus, Column A becomes 2, and Column B becomes $(a)(a)(a)$, or a^3. Now it is easy to see that the relationship must be indeterminate. If a is a fraction, then Column A is greater. If a is a number like 2, then Column B is larger.

18. **(B)** This problem can, of course, be solved using an equation. We know that the laborer worked 8 hours @ $8 per hour, but what we need to know is how much overtime he worked. We let x be the number of overtime hours: (8 hrs. × $8/hr.) + ($x$ hrs. × $12/hr) = $80. The $12/hr. is the laborer's overtime rate—that is, $8 × 1\frac{1}{2}$ = $12. Now it is a fairly simple matter to manipulate the equation:

$$64 + 12x = 80$$
$$12x = 16$$
$$x = \frac{16}{12}$$
$$x = 1\frac{1}{3}$$

Since $\frac{1}{3}$ of an hour is 20 minutes, the laborer worked 1 hour and 20 minutes of overtime, which, when added to the standard 8 hours, gives a total work day of 9 hours and 20 minutes.

Now, it is not absolutely necessary to use an equation. The equation is just a way of formalizing common-sense reasoning, which might have gone like this: Well, I know he made $64 in a regular day. If he made $80 on a given day, $16 must have been overtime pay. His overtime rate is time-and-a-half, that is $1\frac{1}{2}$ times $8/hr, or $12/hr. In the first hour of overtime he made $12, that leaves $4 more. Since $4 is one-third of $12, he had to work another one-third of an hour to make that, which is twenty

minutes. So he worked 8 hours at standard rates for $64, one full hour of overtime for another $12, and another $\frac{1}{3}$ of an overtime hour for $4. So $80 represents 9 hours and 20 minutes of work.

19. **(C)** Since vertical or opposite angles are equal, we know that $4x = x + 30$. Solving for x: $3x = 30$, $x = 10$; so the two columns are equal.

20. **(D)** To find the cost per ounce of the family-size box, we need to know both its size in ounces and its cost. While we know the relationship between the regular and family sizes for both of those items, we do not know the actual size or cost of the regular size and thus cannot use our knowledge of the relationship between the two sizes to any advantage. We wouldn't even know whether the family size or the regular size had the higher cost per ounce of cereal.

21. **(C)** One direct and simple way of solving this problem would be to count on your fingers the actual number of different duos and trios that could be formed from a group of five. The result is ten. A more elegant way of solving the problem is to recognize that $2 + 3 = 5$. In other words, each time a pair is selected to form a duo, three persons from the group have been left behind, and they form a trio. Or each time a different group of three is selected to form a trio, a pair of persons is left behind, and they constitute a duo. So even without calculating the actual number of different trios and duos that could be made, you can reach the conclusion that the number of possible combinations for each is the same.

22. **(A)** This problem is both easy and difficult. Conceptually, the problem is easy to set up. High-risk stocks constitute 8.9% of the total investment of $1,080,192. To find the value of the high-risk stocks we just take 8.9% of $1,080,192. Then the problem becomes slightly difficult because it requires a tedious calculation—or at least it seems to. We say "seems to" because you do not actually have to do the arithmetic. The answer choices are spread fairly far apart; that is, they differ from one another by several thousands of dollars. Round 8.9% off to an even 9%, and $1,080,192 to 1,080,000. Then do the arithmetic in your head: 9% of one million is 90,000, then 9% of 80,000 is 7,200, so you need an answer choice that is close to $97,000—slightly less since you rounded your

percentage (8.9%) in an upward direction. With a bit of practice, you will find that this technique is more efficient than actually doing arithmetic.

23. **(B)** In this problem, the technique of rounding off and estimating is even more useful. The problem is easy enough to set up: Since state-issued bonds constituted 26% of all government bonds and securities, and since government bonds and securities constituted 48.3% of the total investment fund, state-issued bonds must constitute 26% of 48.3% of the total fund. To compute the dollar value of state-issued bonds, we need to find 26% of 48.3% of $1,080,192, but that will require substantial calculation. You can attack it in this way: 26% is close to one-fourth, and one-fourth of 48% would be 12%, so state-issued bonds are 12% of the total. Now, 10% of the total of $1,080,000 (rounded off), would be $108,000, and one-fifth of that (since 2% is one-fifth of 10%) is approximately $20,000. So 12% must be approximately $128,000, answer (B).

24. **(A)** In this problem you can use the method of pairing. Make a rough comparison of answers (A) and (B). If you find that one of the two is clearly the larger, strike the smaller and proceed to compare answer (C) with the larger of (A) and (B). Again, this calculation will be a rough one, and if you find that one of the two is clearly larger, strike the smaller and proceed to compare the larger with (D). Follow this procedure until you have exhausted the list, and one answer remains as the largest. Now, if it turns out that any two answers are too close for a rough estimate to tell them apart, keep them both and compare them to the other answers before actually committing yourself to a detailed calculation, which is unlikely to be necessary. When there are two close answers, it is likely that a later one will supersede both of them.

   In this problem we compare (A) and (B) first. Since both figures are shares of the same pie, we can compare their shares directly. Since the amount invested in municipal bonds with a 7–9% yield is 65%, (A) must be larger than (B) (the other two combined could account for only 35% of the pie), so we strike (B) and hold on to (A). Municipal bonds yielding 7–9% are 65% of all municipal bonds, and since municipal bonds account for 56% of all government bonds and securities, we can determine that

the 7–9% yield municipal bonds account for roughly $\frac{2}{3}$ of the 56% of all government bonds and securities, or slightly less than 40%. This shows that (B) must be larger than (C), since (C) accounts for only 18% of all government bonds and securities—nowhere near 40%. Similarly, we can eliminate (D) from consideration because state-issued bonds account for only 26% of all government bonds and securities—again, that is not even close to 40%. Finally, we compare (A) with (E). Since municipal bonds with a 7–9% yield constitute slightly less than 40% of all government bonds and securities, and since government bonds and securities account for approximately 48% of the entire investment fund, municipal bonds yielding 7–9% must account for 40% of that 48%, or approximately 19% of the total fund. High-risk stocks account for only 8.9% of the total fund, so (E) must be less than (A), and (A) is our answer.

25. **(E)** This question requires a careful reading of the stem. It asks which kind of investment earned the least amount of money, but this group of graphs shows the amount *invested* in types of investment. It cannot be assumed that each type of investment was equally profitable, so we have no way of determining which of the types of investment generated the least income.

26. **(A)** Since *MNOP* is a square, we know that angle *O* must be a right angle, that is, 90°. From that we can conclude that arc *NP* is one-fourth of the entire circle. If arc *NP* is 4 units long, then the circumference of the circle must be 4 times that long, or 16 units. We are now in a position to find the length of the radius of circle *O*, and once we have the radius, we will also know the length of the sides of square *MNOP*, since *ON* and *OP* are both radii. The formula for the circumference of a circle is $C = 2\pi r$, so:

$$2\pi r = 16$$

$$r = \frac{8}{\pi}$$

$$4r = \frac{32}{\pi}$$

So the side of the square *MNOP* must be 8, and its perimeter must be $s + s + s + s$ or $4(8) = 32$.

27. **(C)** The most direct way to solve this problem is first to compute the rate at which the water is filling

the tank. Water is flowing into the tank at 800 cu. ft. per minute, but it is also draining out at the rate of 300 cu. ft. per minute. The net gain each minute, then, is 500 cu. ft. We then divide 3,750 cu. ft. by 500 cu. ft./min., which equals 7.5 minutes. We convert the .5 minutes to 30 seconds, so our answer is 7 min. 30 sec.

28. **(B)** A quick sketch of the information provided in the problem shows that we need to employ the Pythagorean Theorem:

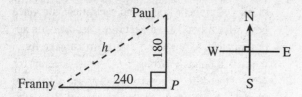

The shortest distance from Paul to Franny is the hypotenuse of this right triangle:

$$180^2 + 240^2 = h^2$$

It is extremely unlikely that the GRE would present a problem requiring such a lengthy calculation. So there must be a shortcut available. The key is to recognize that 180 and 240 are multiples of 60—3×60 and 4×60, respectively. This must be a 3,4,5 right triangle, so our hypotenuse must be $5 \times 60 = 300$.

ANALYTICAL SECTION

Questions 1–6

Arranging the Information

You would probably want to summarize the information:

F > G (F above G)

J > (H & I) (J above both H and I)

K = H + 2 (K is two above H)

F = 3 or 4 (F is 3rd or 4th)

Answering the Questions

1. **(D)** For this question, we need only check each of the choices against the conditions. (A) can be eliminated since K is not ranked two places above H. (B) can be eliminated since J is not ranked above

H and I, and for the further reason that F is out of place. (C) is not acceptable since G is ranked above F. (E) is incorrect since K and H are together, not separated by another person. Only (D) meets all of the requirements for the initial ranking.

2. **(A)** For this question we are given additional information. On the assumption that K is ranked first, we know that H must be ranked third, which in turn places F fourth. Since J must be ranked above H, J must be ranked second. No further conclusion can be definitely drawn about the positions of G and I, so our order is

        1 2 3 4 5 6
        K J H F G/I

At this juncture, we check our deductions against the answer choices. (B) and (C) are contradicted by the diagram. (D) and (E) are possible—not necessary. (A), however, makes a statement that is confirmed by the diagram.

3. **(A)** For this question we assume that F is ranked third. On that assumption, there are only two positions available for K: 2 (with H in 4) and 4 (with H in 6).

    1 2 3 4 5 6   1 2 3 4 5 6
     K F H   F K   H

As for the first possibility, G must be in position 5 with I in 6, or vice versa, for J must be above H, and that means J must be in first position. As for the second possibility, G must be in position 5, which forces J and I to occupy positions 1 and 2, respectively:

    1 2 3 4 5 6   1 2 3 4 5 6
     J K F H I/G   J I F K G H

So there are a total of three possible arrangements. We are looking, however, for a statement that is necessarily true. That is (A), since J is ranked first in all three possibilities. (B) is incorrect since it is only possible, not necessary, that K be second. (C) is incorrect for it makes a false statement. (D) is incorrect for the same reason. Finally, (E) makes a statement that could be true, but is not necessarily true.

4. **(D)** For this question we assume that K is ranked third. This means F is fourth, H is fifth, and G must be sixth. Finally, since J must be above I, J is first, with I second.

1 2 3 4 5 6
J I K F H G

K can challenge only the players one or two ranks above him, and those players are J and I.

5. **(E)** If F is able to issue a challenge to H, this can only be because F is ranked fourth with H third. It is not possible for F to be in the third position with H in the first or second. With H and F in third and fourth, respectively, we are able to deduce the following:

1 2 3 4 5 6
K J H F G/I

K must be in the first position since that is two positions above H, who is in third. Since J must be above H, this means J must be second. Now we check our answer choices. (A), (B), (C), and (D) are all necessarily true as shown by the diagram. (E) is possible, but is not necessary, so (E) is the exception and therefore the correct answer.

6. **(A)** We assume that J challenges K, so K must be ranked above J. But J can be ranked no lower than second, so K must be first with H in third and F in fourth:

1 2 3 4 5 6
K J H F G/I

Checking the answer choices, we see that (A) is necessarily true, while (B), (C), and (D) are necessarily false and (E) only possibly true.

7. **(C)** (C) is an assumption of the psychologist. The psychologist observed the dogs for a certain period of time and found that each time a stranger approached the dogs kept silent. From those observed instances, the psychologist concluded that the dogs never barked at strangers. Obviously this theory would be disproved (or at least it would have to be seriously qualified) if, when the psychologist was not watching, the dogs barked their heads off at strangers. (A) is not an assumption because the speaker makes no value judgment about how dogs ought to be treated. (B) is similar in that no such broad conclusion about "better adjusted" is implied. (D) and (E) are simply confused readings of the speaker's thinking.

8. **(B)** (B) would undermine the psychologist's thesis that "only a beaten dog barks." It cites instances in which the dog was not beaten and still barked at strangers. This would force the psychologist to reconsider the conclusion about the connection between beating and barking. (A) is not like (B). It does not state the dogs were never beaten; it states only that the dogs were not beaten when they barked at strangers. It is conceivable that they were beaten at other times. If they were, then even though they might bark at strangers (and not be beaten at that moment), they would not be counter-examples to the psychologist's theory. (C) is not an assumption of the psychologist, as we saw in the preceding question, so denying it does not affect the strength of the psychologist's argument. The psychologist is concerned with the factual connection between beating a dog and its barking; information about the owners' feelings can hardly be relevant to that factual issue. (D) is an interesting choice, but the fact that some of the dogs also barked at non-strangers doesn't address the connection between discipline and barking at strangers: so they also barked at non-strangers, so what? And (E) is wrong because the analysis depends not on the particular object used but on the notion of physical discipline.

9. **(E)** Another deodorant might also give all-day protection. The ad claims that White Bear is the only deodorant that gives you both protection and scent—a vacuous enough claim since White Bear is probably the only deodorant with the White Bear scent. Of course, (C) is not affected by this point, since the White Bear Company may put its unique scent into many of its products. (B) is also not inconsistent with the ad—that another product is more popular does not say that it has the features the ad claims for the White Bear deodorant. (D) is not inconsistent because the chemical composition is merely "similar." But (E) is inconsistent: the same protection and the same scent.

Questions 10–15

Arranging the Information

Begin by summarizing the initial conditions

1. $H = G$
2. $F+ \neq K+$
3. $(J \neq M)$ or $(J \neq H)$
4. Not $(H+$ and $M+)$
5. $L \neq K$

Answering the Questions

10. **(C)** One of the trio of H, J, and M must vote aye in order to comply with the third condition; and either L or K must vote aye.

11. **(A)** According to the second condition, if F votes aye, then K must also vote aye; but given the fifth condition, L cannot also vote aye.

12. **(D)** If F votes aye, then according to the second condition K also votes aye. And of the trio H, J, and M, at least one must vote aye. For example:

    $+$ F, K, M

    $-$ L, G, H, J

13. **(E)** If G votes aye, then the first condition requires that H also vote aye. But according to the fourth condition, M must vote nay. And given that K votes aye, the fifth condition requires that L vote nay.

14. **(D)** (A) violates the fifth condition; (B) the third; (C) the first; and (E) the second.

15. **(E)** Of the trio H, J, and M, one must vote nay; and of the pair K and L, one must vote nay. If K were to vote nay, then F could not vote aye, and the result would be at least three nay votes—in violation of the additional stipulation made by this question stem. Therefore, K must vote aye and L nay. G and H must both also vote aye. Given that H votes aye, M must vote nay. So the vote will be:

    $+$ K, F, G, H, J

    $-$ L, M

QUESTIONS 16–21

Arranging the Information

Here we have a linear ordering problem, a type now very familiar. We begin by summarizing the information:

$N = 1$ and $P = 7$

$L > K$

$J > M$

$K > O > M$ or $K < O < M$

Answering the Questions

16. **(B)** We begin by processing the additional information. For J and O to be separated by exactly two grades, it must be that they are in grades 2 and 5 or grades 3 and 6, though not necessarily in that order:

1	2	3	4	5	6	7
N	J			O		P
N	O			J		P
N		O			J	P
N	J				O	P

We can eliminate all but the third possibility. The first arrangement is not possible because we cannot honor the requirement $J > M$. The second is not possible because we cannot place O between K and M. The fourth is not possible for the same reason. Using only the third possibility, we know further:

	1	2	3	4	5	6	7
	N	K	O	M	L	J	P
or:	N	K	O	L	M	J	P
or:	N	M	O	K	L	J	P

This proves (B) is necessarily true. The diagram further shows that (A), (C), (D), and (E) are only possibly, though not necessarily, true.

17. **(D)** We begin by processing the additional information:

1	2	3	4	5	6	7
N	M	J	O	K	L	P

With J in grade 3, M must be in grade 2. And we know that L must be higher than K and, further, that O must go between K and M. This means that O, K, and L must be in grades 4, 5, and 6, respectively. The diagram shows that (D) is necessarily true, and that each of the remaining choices is necessarily false.

18. **(D)** Enter the new information on a diagram:

```
1   2   3   4   5   6   7
N   K                   P
```

Next, since K is in grade 2, the three students, O, M, and J must be arranged in that order. So the only question is where to put L:

```
1   2   3   4   5   6   7
N   K   L   O   M   J   P
N   K   O   L   M   J   P
N   K   O   M   L   J   P
N   K   O   M   J   L   P
```

So L, M, or J could be in the fifth grade-but not O.

19. **(A)** We begin by processing the additional information:

```
1 2 3 4 5 6 7
N M J O K L P
```

We separate J from M by one grade by placing J in grade 3, which means that M, to be in a lower grade, must be in grade 2. Next, we reason that for L to be in a grade higher than K's, and yet allowing that O must be between K and M, we have O, K, and L in grades 4 through 6, respectively. The diagram, therefore, proves that (A) is correct while each of the other choices is necessarily false.

20. **(C)** Looking back over the work we have already done, we learned in our discussion of question 13 that O can be in grade 3, and that M can be in grade 4 or grade 5. Our discussion of question 14 shows that O can be in grade 4. So (A), (B), (D), and (E) are all possible. (C), however, is not possible. If O is in the fifth grade, we cannot place either K or M above O without violating one or the other restriction that L > K and that J > M.

21. **(B)** We begin by processing the additional information.

```
1     2     3     4     5     6     7
N   K/M    O   K/M    J     L     P
```

For L to be in the grade ahead of J, they must be in grades 6 and 5 respectively; otherwise it will not be possible to get O between K and M, since both K and M must be in grades lower than those of L and J, respectively. Then, we must put O between K and M, but there is no reason to place K in grade 2 and M in grade 4, as opposed to K in 4 and M in 2. So there are two possible arrangements, as shown by the diagram.

22. **(E)** The argument given in the question stem is circular; that is, it begs the question. It tries to prove that the decision is unfair by claiming that it singles out a group, which is the same thing as discriminating, and then concludes that *since* all discrimination is unfair, so, too, is the court's decision unfair. Of course, the real issue is whether singling out this particular group is unfair. After all, we do make distinctions, e.g., adults are treated differently from children, businesses differently from persons, soldiers differently from executives. The question of fairness cannot be solved by simply noting that the decision singles out some persons. (E) also is circular: It tries to prove this is a beautiful painting because all paintings of this sort are beautiful. (A) is perhaps the second best answer, but notice that it is purely hypothetical in its form: *If* this were true, *then* that would be true. As a consequence, it is not as similar to the question stem as (E), which is phrased in categorical assertions rather than hypothetical statements. (B) moves from the premise that students are not good judges of their needs to a conclusion about the responsibility for planning course work. The conclusion and the premise are not the same so the argument is not circular. (C) is not, technically speaking, even an argument. Remember from the instructional material at the beginning of the book, an argument has premises and a conclusion. These are separate statements. (C) is one long statement, not two short ones. It reads: "A because B"; not "A, therefore B." For example, the statement "I am late because the car broke down" is not an inference but a causal statement. In (D), since the premise (everything after the semicolon) is not the same as the conclusion (the statement before the semicolon), the argument is not a circular argument and so does not parallel the stem argument.

23. **(E)** This is a very sticky question, but it is similar to ones that have been on the GRE. The key here is to keep in mind that you are to pick the *best* answer,

and sometimes you will not be very satisfied with any of them. Here (E) is correct by default of the others. (A) has some merit. After all, the real economist isn't very careful in his statement of his claim. There is no evidence that we have ever been there before, but there is no particular term he uses that we could call ambiguous. (B) is wrong because even though the economist assumes some people take that position (otherwise, against whom would he be arguing?), he does not imply that he alone thinks differently. (C) is like (A), a possible answer, but this interpretation requires additional information. You would have to have said to yourself, "Oh, I see that he is against it. He is probably saying this in an exasperated tone and in the context of a diatribe." If there were such additional information, you would be right, and (C) would be a good answer. But there isn't. (E) does not require this additional speculation and so is truer to the given information. (D) would also require speculation. (E) is not perfect, just best by comparison.

24. **(A)** The main point of the passage is that pregnancy and a child put strain on a young marriage, and that such marriages would have a higher survival rate without the strain of children. It would seem, then, that encouraging such couples not to have children would help them stay married; but that will be possible only if they have not already committed themselves, so to speak, to having a child. If the wife is already pregnant at the time of marriage, the commitment has already been made, so the advice is too late. (B) and (C) are wrong for similar reasons. It is not only the continued presence of the child in the marriage that causes the stress, but the very pregnancy and birth. So (B) and (C) do not address themselves to the *birth* of the child, and that is the factor to which the author attributes the dissolution of the marriage. (D) is wide of the mark. Whether society does or does not have such an interest, the author has shown us a causal linkage, that is, a mere fact of the matter. She states: If this, then fewer divorces. She may or may not believe there should be fewer divorces. (E) is wrong for this reason also, and for the further reason that it says "do not *plan*" to have children. The author's concern is with children during the early part of the marriage. She does not suggest that couples should never have children.

25. **(E)** This question is primarily a matter of careful reading. The phrase "no lower bus fares" must not be read to mean that Flash uniquely has the lowest fare; it means only that no one else has a fare lower than that of Flash. It is conceivable that several companies share the lowest fare. So (B) is not inconsistent with the claim made in the advertisement. (C) is not inconsistent since it mentions the New York City to Boston route, and it is the Washington, D.C., to New York City route that is the subject of the ad's claim. (A) is not inconsistent since it speaks of an *air* fare and the ad's language carefully restricts the claim to *bus* fares. (D) is a bit tricky, but the ad cites only the D.C. to New York trip—(D) talks about the New York to D.C. trip. So there is no contradiction. (E) is clearly a contradiction, and this is a good time to remind you to read all of the choices before selecting one. You might have bitten on (D), but when you see (E), you know that it is a better answer.

QUESTIONS 26–32
ARRANGING THE INFORMATION

This set is a fairly straightforward linear ordering set: Individuals are arranged in a single file from 1 to 7. We summarize the information for easy reference:

K > L (L behind K)

M → N (N directly behind M)

J/O = 1/7 (J and O are first and last or vice versa.)

Answering the Questions

26. **(D)** We know that J finishes first or last, though we do not know which, so (A) and (B) are incorrect. The fourth position is the middle position of the seven. Regardless of whether J finishes first or last, if L is in position 4, L and J are separated by two swimmers. So M and N are 5 and 6. (E) is not possible; (C) is possibly, but not necessarily true.

27. **(B)** We are given no additional information, so the question must be solvable by some general conclusions based on the initial information. We are looking for the one statement that cannot, under any circumstances, be true. Since K finishes ahead of L, and since L cannot be in last place, L can finish at worst sixth, and K can finish at worst fifth. That the remaining statements are possible can be proved by examples.

28. **(D)** Since N finishes directly ahead of K, then M, N, and K finish in that order with L somewhere behind that group. So M could finish only second or third.

29. **(C)** If O and K are to finish one after the other, it must be because O finishes first and K second. Since L finishes after K, K and O cannot finish one after the other if O is seventh. Further, if O is first, J must be seventh.

30. **(B)** If K is fourth, there is only one pair of adjacent finishing positions available for the M-N pairing: second and third. So M finishes second and N third. As for L, we know that L finishes after K, but it is not clear whether it is L or P who finishes in fifth versus sixth position, nor is it established who finishes first and who finishes last.

31. **(C)** If L finishes ahead of N, we know that K finishes somewhere ahead of M. So we have the bloc K . . . M-N . . . L. And it is stipulated that J finishes first, so O finishes last. We have the order: J, K, L, M-N, O. The only unresolved issue is where P goes. There are four possibilities:

P(?)   P(?)   P(?)   P(?)

J   K   L   M-N   O

32. **(E)** We must test each condition. As for (A), knowing the first and last finishers tells us nothing about the order between 2 and 6. As for (B), this establishes nothing about positions 3 through 6. As for (C), this establishes only that N is third and leaves open positions 4, 5, and 6. (D) does tell us that M finishes second, but that is all. (E), however, allows us to infer that M and N finish before L (they must be together); and we know that K finishes before L. This leaves only position 6 for P.

33. **(E)** The author cites a series of similarities between the two diseases, and then, in the last sentence, write, "so . . . ," indicating that the conclusion that the causes of the two diseases are similar rests upon the other similarities listed. Answer (E) correctly describes the basis of the argument. (A) is incorrect, for nothing in the passage indicates that either disease is a public health hazard, much less that one disease is a greater hazard than the other. (B) is unwarranted for the author states only that the scientists are looking for a cure for *aphroditis melancholias*. The author does not state that they will be successful; and even if there is a hint of that

in the argument, we surely would not want to conclude on that basis that scientists will eventually find a cure for *every* disease. (C), like (A), is unrelated to the conclusion the author seeks to establish. All the author wants to maintain is that similarities in the symptoms suggest that scientists should look for similarities in the causes of these diseases. The author offers no opinion of the ultimate goal of modern technology, nor is one needed to complete the argument. (D) is probably the second-best answer, but it is still completely wrong. The author's argument, based on the assumption that similarity of effect depends upon similarity of cause, would neither gain nor lose persuasive force if (D) were true. After all, many diseases occur in both human beings and other animals, but at least (D) has the merit—which (A), (B), and (C) all lack—of trying to say something about the connection between the causes and effects of disease.

34. **(A)** The form of the argument can be represented using letters as:

    (1) All R are either O or W. (All non-Readers are non–Opinion-holders or Wrong.)

    (2) All O are R.

    If (2) is true, (1) might be either false or true, since it is possible that there are some who have not read the report who hold right opinions. That is, even if (2) is true and all O are R, that does not tell us anything about all the R's, only about the O's. The rest of the R's might be W's (wrong opinion-holders) or something else altogether (right opinion-holders). By this reasoning we see that we cannot conclude that (1) is definitely true, so (B) must be wrong. Moreover, we have no ground for believing (1) to be more or less likely true, so (C) can be rejected. As for (D), even if we assume that all the R's are *either* O or W, we are not entitled to conclude that all O's are R's. There may be someone without an opinion who has read the report. Finally, (E), if it is false that all the O's (non–opinion-holders) are R's, that tells us nothing about all R's and their distribution among O and W.

35. **(E)** This advertisement is simply rife with ambiguity. The wording obviously seeks to create the impression that FCBI found jobs for its many graduates and generally does a lot of good for them. But first we should ask how many graduates FCBI

had—one, two, three, a dozen, or a hundred. If it had only twelve or so, finding them jobs might have been easy; but if many people enroll at FCBI, they may not have the same success. Further, we might want to know how many people graduated compared with how many enrolled. Do people finish the program, or does FCBI just take their money and then force them out of the program? So (B) is certainly something we need to know in order to assess the validity of the claim. Now, how many of those who graduated came in looking for help in finding a job? Maybe most people had jobs waiting for them (only a few needed help), in which case the job placement assistance of FCBI is not so impressive. Or perhaps the graduates were so disgusted they did not even seek assistance. So (A) is relevant. (C) is also important. Perhaps FCBI found them jobs sweeping streets—not in business. The ad does not say what jobs FCBI helped its people find. Finally, maybe the ad is truthful—FCBI graduates found jobs—but maybe they did it on their own. So (D) also is a question worth asking. (E), however, is the least problematic. Even if it turns out that the ad was done by a paid, professional actor, so what? That's what you'd expect for an ad.

Practice Examination 4
Answer Sheet

VERBAL SECTION

1. Ⓐ Ⓑ Ⓒ Ⓓ Ⓔ   7. Ⓐ Ⓑ Ⓒ Ⓓ Ⓔ   13. Ⓐ Ⓑ Ⓒ Ⓓ Ⓔ   19. Ⓐ Ⓑ Ⓒ Ⓓ Ⓔ   25. Ⓐ Ⓑ Ⓒ Ⓓ Ⓔ
2. Ⓐ Ⓑ Ⓒ Ⓓ Ⓔ   8. Ⓐ Ⓑ Ⓒ Ⓓ Ⓔ   14. Ⓐ Ⓑ Ⓒ Ⓓ Ⓔ   20. Ⓐ Ⓑ Ⓒ Ⓓ Ⓔ   26. Ⓐ Ⓑ Ⓒ Ⓓ Ⓔ
3. Ⓐ Ⓑ Ⓒ Ⓓ Ⓔ   9. Ⓐ Ⓑ Ⓒ Ⓓ Ⓔ   15. Ⓐ Ⓑ Ⓒ Ⓓ Ⓔ   21. Ⓐ Ⓑ Ⓒ Ⓓ Ⓔ   27. Ⓐ Ⓑ Ⓒ Ⓓ Ⓔ
4. Ⓐ Ⓑ Ⓒ Ⓓ Ⓔ   10. Ⓐ Ⓑ Ⓒ Ⓓ Ⓔ   16. Ⓐ Ⓑ Ⓒ Ⓓ Ⓔ   22. Ⓐ Ⓑ Ⓒ Ⓓ Ⓔ   28. Ⓐ Ⓑ Ⓒ Ⓓ Ⓔ
5. Ⓐ Ⓑ Ⓒ Ⓓ Ⓔ   11. Ⓐ Ⓑ Ⓒ Ⓓ Ⓔ   17. Ⓐ Ⓑ Ⓒ Ⓓ Ⓔ   23. Ⓐ Ⓑ Ⓒ Ⓓ Ⓔ   29. Ⓐ Ⓑ Ⓒ Ⓓ Ⓔ
6. Ⓐ Ⓑ Ⓒ Ⓓ Ⓔ   12. Ⓐ Ⓑ Ⓒ Ⓓ Ⓔ   18. Ⓐ Ⓑ Ⓒ Ⓓ Ⓔ   24. Ⓐ Ⓑ Ⓒ Ⓓ Ⓔ   30. Ⓐ Ⓑ Ⓒ Ⓓ Ⓔ

ANALYTICAL SECTION

1. Ⓐ Ⓑ Ⓒ Ⓓ Ⓔ   8. Ⓐ Ⓑ Ⓒ Ⓓ Ⓔ   15. Ⓐ Ⓑ Ⓒ Ⓓ Ⓔ   22. Ⓐ Ⓑ Ⓒ Ⓓ Ⓔ   29. Ⓐ Ⓑ Ⓒ Ⓓ Ⓔ
2. Ⓐ Ⓑ Ⓒ Ⓓ Ⓔ   9. Ⓐ Ⓑ Ⓒ Ⓓ Ⓔ   16. Ⓐ Ⓑ Ⓒ Ⓓ Ⓔ   23. Ⓐ Ⓑ Ⓒ Ⓓ Ⓔ   30. Ⓐ Ⓑ Ⓒ Ⓓ Ⓔ
3. Ⓐ Ⓑ Ⓒ Ⓓ Ⓔ   10. Ⓐ Ⓑ Ⓒ Ⓓ Ⓔ   17. Ⓐ Ⓑ Ⓒ Ⓓ Ⓔ   24. Ⓐ Ⓑ Ⓒ Ⓓ Ⓔ   31. Ⓐ Ⓑ Ⓒ Ⓓ Ⓔ
4. Ⓐ Ⓑ Ⓒ Ⓓ Ⓔ   11. Ⓐ Ⓑ Ⓒ Ⓓ Ⓔ   18. Ⓐ Ⓑ Ⓒ Ⓓ Ⓔ   25. Ⓐ Ⓑ Ⓒ Ⓓ Ⓔ   32. Ⓐ Ⓑ Ⓒ Ⓓ Ⓔ
5. Ⓐ Ⓑ Ⓒ Ⓓ Ⓔ   12. Ⓐ Ⓑ Ⓒ Ⓓ Ⓔ   19. Ⓐ Ⓑ Ⓒ Ⓓ Ⓔ   26. Ⓐ Ⓑ Ⓒ Ⓓ Ⓔ   33. Ⓐ Ⓑ Ⓒ Ⓓ Ⓔ
6. Ⓐ Ⓑ Ⓒ Ⓓ Ⓔ   13. Ⓐ Ⓑ Ⓒ Ⓓ Ⓔ   20. Ⓐ Ⓑ Ⓒ Ⓓ Ⓔ   27. Ⓐ Ⓑ Ⓒ Ⓓ Ⓔ   34. Ⓐ Ⓑ Ⓒ Ⓓ Ⓔ
7. Ⓐ Ⓑ Ⓒ Ⓓ Ⓔ   14. Ⓐ Ⓑ Ⓒ Ⓓ Ⓔ   21. Ⓐ Ⓑ Ⓒ Ⓓ Ⓔ   28. Ⓐ Ⓑ Ⓒ Ⓓ Ⓔ   35. Ⓐ Ⓑ Ⓒ Ⓓ Ⓔ

MATH SECTION

1. Ⓐ Ⓑ Ⓒ Ⓓ Ⓔ   7. Ⓐ Ⓑ Ⓒ Ⓓ Ⓔ   13. Ⓐ Ⓑ Ⓒ Ⓓ Ⓔ   19. Ⓐ Ⓑ Ⓒ Ⓓ Ⓔ   25. Ⓐ Ⓑ Ⓒ Ⓓ Ⓔ
2. Ⓐ Ⓑ Ⓒ Ⓓ Ⓔ   8. Ⓐ Ⓑ Ⓒ Ⓓ Ⓔ   14. Ⓐ Ⓑ Ⓒ Ⓓ Ⓔ   20. Ⓐ Ⓑ Ⓒ Ⓓ Ⓔ   26. Ⓐ Ⓑ Ⓒ Ⓓ Ⓔ
3. Ⓐ Ⓑ Ⓒ Ⓓ Ⓔ   9. Ⓐ Ⓑ Ⓒ Ⓓ Ⓔ   15. Ⓐ Ⓑ Ⓒ Ⓓ Ⓔ   21. Ⓐ Ⓑ Ⓒ Ⓓ Ⓔ   27. Ⓐ Ⓑ Ⓒ Ⓓ Ⓔ
4. Ⓐ Ⓑ Ⓒ Ⓓ Ⓔ   10. Ⓐ Ⓑ Ⓒ Ⓓ Ⓔ   16. Ⓐ Ⓑ Ⓒ Ⓓ Ⓔ   22. Ⓐ Ⓑ Ⓒ Ⓓ Ⓔ   28. Ⓐ Ⓑ Ⓒ Ⓓ Ⓔ
5. Ⓐ Ⓑ Ⓒ Ⓓ Ⓔ   11. Ⓐ Ⓑ Ⓒ Ⓓ Ⓔ   17. Ⓐ Ⓑ Ⓒ Ⓓ Ⓔ   23. Ⓐ Ⓑ Ⓒ Ⓓ Ⓔ
6. Ⓐ Ⓑ Ⓒ Ⓓ Ⓔ   12. Ⓐ Ⓑ Ⓒ Ⓓ Ⓔ   18. Ⓐ Ⓑ Ⓒ Ⓓ Ⓔ   24. Ⓐ Ⓑ Ⓒ Ⓓ Ⓔ

Practice Examination 4

Verbal Section

30 QUESTIONS • TIME—30 MINUTES

Directions: Each of the questions below contains one or more blank spaces, each blank indicating an omitted word. Each sentence is followed by five (5) words or sets of words. Read and determine the general sense of each sentence. Then choose the word, or set of words that, when inserted in the sentence, best fits the meaning of the sentence.

1. Because of the —— of acupuncture therapy in China, Western physicians are starting to learn the procedure.

   (A) veracity

   (B) manipulation

   (C) liquidity

   (D) effectiveness

   (E) inflation

2. The conclusion of the program was a modern symphony with chords so —— that the piece produced sound similar to the —— one hears as the individual orchestra members tune their instruments before a concert.

   (A) superfluous..melody

   (B) pretentious..roar

   (C) melodious..applause

   (D) versatile..harmony

   (E) discordant..cacophony

3. Black comedy is the combination of that which is humorous with that which would seem —— to humor: the ——.

   (A) apathetic..ignoble

   (B) heretical..salacious

   (C) inferior..grandiose

   (D) extraneous..innocuous

   (E) antithetical..macabre

Directions: Each of the following questions consists of a word printed in capital letters, followed by five words or phrases. Choose the word or phrase that is most nearly opposite in meaning to the word in capital letters. Be sure to consider all the choices before deciding which one is best.

4. PARSIMONY :

   (A) contraband

   (B) stealth

   (C) torpor

   (D) generosity

   (E) defoliation

5. ASPERITY :

   (A) smoothness

   (B) fabrication

   (C) duplicity

   (D) indolence

   (E) intercession

6. IGNOMINIOUS :

   (A) melancholy

   (B) cantankerous

   (C) symmetrical

   (D) honorable

   (E) calamitous

7. EVANESCENT :

   (A) indulgent

   (B) obsequious

   (C) permanent

   (D) illimitable

   (E) serendipitous

369 GO ON TO THE NEXT PAGE

8. SINGER : CHORUS ::

    (A) architect : blueprint

    (B) teacher : student

    (C) author : publisher

    (D) driver : highway

    (E) actor : cast

9. INCISION : SCALPEL ::

    (A) hospital : patient

    (B) playground : swing

    (C) kitchen : knife

    (D) electricity : wire

    (E) cut : saw

10. ALTIMETER : HEIGHT ::

    (A) speedometer : velocity

    (B) observatory : constellation

    (C) racetrack : furlong

    (D) vessel : knots

    (E) metronome : tempo

It would be enormously convenient to have a single, generally accepted index of the economic and social welfare of the people of the United States. A glance at it would tell us how much better or worse off we had
(5) become each year, and we would judge the desirability of any proposed action by asking whether it would raise or lower this index. Some recent discussion implies that such an index could be constructed. Articles in the popular press even criticize the Gross National Product
(10) (GNP) because it is not such a complete index of welfare, ignoring, on the one hand, that it was never intended to be, and suggesting, on the other, that with appropriate changes it could be converted into one.

The output available to satisfy our wants and needs
(15) is one important determinant of welfare. Whatever want, need, or social problem engages our attention, we ordinarily can more easily find resources to deal with it when output is large and growing than when it is not. GNP measures output fairly well, but to evaluate wel-
(20) fare we would need additional measures which would be far more difficult to construct. We would need an index of real costs incurred in production, because we are better off if we get the same output at less cost. Use of just man-hours for welfare evaluation would unrea-
(25) sonably imply that to increase total hours by raising the hours of eight women from 60 to 65 a week imposes no more burden than raising the hours of eight men from 40 to 45 a week, or even than hiring one involuntarily unemployed person for 40 hours a week. A measure of
(30) real costs of labor would also have to consider working conditions. Most of us spend almost half our waking hours on the job and our welfare is vitally affected by the circumstances in which we spend those hours.

To measure welfare we would need a measure of
(35) changes in the need our output must satisfy. One aspect, population change, is now handled by converting output to a per capita basis on the assumption that, other things equal, twice as many people need twice as many goods and services to be equally well off. But an index
(40) of needs would also account for differences in the requirements for living as the population becomes more urbanized and suburbanized; for the changes in national defense requirements; and for changes in the effect of weather on our needs. The index would have to tell us
(45) the cost of meeting our needs in a base year compared with the cost of meeting them equally well under the circumstances prevailing in every other year.

Measures of "needs" shade into measures of the human and physical environment in which we live. We
(50) all are enormously affected by the people around us. Can we go where we like without fear of attack? We are also affected by the physical environment—purity of water and air, accessibility of park land and other conditions. To measure this requires accurate data, but
(55) such data are generally deficient. Moreover, weighting is required: to combine robberies and murders in a crime index; to combine pollution of the Potomac and pollu-tion of Lake Erie into a water pollution index; and then to combine crime and water pollution into some general
(60) index. But there is no basis for weighting these beyond individual preference.

There are further problems. To measure welfare we would need an index of the "goodness" of the distribution of income. There is surely consensus that given the
(65) same total income and output, a distribution with fewer families in poverty would be the better, but what is the ideal distribution? Even if we could construct indexes of output, real costs, needs, and state of the environment, we could not compute a welfare index because we
(70) have no system of weights to combine them.

11. The author's primary concern is to

    (A) refute arguments for a position

    (B) make a proposal and defend it

    (C) attack the sincerity of an opponent

    (D) show defects in a proposal

    (E) review literature relevant to a problem

12. The author implies that man-hours is not an appropriate measure of real cost because it

    (A) ignores the conditions under which the output is generated

    (B) fails to take into consideration the environmental costs of production

    (C) overemphasizes the output of real goods as opposed to services

    (D) is not an effective method for reducing unemployment

    (E) was never intended to be a general measure of welfare

13. It can be inferred from the passage that the most important reason a single index of welfare cannot be designed is

    (A) the cost associated with producing the index would be prohibitive

    (B) considerable empirical research would have to be done regarding output and needs

    (C) any weighting of various measures into a general index would be inherently subjective and arbitrary

    (D) production of the relevant data would require time, thus the index would be only a reflection of past welfare

    (E) accurate statistics on crime and pollution are not yet available

14. The author regards the idea of a general index of welfare as

    (A) an unrealistic dream

    (B) a scientific reality

    (C) an important contribution

    (D) a future necessity

    (E) a desirable change

15. According to the passage, the GNP is

    (A) a fairly accurate measure of output

    (B) a reliable estimate of needs

    (C) an accurate forecaster of welfare

    (D) a precise measure of welfare

    (E) a potential measure of general welfare

16. According to the passage, an adequate measure of need must take into account all of the following EXCEPT

    (A) changing size of the population

    (B) changing effects on people of the weather

    (C) differences in needs of urban and suburban populations

    (D) changing requirements for governmental programs such as defense

    (E) accessibility of park land and other amenities

Directions: Each of the questions below contains one or more blank spaces, each blank indicating an omitted word. Each sentence is followed by five (5) words or sets of words. Read and determine the general sense of each sentence. Then choose the word, or set of words that, when inserted in the sentence, best fits the meaning of the sentence.

17. The press conference did not clarify many issues since the president responded with —— and —— rather than clarity and precision.

    (A) sincerity..humor

    (B) incongruity..candor

    (C) fervor..lucidity

    (D) animation..formality

    (E) obfuscation..vagueness

GO ON TO THE NEXT PAGE

18. It is difficult for a modern audience, accustomed to the —— of film and television, to appreciate opera with its grand spectacle and —— gestures.

    (A) irreverence..hapless

    (B) sophistication..monotonous

    (C) minutiae..extravagant

    (D) plurality..subtle

    (E) flamboyance..inane

19. The sonatas of Beethoven represent the —— of classicism, but they also contain the seed of its destruction, romanticism, which —— the sonata form by allowing emotion rather than tradition to shape the music.

    (A) denigration..perpetuates

    (B) pinnacle..shatters

    (C) plethora..heightens

    (D) fruition..restores

    (E) ignorance..encumbers

Directions: In each of the following questions, you are given a related pair of words or phrases in capital letters. Each capitalized pair is followed by five (5) pairs of words or phrases. Choose the pair that best expresses a relationship similar to that expressed by the original pair.

20. UNGAINLY : ELEGANCE ::

    (A) stately : majesty

    (B) suitable : propriety

    (C) vacuous : temerity

    (D) feckless : sobriety

    (E) perfunctory : attention

21. CONSERVATOR : WASTE ::

    (A) sentinel : vigilance

    (B) monarch : subject

    (C) demagogue : benevolence

    (D) chaperon : transgression

    (E) minister : profanity

22. POLEMICIST : CONTROVERSY ::

    (A) dilettante : virtuosity

    (B) visionary : dream

    (C) pundit : sophistry

    (D) zealot : benevolence

    (E) bigot : equanimity

23. PROSELYTIZE : CONVERT ::

    (A) argue : persuade

    (B) digress : disturb

    (C) abide : forego

    (D) deflect : condone

    (E) dissemble : abet

Directions: The passage below is followed by questions based on its content. Choose the best answer to each question.

In a sense the university has failed. It has stored great quantities of knowledge; it teaches more people; and despite its failures, it teaches them better. It is in the application of this knowledge that the failure has come.
(5) Of the great branches of knowledge—the sciences, the social sciences and humanities—the sciences are applied. Strenuous and occasionally successful efforts are made to apply the social sciences, but almost never are the humanities well applied. We do not use philosophy
(10) in defining our conduct. We do not use literature as a source of real and vicarious experience. The great task of the university in the next generation is to learn to use the knowledge we have for the questions that come before us. The university should organize courses around
(15) primary problems. The difference between a primary problem and a secondary or even tertiary problem is that primary problems tend to be around for a long time, whereas the less important ones get solved.

One primary problem is that of interfering with bio-
(20) logical development. The next generation, and perhaps this one, will be able to interfere chemically with the actual development of an individual and perhaps biologically by interfering with an individual's genes. Obviously, there are benefits both to individuals and to society
(25) from eliminating, or at least improving, mentally and physically deformed persons. On the other hand, there could be very serious consequences if this knowledge were used with premeditation to produce superior and

subordinate classes, each genetically prepared to carry
(30) out a predetermined mission. This can be done, but what
happens to free will and the rights of the individual? Here
we have a primary problem that will still exist when we
are all dead. Of course, the traditional faculty members
would say, "But the students won't learn enough to go to
(35) graduate school." And certainly they would not learn
everything we are in the habit of making them learn, but
they would learn some other things.

24. The author suggests that the university's greatest
shortcoming is its failure to

(A) attempt to provide equal opportunity for all

(B) offer courses in philosophy and the
humanities

(C) prepare students adequately for professional studies

(D) help students see the relevance of the
humanities to real problems

(E) require students to include in their cur-
ricula liberal arts courses

25. It can be inferred that the author presupposes that the
reader will regard a course in literature as a course

(A) with little or no practical value

(B) of interest only to academic scholars

(C) required by most universities for graduation

(D) uniquely relevant to today's primary problems

(E) used to teach students good writing skills

26. Which of the following questions would the
author most likely consider a primary question?

(A) Should Congress increase the level of
Social Security benefits?

(B) Is it appropriate for the state to use capital
punishment?

(C) Who is the best candidate for president in
the next presidential election?

(D) At what month can the fetus be considered
medically viable outside the mother's womb?

(E) What measures should be taken to solve
the problem of world hunger?

27. VILIFY :

(A) thwart
(B) purport
(C) abound
(D) circumscribe
(E) laud

28. TENDER :

(A) demote
(B) truncate
(C) retract
(D) emancipate
(E) besiege

29. FUNGIBLE :

(A) corrosive
(B) iridescent
(C) unique
(D) retrograde
(E) discursive

30. SPLENETIC :

(A) taciturn
(B) enigmatic
(C) complacent
(D) contrite
(E) mischievous

WARNING

IF YOU FINISHED THIS SECTION BEFORE TIME EXPIRED, GO
IMMEDIATELY TO THE NEXT SECTION. YOU MAY NOT CON-
TINUE TO WORK ON THIS SECTION AFTER TIME HAS EXPIRED.

Analytical Section

35 QUESTIONS • TIME—40 MINUTES

Directions: Each of the following questions or groups of questions is based on a short passage or a set of propositions. In answering these questions it may sometimes be helpful to draw a simple picture or chart.

Questions 1–6

On a certain railway route, five trains each day operate between City X and City Y: the Meteor, the Comet, the Flash, the Streak, and the Rocket. Each train consists of exactly five cars, and each car is either a deluxe-class car or a coach car.

On the Meteor, only the first, second, and fifth cars are coach.

On the Comet, only the second and third cars are coach.

On the Flash, only the second car is coach.

On the Streak, only the third and fourth cars are coach.

On the Rocket, all cars are coach.

1. On a typical day, which of the following must be true of the railway's trains operating between City X and City Y?

   (A) More deluxe cars than coach cars are used as first cars.

   (B) More deluxe cars than coach cars are used as second cars.

   (C) Every train uses a deluxe car for the fifth car.

   (D) More deluxe cars are used than coach cars.

   (E) More deluxe cars are used on the Rocket and the Streak combined than on the Flash and the Comet combined.

2. Which of the following cars cannot both be deluxe cars on the same train?

   (A) First and second

   (B) First and third

   (C) Second and third

   (D) Third and fourth

   (E) Fourth and fifth

3. To determine which train is the Streak, correct information on whether a car is deluxe or coach is needed for which car or cars?

   (A) First

   (B) Second

   (C) Third

   (D) First and fifth

   (E) Third and fifth

4. If a train has a coach car as the second car, then that train could be any train EXCEPT the

   (A) Meteor

   (B) Comet

   (C) Flash

   (D) Streak

   (E) Rocket

5. If a train has deluxe cars as the first and third cars of the train, that train must be the

   (A) Meteor

   (B) Comet

   (C) Flash

   (D) Streak

   (E) Rocket

6. If only one of the third, fourth, and fifth cars of a train is a deluxe car, then that train must be the

   (A) Meteor

   (B) Comet

   (C) Flash

   (D) Streak

   (E) Rocket

Questions 7 and 8

During the 1970s the number of clandestine CIA agents posted to foreign countries increased 25 percent and the number of CIA employees not assigned to field work increased by 21 percent. In the same period, the number of FBI agents assigned to case investigation rose by 18 percent, but the number of noncase-working agents rose by only 3 percent.

7. The statistics best support which of the following claims?

(A) More agents are needed to administer the CIA than are needed for the FBI.

(B) The CIA needs more people to accomplish its mission than does the FBI.

(C) The number of field agents tends to increase more rapidly than the number of non-field agents in both the CIA and the FBI.

(D) The rate of change in the number of supervisory agents in an intelligence-gathering agency or a law-enforcement agency is proportional to the percentage change in the results produced by the agency.

(E) At the end of the 1960s, the CIA was more efficiently administered than was the FBI.

8. In response to the allegation that it was more overstaffed with support and supervisory personnel than the FBI, the CIA could best argue:

(A) The FBI is less useful than the CIA in gathering intelligence against foreign powers.

(B) The rate of pay for a CIA non-field agent is less than the rate of pay for a non-investigating FBI agent.

(C) The number of FBI agents should not rise as rapidly as the number of CIA agents, given the longer tenure of an FBI agent.

(D) A CIA field agent working in a foreign country requires more back-up support than does an FBI investigator working domestically.

(E) The number of CIA agents is determined by the Congress each year when they appropriate funds for the agency, and the Congress is very sensitive to changes in the international political climate.

9. All effective administrators are concerned about the welfare of their employees, and all administrators who are concerned about the welfare of their employees are liberal in granting time off for personal needs; therefore, all administrators who are not liberal in granting time off for their employees' personal needs are not effective administrators.

If the argument above is valid, then it must be true that

(A) no ineffective administrators are liberal in granting time off for their employees' personal needs

(B) no ineffective administrators are concerned about the welfare of their employees

(C) some effective administrators are not liberal in granting time off for their employees' personal needs

(D) all effective administrators are liberal in granting time off for their employees' personal needs

(E) all time off for personal needs is granted by effective administrators

Questions 10–15

The principal of a high school is selecting a committee of students to attend an annual student leadership conference. The students eligible for selection are P, Q, R, S, T, U, and V. The committee must be selected in accordance with the following considerations:

If V is selected, R must be selected.

If both R and Q are selected, then P cannot be selected.

If both Q and P are selected, then T cannot be selected.

If P is selected, then either S or U must be selected; but S and U cannot both be selected.

Either S or T must be selected, but S and T cannot both be selected.

GO ON TO THE NEXT PAGE

10. If neither S nor U is selected, what is the largest number of students who can be selected for the conference?

    (A) 2

    (B) 3

    (C) 4

    (D) 5

    (E) 6

11. If both P and V are selected, what is the smallest number of students who can be selected for the conference?

    (A) 3

    (B) 4

    (C) 5

    (D) 6

    (E) 7

12. If both P and U are selected, which of the following must be true?

    (A) Q must be selected.

    (B) S must be selected.

    (C) T must be selected.

    (D) R cannot be selected.

    (E) V cannot be selected.

13. Which of the following is an acceptable delegation to the conference if only three students are selected?

    (A) P, Q, and S

    (B) P, Q, and T

    (C) P, R, and V

    (D) R, S, and T

    (E) R, S, and U

14. If both P and T are chosen, which of the following CANNOT be true?

    (A) The committee consists of three students.

    (B) The committee consists of four students.

    (C) The committee consists of five students.

    (D) U is not chosen.

    (E) V is not chosen.

15. If U and three other students are selected, which of the following groups can accompany U?

    (A) P, Q, and T

    (B) P, R, and T

    (C) P, Q, and V

    (D) P, V, and S

    (E) R, S, and V

Questions 16–21

A farm is divided into four fields designated as the North Field, the East Field, the South Field, and the West Field. For the new growing season, each of the fields will be planted with exactly one of four crops—corn, beans, barley, or oats—according to the following plan:

The West Field must be planted with either barley or beans.

At least one field must be planted with corn.

If, in the previous year, a field was planted with beans, then it must be planted with beans again.

If, in the previous year, a field was planted with either wheat or alfalfa, then it must be planted with oats.

16. Which of the following could be the crops planted?

	North	East	South	West
(A)	beans	corn	barley	oats
(B)	beans	barley	oats	beans
(C)	wheat	barley	oats	beans
(D)	oats	barley	corn	beans
(E)	alfalfa	corn	beans	beans

17. If, in one year, the East Field is planted with wheat and the South Field is planted with beans, which of the following must be true of the year immediately following?

    (A) The North Field is planted with barley.

    (B) The North Field is planted with corn.

    (C) The West Field is planted with barley.

    (D) The South Field is planted with oats.

    (E) The East Field is planted with beans.

18. In the previous growing season, the West Field could have been planted with any of the following crops EXCEPT

    (A) alfalfa

    (B) beans

    (C) barley

    (D) oats

    (E) corn

19. If, in the previous growing season, the West Field was planted with corn and the other three fields were planted with oats, what is the minimum number of fields that must be planted with crops that are different from those planted there for the previous growing season?

    (A) None

    (B) One

    (C) Two

    (D) Three

    (E) Four

20. If three of the four fields were planted with beans for the previous growing season, which of the following could also have been true of the previous growing season?

    (A) Barley was planted in the West Field.

    (B) Corn was planted in the West Field.

    (C) The fourth field was planted with oats.

    (D) The fourth field was planted with wheat.

    (E) The fourth field was planted with beans.

21. If, for the previous growing season, the North Field was planted with oats, the East Field was planted with beans, and the South Field was planted with alfalfa, which of the following must be true of the new growing season?

    (A) Corn is planted in the North Field.

    (B) Oats are planted in the North Field.

    (C) Barley is planted in the East Field.

    (D) Barley is planted in the West Field.

    (E) Beans are planted in the West Field.

22. Opponents to the mayor's plan for express bus lanes on the city's major commuter arteries objected that people could not be lured out of their automobiles in that way. The opponents were proved wrong; following implementation of the plan, bus ridership rose dramatically, and there was a corresponding drop in automobile traffic. Nonetheless, the plan failed to achieve its stated objective of reducing average commuting time.

    Which of the following sentences would be the most logical continuation of this argument?

    (A) The plan's opponents failed to realize that many people would take advantage of improved bus transportation.

    (B) Unfortunately, politically attractive solutions do not always get results.

    (C) The number of people a vehicle can transport varies directly with the size of the passenger compartment of the vehicle.

    (D) Opponents cited an independent survey of city commuters showing that before the plan's adoption only one out of every seven used commuter bus lines.

    (E) With the express lanes closed to private automobile traffic, the remaining cars were forced to use too few lanes and this created gigantic traffic tie-ups.

23. Clark must have known that his sister Janet and not the governess pulled the trigger, but he silently stood by while the jury convicted the governess. Any person of clear conscience would have felt terrible for not having come forward with the information about his sister, and Clark lived with that information until his death thirty years later. Since he was an extremely happy man, however, I conclude that he must have helped Janet commit the crime.

Which of the following assumptions must underlie the author's conclusion of the last sentence?

(A) Loyalty to members of one's family is conducive to contentment.

(B) Servants are not to be treated with the same respect as members of the peerage.

(C) Clark never had a bad conscience over his silence because he was also guilty of the crime.

(D) It is better to be a virtuous man than a happy one.

(E) It is actually better to be content in life than to behave morally towards one's fellow humans.

24. "Whom did you pass on the road?" the King went on, holding his hand out to the messenger for some hay.

"Nobody," said the messenger.

"Quite right," said the King. "This young lady saw him, too. So, of course, Nobody walks slower than you."

The King's response shows that he believes

(A) the messenger is a very good messenger

(B) "Nobody" is a person who might be seen

(C) the young lady's eyesight is better than the messenger's

(D) the messenger is not telling him the truth

(E) there was a person actually seen by the messenger on the road

25. New Evergreen Gum has twice as much flavor for your money as Spring Mint Gum, and we can prove it. You see, a stick of Evergreen Gum is twice as large as a stick of Spring Mint Gum, and the more gum, the more flavor.

All BUT which of the following would tend to weaken the argument above?

(A) A package of Spring Mint Gum contains twice as many sticks as a package of Evergreen Gum.

(B) Spring Mint Gum has more concentrated flavor than Evergreen Gum.

(C) A stick of Evergreen Gum weights only 50 percent as much as a stick of Spring Mint Gum.

(D) A package of Evergreen Gum costs twice as much as a package of Spring Mint Gum.

(E) People surveyed indicated a preference for Evergreen Gum over Spring Mint Gum.

Questions 26–32

Nine people, J, K, L, M, N, O, P, Q, and R, have rented a small hotel for a weekend. The hotel has five floors, numbered consecutively 1 (bottom) to 5 (top). The top floor has only one room while floors 1 through 4 each have two rooms. Each person will occupy one and only one room for the weekend.

Q and R will occupy the rooms on the third floor.

P will stay on a lower floor than M.

K will stay on a lower floor than N.

K will stay on a lower floor than L.

J and L will occupy rooms on the same floor.

26. Which of the following CANNOT be true?

(A) J stays on the first floor.

(B) K stays on the first floor.

(C) O stays on the second floor.

(D) M stays on the fourth floor.

(E) N stays on the fifth floor.

27. If M occupies a room on the second floor, which of the following must be true?

    (A) J stays on the fifth floor.

    (B) N stays on the fifth floor.

    (C) J stays on the fourth floor.

    (D) K stays on the second floor.

    (E) O stays on the first floor.

28. Which of the following CANNNOT be true?

    (A) K stays on the fifth floor.

    (B) M stays on the fifth floor.

    (C) J stays on the fourth floor.

    (D) R stays on the third floor.

    (E) L stays on the second floor.

29. Which of the following is a complete and accurate list of the persons who could stay on the first floor?

    (A) K, O

    (B) M, N

    (C) M, O

    (D) K, M, O

    (E) K, O, P

30. If M occupies a room on the fourth floor, which of the following must be true?

    (A) J stays on the first floor.

    (B) K stays on the first floor.

    (C) O stays on the fourth floor.

    (D) O stays on the fifth floor.

    (E) N stays on the fifth floor.

31. If K and M stay in rooms on the same floor, which of the following is a complete and accurate list of the floors on which they could stay?

    (A) 1

    (B) 2

    (C) 4

    (D) 1 and 4

    (E) 2 and 4

32. Which of the following, if true, provides sufficient additional information to determine on which floor each person will stay?

    (A) P stays on the first floor.

    (B) M stays on the second floor.

    (C) K stays on the second floor.

    (D) M stays on the fourth floor.

    (E) N stays on the fifth floor.

33. Some judges have allowed hospitals to disconnect life-support equipment of patients who have no prospects for recovery. But I say that is cold-blooded murder. Either we put a stop to this practice now or we will soon have programs of euthanasia for the old and infirm as well as others who might be considered a burden. Rather than disconnecting life-support equipment, we should let nature take its course.

    Which of the following objections is the LEAST effective criticism of the argument above?

    (A) It is internally inconsistent.

    (B) It employs emotionally charged terms.

    (C) It presents a false dilemma.

    (D) It oversimplifies a complex moral situation.

    (E) It fails to cite an authority for its conclusion.

GO ON TO THE NEXT PAGE

34. The main ingredient in this bottle of Dr. John's Milk of Magnesia is used by nine out of ten hospitals across the country as an antacid and laxative.

If this advertising claim is true, which of the following statements must also be true?

(A) Nine out of ten hospitals across the country use Dr. John's Milk of Magnesia for some ailments.

(B) Only one out of ten hospitals in the country does not treat acid indigestion and constipation.

(C) Only one out of ten hospitals across the country does not recommend Dr. John's Milk of Magnesia for patients who need milk of magnesia.

(D) Only one of ten hospitals across the country uses a patent medicine other than Dr. John's Milk of Magnesia as an antacid and laxative.

(E) Nine out of ten hospitals across the country use the main ingredient in Dr. John's Milk of Magnesia as an antacid and laxative.

35. A study published by the Department of Education shows that children in the central cities lag far behind students in the suburbs and the rural areas in reading skills. The report blamed this differential on the overcrowding in the classrooms of city schools. I maintain, however, that the real reason that city children are poorer readers than non-city children is that they do not get enough fresh air and sunshine.

Which of the following would LEAST strengthen the author's point in the argument above?

(A) Medical research that shows a correlation between air pollution and learning disabilities

(B) A report by educational experts demonstrating there is no relationship between the number of students in a classroom and a student's ability to read

(C) A notice released by the Department of Education retracting that part of their report that mentions overcrowding as the reason for the differential

(D) The results of a federal program that indicates that city students show significant improvement in reading skills when they spend the summer in the country

(E) A proposal by the federal government to fund emergency programs to hire more teachers for central city schools in an attempt to reduce overcrowding in the classrooms

WARNING

IF YOU FINISHED THIS SECTION BEFORE TIME EXPIRED, GO IMMEDIATELY TO THE NEXT SECTION. YOU MAY NOT CONTINUE TO WORK ON THIS SECTION AFTER TIME HAS EXPIRED.

Math Section

28 QUESTIONS • TIME—45 MINUTES

Directions: For each of these questions, select the best of the answer choices given.

Numbers: All numbers used are real numbers.

Figures: Assume that the position of points, angles, regions, and so forth are in the order shown. Figures are assumed to lie in a plane unless otherwise indicated. Figures accompanying questions are intended to provide information you can use in answering the questions. However, unless a note states that a figure is drawn to scale, you should solve the problems by using your knowledge of mathematics and not by estimating sizes by sight or measurement.

Lines: Assume that lines shown as straight are indeed straight.

Directions: For each of the following questions two quantities are given, one in Column A and one in Column B. Compare the two quantities and choose

   A: if the quantity in Column A is the greater
   B: if the quantity in Column B is the greater
   C: if the two quantities are equal
   D: if the relationship cannot be determined
      from the information given.

Common Information: In any question, information applying to both columns is centered between the columns and above the quantities in columns A and B. Any symbol that appears in both columns represents the same idea or quantity in both columns.

Column A	Column B
	$x = -y$	

	Column A	Column B
1.	x	y
2.	$\dfrac{1}{100}$	.01%

Column A	Column B
The price of paper increased from $1.23 per ream to $1.48 per ream.	

3. The percent increase   20%
   in the price of paper

M is the average (arithmetic mean) of x and y.

4. $\dfrac{M+x+y}{3}$ $\dfrac{x+y}{2}$

5. $(a+2)(b+3)$ $(a+3)(b+2)$

Directions: For each of these questions, select the best of the answer choices given.

6. $\dfrac{3}{4} + \dfrac{4}{5} =$

(A) $\dfrac{7}{20}$

(B) $\dfrac{3}{5}$

(C) $\dfrac{7}{9}$

(D) $\dfrac{12}{9}$

(E) $\dfrac{31}{20}$

7. If $x + 6 = 3$, then $x + 3 =$

(A) -9

(B) -3

(C) 0

(D) 3

(E) 9

GO ON TO THE NEXT PAGE

8. A person is standing on a staircase. He walks down 4 steps, up 3 steps, down 6 steps, up 2 steps, up 9 steps, and down 2 steps. Where is he standing in relation to the step on which he started?

(A) 2 steps above

(B) 1 step above

(C) the same place

(D) 1 step below

(E) 2 steps below

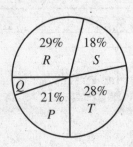

9. What portion of the circle graph above belongs to sector Q?

(A) 4%

(B) 5%

(C) 6%

(D) 75%

(E) 96%

10. $326(31) - 326(19) =$

(A) 3,912

(B) 704

(C) 100

(D) 32.6

(E) 10

Directions: For each of the following questions two quantities are given, one in Column A and one in Column B. Compare the two quantities and choose

A: if the quantity in Column A is the greater

B: if the quantity in Column B is the greater

C: if the two quantities are equal

D: if the relationship cannot be determined from the information given.

Column A	Column B
11. The average (arithmetic mean) of the number of degrees in the angles of a pentagon.	The average (arithmetic mean) of the number of degrees in the angles of a hexagon.

A bookshelf contains 16 books written in French and 8 books written in Italian and no other books. 75% of the books written in French and 50% of the books written in Italian are removed from the bookshelf.

12. The proportion of the original number of books remaining on the shelf	$\dfrac{2}{3}$

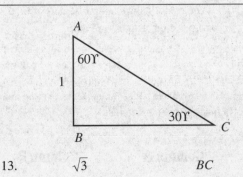

13. $\sqrt{3}$	BC

$$x^2 - 1 = 0$$

14. x	1

Tickets to a concert cost $25 and $13. An agent sells 11 tickets for a total price of $227.

15. The number of $25 tickets sold	The number of $13 tickets sold

Questions 16–20 are based on the following figure.

Directions: For each of these questions, select the best of the answer choices given.

Sales and Earnings of Company *K*

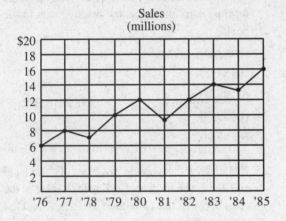

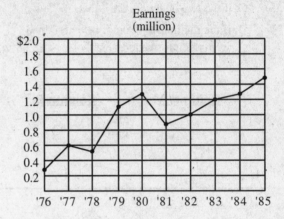

16. From 1977 to 1983, inclusive, what was the amount of the greatest increase in earnings from one year to the next?

    (A) $300,000
    (B) $600,000
    (C) $750,000
    (D) $1,000,000
    (E) $1,200,000

17. From 1980 to 1984, inclusive, in which year did sales change by the greatest percent over the previous year?

    (A) 1980
    (B) 1981
    (C) 1982
    (D) 1983
    (E) 1984

18. For the years 1981 to 1985, inclusive, average earnings of Company K were approximately

    (A) $1,180,000
    (B) $998,000
    (C) $920,000
    (D) $880,000
    (E) $720,000

19. From 1976 to 1985, earnings of Company K increased by what percent?

    (A) 150%
    (B) 200%
    (C) $233\frac{1}{3}\%$
    (D) 400%
    (E) 500%

20. In how many of the years shown were earnings equal to or greater than 10 percent of sales?

    (A) 3
    (B) 4
    (C) 5
    (D) 6
    (E) 7

GO ON TO THE NEXT PAGE

Directions: For each of the following questions two quantities are given, one in Column A and one in Column B. Compare the two quantities and choose

A: if the quantity in Column A is the greater

B: if the quantity in Column B is the greater

C: if the two quantities are equal

D: if the relationship cannot be determined from the information given.

Directions: For each of these questions, select the best of the answer choices given.

24. A child withdraws from his piggy bank 10% of the original sum in the bank. If he must add 90¢ to bring the amount in the bank back up to the original sum, what was the original sum in the bank?

(A) $1.00

(B) $1.90

(C) $8.10

(D) $9.00

(E) $9.90

Column A	Column B

$$x - y \neq 0$$

21. $\dfrac{x^2 - y^2}{x - y}$ $x + y$

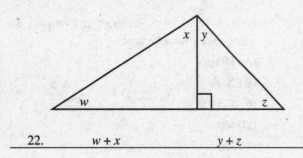

22. $w + x$ $y + z$

25. If cylinder P has a height twice that of cylinder Q and a radius half that of cylinder Q, what is the ratio between the volume of cylinder P and the volume of cylinder Q?

(A) 1 : 8

(B) 1 : 4

(C) 1 : 2

(D) 1 : 1

(E) 2 : 1

Planes X and Y are 300 miles apart and flying toward each other on a direct course and at constant speeds. X is flying at 150 miles per hour. After 40 minutes, they pass one another.

23.   Speed of plane Y 150 miles per hour

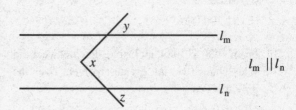

26. In the figure above, which of the following is true?

(A) $y + z = x$

(B) $y = 90°$

(C) $x + y + z = 180°$

(D) $y = x + z$

(E) $z = x + y$

27. If the width of a rectangle is increased by 25% while the length remains constant, the resulting area is what percent of the original area?

(A) 25%

(B) 75%

(C) 125%

(D) 225%

(E) Cannot be determined from the information given.

28. The sum of four consecutive odd positive integers is always

(A) an odd number

(B) divisible by 4

(C) a prime number

(D) a multiple of 3

(E) greater than 24

WARNING

IF YOU FINISHED THIS SECTION BEFORE TIME EXPIRED, GO IMMEDIATELY TO THE NEXT SECTION. YOU MAY NOT CONTINUE TO WORK ON THIS SECTION AFTER TIME HAS EXPIRED.

Answer Key

VERBAL SECTION

1. D	7. C	13. C	19. B	25. A
2. E	8. E	14. A	20. E	26. B
3. E	9. E	15. A	21. D	27. E
4. D	10. A	16. E	22. B	28. C
5. A	11. D	17. E	23. A	29. C
6. D	12. A	18. C	24. D	30. C

ANALYTICAL SECTION

1. A	8. D	15. B	22. E	29. E
2. C	9. D	16. D	23. C	30. B
3. B	10. C	17. B	24. B	31. B
4. D	11. B	18. A	25. E	32. C
5. C	12. C	19. C	26. A	33. E
6. D	13. A	20. C	27. C	34. E
7. C	14. D	21. A	28. A	35. E

MATH SECTION

1. D	7. C	13. C	19. D	25. C
2. A	8. A	14. D	20. B	26. A
3. A	9. A	15. A	21. C	27. C
4. C	10. A	16. B	22. C	28. B
5. D	11. B	17. C	23. A	
6. E	12. B	18. A	24. D	

Practice Examination 4

Explanatory Answers

VERBAL SECTION

1. **(D)** This is basically a vocabulary question. You do, however, have one clue to the meaning of the sentence. The sentence tells you that Western physicians are learning a procedure. Logically, they are doing this because it is desirable, so you should look for the noun that has a positive connotation. This eliminates (B) and (E). If you substitute (A) or (C), you have a meaningless sentence. So the answer must be (D).

2. **(E)** The second blank is an extension of the first idea. You can eliminate (A) because the idea of hearing a melody does not explain why a chord is superfluous. You can eliminate (B) because the idea of hearing a roar doesn't explain why a chord might be pretentious. You can eliminate (C) because the idea of hearing applause doesn't explain why a chord might be melodious. And you can eliminate (D) because hearing harmony doesn't explain why a chord might be versatile. (E) preserves the sense and logic of the sentence. "Hearing cacophony" indicates that the chord is discordant.

3. **(E)** The best way to attack this question is to substitute each pair until you find one that works. You can immediately eliminate (A) on the grounds of usage, as "*apathetic* to humor" makes no sense. Next, the *salacious* is not *heretical* to humor, so eliminate (B). The *grandiose* is not *inferior* to humor, so eliminate (C). The *innocuous* is not *extraneous* to humor, so eliminate (D). You are left with (E), which does make sense. The *macabre* might be *antithetical* to humor.

4. **(D)** *Parsimony* means "frugality or stinginess," so *generosity* is a good opposite.

5. **(A)** *Asperity* means "roughness or unevenness"; therefore, a good antonym is *smoothness*.

6. **(D)** *Ignominious* means "dishonorable or disgraceful." *Honorable* is a precise antonym.

7. **(C)** *Evanescent* means "vanishing, fleeting, or passing away." A good opposite is *permanent*.

8. **(E)** This is a part to whole analogy. A SINGER is part of a CHORUS, and an *actor* is part of a *cast*.

9. **(E)** This analogy falls into the "tool" category. An INCISION is made with a SCALPEL, or a scalpel is the tool used to make an incision. A *cut* is made with a *saw*, or a saw is the tool used to cut.

10. **(A)** This analogy is fairly straightforward. An ALTIMETER measures HEIGHT, and a *speedometer* measures *velocity*.

11. **(D)** This is a main idea question. The author begins by stating that it would be useful to have a general index to measure welfare and notes that some have even suggested the GNP might be adapted for that purpose. The author then proceeds to demonstrate why such an index cannot be constructed. Generally, then, the author shows the defects in a proposal for a general index of welfare, and (D) nicely describes this development. (A) is incorrect for the author never produces any arguments for the position being attacked. And even when the author raises points such as the suggestion that hours worked might be a measure of cost of production, the author is not citing arguments for that position, but only mentioning the position to attack it. (B) is incorrect since the author is attacking and not defending the proposal discussed. (C) is easily eliminated because the author never attacks the sincerity of opponents. Finally, (E) is wrong, for the author never reviews any literature on the subject being discussed.

12. **(A)** This is an inference question. We turn to the second paragraph. There the author mentions that a general index of welfare would have to include some measure of the cost of producing the output. The author suggests that someone might think hours worked would do the trick, but rejects that position by noting that hours worked, as a statistic, does not take into account the quality of the work time, e.g., long hours versus short hours, working conditions, satisfaction of workers. Answer (A) best describes this argument. (B) is incorrect, for the author discusses environmental costs in connection with another aspect of a general index. (C) is incorrect since this distinction is never used by the author. (D) is incorrect since this is not mentioned as a goal of such a measure. Finally, (E)

confuses the GNP, mentioned in the first part of the paragraph, with the index to measure real costs.

13. **(C)** This is an inference question that asks about the main point of the passage. The author adduces several objections to the idea of a general index of welfare. Then the final blow is delivered in the last paragraph: Even if you could devise measures for these various components of a general index, any combination or weighting of the individual measures would reflect only the judgment (personal preference) of the weighter. For this reason alone, argues the author, the entire idea is unworkable. (C) makes this point. (A) and (D) can be eliminated since the author never uses cost or time as arguments against the index. (B) can be eliminated on similar ground. The author may recognize that considerable research would be needed to attempt such measures, yet does not bother to use that as an objection. (E) can be eliminated for a similar reason. The author may have some arguments against the way such statistics are gathered now, but does not bother to make them. The author's argument has the structure: Even assuming there are such data, we cannot combine these statistics to get a general measure of the quality of the environment.

14. **(A)** This is a tone question, and the justification for (A) is already implicit in the discussion thus far. The author sees fatal theoretical weaknesses inherent in the idea of an index of welfare. So we might say that the author regards such a notion as an unrealistic, that is, unachievable, dream. (B) is incorrect because the author does not believe the idea can ever be implemented. (C), (D), and (E) can be eliminated on substantially the same ground.

15. **(A)** This is an explicit idea question. The second paragraph acknowledges that the GNP is a fairly accurate measure of output. The author never suggests that the GNP can estimate needs, predict welfare, or measure welfare generally. So we can eliminate the remaining choices.

16. **(E)** This is an explicit idea question, with a thought-reverser. (A), (B), (C), and (D) are all mentioned in the third paragraph as aspects of a needs index. The fourth paragraph does not treat the idea of a needs index but the idea of a physical environment index. That is where the author discusses the items mentioned in (E). So the author does mention the

items covered by (E), but not as part of a needs index.

17. **(E)** This entire sentence is a thought-reverser. The president responded with something other than clarity and precision. You should immediately look for opposites of these words for the blanks. (E), *obfuscation* and *vagueness*, do the job.

18. **(C)** This sentence contains a thought-reverser and a thought-extender. The first blank requires a word that will reverse the idea of grand spectacle, since we know that the modern audience has learned to appreciate the opposite of grand spectacle. The second blank requires a word that extends the idea of grand spectacle. (A) is not possible, since *irreverence* is not the opposite of grand spectacle and hapless does not extend that idea. (B) might seem plausible, since one could say that film and television are *sophisticated*, but *monotonous* is hardly the word one would use to describe grand spectacle. (C) is correct because the idea of *minutiae*, or details, is in direct opposition to the idea of something large or grand like opera. The second word also fits nicely, since *extravagant* extends the idea of grand spectacle. As for (D), the first word fails to make a meaningful sentence, and (E) cannot be correct since *flamboyance* extends the idea of grand spectacle instead of reversing it.

19. **(B)** This sentence contains a thought-reverser and a thought-extender. The first blank requires a word that reverses the idea of destruction of classicism and the second blank requires a word that extends the idea of destruction. (A) may appear possible at first, but the second word, *perpetuates*, makes the choice impossible since it does not extend the idea of destruction. (B) is correct because "pinnacle of classicism" is the opposite of the concept of its destruction, and *shatters* perfectly extends the idea of destruction. (C) is wrong because it fails to make a meaningful sentence. (D) appears plausible, because *fruition* certainly reverses the notion of destruction, but *restores* does not extend the idea of destruction. As for (E), if the sonatas represent an ignorance of classicism, then they could not also contain the seeds of its destruction.

20. **(E)** This analogy fits into the "lack of" category. That which is UNGAINLY lacks ELEGANCE, and that which is *perfunctory* lacks *attention*.

21. **(D)** This is a variation on the "defining characteristic" analogy. A CONSERVATOR is one who prevents WASTE and a *chaperon* is one who prevents *transgression*.

22. **(B)** This is another "defining characteristic" analogy. A POLEMICIST is involved in CONTROVERSY and a *visionary* in *dreams*.

23. **(A)** To PROSELYTIZE is to try to CONVERT; to *argue* is to try to *persuade*.

24. **(D)** This is a fairly easy inference question. We are asked to determine which of the problems mentioned by the author is the most important. (B) can be eliminated because the author's criticism is not that such courses are not offered, nor even that such courses are not required. So we eliminate (E) as well. The most important shortcoming, according to the author, is that students have not been encouraged to apply the principles learned in the humanities. As for (C), this is not mentioned by the author as a weakness in the present curriculum structure. Rather, the author anticipates that this is a possible objection to the proposal to require students to devote part of their time to the study of primary problems. Finally, as for (A), the author does not mention the university's failure to achieve complete equality of opportunity as a serious problem.

25. **(A)** This is an inference question as well, though of a greater degree of difficulty. It seems possible to eliminate (C) and (E) as fairly implausible. The author's remarks about literature, addressed to us as readers, do not suggest that we believe literature is required, nor that it is used to teach writing. As for (D), the author apparently presupposes that we, the readers, do not see the relevance of literature to real problems, for that it is relevant is at least part of the burden of the author's argument. (B) is perhaps the second best answer. It may very well be that most people regard literature as something scholarly, but that does not prove that (B) is a presupposition of the argument. The author states that literature is a source of real and vicarious experience. What is the value of that? The author is trying to show that literature has a real, practical value. The crucial question, then, is why the author is attempting to prove that literature has real value. The answer is because the author presupposes that we disagree with this conclusion. There is a subtle but important difference between a presupposition that literature is scholarly and a presupposition that literature has no practical value. After all, there are many non-scholarly undertakings that may lack practical value.

26. **(B)** This is an application question. The author uses the term "primary problems" to refer to questions of grave importance that are not susceptible to easy answers. Each of the incorrect answers poses a question that can be answered with a short answer. (A) can be answered with a yes or no. (C) can be answered with a name. (D) can be answered with a date. (E) can be answered with a series of proposals. And even if the answers are not absolutely indisputable, the questions will soon become dead issues. The only problem that is likely to still be around after we are all dead is the one of capital punishment.

27. **(E)** To *vilify* is to slander, defile, or defame. *Laud*, which means "praise," is a fine opposite.

28. **(C)** As a verb, *tender* means "to present for acceptance" or "to offer." Therefore, *retract* is a good antonym.

29. **(C)** Since *fungible* means "capable of being used in place of something else," *unique* is a good opposite.

30. **(C)** Since *splenetic* means "bad-tempered or irritable," *complacent* is the best opposite.

ANALYTICAL SECTION

Questions 1–6

Arranging the Information

With a set such as this, the main task is organizing the information. We will use a matrix:

Cars

	1	2	3	4	5
Meteor	C	C	D	D	C
Comet	D	C	C	D	D
Flash	D	C	D	D	D
Streak	D	D	C	C	D
Rocket	C	C	C	C	C

D=Deluxe   C=Coach

1. **(A)** This is seen to be true by our matrix. Three of the five trains use deluxe cars in the first position. The matrix shows that (B) is false since the ratio of deluxe to coach here is only one to four. (C) is also seen to be false since the Meteor and the Rocket have coach cars in the fifth position. (D) is proved false by a quick count. In a typical day, 12 deluxe cars and 13 coach cars are used. Finally, (E) is incorrect since the Rocket and the Streak together use only three deluxe cars, while the Flash and the Comet use seven deluxe cars.

2. **(C)** No train has deluxe cars in positions 2 and 3. As for (A), the Streak has deluxe cars first and second. As for (B), the Flash has deluxe cars first and third. As for (D), the Flash has deluxe cars third and fourth. And as for (E), the Flash also has deluxe cars fourth and fifth.

3. **(B)** If we know correctly that the second car of a train is a deluxe car, this establishes that train as the Streak—as shown by the matrix. As for (A), knowing the first car to be deluxe does not distinguish the Streak from the Comet or the Flash. As for (C), knowing the third car to be a coach car leaves open the possibility that the train might be the Comet, the Streak, or the Rocket. As for (D), although the Streak has deluxe as its first and fifth cars, this is also true of the Comet and the Flash. Finally, as for (E), the Streak has coach and deluxe in places 3 and 5, but this is also true of the Comet.

4. **(D)** As the matrix shows, the Meteor, the Comet, the Flash, and the Rocket all have coach cars as the second car. Only the Streak has a deluxe car in the second position.

5. **(C)** A quick look at the matrix shows that only one train, the Flash, has deluxe cars as the first and third cars of the train.

6. **(D)** Again, a quick glance at the matrix gives us the needed information. For the Streak, of the last three cars, only the fifth is a deluxe car. For the Meteor, two of the three last cars are deluxe cars. The same is true for the Comet. For the Flash, the last three cars are all deluxe cars, while for the Rocket none of the last three cars is a deluxe car.

7. **(C)** You should remember that there is a very important distinction to be drawn between numbers and percentages. For example, an increase from one murder per year to two murders per year can be described as a "whopping big 100% increase." The argument speaks only of percentages, so we would not want to conclude anything about the numbers underlying those percentages. Therefore, both (A) and (B) are incorrect. They speak of "more agents" and "more people," and those are numbers rather than percentages. Furthermore, if we would not want to draw a conclusion about numbers from data given in percentage terms, we surely would not want to base a conclusion about efficiency or work accomplished on percentages. Thus, (D) and (E) are incorrect. What makes (C) the best answer of the five is the possibility of making percentage comparisons *within* each agency. Within both agencies, the number of field agents increased by a greater *percentage* than the number of non-field agents.

8. **(D)** Keeping in mind our comments about (D) and (E) in the preceding question, (A) must be wrong. We do not want to conclude from sheer number of employees anything about the actual work accomplished. (B) and (E) are incorrect for pretty much the same reason. The question stem asks us to give an argument defending the CIA against the claim that it is overstaffed. Neither rate of pay nor appropriations has anything to do with whether or not there are too many people on the payroll. (C) is the second-best answer, but it fails because it does not keep in mind the ratio of non-field to field agents. Our concern is not with the number of agents generally, but the number of support and supervisory workers (reread the question stem). (D) focuses on this nicely by explaining why the CIA should experience a faster increase (which is to say, a greater percentage increase) in the number.

9. **(D)** Let us use letters to represent the categories. "All effective administrators" will be A. "Concerned about welfare" will be C. "Are liberal" will be L. The three propositions can now be represented as:

1. All A are W.
2. All W are L.
3. All non-L are not A.

Proposition 3 is equivalent to "all A are not non-L, and that is in turn equivalent to "all A are L. Thus, (D) follows fairly directly as a matter of logic. (A) is incorrect, for while we know that "all A are L," we would not want to conclude that "no L are A"—there might be some ineffective administrators who grant time off. They could be ineffective for other reasons. (B) is incorrect for the same reason. Even though all effective administrators are concerned about their employees' welfare, this does not mean that an ineffective administrator could not be concerned. The administrator might be concerned, but ineffective for another reason. (C) is clearly false, given our propositions: We know that all effective administrators are liberal. Finally, (E) is not inferable. Just because all effective administrators grant time off does not mean that all the time off granted is granted by effective administrators.

Questions 10–15

Arranging the Information

This is a selection set, and we begin by setting up the information in more usable form:

(1) V → R

(2) (R & Q) → ~P

(3) (Q & P) → ~T

(4a) P → (S v U)

(4b) ~ (S & U)

(5a) (S v T)

(5b) ~ (S & T)

The numbered statements (1) through (5b) correspond to the five conditions given in the set. We have broken the fourth and fifth conditions down into two statements because each of those conditions is actually two conditions. So (4a) corresponds to "If P is selected, then either S or U must be selected," and (4b) corresponds to "S and U cannot both be selected." (5) is treated in similar fashion.

Answering the Questions

10. **(C)** If neither S nor U is selected, then we know by (5a) that T is selected and by (4a) that P is not selected. Thus far we have eliminated S and U (by stipulation) and P, and we have selected T, which leaves Q, R, and V for consideration. Since P is not selected, we may include both R and Q without violating (2). And having chosen R, we may include V without violating (1). So, on the assumption that neither S nor U is selected, the largest delegation would consist of T, R, Q, and V.

11. **(B)** If V is selected, then by (1) R must also be selected. Further, if P is selected, by (4a) either S or U must be selected. But we also have (5a), and either S or T must be selected. Since we have both (S or U) and (S or T), we will minimize the number selected if we choose S rather than U or T. So the smallest delegation that includes both P and V will also include R and S.

12. **(C)** If P is selected, then by (4a) either S or U must be selected. Since by (4b) we cannot choose both S and U, S cannot be selected. But we know by (5a) that either S or T must be chosen, so we must pick T. As for the incorrect answers, this reasoning eliminates (B) as definitely false. As for (A), we cannot choose Q, for to choose Q along with P would mean we could not select T [by (3)]. But we have already learned that we must choose T because S cannot be chosen. As for (D) and (E), it is possible to choose R or V and R: since Q cannot be selected [see rejection of (A)], this effectively isolates R and V from the other students by breaking the only connection with R and V, which is (2).

13. **(A)** P, Q, and S are a possible three-student delegation. Selecting P requires that we have either S or U (4a), and that condition is satisfied by including S. Having P and Q together means only that we may not have T (3), but that can be avoided if we choose S to satisfy (5a). As for (B), P, Q, and T are not a possible delegation, since Q and P together require that T not be chosen, by (3). As for (C), P, R, and V are not acceptable because, by (5a), we must have either S or T. As for (D), R, S, and T are not permissible because this violates (5b). Finally, (E) is incorrect since the group R, S, and U violates (4b).

14. **(D)** If P is selected, then either S or U must also be selected, by (4a). But if T is chosen, then S cannot be chosen, by (5b), which means that U must be chosen. So it is not possible that U is not chosen. Then, since T and P are chosen, we cannot choose Q, by (3). R and/or V may be chosen, so the committee could consists of 3, 4, or 5 students.

15. **(B)** P, R, and T accompanied by U will satisfy all of the requirements. Choosing T satisfies (5a). Then, P and U together satisfy (4a). We do not have

S, so both (4b) and (5b) are respected. And since we do not have Q, (2) and (3) are satisfied. Finally, without V, we have no problem with (1). As for (A), P and Q cannot accompany T; that is a violation of (3). As for (C), V must be accompanied by R, by (1); and (D) can be eliminated on the same ground. Finally, as for (E), S and U violates (4b).

Questions 16–21

Arranging the Information

We will begin by summarizing the initial conditions.

1. crn, bns, bar, oats
2. W = bar or bns
3. At least 1 crn
4. beans → beans
5. (wht or alf) → oats

Answering the Questions

16. **(D)** Use the initial conditions to eliminate choices. Using condition 1, we can eliminate (E). Using condition 2, we can eliminate (A). And using condition 3, we can eliminate (B) and (C).

17. **(B)** Given the additional information, for the new growing season the East Field will have oats and the South Field will have beans. Then, given conditions 2 and 3, we infer that the North Field must have corn.

18. **(A)** A field planted with alfalfa in the previous growing season would have to be planted with oats for the new season, but initial condition 2 states that the West Field will be planted with either barley or beans.

19. **(C)** Given condition 2, the West Field will have a different crop; and given condition 3, at least one of the remaining fields will shift crops.

20. **(C)** Given the additional information, we can conclude that three of the four fields will contain beans for the new growing season. The fourth must have corn, so (D) and (E) are not possible. (For the new growing season, the fourth field would have oats or beans, respectively.) Then neither (A) nor (B) is possible because the other three fields will have beans for the new growing season, and no field will have corn.

21. **(A)** Given the additional information, we can deduce that beans must be planted in the East Field and oats in the South Field. Since the West Field will be planted with either barley or beans, the North Field must be planted with corn.

22. **(E)** What we are looking for here is an intervening causal link that caused the plan to be unsuccessful. The projected train of events was: (1) Adopt express lanes, (2) fewer cars, and (3) faster traffic flow. Between the first and the third steps, however, something went wrong. (E) alone supplies that unforeseen side effect. Since the cars backed up on too few lanes, total flow of traffic was actually slowed, not speeded up. (A) is irrelevant since it does not explain what went wrong after the plan was adopted. (B) does not even attempt to address the sequence of events that we have just outlined. Although (C) is probably true and was something the planners likely considered in their projections, it does not explain the plan's failure. Finally, (D) might have been relevant in deciding whether or not to adopt the plan, but given that the plan was adopted, (D) cannot explain why it then failed.

23. **(C)** Clark was unhappy if he had a clear conscience but knew, or Clark was happy if he knew but had an unclear conscience. It is not the case that Clark was unhappy, so he must have been happy. Since he knew, however, his happiness must stem from an unclear conscience. (A), (D), and (E) are incorrect because they make irrelevant value judgments. As was just shown, the author's point can be analyzed as a purely logical one. (B) is just distraction, playing on the connection between "governess" and "servant," which, of course, are not the same thing.

24. **(B)** The key here is that the word *nobody* is used in a cleverly ambiguous way—and, as many of you probably know, the "young lady" in the story is Lewis Carroll's Alice. This is fairly representative of his word play. (E) must be incorrect since it misses completely the little play on words: "I saw Nobody," encouraging a response such as "Oh, is he a handsome man?" (D) is beside the point, for the King is not interested in the messenger's veracity. He may be interested in his reliability (A); but, if anything, we should conclude the King finds the

messenger unreliable since "nobody walks slower" than the messenger. (C) is wrong because the question is not a matter of eyesight. The King does not say, "If you had better eyes, you might have seen Nobody."

25. **(E)** The advertisement employs the term "more" in an ambiguous manner. In the context, one might expect the phrase more flavor to mean more highly concentrated flavor, that is, more flavor per unit weight. What the ad actually says, however, is that the sticks of Evergreen are larger, so if they are larger, there must be more total flavor. As for (A), it is possible to beat the ad at its own game: Want more flavor? Chew more sticks. As for (B), more highly concentrated favor means more flavor per stick, so size is not important. As for (C), a bigger stick doesn't necessarily mean more flavor. And (D), of course, cuts to the heart of the claim: money or value. (E), however, if anything would add to the appeal of the ad: Do what most people do.

Questions 26–32

Arranging the Information

Here we have an ordering set that is not strictly linear, that is, the individuals are not aligned in a single file. We begin by summarizing the information:

$$(Q \& R) = 3$$
$$P < M$$
$$K < N$$
$$K < L$$
$$J = L$$

A moment's study will lead us to one or two further conclusions. If K is lower than L, then, of course, K cannot occupy the top floor. Further, since J and L occupy the same floor, and since the fifth floor has only one room, J and L cannot occupy a floor higher than the fourth floor, which means that K cannot occupy a floor higher than the second floor. (Remember that Q and R must occupy the third floor.) With these preliminary conclusions in mind, we can turn to the questions.

Answering the Questions

26. **(A)** Since K must stay below J, J cannot occupy the first floor. (A), as the exception, must be the correct answer. The other choices could be true, as illustrated by the diagram:

5	M/N			5	O
4	J L			4	M N
3	Q R	or		3	Q R
2	O(N/M)			2	J L
1	K P			1	K P

27. **(C)** We begin by processing the additional information. With M entered on the second floor, we deduce

5	
4	J L
3	Q R
2	M
1	P

With M on the second floor, P must be on the first floor. Then, with floors 1, 2, and 3 occupied, J and L must occupy floor 4 because the fifth floor has only one room. This seems as far as we can go. We know that K must occupy either 2 or 1, but that is not very helpful. So we look to the choices. We see that (A) is definitely incorrect, since (C) is proved by the diagram. (B) is possibly, though not necessarily, true. As we just noted, (D) is also only possible. Finally, (E) is also just a possibility, since O might also be on floor 5 or 2.

28. **(A)** As we deduced in the overview, K cannot stay on a floor higher than two. For the other possibility, revisit the explanation for #26, above.

29. **(E)** We have the list of people, J, K, L, M, N, O, P, Q, R, and we eliminate people as first-floor occupants as follows. Q and R must occupy the third floor. J and L occupy a floor together above that of K. M occupies a floor above P, and so cannot occupy floor 1. And the same reasoning applies to N. So we eliminate J, L, M, N, Q, and R, leaving K, O, and P.

30. **(B)** We begin by assimilating the additional information. With M on floor 4 we have:

5	
4	M
3	Q and R
2	J and L
1	K and P

With M on 4, we must put J and L on 2 for that is the only floor above floor 1 that remains open and has two rooms. Then, K must be on 1 (below L) and P must be on 1 (to be below M). As for N and O, they must occupy floors 4 and 5, though not necessarily in that order.

31. **(B)** We know that K and M, if they are together, cannot occupy floor 3 (because of Q and R) nor floor 5 (which has only one room). Nor can M occupy floor 1. K must be below J and L so K cannot occupy 4. The only floor for K and M together is 2.

32. **(C)** The additional information provided in (C) proves the following:

    5   N
    4   J and L
    3   Q and R
    2   K and M
    1   P and O

With K on 2, J and L must be on 4 (since L must be above K). Then, since K is lower than N, N must occupy 5. Next, since P < M, P must occupy 1 and M must occupy 2. And this leaves only O to occupy the other room on 1. The other answers will not do the trick. As for (A), putting P on 1 does not force J and L onto a floor. They might occupy either 2 or 4. As for (B), putting M on 2 means that J and L will occupy 4 and that P will occupy 1, but this leaves several individuals unplaced. Placing N on the top floor does not place J and K, and that is critical to fixing a definite order.

33. **(E)** Perhaps the most obvious weakness in the argument is that it oversimplifies matters. The author argues, in effect: Either we put a stop to this now, or there will be no stopping it. This argument ignores the many intermediate positions one might take. (C) is one way of describing this shortcoming: The dilemma posed by the author is a false one because it overlooks positions between the two extremes. (B) is also a weakness of the argument: "Cold-blooded murder" is obviously a phrase calculated to excite negative feelings. Finally, the whole argument is also internally inconsistent. The conclusion is that we should allow nature to take its course. How? By prolonging life with artificial means. But the failure of an argument to cite an authority is not necessarily a weakness. To be sure, the argument is subject to criticism; but, in general, unless the argument is one that requires an authority (say, for some key detail), the failure to cite an authority is not a defect.

34. **(E)** The ad is a little deceptive. It tries to create the impression that if hospitals are using Dr. John's Milk of Magnesia, people will believe it is a good product. But what the ad actually says is that Dr. John uses the same *ingredient* that hospitals use (milk of magnesia is a simple suspension of magnesium hydroxide in water). The ad is something like an ad for John's Vinegar that claims it has "acetic acid," which is vinegar. (A), (B), (C), and (D), in various ways, fall into the trap of the inviting wording, and those statements are not conclusions that can be logically inferred. Statement (E), however, is logically inferable: from 9 of 10 X are Y, you can infer that it is true that Y is X 9 out of 10 times.

35. **(E)** The question stem asks us to find the one item that will not strengthen the author's argument. That is (E). Remember, the author's argument is an attempt (to be sure, a weak one) to develop an alternative causal explanation. (A) would provide some evidence that the author's claim—which at first glance seems a bit far-fetched—actually has some empirical foundation. While (B) does not add any strength to the author's own explanation of the phenomenon being studied, it does strengthen the author's overall position by undermining the explanation given in the report. (C) strengthens the author's position for the same reason that (B) does: It weakens the position he is attacking. (D) strengthens the argument in the same way that (A) does, by providing some empirical support for the otherwise seemingly far-fetched explanation.

MATH SECTION

1. **(D)** Since no information is given directly about x or y, we cannot determine the relationship. Do not assume that since $x = -y$, y will be greater than $-y$ and thus greater than x. It is possible that y is a negative number, in which case x is a positive number and greater than y. Also, x and y could both be equal to zero.

2. **(A)** $\frac{1}{100}$ is equal to 1%, so Column A is greater. .01% expressed as a fraction is $\frac{1}{10,000}$.

3. **(A)** To compute a percentage increase, it is necessary to create a fraction: $\frac{\text{difference}}{\text{starting point}}$. In this problem, the price of paper increased from $1.23 to $1.48, for a difference of $0.25. Thus, our fraction is $\frac{.25}{1.23}$. If we actually needed to calculate the

percentage increase, we would then divide 1.23 into .25 and multiply that quotient by 100 (to convert the decimal to a percent). For purposes of answering the quantitative comparison question, however, a rough estimate will be sufficient. The percentage increase in the price is more than $25 \div 125$, and that would be a $\frac{1}{5}$ or 20% increase. Thus Column A is slightly greater than 20%, so Column A must be greater.

4. **(C)** The intuitive way of solving this problem is to reason that $\frac{M+x+y}{3}$ is the average of M, x, and y, and that $\frac{x+y}{2}$ is the average of x and y. Since the average of any number and itself is itself—that is, the average of x and x is x—Column A must be equal to Column B. The same conclusion can be more rigorously demonstrated by substituting $\frac{x+y}{2}$ for M in column A:

$$\frac{\frac{x+y}{2}+x+y}{3} = \frac{\frac{x+y+2(x+y)}{2}}{3} = \frac{3x+3y}{6} = \frac{x+y}{2}$$

5. **(D)** The natural starting point for solving this problem is to perform the indicated operations—that is, to multiply the expressions:

$(a+2)(b+3)=$ $(a+3)(b+2)=$
$ab+3a+2b+6$ $ab+2a+3b+6$

Of course, since ab and 6 are common to both expressions, those terms cannot make any difference in the comparison of the two columns. After we strip away the ab terms and 6, we are left with $3a+2b$ in Column A and $2a+3b$ in Column B. Since no information is given about the relative magnitudes of a and b, the answer must be (D).

6. **(E)** A simple method for adding any two fractions is:

Step A: Find the new denominator by multiplying the old ones.
Step B: Multiply the numerator of the first fraction by the denominator of the second.
Step C: Multiply the denominator of the first fraction by the numerator of the second.
Step D: Add the results of B and C.
Step E: Reduce, if necessary.

The process is more easily comprehended when presented in the following way:

$$\frac{a}{b}+\frac{c}{d}=\frac{ad+bc}{bd}$$

Here, we have:

$$\frac{3}{4}+\frac{4}{5}=\frac{15+16}{20}=\frac{13}{20}$$

7. **(C)** Since $x+6=3$, $x=-3$. Then, substituting -3 for x in the second expression, $x+3$ is $-3+3=0$.

8. **(A)** Probably the easiest way to solve this problem is just to count the steps on your fingers, but the same process can be expressed mathematically. Let those steps he walks down be assigned negative values, and those steps he walks up be positive. We then have: $-4+3-6+2+9-2=+2$. So the person comes to rest two steps above where he started.

9. **(A)** In a circle graph such as this, the sectors must total 100%. The sectors P, R, S, and T account for 21%, 29%, 18%, and 28%, respectively, for a total of 96%. So Q must be 4%.

10. **(A)** The easiest way to solve this problem is to factor the 326 from both terms of the expression:

$$326(31-19)=326(12)=3{,}912$$

Of course, you might actually do the arithmetic by multiplying first 326 by 31 and then 326 by 19 and then subtracting the smaller total from the larger. That takes quite a bit longer! But if you did not see the first way (factoring) and can manage the arithmetic in thirty or forty seconds, you should proceed with the one way you know to get the correct answer. However, the better approach by far is to find a way of avoiding the calculation.

11. **(B)** The sum of the interior angles of a pentagon is 540°, and that of a hexagon is 720°. If you did not recall this, you could have computed the sum in the following way:

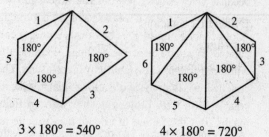

$3 \times 180° = 540°$ $4 \times 180° = 720°$

(Notice that the sum of the interior angles is unrelated to the relative lengths of the sides.)

The average size of the angles of the pentagon, then, is 540 divided by 5, or 108°. And the average size of the angles of the hexagon is 720° divided by 6, or 120°. The general rule is: The average size of the angle grows as the number of sides in the polygon increases.

12. **(B)** The shelf originally contains 24 books. We remove 75% of the 16 French books, or 12, which leaves 4 French books remaining on the shelf. Then we remove 50% of the 8 Italian books, leaving 4 Italian books. Only 8 books remain on the shelf—that is, $\frac{1}{3}$ of the total.

13. **(C)** In a right triangle in which the angles are 90°, 60°, and 30°, the length of the side opposite the 30° angle is one-half the length of the hypotenuse, and the length of the side opposite the 60° angle is one-half the length of the hypotenuse times $\sqrt{3}$. Since two of the angles of this triangle total 90°, and there are 180° in a triangle, angle B must equal 90°, and this is a right triangle. Side AB is opposite the 30° angle, and so must be one-half the hypotenuse. AB is 1; therefore, AC must be 2. BC, then, will be one-half the length of the hypotenuse times $\sqrt{3}$. So BC will be $\sqrt{3}$.

14. **(D)** There are several ways of solving this problem. One way is to manipulate the centered equation so that $x^2 = 1$. Then it should be clear that $x = \pm1$, and so x might be +1 or −1. Similarly, one might factor $x^2 - 1$ to get $(x+1)(x-1) = 0$, showing that there are two values for x, only one of which is +1.

15. **(A)** This problem can be solved using simultaneous equations. Let x be the number of $13 tickets and y the number of $25 tickets.

Then: $x + y = 11$
And: $13x + 25y = 227$
By the first equation: $x = 11 - y$
Substitute: $13(11 - y) + 25y = 227$
Then manipulate: $143 - 13y + 25y = 227$
                       $12y = 84$
                       $y = 7$

And if the number of $25 tickets is equal to 7, the number of $13 tickets is only 4, so Column A is greater. An easier and therefore a better way of solving the problem is to recognize that the average value of the tickets must be approximately $20. If

an equal number of tickets had been sold (impossible, of course, since an odd number of tickets was sold), the average would have been midway between $13 and $25, or $19. Since the average is above $19, more of the expensive tickets must have been sold.

16. **(B)** The greatest increase occurred from 1978 to 1979. It was:

1979 Earnings − 1978 Earnings = 1.1 − 0.5 = 0.6 million = $600,000

17. **(C)** This question asks about percent change, so use the "change over" strategy. To make the task easier, try to work with the fractions you create directly and avoid changing them to percents.

(A) $\dfrac{1980 - 1979}{1979} = \dfrac{12 - 10}{10} = \dfrac{2}{10} = \dfrac{1}{5}$

(B) $\dfrac{1981 - 1980}{1980} = \dfrac{9 - 12}{12} = -\dfrac{3}{12} = -\dfrac{1}{4}$
(decrease)

(C) $\dfrac{1982 - 1981}{1981} = \dfrac{12 - 9}{9} = \dfrac{3}{9} = \dfrac{1}{3}$

(D) $\dfrac{1983 - 1982}{1982} = \dfrac{14 - 12}{12} = \dfrac{2}{12} = \dfrac{1}{6}$

(E) $\dfrac{1984 - 1983}{1983} = \dfrac{13 - 14}{14} = -\dfrac{1}{14}$
(decrease)

18. **(A)** Just calculate the average:

$(0.9 + 1.0 + 1.2 + 1.3 + 1.5) \div 5 = 5.9 \div 5 = 1.18 = $1,180,000$

19. **(D)** Since this question asks for percent change, use the "change over" strategy.

$\dfrac{1985 - 1976}{1976} = \dfrac{1.5 - 0.3}{0.3} = \dfrac{1.2}{0.3} = 4 = 400\%$

20. **(B)** If you try to solve this problem by writing out a calculation for each of the years, you'll run out of time before you can get halfway through. Instead, you should do the math in your head. You can find 10 percent of a number just by moving the decimal point one place to the left. Take 1976, for example. Ten percent of 6 million is 0.6 million, which is larger than 0.3 million, so in that year earnings were not equal to or greater than 10 percent of sales. Work your way quickly through the other years.

You will find that in four years, earnings were either equal to or greater than 10 percent of sales: 1979, 1980, 1981, and 1984.

21. **(C)** This problem requires that the expression in Column A be factored. From basic algebra you will recall that $(x+y)(x-y) = x^2 - y^2$. So the denominator of Column A can be factored into $(x+y)(x-y)$. Then the $x - y$ can be cancelled, leaving $x + y$ for both columns.

22. **(C)** To make the explanation easier to grasp, we add the following notation:

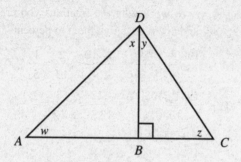

Since BD is perpendicular to AC, both triangle ABD and triangle CBD are right triangles. Consequently:

$w + x + 90° = 180°$ and $y + z + 90° = 180°$

so: $w + x = 90°$ and $y + z = 90°$

23. **(A)** The two planes converge on each other at the rate of 300 miles/40 minutes, or 300 miles/$\frac{2}{3}$ hr. That is a rate of 450 miles per hour—the *sum* of their speeds. Since plane X is flying at 150 MPH, plane Y must be flying at 300 MPH. Another way of solving the problem would be to reason that *if* plane Y were flying at 150 MPH, the two planes would be converging at the rate of 300 MPH and it would take a full hour, not 40 minutes, for them to pass. This shows that plane Y must be flying at a speed faster than 150 MPH.

24. **(D)** In simple English, the 90¢ the child must replace to bring the amount back up to its original amount is 10% of the original amount. Expressed in notation, that is:

$90¢ = .10$ of x

$\$9.00 = x$

25. **(C)** Let us begin by assigning letters to the height and radius of each cylinder. Since most people find it easier to deal with whole numbers instead of fractions, let us say that cylinder Q has a radius of $2r$, so that cylinder P can have a radius of r. Then, we assign cylinder Q a height of h so that P can have a height of $2h$. Now, the formula for the volume of a cylinder is $\pi r^2 \times h$. So P and Q have volumes:

Volume $P = \pi(r)^2 \times 2h$ Volume $Q = (2\pi r)^2 \times h$

$P = 2\pi r^2 h$ $Q = 4\pi r^2 h$

Thus, the ratio of P:Q is $\dfrac{2\pi r^2 h}{4\pi r^2 h} = \dfrac{2}{4} = \dfrac{1}{2}$.

26. **(A)** We begin by extending the lines to give this picture:

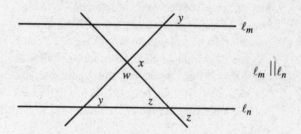

Then we add another angle y (lines l_m and l_n are parallel, so alternate interior angles are equal) and another z (opposite angles are equal). We know that $x + w = 180°$, and we know that $y + z + w = 180°$. So, $x + w = y + z + w$, and $x = y + z$.

27. **(C)** Let us begin by drawing the rectangle:

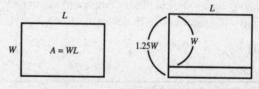

$A = 1.25W \times L = 1.25WL$

The original area is WL. The width of the new rectangle is $W + .25W$ or $1.25W$. So the new area is $1.25WL$. It then follows that the new area is $\frac{1.25WL}{WL}$, or 125% of the old area.

28. **(B)** Let us take any odd integer, m. The next consecutive odd integer will be two more than m, or $m + 2$. The third integer in the series will be $m + 4$, and the fourth integer in the series will be $m + 6$. The sum of the four is: $(m) + (m + 2) + (m + 4) +$

$(m + 6) = 4m + 12$. And when $(4m + 12)$ is divided by 4, the result is: $\frac{4m+12}{4} = m + 3$. So the sum of four consecutive odd/positive integers is always evenly divisible by 4.

Answer Sheet

MATH SECTION

1. Ⓐ Ⓑ Ⓒ Ⓓ Ⓔ 7. Ⓐ Ⓑ Ⓒ Ⓓ Ⓔ 13. Ⓐ Ⓑ Ⓒ Ⓓ Ⓔ 19. Ⓐ Ⓑ Ⓒ Ⓓ Ⓔ 25. Ⓐ Ⓑ Ⓒ Ⓓ Ⓔ
2. Ⓐ Ⓑ Ⓒ Ⓓ Ⓔ 8. Ⓐ Ⓑ Ⓒ Ⓓ Ⓔ 14. Ⓐ Ⓑ Ⓒ Ⓓ Ⓔ 20. Ⓐ Ⓑ Ⓒ Ⓓ Ⓔ 26. Ⓐ Ⓑ Ⓒ Ⓓ Ⓔ
3. Ⓐ Ⓑ Ⓒ Ⓓ Ⓔ 9. Ⓐ Ⓑ Ⓒ Ⓓ Ⓔ 15. Ⓐ Ⓑ Ⓒ Ⓓ Ⓔ 21. Ⓐ Ⓑ Ⓒ Ⓓ Ⓔ 27. Ⓐ Ⓑ Ⓒ Ⓓ Ⓔ
4. Ⓐ Ⓑ Ⓒ Ⓓ Ⓔ 10. Ⓐ Ⓑ Ⓒ Ⓓ Ⓔ 16. Ⓐ Ⓑ Ⓒ Ⓓ Ⓔ 22. Ⓐ Ⓑ Ⓒ Ⓓ Ⓔ 28. Ⓐ Ⓑ Ⓒ Ⓓ Ⓔ
5. Ⓐ Ⓑ Ⓒ Ⓓ Ⓔ 11. Ⓐ Ⓑ Ⓒ Ⓓ Ⓔ 17. Ⓐ Ⓑ Ⓒ Ⓓ Ⓔ 23. Ⓐ Ⓑ Ⓒ Ⓓ Ⓔ
6. Ⓐ Ⓑ Ⓒ Ⓓ Ⓔ 12. Ⓐ Ⓑ Ⓒ Ⓓ Ⓔ 18. Ⓐ Ⓑ Ⓒ Ⓓ Ⓔ 24. Ⓐ Ⓑ Ⓒ Ⓓ Ⓔ

VERBAL SECTION

1. Ⓐ Ⓑ Ⓒ Ⓓ Ⓔ 7. Ⓐ Ⓑ Ⓒ Ⓓ Ⓔ 13. Ⓐ Ⓑ Ⓒ Ⓓ Ⓔ 19. Ⓐ Ⓑ Ⓒ Ⓓ Ⓔ 25. Ⓐ Ⓑ Ⓒ Ⓓ Ⓔ
2. Ⓐ Ⓑ Ⓒ Ⓓ Ⓔ 8. Ⓐ Ⓑ Ⓒ Ⓓ Ⓔ 14. Ⓐ Ⓑ Ⓒ Ⓓ Ⓔ 20. Ⓐ Ⓑ Ⓒ Ⓓ Ⓔ 26. Ⓐ Ⓑ Ⓒ Ⓓ Ⓔ
3. Ⓐ Ⓑ Ⓒ Ⓓ Ⓔ 9. Ⓐ Ⓑ Ⓒ Ⓓ Ⓔ 15. Ⓐ Ⓑ Ⓒ Ⓓ Ⓔ 21. Ⓐ Ⓑ Ⓒ Ⓓ Ⓔ 27. Ⓐ Ⓑ Ⓒ Ⓓ Ⓔ
4. Ⓐ Ⓑ Ⓒ Ⓓ Ⓔ 10. Ⓐ Ⓑ Ⓒ Ⓓ Ⓔ 16. Ⓐ Ⓑ Ⓒ Ⓓ Ⓔ 22. Ⓐ Ⓑ Ⓒ Ⓓ Ⓔ 28. Ⓐ Ⓑ Ⓒ Ⓓ Ⓔ
5. Ⓐ Ⓑ Ⓒ Ⓓ Ⓔ 11. Ⓐ Ⓑ Ⓒ Ⓓ Ⓔ 17. Ⓐ Ⓑ Ⓒ Ⓓ Ⓔ 23. Ⓐ Ⓑ Ⓒ Ⓓ Ⓔ 29. Ⓐ Ⓑ Ⓒ Ⓓ Ⓔ
6. Ⓐ Ⓑ Ⓒ Ⓓ Ⓔ 12. Ⓐ Ⓑ Ⓒ Ⓓ Ⓔ 18. Ⓐ Ⓑ Ⓒ Ⓓ Ⓔ 24. Ⓐ Ⓑ Ⓒ Ⓓ Ⓔ 30. Ⓐ Ⓑ Ⓒ Ⓓ Ⓔ

ANALYTICAL SECTION

1. Ⓐ Ⓑ Ⓒ Ⓓ Ⓔ 8. Ⓐ Ⓑ Ⓒ Ⓓ Ⓔ 15. Ⓐ Ⓑ Ⓒ Ⓓ Ⓔ 22. Ⓐ Ⓑ Ⓒ Ⓓ Ⓔ 29. Ⓐ Ⓑ Ⓒ Ⓓ Ⓔ
2. Ⓐ Ⓑ Ⓒ Ⓓ Ⓔ 9. Ⓐ Ⓑ Ⓒ Ⓓ Ⓔ 16. Ⓐ Ⓑ Ⓒ Ⓓ Ⓔ 23. Ⓐ Ⓑ Ⓒ Ⓓ Ⓔ 30. Ⓐ Ⓑ Ⓒ Ⓓ Ⓔ
3. Ⓐ Ⓑ Ⓒ Ⓓ Ⓔ 10. Ⓐ Ⓑ Ⓒ Ⓓ Ⓔ 17. Ⓐ Ⓑ Ⓒ Ⓓ Ⓔ 24. Ⓐ Ⓑ Ⓒ Ⓓ Ⓔ 31. Ⓐ Ⓑ Ⓒ Ⓓ Ⓔ
4. Ⓐ Ⓑ Ⓒ Ⓓ Ⓔ 11. Ⓐ Ⓑ Ⓒ Ⓓ Ⓔ 18. Ⓐ Ⓑ Ⓒ Ⓓ Ⓔ 25. Ⓐ Ⓑ Ⓒ Ⓓ Ⓔ 32. Ⓐ Ⓑ Ⓒ Ⓓ Ⓔ
5. Ⓐ Ⓑ Ⓒ Ⓓ Ⓔ 12. Ⓐ Ⓑ Ⓒ Ⓓ Ⓔ 19. Ⓐ Ⓑ Ⓒ Ⓓ Ⓔ 26. Ⓐ Ⓑ Ⓒ Ⓓ Ⓔ 33. Ⓐ Ⓑ Ⓒ Ⓓ Ⓔ
6. Ⓐ Ⓑ Ⓒ Ⓓ Ⓔ 13. Ⓐ Ⓑ Ⓒ Ⓓ Ⓔ 20. Ⓐ Ⓑ Ⓒ Ⓓ Ⓔ 27. Ⓐ Ⓑ Ⓒ Ⓓ Ⓔ 34. Ⓐ Ⓑ Ⓒ Ⓓ Ⓔ
7. Ⓐ Ⓑ Ⓒ Ⓓ Ⓔ 14. Ⓐ Ⓑ Ⓒ Ⓓ Ⓔ 21. Ⓐ Ⓑ Ⓒ Ⓓ Ⓔ 28. Ⓐ Ⓑ Ⓒ Ⓓ Ⓔ 35. Ⓐ Ⓑ Ⓒ Ⓓ Ⓔ

TEAR HERE

Practice Examination 5

Math Section

28 QUESTIONS • TIME—45 MINUTES

Directions: For each of these questions, select the best of the answer choices given.

Numbers: All numbers used are real numbers.

Figures: Assume that the position of points, angles, regions and so forth are in the order shown. Figures are assumed to lie in a plane unless otherwise indicated. Figures accompanying questions are intended to provide information you can use in answering the questions. However, unless a note states that a figure is drawn to scale, you should solve the problems by using your knowledge of mathematics and not by estimating sizes by sight or measurement.

Lines: Assume that lines shown as straight are indeed straight.

Directions: For each of the following questions two quantities are given, one in Column A and one in Column B. Compare the two quantities and choose

A: if the quantity in Column A is the greater

B: if the quantity in Column B is the greater

C: if the two quantities are equal

D: if the relationship cannot be determined from the information given.

Common Information: In any question, information applying to both columns is centered between the columns and above the quantities in columns A and B. Any symbol that appears in both columns represents the same idea or quantity in both columns.

	Column A	Column B

| 1. | x | y |

$$x > 0$$
$$y > 0$$

2.	$x\%$ of $y\%$ of 100	$y\%$ of $x\%$ of 100
3.	0.3	$\sqrt{0.9}$
4.	$(x + y)^2$	$x(x + y) + y(x + y)$
5.	$\dfrac{17}{8,786}$	$\dfrac{17}{8,787}$

401

Directions: For each of these questions, select the best of the answer choices given.

6. If $(x - y)^2 = 12$ and $xy = 1$, then $x^2 + y^2 =$

   (A) 14

   (B) 13

   (C) 12

   (D) 11

   (E) 10

7.

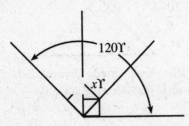

(*Note*: Figure not drawn to scale.)

What is the measure of angle x?

   (A) 30°

   (B) 45°

   (C) 60°

   (D) 90°

   (E) 240°

8. If n is a positive integer and 95 and 135 are divided by n, and the remainders are 5 and 3 respectively, then $n =$

   (A) 6

   (B) 8

   (C) 10

   (D) 15

   (E) 21

9. A student conducts an experiment in biology lab and discovers that the ratio of the number of insects in a given population having characteristic X to the number of insects in the population not having characteristic X is 5:3, and that $\frac{3}{8}$ of the insects having characteristic X are male insects. What proportion of the total insect population are male insects having the characteristic X?

   (A) 1

   (B) $\frac{5}{8}$

   (C) $\frac{6}{13}$

   (D) $\frac{15}{64}$

   (E) $\frac{1}{5}$

10. If the following were arranged in order of magnitude, which term would be the middle number in the series?

   (A) $\frac{3^8}{5^6}$

   (B) $3^3 - 1$

   (C) 3^0

   (D) 3^{27}

   (E) $3(3^2)$

Directions: For each of the following questions two quantities are given, one in Column A and one in Column B. Compare the two quantities and choose

   A: if the quantity in Column A is the greater

   B: if the quantity in Column B is the greater

   C: if the two quantities are equal

   D: if the relationship cannot be determined from the information given.

Column A	Column B

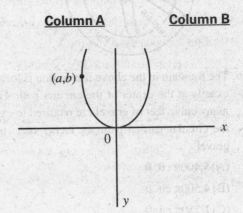

11. a b

	Column A	Column B
12.	$3x + 5$	$2x + 3$

$$x < 0$$

	Column A	Column B
13.	$(x^3)^5$	$x^3 \cdot x^5$

A man buys 16 shirts. Some of them cost $13 each, while the remainder cost $10 each. The cost of all 16 shirts is $187.

14.	The number of $13 shirts purchased	The number of $10 shirts purchased

15.	The volume of a sphere with a radius of 5	The volume of a cube with a side of 10

Directions: For each of these questions, select the best of the answer choices given.

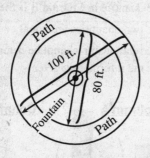

16. The fountain in the above illustration is located exactly at the center of the circular path. How many cubic feet of gravel are required to cover the circular garden path six inches deep with gravel?

    (A) $5,400\pi$ cu. ft.

    (B) $4,500\pi$ cu. ft.

    (C) $1,250\pi$ cu. ft.

    (D) 450π cu. ft.

    (E) 5π cu. ft.

17. A business firm reduces the number of hours its employees work from 40 hours per week to 36 hours per week while continuing to pay the same amount of money. If an employee earned x dollars per hour before the reduction in hours, how much does he earn per hour under the new system?

    (A) $\dfrac{1}{10}$

    (B) $\dfrac{x}{9}$

    (C) $\dfrac{9x}{10}$

    (D) $\dfrac{10x}{9}$

    (E) $9x$

18. A ceiling is supported by two parallel columns as shown in the following drawing:

    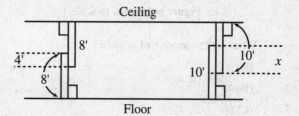

    What is the length of segment x in feet?

    (A) 10

    (B) 8

    (C) 6

    (D) 4

    (E) Cannot be determined from the information given.

19. A painter has painted one-third of a rectangular wall which is ten feet high. When she has painted another 75 square feet of wall, she will be three-quarters finished with the job. What is the length (the horizontal dimension) of the wall?

    (A) 18 feet

    (B) 12 feet

    (C) 10 feet

    (D) 9 feet

    (E) 6 feet

Directions: For each of the following questions two quantities are given, one in Column A and one in Column B. Compare the two quantities and choose

    A: if the quantity in Column A is the greater

    B: if the quantity in Column B is the greater

    C: if the two quantities are equal

    D: if the relationship cannot be determined from the information given.

Column A	Column B
20. $-(3^6)$	$(-3)^6$

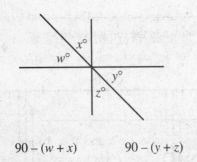

21. $90 - (w + x)$	$90 - (y + z)$

Directions: For each of these questions, select the best of the answer choices given.

Questions 22–25 refer to the graph below.

22. From 1972 to 1977, inclusive, the total number of fares collected for subways was approximately how many million?

  (A) 1,900

  (B) 1,700

  (C) 1,500

  (D) 1,300

  (E) 1,100

23. From 1975 to 1977, the number of fares collected for subways dropped by approximately what percent?

  (A) 90

  (B) 35

  (C) 25

  (D) 15

  (E) 9

PUBLIC TRANSPORTATION IN METROPOLITAN AREA P

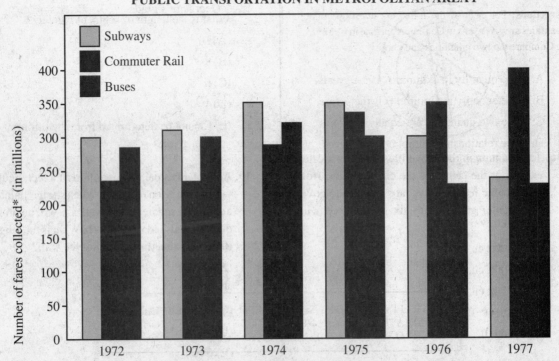

* One passenger paying one fare for one trip

24. If in 1974 the average subway fare collected was 50¢ and the average bus fare collected was 30¢, then the ratio of the total dollar amount of subway fares collected to the total dollar amount of bus fares was approximately

   (A) $\dfrac{1}{4}$

   (B) $\dfrac{1}{3}$

   (C) $\dfrac{3}{5}$

   (D) 1

   (E) $\dfrac{7}{4}$

25. The number of commuter rail fares collected in 1977 accounted for approximately what percent of all fares collected on subways, buses, and commuter rail in that year?

   (A) 200%

   (B) 100%

   (C) 50%

   (D) 28%

   (E) 12%

Directions: For each of the following questions two quantities are given, one in Column A and one in Column B. Compare the two quantities and choose

   A: if the quantity in Column A is the greater

   B: if the quantity in Column B is the greater

   C: if the two quantities are equal

   D: if the relationship cannot be determined from the information given.

Column A	Column B

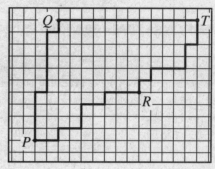

All angles are right angles

	Column A	Column B
26.	Distance from P to T via Q	Distance from P to T via R
27.	The length of side of any equilateral polygon inscribed in circle O	The length of the diameter of circle O

Peter's grade was higher than that of Victor, and Victor's grade was less than that of Georgette.

	Column A	Column B
28.	Georgette's grade	Peter's grade

WARNING

IF YOU FINISHED THIS SECTION BEFORE TIME EXPIRED, GO IMMEDIATELY TO THE NEXT SECTION. YOU MAY NOT CONTINUE TO WORK ON THIS SECTION AFTER TIME HAS EXPIRED.

Verbal Section

30 QUESTIONS • TIME—30 MINUTES

Directions: Each of the questions below contains one or more blank spaces, each blank indicating an omitted word. Each sentence is followed by five (5) words or sets of words. Read and determine the general sense of each sentence. Then choose the word, or set of words that, when inserted in the sentence, best fits the meaning of the sentence.

1. The history book, written in 1880, was tremendously ——, unfairly blaming the South for the Civil War.

   (A) biased

   (B) objective

   (C) suppressed

   (D) questionable

   (E) complicated

2. In the Middle Ages, scientists and clergymen thought the universe was well-ordered and ——; today scientists are more likely to see the world as ——.

   (A) baffling..dogmatic

   (B) harmonious..chaotic

   (C) transient..predictable

   (D) emancipated..intriguing

   (E) divergent..galling

3. Hot milk has long been a standard cure for insomnia because of its —— quality.

   (A) malevolent

   (B) amorphous

   (C) soporific

   (D) plaintive

   (E) desultory

Directions: In each of the following questions, you are given a related pair of words or phrases in capital letters. Each capitalized pair is followed by five (5) pairs of words or phrases. Choose the pair that best expresses a relationship similar to that expressed by the original pair.

4. DISLIKABLE : ABHORRENT ::

   (A) trustworthy : helpful

   (B) difficult : arduous

   (C) silly : young

   (D) tender : hard

   (E) ugly : beautiful

5. UNIFORM : SOLDIER ::

   (A) silks : jockey

   (B) leash : dog

   (C) pasture : cow

   (D) farmer : tractor

   (E) costume : scenery

6. MURAL : WALL ::

   (A) pen : letter

   (B) tree : forest

   (C) painting : canvas

   (D) tobacco : smoke

   (E) museum : curator

Directions: The passage below is followed by questions based on its content. Choose the best answer to each question.

One continuing problem in labor-management relations is the "us/them" mentality. In addition to fiscal constraints, continuing problems with the Fair Labor Standards Act, bad-faith negotiations, bad management (5) practices, poor union leadership, and a continued loss of management prerogatives will all combine to produce forces that will cause a significant increase in disruptive job actions in the near future. Neither side is blameless. The tragedy of the situation is that the impact of poor (10) labor-management relations is relatively predictable and is thus avoidable.

Since the economic situation will not improve significantly in the next few years, the pressure on the part of

union leaders to obtain more benefits for their members
(15) will be frustrated. As a result of the PATCO strike,
management has learned that times are conducive to
regaining prerogatives lost during the previous decade.
The stage for confrontation between labor and management in the public sector is set, and in many areas, only
(20) requires an incident to force disruptive job actions. The
only solution to this seemingly intractable problem lies in
the area of skilled negotiations and good-faith bargaining.
This requires commitment on the part of management and
labor to live up to the terms of existing contracts.

7. It can be inferred that the PATCO strike (lines 15–16)

   (A) was an example of bad-faith negotiations

   (B) lasted only a brief period

   (C) was the fault of incompetent management

   (D) violated the provisions of the Fair Labor Standards Act

   (E) resulted in a victory for management

8. The author's discussion of labor-management relations can best be described as

   (A) extremely pro-labor

   (B) mildly pro-labor

   (C) neutral

   (D) mildly pro-management

   (E) extremely pro-management

9. The author implies that if the economic conditions improve

   (A) management will lose much of its power

   (B) labor leaders will not seek more benefits

   (C) labor-management tensions will decline

   (D) the Fair Labor Standards Act will be repealed

   (E) labor will win a voice in management

10. The author mentions all of the following as factors that might contribute to disruptive job actions EXCEPT:

    (A) unsatisfactory union leadership

    (B) loss of management control

    (C) bad-faith negotiations

    (D) poor management practices

    (E) low interest rates

Directions: In each of the following questions, you are given a related pair of words or phrases in capital letters. Each capitalized pair is followed by five (5) pairs of words or phrases. Choose the pair that best expresses a relationship similar to that expressed by the original pair.

11. COMMENCE : PROCRASTINATION ::

    (A) terminate : prolongation

    (B) show : demonstration

    (C) frighten : terror

    (D) guarantee : refund

    (E) capture : torture

12. BUCOLIC : URBAN ::

    (A) dense : sparse

    (B) rural : ephemeral

    (C) elastic : plastic

    (D) mist : smog

    (E) rustic : toxic

13. REGRETTABLE : LAMENT ::

    (A) praiseworthy : applaud

    (B) verbose : rejoice

    (C) incongruous : detect

    (D) reliable : defend

    (E) obnoxious : boast

14. FASTIDIOUS : CLEANLINESS ::

    (A) pliant : fabrication

    (B) meticulous : detail

    (C) timorous : hostility

    (D) bereft : animosity

    (E) enervated : activity

15. DISAPPROBATION : CONDEMN ::

    (A) solvency : deploy

    (B) calumny : praise

    (C) enigma : enlighten

    (D) fallacy : disseminate

    (E) exhortation : urge

GO ON TO THE NEXT PAGE

16. In the Middle Ages, the Benedictine monasteries were often —— of civilization and a refuge for science in an otherwise —— and superstitious world.

    (A) arbiters..scholarly

    (B) brethren..sanctimonious

    (C) forerunners..erudite

    (D) conservators..barbarous

    (E) advocates..rarefied

17. Both coffee and tea have beneficial as well as —— side-effects: while they stimulate the heart and help overcome fatigue, they also —— insomnia and other nervous disorders.

    (A) injurious..exacerbate

    (B) malignant..interrupt

    (C) salutary..heighten

    (D) negligible..forestall

    (E) specious..prevent

18. GUILE :

    (A) abundance

    (B) forbidden

    (C) treasure

    (D) naïveté

    (E) impression

19. MALIGN :

    (A) refuse

    (B) constrain

    (C) praise

    (D) demand

    (E) reply

20. INCITE :

    (A) forget

    (B) calm

    (C) change

    (D) involve

    (E) produce

At the present time, 98 percent of the world energy consumption comes from stored sources, such as fossil fuels or nuclear fuel. Only hydroelectric and wood energy represent completely renewable sources on or-
(5) dinary time scales. Discovery of large additional fossil fuel reserves, solution of the nuclear safety and waste disposal problems, or the development of controlled thermonuclear fusion will provide only a short-term solution to the world's energy crisis. Within about 100
(10) years, the thermal pollution resulting from our in-creased energy consumption will make solar energy a necessity at any cost.

Man's energy consumption is currently about one part in ten thousand that of the energy we receive from
(15) the sun. However, it is growing at a 5 percent rate, of which about 2 percent represents a population growth and 3 percent a per capita energy increase. If this growth continues, within 100 years our energy consumption will be about 1 percent of the absorbed solar energy,
(20) enough to increase the average temperature of the earth by about one degree centigrade if stored energy contin-ues to be our predominant source. This will be the point at which there will be significant effects in our climate, including the melting of the polar ice caps, a phenom-
(25) enon which will raise the level of the oceans and flood parts of our major cities. There is positive feedback associated with this process, since the polar ice cap contributes to the partial reflectivity of the energy

arriving from the sun: As the ice caps begin to melt, the
(30) reflectivity will decrease, thus heating the earth still
further.

It is often stated that the growth rate will decline or
that energy conservation measures will preclude any
long-range problem. Instead, this only postpones the
(35) problem by a few years. Conservation by a factor of two
together with a maintenance of the 5 percent growth rate
delays the problem by only 14 years. Reduction of the
growth rate to 4 percent postpones the problem by only
25 years; in addition, the inequities in standards of
(40) living throughout the world will provide pressure toward an increase in growth rate, particularly if cheap
energy is available. The problem of a changing climate
will not be evident until perhaps ten years before it
becomes critical due to the nature of an exponential
(45) growth rate together with the normal annual weather
variations. This may be too short a period to circumvent
the problem by converting to other energy sources, so
advance planning is a necessity.

The only practical means of avoiding the problem of
(50) thermal pollution appears to be the use of solar energy.
(Schemes to "air-condition" the earth do not appear to
be feasible before the twenty-second century.) Using
the solar energy before it is dissipated to heat does not
increase the earth's energy balance. The cost of solar
(55) energy is extremely favorable now, particularly when
compared to the cost of relocating many of our major
cities.

21. The author is primarily concerned with

(A) describing a phenomenon and explaining
its causes

(B) outlining a position and supporting it with
statistics

(C) isolating an ambiguity and clarifying it by
definition

(D) presenting a problem and advocating a
solution for it

(E) citing a counter-argument and refuting it

22. According to the passage, all of the following are
factors that will tend to increase thermal pollution EXCEPT

(A) the earth's increasing population

(B) melting of the polar ice caps

(C) increase in per capita energy consumption

(D) pressure to redress standard of living
inequities by increasing energy consumption

(E) expected anomalies in weather patterns

23. The positive feedback mentioned in lines 26–27
means that the melting of the polar ice caps will

(A) reduce per capita energy consumption

(B) accelerate the transition to solar energy

(C) intensify the effects of thermal pollution

(D) necessitate a shift to alternative energy
sources

(E) result in the inundations of major cities.

24. The possibility of energy conservation is mentioned (lines 32–34) in order to

(A) preempt and refute a possible objection to
the author's position

(B) support directly the central thesis of the
passage

(C) minimize the significance of a contradiction in the passage

(D) prove that such measures are ineffective
and counterproductive

(E) supply the reader with additional background information

25. It can be inferred that the "air-conditioning" of
the earth (line 51) refers to proposals to

(A) distribute frigid air from the polar ice caps
to coastal cities as the temperature increases due to thermal pollution

(B) dissipate the surplus of the release of
stored solar energy over absorbed solar
energy into space

(C) conserve completely renewable energy
sources by requiring that industry replace
these resources

(D) avoid further thermal pollution by converting to solar energy as opposed to conven-
tional and nuclear sources

(E) utilize hydroelectric and wood energy to
replace non-conventional energy sources
such as nuclear energy

GO ON TO THE NEXT PAGE

26. Since the results of the experiment were —— the body of research already completed, the committee considered the results to be ——.

    (A) similar to..speculative

    (B) inconsistent with..anomalous

    (C) compounded by..heretical

    (D) dispelled by..convincing

    (E) contradicted by..redundant

27. Psychologists believe that modern life —— neurosis because of the —— of traditional values that define acceptable behavior.

    (A) copes with..inundation

    (B) strives for..condoning

    (C) concentrates on..plethora

    (D) fosters..disappearance

    (E) corroborates..dispelling

28. CONTROVERT :

    (A) predict

    (B) bemuse

    (C) intend

    (D) agree

    (E) rectify

29. LANGUOROUS :

    (A) frenetic

    (B) corporeal

    (C) explicit

    (D) recondite

    (E) anomalous

30. PERSPICACIOUS :

    (A) of indefinite duration

    (B) lacking intrinsic value

    (C) insufficiently precise

    (D) condemnatory

    (E) dull-witted

WARNING

Analytical Section

35 QUESTIONS • TIME—40 MINUTES

Directions: Each of the following questions or groups of questions is based on a short passage or a set of propositions. In answering these questions it may sometimes be helpful to draw a simple picture or chart.

Questions 1–7

A music student is composing a musical phrase from six notes —J, K, L, M, N, and O. Each note will be played exactly once in the phrase according to the following conditions:

Both J and O must be played after N.

J must be played before M.

K is the third note.

1. Which of the following could be the order in which the notes are played?
   (A) K, L, N, O, M, J
   (B) K, N, O, J, M, L
   (C) M, J, K, O, L, N
   (D) N, L, K, J, O, M
   (E) N, O, J, M, K, L

2. Which of the following must be true of the order in which the notes are played?
   (A) K is played before L.
   (B) N is played before M.
   (C) K is played before N.
   (D) M is played before O.
   (E) J is played before O.

3. Which of the following could be true?
   (A) The first note is K.
   (B) The second note is M.
   (C) The third note is N.
   (D) The sixth note is J.
   (E) The sixth note is O.

4. If L is the first note in the phrase, then the second note must be
   (A) J
   (B) K
   (C) M
   (D) N
   (E) O

5. If M is played immediately before O and immediately after L, then J must be played
   (A) first
   (B) second
   (C) fourth
   (D) fifth
   (E) sixth

6. If L is the sixth note in the phrase, which of the following could be the first and second notes, respectively?

   I. N and J
   II. N and O
   III. J and O

   (A) I only
   (B) II only
   (C) I and II only
   (D) II and III only
   (E) I, II, and III

7. All of the following could be played immediately after K EXCEPT
   (A) J
   (B) L
   (C) M
   (D) N
   (E) O

GO ON TO THE NEXT PAGE

Questions 8–9

New Weight Loss Salons invites all of you who are dissatisfied with your present build to join our Exercise for Lunch Bunch. Instead of putting on even more weight by eating lunch, you actually cut down on your daily caloric intake by exercising rather than eating. Every single one of us has potential to be thin, so take the initiative and begin losing excess pounds today. Don't eat! Exercise! You'll lose weight and be healthier, happier, and more attractive.

8. Which of the following, if true, would weaken the logic of the argument made by the advertisement?

    I. Most people will experience increased desire for food as a result of the exercise and will lose little weight as a result of enrolling in the program.

    II. Nutritionists agree that skipping lunch is not a healthy practice.

    III. In our society, obesity is regarded as unattractive.

    IV. A person who is too thin is probably not in good health.

    (A) I only
    (B) I and II only
    (C) II and III only
    (D) III and IV only
    (E) I, II, and III

9. A person hearing this advertisement countered, "I know some people who are not overweight and are still unhappy and unattractive." The author of the advertisement could logically and consistently reply to this objection by pointing out that the ad never claimed that

    (A) being overweight is always caused by unhappiness

    (B) being overweight is the only cause of unhappiness and unattractiveness

    (C) unhappiness and unattractiveness can cause someone to be overweight

    (D) unhappiness necessarily leads to being overweight

    (E) unhappiness and unattractiveness are always found together

10. Clara prefers English Literature to Introductory Physics. She likes English Literature, however, less than she likes Basic Economics. She actually finds Basic Economics preferable to any other college course, and she dislikes Physical Education more than she dislikes Introductory Physics.

    All of the following statements can be inferred from the information given above EXCEPT

    (A) Clara prefers Basic Economics to English Literature

    (B) Clara likes English Literature better than she likes Physical Education

    (C) Clara prefers Basic Economics to Advanced Calculus

    (D) Clara likes World History better than she likes Introductory Physics

    (E) Clara likes Physical Education less than she likes English Literature.

Questions 11–16

Six people—Hector, Ira, Jerome, Kurt, Lenny, and Mo—must be seated at the head table at an awards ceremony.

Three people will be seated to the left of the speaker's stand and three will be seated to the right of the speaker's stand.

Lenny and Mo cannot be seated on the same side.

Either Hector or Ira must sit on the same side as Jerome.

11. Which of the following groups could sit on the left side of speaker's stand?

(A) Hector, Ira, Lenny

(B) Hector, Ira, Mo

(C) Hector, Jerome, Ira

(D) Ira, Lenny, Mo

(E) Jerome, Ira, Mo

12. If Jerome and Mo sit on the left side of the speaker's stand, then which of the following pairs must sit on the right side of the speaker's stand?

(A) Hector and Ira

(B) Hector and Kurt

(C) Hector and Lenny

(D) Ira and Lenny

(E) Kurt and Lenny

13. If Kurt and Mo sit on the left side of the speaker's stand, then which of the following pairs must sit on the right side of the speaker's stand?

(A) Hector and Jerome

(B) Hector and Lenny

(C) Ira and Jerome

(D) Ira and Lenny

(E) Jerome and Lenny

14. Which of the following pairs CANNOT sit on the same side of the speaker's stand?

(A) Hector and Ira

(B) Hector and Kurt

(C) Jerome and Mo

(D) Kurt and Lenny

(E) Kurt and Mo

15. If Hector and Kurt are seated on opposite sides of the speaker's stand, then which of the following must be true?

I. Ira and Kurt are seated on the same side of the speaker's stand.

II. Jerome and Lenny are seated on the same side of the speaker's stand.

III. Hector and Lenny are seated on the same side of the speaker's stand.

(A) I only

(B) II only

(C) I and II only

(D) II and III only

(E) I, II, and III

16. If Hector and Jerome are seated to the left of the speaker's stand, then which of the following must be true?

I. Ira and Kurt are seated on the same side of the speaker's stand.

II. Kurt and Lenny are seated on the same side of the speaker's stand.

III. Hector and Mo are seated on the same side of the speaker's stand.

(A) I only

(B) II only

(C) III only

(D) I and III only

(E) II and III only

Questions 17–22

The Dean of a college must appoint a committee consisting of at least three students but no more than five students to prepare a report on the college's freshman orientation program. The list of candidates includes three women who are juniors, two women who are seniors, one man who is a junior, and one man who is a senior.

The committee must include at least one man.

The committee must include at least one senior.

The committee cannot include all three seniors.

The committee cannot include all four juniors.

If the committee includes the man who is a junior, then it must also include at least one of the women who are juniors.

GO ON TO THE NEXT PAGE

17. Which of the following is an acceptable committee?

    (A) Three women who are juniors

    (B) Two women who are juniors and the two women who are seniors

    (C) The two women who are juniors and the man who is a junior

    (D) Two women who are juniors, the man who is a junior, and one woman who is a senior

    (E) The two women who are seniors, the man who is a senior, and one woman who is a junior

18. If exactly five students are selected for the committee, the committee must include exactly

    (A) one woman who is a senior

    (B) two seniors

    (C) two men

    (D) three juniors who are women

    (E) four juniors

19. If the only man selected for the committee is the senior, which of the following must be true?

    (A) The committee consists of exactly four students.

    (B) The remaining members of the committee are juniors.

    (C) The committee includes one woman who is a senior plus the three women who are juniors.

    (D) Either the committee includes one woman who is a senior and at least one woman who is a junior, or the committee includes at least two women who are juniors.

    (E) Either the committee includes two women who are juniors and one of the two women seniors, or the committee includes exactly three women who are juniors.

20. If the three women who are juniors are selected for the committee, which of the following must also be included?

    (A) The man who is a junior

    (B) The man who is a senior

    (C) One woman who is a senior

    (D) One woman who is a senior and the man who is a senior

    (E) One woman who is a senior and the man who is a junior

21. An acceptable committee can consist of the two men and any of the following combinations EXCEPT

    (A) one woman who is a junior

    (B) two women who are juniors

    (C) all three women who are juniors

    (D) one woman who is a senior and one woman who is a junior

    (E) one woman who is a senior and two women who are juniors

22. An acceptable committee can consist of the man who is a junior, a woman who is a senior, and any of the following combinations EXCEPT

    (A) one woman who is a junior

    (B) two women who are juniors

    (C) the other woman who is a senior

    (D) the other woman who is a senior and one woman who is a junior

    (E) the other woman who is a senior and two women who are juniors

23. There is something irrational about our system of laws. The criminal law punishes a person more severely for having successfully committed a crime than it does a person who fails in his attempt to commit the same crime—even though the same evil intention is present in both cases. But under the civil law a person who attempts to defraud his victim but is unsuccessful is not required to pay damages.

Which of the following, if true, would most weaken the author's argument?

(A) Most persons who are imprisoned for crimes will commit another crime if they are ever released from prison.

(B) A person is morally culpable for his evil thoughts as well as for his evil deeds.

(C) There are more criminal laws on the books than there are civil laws on the books.

(D) A criminal trial is considerably more costly to the state than a civil trial.

(E) The goal of the criminal law is to punish the criminal, but the goal of the civil law is to compensate the victim.

24. An independent medical research team recently did a survey at a mountain retreat founded to help heavy smokers quit or cut down on their cigarette smoking. Eighty percent of those persons smoking three packs a day or more were able to cut down to one pack a day after they began to take End-Smoke with its patented desire suppressant. Try End-Smoke to help you cut down significantly on your smoking.

Which of the following could be offered as valid criticism of the above advertisement?

 I. Heavy smokers may be physically as well as psychologically addicted to tobacco.

 II. A medicine that is effective for very heavy smokers may not be effective for the population of smokers generally.

 III. A survey conducted at a mountain retreat to aid smokers may yield different results than one would expect under other circumstances.

(A) I only
(B) II only
(C) III only
(D) II and III only
(E) I, II, and III

25. In his most recent speech, my opponent, Governor Smith, accused me of having distorted the facts, misrepresenting his position, suppressing information, and deliberately lying to the people.

Which of the following possible responses by this speaker would be LEAST relevant to his dispute with Governor Smith?

(A) Governor Smith would not have begun to smear me if he did not sense that his own campaign was in serious trouble.

(B) Governor Smith apparently misunderstood my characterization of his position, so I will attempt to state more clearly my understanding of it.

(C) At the time I made those remarks, certain key facts were not available, but new information uncovered by my staff does support the position I took at that time.

(D) I can only wish Governor Smith had specified those points he considered to be lies so that I could have responded to them now.

(E) With regard to the allegedly distorted facts, the source of my information is a Department of Transportation publication entitled "Safe Driving."

Questions 26–32

The planning committee of an academic conference is planning a series of panels using eight professors, M, N, Q, R, S, T, U, and V. Each panel must be put together in accordance with the following conditions:

N, T, and U cannot all appear on the same panel.

M, N, and R cannot all appear on the same panel.

Q and V cannot appear on the same panel.

If V appears on a panel, at least two professors of the trio M, S, and U must also appear on the panel.

Neither R nor Q can appear on a panel unless the other also appears on the panel.

If S appears on a panel, both N and V must also appear on that panel.

GO ON TO THE NEXT PAGE

26. Which of the following CANNOT appear on a panel with R?

(A) M

(B) N

(C) Q

(D) S

(E) T

27. Exactly how many of the professors can appear on a panel alone?

(A) 1

(B) 2

(C) 3

(D) 4

(E) 5

28. If neither V nor N appears on a panel, then which of the following must be true?

(A) M appears on the panel.

(B) Q appears on the panel.

(C) T appears on the panel.

(D) S does not appear on the panel.

(E) U does not appear on the panel.

29. If S appears on a panel, that panel must consist of at least how many professors?

(A) 3

(B) 4

(C) 5

(D) 6

(E) 7

30. Which of the following is an acceptable group of professors for a panel?

(A) M, N, Q, R

(B) M, Q, R, T

(C) M, R, T, U

(D) M, S, U, V

(E) N, R, T, U

31. Which of the following groups of professors can form an acceptable panel by doing nothing more than adding one more professor to the group?

(A) M, R, T

(B) N, Q, M

(C) Q, R, S

(D) Q, R, V

(E) V, R, N

32. Of the group N, S, T, U, V, which professor will have to be removed to form an acceptable panel?

(A) N

(B) S

(C) T

(D) U

(E) V

33.   SPEAKER: The great majority of people in the United States have access to the best medical care available anywhere in the world.

OBJECTOR: There are thousands of poor in this country who cannot afford to pay to see a doctor.

A possible objection to the speaker's comments would be to point to the existence of

(A) a country that has more medical assistants than the United States

(B) a nation where medical care is provided free of charge by the government

(C) a country in which the people are given better medical care than Americans

(D) government hearings in the United States on the problems poor people have getting medical care

(E) a country that has a higher hospital bed per person ratio than the United States

34. Statistics published by the State Department of Traffic and Highway Safety show that nearly 80% of all traffic fatalities occur at speeds under 35 miles per hour and within 25 miles of home.

Which of the following would be the most reasonable conclusion to draw from these statistics?

(A) One is less likely to have a fatal accident if one always drives over 35 miles per hour and always at distances greater than 25 miles from home.

(B) There is a direct correlation between distance driven and the likelihood of a fatal accident.

(C) The greater the likelihood that one is about to be involved in a fatal accident, the more likely it is that one is driving close to home at a speed less than 35 miles per hour.

(D) If it were not the case that one were about to be involved in a fatal traffic accident, then one would not have been driving at the speed or in the location one was, in fact, driving.

(E) Most driving is done at less than 35 miles per hour and within 25 miles of home.

35. It is sometimes argued that we are reaching the limits of the Earth's capacity to supply our energy needs with fossil fuels. In the past ten years, however, as a result of technological progress making it possible to extract resources from even marginal wells and mines, yields from oil and coal fields have increased tremendously. There is no reason to believe that there is a limit to the Earth's capacity to supply our energy needs.

Which of the following statements most directly contradicts the conclusion drawn above?

(A) Even if we exhaust our supplies of fossil fuel, the earth can still be mined for uranium for nuclear fuel.

(B) The technology needed to extract fossil fuels from marginal sources is very expensive.

(C) Even given the improvements in technology, oil and coal are not renewable resources, so we will sometime exhaust our supplies of them.

(D) Most of the land under which marginal oil and coal supplies lie is more suitable to cultivation or pasturing than to production of fossil fuels.

(E) The fuels that are yielded by marginal sources tend to be high in sulfur and other undesirable elements that aggravate the air pollution problem.

WARNING

IF YOU FINISHED THIS SECTION BEFORE TIME EXPIRED, GO IMMEDIATELY TO THE NEXT SECTION. YOU MAY NOT CONTINUE TO WORK ON THIS SECTION AFTER TIME HAS EXPIRED.

Practice Examination 5

Answer Key

MATH SECTION

1. D	7. C	13. B	19. A	25. C
2. C	8. A	14. A	20. B	26. C
3. B	9. D	15. B	21. C	27. B
4. C	10. B	16. D	22. A	28. D
5. A	11. B	17. D	23. C	
6. A	12. D	18. B	24. E	

VERBAL SECTION

1. A	7. E	13. A	19. C	25. B
2. B	8. C	14. B	20. B	26. B
3. C	9. C	15. E	21. D	27. D
4. B	10. E	16. D	22. E	28. D
5. A	11. A	17. A	23. C	29. A
6. C	12. D	18. D	24. A	30. E

ANALYTICAL SECTION

1. D	8. B	15. A	22. C	29. B
2. B	9. B	16. A	23. E	30. B
3. E	10. D	17. D	24. D	31. A
4. D	11. E	18. B	25. A	32. C
5. B	12. E	19. D	26. D	33. C
6. C	13. E	20. B	27. D	34. E
7. D	14. A	21. C	28. D	35. C

Practice Examination 5

Explanatory Answers

MATH SECTION

1. **(D)** Although this is a right triangle, and though the hypotenuse has length $\sqrt{2}$, the triangle need not be a 45°-45°-90° triangle. The easiest way to show this is with a drawing:

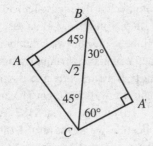

2. **(C)** Since it makes no difference in which order the elements are multiplied, Column A is equivalent to Column B.

3. **(B)** It is important to remember that the square root of a number between 0 and 1, whether expressed as a decimal or as a fraction, is *larger* than the number itself. For example $\sqrt{\frac{1}{4}} = \frac{1}{2}$, but $\frac{1}{2} > \frac{1}{4}$. So, too, here $\sqrt{0.9}$ is actually greater than 0.9. Another method for solving the problem is to square both sides of the comparison. If the two quantities were originally equal, then squaring both sides will not upset the balance. Further, if either of the two quantities is greater than the other, squaring both sides will not interfere with the *direction* of the inequality. (It will interfere with the *magnitude* of the inequality, but the quantitative comparison question is a "yes or no" exercise: which is larger, *not* how much larger.) Squaring both sides:

$$(0.3)^2 \qquad \left(\sqrt{0.9}\right)^2$$
$$.09 \qquad 0.9$$

Clearly, Column B is larger.

4. **(C)** Performing the multiplication in each column is the simplest approach to the question:

$$(x+y)^2 \qquad x(x+y)+y(x+y)$$
$$(x+y)(x+y) \qquad x^2+xy+xy+y^2$$
$$x^2+xy+xy+y^2 \qquad x^2+2xy+y^2$$
$$x^2+2xy+y2$$

5. **(A)** One property of positive fractions is that, given the same denominator, the larger numerator makes the larger fraction and, conversely, given the same numerator, the larger denominator makes the *smaller* fraction. In this question, the numerators are equal. The fraction in Column B has the larger denominator, so it is actually smaller than the fraction in Column A.

6. **(A)** We begin by multiplying $(x-y)^2$:

$$(x-y)(x-y) = x^2 - 2xy + y^2 = 12$$

Then we substitute 1 for xy:

$$x^2 - 2(1) + y^2 = 12$$
$$x^2 + y^2 = 14$$

7. **(C)** Let us begin by adding the following notation:

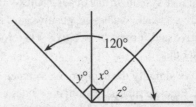

Since the entire angle is 120°, $y + 90 = 120$, so $y = 30$. Similarly, $z + 90 = 120$, so $z = 30$. Since $x + y + z = 120$, $x + 30 + 30 = 120$, so $x = 60$.

8. **(A)** Certainly the easiest and most direct way to solve this problem is to test each of the integers. There is no reason to try and find some fancy mathematical equation to describe the problem when a simple substitution of answer choices will do. When 95 is divided by 6, 10, and 15—answers (A), (C), and (D)—the remainder in each case is 5. And when 135 is divided by 10, the remainder is 5, not 3; and when 135 is divided by 15 there is a remainder of 0. When 135 is divided by 6, the remainder is 3. So only 6 fits both the conditions for n.

9. **(D)** Since the ratio of insects with X to those without X is 5:3, we know that $\frac{5}{8}$ of the population has X. (There are 8 equal units—$5 + 3$—5 of which are insects with X.) Then, of those $\frac{5}{8}$, $\frac{3}{8}$ are male. So we take $\frac{3}{8}$ of the $\frac{5}{8}\left(\frac{3}{8} \times \frac{5}{8}\right)$ and that tells us that $\frac{15}{64}$ of the total population are male insects with X.

419

10. **(B)** We can order the elements by clarifying the exponents:

(A) $\dfrac{3^8}{3^6} = 3^{8-6} = 3^2 = 9$

(B) $3^3 - 1 = 27 - 1 = 26$

(C) $3^0 = 1$

(D) 3^{27} is too large to compute here, but is obviously the greatest quantity in the group.

(E) $3(3^2) = 3^3 = 27$

The order is (C), (A), (B), (E), (D); so (B) is the middle term.

11. **(B)** The parabola drawn on the graph actually adds no information needed for solving the problem. Regardless of what figure is drawn through point (a, b), and there are of course an infinite number of different ones, point (a, b) is in the second quadrant—that is, the upper left-hand section of the coordinate system. In that quadrant all x-values are negative and all y-values are positive, so a must be negative and b must be positive. Therefore, b is greater than a.

12. **(D)** We simplify the comparison as much as possible. First we subtract 3 from both sides and then we subtract $2x$ from both sides. This reduces Column A to $x + 2$ and Column B to 0. We can now ask the simpler question: Which is greater, $x + 2$ or 0? This is simpler because we can immediately see that the answer will depend on the value of x, information we lack.

13. **(B)** First, let us perform the indicated operations. In Column A we find a power raised to a power, and that calls for the multiplication of the two exponents: $(x^3)5 = x^{3 \cdot 5} = x^{15}$. In Column B we find multiplication of like bases, so we add the exponents: $x^3 \cdot x^5 = x^{3 \cdot 5} = x^8$. The centered information states that x is negative. Since a negative number raised to a power that is odd yields a negative number (negative times negative times negative . . . yields a negative number), Column A is negative. Column B, however, must be positive since it is raised to an even power. Consequently, whatever x might be, Column A is negative, Column B is positive; therefore, Column B must be greater than Column A.

14. **(A)** The problem can be worked out using simultaneous equations, but that is not the most efficient way of solving it. For that reason we will set up the equations (for the "aficionados"), but we will not actually solve for x and y. Let x be the number of shirts costing \$13 and y the number costing \$10.

$$x + y = 16$$
$$13x + 10y = 187$$

Final solution: $x = 9$ and $y = 7$

We have omitted the detailed calculations because there is a simpler method. Let us assume, for the sake of argument, that the two columns are equal—that is, that the man bought equal numbers of both types of shirts. If we are correct in assuming that he bought eight \$13 shirts and eight \$10 shirts, then $(8 \times 13) + (8 \times 10)$ ought to equal \$187. When we do the multiplication, we get the result \$184. That tells us our original assumption of equal numbers was incorrect and, further, that the answer to the question is not (C). We should then make a second assumption, but should we assume that he bought more expensive shirts than we first guessed, or fewer? A moment of reflection will show that we should adjust our initial assumption to include a greater number of expensive shirts, for only by increasing that number will we add to the \$184 which was the result of our original assumption. So we would next assume—again for the purposes of argument—that the man bought nine \$13 shirts and only seven \$10 shirts. But at this point we have already solved the problem! We do not need to know the precise ratio, e.g., whether 9:7, 10:6, 11:5, 12:4, 13:3, 14:2, or 15:1; we have already determined that the ratio is one of those listed, and so it must be the case that Column A is larger.

15. **(B)** This problem, too, can be solved with a little gimmick. It is not necessary to actually calculate the volumes in question. You need only recognize that the sphere will have a diameter of 10 and that this is equal to the side of the cube. This means that the sphere can be placed within the cube, so the cube must have a greater volume.

16. **(D)** The proper way to "visualize" this problem is to imagine that the gravel-covered walk will be a very squat-shaped cylinder with a donut hole removed (the circular region inside the walk). Expressed more abstractly, we need to compute the

volume of a cylinder with a radius of 50 feet ($\frac{1}{2}$ of $100 = 50$) and a height of 6 inches, or $\frac{1}{2}$ foot. Then we compute the volume of a cylinder with a radius of 40 feet ($\frac{1}{2}$ of $80 = 40$) and a height of 6 inches, or $\frac{1}{2}$ foot. Then we subtract the second from the first and what is left is the volume we seek. Now, since both cylinders have the same height, it will be easier to compute the areas of the bases first and subtract before multiplying by $\frac{1}{2}$ foot.

Area of larger circle: Area $= \pi r^2 = \pi(50)^2 = 2{,}500\pi$.

Area of smaller circle: Area $= \pi r^2 = \pi(40)^2 = 1{,}600\pi$.

By subtracting $1{,}600\pi$ from $2{,}500\pi$, we determine that the area of the garden path is 900π square feet. To determine the volume of gravel we need, we then multiply that figure by $\frac{1}{2}$ foot (the depth of the gravel), and arrive at our answer: 450π cu. ft.

17. **(D)** Let d stand for the hourly rate under the new system. Since the employee is to make the same amount per week under both systems, it must be the case that:

$$\frac{\$x}{\text{hr.}} \times 40 \text{ hrs.} = \frac{\$d}{\text{hr.}} \times 36 \text{ hrs.}$$

Now we must solve for d:

$$40x = 36d$$

$$d = \frac{10x}{9}$$

The problem can also be solved in an intuitive way. Since the employee is working less time yet making the same weekly total, he must be earning slightly more per hour under the new system than under the old. Answer (A) is just the naked fraction $\frac{1}{10}$, without making reference to monetary units. Answer (B) implies that the employee is making $\frac{1}{9}$ as much per hour under the new system as under the old—that would be a decrease in the hourly rate. Similarly, (C) says that the employee is making only 90% of his old hourly rate and that, too, is a decrease. Finally, (E) says that the employee is making 9 *times* the hourly rate he made under the old system, a figure that is obviously out of line. The only reasonable choice is (D). The moral is: Even if you cannot set up the math in a technically correct way, use a little common sense.

18. **(B)** Since the columns are perpendicular to both ceiling and floor, we know that they are parallel. The left-hand column must be 12 feet long: If the two 8-foot pieces were laid end to end, they would total 16 feet, but there is a 4-foot overlap, so the length of the column is 16 feet minus 4 feet, or 12 feet. The right-hand column must also be 12 feet long. But the two 10-foot pieces, if laid end to end, would form a column 20 feet long. Therefore, the overlap, x, must be 8 feet ($20 - x = 12$).

19. **(A)** This problem must be solved in two stages. First, we need to calculate the total area of the wall. The information given in the problem states that $\frac{1}{3}$ of the job plus another 75 square feet equals $\frac{3}{4}$ of the job. In algebraic notation, this is:

$$\frac{1}{3}x + 75 = \frac{3}{4}x$$

$$75 = \frac{3}{4}x - \frac{1}{3}x$$

$$75 = \frac{5}{12}x$$

$$x = 180$$

So the entire wall is 180 square feet—that is, $W \times L = 180$. We know that the height of the wall is 10 feet; so $10 \times L = 180$, and $L = 18$.

20. **(B)** A quick glance at the two expressions shows that Column A must be negative and Column B positive. Whatever the absolute value of the number 3^6, in Column A it will be negative since it is prefixed with the minus sign. Column B, however, will be positive. The minus sign is enclosed within the parentheses. This indicates that we are raising minus three to the sixth power. Since six is an even number, the final result will be positive (negative times negative times negative times negative times negative times negative yields a positive).

21. **(C)** We should notice first that we are definitely not in a position to say that the magnitude of the unlabeled angles is 90°. But we need not make the assumption! We know that $w = y$ and $x = z$ because vertical angles are equal. Therefore, $w + x = y + z$. We can drop these expressions from both sides of our comparison. In effect, we are subtracting equals from both sides of the comparison, a maneuver which, as we have already seen, will neither upset

the balance of the original equality nor interfere with the direction of the inequality. This leaves us with 90 on both sides of the comparison, so we conclude that the original comparison must have been an equality.

22. **(A)** This is just a matter of adding up the total fares collected for subways in the six years:

1972:	300 million
1973:	310 million
1974:	350 million
1975:	350 million
1976:	310 million
1977:	250 million

1,870

23. **(C)** The number of fares collected in 1975 was 350 million, and the number of fares collected in 1977 was 250 million. The number of fares dropped by 100 million, but we are looking for the rate, or percentage, of decrease. So we set our fraction up, difference over starting amount, $\frac{100}{350}$ = 28.6%, which is closest to 25%.

24. **(E)** The number of subway fares collected in 1974 was 350 million; the number of bus fares collected in that year was 315 million. Our ratio then is $\frac{50\times350}{30\times315}$, which we then reduce by a factor of 10, $\frac{5\times350}{3\times315}$, and again by a factor of 5, $\frac{5\times70}{3\times63}$; then we can do the arithmetic a little more easily: $\frac{350}{189}$. If we round 189 off to 200 and reduce again by a factor of 10, we get $\frac{35}{20}$, or $\frac{7}{4}$ as a good approximation of the ratio. Actually, we need not do all of this arithmetic. We can see at a glance that more subway fares were collected than bus fares; so, given that the subway fares are more expensive, we can conclude that the revenues derived from subway fares were greater than those for bus fares, and that means our ratio must be greater than 1. Only (E) is possible.

25. **(C)** In 1977, the total number of fares collected was 240 (subways) + 400 (commuter rail) + 235 (bus) = 875 total. Of the 875 million fares collected, 400 were commuter rail fares, so the commuter rail fares accounted for about $\frac{1}{2}$, or 50%, of all the fares collected in that year.

26. **(C)** At first glance, the problem appears to be a difficult one. A closer look, however, shows that it is actually quite simple. Both paths cover the same vertical distance of 10 units and the same horizontal distance of 14 units. Since it makes no difference whether one moves vertically or horizontally first, the two paths are equal. Notice further that each path covers a distance of 24 units. That is equal to the sum of one width and one length of a rectangle with dimension 10 and 14 that could be constructed using P and T as vertices.

27. **(B)** Let us begin by inscribing an equilateral triangle in a circle:

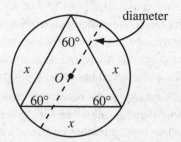

Since the longest chord of any circle is the chord drawn through the center of the circle (that is, the diameter of the circle), and since no side of the triangle can pass through the center, the side of the equilateral triangle must be shorter than the diameter of the circle in which it is inscribed. Having determined that, we then proceed to ask whether the length of the side of a square inscribed in the same circle is longer or shorter than that of the side of the equilateral triangle.

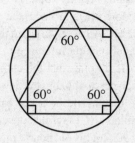

The side of the square is shorter, and we can see that the greater the number of sides, the shorter will be the length of those sides. From this we can conclude that for all equilateral polygons inscribed in circles, the side of the polygon will be shorter than the diameter of the circle.

28. **(D)** Using P, V, and G to represent Peter's, Victor's, and Georgette's grades, respectively, the centered information tells us: P > V and G > V. But we have no information regarding the relationship between P and G.

VERBAL SECTION

1. **(A)** The sentence gives you a very strong clue with the word *unfairly*. You can eliminate (B) since something that is unfair could not be objective. You can also eliminate (C) and (D) because they do not create meaningful sentences. (A), *biased*, is the best word to convey the idea that the book blamed the South unfairly.

2. **(B)** This sentence contains both a thought-extender and a thought-reverser. The first blank extends the thought that the universe was well-ordered. You can eliminate (A) since it is not logical that something would be well-ordered and baffling. (C), (D), and (E) are not words you would use to describe the universe. This leaves you with (B). There is a *but* or *yet* understood in this sentence, so the word in the next blank will have the opposite meaning of *harmonious*. The second element of (B) works because *chaotic* is the opposite of *harmonious*.

3. **(C)** This is a vocabulary question. You must know that something that cures insomnia is a soporific—something that induces sleep.

4. **(B)** To be ABHORRENT is to be extremely DISLIKABLE; to be *arduous* is to be extremely *difficult*.

5. **(A)** This analogy does not fit a category, but the relationship is quite clear. A SOLDIER wears a UNIFORM, and a *jockey* wears *silks*.

6. **(C)** Here there is a clear relationship. A MURAL is painted on a WALL and a *painting* is painted on a *canvas*.

7. **(E)** This is an inference question. The author states that a result of the PATCO strike is that management can now expect to regain some of the power it gave up to labor in earlier decades. So you may infer that the outcome of that strike was favorable to management. This is the description given by (E). As for (A), though the author mentions bad-faith negotiations in the first paragraph, there is nothing to connect that concept with the example

mentioned in the second paragraph. As for (B), nothing in the passage supports a conclusion one way or the other about the length of the strike, as opposed to its outcome. (C) and (D) make the same mistake as (A). Though they are ideas mentioned in the passage, there is nothing to connect them with the example of the PATCO strike.

8. **(C)** This is an attitude question, and the choices have already been arranged for you on a spectrum. You can eliminate all but (C) because there is nothing to indicate a preference for one side over the other. In fact, statements such as "neither side is blameless" specifically attest to the author's neutrality.

9. **(C)** This is an implied idea question. The first sentence of the second paragraph states that since the economic situation will not improve, union leaders will be frustrated. So the stage is set for confrontation. We may infer, therefore, that if economic conditions were better, labor would be happier, and tensions would be lessened. This is choice (C). (A) carries this line of reasoning too far. We can infer that better economic conditions would prevent management from recouping its losses, but we cannot infer that better economic conditions will cause further erosion of management's position. As for (B), the opposite conclusion seems inferable. When economic circumstances are good, labor demands more. As for (E), there is nothing to connect this idea mentioned in the first paragraph with the line of reasoning in the second. Finally, (D) makes the same mistake as (A).

10. **(E)** This is an explicit detail question. The ideas suggests by (A) through (D) are all explicitly mentioned in the selection. At no point, however, does the author mention low interest rates.

11. **(A)** This is a variation on the "lack of" relationship. PROCRASTINATION is a lack of COMMENCEMENT, and *prolongation* is a lack of *termination*. Note that in this analogy it is helpful to change the parts of speech.

12. **(D)** BUCOLIC relates to rural life and suggests the natural; URBAN implies the manufactured. *Mist* is a natural occurrence; *smog* is fog made foul by smoke and chemical fumes.

13. **(A)** This is a "defining characteristic" analogy. By definition, that which is LAMENTED is REGRETTABLE, and that which is *applauded* is *praiseworthy*.

14. **(B)** This is an analogy of degree. To be FASTIDIOUS is to be extremely preoccupied with CLEANLINESS, and to be *meticulous* is to be extremely preoccupied with *detail*.

15. **(E)** This is a "defining characteristic" analogy. CONDEMNING presupposes DISAPPROBATION, and *urging* presupposes *exhortation*.

16. **(D)** This sentence contains two thought-extenders. The first blank extends the idea of refuge for science," and it should also be the reverse of the idea of *superstitious*. The second blank extends the idea of *superstitious*. (A) cannot be correct, for although the first word makes some sense, it makes no sense to say that the world was both scholarly and superstitious since that is a contradiction. (B) does not make a meaningful statement, nor does (C). (D) makes sense because the idea that the monks were conservators of civilization extends the idea that the monasteries were a refuge for science, and the adjective *barbarous* goes well with *superstitious* to produce an idea that is more or less the opposite of *civilized*. (E) looks plausible because one might describe the monks as "advocates of civilization," but *rarefied* does not extend the idea of *superstitious*.

17. **(A)** The logical structure of this sentence is fairly clear; the first blank must be a word that is more or less the opposite of *beneficial*. The word *while* gives you the clue that the second blank must be a word with negative overtones since the first example of what coffee and tea do is beneficial. The construction is "while they are (beneficial) they are also (harmful)." (A) looks possible because *injurious* is certainly the opposite of *beneficial*. The second word also works well. Coffee and tea exacerbate problems. This seems to be the correct choice. The best thing to do here is to test the other responses to make certain that (A) is the best choice. (B) doesn't work because although the first word is possible, if coffee and tea interrupted nervous disorders, they would be beneficial, not harmful. (C) is wrong because *salutary* is almost a synonym for *beneficial*, and we are looking for a

word that is almost an opposite. (D) is wrong because *negligible* is not the opposite of *beneficial*, and again, if coffee and tea forestalled nervous disorders, that would be beneficial. (E) also fails because of the second word. Preventing nervous disorders is positive, not negative.

18. **(D)** Since *guile* means "craft or cunning, "*naïve* is a good opposite.

19. **(C)** To *malign* is to speak evil of or to slander; *praise* is a precise opposite.

20. **(B)** To *incite* is to arouse or move to action. *Calm* is an opposite.

21. **(D)** This is a main idea question. This passage does two things: It describes the problem of increasing thermal pollution and it suggests that solar energy will solve the problem. (D) neatly describes this double development. (A) is incorrect, for the author not only describes the phenomenon of thermal pollution and its causes, but also proposes a solution. (B) is incorrect since it fails to make reference to the fact that an important part of the passage is the description of a problem. It can be argued that (B) does make an attempt to describe the development of the passage, but it does not do as nicely as (D) does. (C) is easily eliminated since no ambiguity is mentioned. Finally, (E) is incorrect since the author never cites and then refutes a counter-argument.

22. **(E)** This is an explicit idea question. (A), (B), and (C) are mentioned in the second paragraph as factors contributing to thermal pollution. (D) is mentioned in the third paragraph as a pressure increasing thermal pollution. (E) is mentioned in the third paragraph—but not as a factor contributing to thermal pollution. Unpredictable weather patterns make it difficult to predict when the thermal pollution problem will reach the critical stage, but the patterns do not contribute to thermal pollution.

23. **(C)** This is an inference question. In discussing the melting of the polar ice caps, the author notes that there is a positive feedback mechanism: Since the ice caps reflect sunlight and therefore dissipate solar energy that would otherwise be absorbed by the earth, the melting of the ice caps increases the amount of energy captured by the earth, which in turn contributes to the melting of the ice caps, and

so on. (C) correctly describes this as intensifying the effects of thermal pollution. (A) is easily eliminated since this feedback mechanism has nothing to do with a possible reduction in per capita energy consumption. (B) is incorrect, for though this feedback loop increases the problem, and thereby the urgency for the changeover to solar energy, the loop itself will not cause a change in policy. (D) is incorrect for the same reason. Finally, though the melting of the polar ice caps will result in flooding, this flooding is not an explanation of the feedback loop. Rather it is the result of the general phenomenon of the melting of the ice caps.

24. **(A)** This is a logical detail question. Why does the author discuss energy conservation? Conservation may appear as a possible alternative to solar energy. The author argues, however, that a closer examination shows that conservation cannot avert but only postpone the crisis. In terms of tactics, the author's move is to raise a possible objection and give an answer to it—as stated in (A). (B) is incorrect, for the refutation of a possible objection does not support the central thesis directly, only indirectly by eliminating a possible counter-argument. (C) is incorrect since the author never acknowledges any contradiction. (D) is incorrect since it overstates the case. The author admits that conservation has a beneficial effect, but denies that conservation obviates the need for solar energy. Finally, (E) is incorrect since the point is argumentative and not merely informational.

25. **(B)** This is an inference question. In the final paragraph the author makes references to the possibility of "air-conditioning" the earth. The quotation marks indicate that the word is being used in a non-standard way. Ordinarily, we use the word "air-condition" to mean to cool, say, a room or an entire building. Obviously, the author is not referring to some gigantic air-conditioning unit mounted, say, on top of the earth. But the general idea of removing heat seems to be what the term means in this context. This is consonant with the passage as well. Thermal pollution is the buildup of energy, and we are showing a positive buildup because fossil fuel and other sources of energy release energy that was only stored. So this, coupled with the sun's energy, which comes in each moment,

gives us a positive (though not desirable) balance of energy retention over loss. The idea of air-conditioning the earth, though not feasible according to the passage, must refer to schemes to get rid of this energy, say, into outer space. This is the idea presented in (B). As for (A), redistribution of thermal energy within the earth's energy system will not solve the problem of accumulated energy, so that cannot be what proponents of "air-conditioning" have in mind. (C) is a good definition of conservation, but not air-conditioning." (D) is the recommendation given by the author, but that is not a response to this question. Finally, (E) is incorrect for the reason that burning wood is not going to cool the earth.

26. **(B)** Given that there is a body of research already existing, the results can only be irrelevant to it, consistent with it, or inconsistent with it. This eliminates choice (C). Then you have to substitute both words of the remaining choices in order to determine the correct answer. (A) cannot be correct, since results would not be speculative if they were similar to the research already done. (D) is not possible because the body of research would not be dispelled by convincing results. (E) makes no sense because if the results were redundant, then they would not contradict the existing research. This leaves you with (B), which works very well. Results might be considered anomalous if they were inconsistent with the research already done.

27. **(D)** The logical clue here is a thought-extender. But the order in which the ideas are presented in the sentence makes this difficult to see. The idea that follows the *because* specifies the cause of the first idea: "The —— of traditional values" causes modern life to "—— neurosis." Substitute each of the choices into this new sentence. Only (D) produces a sentence that fits the logical structure.

28. **(D)** To *controvert* is to dispute or deny, so *agree* is a good opposite.

29. **(A)** *Languorous* means "characterized by lack of vigor or weakness," so frenetic is a good opposite.

30. **(E)** Since *perspicacious* means "having keen insight or understanding," *dull-witted* is a good antonym.

ANALYTICAL SECTION

1. **(D)** The first condition eliminates (C); the second condition eliminates (A); and the third condition eliminates both (B) and (E).

2. **(B)** Since N comes before J and J before M, N must come before M.

3. **(E)** The third condition eliminates (A) and (C). Then, (B) is not possible because both N and J must come before M. Finally, (D) is not possible because J must come before M.

4. **(D)** N must come before J, M, and O. So if L is the first note (and K the third), N must be the second note.

5. **(B)** If L-M-O are played consecutively in that order, then they must be the fourth, fifth, and sixth notes of the phrase. Then since N must be played before J, N must be the first note and J the second.

6. **(C)** If L is the sixth note, then there are exactly three possible phrases:

1	2	3	4	5	6
N	J	K	M	O	L
N	J	K	O	M	L
N	O	K	J	M	L

7. **(D)** N cannot be played as the fourth note, because N must be played before J, O, and M.

8. **(B)** Statement I would undermine the advertisement considerably. Since the point of the ad is that you will lose weight, any unforeseen effects that would make it impossible to lose weight would defeat the purposes of the program. Statement II is less obvious, but it does weaken the ad somewhat. Although the ad does not specifically say you will be healthier for having enrolled in the program, surely the advantages of the program are less significant if you have to pay an additional, hidden cost, i.e., health. Statement III, if anything, supports the advertisement. Statement IV is irrelevant since the ad does not claim you will become too thin.

9. **(B)** This question is like one of those simple conversation questions: "X: All bats are mammals. Y: Not true, whales are mammals too." In this little exchange, B misunderstands A to have said that "All mammals are bats." Here, the objection must be based on a misunderstanding. The objector must think that the ad has claimed that the only cause of unhappiness, etc., is being overweight, otherwise he would not have offered his counter-example. (A) is wrong because the ad never takes a stand on the *causes* of overweight conditions—only on a possible cure. This reasoning invalidates (C) and (D) as well. (E) makes a similar error, but about effects not about causes. The ad does not say everyone who is unhappy is unattractive, or vice versa.

10. **(D)** The easiest way to set this problem up is to draw a relational line:

    PE   IP   EL   BE

    Dislikes ——————————→ Likes

    We note that Clara likes Basic Economics better than anything else, which means she must like it better than Advanced Calculus. So even though Advanced Calculus does not appear on our line, since we know that Basic Economics is the maximum, Clara must like Advanced Calculus less than Basic Economics. So (C) can be inferred. But we do not know where World History ranks on the preference line, and since Introductory Physics is not a maximal or a minimal value, we can make no judgment regarding it and an unplaced course. Quick reference to the line will show that (A), (B), and (E) are inferable.

11. **(E)** The first condition eliminates both (C) and (D), while the second condition eliminates (A) and (B).

12. **(E)** If Jerome and Mo are sitting on the same side of the speaker's stand, then the third person on that side must be either Hector or Ira. Thus, Kurt and Lenny must be seated on the other side. Thus (A) is not possible, while (B), (C), and (D) are merely possible.

13. **(E)** If Kurt and Mo are seated to the left of the speaker's stand, then Lenny must be seated to the right along with Jerome and either Hector or Ira.

14. **(A)** If Hector and Ira were seated on the same side of the speaker's stand, then Jerome would also be seated there; but that would leave both Lenny and Mo together on the other side.

15. **(A)** If Hector and Kurt are seated on opposite sides of the speaker's stand, then (given that Lenny and Mo are also on opposite sides), Jerome and Ira are

to be on opposite sides as well. But since Jerome must be on a side with either Hector or Ira, Jerome must be on the same side as Hector and Kurt on the same side as Ira. Nothing, however, determines the position of Lenny and Mo with regard to the other four.

16. **(A)** If Hector and Jerome are seated on the same side of the speaker's stand, then (since Lenny and Mo are on opposite sides) Ira and Kurt are seated on the other side.

17. **(D)** The first condition eliminates both (A) and (B). The second condition eliminates (C). And the third condition eliminates (E).

18. **(B)** If exactly five students are selected for the committee, the committee must include three of the four juniors (it cannot include all four) and two of the three seniors (it cannot include all three).

19. **(D)** If the senior man is selected for the committee and the junior man is not, then the committee must include *either* one of the two senior women (but not both for that would have all three seniors on the committee) plus one or more women from the junior class or two or more women from the junior class.

20. **(B)** If the three women who are juniors are on the committee, then the man who is a junior cannot be on the committee. Thus, the man who is a senior must be on the committee.

21. **(C)** If both men are selected, then the junior man is on the committee and the other three juniors cannot be included.

22. **(C)** One of the initial conditions stipulates that if the man who is a junior is used on the committee, then at least one of the women who is a junior must also be used.

23. **(E)** The point of the passage is that there is a seeming contradiction in our body of laws. Sometimes a person pays for attempted misdeeds, and other times he does not pay for them. If there could be found a good reason for this difference, then the contradiction could be explained away. This is just what (E) does. It points out that the law treats the situations differently because it has different goals: Sometimes we drive fast because we are in a hurry, other times we drive slowly because we want to enjoy the scenery. (B) would not weaken the argument for it only intensifies the contradiction. (D) makes an attempt to reconcile the seemingly conflicting positions by hinting at a possible goal of one action that is not a goal of the other. But, if anything, it intensifies the contradiction because one might infer that we should not try persons for attempted crimes because criminal trials are expensive, but we should allow compensation for attempted frauds because civil trials are less expensive. (C) and (A) are just distractions. Whether there are more laws of one kind than another on the books has nothing to do with the seeming contradiction. And whether persons are more likely to commit a second crime after they are released from prison does not speak to the issue of whether an unsuccessful attempt to commit a crime should be a crime in the first place.

24. **(D)** The ad is weak for two reasons. First, although it is addressed to smokers in general, the evidence it cites is restricted to heavy (three-packs-a-day) smokers. Second, the success achieved by the product was restricted to a highly specific and unusual location—the mountain retreat of a clinic with a population trying hard to quit smoking. Thus, II will undermine the appeal of the advertisement because it cites the first of the weaknesses. III also will tell against the ad since it mentions the second of these weaknesses. I, however, is irrelevant to the ad's appeal since the cause of a smoker's addiction plays no role in the claim of this ad to assist smokers in quitting or cutting down.

25. **(A)** The question stem asks us to focus on the "dispute" between the two opponents. What will be relevant to it will be those items that affect the merits of the issues, or perhaps those that affect the credibility of the parties. (C) and (E) both mention items—facts and their source—that would be relevant to the substantive issues. (B) and (D) are legitimate attempts to clarify the issues and so are relevant. (A) is not relevant to the issues nor is it relevant to the credibility (e.g., where did the facts come from) of the debaters. (A) is the least relevant because it is an *ad hominem* attack of the illegitimate sort.

Questions 26–32

Arranging the Information

Here we have a selection problem, and we begin by using a notational system to summarize the information:

(1) $\sim (N \& T \& U)$

(2) $\sim (M \& N \& R)$

(3) $Q \neq V$

(4) $V \supset [(M \& S) \vee (M \& U) \vee (S \& U) \vee (M \& S \& U)]$

(5) $R = Q$

(6) $S \supset (N \& V)$

Perhaps (4) requires some clarification. The statement given in the problem structure is logically equivalent to: If V is selected, then either (a) M and S are selected, or (b) M and U are selected, or (c) S and U are selected, or (d) all three are selected.

Answering the Questions

26. **(D)** If R appears, then Q must appear (5). And if Q appears, then V cannot appear (3). But if V does not appear, then S cannot appear (6). So (D) is the correct answer. As for the remaining choices, we could have:

    (A) R, Q, and M

    (B) R, Q, and N

    (C) R and Q

    (E) R, Q, and T

27. **(D)** There are four professors who must be accompanied by other professors: V (4), R and Q (5), and S (6). Every other professor, M, N, T, and U, can appear without the necessity of including any other professor.

28. **(D)** Given the sixth condition, if neither N nor V appears, then S cannot appear.

29. **(B)** If S appears, then both N and V must also appear (6). And if V appears, then two of the three, M, S, and U, must appear. Since S is already included (by stipulation), we need choose only one of the pair M and U. Thus, at minimum, we have S, N, V, and either M or U, for a total of four.

30. **(B)** We handle this question by the process of elimination, checking each of the available choices against the restrictions established in the initial set

of conditions. (A) can be eliminated because it violates (2). (C) violates (5) since Q is not there to accompany R. (D) can be eliminated because we have S without N, in violation of (6). And (E) violates (5) because we have R without Q.

31. **(A)** This question, too, is solved in a manner similar to that used for question 21. But here we must check each choice against the initial conditions in an effort to add exactly one more professor to obtain a permissible grouping. (A) can be turned into an acceptable grouping just by adding Q: M, R, T, and Q. (B) can be eliminated since Q requires R (5), but N, M, and R cannot appear together (2). (C) can be eliminated since S will require the addition of both N and V (6), two professors, not just one. (D) can be eliminated since V requires the addition of two out of three from the trio M, S, and U (4). Finally, (E) is incorrect since R requires Q (5) and V requires other professors (4).

32. **(C)** Removing T from the group eliminates the violation of (1), without violating any other restriction. As for (A), removing N eliminates the violation of (1), but this places the group in violation of (6) (S without N). As for (D), removing U corrects the violation of (1), but the resulting group violates (4) because V is included without two out of three from the group M, S, or U. Finally, eliminating V runs afoul of (5).

33. **(C)** There are really two parts to the speaker's claim. First, the speaker maintains that the majority of Americans can get access to the medical care in this country; and, second, that the care they have access to is the best in the world. As for the second, good medical care is a function of many variables: number and location of facilities, availability of doctors, quality of education, etc. (A) and (E) may both be consistent with the speaker's claim. Even though we have fewer assistants (A) than some other country, we have more doctors and that more than makes up for the fewer assistants. Or, perhaps, we have such good preventive medicine that people do not need to go into the hospital as frequently as the citizens of other nations (E). (B) is wrong for a similar reason. Although it suggests there is a country in which people have greater access to the available care, it does not come to grips with the second element of the speaker's claim: that the care we get is the best. (C), however, does meet both

because it cites the existence of a country in which people are given (that is the first element) *better* (the second element) care. (D) hardly counts against the speaker's claim since the speaker has implicitly conceded that some people do not have access to the care.

34. **(E)** Common sense dictates that where one is driving in relationship to one's home (within or without a 25-mile radius) has little or nothing to do with the safety factor. Moreover, common sense also says that a person driving under 35 miles per hour is (usually) safer than one driving at 60 miles per hour. The explanation, then, for the fact that most traffic fatalities occur under conditions contrary to those that would be suggested by common sense is that more driving is done under those conditions. Just as common sense indicates, the driving is safer per mile, but there are so many more miles driven under those conditions that there are many fatalities. (A) is obviously inconsistent with common sense. And the directions for the Logical Reasoning section explicitly say that the BEST answer will be one that does not require you to make such assumptions. (B) is incorrect since the statistics mention the location of the accident—how far away from home—not how far the driver had driven at the time of the accident. Even though the accident occurred, say, 26 miles from home, you would not want to conclude the driver had driven 26 miles. (C) compounds the error made by (A). Not only does it take the general conclusion regarding fatalities and attempt to apply it to a specific case without regard to the individual variety of those cases, but it commits the further error of conditioning the speed of driving on the occurrence of an accident. (D) does exactly the same thing and is also wrong.

35. **(C)** The author claims that we have unbounded resources, and tries to prove this by showing that we are getting better and better at extracting those resources from the ground. But that is like saying "I have found a way of getting the last little bit of toothpaste out of the tube; therefore, the tube will never run out." (C) calls our attention to this oversight. (A) does not contradict the author's claim. In fact, it seems to support it. The author might suggest, "Even if we run out of fossil fuels, we still have uranium for nuclear power." Now, this is not to suggest that the author would actually make such a suggestion, but only to show that (A) supports rather than undermines the author's contention. (B) is an attack on the author's general stance, but it does not really *contradict* the particular conclusion drawn. The author says, "We have enough." (B) says, "It is expensive." Both could very well be true, so they cannot contradict one another. (D) is similar to (B). Yes, you may be correct, the technology is expensive or, in this case, wasteful, but it will still get us the fuel we need. Finally, (E) is incorrect for pretty much these same reasons. Yes, the energy will have unwanted side effects, but the author claimed only that we could get the energy. The difficulty with (B), (D), and (E) is that though they attack the author's general *position,* they do not *contradict* the *conclusion.*

SEVEN

GRE Math Review

PREVIEW ➔

TIME MANAGER
STUDY PLANS

PLAN A: ACCELERATED

- *Read* each topic
- *Study* the examples
- *Work* the last two items in each set of Practice Problems and check your answers
- *If* you get the problems right, move on. If not, work the rest of the Practice Problems

PLAN B: TOP SPEED

- *Skim* each topic
- *Study* the examples

GRE Math Review

In order to solve a mathematical problem, it is essential to know the mathematical meaning of the words used. There are many expressions having the same meaning in mathematics. These expressions may indicate a relationship between quantities or an operation (addition, subtraction, multiplication, division) to be performed. This chapter will help you to recognize some of the mathematical synonyms commonly found in word problems.

Expressions

Equality

The following expressions all indicate that two quantities are equal (=):

> is equal to
> is the same as
> the result is
> yields
> gives

Also, the word "is" is often used to mean "equals," as in "8 *is* 5 more than 3," which translates to "8 = 5 + 3."

Addition

The following expressions all indicate that the numbers A and B are to be added:

$A + B$	$2 + 3$
the sum of A and B	the sum of 2 and 3
the total of A and B	the total of 2 and 3
A added to B	2 added to 3
A increased by B	2 increased by 3
A more than B	2 more than 3
A greater than B	2 greater than 3

Subtraction

The following expressions all indicate that the number B is to be subtracted from the number A:

$A - B$	$10 - 3$
A minus B	10 minus 3
A less B	10 less 3
the difference of A and B	the difference of 10 and 3
from A subtract B	from 10 subtract 3
A take away B	10 take away 3
A decreased by B	10 decreased by 3
A diminished by B	10 diminished by 3
B is subtracted from A	3 is subtracted from 10
B less than A	3 less than 10

Multiplication

If the numbers A and B are to be multiplied ($A \times B$), the following expressions may be used:

$A \times B$	2×3
A multiplied by B	2 multiplied by 3
the product of A and B	the product of 2 and 3

The parts of a multiplication problem are indicated in the example below:

$$15 \quad \text{(multiplicand)}$$
$$\underline{\times 10} \quad \text{(multiplier)}$$
$$150 \quad \text{(product)}$$

Other ways of indicating multiplication are:

Parentheses: $A \times B = (A)(B)$

Dots: $A \times B = A \bullet B$

In algebra, letters next to each other: $A \times B = AB$

A **coefficient** is a number by which to multiply a variable, such as in $3B$, where 3 is the coefficient.

Inequalities

When two numbers are not necessarily equal to each other, this idea can be expressed by using the "greater than" symbol (>) or the "less than" symbol (<). The wider part of the wedge is always towards the greater number.

A is greater than B	A is less than B
$A > B$	$A < B$
A is greater than or equal to B	A is less than or equal to B
$A \geq B$	$A \leq B$

An **integer** can be defined informally as a whole number, either positive or negative, including zero, e.g., +5, –10, 0, +30, –62, etc.

A **prime number** can be defined informally as a whole number (positive only) that is evenly divisible only by itself and 1, e.g., 1, 2, 3, 5, 7, 11, 13, 17, 19, etc.

Division

Division of the numbers A and B (in the order $A \div B$) may be indicated in the following ways. (See also the discussion of fractions.)

$A \div B$	$14 \div 2$
A divided by B	14 divided by 2
the quotient of A and B	the quotient of 14 and 2

The parts of a division problem are indicated in the example below:

$$
\begin{array}{r}
5\frac{1}{7} \text{ (quotient)} \\
\text{(divisor) } 7\overline{)36} \text{ (dividend)} \\
\underline{35} \\
1 \text{ (remainder)}
\end{array}
$$

Factors and Divisors

The relationship $A \times B = C$, for any whole numbers A, B, and C, may be expressed as:

$A \times B = C$	$2 \times 3 = 6$
A and B are factors of C	2 and 3 are factors of 6
A and B are divisors of C	2 and 3 are divisors of 6
C is divisible by A and by B	6 is divisible by 2 and by 3
C is a multiple of A and of B	6 is a multiple of 2 and of 3

Symbols

Common symbols used on the exam are*:

$\neq$	is not equal to
$>$	is greater than ($3 > 2$)
$<$	is less than ($2 < 3$)
$\geq$	is greater than or equal to
$\leq$	is less than or equal to
: and ::	is to; the ratio to (see also section on ratios)
$\sqrt{}$	radical sign—used without a number, it indicates the square root of ($\sqrt{9} = 3$) or with an index above the sign to indicate the root to be taken if the root is not a square root ($\sqrt[3]{8} = 2$) (see also section on powers and roots)
$\lvert x \rvert$	absolute value of (in this case x) (see section on basic properties of numbers, item 6)

Basic Properties of Numbers

1. A number greater than zero is called a **positive number.**

2. A number smaller than zero is called a **negative number.**

3. When a negative number is added to another number, this is the same as subtracting the equivalent positive number.

   Example: $2 + (-1) = 2 - 1 = 1$.

4. When two numbers of the same sign are multiplied together, the result is a positive number.

   Example: $2 \times 2 = 4$.
   Example: $(-2)(-3) = +6$.

5. When two numbers of different signs are multiplied together, the result is a negative number.

   Example: $(+5)(-10) = -50$.
   Example: $(-6)(+8) = -48$.

6. The **absolute value** of a number is the equivalent positive value.

   Example: $\lvert +2 \rvert = +2$.
   Example: $\lvert -3 \rvert = +3$.

*Geometric symbols are reviewed in the section on geometry.

7. An **even number** is an integer that is divisible evenly by two. Zero would be considered an even number for practical purposes.

8. An **odd number** is an integer that is not an even number.

9. An even number times any integer will yield an even number.

10. An odd number times an odd number will yield an odd number.

11. Two even numbers or two odd numbers added together will yield an even number.

12. An odd number added to an even number will yield an odd number.

Fractions

Fractions and Mixed Numbers

1. A **fraction** is part of a unit.

   a. A fraction has a **numerator** and a **denominator**.

   Example: In the fraction $\frac{3}{4}$, 3 is the numerator and 4 is the denominator.

   b. In any fraction, the numerator is being divided by the denominator.

   Example: The fraction $\frac{2}{7}$ indicates that 2 is being divided by 7.

   c. The whole quantity 1 may be expressed by a fraction in which the numerator and denominator are the same number.

   Example: If the problem involves $\frac{1}{8}$ of a quantity, then the whole quantity is $\frac{8}{8}$, or 1.

2. A **mixed number** is an integer together with a fraction such as $2\frac{3}{5}$, $7\frac{7}{8}$, etc. The integer is the integral part, and the fraction is the fractional part.

3. An **improper fraction** is one in which the numerator is equal to or greater than the denominator, such as $\frac{19}{6}$, $\frac{25}{4}$, or $\frac{10}{10}$.

4. To change a mixed number to an improper fraction:

   a. Multiply the denominator of the fraction by the integer.

   b. Add the numerator to this product.

   c. Place this sum over the denominator of the fraction.

   Illustration: Change $3\frac{4}{7}$ to an improper fraction.

   SOLUTION:
   $$7 \times 3 = 21$$
   $$21 + 4 = 25$$
   $$3\frac{4}{7} = \frac{25}{7}$$

   Answer: $\frac{25}{7}$

5. To change an improper fraction to a mixed number:

   a. Divide the numerator by the denominator. The quotient, disregarding the remainder, is the integral part of the mixed number.

   b. Place the remainder, if any, over the denominator. This is the fractional part of the mixed number.

   Illustration: Change $\frac{36}{13}$ to a mixed number.

   SOLUTION:
   $$13\overline{)36}$$
   $$\frac{26}{10} \text{ remainder}$$
   $$\frac{36}{16} = 2\frac{10}{13}$$

   Answer: $2\frac{10}{13}$

6. The numerator and denominator of a fraction may be changed, without affecting the value of the fraction, by multiplying both by the same number.

   Example: The value of the fraction $\frac{2}{3}$ will not be altered if the numerator and the denominator are multiplied by 2, to result in $\frac{4}{6}$.

7. The numerator and the denominator of a fraction may be changed, without affecting the value of the fraction, by dividing both by the same

number. This process is called **reducing the fraction.** A fraction that has been reduced as much as possible is said to be in **lowest terms.**

Example: The value of the fraction $\dfrac{3}{12}$ will not be altered if the numerator and denominator are divided by 3, to result in $\dfrac{1}{4}$.

Example: If $\dfrac{6}{30}$ is reduced to lowest terms (by dividing both numerator and denominator by 6), the result is $\dfrac{1}{5}$.

8. As a final answer to an exam question, it may be necessary to:

    a. reduce a fraction to lowest terms

    b. convert an improper fraction to a mixed number

    c. convert a mixed number to an improper fraction

Addition of Fractions

9. Fractions cannot be added unless the denominators are all the same.

    a. If the denominators are the same, add all the numerators and place this sum over the common denominator. In the case of mixed numbers, follow the above rule for the fractions and then add the integers.

    Example: The sum of $2\dfrac{3}{8} + 3\dfrac{1}{8} + \dfrac{3}{8} = 5\dfrac{7}{8}$.

    b. If the denominators are not the same, the fractions, in order to be added, must be converted to ones having the same denominator. The lowest common denominator is often the most convenient common denominator to find, but any common denominator will work. You can cancel out the extra numbers after the addition.

10. The **lowest common denominator** (henceforth called the **L.C.D.**) is the lowest number that can be divided evenly by all the given denominators. If no two of the given denominators can be divided by the same number, then the L.C.D. is the product of all the denominators.

    Example: The L.C.D. of $\dfrac{1}{2}, \dfrac{1}{3}$, and $\dfrac{1}{5}$ is $2 \times 3 \times 5 = 30$.

11. To find the L.C.D. when two or more of the given denominators can be divided by the same number:

    a. Write down the denominators, leaving plenty of space between the numbers.

    b. Select the smallest number (other than 1) by which one or more of the denominators can be divided evenly.

    c. Divide the denominators by this number, copying down those that cannot be divided evenly. Place this number to one side.

    d. Repeat this process, placing each divisor to one side until there are no longer any denominators that can be divided evenly by any selected number.

    e. Multiply all the divisors to find the L.C.D.

    Illustration: Find the L.C.D. of $\dfrac{1}{5}, \dfrac{1}{7}, \dfrac{1}{10}$, and $\dfrac{1}{14}$.

$$
\begin{array}{l|cccc}
SOLUTION: & & & & \\
2\,) & 5 & 7 & 10 & 14 \\ \hline
5\,) & 5 & 7 & 5 & 7 \\ \hline
7\,) & 1 & 7 & 1 & 7 \\ \hline
& 1 & 1 & 1 & 1
\end{array}
$$

$$7 \times 5 \times 2 = 70$$

Answer: The L.C.D. is 70.

12. To add fractions having different denominators:

    a. Find the L.C.D. of the denominators.

    b. Change each fraction to an equivalent fraction having the L.C.D. as its denominator.

    c. When all of the fractions have the same denominator, they may be added, as in the example following item 9a.

Illustration: Add $\dfrac{1}{4}, \dfrac{3}{10}$, and $\dfrac{2}{5}$.

SOLUTION: Find the L.C.D.:

$$
\begin{array}{l|ccc}
2\,) & 4 & 10 & 5 \\ \hline
5\,) & 2 & 5 & 5 \\ \hline
2\,) & 2 & 1 & 1 \\ \hline
& 1 & 1 & 1
\end{array}
$$

$$\text{L.C.D.} = 2 \times 5 \times 2 = 20$$

$$\frac{1}{4} = \frac{5}{20}$$
$$\frac{3}{10} = \frac{6}{20}$$
$$+\frac{2}{5} = +\frac{8}{20}$$
$$\frac{19}{20}$$

Answer: $\frac{19}{20}$

13. To add mixed numbers in which the fractions have different denominators, add the fractions by following the rules in item 12 above, then add the integers.

Illustration: Add $2\frac{5}{7}$, $5\frac{1}{2}$, and 8.

SOLUTION: L.C.D. = 14

$$2\frac{5}{7} = 2\frac{10}{14}$$
$$5\frac{1}{2} = 5\frac{7}{14}$$
$$+8 = +8$$
$$15\frac{17}{14} = 16\frac{3}{14}$$

Answer: $16\frac{3}{14}$

Subtraction of Fractions

14. a. Unlike addition, which may involve adding more than two numbers at the same time, subtraction involves only two numbers.

   b. In subtraction, as in addition, the denominators must be the same.

15. To subtract fractions:

   a. Find the L.C.D.

   b. Change both fractions so that each has the L.C.D. as the denominator.

   c. Subtract the numerator of the second fraction from the numerator of the first, and place this difference over the L.C.D.

   d. Reduce, if possible.

Illustration: Find the difference of $\frac{5}{8}$ and $\frac{1}{4}$.

SOLUTION: L.C.D. = 8

$$\frac{5}{8} = \frac{5}{8}$$
$$-\frac{1}{4} = -\frac{2}{8}$$
$$\frac{3}{8}$$

Answer: $\frac{3}{8}$

16. To subtract mixed numbers:

   a. It may be necessary to "borrow," so that the fractional part of the first term is larger than the fractional part of the second term.

   b. Subtract the fractional parts of the mixed numbers and reduce.

   c. Subtract the integers.

Illustration: Subtract $16\frac{4}{5}$ from $29\frac{1}{3}$.

SOLUTION: L.C.D. = 15

$$29\frac{1}{3} = 29\frac{5}{15}$$
$$-16\frac{4}{5} = -16\frac{12}{15}$$

Note that $\frac{5}{15}$ is less than $\frac{12}{15}$. Borrow 1 from 29, and change to $\frac{15}{15}$.

$$29\frac{5}{15} = 28\frac{20}{15}$$
$$-16\frac{12}{15} = -16\frac{12}{15}$$
$$12\frac{8}{15}$$

Answer: $12\frac{8}{15}$

Multiplication of Fractions

17. a. To be multiplied, fractions need not have the same denominators.

   b. A whole number can be thought of as having a denominator of 1: $3 = \frac{3}{1}$.

18. To multiply fractions:

   a. Change the mixed numbers, if any, to improper fractions.

   b. Multiply all the numerators, and place this product over the product of the denominators.

   c. Reduce, if possible.

Illustration: Multiply $\frac{2}{3} \times 2\frac{4}{7} \times \frac{5}{9}$.

SOLUTION: $2\frac{4}{7} = \frac{18}{7}$

$$\frac{2}{3} \times \frac{18}{7} \times \frac{5}{9} = \frac{180}{189}$$
$$= \frac{20}{21}$$

Answer: $\frac{20}{21}$

19. a. **Cancellation** is a device to facilitate multiplication. To cancel means to divide a numerator and a denominator by the same number in a multiplication problem.

    Example: In the problem $\dfrac{4}{7} \times \dfrac{5}{6}$, the numerator 4 and the denominator 6 may be divided by 2.

    $$\dfrac{\overset{2}{4}}{7} \times \dfrac{5}{\underset{3}{6}} = \dfrac{10}{12}$$

    b. With fractions (and percentages), the word "of" is often used to mean "multiply."

    Example: $\dfrac{1}{2}$ of $\dfrac{1}{2} = \dfrac{1}{2} \times \dfrac{1}{2} = \dfrac{1}{4}$

20. To multiply a whole number by a mixed number:

    a. Multiply the whole number by the fractional part of the mixed number.

    b. Multiply the whole number by the integral part of the mixed number.

    c. Add both products.

    Illustration: Multiply $23\dfrac{3}{4}$ by 95.

    SOLUTION: $\dfrac{95}{1} \times \dfrac{3}{4} = \dfrac{285}{4}$

    $$= 71\dfrac{1}{4}$$

    $$95 \times 23 = 2185$$

    $$2185 + 71\dfrac{1}{4} = 2256\dfrac{1}{4}$$

    Answer: $2256\dfrac{1}{4}$

Division of Fractions

21. The **reciprocal** of a fraction is that fraction inverted.

    a. When a fraction is inverted, the numerator becomes the denominator and the denominator becomes the numerator.

    Example: The reciprocal of $\dfrac{3}{8}$ is $\dfrac{8}{3}$.

    Example: The reciprocal of $\dfrac{1}{3}$ is $\dfrac{3}{1}$, or simply 3.

    b. Since every whole number has the denominator 1 understood, the reciprocal of a whole number is a fraction having 1 as the numerator and the number itself as the denominator.

    Example: The reciprocal of 5 (expressed fractionally as $\dfrac{5}{1}$) is $\dfrac{1}{5}$.

22. To divide fractions:

    a. Change all the mixed numbers, if any, to improper fractions.

    b. Invert the second fraction and multiply.

    c. Reduce, if possible.

    Illustration: Divide $\dfrac{2}{3}$ by $2\dfrac{1}{4}$.

    SOLUTION: $2\dfrac{1}{4} = \dfrac{9}{4}$

    $$\dfrac{2}{3} \div \dfrac{9}{4} = \dfrac{2}{3} \times \dfrac{4}{9}$$

    $$= \dfrac{8}{27}$$

    Answer: $\dfrac{8}{27}$

23. A **complex fraction** is one that has a fraction as the numerator, or as the denominator, or as both.

    Example: $\dfrac{\frac{2}{3}}{5}$ is a complex fraction.

24. To clear (simplify) a complex fraction:

    a. Divide the numerator by the denominator.

    b. Reduce, if possible.

    Illustration: Clear $\dfrac{\frac{3}{7}}{\frac{5}{14}}$.

    SOLUTION: $\dfrac{3}{7} \div \dfrac{5}{14} = \dfrac{3}{7} \times \dfrac{14}{5} = \dfrac{42}{35}$

    $$= \dfrac{6}{5}$$

    $$= 1\dfrac{1}{5}$$

    Answer: $1\dfrac{1}{5}$

Comparing Fractions

25. If two fractions have the same denominator, the one having the larger numerator is the greater fraction.

    Example: $\dfrac{3}{7}$ is greater than $\dfrac{2}{7}$.

26. If two fractions have the same numerator, the one having the larger denominator is the smaller fraction.

Example: $\dfrac{5}{12}$ is smaller than $\dfrac{5}{11}$.

27. To compare two fractions having different numerators and different denominators:

a. Change the fractions to equivalent fractions having their L.C.D. as their new denominator.

b. Compare, as in the example following item 25, for the largest numerator.

Illustration: Compare $\dfrac{4}{7}$ and $\dfrac{5}{8}$.

SOLUTION: L.C.D. $= 7 \times 8 = 56$

$$\frac{4}{7} = \frac{32}{56}$$

$$\frac{5}{8} = \frac{35}{56}$$

Answer: Since $\dfrac{35}{56}$ is larger than $\dfrac{32}{56}$, $\dfrac{5}{8}$ is larger than $\dfrac{4}{7}$.

Note: Actually, any common denominator will work, not only the L.C.D.

28. To compare two fractions, multiply the denominator of the left fraction by the numerator of the right fraction and write the result above the right fraction. Then multiply the denominator of the right fraction by the numerator of the left fraction and write the result over the left fraction. If the number over the left fraction is larger than the number over the right fraction, the left fraction is larger. If the number over the right fraction is larger, the right fraction is larger. If the numbers over the two fractions are equal, the fractions are equal.

Illustration: Compare $\dfrac{5}{7}$ and $\dfrac{3}{4}$.

SOLUTION: 20 21

$$\frac{5}{7} \diagup \diagdown \frac{3}{4}$$

$3 \times 7 = 21$
$4 \times 5 = 20$
$20 < 21$

Answer: $\dfrac{5}{7} < \dfrac{3}{4}$. This method will only determine which fraction is larger. It cannot be used to tell you the size of the difference.

Fraction Problems

29. Most fraction problems can be arranged in the form: "What fraction of a number is another number?" This form contains three important parts:

• The fractional part
• The number following "of "
• The number following "is"

a. If the fraction and the "of " number are given, multiply them to find the "is" number.

Illustration: What is $\dfrac{3}{4}$ of 20?

SOLUTION: Write the question as " $\dfrac{3}{4}$ of 20 is what number?" Then multiply the fraction $\dfrac{3}{4}$ by the "of " number, 20:

$$\frac{3}{4} \times \overset{5}{\cancel{20}} = 15$$
$$\hspace{3.5em}{}_{1}$$

Answer: 15

b. If the fractional part and the "is" number are given, divide the "is" number by the fraction to find the "of " number.

Illustration: $\dfrac{4}{5}$ of what number is 40?

SOLUTION: To find the "of " number, divide 40 by $\dfrac{4}{5}$:

$$40 \div \frac{4}{5} = \frac{\overset{10}{\cancel{40}}}{1} \times \frac{5}{\underset{1}{\cancel{4}}} = 50$$

Answer: 50

c. To find the fractional part when the other two numbers are known, divide the "is" number by the "of " number.

Illustration: What part of 12 is 9?

SOLUTION: $9 \div 12 = \dfrac{9}{12} = \dfrac{3}{4}$

Answer: $\dfrac{3}{4}$

Practice Problems Involving Fractions

1. Reduce to lowest terms: $\dfrac{60}{108}$.

   (A) $\dfrac{1}{48}$

   (B) $\dfrac{1}{3}$

   (C) $\dfrac{1}{9}$

   (D) $\dfrac{5}{9}$

   (E) $\dfrac{15}{59}$

2. Change $\dfrac{27}{7}$ to a mixed number.

   (A) $2\dfrac{1}{7}$

   (B) $3\dfrac{6}{7}$

   (C) $6\dfrac{1}{3}$

   (D) $7\dfrac{1}{2}$

   (E) $8\dfrac{1}{7}$

3. Change $4\dfrac{2}{3}$ to an improper fraction.

   (A) $\dfrac{10}{3}$

   (B) $\dfrac{11}{3}$

   (C) $\dfrac{14}{3}$

   (D) $\dfrac{24}{3}$

   (E) $\dfrac{42}{3}$

4. Find the L.C.D. of $\dfrac{1}{6}$, $\dfrac{1}{10}$, $\dfrac{1}{18}$, and $\dfrac{1}{21}$.

   (A) 160
   (B) 330
   (C) 630
   (D) 890
   (E) 1260

5. Add $16\dfrac{3}{8}$, $4\dfrac{4}{5}$, $12\dfrac{3}{4}$, and $23\dfrac{5}{6}$.

   (A) $57\dfrac{91}{120}$

   (B) $57\dfrac{1}{4}$

   (C) 58

   (D) 59

   (E) $59\dfrac{91}{120}$

6. Subtract $27\dfrac{5}{14}$ from $43\dfrac{1}{6}$.

   (A) 15

   (B) $15\dfrac{5}{84}$

   (C) $15\dfrac{8}{21}$

   (D) $15\dfrac{15}{20}$

   (E) $15\dfrac{17}{21}$

7. Multiply $17\dfrac{5}{8}$ by 128.

   (A) 2256
   (B) 2305
   (C) 2356
   (D) 2368
   (E) 2394

8. Divide $1\dfrac{2}{3}$ by $1\dfrac{1}{9}$.

   (A) $\dfrac{2}{3}$

   (B) $1\dfrac{1}{2}$

   (C) $1\dfrac{23}{27}$

   (D) 4

   (E) 6

9. What is the value of $12\dfrac{1}{6} - 2\dfrac{3}{8} - 7\dfrac{2}{3} + 19\dfrac{3}{4}$?

   (A) 21

   (B) $21\dfrac{7}{8}$

   (C) $21\dfrac{1}{8}$

   (D) 22

   (E) $22\dfrac{7}{8}$

10. Simplify the complex fraction $\dfrac{\frac{4}{9}}{\frac{2}{5}}$.

   (A) $\dfrac{1}{2}$

   (B) $\dfrac{9}{10}$

   (C) $\dfrac{2}{5}$

   (D) 1

   (E) $1\dfrac{1}{9}$

11. Which fraction is largest?

   (A) $\dfrac{9}{16}$

   (B) $\dfrac{7}{10}$

   (C) $\dfrac{5}{8}$

   (D) $\dfrac{4}{5}$

   (E) $\dfrac{1}{2}$

12. One brass rod measures $3\dfrac{5}{16}$ inches long and another brass rod measures $2\dfrac{3}{4}$ inches long. Together their length is

   (A) $6\dfrac{9}{16}$ in.

   (B) $6\dfrac{1}{16}$ in.

   (C) $5\dfrac{1}{2}$ in.

   (D) $5\dfrac{1}{16}$ in.

   (E) $5\dfrac{1}{32}$ in.

13. The number of half-pound packages of tea that can be weighed out of a box that holds $10\dfrac{1}{2}$ lb. of tea is

   (A) 5

   (B) $10\dfrac{1}{2}$

   (C) 11

   (D) $20\dfrac{1}{2}$

   (E) 21

14. If each bag of tokens weighs $5\dfrac{3}{4}$ pounds, how many pounds do 3 bags weigh?

   (A) $7\dfrac{1}{4}$

   (B) $15\dfrac{3}{4}$

   (C) $16\dfrac{1}{2}$

   (D) $17\dfrac{1}{4}$

   (E) $17\dfrac{1}{2}$

15. During one week, a man traveled $3\dfrac{1}{2}, 1\dfrac{1}{4}, 1\dfrac{1}{6},$ and $2\dfrac{3}{8}$ miles. The next week he traveled $\dfrac{1}{4}, \dfrac{3}{8}, \dfrac{9}{16}, 3\dfrac{1}{16}, 2\dfrac{5}{8},$ and $3\dfrac{3}{16}$ miles. How many more miles did he travel the second week than the first week?

   (A) $1\dfrac{37}{48}$

   (B) $1\dfrac{1}{2}$

   (C) $1\dfrac{3}{4}$

   (D) 1

   (E) $\dfrac{47}{48}$

16. A certain type of board is sold only in lengths of multiples of 2 feet. The shortest board sold is 6 feet and the longest is 24 feet. A builder needs a large quantity of this type of board in $5\dfrac{1}{2}$-foot lengths. For minimum waste the lengths to be ordered should be

   (A) 6 ft.
   (B) 12 ft.
   (C) 22 ft.
   (D) 24 ft.
   (E) 26 ft.

17. A man spent $\frac{15}{16}$ of his entire fortune in buying a car for $7500. How much money did he possess?

    (A) $6000
    (B) $6500
    (C) $7000
    (D) $8000
    (E) $8500

18. The population of a town was 54,000 in the last census. It has increased $\frac{2}{3}$ since then. Its present population is

    (A) 18,000
    (B) 36,000
    (C) 72,000
    (D) 90,000
    (E) 108,000

19. If $\frac{1}{3}$ of the liquid contents of a can evaporates on the first day and $\frac{3}{4}$ of the remainder evaporates on the second day, the fractional part of the original contents remaining at the close of the second day is

    (A) $\frac{5}{12}$

    (B) $\frac{7}{12}$

    (C) $\frac{1}{6}$

    (D) $\frac{1}{2}$

    (E) $\frac{4}{7}$

20. A car is run until the gas tank is $\frac{1}{8}$ full. The tank is then filled to capacity by putting in 14 gallons. The capacity of the gas tank of the car is

    (A) 14 gal.
    (B) 15 gal.
    (C) 16 gal.
    (D) 17 gal.
    (E) 18 gal.

Fraction Problems—Correct Answers

1. (C)   6. (E)   11. (D)   16. (C)
2. (B)   7. (A)   12. (B)   17. (D)
3. (C)   8. (B)   13. (E)   18. (D)
4. (C)   9. (B)   14. (D)   19. (C)
5. (A)   10. (E)   15. (A)   20. (C)

Problem Solutions—Fractions

1. Divide the numerator and denominator by 12:

$$\frac{60 \div 12}{108 \div 12} = \frac{5}{9}$$

One alternate method (there are several) is to divide the numerator and denominator by 6 and then by 2:

$$\frac{60 \div 6}{108 \div 6} = \frac{10}{18}$$

$$\frac{10 \div 2}{18 \div 2} = \frac{5}{9}$$

Answer: **(C)** $\frac{5}{9}$

2. Divide the numerator (27) by the denominator (7):

$$7\overline{)27}$$
$$\underline{21}$$
$$6 \text{ remainder}$$

$$\frac{27}{7} = 3\frac{6}{7}$$

Answer: **(B)** $3\frac{6}{7}$

3. $4 \times 3 = 12$
    $12 + 2 = 14$
    $4\frac{2}{3} = \frac{14}{3}$

Answer: **(C)** $\frac{14}{3}$

4. 2) 6   10   18   21   (2 is a divisor of 6, 10, and 18)

    3) 3   5   9   21   (3 is a divisor of 3, 9, and 21)

    3) 1   5   3   7   (3 is a divisor of 3)

    5) 1   5   1   7   (5 is a divisor of 5)

    7) 1   1   1   7   (7 is a divisor of 7)

        1   1   1   1

L.C.D. $= 2 \times 3 \times 3 \times 5 \times 7 = 630$

Answer: **(C)** 630

5. L.C.D. = 120

$$16\frac{3}{8} = 16\frac{45}{120}$$
$$4\frac{4}{5} = 4\frac{96}{120}$$
$$12\frac{3}{4} = 12\frac{90}{120}$$
$$23\frac{5}{6} = +23\frac{100}{120}$$
$$55\frac{331}{120} = 57\frac{91}{120}$$

Answer: (A) $57\frac{91}{120}$

6. L.C.D. = 42

$$43\frac{1}{6} = 43\frac{7}{42} = 42\frac{49}{42}$$
$$-27\frac{5}{14} = -27\frac{15}{42} = -27\frac{15}{42}$$
$$15\frac{34}{42} = 15\frac{17}{21}$$

Answer: (E) $15\frac{17}{21}$

7. $17\frac{5}{8} = \frac{141}{8}$

$$\frac{141}{\cancel{8}_1} \times \frac{\overset{16}{\cancel{128}}}{1} = 2256$$

Answer: (A) 2256

8. $1\frac{2}{3} \div 1\frac{1}{9} = \frac{5}{3} \div \frac{5}{3}$

$$= \frac{\cancel{5}^1}{\cancel{3}_1} \times \frac{\cancel{9}^3}{\cancel{10}_2}$$
$$= \frac{3}{2}$$
$$= 1\frac{1}{2}$$

Answer: (B) $1\frac{1}{2}$

9. L.C.D. = 24

$$12\frac{1}{6} = 12\frac{4}{24} = 11\frac{28}{24}$$
$$-2\frac{3}{8} = -2\frac{9}{24} = -2\frac{9}{24}$$
$$9\frac{19}{24} = 9\frac{19}{24}$$

$$-7\frac{2}{3} = -7\frac{16}{24}$$
$$2\frac{3}{24} = 2\frac{3}{24}$$

$$+19\frac{3}{4} = +19\frac{18}{24}$$
$$21\frac{21}{24}$$

$$21\frac{21}{24} = 21\frac{7}{8}$$

Answer: (B) $21\frac{7}{8}$

10. To simplify a complex fraction, divide the numerator by the denominator:

$$\frac{4}{9} \div \frac{2}{5} = \frac{\overset{2}{\cancel{4}}}{9} \times \frac{5}{\underset{1}{\cancel{2}}}$$
$$= \frac{10}{9}$$
$$= 1\frac{1}{9}$$

Answer: (E) $1\frac{1}{9}$

11. Write all of the fractions with the same denominator. L.C.D. = 80

$$\frac{9}{16} = \frac{45}{80}$$
$$\frac{7}{10} = \frac{56}{80}$$
$$\frac{5}{8} = \frac{50}{80}$$
$$\frac{4}{5} = \frac{64}{80}$$
$$\frac{1}{2} = \frac{40}{80}$$

Answer: (D) $\frac{4}{5}$

12.
$$3\frac{5}{16} = 3\frac{5}{16}$$
$$+2\frac{3}{4} = +2\frac{12}{16}$$
$$5\frac{17}{16}$$
$$= 6\frac{1}{16}$$

Answer: (B) $6\frac{1}{16}$ in.

13.
$$10\frac{1}{2} \div \frac{1}{2} = \frac{21}{2} \div \frac{1}{2}$$
$$= \frac{21}{2} \times \frac{2}{1}$$
$$= 21$$

Answer: (E) 21

14.
$$5\frac{3}{4} \times 3 = \frac{23}{4} \times \frac{3}{1}$$
$$= \frac{69}{4}$$
$$= 17\frac{1}{4}$$

Answer: (D) $17\frac{1}{4}$

15. First week:

    L.C.D. = 24

    $$3\frac{1}{2} = 3\frac{12}{24} \text{ miles}$$

    $$1\frac{1}{4} = 1\frac{6}{24}$$

    $$1\frac{1}{6} = 1\frac{4}{24}$$

    $$+2\frac{3}{8} = +2\frac{9}{24}$$

    $$7\frac{31}{24} = 8\frac{7}{24} \text{ miles}$$

    Second week:

    L.C.D. = 16

    $$\frac{1}{4} = \frac{4}{16} \text{ miles}$$

    $$\frac{3}{8} = \frac{6}{16}$$

    $$\frac{9}{16} = \frac{9}{16}$$

    $$3\frac{1}{16} = 3\frac{1}{16}$$

    $$2\frac{5}{8} = 2\frac{10}{16}$$

    $$+3\frac{3}{16} = +3\frac{3}{16}$$

    $$8\frac{33}{16} = 10\frac{1}{16} \text{ miles}$$

    L.C.D. = 48

    $$10\frac{1}{16} = 9\frac{51}{48} \text{ miles second week}$$

    $$-8\frac{7}{24} = -8\frac{14}{48} \text{ miles first week}$$

    $$1\frac{37}{48} \text{ more miles traveled}$$

    Answer: **(A)** $1\frac{37}{48}$

16. Consider each choice:

    Each 6-ft. board yields one $5\frac{1}{2}$-ft. board with $\frac{1}{2}$ ft. waste.

    Each 12-ft. board yields two $5\frac{1}{2}$-ft. boards with 1 ft. waste $(2 \times 5\frac{1}{2} = 11; 12 - 11 = 1 \text{ ft. waste})$.

    Each 24-ft. board yields four $5\frac{1}{2}$-ft. boards with 2 ft. waste $(4 \times 5\frac{1}{2} = 22; 24 - 22 = 2 \text{ ft. waste})$.

    Each 22 ft. board may be divided into four $5\frac{1}{2}$-ft. boards with no waste $(4 \times 5\frac{1}{2} = 22 \text{ exactly})$.

    Answer: **(C)** 22 ft.

17. $\frac{15}{16}$ of his fortune is $7500.

    Therefore, his fortune $= 7500 \div \frac{15}{16}$

    $$= \frac{\overset{500}{\cancel{7500}}}{1} \times \frac{16}{\underset{.1}{\cancel{15}}}$$

    $$= 8000$$

    Answer: **(D)** $8000

18. $\frac{2}{3}$ of 54,000 = increase

    $$\text{Increase} = \frac{2}{\cancel{3}} \times \overset{18,000}{\cancel{54,000}}$$

    $$= 36,000$$

    $$\text{Present population} = 54,000 + 36,000$$

    $$= 90,000$$

    Answer: **(D)** 90,000

19. First day: $\frac{1}{3}$ evaporates

    $\frac{2}{3}$ remains

    Second day: $\frac{3}{4}$ of $\frac{2}{3}$ evaporates

    $\frac{1}{4}$ of $\frac{2}{3}$ remains

    The amount remaining is

    $$\frac{1}{\underset{2}{\cancel{4}}} \times \frac{\overset{1}{\cancel{2}}}{3} = \frac{1}{6} \text{ of original contents}$$

    Answer: **(C)** $\frac{1}{6}$

20. $\frac{7}{8}$ of capacity = 14 gal.

    Therefore, capacity $= 14 \div \frac{7}{8}$

    $$= \frac{\overset{2}{\cancel{14}}}{1} \times \frac{8}{\underset{1}{\cancel{7}}}$$

    $$= 16 \text{ gal.}$$

    Answer: **(C)** 16 gal.

Decimals

1. A **decimal,** which is a number with a decimal point (.), is actually a fraction, the denominator of which is understood to be 10 or some power of 10.

    a. The number of digits, or places, after a decimal point determines which power of 10 the denominator is. If there is one digit, the denominator is understood to be 10; if there are two digits, the denominator is understood to be 100, etc.

    Example: $.3 = \dfrac{3}{10}$; $.57 = \dfrac{57}{100}$; $.643 = \dfrac{643}{1000}$.

    b. The addition of zeros after a decimal point does not change the value of the decimal. The zeros may be removed without changing the value of the decimal.

    Example: $.7 = .70 = .700$, and vice versa: $.700 = .70 = .7$.

    c. Since a decimal point is understood to exist after any whole number, the addition of any number of zeros after such a decimal point does not change the value of the number.

    Example: $2 = 2.0 = 2.00 = 2.000$.

Addition of Decimals

2. Decimals are added in the same way that whole numbers are added, with the provision that the decimal points must be kept in a vertical line, one under the other. This determines the place of the decimal point in the answer.

    Illustration: Add 2.31, .037, 4, and 5.0017.

    SOLUTION:
    ```
       2.3100
        .0370
       4.0000
    +  5.0017
      11.3487
    ```

    Answer: 11.3487

Subtraction of Decimals

3. Decimals are subtracted in the same way that whole numbers are subtracted, with the provision that, as in addition, the decimal points must be kept in a vertical line, one under the other. This determines the place of the decimal point in the answer.

    Illustration: Subtract 4.0037 from 15.3.

    SOLUTION:
    ```
      15.3000
    -  4.0037
      11.2963
    ```

    Answer: 11.2963

Multiplication of Decimals

4. Decimals are multiplied in the same way that whole numbers are multiplied.

    a. The number of decimal places in the product equals the sum of the decimal places in the multiplicand and in the multiplier.

    b. If there are fewer places in the product than this sum, then a sufficient number of zeros must be added in front of the product to equal the number of places required, and a decimal point is written in front of the zeros.

    Illustration: Multiply 2.372 by .012.

    SOLUTION:
    ```
         2.372
    ×     .012
          4744
         2372
       .028464
    ```

    Answer: .028464

5. A decimal can be multiplied by a power of 10 by moving the decimal point to the *right* as many places as indicated by the power. If multiplied by 10, the decimal point is moved one place to the right; if multiplied by 100, the decimal point is moved two places to the right, etc.

    Example:
    $$.235 \times 10 = 2.35$$
    $$.235 \times 100 = 23.5$$
    $$.235 \times 1000 = 235$$

Division of Decimals

6. There are four types of division involving decimals:

- When the dividend only is a decimal.
- When the divisor only is a decimal.
- When both are decimals.
- When neither dividend nor divisor is a decimal.

   a. When the dividend only is a decimal, the division is the same as that of whole numbers, except that a decimal point must be placed in the quotient exactly above that in the dividend.

Illustration: Divide 12.864 by 32.

$$\text{SOLUTION: } 32\overline{)12.864} \to .402$$

$$\begin{array}{r} .402 \\ 32\overline{)12.864} \\ \underline{12\,8} \\ 64 \\ \underline{64} \end{array}$$

Answer: .402

   b. When the divisor only is a decimal, the decimal point in the divisor is omitted and as many zeros are placed to the right of the dividend as there were decimal places in the divisor.

Illustration: Divide 211,327 by 6.817.

SOLUTION:

$$6.817\overline{)211327}$$
(3 decimal places)

$$= 6817\overline{)211327000} \to 31000$$

$$\begin{array}{r} 31000 \\ 6817\overline{)211327000} \\ \underline{20451} \\ 6817 \\ \underline{6817} \end{array}$$

Answer: 31,000

   c. When both divisor and dividend are decimals, the decimal point in the divisor is omitted and the decimal point in the dividend must be moved to the right as many decimal places as there were in the divisor. If there are not enough places in the dividend, zeros must be added to make up the difference.

Illustration: Divide 2.62 by .131.

$$\text{SOLUTION: } .131\overline{)2.62} = 131\overline{)2620} \to 20$$

$$\begin{array}{r} 20 \\ 131\overline{)2620} \\ \underline{262} \end{array}$$

Answer: 20

   d. In instances when neither the divisor nor the dividend is a decimal, a problem may still involve decimals. This occurs in two cases: when the dividend is a smaller number than the divisor, and when it is required to work out a division to a certain number of decimal places. In either case, write in a decimal point after the dividend, add as many zeros as necessary, and place a decimal point in the quotient above that in the dividend.

Illustration: Divide 7 by 50.

$$\text{SOLUTION: } \begin{array}{r} .14 \\ 50\overline{)7.00} \\ \underline{5\,0} \\ 2\,00 \\ \underline{2\,00} \end{array}$$

Answer: .14

Illustration: How much is 155 divided by 40, carried out to 3 decimal places?

$$\text{SOLUTION: } \begin{array}{r} 3.875 \\ 40\overline{)155.000} \\ \underline{120} \\ 350 \\ \underline{320} \\ 300 \\ \underline{280} \\ 200 \end{array}$$

Answer: 3.875

7. A decimal can be divided by a power of 10 by moving the decimal to the *left* as many places as indicated by the power. If divided by 10, the decimal point is moved one place to the left; if divided by 100, the decimal point is moved two places to the left, etc. If there are not enough places, add zeros in front of the number to make up the difference and add a decimal point.

Example: .4 divided by 10 = .04
            .4 divided by 100 = .004

Rounding Decimals

8. To round a number to a given decimal place:

   a. Locate the given place.

   b. If the digit to the right is less than 5, omit all digits following the given place.

   c. If the digit to the right is 5 or more, raise the given place by 1 and omit all digits following the given place.

   Examples:

      4.27   = 4.3 to the nearest tenth

      .71345 = .713 to the nearest thousandth

9. In problems involving money, answers are usually rounded to the nearest cent.

Conversion of Fractions to Decimals

10. A fraction can be changed to a decimal by dividing the numerator by the denominator and working out the division to as many decimal places as required.

    Illustration: Change $\dfrac{5}{11}$ to a decimal of 2 places.

    SOLUTION:
    $$\frac{5}{11} = 11\overline{)5.00}^{\,.45\frac{5}{11}}$$
    $$\begin{array}{r} \underline{44} \\ 60 \\ \underline{55} \\ 5 \end{array}$$

    Answer: $.45\dfrac{5}{11}$

11. To clear fractions containing a decimal in either the numerator or the denominator, or in both, divide the numerator by the denominator.

    Illustration: What is the value of $\dfrac{2.34}{.6}$?

    SOLUTION: $\dfrac{2.34}{.6} = .6\overline{)2.34} = 6\overline{)23.4}^{\,3.9}$
    $$\begin{array}{r} \underline{18} \\ 54 \\ \underline{54} \end{array}$$

    Answer: 3.9

Conversion of Decimals to Fractions

12. Since a decimal point indicates a number having a denominator that is a power of 10, a decimal can be expressed as a fraction, the numerator of which is the number itself and the denominator of which is the power indicated by the number of decimal places in the decimal.

    Examples: $.3 = \dfrac{3}{10}$, $.47 = \dfrac{47}{100}$.

13. When the decimal is a mixed number, divide by the power of 10 indicated by its number of decimal places. The fraction does not count as a decimal place.

    Illustration: Change $.25\dfrac{1}{3}$ to a fraction.

    SOLUTION: $.25\frac{1}{3} = 25\frac{1}{3} \div 100$
    $$= \tfrac{76}{3} \times \tfrac{1}{100}$$
    $$= \tfrac{76}{300} = \tfrac{19}{75}$$

    Answer: $\dfrac{19}{75}$

14. When to change decimals to fractions:

    a. When dealing with whole numbers, do not change the decimal.

    Example: In the problem $12 \times .14$, it is better to keep the decimal:

    $$12 \times .14 = 1.68$$

    b. When dealing with fractions, change the decimal to a fraction.

    Example: In the problem $\dfrac{3}{5} \times .17$, it is best to change the decimal to a fraction:

    $$\frac{3}{5} \times .17 = \frac{3}{5} \times \frac{17}{100} = \frac{51}{500}$$

15. Because decimal equivalents of fractions are often used, it is helpful to be familiar with the most common conversions.

$\dfrac{1}{2} = .5$	$\dfrac{1}{3} = .3333$
$\dfrac{1}{4} = .25$	$\dfrac{2}{3} = .6667$
$\dfrac{3}{4} = .75$	$\dfrac{1}{6} = .1667$
$\dfrac{1}{5} = .2$	$\dfrac{1}{7} = .1429$
$\dfrac{1}{8} = .125$	$\dfrac{1}{9} = .1111$
$\dfrac{1}{16} = .0625$	$\dfrac{1}{12} = .0833$

    Note that the left column contains exact values The values in the right column have been rounded to the nearest ten-thousandth.

Practice Problems Involving Decimals

1. Add 37.03, 11.5627, 3.4005, 3423, and 1.141.

   _____

2. Subtract 4.64324 from 7. _____

3. Multiply 27.34 by 16.943. _____

4. How much is 19.6 divided by 3.2, carried out to 3 decimal places? _____

5. What is $\dfrac{5}{11}$ in decimal form (to the nearest hundredth)? _____

6. What is $.64\dfrac{2}{3}$ in fraction form? _____

7. What is the difference between $\dfrac{3}{5}$ and $\dfrac{9}{8}$ expressed decimally? _____

8. A boy saved up $4.56 the first month, $3.82 the second month, and $5.06 the third month. How much did he save altogether? _____

9. The diameter of a certain rod is required to be 1.51 ± .015 inches. The rod's diameter must be between _____ and _____ .

10. After an employer figures out an employee's salary of $190.57, he deducts $3.05 for social security and $5.68 for pension. What is the amount of the check after these deductions? _____

11. If the outer radius of a metal pipe is 2.84 inches and the inner radius is 1.94 inches, the thickness of the metal is _____ .

12. A boy earns $20.56 on Monday, $32.90 on Tuesday, and $20.78 on Wednesday. He spends half of all that he earned during the three days. How much has he left? _____

13. The total cost of $3\dfrac{1}{2}$ pounds of meat at $1.69 a pound and 20 lemons at $.60 a dozen will be

   _____ .

14. A reel of cable weighs 1279 lb. If the empty reel weighs 285 lb and the cable weighs 7.1 lb per foot, the number of feet of cable on the reel is _____ .

15. 345 fasteners at $4.15 per hundred will cost

   _____ .

Problem Solutions—Decimals

1. Line up all the decimal points one under the other. Then add:

$$
\begin{array}{r}
37.03 \\
11.5627 \\
3.4005 \\
3423.0000 \\
+\ \ 1.141 \\
\hline
3476.1342
\end{array}
$$

   Answer: 3476.1342

2. Add a decimal point and five zeros to the 7. Then subtract:

$$
\begin{array}{r}
7.00000 \\
-4.64324 \\
\hline
2.35676
\end{array}
$$

   Answer: 2.35676

3. Since there are two decimal places in the multiplicand and three decimal places in the multiplier, there will be 2 + 3 = 5 decimal places in the product.

$$
\begin{array}{r}
27.34 \\
\times 16.943 \\
\hline
8202 \\
10936 \\
24606 \\
16404 \\
2734 \\
\hline
463.22162
\end{array}
$$

   Answer: 463.22162

4. Omit the decimal point in the divisor by moving it one place to the right. Move the decimal point in the dividend one place to the right and add three zeros in order to carry your answer out to three decimal places, as instructed in the problem.

$$
\begin{array}{r}
6.125 \\
3.2\,)\overline{19.6\,000} \\
19\ 2\ \ \ \ \ \\
\hline
4\ 0\ \ \ \\
3\ 2\ \ \ \\
\hline
80\ \ \\
64\ \ \\
\hline
160 \\
160 \\
\hline
\end{array}
$$

   Answer: 6.125

5. To convert a fraction to a decimal, divide the numerator by the denominator:

$$
\begin{array}{r}
.454 \\
11\overline{)5.000} \\
44 \\
\hline
60 \\
55 \\
\hline
50 \\
44 \\
\hline
6
\end{array}
$$

Answer: .45 to the nearest hundredth

6. To convert a decimal to a fraction, divide by the power of 10 indicated by the number of decimal places. (The fraction does not count as a decimal place.)

$$
\begin{aligned}
64\tfrac{2}{3} \div 100 &= \tfrac{194}{3} \div \tfrac{100}{1} \\
&= \tfrac{194}{3} \times \tfrac{1}{100} \\
&= \tfrac{194}{300} \\
&= \tfrac{97}{150}
\end{aligned}
$$

Answer: $\dfrac{97}{150}$

7. Convert each fraction to a decimal and subtract to find the difference:

$$
\frac{9}{8} = 1.125 \qquad \frac{3}{5} = .60 \qquad
\begin{array}{r}
1.125 \\
-\ .60 \\
\hline
.525
\end{array}
$$

Answer: .525

8. Add the savings for each month:

$$
\begin{array}{r}
\$4.56 \\
3.82 \\
+\ 5.06 \\
\hline
\$13.44
\end{array}
$$

Answer: \$13.44

9.
$$
\begin{array}{r}
1.51 \\
+\ .015 \\
\hline
1.525
\end{array}
\qquad
\begin{array}{r}
1.510 \\
-\ .015 \\
\hline
1.495
\end{array}
$$

Answer: The rod may have a diameter of from 1.495 inches to 1.525 inches inclusive.

10. Add to find total deductions:

$$
\begin{array}{r}
\$3.05 \\
+\ 5.68 \\
\hline
\$8.73
\end{array}
$$

Subtract total deductions from salary to find amount of check:

$$
\begin{array}{r}
\$190.57 \\
-\ 8.73 \\
\hline
\$181.84
\end{array}
$$

Answer: \$181.84

11. Outer radius minus inner radius equals thickness of metal:

$$
\begin{array}{r}
2.84 \\
-1.94 \\
\hline
.90
\end{array}
$$

Answer: .90 in.

12. Add daily earnings to find total earnings:

$$
\begin{array}{r}
\$20.56 \\
32.90 \\
+\ 20.78 \\
\hline
\$74.24
\end{array}
$$

Divide total earnings by 2 to find out what he has left:

$$
\begin{array}{r}
\$37.12 \\
2\overline{)\$74.24}
\end{array}
$$

Answer: \$37.12

13. Find cost of $3\tfrac{1}{2}$ pounds of meat:

$$
\begin{array}{r}
\$1.69 \\
\times\ 3.5 \\
\hline
845 \\
5\ 07 \\
\hline
\end{array}
$$

$5.915 = $5.92 to the nearest cent

Find cost of 20 lemons:
$.60 \div 12 = $.05 (for 1 lemon)
$.05 \times 20 = $1.00 (for 20 lemons)

Add cost of meat and cost of lemons:

$$
\begin{array}{r}
\$5.92 \\
+\ 1.00 \\
\hline
\$6.92
\end{array}
$$

Answer: \$6.92

14. Subtract weight of empty reel from total weight to find weight of cable:

$$
\begin{array}{r}
1279 \text{ lb} \\
- 285 \text{ lb} \\
\hline
994 \text{ lb}
\end{array}
$$

Each foot of cable weighs 7.1 lb. Therefore, to find the number of feet of cable on the reel, divide 994 by 7.1:

$$
\begin{array}{r}
14\ 0. \\
7.1\,\overline{)994.\,0.} \\
\underline{71} \\
284 \\
\underline{284} \\
0\ 0
\end{array}
$$

Answer: 140

15. Each fastener costs:

$$\$4.15 \div 100 = \$.0415$$

345 fasteners cost:

$$
\begin{array}{r}
345 \\
\times\,.0415 \\
\hline
1725 \\
345 \\
13\ 80 \\
\hline
14.3175
\end{array}
$$

Answer: $14.32

Percents

1. The **percent symbol** (%) means "parts out of a hundred." Thus a percent is really a fraction—25% is 25 parts out of a hundred, or $\frac{25}{100}$, which reduces or simplifies to $\frac{1}{4}$, or one part out of four. Some problems involve expressing a fraction or a decimal as a percent. In other problems it is necessary to express a percent as a fraction or decimal in order to perform the calculations efficiently. When you have a percent (or decimal) which converts to a common fraction (25% = .25 = $\frac{1}{4}$), it is usually best to do any multiplying or dividing by first converting the percent or decimal to the common fraction, since the numbers are usually smaller and will work better. For adding and subtracting, percentages and decimals are often easier.

2. To change a whole number or a decimal to a percent:

   a. Multiply the number by 100.

   b. Affix a % sign.

   Illustration: Change 3 to a percent.

   SOLUTION: $3 \times 100 = 300$
   $$3 = 300\%$$

   Answer: 300%

   Illustration: Change .67 to a percent.

   SOLUTION: $.67 \times 100 = 67$
   $$.67 = 67\%$$

   Answer: 67%

3. To change a fraction or a mixed number to a percent:

   a. Multiply the fraction or mixed number by 100.

   b. Reduce, if possible.

   c. Affix a % sign.

   Illustration: Change $\frac{1}{7}$ to a percent.

   SOLUTION: $\frac{1}{7} \times 100 = \frac{100}{7}$
   $$= 14\frac{2}{7}$$
   $$\frac{1}{7} = 14\frac{2}{7}\%$$

   Answer: $14\frac{2}{7}\%$

   Illustration: Change $4\frac{2}{3}$ to a percent.

   SOLUTION: $4\frac{2}{3} \times 100 = \frac{14}{3} \times 100 = \frac{1400}{3}$
   $$= 466\frac{2}{3}$$
   $$4\frac{2}{3} = 466\frac{2}{3}\%$$

   Answer: $466\frac{2}{3}\%$

4. To remove a % sign attached to a decimal, divide the decimal by 100. If necessary, the resulting decimal may then be changed to a fraction.

   Illustration: Change .5% to a decimal and to a fraction.

SOLUTION: $.5\% = .5 \div 100 = .005$

$.005 = \frac{5}{1000} = \frac{1}{200}$

Answer: $.5\% = .005$

$.5\% = \frac{1}{200}$

5. To remove a % sign attached to a fraction or mixed number, divide the fraction or mixed number by 100, and reduce, if possible. If necessary, the resulting fraction may then be changed to a decimal.

Illustration: Change $\frac{3}{4}\%$ to a fraction and to a decimal.

SOLUTION: $\frac{3}{4}\% = \frac{3}{4} \div 100 = \frac{3}{4} \times \frac{1}{100}$

$= \frac{3}{400}$

$\frac{3}{400} = 400\overline{)3.0000}^{\,.0075}$

Answer: $\frac{3}{4}\% = \frac{3}{400}$

$\frac{3}{4}\% = .0075$

6. To remove a % sign attached to a decimal that includes a fraction, divide the decimal by 100. If necessary, the resulting number may then be changed to a fraction.

Illustration: Change $.5\frac{1}{3}\%$ to a fraction.

SOLUTION: $.5\frac{1}{3}\% = .005\frac{1}{3}$

$= \frac{5\frac{1}{3}}{1000}$

$= 5\frac{1}{3} \div 1000$

$= \frac{16}{3} \times \frac{1}{1000}$

$= \frac{16}{3000}$

$= \frac{2}{375}$

Answer: $.5\frac{1}{3}\% = \frac{2}{375}$

7. Some fraction-percent equivalents are used so frequently that it is helpful to be familiar with them.

$\frac{1}{25} = 4\%$ $\frac{1}{5} = 20\%$

$\frac{1}{20} = 5\%$ $\frac{1}{4} = 25\%$

$\frac{1}{12} = 8\frac{1}{3}\%$ $\frac{1}{3} = 33\frac{1}{3}\%$

$\frac{1}{10} = 10\%$ $\frac{1}{2} = 50\%$

$\frac{1}{8} = 12\frac{1}{2}\%$ $\frac{2}{3} = 66\frac{2}{3}\%$

$\frac{1}{6} = 16\frac{2}{3}\%$ $\frac{3}{4} = 75\%$

Solving Percent Problems

8. Most percent problems involve three quantities:

- The rate, R, which is followed by a % sign.
- The base, B, which follows the word "of."
- The amount of percentage, P, which usually follows the word "is."

a. If the rate (R) and the base (B) are known, then the percentage $(P) = R \times B$.

Illustration: Find 15% of 50.

SOLUTION: Rate = 15%

Base = 50

$P = R \times B$
$P = 15\% \times 50$
$= .15 \times 50$
$= 7.5$

Answer: 15% of 50 is 7.5.

b. If the rate (R) and the percentage (P) are known, then the base $(B) = \frac{P}{R}$.

Illustration: 7% of what number is 35?

SOLUTION: Rate = 7%

Percentage = 35

$B = \frac{P}{R}$

$B = \frac{35}{7\%}$

$= 35 \div .07$

$= 500$

Answer: 7% of 500 is 35.

c. If the percentage (P) and the base (B) are known, the rate $(R) = \frac{P}{B}$.

Illustration: There are 96 men in a group of 150 people. What percent of the group is men?

SOLUTION: Base $= 150$
Percentage $= 96$
Rate $= \frac{96}{150}$
$= .64$
$= 64\%$

Answer: 64% of the group are men.

Illustration: In a tank holding 20 gallons of solution, 1 gallon is alcohol. What is the strength of the solution in percent?

SOLUTION: Percentage (amount) $= 1$ gallon
Base $= 20$ gallons
Rate $= \frac{1}{20}$
$= .05$
$= 5\%$

Answer: The solution is 5% alcohol.

9. In a percent problem, the whole is 100%.

Example: If a problem involves 10% of a quantity, the rest of the quantity is 90%.

Example: If a quantity has been increased by 5%, the new amount is 105% of the original quantity.

Example: If a quantity has been decreased by 15%, the new amount is 85% of the original quantity.

10. Percent change, percent increase, and percent decrease are special types of percent problems in which the difficulty is in making sure to use the right numbers to calculate the percent. The full formula is:

$$\frac{\text{(New Amount)} - \text{(Original Amount)}}{\text{(Original Amount)}} \times 100 = \text{Percent Change}$$

Where the new amount is less than the original amount, the number on top will be a negative number and the result will be a **percent decrease.** When a percent decrease is asked for, the negative sign is omitted. Where the new amount is greater than the original amount, the percent change is positive and is called a **percent increase.**

The percent of increase or decrease is found by putting the amount of increase or decrease over the original amount and changing this fraction to a percent by multiplying by 100.

Illustration: The number of automobiles sold by the Cadcoln Dealership increased from 300 one year to 400 the following year. What was the percent of increase?

SOLUTION: There was an increase of 100, which must be compared to the original 300.

$$\frac{100}{300} = \frac{1}{3} = 33\frac{1}{3}\%$$

Answer: $33\frac{1}{3}\%$

Practice Problems Involving Percents

1. 10% written as a decimal is

(A) 1.0
(B) 0.1
(C) 0.01
(D) 0.010
(E) 0.001

2. What is 5.37% in fraction form?

(A) $\dfrac{537}{10,000}$

(B) $\dfrac{537}{1,000}$

(C) $5\dfrac{37}{10,000}$

(D) $5\dfrac{37}{100}$

(E) $\dfrac{537}{10}$

3. What percent is $\dfrac{3}{4}$ of $\dfrac{5}{6}$?

(A) 60%
(B) 75%
(C) 80%
(D) 90%
(E) 111%

4. What percent is 14 of 24?

(A) $62\dfrac{1}{4}\%$

(B) $58\dfrac{1}{3}\%$

(C) $41\dfrac{2}{3}\%$

(D) $33\dfrac{3}{5}\%$

(E) 14%

5. 200% of 800 equals

   (A) 4
   (B) 16
   (C) 200
   (D) 800
   (E) 1600

6. If John must have a mark of 80% to pass a test of 35 items, the number of items he may miss and still pass the test is

   (A) 7
   (B) 8
   (C) 11
   (D) 28
   (E) 35

7. The regular price of a TV set that sold for $118.80 at a 20% reduction sale is

   (A) $158.60
   (B) $148.50
   (C) $138.84
   (D) $95.04
   (E) $29.70

8. A circle graph of a budget shows the expenditure of 26.2% for housing, 28.4% for food, 12% for clothing, 12.7% for taxes, and the balance for miscellaneous items. The percent for miscellaneous items is

   (A) 79.3
   (B) 70.3
   (C) 68.5
   (D) 29.7
   (E) 20.7

9. Two dozen shuttlecocks and four badminton rackets are to be purchased for a playground. The shuttlecocks are priced at $.35 each and the rackets at $2.75 each. The playground receives a discount of 30% from these prices. The total cost of this equipment is

   (A) $7.29
   (B) $11.43
   (C) $13.58
   (D) $18.60
   (E) $19.40

10. A piece of wood weighing 10 ounces is found to have a weight of 8 ounces after drying. The moisture content was

    (A) 80%
    (B) 40%
    (C) $33\frac{1}{3}\%$
    (D) 25%
    (E) 20%

11. A bag contains 800 coins. Of these, 10 percent are dimes, 30 percent are nickels, and the rest are quarters. The amount of money in the bag is

    (A) less than $150
    (B) between $150 and $300
    (C) between $301 and $450
    (D) between $450 and $800
    (E) more than $800

12. Six quarts of a 20% solution of alcohol in water are mixed with 4 quarts of a 60% solution of alcohol in water. The alcoholic strength of the mixture is

    (A) 80%
    (B) 40%
    (C) 36%
    (D) $33\frac{1}{3}\%$
    (E) 10%

13. A man insures 80% of his property and pays a $2\frac{1}{2}\%$ premium amounting to $348. What is the total value of his property?

    (A) $19,000
    (B) $18,400
    (C) $18,000
    (D) $17,400
    (E) $13,920

14. A clerk divided his 35-hour work week as follows: $\frac{1}{5}$ of his time was spent in sorting mail; $\frac{1}{2}$ of his time in filing letters; and $\frac{1}{7}$ of his time in reception work. The rest of his time was devoted to messenger work. The percent of time spent on messenger work by the clerk during the week was most nearly

    (A) 6%
    (B) 10%
    (C) 14%
    (D) 16%
    (E) 20%

15. In a school in which 40% of the enrolled students are boys, 80% of the boys are present on a certain day. If 1152 boys are present, the total school enrollment is

    (A) 1440
    (B) 2880
    (C) 3600
    (D) 5400
    (E) 5760

16. Mrs. Morris receives a salary raise from $25,000 to $27,500. Find the percent of increase.

    (A) 9
    (B) 10
    (C) 90
    (D) 15 $\frac{1}{2}$
    (E) 12 $\frac{1}{2}$

17. The population of Stormville has increased from 80,000 to 100,000 in the last 20 years. Find the percent of increase.

    (A) 20
    (B) 25
    (C) 80
    (D) 60
    (E) 10

18. The value of Super Company Stock dropped from $25 a share to $21 a share. Find the percent of decrease.

    (A) 4
    (B) 8
    (C) 12
    (D) 16
    (E) 20

19. The Rubins bought their home for $30,000 and sold it for $60,000. What was the percent of increase?

    (A) 100
    (B) 50
    (C) 200
    (D) 300
    (E) 150

20. During the pre-holiday rush, Martin's Department Store increased its sales staff from 150 to 200 persons. By what percent must it now decrease its sales staff to return to the usual number of salespersons?

    (A) 25
    (B) 33 $\frac{1}{3}$
    (C) 20
    (D) 40
    (E) 75

Percent Problems—Correct Answers

1. **(B)**	6. **(A)**	11. **(A)**	16. **(B)**
2. **(A)**	7. **(B)**	12. **(C)**	17. **(B)**
3. **(D)**	8. **(E)**	13. **(D)**	18. **(D)**
4. **(B)**	9. **(C)**	14. **(D)**	19. **(A)**
5. **(E)**	10. **(E)**	15. **(C)**	20. **(A)**

Problem Solutions—Percents

1. $10\% = .10 = .1$

   Answer: **(B)** 0.1

2. $5.37\% = .0537 = \dfrac{537}{10,000}$

   Answer: **(A)** $\dfrac{537}{10,000}$

3. Base (number following "of ") $= \dfrac{5}{6}$

   Percentage (number following "is") $= \dfrac{3}{4}$

   Rate $= \dfrac{\text{Percentage}}{\text{Base}}$

   $=$ Percentage ÷ Base

   Rate $= \dfrac{3}{4} \div \dfrac{5}{6}$

   $= \dfrac{3}{\underset{2}{\cancel{4}}} \times \dfrac{\overset{3}{\cancel{6}}}{5}$

   $= \dfrac{9}{10}$

   $\dfrac{9}{10} = .9 = 90\%$

   Answer: **(D)** 90%

4. Base (number following "of ") $= 24$

   Percentage (number following "is") $= 14$

   Rate $=$ Percentage ÷ Base

   Rate $= 14 \div 24$

   $= .58 \frac{1}{3}$

   $= 58 \frac{1}{3}\%$

   Answer: **(B)** $58 \frac{1}{3}\%$

5. 200% of 800 = 2.00 × 800
    = 1600

    Answer: **(E)** 1600

6. He must answer 80% of 35 correctly. Therefore, he may miss 20% of 35.

    20% of 35 = .20 × 35
    = 7

    Answer: **(A)** 7

7. Since $118.80 represents a 20% reduction, $118.80 = 80% of the regular price.

    Regular price $=\frac{\$118.80}{80\%}$

    $= \$118.80 \div .80$

    $= \$148.50$

    Answer: **(B)** $148.50

8. All the items in a circle graph total 100%. Add the figures given for housing, food, clothing, and taxes:

    $$\begin{array}{r} 26.2\% \\ 28.4\% \\ 12\ \ \% \\ +12.7\% \\ \hline 79.3\% \end{array}$$

    Subtract this total from 100% to find the percent for miscellaneous items:

    $$\begin{array}{r} 100.0\% \\ -\ 79.3\% \\ \hline 20.7\% \end{array}$$

    Answer: **(E)** 20.7%

9. Price of shuttlecocks = 24 × $.35 = $8.40
    Price of rackets   = 4 × $2.75 = $11.00
    Total price   = $19.40

    Discount is 30%, and 100% − 30% = 70%

    Actual cost = 70% of 19.40
    = .70 × 19.40
    = 13.58

    Answer: **(C)** $13.58

10. Subtract weight of wood after drying from original weight of wood to find amount of moisture in wood:

    $$\begin{array}{r} 10 \\ -\ 8 \\ \hline 2 \end{array}$$ ounces of moisture in wood

    Moisture content $= \frac{2\text{ ounces}}{10\text{ ounces}} = .2 = 20\%$

    Answer: **(E)** 20%

11. Find the number of each kind of coin:

    10% of 800 = .10 × 800 = 80 dimes
    30% of 800 = .30 × 800 = 240 nickels
    60% of 800 = .60 × 800 = 480 quarters

    Find the value of the coins:

    $$\begin{array}{l} 80\text{ dimes} = \ \ 80 \times .10 = \ \ \$8.00 \\ 240\text{ nickels} = 240 \times .05 = \ \ 12.00 \\ 480\text{ quarters} = 480 \times .25 = \underline{120.00} \end{array}$$

    Total $140.00

    Answer: **(A)** less than $150

12. First solution contains 20% of 6 quarts of alcohol.

    Alcohol content = .20 × 6
    = 1.2 quarts

    Second solution contains 60% of 4 quarts of alcohol.

    Alcohol content = .60 × 4
    = 2.4 quarts

    Mixture contains: 1.2 + 2.4 = 3.6 quarts alcohol

    6 + 4 = 10 quarts liquid

    Alcoholic strength of mixture $= \frac{3.6}{10} = 36\%$

    Answer: **(C)** 36%

13. $2\frac{1}{2}\%$ of insured value = $348

    Insured value $= \dfrac{348}{2\frac{1}{2}\%}$

    $= 348 \div .025$

    $= 13,920$

$13,920 is 80% of total value

$$\text{Total value} = \frac{\$13,920}{80\%}$$
$$= \$13,920 \div .80$$
$$= \$17,400$$

Answer: **(D)** $17,400

14. $\frac{1}{5} \times 35 =$ 7   hr. sorting mail

     $\frac{1}{2} \times 35 =$ $17\frac{1}{2}$ hr. filing

     $\frac{1}{7} \times 35 =$ 5   hr. reception

           $29\frac{1}{2}$ hr. accounted for

$35 - 29\frac{1}{2} = 5\frac{1}{2}$ hr. left for messenger work

% spent on messenger work:

$$= \frac{5\frac{1}{2}}{35}$$
$$= 5\frac{1}{2} \div 35$$
$$= \frac{11}{2} \times \frac{1}{35}$$
$$= \frac{11}{70}$$
$$= .15\frac{5}{7}$$
$$= 15\frac{5}{7}\%$$

Answer: **(D)** most nearly 16%

15. 80% of the boys = 1152

$$\text{Number of boys} = \frac{1152}{80\%}$$
$$= 1152 \div .80$$
$$= 1440$$

40% of students = 1440

$$\text{Total number of students} = \frac{1440}{40\%}$$
$$= 1440 \div .40$$
$$= 3600$$

Answer: **(C)** 3600

16. Amount of increase = $2500

$$\text{Percent of increase} = \frac{\text{amount of increase}}{\text{original}}$$

$$\frac{2500}{25,000} = \frac{1}{10} = 10\%$$

Answer: **(B)** 10%

17. Amount of increase = 20,000

$$\text{Percent of increase} = \frac{20,000}{80,000} = \frac{1}{4} = 25\%$$

Answer: **(B)** 25%

18. Amount of decrease = $4

$$\text{Percent of decrease} = \frac{4}{25} = \frac{16}{100} = 16\%$$

Answer: **(D)** 16%

19. Amount of increase = $30,000

$$\text{Percent of increase} = \frac{30,000}{30,000} = 1 = 100\%$$

Answer: **(A)** 100%

20. Amount of decrease = 50

$$\text{Percent of decrease} = \frac{50}{200} = \frac{1}{4} = 25\%$$

Answer: **(A)** 25%

Shortcuts in Multiplication and Division

There are several shortcuts for simplifying multiplication and division. Following the description of each shortcut, practice problems are provided.

Dropping Final Zeros

1. a. A zero in a whole number is considered a "final zero" if it appears in the units column or if all columns to its right are filled with zeros. A final zero may be omitted in certain kinds of problems.

   b. In decimal numbers, a zero appearing in the extreme right column may be dropped with no effect on the solution of a problem.

2. In multiplying whole numbers, the final zero(s) may be dropped during computation and simply transferred to the answer.

Examples:

$$
\begin{array}{r}
2310 \\
\times\ 150 \\
\hline
1155 \\
231 \\
\hline
346500
\end{array}
\qquad
\begin{array}{r}
129 \\
\times\ 210 \\
\hline
129 \\
258 \\
\hline
27090
\end{array}
$$

$$
\begin{array}{r}
1760 \\
\times\ 205 \\
\hline
880 \\
352 \\
\hline
360800
\end{array}
$$

Practice Problems

Solve the following multiplication problems, dropping the final zeros during computation.

1. $\begin{array}{r} 230 \\ \times\ 12 \\ \hline \end{array}$ 6. $\begin{array}{r} 132 \\ \times 310 \\ \hline \end{array}$

2. $\begin{array}{r} 175 \\ \times 130 \\ \hline \end{array}$ 7. $\begin{array}{r} 350 \\ \times\ 24 \\ \hline \end{array}$

3. $\begin{array}{r} 203 \\ \times\ 14 \\ \hline \end{array}$ 8. $\begin{array}{r} 520 \\ \times 410 \\ \hline \end{array}$

4. $\begin{array}{r} 621 \\ \times 140 \\ \hline \end{array}$ 9. $\begin{array}{r} 634 \\ \times 120 \\ \hline \end{array}$

5. $\begin{array}{r} 430 \\ \times 360 \\ \hline \end{array}$ 10. $\begin{array}{r} 431 \\ \times 230 \\ \hline \end{array}$

Solutions to Practice Problems

1. $\begin{array}{r} 230 \\ \times\ 12 \\ \hline 46 \\ 23 \\ \hline 2760 \end{array}$ 6. $\begin{array}{r} 132 \\ \times\ 310 \\ \hline 132 \\ 396 \\ \hline 40920 \end{array}$

2. $\begin{array}{r} 175 \\ \times 130 \\ \hline 525 \\ 175 \\ \hline 22750 \end{array}$ 7. $\begin{array}{r} 350 \\ \times\ 24 \\ \hline 140 \\ 70 \\ \hline 8400 \end{array}$

3. $\begin{array}{r} 203 \\ \times\ 14 \\ \hline 812 \\ 203 \\ \hline 2842 \end{array}$ 8. $\begin{array}{r} 520 \\ \times\ 410 \\ \hline 52 \\ 208 \\ \hline 213200 \end{array}$

   (no final zeros)

4. $\begin{array}{r} 621 \\ \times 140 \\ \hline 2484 \\ 621 \\ \hline 86940 \end{array}$ 9. $\begin{array}{r} 634 \\ \times\ 120 \\ \hline 1268 \\ 634 \\ \hline 76080 \end{array}$

5. $\begin{array}{r} 430 \\ \times\ 360 \\ \hline 258 \\ 129 \\ \hline 154800 \end{array}$ 10. $\begin{array}{r} 431 \\ \times\ 230 \\ \hline 1293 \\ 862 \\ \hline 99130 \end{array}$

Multiplying Whole Numbers by Decimals

3. In multiplying a whole number by a decimal number, if there are one or more final zeros in the multiplicand, move the decimal point in the multiplier to the right the same number of places as there are final zeros in the multiplicand. Then cross out the final zero(s) in the multiplicand.

Examples:

$$
\begin{array}{r} 27500 \\ \times\ .15 \\ \hline \end{array}
=
\begin{array}{r} 275 \\ \times\ 15 \\ \hline \end{array}
$$

$$
\begin{array}{r} 1250 \\ \times\ .345 \\ \hline \end{array}
=
\begin{array}{r} 125 \\ \times\ 3.45 \\ \hline \end{array}
$$

Practice Problems

Rewrite the following problems, dropping the final zeros and moving decimal points the appropriate number of spaces. Then compute the answers.

1. 2400
    × .02

2. 620
    × .04

3. 800
    × .005

4. 600
    × .002

5. 340
    × .08

6. 480
    × .4

7. 400
    × .04

8. 5300
    × .5

9. 930
    × .3

10. 9000
    ×.001

Solutions to Practice Problems

The rewritten problems are shown, along with the answers.

1. 24
    × 2
    ——
    48

2. 62
    × .4
    ——
    24.8

3. 8
    × .5
    ——
    4.0

4. 6
    × .2
    ——
    1.2

5. 34
    × .8
    ——
    27.2

6. 48
    × 4
    ——
    192

7. 4
    × 4
    ——
    16

8. 530
    × 5
    ——
    2650

9. 93
    × 3
    ——
    279

10. 9
    × 1
    ——
    9

Dividing by Whole Numbers

4. a. When there are final zeros in the divisor but no final zeros in the dividend, move the decimal point in the dividend to the left as many places as there are final zeros in the divisor, then omit the final zeros.

Example: $2700.\overline{)37523.} = 27.\overline{)375.23}$

b. When there are fewer final zeros in the divisor than there are in the dividend, drop the same number of final zeros from the dividend as there are final zeros in the divisor.

Example: $250.\overline{)45300.} = 25.\overline{)4530.}$

c. When there are more final zeros in the divisor than there are in the dividend, move the decimal point in the dividend to the left as many places as there are final zeros in the divisor; then omit the final zeros.

Example: $2300.\overline{)690.} = 23.\overline{)6.9}$

d. When there are no final zeros in the divisor, no zeros can be dropped in the dividend.

Example: $23.\overline{)690.} = 23.\overline{)690.}$

Practice Problems

Rewrite the following problems, dropping the final zeros and moving the decimal points the appropriate number of places. Then compute the quotients.

1. $600.\overline{)72.}$

2. $310.\overline{)6200.}$

3. $7600\overline{)1520.}$

4. $46.\overline{)920.}$

5. $11.0\overline{)220.}$

6. $700.\overline{)84.}$

7. $90.\overline{)8100.}$

8. $8100.\overline{)1620.}$

9. $25.\overline{)5250.}$

10. $41.0\overline{)820.}$

11. $800.\overline{)96.}$

12. $650.\overline{)1300.}$

13. $5500.\overline{)110.}$

14. $36.\overline{)720.}$

15. $87.0\overline{)1740.}$

Rewritten Practice Problems

1. $6.\overline{)\,.72}$

2. $31.\overline{)\,620.}$

3. $76.\overline{)\,15.2}$

4. $46.\overline{)\,920.}$

5. $11.\overline{)\,220.}$

6. $7.\overline{)\,.84}$

7. $9.\overline{)\,810.}$

8. $81.\overline{)\,16.2}$

9. $25.\overline{)\,5250.}$

10. $41.\overline{)\,820.}$

11. $8.\overline{)\,.96}$

12. $65.\overline{)\,130.}$

13. $55.\overline{)\,1.1}$

14. $36.\overline{)\,720.}$

15. $87.\overline{)\,1740.}$

Solutions to Practice Problems

1. $6.\overset{.12}{\overline{)\,.72}}$

2. $31.\overset{20}{\overline{)\,620.}}$ $\;\;\dfrac{62}{00}$

3. $76.\overset{.2}{\overline{)\,15.2}}$ $\;\;\dfrac{15\;2}{0\;0}$

4. $46.\overset{20}{\overline{)\,920.}}$ $\;\;\dfrac{92}{00}$

5. $11.\overset{20}{\overline{)\,220.}}$ $\;\;\dfrac{22}{00}$

6. $7.\overset{.12}{\overline{)\,.84}}$

7. $9.\overset{90}{\overline{)\,810.}}$ $\;\;\dfrac{81}{00}$

8. $81.\overset{.2}{\overline{)\,16.2}}$ $\;\;\dfrac{16.2}{0\;0}$

9. $25.\overset{210}{\overline{)\,5250.}}$ $\;\;\dfrac{50}{25}$ $\dfrac{25}{00}$

10. $41.\overset{20}{\overline{)\,820.}}$ $\;\;\dfrac{82}{00}$

11. $8.\overset{.12}{\overline{)\,.96}}$

12. $65.\overset{2}{\overline{)\,130.}}$ $\;\;\dfrac{130}{00}$

13. $55.\overset{.02}{\overline{)\,1.10}}$ $\;\;\dfrac{1\;10}{00}$

14. $36.\overset{20}{\overline{)\,720.}}$ $\;\;\dfrac{72}{00}$

15. $87.\overset{20}{\overline{)\,1740.}}$ $\;\;\dfrac{174}{00}$

Division by Multiplication

5. Instead of dividing by a particular number, the same answer is obtained by multiplying by the equivalent multiplier.

6. To find the equivalent multiplier of a given divisor, divide 1 by the divisor.

   Example: The equivalent multiplier of $12\frac{1}{2}$ is $1 \div 12\frac{1}{2}$ or .08. The division problem $100 \div 12\frac{1}{2}$ may be more easily solved as the multiplication problem $100 \times .08$. The answer will be the same. This can be helpful when you are estimating answers.

7. Common divisors and their equivalent multipliers are shown below:

Divisor	Equivalent Multiplier
$11\frac{1}{9}$	.09
$12\frac{1}{2}$	.08
$14\frac{2}{7}$	.07
$16\frac{2}{3}$	.06
20	.05
25	.04
$33\frac{1}{3}$	.03
50	.02

8. A divisor may be multiplied or divided by any power of 10, and the only change in its equivalent multiplier will be in the placement of the decimal point, as may be seen in the following table:

Divisor	Equivalent Multiplier
.025	40.
.25	4.
2.5	.4
25.	.04
250.	.004
2500.	.0004

Practice Problems

Rewrite and solve each of the following problems by using equivalent multipliers. Drop the final zeros where appropriate.

1. $100 \div 16\frac{2}{3} =$

2. $200 \div 25 =$

3. $300 \div 33\frac{1}{3} =$

4. $250 \div 50 =$

5. $80 \div 12\frac{1}{2} =$

6. $800 \div 14\frac{2}{7} =$

7. $620 \div 20 =$

8. $500 \div 11\frac{1}{9} =$

9. $420 \div 16\frac{2}{3} =$

10. $1200 \div 33\frac{1}{3} =$

11. $955 \div 50 =$

12. $900 \div 33\frac{1}{3} =$

13. $275 \div 12\frac{1}{2} =$

14. $625 \div 25 =$

15. $244 \div 20 =$

16. $350 \div 16\frac{2}{3} =$

17. $400 \div 33\frac{1}{3} =$

18. $375 \div 25 =$

19. $460 \div 20 =$

20. $250 \div 12\frac{1}{2} =$

Solutions to Practice Problems

The rewritten problems and their solutions appear below:

1. $100 \times .06 = 1 \times 6 = 6$

2. $200 \times .04 = 2 \times 4 = 8$

3. $300 \times .03 = 3 \times 3 = 9$

4. $250 \times .02 = 25 \times .2 = 5$

5. $80 \times .08 = 8 \times .8 = 6.4$

6. $800 \times .07 = 8 \times 7 = 56$

7. $620 \times .05 = 62 \times .5 = 31$

8. $500 \times .09 = 5 \times 9 = 45$

9. $420 \times .06 = 42 \times .6 = 25.2$

10. $1200 \times .03 = 12 \times 3 = 36$

11. $955 \times .02 = 19.1$

12. $900 \times .03 = 9 \times 3 = 27$

13. $275 \times .08 = 22$

14. $625 \times .04 = 25$

15. $244 \times .05 = 12.2$

16. $350 \times .06 = 35 \times .6 = 21$

17. $400 \times .03 = 4 \times 3 = 12$

18. $375 \times .04 = 15$

19. $460 \times .05 = 46 \times .5 = 23$

20. $250 \times .08 = 25 \times .8 = 20$

Multiplication by Division

9. Just as some division problems are made easier by changing them to equivalent multiplication problems, certain multiplication problems are made easier by changing them to equivalent division problems.
10. Instead of arriving at an answer by multiplying by a particular number, the same answer is obtained by dividing by the equivalent divisor.
11. To find the equivalent divisor of a given multiplier, divide 1 by the multiplier.
12. Common multipliers and their equivalent divisors are shown below:

Multiplier	Equivalent Divisor
$11\frac{1}{9}$	.09
$12\frac{1}{2}$	.08
$14\frac{2}{7}$	.07
$16\frac{2}{3}$	.06
20	.05
25	.04
$33\frac{1}{3}$	.03
50	.02

Notice that the multiplier-equivalent divisor pairs are the same as the divisor-equivalent multiplier pairs given earlier.

Practice Problems

Rewrite and solve each of the following problems by using division. Drop the final zeros where appropriate.

1. $77 \times 14\frac{2}{7} =$
2. $81 \times 11\frac{1}{9} =$
3. $475 \times 20 =$
4. $42 \times 50 =$
5. $36 \times 33\frac{1}{3} =$
6. $96 \times 12\frac{1}{2} =$
7. $126 \times 16\frac{2}{3} =$
8. $48 \times 25 =$
9. $33 \times 33\frac{1}{3} =$
10. $84 \times 14\frac{2}{7} =$
11. $99 \times 11\frac{1}{9} =$
12. $126 \times 33\frac{1}{3} =$
13. $168 \times 12\frac{1}{2} =$
14. $654 \times 16\frac{2}{3} =$
15. $154 \times 14\frac{2}{7} =$
16. $5250 \times 50 =$
17. $324 \times 25 =$
18. $625 \times 20 =$
19. $198 \times 11\frac{1}{9} =$
20. $224 \times 14\frac{2}{7} =$

Solutions to Practice Problems

The rewritten problems and their solutions appear below:

1. $.07\overline{)77.} = 7\overline{)7700.}$ quotient $1100.$
2. $.09\overline{)81.} = 9\overline{)8100.}$ quotient $900.$
3. $.05\overline{)475.} = 5\overline{)47500.}$ quotient $9500.$
4. $.02\overline{)42.} = 2\overline{)4200.}$ quotient $2100.$
5. $.03\overline{)36.} = 3\overline{)3600.}$ quotient $1200.$

6. $.08 \overline{) 96.} = 8 \overline{) 9600.} \quad \overset{1200.}{}$

7. $.06 \overline{) 126.} = 6 \overline{) 12600.} \quad \overset{2100.}{}$

8. $.04 \overline{) 48.} = 4 \overline{) 4800.} \quad \overset{1200.}{}$

9. $.03 \overline{) 33.} = 3 \overline{) 3300.} \quad \overset{1100.}{}$

10. $.07 \overline{) 84.} = 7 \overline{) 8400.} \quad \overset{1200.}{}$

11. $.09 \overline{) 99.} = 9 \overline{) 9900.} \quad \overset{1100.}{}$

12. $.03 \overline{) 126.} = 3 \overline{) 12600.} \quad \overset{4200.}{}$

13. $.08 \overline{) 168.} = 8 \overline{) 16800.} \quad \overset{2100.}{}$

14. $.06 \overline{) 654.} = 6 \overline{) 65400.} \quad \overset{10900.}{}$

15. $.07 \overline{) 154.} = 7 \overline{) 15400.} \quad \overset{2200.}{}$

16. $.02 \overline{) 5250.} = 2 \overline{) 525000.} \quad \overset{262500.}{}$

17. $.04 \overline{) 324.} = 4 \overline{) 32400.} \quad \overset{8100.}{}$

18. $.05 \overline{) 625.} = 5 \overline{) 62500.} \quad \overset{12500.}{}$

19. $.09 \overline{) 198.} = 9 \overline{) 19800.} \quad \overset{2200.}{}$

20. $.07 \overline{) 224.} = 7 \overline{) 22400.} \quad \overset{3200.}{}$

Averages

1. a. The term average can technically refer to a variety of mathematical ideas, but on the test it refers to the **arithmetic mean.** It is found by adding the numbers given and then dividing this sum by the number of items being averaged.

   Illustration: Find the arithmetic mean of 2, 8, 5, 9, 6, and 12.

   SOLUTION: There are 6 numbers.

   $$\text{Arithmetic mean} = \frac{2+8+5+9+6+12}{6}$$

   $$= \frac{42}{6}$$

   $$= 7$$

   Answer: The arithmetic mean is 7.

   b. If a problem calls for simply the average or the mean, it is referring to the arithmetic mean.

2. If a group of numbers is arranged in order, the middle number is called the **median.** If there is no single middle number (this occurs when there is an even number of items), the median is found by computing the arithmetic mean of the two middle numbers.

   Example: The median of 6, 8, 10, 12, 14, and 16 is 11.

   Example: The median of 6, 8, 10, 12, 14, and 16 is the arithmetic mean of 10 and 12.

   $$\frac{10+12}{2} = \frac{22}{2} = 11$$

3. The **mode** of a group of numbers is the number that appears most often.

   Example: The mode of 10, 5, 7, 9, 12, 5, 10, 5, and 9 is 5.

4. When some numbers among terms to be averaged occur more than once, they must be given the appropriate weight. For example, if a student received four grades of 80 and one of 90, his average would not be the average of 80 and 90, but rather the average of 80, 80, 80, 80, and 90.

To obtain the average of quantities that are weighted:

a. Set up a table listing the quantities, their respective weights, and their respective values.

b. Multiply the value of each quantity by its respective weight.

c. Add up these products.

d. Add up the weights.

e. Divide the sum of the products by the sum of the weights.

Illustration: Assume that the weights for the following subjects are: English 3, History 2, Mathematics 2, Foreign Languages 2, and Art 1. What would be the average of a student whose marks are: English 80, History 85, Algebra 84, Spanish 82, and Art 90?

SOLUTION: Subject	Weight	Mark
English	3	80
History	2	85
Algebra	2	84
Spanish	2	82
Art	1	90
English	$3 \times 80 = 240$	
History	$2 \times 85 = 170$	
Algebra	$2 \times 84 = 168$	
Spanish	$2 \times 82 = 164$	
Art	$1 \times 90 = \underline{90}$	
	832	

Sum of the weights: $3 + 2 + 2 + 2 + 1 = 10$
$$832 \div 10 = 83.2$$

Answer: Average = 83.2

Note: On the test, you might go directly to a list of the weighted amounts, here totalling 832, and divide by the number of weights; or you might set up a single equation.

Illustration: Mr. Martin drove for 6 hours at an average rate of 50 miles per hour and for 2 hours at an average rate of 60 miles per hour. Find his average rate for the entire trip.

SOLUTION:
$$\frac{6(50) + 2(60)}{8} = \frac{300 + 120}{8} = \frac{420}{8} = 52\frac{1}{2}$$
Answer: $52\frac{1}{2}$

Since he drove many more hours at 50 miles per hour than at 60 miles per hour, his average rate should be closer to 50 than to 60, which it is. In general, average rate can always be found by dividing the total distance covered by the time spent traveling.

Practice Problems Involving Averages

1. The arithmetic mean of 73.8, 92.2, 64.7, 43.8, 56.5, and 46.4 is

   (A) 60.6
   (B) 62.9
   (C) 64.48
   (D) 75.48
   (E) 82.9

2. The median of the numbers 8, 5, 7, 5, 9, 9, 1, 8, 10, 5, and 10 is

   (A) 5
   (B) 7
   (C) 8
   (D) 9
   (E) 10

3. The mode of the numbers 16, 15, 17, 12, 15, 15, 18, 19, and 18 is

   (A) 15
   (B) 16
   (C) 17
   (D) 18
   (E) 19

4. A clerk filed 73 forms on Monday, 85 forms on Tuesday, 54 on Wednesday, 92 on Thursday, and 66 on Friday. What was the average number of forms filed per day?

   (A) 60
   (B) 72
   (C) 74
   (D) 92
   (E) 370

5. The grades received on a test by twenty students were: 100, 55, 75, 80, 65, 65, 85, 90, 80, 45, 40, 50, 85, 85, 85, 80, 80, 70, 65, and 60. The average of these grades is

   (A) 70
   (B) 72
   (C) 77
   (D) 80
   (E) 100

6. A buyer purchased 75 six-inch rulers costing 15¢ each, 100 one-foot rulers costing 30¢ each, and 50 one-yard rulers costing 72¢ each. What was the average price per ruler?

   (A) $26\frac{1}{8}$¢
   (B) $34\frac{1}{3}$¢
   (C) 39¢
   (D) 42¢
   (E) $77\frac{1}{4}$¢

7. What is the average of a student who received 90 in English, 84 in Algebra, 75 in French, and 76 in Music, if the subjects have the following weights: English 4, Algebra 3, French 3, and Music 1?

   (A) 81
   (B) $81\frac{1}{2}$
   (C) 82
   (D) $82\frac{1}{2}$
   (E) 83

Questions 8–10 refer to the following information.

A census shows that on a certain block the number of children in each family is 3, 4, 4, 0, 1, 2, 0, 2, and 2, respectively.

8. Find the average number of children per family.

   (A) 4
   (B) 3
   (C) $3\frac{1}{2}$
   (D) 2
   (E) $1\frac{1}{2}$

9. Find the median number of children.

   (A) 1
   (B) 2
   (C) 3
   (D) 4
   (E) 5

10. Find the mode of the number of children.

   (A) 0
   (B) 1
   (C) 2
   (D) 3
   (E) 4

Averages Problems—Correct Answers

1. **(B)**	6. **(B)**
2. **(C)**	7. **(E)**
3. **(A)**	8. **(D)**
4. **(C)**	9. **(B)**
5. **(B)**	10. **(C)**

Problem Solutions—Averages

1. Find the sum of the values:

   $73.8 + 92.2 + 64.7 + 43.8 + 56.5 + 46.4 = 377.4$

   There are 6 values.

   $$\text{Arithmetic mean} = \frac{377.4}{6} = 62.9$$

   Answer: **(B)** 62.9

2. Arrange the numbers in order:

   1, 5, 5, 5, 7, 8, 8, 9, 9, 10, 10

   The middle number, or median, is 8.

   Answer: **(C)** 8

3. The mode is that number appearing most frequently. The number 15 appears three times.

   Answer: **(A)** 15

4. Average $= \dfrac{73 + 85 + 54 + 92 + 66}{5}$

   $= \dfrac{370}{5}$

   $= 74$

   Answer: **(C)** 74

5. Sum of the grades = 1440.

$$\frac{1440}{20} = 72$$

Answer: **(B)** 72

6. $75 \times 15¢ = 1125¢$
    $100 \times 30¢ = 3000¢$
    $\underline{50 \times 72¢ = 3600¢}$
   225   7725¢

$$\frac{7725¢}{225} = 34\frac{1}{3}¢$$

Answer: **(B)** $34\frac{1}{3}¢$

7.

Subject	Grade	Weight
English	90	4
Algebra	84	3
French	75	3
Music	76	1

$(90 \times 4) + (84 \times 3) + (75 \times 3) + (76 \times 1) =$
$360 + 252 + 225 + 76 = 913$
Weight $= 4 + 3 + 3 + 1 = 11$
$913 \div 11 = 83$ average

Answer: **(E)** 83

8. Average $= \dfrac{3+4+4+0+1+2+0+2+2}{9}$

$$= \frac{18}{9}$$

$$= 2$$

Answer: **(D)** 2

9. Arrange the numbers in order:

$$0, 0, 1, 2, 2, 2, 3, 4, 4$$

Of the 9 numbers, the fifth (middle) number is 2.

Answer: **(B)** 2

10. The number appearing most often is 2.

Answer: **(C)** 2

Ratio and Proportion

Ratio

1. A **ratio** expresses the relationship between two (or more) quantities in terms of numbers. The mark used to indicate a ratio is the colon (:) and is read "to."

   Example: The ratio 2:3 is read "2 to 3."

2. A ratio also represents division. Therefore, any ratio of two terms may be written as a fraction, and any fraction may be written as a ratio.

   Example: $3:4 = \dfrac{3}{4}$

   $\dfrac{5}{6} = 5:6$

3. To simplify any complicated ratio of two terms containing fractions, decimals, or percents:

   a. Divide the first term by the second.

   b. Write as a fraction in lowest terms.

   c. Write the fraction as a ratio.

   Illustration: Simplify the ratio $\dfrac{5}{6} : \dfrac{7}{8}$.

   SOLUTION: $\dfrac{5}{6} \div \dfrac{7}{8} = \dfrac{5}{6} \times \dfrac{8}{7} = \dfrac{40}{42} = \dfrac{20}{21}$

   $$\frac{20}{21} = 20:21$$

   Answer: 20:21

4. To solve problems in which the ratio is given:

   a. Add the terms in the ratio.

   b. Divide the total amount that is to be put into a ratio by this sum.

   c. Multiply each term in the ratio by this quotient.

   Illustration: The sum of $360 is to be divided among three people according to the ratio 3:4:5. How much does each one receive?

   SOLUTION: $3 + 4 + 5 = 12$
               $360 \div 12 = 30
                 $30 \times 3 = 90
                 $30 \times 4 = 120
                 $30 \times 5 = 150

   Answer: The money is divided thus: $90, $120, $150.

Proportion

5. a. A **proportion** indicates the equality of two ratios.

   Example: 2:4 = 5:10 is a proportion. This is read "2 is to 4 as 5 is to 10."

   b. In a proportion, the two outside terms are called the **extremes,** and the two inside terms are called the **means.**

   Example: In the proportion 2:4 = 5:10, 2 and 10 are the extremes, and 4 and 5 are the means.

   c. Proportions are often written in fractional form.

   Example: The proportion 2:4 = 5:10 may be written $\frac{2}{4} = \frac{5}{10}$.

   d. In any proportion, the product of the means equals the product of the extremes. If the proportion is a fractional form, the products may be found by cross-multiplication.

   Example: In $\frac{2}{4} = \frac{5}{10}$, $4 \times 5 = 2 \times 10$.

   e. The product of the extremes divided by one mean equals the other mean; the product of the means divided by one extreme equals the other extreme.

6. Many problems in which three terms are given and one term is unknown can be solved by using proportions. To solve such problems:

   a. Formulate the proportion very carefully according to the facts given. (If any term is misplaced, the solution will be incorrect.) Any symbol may be written in place of the missing term.

   b. Determine by inspection whether the means or the extremes are known. Multiply the pair that has both terms given.

   c. Divide this product by the third term given to find the unknown term.

Illustration: The scale on a map shows that 2 cm. represents 30 miles of actual length. What is the actual length of a road that is represented by 7 cm on the map?

SOLUTION: The map lengths and the actual lengths are in proportion—that is, they have equal ratios. If m stands for the unknown length, the proportion is:

$$\frac{2}{7} = \frac{30}{m}$$

As the proportion is written, m is an extreme and is equal to the product of the means, divided by the other extreme:

$$m = \frac{7 \times 30}{2}$$
$$m = \frac{210}{2}$$
$$m = 105$$

Answer: 7 cm. on the map represents 105 miles.

Illustration: If a money bag containing 500 nickels weighs 6 pounds, how much will a money bag containing 1600 nickels weigh?

SOLUTION: The weights of the bags and the number of coins in them are proportional. Suppose w represents the unknown weight. Then

$$\frac{6}{w} = \frac{500}{1600}$$

The unknown is a mean and is equal to the product of the extremes, divided by the other mean:

$$w = \frac{6 \times 1600}{500}$$
$$w = 19.2$$

Answer: A bag containing 1600 nickels weighs 19.2 pounds.

Practice Problems Involving Ratio and Proportion

1. The ratio of 24 to 64 is

   (A) 1:64
   (B) 1:24
   (C) 20:100
   (D) 24:100
   (E) 3:8

2. The Baltimore Colts won 8 games and lost 3. The ratio of games won to games played is

   (A) 11:8
   (B) 8:3
   (C) 8:11
   (D) 3:8
   (E) 3:11

3. The ratio of $\frac{1}{4}$ to $\frac{3}{5}$ is

   (A) 1 to 3
   (B) 3 to 20
   (C) 5 to 12
   (D) 3 to 4
   (E) 5 to 4

4. If there are 16 boys and 12 girls in a class, the ratio of the number of girls to the number of children in the class is

   (A) 3 to 4
   (B) 3 to 7
   (C) 4 to 7
   (D) 4 to 3
   (E) 7 to 4

5. 259 is to 37 as

   (A) 5 is to 1
   (B) 63 is to 441
   (C) 84 is to 12
   (D) 130 is to 19
   (E) 25 is to 4

6. 2 dozen cans of dog food at the rate of 3 cans for $1.45 would cost

   (A) $10.05
   (B) $10.20
   (C) $11.20
   (D) $11.60
   (E) $11.75

7. A snapshot measures $2\frac{1}{2}$ inches by $1\frac{7}{8}$ inches. It is to be enlarged so that the longer dimension will be 4 inches. The length of the enlarged shorter dimension will be

   (A) $2\frac{1}{2}$ in.
   (B) 3 in.
   (C) $3\frac{3}{8}$ in.
   (D) 4 in.
   (E) 5 in.

8. Men's white handkerchiefs cost $2.29 for 3. The cost per dozen handkerchiefs is

   (A) $27.48
   (B) $13.74
   (C) $9.16
   (D) $6.87
   (E) $4.58

9. A certain pole casts a shadow 24 feet long. At the same time another pole 3 feet high casts a shadow 4 feet long. How high is the first pole, given that the heights and shadows are in proportion?

   (A) 18 ft.
   (B) 19 ft.
   (C) 20 ft.
   (D) 21 ft.
   (E) 24 ft.

10. The actual length represented by $3\frac{1}{2}$ inches on a drawing having a scale of $\frac{1}{8}$ inch to the foot is

    (A) 3.5 ft.
    (B) 7 ft.
    (C) 21 ft.
    (D) 28 ft.
    (E) 120 ft.

11. Aluminum bronze consists of copper and aluminum, usually in the ratio of 10:1 by weight. If an object made of this alloy weighs 77 lb., how many pounds of aluminum does it contain?

    (A) 0.7
    (B) 7.0
    (C) 7.7
    (D) 70.7
    (E) 77.0

12. It costs 31 cents a square foot to lay vinyl flooring. To lay 180 square feet of flooring, it will cost

   (A) $16.20
   (B) $18.60
   (C) $55.80
   (D) $62.00
   (E) $180.00

13. If a per diem worker earns $352 in 16 days, the amount that he will earn in 117 days is most nearly

   (A) $3050
   (B) $2575
   (C) $2285
   (D) $2080
   (E) $1170

14. Assuming that on a blueprint $\frac{1}{8}$ inch equals 12 inches of actual length, the actual length in inches of a steel bar represented on the blueprint by a line $3\frac{3}{4}$ inches long is

   (A) $3\frac{3}{4}$

   (B) 30

   (C) 36

   (D) 360

   (E) 450

15. A, B, and C invested $9,000, $7,000, and $6,000, respectively. Their profits were to be divided according to the ratio of their investment. If B uses his share of the firm's profit of $825 to pay a personal debt of $230, how much will he have left?

   (A) $30.50
   (B) $32.50
   (C) $34.50
   (D) $36.50
   (E) $37.50

Ratio and Proportion Problems— Correct Answers

1. (E)	6. (D)	11. (B)
2. (C)	7. (B)	12. (C)
3. (C)	8. (C)	13. (B)
4. (B)	9. (A)	14. (D)
5. (C)	10. (D)	15. (B)

Problem Solutions—Ratio and Proportion

1. The ratio 24 to 64 may be written 24:64 or $\frac{24}{64}$. In fraction form, the ratio can be reduced:

   $$\frac{24}{64} = \frac{3}{8} \text{ or } 3:8$$

   Answer: **(E)** 3:8

2. The number of games played was $3 + 8 = 11$. The ratio of games won to games played is 8:11.

   Answer: **(C)** 8:11

3. $\frac{1}{4}:\frac{3}{5} = \frac{1}{4} \div \frac{3}{5}$

   $$= \frac{1}{4} \times \frac{5}{3}$$

   $$= \frac{5}{12}$$

   $$= 5:12$$

   Answer: **(C)** 5 to 12

4. There are $16 + 12 = 28$ children in the class. The ratio of number of girls to number of children is 12:28.

   $$\frac{12}{28} = \frac{3}{7}$$

   Answer: **(B)** 3 to 7

5. The ratio $\frac{259}{37}$ reduces by 37 to $\frac{7}{1}$. The ratio also reduces to $\frac{7}{1}$. Therefore, $\frac{259}{37} = \frac{84}{12}$ is a proportion.

   Answer: **(C)** 84 is to 12

6. The number of cans is proportional to the price. Let p represent the unknown price:

   Then $\frac{3}{24} = \frac{1.45}{p}$

   $$p = \frac{1.45 \times 24}{3}$$

   $$p = \frac{34.80}{3}$$

   $$= \$11.60$$

   Answer: **(D)** $11.60

7. Let s represent the unknown shorter dimension:

$$\frac{2\frac{1}{2}}{4}=\frac{1\frac{7}{8}}{s}$$

$$s=\frac{4\times1\frac{7}{8}}{2\frac{1}{2}}$$

$$=\frac{{}^{1}\!4\times\frac{15}{8_2}}{2\frac{1}{2}}$$

$$=\frac{15}{2}\div2\frac{1}{2}$$

$$=\frac{15}{2}\div\frac{5}{2}$$

$$=\frac{15}{2}\times\frac{2}{5}$$

Answer: **(B)** 3 in.

8. If p is the cost per dozen (12):

$$\frac{3}{12}=\frac{2.29}{p}$$

$$p=\frac{{}^{4}\!12\times2.29}{3_1}$$

$$p=9.16$$

Answer: **(C)** $9.16

9. If f is the height of the first pole, the proportion is:

$$\frac{f}{24}=\frac{3}{4}$$

$$f=\frac{{}^{6}\!24\times3}{4_1}$$

$$=18$$

Answer: **(A)** 18 ft.

10. If y is the unknown length:

$$\frac{3\frac{1}{2}}{\frac{1}{8}}=\frac{y}{1}$$

$$y=\frac{3\frac{1}{2}\times1}{\frac{1}{8}}$$

$$=3\frac{1}{2}\div\frac{1}{8}$$

$$=\frac{7}{{}_1 2}\times\frac{8^4}{1}$$

$$=28$$

Answer: **(D)** 28 ft.

11. Since only two parts of a proportion are known (77 is total weight), the problem must be solved by the ratio method. The ratio 10:1 means that if the alloy were separated into equal parts, 10 of those parts would be copper and 1 would be aluminum, for a total of $10 + 1 = 11$ parts.

$$77 \div 11 = 7 \text{ lb. per part}$$

The alloy has 1 part aluminum.

$$7 \times 1 = 7 \text{ lb. aluminum}$$

Answer: **(B)** 7.0

12. The cost (c) is proportional to the number of square feet.

$$\frac{\$.31}{c}=\frac{1}{180}$$

$$c=\frac{\$.31\times180}{1}$$

$$=\$55.80$$

Answer: **(C)** $55.80

13. The amount earned is proportional to the number of days worked. If a is the unknown amount:

$$\frac{\$352}{a}=\frac{16}{117}$$

$$a=\frac{\$352\times117}{16}$$

$$a=\$2574$$

Answer: **(B)** $2575

14. If n is the unknown length:

$$\frac{\frac{1}{8}}{3\frac{3}{4}}=\frac{12}{n}$$

$$n=\frac{12\times3\frac{3}{4}}{\frac{1}{8}}$$

$$=\frac{{}^{3}\!12\times\frac{15}{4_1}}{\frac{1}{8}}$$

$$=\frac{45}{\frac{1}{8}}$$

$$=45\div\frac{1}{8}$$

$$=45\times\frac{8}{1}$$

$$=360$$

Answer: **(D)** 360

15. The ratio of investment is:

9,000:7,000:6,000 or 9:7:6

$9 + 7 + 6 = 22$
$825 \div 22 = \$37.50$ each share of profit
$7 \times \$37.50 = \$262.50$, B's share of profit

$$\begin{array}{r} \$\ 262.50 \\ -\ 230.00 \\ \hline \$\ \ 32.50, \text{ amount B has left} \end{array}$$

Answer: **(B)** $32.50

Powers and Roots

1. The numbers that are multiplied to give a product are called the **factors** of the product.

   Example: In $2 \times 3 = 6$, 2 and 3 are factors.

2. If the factors are the same, an **exponent** may be used to indicate the number of times the factor appears.

   Example: In $3 \times 3 = 3^2$, the number 3 appears as a factor twice, as is indicated by the exponent 2.

3. When a product is written in exponential form, the number the exponent refers to is called the **base.** The product itself is called the **power.**

   Example: In 2^5, the number 2 is the base and 5 is the exponent.
   $2^5 = 2 \times 2 \times 2 \times 2 \times 2 = 32$, so 32 is the power.

4. a. If the exponent used is 2, we say that the base has been **squared,** or raised to the second power.

   Example: 6^2 is read "six squared" or "six to the second power."

   b. If the exponent used is 3, we say that the base has been **cubed,** or raised to the third power.

   Example: 5^3 is read "five cubed" or "five to the third power."

   c. If the exponent is 4, we say that the base has been raised to the fourth power. If the exponent is 5, we say the base has been raised to the fifth power, etc.

   Example: 2^8 is read "two to the eighth power."

5. A number that is the product of a whole number squared is called a **perfect square.**

   Example: 25 is a perfect square because $25 = 5^2$.

6. a. If a number has exactly two equal factors, each factor is called the **square root** of the number.

   Example: $9 = 3 \times 3$; therefore, 3 is the square root of 9.

   b. The symbol $\sqrt{}$ is used to indicate square root.

   Example: $\sqrt{9} = 3$ means that the square root of 9 is 3, or $3 \times 3 = 9$.

   c. In principle, all numbers have a square root. Although many square roots cannot be calculated exactly, they can be found to whatever degree of accuracy is needed (see item 8). Thus the square root of 10, $\sqrt{10}$, is *by definition* the number that equals 10 when it is squared—$\sqrt{10} \times \sqrt{10} = 10$.

   d. If a number has exactly three equal factors, each factor is called a **cube root.** The symbol $\sqrt[3]{}$ is used to indicate a cube root.

   Example: $8 = 2 \times 2 \times 2$; thus $2 = \sqrt[3]{8}$

   e. In general, the *nth* root is indicated as $\sqrt[n]{}$.

7. The square root of the most common perfect squares may be found by using the following table, or by trial and error; that is, by finding the number that, when squared, yields the given perfect square.

Number	Perfect Square	Number	Perfect Square
1	1	10	100
2	4	11	121
3	9	12	144
4	16	13	169
5	25	14	196
6	36	15	225
7	49	20	400
8	64	25	625
9	81	30	900

Example: To find $\sqrt{81}$, note that 81 is the perfect square of 9, or $9^2 = 81$. Therefore, $\sqrt{81} = 9$.

8. On the GRE you will only rarely have to find the square root of a number that is not a perfect square. The two most common square roots you will have to deal with are $\sqrt{2}$, which equals approximately 1.4, and $\sqrt{3}$, which equals approximately 1.7. Most times you will not have to convert these square roots to their equivalents since the answer choices will be in terms of the square roots, e.g., (A) $4\sqrt{3}$, etc.

The following method is the way to compute square roots of numbers that are not perfect squares. It is very effective, but it is long and you are unlikely to actually need it on the GRE.

a. Locate the decimal point.

b. Mark off the digits in groups of two in both directions beginning at the decimal point.

c. Mark the decimal point for the answer just above the decimal point of the number whose square root is to be taken.

d. Find the largest perfect square contained in the left-hand group of two.

e. Place its square root in the answer. Subtract the perfect square from the first digit or pair of digits.

f. Bring down the next pair.

g. Double the partial answer.

h. Add a trial digit to the right of the doubled partial answer. Multiply this new number by the trial digit. Place the correct new digit in the answer.

i. Subtract the product.

j. Repeat steps f to i as often as necessary.

You will notice that you get one digit in the answer for every group of two you marked off in the original number.

Illustration: Find the square root of 138,384.

SOLUTION:

$$\begin{array}{r} 3 \\ \sqrt{13'\,83'\,84.} \end{array}$$
$$3^2 = \quad 9$$
$$\overline{\quad 4\ \ 83}$$

$$\begin{array}{r} 3\ \ 7\ \ 2. \\ \sqrt{13'\,83'\,84.} \end{array}$$
$$3^2 = \quad 9$$
$$\overline{\quad 4\ 83}$$

$$7 \times 67 = \quad \underline{469}$$
$$1484$$
$$2 \times 742 = \quad \underline{1484}$$

The number must first be marked off in groups of two figures each, beginning at the decimal point, which, in the case of a whole number, is at the right. The number of figures in the root will be the same as the number of groups so obtained.

The largest square less than 13 is 9. $\sqrt{9} = 3$

Place its square root in the answer. Subtract the perfect square from the first digit or pair of digits. Bring down the next pair. To form our trial divisor, annex 0 to this root "3" (making 30) and multiply by 2.

$483 \div 60 = 8$. Multiplying the trial divisor 68 by 8, we obtain 544, which is too large. We then try multiplying 67 by 7. This is correct. Add the trial digit to the right of the doubled partial answer. Place the new digit in the answer. Subtract the product. Bring down the final group. Annex 0 to the new root 37 and multiply by 2 for the trial divisor:

$$2 \times 370 = 740$$
$$1484 \div 740 = 2$$

Place the 2 in the answer.

Answer: The square root of 138,384 is 372.

Illustration: Find the square root of 3 to the nearest hundredth.

SOLUTION:

$$\begin{array}{r} 1.\ 7\ 3\ 2 \\ \sqrt{3.00'\ 00'\ 00} \end{array}$$

$$1^2 = \underline{1}$$

$$20 \qquad 2\ 00$$

$$7 \times 27 = \underline{1\ 89}$$

$$340 \qquad 11\ 00$$

$$3 \times 343 = \qquad \underline{10\ 29}$$

$$3460 \qquad 71\ 00$$

$$2 \times 3462 = \qquad \underline{69\ 24}$$

Answer: The square root of 3 is 1.73 to the nearest hundredth.

9. When more complex items are raised to powers, the same basic rules apply.

   a. To find the power of some multiplied item, find the power of each multiplicand and multiply those powers together.

   Example: $(4x)^2 = (4x)(4x) = (4)(4)(x)(x)$
   $= (4x)^2(x)^2 = 16x^2$

   Example: $(2xy)^4 = (2)^4(x)^4(y)^4 = 16x^4y^4$

   b. To find the power of some divided item or fraction, find the power of each part of the fraction and then divide in the manner of the original fraction.

   Example: $\left(\dfrac{2}{x}\right)^2 = \left(\dfrac{2}{x}\right)\left(\dfrac{2}{x}\right) = \left(\dfrac{4}{x^2}\right)$

   c. To find the result when two powers of the same base are multiplied together, *add* the exponents. You add the exponents because you are adding to the length of the string of the same base all being multiplied together.

   Example: $(x^2)(x^3) = (x)(x) \bullet (x)(x)(x) = xxxxx$
   $= x^{(2+3)} = x^5$

   Example: $2^a \bullet 2^b = 2^{(a+b)}$

   d. To find the result when a power is raised to an exponent, *multiply* the exponents. You multiply the exponents together because you are multiplying the length of the string of the same base all being multiplied together.

Example:

$$(x^2)^3 = (x^2)(x^2)(x^2) = xxxxxx = x^{(2\bullet3)} = x^6$$

   e. When a power is divided by another power of the same base, the result is found by subtracting the exponent in the denominator (bottom) from the exponent in the numerator (top).

   Example: $\dfrac{x^3}{x^2} = \dfrac{xxx}{xx} = x^{(3-2)} = x^1 = x$

   Note: Any base to the first power, x^1, equals the base.

   Example: $\dfrac{x^9}{x^6} = x^{(9-6)} = x^3$

   Example: $\dfrac{x^2}{x^2} = \dfrac{xx}{xx} = x^{(2-2)} = x^0 = 1$

   Note: Any base to the "zero-th" power, x^0, equals 1.

   Example: $\dfrac{x^3}{x^4} = \dfrac{xxx}{xxxx} = \dfrac{1}{x} = x^{(3-4)} = x^{-1}$

   f. A **negative exponent** is a reciprocal, as discussed in the earlier section on fractions.

   Example: $z^{-3} = \left(\dfrac{z}{1}\right)^{-3} = \left(\dfrac{1}{z}\right)^{+3} = \dfrac{1^3}{z^3} = \dfrac{1}{z^3}$

   Example: $(3p)^{-2} = \dfrac{1}{(3p)^{+2}} = \dfrac{1}{9p^2}$

   Example: $(r^{-3})^{-6} = \dfrac{1}{(r^{-3})^{+6}} = \dfrac{1}{\left(\dfrac{1}{r^3}\right)^6} = \dfrac{1}{\dfrac{1}{r^{18}}}$

   $$= (1)\left(\dfrac{r^{18}}{1}\right) = r^{18}$$

   or $(r^{-3})^{-6} = r^{(-3x-6)} = r^{+18}$

10. Some problems require that different powers be grouped together. Depending on the relationships, they can be grouped by doing the processes explained in #9 in the reverse direction.

   Example: $9x^2 = 3^2 \bullet x^2 = (3x)^2$

   Example: $\dfrac{81}{y^2} = \dfrac{9^2}{y^2} = \left(\dfrac{9}{y}\right)^2$

Example: $m^{12} = (m^5)(m^7)$ or $(m^{10})(m^2)$, etc.

Example: $z^{24} = (z^6)^4$ or $(z^8)^3$, etc.

11. The conditions under which radicals can be added or subtracted are much the same as the conditions for letters in an algebraic expression. The radicals act as a label, or unit, and must therefore be exactly the same. In adding or subtracting, we add or subtract the coefficients, or rational parts, and carry the radical along as a label, which does not change.

Example: $\sqrt{2} + \sqrt{3}$ cannot be added

            $\sqrt{2} + 3\sqrt{2}$ can be added

            $4\sqrt{2} + 5\sqrt{2} = 9\sqrt{2}$

Often, when radicals to be added or subtracted are not the same, simplification of one or more radicals will make them the same. To simplify a radical, we remove any perfect square factors from underneath the radical sign.

Example: $\sqrt{12} = \sqrt{4}\sqrt{3} = 2\sqrt{3}$

            $\sqrt{27} = \sqrt{9}\sqrt{3} = 3\sqrt{3}$

If we wish to add $\sqrt{12} + \sqrt{27}$, we must first simplify each one. Adding the simplified radicals gives a sum of $5\sqrt{3}$.

Illustration: $\sqrt{125} + \sqrt{20} - \sqrt{500}$

SOLUTION:

$\sqrt{25}\sqrt{5} + \sqrt{4}\sqrt{5} - \sqrt{100}\sqrt{5} =$
$5\sqrt{5} + 2\sqrt{5} - 10\sqrt{5} =$
$-3\sqrt{5}$

Answer: $-3\sqrt{5}$

12. In multiplication and division we again treat the radicals as we would letters in an algebraic expression. They are factors and must be treated as such.

Example: $(\sqrt{2})(\sqrt{3}) = \sqrt{(2)\,(3)} = \sqrt{6}$

Example: $4\sqrt{2} \cdot 5\sqrt{3} = 20 \cdot \sqrt{6}$

Example: $(3\sqrt{2})^2 = 3\sqrt{2} \cdot 3\sqrt{2} = 9 \cdot 2 = 18$

Example: $\dfrac{\sqrt{8}}{\sqrt{2}} = \sqrt{4} = 2$

Example: $\dfrac{10\sqrt{20}}{\sqrt{4}} = \dfrac{\overset{5}{10}\sqrt{20}}{2} = 5\sqrt{20} = 5\sqrt{4}\sqrt{5} = 10\sqrt{5}$

Example: $\sqrt{2}(\sqrt{8} + \sqrt{18}) = \sqrt{16} + \sqrt{36}$
                      $= 4 + 6 = 10$

13. In simplifying radicals that contain several terms under the radical sign, we must combine terms before taking the square root.

Example: $\sqrt{16 + 9} = \sqrt{25} = 5$

    Note: It is not true that $\sqrt{16 + 9} = \sqrt{16} + \sqrt{9}$, which would be $4 + 3$, or 7.

Example:
$$\sqrt{\dfrac{x^2}{16} - \dfrac{x^2}{25}} = \sqrt{\dfrac{25x^2 - 16x^2}{400}}$$
$$= \sqrt{\dfrac{9x^2}{400}} = \dfrac{3|x|}{20}$$

Practice Problems Involving Roots

1. Combine $4\sqrt{27} - 2\sqrt{48} + \sqrt{147}$

   (A) $27\sqrt{3}$

   (B) $-3\sqrt{3}$

   (C) $9\sqrt{3}$

   (D) $10\sqrt{3}$

   (E) $11\sqrt{3}$

2. Combine $\sqrt{80} + \sqrt{45} - \sqrt{20}$

   (A) $9\sqrt{5}$

   (B) $5\sqrt{5}$

   (C) $-\sqrt{5}$

   (D) $3\sqrt{5}$

   (E) $-2\sqrt{5}$

3. Combine $6\sqrt{5} + 3\sqrt{2} - 4\sqrt{5} + \sqrt{2}$

(A) 8

(B) $2\sqrt{5} + 3\sqrt{2}$

(C) $2\sqrt{5} + 4\sqrt{2}$

(D) $5\sqrt{7}$

(E) 5

4. Combine $\frac{1}{2}\sqrt{180} + \frac{1}{3}\sqrt{45} - \frac{2}{5}\sqrt{20}$

(A) $3\sqrt{10} + \sqrt{15} + 2\sqrt{2}$

(B) $\frac{16}{5}\sqrt{5}$

(C) $\sqrt{97}$

(D) $\frac{24}{5}\sqrt{5}$

(E) none of these

5. Combine $5\sqrt{mn} - 3\sqrt{mn} - 2\sqrt{mn}$

(A) 0

(B) 1

(C) $\sqrt{mn}$

(D) mn

(E) $-\sqrt{mn}$

6. Multiply and simplify: $2\sqrt{18} \cdot 6\sqrt{2}$

(A) 72

(B) 48

(C) $12\sqrt{6}$

(D) $8\sqrt{6}$

(E) 36

7. Find $(3\sqrt{3})^3$

(A) $27\sqrt{3}$

(B) $81\sqrt{3}$

(C) 81

(D) $9\sqrt{3}$

(E) 243

8. Multiply and simplify: $\frac{1}{2}\sqrt{2}(\sqrt{6} + \frac{1}{2}\sqrt{2})$

(A) $\sqrt{3} + \frac{1}{2}$

(B) $\frac{1}{2}\sqrt{3}$

(C) $\sqrt{6} + 1$

(D) $\sqrt{6} + \frac{1}{2}$

(E) $\sqrt{6} + 2$

9. Divide and simplify: $\dfrac{\sqrt{32b^3}}{\sqrt{8b}}$

(A) $2\sqrt{b}$

(B) $\sqrt{2b}$

(C) $2b$

(D) $\sqrt{2b^2}$

(E) $b\sqrt{2b}$

10. Divide and simplify: $\dfrac{15\sqrt{96}}{5\sqrt{2}}$

(A) $7\sqrt{3}$

(B) $7\sqrt{12}$

(C) $11\sqrt{3}$

(D) $12\sqrt{3}$

(E) $40\sqrt{3}$

11. Simplify $\sqrt{\dfrac{x^2}{9} + \dfrac{x^2}{16}}$

(A) $\dfrac{25x^2}{144}$

(B) $\dfrac{5|x|}{12}$

(C) $\dfrac{5x^2}{12}$

(D) $\dfrac{|x|}{7}$

(E) $\dfrac{7|x|}{12}$

12. Simplify $\sqrt{36y^2 + 64x^2}$

(A) $6y + 8x$

(B) $10xy$

(C) $6y^2 + 8x^2$

(D) $10x^2y^2$

(E) $2\sqrt{9y^2 + 16x^2}$

13. Simplify $\sqrt{\dfrac{x^2}{64} - \dfrac{x^2}{100}}$

(A) $\dfrac{x}{40}$

(B) $-\dfrac{x}{2}$

(C) $\dfrac{x}{2}$

(D) $\dfrac{3|x|}{40}$

(E) $\dfrac{3x}{80}$

14. Simplify $\sqrt{\dfrac{y^2}{2} - \dfrac{y^2}{18}}$

(A) $\dfrac{2|y|}{3}$

(B) $\dfrac{|y|\sqrt{5}}{3}$

(C) $\dfrac{10|y|}{3}$

(D) $\dfrac{|y|\sqrt{3}}{6}$

(E) cannot be simplified

15. $\sqrt{a^2 + b^2}$ is equal to

(A) $a + b$

(B) $a - b$

(C) $\sqrt{a^2} + \sqrt{b^2}$

(D) $(a + b)(a - b)$

(E) none of these

16. Which of the following square roots can be found exactly?

(A) $\sqrt{.4}$

(B) $\sqrt{.9}$

(C) $\sqrt{.09}$

(D) $\sqrt{.02}$

(E) $\sqrt{.025}$

Root Problems—Correct Answers

1. **(E)**	9. **(C)**
2. **(B)**	10. **(D)**
3. **(C)**	11. **(B)**
4. **(B)**	12. **(E)**
5. **(A)**	13. **(D)**
6. **(A)**	14. **(A)**
7. **(B)**	15. **(E)**
8. **(A)**	16. **(C)**

Problem Solutions—Roots

1. $4\sqrt{27} = 4\sqrt{9}\sqrt{3} = 12\sqrt{3}$

   $2\sqrt{48} = 2\sqrt{16}\sqrt{3} = 8\sqrt{3}$

   $\sqrt{147} = \sqrt{49}\sqrt{3} = 7\sqrt{3}$

   $12\sqrt{3} - 8\sqrt{3} + 7\sqrt{3} = 11\sqrt{3}$

   Answer: **(E)** $11\sqrt{3}$

2. $\sqrt{80} = \sqrt{16}\sqrt{5} = 4\sqrt{5}$

   $\sqrt{45} = \sqrt{9}\sqrt{5} = 3\sqrt{5}$

   $\sqrt{20} = \sqrt{4}\sqrt{5} = 2\sqrt{5}$

   $4\sqrt{5} + 3\sqrt{5} - 2\sqrt{5} = 5\sqrt{5}$

   Answer: **(B)** $5\sqrt{5}$

3. Only terms with the same radical may be combined.

   $6\sqrt{5} - 4\sqrt{5} = 2\sqrt{5}$

   $3\sqrt{2} + \sqrt{2} = 4\sqrt{2}$

   Therefore, we have $2\sqrt{5} + 4\sqrt{2}$

   Answer: **(C)** $2\sqrt{5} + 4\sqrt{2}$

4. $\dfrac{1}{2}\sqrt{80} = \dfrac{1}{2}\sqrt{36}\sqrt{5} = 3\sqrt{5}$

   $\dfrac{1}{3}\sqrt{45} = \dfrac{1}{3}\sqrt{9}\sqrt{5} = \sqrt{5}$

   $\dfrac{2}{5}\sqrt{20} = \dfrac{2}{5}\sqrt{4}\sqrt{5} = \dfrac{4}{5}\sqrt{5}$

   $3\sqrt{5} + \sqrt{5} - \dfrac{4}{5}\sqrt{5} = 4\sqrt{5} - \dfrac{4}{5}\sqrt{5} = 3\dfrac{1}{5}\sqrt{5} =$

   $\dfrac{16}{5}\sqrt{5}$

   Answer: **(B)** $\dfrac{16}{5}\sqrt{5}$

5. $5\sqrt{mn} - 5\sqrt{mn} = 0$

   Answer: **(A)** 0

6. $2\sqrt{18} \cdot 6\sqrt{2} = 12\sqrt{36} = 12 \cdot 6 = 72$

   Answer: **(A)** 72

7. $3\sqrt{3} \cdot 3\sqrt{3} \cdot 3\sqrt{3} = 27(3\sqrt{3}) = 81\sqrt{3}$

   Answer: **(B)**

8. Using the distributive law, we have

   $\frac{1}{2}\sqrt{12} + \frac{1}{4} \cdot 2 = \frac{1}{2}\sqrt{4}\sqrt{3} + \frac{1}{2} = \sqrt{3} + \frac{1}{2}$

   Answer: **(A)** $\sqrt{3} + \frac{1}{2}$

9. Dividing the numbers in the radical sign, we have
   $\sqrt{4b^2} = 2b$

   Answer: **(C)** $2b$

10. $3\sqrt{48} = 3\sqrt{16}\sqrt{3} = 12\sqrt{3}$

    Answer: **(D)** $12\sqrt{3}$

11. $\sqrt{\frac{16x^2 + 9x^2}{144}} = \sqrt{\frac{25x^2}{144}} = \frac{5x}{12}$

    Answer: **(B)** $\frac{5x}{12}$

12. The terms cannot be combined, and it is not possible to take the square root of separated terms.

    Answer: **(E)** cannot be simplified

13. $\sqrt{\frac{100x^2 - 64x^2}{6400}} = \sqrt{\frac{36x^2}{6400}} = \frac{6x}{80} = \frac{3x}{40}$

    Answer: **(D)** $\frac{3x}{40}$

14. $\sqrt{\frac{18y^2 - 2y^2}{36}} = \sqrt{\frac{16y^2}{36}} = \frac{4y}{6} = \frac{2y}{3}$

    Answer: **(A)** $\frac{2y}{3}$

15. It is not possible to find the square root of separate terms.

    Answer: **(E)** none of these

16. In order to take the square root of a decimal, it must have an even number of decimal places so that its square root will have exactly half as many. In addition to this, the digits must form a perfect square $\left(\sqrt{.09} = .3\right)$.

    Answer: **(C)** $\sqrt{.09}$

Algebraic Fractions

1. In reducing algebraic fractions, we must divide the numerator and denominator by the same factor, just as we do in arithmetic. We can never cancel terms, as this would be adding or subtracting the same number from the numerator and denominator, which changes the value of the fraction. When we reduce $\frac{6}{8}$ to $\frac{3}{4}$, we are really saying that $\frac{6}{8} = \frac{2 \cdot 3}{2 \cdot 4}$ and then dividing numerator and denominator by 2. We do not say $\frac{6}{8} = \frac{3+3}{3+5}$ and then say $\frac{6}{8} = \frac{3}{5}$. This is faulty reasoning in algebra as well. If we have $\frac{6t}{8t}$, we can divide numerator and denominator by 2t, giving $\frac{3}{4}$ as an answer. However, if we have $\frac{6+t}{8+t}$, we can do no more, as there is no factor that divides into the *entire* numerator as well as the *entire* denominator. Cancelling terms is one of the most frequent student errors. Don't get caught! Be careful!

   Illustration: Reduce $\frac{3x^2 + 6x}{4x^3 + 8x^2}$ to its lowest terms.

   SOLUTION: Factoring the numerator and denominator, we have $\frac{3x(x+2)}{4x^2(x+2)}$. The factors common to both numerator and denominator are x and $(x + 2)$. Dividing these out, we arrive at $\frac{3}{4x}$.

   Answer: $\frac{3}{4x}$

2. In adding or subtracting fractions, we must work with a common denominator and the same short-cuts we used in arithmetic.

Illustration: Find the sum of $\dfrac{1}{a}$ and $\dfrac{1}{b}$.

SOLUTION: Remember to add the two cross-products and put the sum over the denominator product.

Answer: $\dfrac{b+a}{ab}$

Illustration: Add: $\dfrac{2n}{3}+\dfrac{3n}{2}$

SOLUTION: $\dfrac{4n+9n}{6}=\dfrac{13n}{6}$

Answer: $\dfrac{13n}{6}$

3. In multiplying or dividing fractions, we may cancel a factor common to any numerator and any denominator. Always remember to invert the fraction following the division sign. Where exponents are involved, they are added in multiplication and subtracted in division.

Illustration: Find the product of $\dfrac{a^3}{b^2}$ and $\dfrac{b^3}{a^2}$.

SOLUTION: We divide a^2 into the first numerator and second denominator, giving $\dfrac{a}{b^2}\cdot\dfrac{b^3}{1}$. Then we divide b^2 into the first denominator and second numerator, giving $\dfrac{a}{1}\cdot\dfrac{b}{1}$. Finally, we multiply the resulting fractions, giving an answer of ab.

Answer: ab

Illustration: Divide $\dfrac{6x^2y}{5}$ by $2x^3$.

SOLUTION: $\dfrac{6x^2y}{5}\cdot\dfrac{1}{2x^3}$. Divide the first numerator and second denominator by $2x^2$, giving $\dfrac{3y}{5}\cdot\dfrac{1}{x}$. Multiplying the resulting fractions, we get $\dfrac{3y}{5x}$.

Answer: $\dfrac{3y}{5x}$

4. Complex algebraic fractions are simplified by the same methods used in arithmetic. Multiply *each term* of the complex fraction by the lowest quantity that will eliminate the fraction within the fraction.

Illustration: $\dfrac{\dfrac{1}{a}+\dfrac{1}{b}}{ab}$

SOLUTION: We must multiply *each term* by ab, giving $\dfrac{b+a}{a^2b^2}$. Since no reduction beyond this is possible, $\dfrac{b+a}{a^2b^2}$ is our final answer. Remember *never* to cancel terms unless they apply to the entire numerator or the entire denominator.

Answer: $\dfrac{b+a}{a^2b^2}$

Practice Problems Involving Algebraic Fractions

1. Find the sum of $\dfrac{n}{6}+\dfrac{2n}{5}$.

   (A) $\dfrac{13n}{30}$

   (B) $17n$

   (C) $\dfrac{3n}{30}$

   (D) $\dfrac{17n}{30}$

   (E) $\dfrac{3n}{11}$

2. Combine into a single fraction: $1-\dfrac{x}{y}$

(A) $\dfrac{1-x}{y}$

(B) $\dfrac{y-x}{y}$

(C) $\dfrac{x-y}{y}$

(D) $\dfrac{1-x}{1-y}$

(E) $\dfrac{y-x}{xy}$

3. Divide $\dfrac{x-y}{x+y}$ by $\dfrac{y-x}{y+x}$

(A) 1

(B) -1

(C) $\dfrac{(x-y)^2}{(x+y)^2}$

(D) $-\dfrac{(x-y)^2}{(x+y)^2}$

(E) 0

4. Simplify: $\dfrac{1+\frac{1}{x}}{\frac{y}{x}}$

(A) $\dfrac{x+1}{y}$

(B) $\dfrac{x+1}{x}$

(C) $\dfrac{x+1}{xy}$

(D) $\dfrac{x^2+1}{xy}$

(E) $\dfrac{y+1}{y}$

5. Find an expression equivalent to $\left(\dfrac{2x^2}{y}\right)^3$

(A) $\dfrac{8x^5}{3y}$

(B) $\dfrac{6x^6}{y^3}$

(C) $\dfrac{6x^5}{y^3}$

(D) $\dfrac{8x^5}{y^3}$

(E) $\dfrac{8x^6}{y^3}$

6. Simplify: $\dfrac{\frac{1}{x}+\frac{1}{y}}{3}$

(A) $\dfrac{3x+3y}{xy}$

(B) $\dfrac{3xy}{x+y}$

(C) $\dfrac{xy}{3}$

(D) $\dfrac{y+x}{3xy}$

(E) $\dfrac{y+x}{3}$

7. $\dfrac{1}{a}+\dfrac{1}{b}=7$ and $\dfrac{1}{a}-\dfrac{1}{b}=3$.

Find $\dfrac{1}{a^2}-\dfrac{1}{b^2}$.

(A) 10

(B) 7

(C) 3

(D) 21

(E) 4

Algebraic Fractions—Correct Answers

1. **(D)**	5. **(E)**
2. **(B)**	6. **(D)**
3. **(B)**	7. **(D)**
4. **(A)**	

Solutions—Algebraic Fractions

1. $\dfrac{n}{6}+\dfrac{2n}{5}=\dfrac{5n+12n}{30}=\dfrac{17n}{30}$

Answer: **(D)** $\dfrac{17n}{30}$

2. $\dfrac{1}{1}-\dfrac{x}{y}=\dfrac{y-x}{y}$

Answer: **(B)** $\dfrac{y-x}{y}$

3. $\dfrac{x-y}{x+y} \cdot \dfrac{y+x}{y-x}$

Since addition is commutative, we may cancel $x + y$ with $y + x$, as they are the same quantity. However, subtraction is not commutative, so we may not cancel $x - y$ with $y - x$, as they are *not* the same quantity. We can change the form of $y - x$ by factoring out a -1. Thus, $y - x = (-1)(x - y)$. In this form, we can cancel $x - y$, leaving an answer of $\dfrac{1}{-1}$, or -1.

Answer: **(B)** -1

4. Multiply every term in the fraction by x, giving $\dfrac{x+1}{y}$.

Answer: **(A)** $\dfrac{x+1}{y}$

5. $\dfrac{2x^2}{y} \cdot \dfrac{2x^2}{y} \cdot \dfrac{2x^2}{y} = \dfrac{8x^6}{y^3}$

Answer: **(E)** $\dfrac{8x^6}{y^3}$

6. Multiply every term of the fraction by xy, giving $\dfrac{y+x}{3xy}$.

Answer: **(D)** $\dfrac{y+x}{3xy}$

7. $\dfrac{1}{a^2} - \dfrac{1}{b^2}$ is equivalent to $\left(\dfrac{1}{a} + \dfrac{1}{b}\right)\left(\dfrac{1}{a} - \dfrac{1}{b}\right)$.

We therefore multiply 7 by 3 for an answer of 21.

Answer: **(D)** 21

Problem-Solving in Algebra

1. In solving verbal problems, the most important technique is to read accurately. Be sure you understand clearly what you are asked to find. Then try to evaluate the problem in common sense terms; use this to eliminate answer choices.

Example: If two people are working together, their combined speed is greater than either one, but not more than twice as fast as the fastest one.

Example: The total number of the correct answers cannot be greater than the total number of answers. Thus if x questions are asked and you are to determine from other information how many correct answers there were, they cannot come to $2x$.

2. The next step, when common sense alone is not enough, is to translate the problem into algebra. Keep it as simple as possible.

Example: 24 is what percent of 12?
Translation: $24 = x\% \cdot 12$

$$\text{or } 24 = x \tfrac{1}{100} \cdot 12$$
$$\text{or } 24 = \tfrac{x}{100} \cdot \tfrac{12}{1}$$

Divide both sides by 12.

$$2 = \tfrac{x}{100}$$

Multiply both sides by 100.

$$200 = x$$

3. Be alert for the "hidden equation." This is some necessary information so obvious in the stated situation that the question assumes that you know it.

Example: Boys plus girls = total class.

Example: Imported wine plus domestic wine = all wine.

Example: The wall and floor, or the shadow and the building, make a right angle (thus permitting use of the Pythagorean Theorem).

4. Always remember that a variable (letter) can have any value whatsoever within the terms of the problem. Keep the possibility of fractional and negative values constantly in mind.

5. **Manipulating Equations.** You can perform any mathematical function you think helpful to one side of the equation, *provided* you do precisely the same thing to the other side of the equation. You can also substitute one side of an equality for the other in another equation.

6. **Manipulating Inequalities.** You can add to or subtract from both sides of an inequality without changing the direction of the inequality.

   Example: $8 > 5$
   $8 + 10 > 5 + 10$
   $18 > 15$

   Example: $3x > y + z$
   $3x + 5 > y + z + 5$

   You can also multiply or divide both sides of the inequality by any POSITIVE number without changing the direction of the inequality.

   Example: $12 > 4$
   $3(12) > 3(4)$
   $36 > 12$

   Example: $x > y$
   $3x > 3y$

   If you multiply or divide an inequality by a NEGATIVE number, you REVERSE the direction of the inequality.

   Example: $4 > 3$
   $(-2)(4) < (-2)(3)$
   $-8 < -6$

   Example: $x^2 y > z^2 x$
   $-3(x^2 y) < -3(z^2 x)$

7. **Solving Equations.** The first step is to determine what quantity or letter you wish to isolate. Solving an equation for x means getting x on one side of the equal sign and everything else on the other.

   Example: $5x + 3 = y$
   Subtract 3.
   $5x = y - 3$
   Divide by 5.
   $x = \dfrac{y - 3}{5}$

8. If there are two variables in an equation, it may be helpful to put all expressions containing one variable on one side and all the others on the other.

9. Expressing x in terms of y means having an equation with x alone on one side and some expression of y on the other, such as $x = 4y^2 + 3y + 4$.

10. We will review some of the frequently encountered types of algebra problems, although not every problem you may get will fall into one of these categories. However, thoroughly familiarizing yourself with the types of problems that follow will help you to translate and solve all kinds of verbal problems.

A. Coin Problems

In solving coin problems, it is best to change the value of all monies involved to cents before writing an equation. Thus, the number of nickels must be multiplied by 5 to give their value in cents; dimes must be multiplied by 10; quarters by 25; half-dollars by 50; and dollars by 100.

Illustration: Richard has $3.50 consisting of nickels and dimes. If he has 5 more dimes than nickels, how many dimes does he have?

SOLUTION:

Let x = the number of nickels
$x + 5$ = the number of dimes
$5x$ = the value of the nickels in cents
$10x + 50$ = the value of the dimes in cents
350 = the value of the money he has in cents
$5x + 10x + 50 = 350$
$15x = 300$
$x = 20$

Answer: He has 20 nickels and 25 dimes.

In a problem such as this, you can be sure that 20 would be among the multiple-choice answers. You must be sure to read carefully what you are asked to find and then continue until you have found the quantity sought.

B. Consecutive Integer Problems

Consecutive integers are one apart and can be represented by $x, x + 1, x + 2$, etc. Consecutive even or odd integers are two apart and can be represented by $x, x + 2, x + 4$, etc.

Illustration: Three consecutive odd integers have a sum of 33. Find the average of these integers.

SOLUTION: Represent the integers as x, $x + 2$, and $x + 4$. Write an equation indicating the sum is 33.

$$3x + 6 = 33$$
$$3x = 27$$
$$x = 9$$

The integers are 9, 11, and 13. In the case of evenly spaced numbers such as these, the average is the middle number, 11. Since the sum of the three numbers was given originally, all we really had to do was to divide this sum by 3 to find the average, without ever knowing what the numbers were.

Answer: 11

C. Age Problems

Problems of this type usually involve a comparison of ages at the present time, several years from now, or several years ago. A person's age x years from now is found by adding x to his present age. A person's age x years ago is found by subtracting x from his present age.

Illustration: Michelle was 12 years old y years ago. Represent her age b years from now.

SOLUTION: Her present age is $12 + y$. In b years, her age will be $12 + y + b$.

Answer: $12 + y + b$

D. Interest Problems

The annual amount of interest paid on an investment is found by multiplying the amount of prin-cipal invested by the rate (percent) of interest paid.

$$\text{Principal} \cdot \text{Rate} = \text{Interest income}$$

Illustration: Mr. Strauss invests $4,000, part at 6% and part at 7%. His income from these investments in one year is $250. Find the amount invested at 7%.

SOLUTION: Represent each investment.

Let $x =$ the amount invested at 7%. Always try to let x represent what you are looking for.
$4000 - x =$ the amount invested at 6%
$.07x =$ the income from the 7% investment
$.06(4000 - x) =$ the income from the 6% investment
$.07x + .06(4000 - x) = 250$
$$7x + 6(4000 - x) = 25000$$
$$7x + 24000 - 6x = 25000$$
$$x = 1000$$
Answer: He invested $1,000 at 7%.

E. Mixture

There are two kinds of mixture problems with which you could be familiar. These problems are rare, so this is best regarded as an extra-credit section and not given top priority. The first is sometimes referred to as dry mixture, in which we mix dry ingredients of different values, such as nuts or coffee. Also solved by the same method are problems such as those dealing with tickets at different prices. In solving this type of problem, it is best to organize the data in a chart of three rows and three columns labeled as illustrated in the following problem.

Illustration: A dealer wishes to mix 20 pounds of nuts selling for 45 cents per pound with some more expensive nuts selling for 60 cents per pound, to make a mixture that will sell for 50 cents per pound. How many pounds of the more expensive nuts should he use?

SOLUTION:

	No. of lbs. $\times$	Price/lb. $=$	Total Value
Original	20	.45	.45(20)
Added	x	.60	.60(x)
Mixture	$20 + x$	.50	.50(20+x)

The value of the original nuts plus the value of the added nuts must equal the value of the mixture. Almost all mixture problems require an equation that comes from adding the final column.

$$.45(20) + .60(x) = .50(20 + x)$$

Multiply by 100 to remove decimals.

$$45(20) + 60(x) = 50(20 + x)$$
$$900 + 60x = 1000 + 50x$$
$$10x = 100$$
$$x = 10$$

Answer: He should use 10 lbs. of 60-cent nuts.

In solving the second type, or chemical, mixture problem, we are dealing with percents rather than prices, and amounts instead of value.

Illustration: How much water must be added to 20 gallons of solution that is 30% alcohol to dilute it to a solution that is only 25% alcohol?

SOLUTION:

	No. of gals.	% alcohol	= Amt. alcohol
Original	20	.30	.30(20)
Added	x	0	0
Mixture	$20 + x$	.25	.25(20+x)

Note that the percent of alcohol in water is 0. Had we added pure alcohol to strengthen the solution, the percent would have been 100. The equation again comes from the last column. The amount of alcohol added (none in this case) plus the amount we had to start with must equal the amount of alcohol in the new solution.

$$.30(20) = .25(20 + x)$$
$$30(20) = 25(20 + x)$$
$$600 = 500 + 25x$$
$$100 = 25x$$
$$x = 4$$

Answer: 4 gallons.

F. Motion Problems

The fundamental relationship in all motion problems is that Rate • Time = Distance. The problems at the level of this examination usually derive their equation from a relationship concerning distance. Most problems fall into one of three types.

Motion in opposite directions. When two objects start at the same time and move in opposite directions, or when two objects start at points at a given distance apart and move toward each other until they meet, then the distance the second travels will equal one-half the total distance covered.

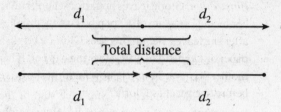

In either of the above cases, $d_1 + d_2 =$ Total distance.

Motion in the same direction. This type of problem is sometimes called the "catch-up" problem. Two objects leave the same place at different times and different rates, but one "catches up" to the other. In such a case, the two distances must be equal.

Round trip. In this type of problem, the rate going is usually different from the rate returning. The times are also different. But if we go somewhere and then return to the starting point, the distances must be the same.

To solve any motion problem, it is helpful to organize the data in a box with columns for rate, time, and distance. A separate line should be used for each moving object. Remember that if the rate is given in *miles per hour,* the time must be in *hours* and the distance in *miles.*

Illustration: Two cars leave a restaurant at 1 P.M., with one car traveling east at 60 miles per hour and the other west at 40 miles per hour along a straight highway. At what time will they be 350 miles apart?

SOLUTION:

	Rate ×	Time =	Distance
Eastbound	60	x	$60x$
Westbound	40	x	$40x$

Notice that the time is unknown, since we must discover the number of hours traveled. However, since the cars start at the same time and stop when they are 350 miles apart, their times are the same.

$$60x + 40x = 350$$
$$100x = 350$$
$$x = 3\frac{1}{2}$$

Answer: In $3\frac{1}{2}$ hours, it will be 4:30 P.M.

Illustration: Gloria leaves home for school, riding her bicycle at a rate of 12 m.p.h. Twenty minutes after she leaves, her mother sees Gloria's English paper on her bed and leaves to bring it to her. If her mother drives at 36 m.p.h, how far must she drive before she reaches Gloria?

SOLUTION:

	Rate $\times$	Time $=$	Distance
Gloria	12	x	$12x$
Mother	36	$x - \frac{1}{3}$	$36(x - \frac{1}{3})$

Notice that 20 minutes has been changed to $\frac{1}{3}$ of an hour. In this problem the times are not equal, but the distances are.

$$12x = 36(x - \frac{1}{3})$$
$$12x = 36x - 12$$
$$12 = 24x$$
$$x = \frac{1}{2}$$

Answer: If Gloria rode for $\frac{1}{2}$ hour at 12 m.p.h., the distance covered was 6 miles.

Illustration: Judy leaves home at 11 A.M. and rides to Mary's house to return her bicycle. She travels at 12 miles per hour and arrives at 11:30 a.m. She turns right around and walks home. How fast does she walk if she returns home at 1 P.M.?

SOLUTION:

	Rate $\times$	Time $=$	Distance
Going	12	$\frac{1}{2}$	6
Return	x	$1\frac{1}{2}$	$\frac{3}{2}x$

The distances are equal.

$$6 = \frac{3}{2}x$$
$$12 = 3x$$
$$x = 4$$

Answer: She walked at 4 m.p.h.

G. Work Problems

In most work problems, a complete job is broken into several parts, each representing a fractional part of the entire job. For each fractional part, which represents the portion completed by one man, one machine, one pipe, etc., the numerator should represent the time actually spent working, while the denominator should represent the total time needed to do the entire job alone. The sum of all the individual fractions should be 1.

Illustration: John can wax his car in 3 hours. Jim can do the same job in 5 hours. How long will it take them if they work together?

SOLUTION: If multiple-choice answers are given, you should realize that the correct answer must be smaller than the shortest time given, for no matter how slow a helper may be, he does do part of the job and therefore it will be completed in less time.

$$\frac{\text{Time spent}}{\text{Total time needed to do job alone}} \quad \overset{\text{John}}{\frac{x}{3}} + \overset{\text{Jim}}{\frac{x}{5}} = 1$$

Multiply by 15 to eliminate fractions.

$$5x + 3x = 15$$
$$8x = 15$$
$$x = 1\frac{7}{8} \text{ hours}$$

1. In general, you need as many equations as you have unknowns in order to get a unique numerical solution.

2. The two methods for coping with two or more equations are called **substitution** and **simultaneous.** They overlap. You have used both many times.

   Substitution. Whenever one unknown equals something, you can substitute that something for it.

Example: (1) $2x + 3y = 14$
              (2) $x = 2y$ } given

Substitute $2y$ for x in first equation.

$$2(2y) + 3y = 14$$
$$4y + 3y = 14$$

Add up y's; divide by 7.

$$7y = 14$$
$$y = 2$$

Substitute for y in second equation.

$$x = 2(2)$$
$$x = 4$$

Simultaneous. Sometimes adding or subtracting whole equations is shorter.

Example: (1) $5x + 3y = 13$
              (2) $2x + 3y = 7$

Subtract (2) from (1).

$$5x + 3y = 13$$
$$-[2x + 3y = 7]$$

$$\overline{[5x - 2x] + [3y - 3y] = [13 - 7]}$$

$$3x = 6$$

Divide by 3.

$$x = 2$$
$$y = 1 \text{ by substitution}$$

Practice Problems—Algebra

1. Sue and Nancy wish to buy a gift for a friend. They combine their money and find they have $4.00, consisting of quarters, dimes, and nickels. If they have 35 coins and the number of quarters is half the number of nickels, how many quarters do they have?

   (A) 5
   (B) 10
   (C) 20
   (D) 3
   (E) 6

2. Three times the first of three consecutive odd integers is 3 more than twice the third. Find the third integer.

   (A) 9
   (B) 11
   (C) 13
   (D) 15
   (E) 7

3. Robert is 15 years older than his brother Stan. However, y years ago Robert was twice as old as Stan. If Stan is now b years old and $b > y$, find the value of $b - y$.

   (A) 13
   (B) 14
   (C) 15
   (D) 16
   (E) 17

4. How many ounces of pure acid must be added to 20 ounces of a solution that is 5% acid to strengthen it to a solution that is 24% acid?

   (A) $2\frac{1}{2}$
   (B) 5
   (C) 6
   (D) $7\frac{1}{2}$
   (E) 10

5. A dealer mixes a lbs. of nuts worth b cents per pound with c lbs. of nuts worth d cents per pound. At what price should he sell a pound of the mixture if he wishes to make a profit of 10 cents per pound?

   (A) $\dfrac{ab + cd}{a + c} + 10$
   (B) $\dfrac{ab + cd}{a + c} + .10$
   (C) $\dfrac{b + d}{a + c} + 10$
   (D) $\dfrac{b + d}{a + c} + .10$
   (E) $\dfrac{b + d + 10}{a + c}$

6. Barbara invests $2,400 in the Security National Bank at 5%. How much additional money must she invest at 8% so that the total annual income will be equal to 6% of her entire investment?

   (A) $2,400
   (B) $3,600
   (C) $1,000
   (D) $3,000
   (E) $1,200

7. Frank left Austin to drive to Boxville at 6:15 p.m. and arrived at 11:45 P.M. If he averaged 30 miles per hour and stopped one hour for dinner, how far is Boxville from Austin?

(A) 120
(B) 135
(C) 180
(D) 165
(E) 150

8. A plane traveling 600 miles per hour is 30 miles from Kennedy Airport at 4:58 P.M. At what time will it arrive at the airport?

(A) 5:00 P.M.
(B) 5:01 P.M.
(C) 5:02 P.M.
(D) 5:20 P.M.
(E) 5:03 P.M.

9. Mr. Bridges can wash his car in 15 minutes, while his son Dave takes twice as long to do the same job. If they work together, how many minutes will the job take them?

(A) 5
(B) $7\frac{1}{2}$
(C) 10
(D) $22\frac{1}{2}$
(E) 30

10. The value of a fraction is $\frac{2}{5}$. If the numerator is decreased by 2 and the denominator increased by 1, the resulting fraction is equivalent to $\frac{1}{4}$. Find the numerator of the original fraction.

(A) 3
(B) 4
(C) 6
(D) 10
(E) 15

Algebra Problem-Solving— Correct Answers

1. (B)	6. (E)
2. (D)	7. (B)
3. (C)	8. (B)
4. (B)	9. (C)
5. (A)	10. (C)

Problem Solutions—Algebra Problem-Solving

1. Let x = number of quarters
    $2x$ = number of nickels
    $35 - 3x$ = number of dimes
    Write all money values in cents.
    $$25(x) + 5(2x) + 10(35 - 3x) = 400$$
    $$25x + 10x + 350 - 30x = 400$$
    $$5x = 50$$
    $$x = 10$$

Answer: (**B**) 10

2. Let x = first integer
    $x + 2$ = second integer
    $x + 4$ = third integer
    $$3(x) = 3 + 2(x + 4)$$
    $$3x = 3 + 2x + 8$$
    $$x = + 11$$
    The third integer is 15.

Answer: (**D**) 15

3. b = Stan's age now
    $b + 15$ = Robert's age now
    $b - y$ = Stan's age y years ago
    $b + 15 - y$ = Robert's age y years ago
    $$b + 15 - y = 2(b - y)$$
    $$b + 15 - y = 2b - 2y$$
    $$15 = b - y$$

Answer: (**C**) 15

4.

	No. of oz.	× % acid	÷ 100 = Amt. acid
Original	20	.05	1
Added	x	1.00	x
Mixture	$20 + x$	.24	$.24(20+x)$

$1 + x = .24(20 + x)$. Multiply by 100 to eliminate decimal.

$$100 + 100x = 480 + 24x$$
$$76x = 380$$
$$x = 5$$

Answer: (**B**) 5

5. The a lbs. of nuts are worth a total of ab cents. The c lbs. of nuts are worth a total of cd cents. The value of the mixture is $ab + cd$ cents. Since there are $a + c$ pounds, each pound is worth $\frac{ab+cd}{a+c}$ cents.

Since the dealer wants to add 10 cents to each pound for profit, and the value of each pound is in cents, we add 10 to the value of each pound.

Answer: **(A)** $\frac{ab+cd}{a+c} + 10$

6. If Barbara invests x additional dollars at 8%, her total investment will amount to $2400 + x$ dollars.

$$.05(2400) + .08(x) = .06(2400 + x)$$
$$5(2400) + 8(x) = 6(2400 + x)$$
$$12,000 + 8x = 14400 + 6x$$
$$2x = 2400$$
$$x = 1200$$

Answer: **(E)** $1,200

7. Total time elapsed is $5\frac{1}{2}$ hours. However, one hour was used for dinner. Therefore, Frank drove at 30 m.p.h. for $4\frac{1}{2}$ hours, covering 135 miles.

Answer: **(B)** 135

8. Time $= \dfrac{\text{Distance}}{\text{Rate}} = \dfrac{30}{600} = \dfrac{1}{20}$ hour, or 3 minutes.

Answer: **(B)** 5:01 P.M.

9. Dave takes 30 minutes to wash the car alone.
$$\frac{x}{15} + \frac{x}{30} = 1$$
$$2x + x = 30$$
$$3x = 30$$
$$x = 10$$

Answer: **(C)** 10

10. Let $2x$ = original numerator
    $5x$ = original denominator
$$\frac{2x-2}{5x+1} = \frac{1}{4} \quad \text{Cross-multiply}$$
$$8x - 8 = 5x + 1$$
$$3x = 9$$
$$x = 3$$
Original numerator is $2(3)$, or 6.

Answer: (C) 6

Polynomial Multiplication and Factoring

1. A polynomial is any expression with two or more terms, such as $2x + y$ or $3z + 9m^2$.

2. A single term multiplied by another expression must multiply *every* term in the second expression.

    Example: $4(x + y + 2z) = 4x + 4y + 8z$

3. The same holds true for division.

    Example: $\dfrac{(a+b+3c)}{3} = \dfrac{a}{3} + \dfrac{b}{3} + \dfrac{3c}{3}$
    $= \dfrac{a}{3} + \dfrac{b}{3} + c$

4. The FOIL method should be used when multiplying two binomials together.

    Example: $(x + y)(x + y)$

    First $\quad (x + y)(x + y) = x^2$

    Outer $\quad (x + y)(x + y) = xy$

    Inner $\quad (x + y)(x + y) = xy$

    Last $\quad (x + y)(x + y) = y^2$
    $\quad\quad\quad (x + y)(x + y) = x^2 + 2xy + y^2$

5. You should know these three equivalencies by heart for the GRE.

    $(x + y)^2 = (x + y)(x + y) = x^2 + 2xy + y^2$
    $(x - y)^2 = (x - y)(x - y) = x^2 - 2xy + y^2$
    $(x + y)(x - y) = x^2 - y^2$

    Work all three out with the FOIL method. The x or y could stand for a letter, a number, or an expression.

    Example: $(m + 3)^2 = m^2 + 2 \cdot 3 \cdot m + 3^2$
    $= m^2 + 6m + 9$

    Example: $(2k - p)^2 = (2k)^2 - 2 \cdot 2k \cdot p + p^2$
    $= 4k^2 - 4kp + p^2$

6. You will not need much factoring on the exam. Most of what you do need was covered in the preceding points—if you just reverse the process of multiplication.

Example: $3x + 6xy = 3x(1 + 2y)$

Example: $2xyz + 4xy = 2xy(z + 2)$

7. One special situation (called a quadratic equation) occurs when an algebraic multiplication equals zero. Since zero can only be achieved in multiplication by multiplying by zero itself, one of the factors must be zero.

Example: $(x + 1)(x + 2) = 0$
Therefore, either $x + 1 = 0, x = -1$
$\qquad$ or $x + 2 = 0, x = -2$.

In such a situation you simply have to live with two possible answers. This uncertainty may be important in Quantitative Comparison questions.

8. You may also need to factor to achieve a quadratic format.

Example: $x^2 + 2x + 1 \qquad = 0$
$\qquad (x + 1)(x + 1) = 0$

Thus, $x + 1 = 0$
$\qquad x = -1$ since both factors are the same.

Geometry

Symbols

The most common symbols used in GRE geometry problems are listed below. The concepts behind the symbols will be explained in this section.

Angles
$\angle$ or $\measuredangle$ angle ($\angle C$ = angle C or $\measuredangle C$ = angle C)
$\llcorner$ right angle (90°)

Lines
$\perp$ perpendicular, at right angles to
$\parallel$ parallel (line B $\parallel$ line C)
$\overline{BD}$ line or line segment BD

Circles
$\odot$ circle
$\overset{\frown}{AC}$ arc AC

Angles

1. a. An **angle** is the figure formed by two lines meeting at a point.

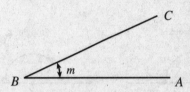

b. The point B is the **vertex** of the angle and the lines BA and BC are the **sides** of the angle.

2. There are three common ways of naming an angle:

a. By a small letter or figure written within the angle, as $\angle m$.

b. By a capital letter at its vertex, as $\angle B$.

c. By three capital letters, the middle letter being the vertex letter, as $\angle ABC$.

3. a. When two straight lines intersect (cut each other), four angles are formed. If these four angles are equal, each angle is a **right angle** and contains 90°. The symbol $\llcorner$ is used to indicate a right angle.

Example

$\measuredangle ABC$ is a right angle.

b. An angle less than a right angle is an **acute angle.**

c. If the two sides of an angle extend in opposite directions forming a straight line, the angle is a **straight angle** and contains 180°.

d. An angle greater than a right angle (90°) and less than a straight angle (180°) is an **obtuse angle.**

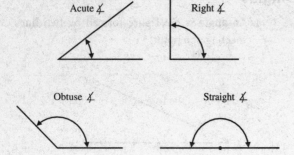

Acute ∡   Right ∡

Obtuse ∡   Straight ∡

4. a. Two angles are **complementary** if their sum is 90°.

b. To find the complement of an angle, subtract the given number of degrees from 90°.

Example: The complement of 60° is 90° – 60° = 30°.

5. a. Two angles are **supplementary** if their sum is 180°.

b. To find the supplement of an angle, subtract the given number of degrees from 180°.

Example: The supplement of 60° is 180° – 60° = 120°.

Lines

6. a. Two lines are **perpendicular** to each other if they meet to form a right angle. The symbol ⊥ is used to indicate that the lines are perpendicular.

Example: ∠ABC is a right angle. Therefore, AB ⊥ BC.

b. Lines that do not meet no matter how far they are extended are called **parallel lines.** Parallel lines are always the same perpendicular distance from each other. The symbol ∥ is used to indicate that two lines are parallel.

Example: AB ∥ CD

Triangles

7. A **triangle** is a closed, three-sided figure. The figures below are all triangles.

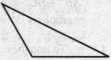

8. a. The sum of the three angles of a triangle is 180°.

b. To find an angle of a triangle when you are given the other two angles, add the given angles and subtract their sum from 180°.

Illustration: Two angles of a triangle are 60° and 40°. Find the third angle.

SOLUTION: 60° + 40° = 100°
180° – 100° = 80°

Answer: The third angle is 80°.

9. a. A triangle that has two equal sides is called an **isosceles triangle.**

b. In an isosceles triangle, the angles opposite the equal sides are also equal.

10. a. A triangle that has all three sides equal is called an **equilateral triangle.**

b. Each angle of an equilateral triangle is 60°.

11. a. A triangle that has a right angle is called a **right triangle.**

b. In a right triangle, the two acute angles are complementary.

c. In a right triangle, the side opposite the right angle is called the **hypotenuse** and is the longest side. The other two sides are called **legs.**

Example: AC is the hypotenuse.
AB and BC are the legs.

12. The **Pythagorean Theorem** states that in a right triangle the square of the hypotenuse equals the sum of the squares of the legs. In the triangle above, this would be expressed as $\overline{AB}^2 + \overline{BC}^2 = \overline{AC}^2$. The simplest whole number example is $3^2 + 4^2 = 5^2$.

13. a. To find the hypotenuse of a right triangle when given the legs:

    1. Square each leg.

    2. Add the squares.

    3. Extract the square root of this sum.

    Illustration: In a right triangle the legs are 6 inches and 8 inches. Find the hypotenuse.

    SOLUTION: $6^2 = 36$ $8^2 = 64$
    $$36 + 64 = 100$$
    $$\sqrt{100} = 10$$

    Answer: The hypotenuse is 10 inches.

    b. To find a leg when given the other leg and the hypotenuse of a right triangle:

    1. Square the hypotenuse and the given leg.

    2. Subtract the square of the leg from the square of the hypotenuse.

    3. Extract the square root of this difference.

    Illustration: One leg of a right triangle is 12 feet and the hypotenuse is 20 feet. Find the other leg.

    SOLUTION: $12^2 = 144$ $20^2 = 400$
    $$400 - 144 = 256$$
    $$\sqrt{256} = 16$$

    Answer: The other leg is 16 feet.

14. Within a given triangle, the largest side is opposite the largest angle; the smallest side is opposite the smallest angle; and equal sides are opposite equal angles.

Quadrilaterals

15. a. A **quadrilateral** is a closed, four-sided figure in two dimensions. Common quadrilaterals are the **parallelogram, rectangle,** and **square.**

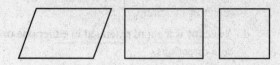

    b. The sum of the four angles of a quadrilateral is 360°.

16. a. A **parallelogram** is a quadrilateral in which both pairs of opposite sides are parallel.

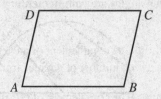

    b. Opposite sides of a parallelogram are also equal.

    c. Opposite angles of a parallelogram are equal.

17. A **rectangle** has all of the properties of a parallelogram. In addition, all four of its angles are right angles.

18. A **square** is a rectangle having the additional property that all four of its sides are equal.

Circles

19. A **circle** is a closed plane curve, all points of which are equidistant from a point within called the **center.**

20. a. A **complete circle** contains 360°.

    b. A **semicircle** contains 180°.

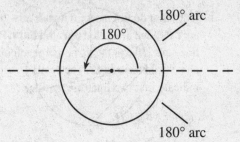

21. a. A **chord** is a line segment connecting any two points on the circle.

b. A **radius** of a circle is a line segment connecting the center with any point on the circle.

c. A **diameter** is a chord passing through the center of the circle.

d. A **secant** is a chord extended in either one or both directions.

e. A **tangent** is a line touching a circle at one and only one point.

f. The **circumference** is the curved line bounding the circle.

g. An **arc** of a circle is any part of the circumference.

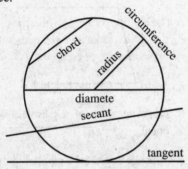

Note: The terms *secant* and *chord* are rarely used on the test.

22. a. A **central angle**, as ∠AOB in the next figure, is an angle whose vertex is the center of the circle and whose sides are radii. A central angle is equal to, or has the same number of degrees as, its intercepted arc.

b. An **inscribed angle,** as ∠MNP, is an angle whose vertex is on the circle and whose sides are chords. An inscribed angle has half the number of degrees of its intercepted arc. ∠MNP intercepts arc MP and has half the degrees of arc MP.

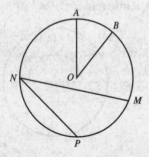

Perimeter

23. The **perimeter** of a two-dimensional figure is the distance around the figure.

Example: The perimeter of the figure above is 9 + 8 + 4 + 3 + 5 = 29.

24. a. The perimeter of a triangle is found by adding all of its sides.

Example: If the sides of a triangle are 4, 5, and 7, its perimeter is 4 + 5 + 7 = 16.

b. If the perimeter and two sides of a triangle are given, the third side is found by adding the two given sides and subtracting this sum from the perimeter.

Illustration: Two sides of a triangle are 12 and 15, and the perimeter is 37. Find the other side.

SOLUTION: 12 + 15 = 27
37 − 27 = 10

Answer: The third side is 10.

25. The perimeter of a rectangle equals twice the sum of the length and the width. The formula is $P = 2(l + w)$.

Example: The perimeter of a rectangle whose length is 7 feet and width is 3 feet equals 2×10 = 20 feet.

26. The perimeter of a square equals one side multiplied by 4. The formula is $P = 4s$.

Example: The perimeter of a square, one side of which is 5 feet, is 4×5 feet = 20 feet.

27. a. The circumference of a circle is equal to the product of the diameter multiplied by π. The formula is $C = \pi d$.

   b. The number π (pi) is approximately equal to $\frac{22}{7}$, or 3.14 (3.1416 for greater accuracy). A problem will usually state which value to use; otherwise, express the answer in terms of "pi," π.

   Example: The circumference of a circle whose diameter is 4 inches = 4π inches; or, if it is stated that $\pi = \frac{22}{7}$, the circumference is $4 \times \frac{22}{7} = \frac{88}{7} = 12\frac{4}{7}$ inches.

   c. Since the diameter is twice the radius, the circumference equals twice the radius multiplied by π. The formula is $C = 2\pi r$.

   Example: If the radius of a circle is 3 inches, then the circumference = 6π inches.

   d. The diameter of a circle equals the circumference divided by π.

   Example: If the circumference of a circle is 11 inches, then, assuming $\pi = \frac{22}{7}$,

   $$\text{diameter} = 11 \div \frac{22}{7} \text{ inches}$$
   $$= {}^1\!\!\not{11} \times \frac{7}{\not{22}_2} \text{ inches}$$
   $$= \frac{7}{2} \text{ inches, or } 3\frac{1}{2} \text{ inches}$$

Area

28. a. In a figure of two dimensions, the total space within the figure is called the **area.**

   b. Area is expressed in square denominations, such as square inches, square centimeters, and square miles.

   c. In computing area, all dimensions must be expressed in the same denomination.

29. The area of a square is equal to the square of the length of any side. The formula is $A = s^2$.

   Example: The area of a square, one side of which is 6 inches, is $6 \times 6 = 36$ square inches.

30. a. The area of a rectangle equals the product of the length multiplied by the width. The length is any side; the width is the side next to the length. The formula is $A = l \times w$.

   Example: If the length of a rectangle is 6 feet and its width 4 feet, then the area is $6 \times 4 = 24$ square feet.

   b. If given the area of a rectangle and one dimension, divide the area by the given dimension to find the other dimension.

   Example: If the area of a rectangle is 48 square feet and one dimension is 4 feet, then the other dimension is $48 \div 4 = 12$ feet.

31. a. The altitude, or height, of a parallelogram is a line drawn from a vertex perpendicular to the opposite side, or base.

   Example: DE is the height.
   AB is the base.

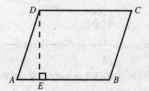

   b. The area of a parallelogram is equal to the product of its base and its height: $A = b \times h$.

   Example: If the base of a parallelogram is 10 centimeters and its height is 5 centimeters, its area is $5 \times 10 = 50$ square centimeters.

   c. If given one of these dimensions and the area, divide the area by the given dimension to find the base or the height of a parallelogram.

   Example: If the area of a parallelogram is 40 square inches and its height is 8 inches, its base is $40 \div 8 = 5$ inches.

32. a. The altitude, or height, of a triangle is a line drawn from a vertex perpendicular to the opposite side, called the base. Each triangle has three sets of altitudes and bases.

b. The area of a triangle is equal to one-half the product of the base and the height: $A = \frac{1}{2} b \times h$.

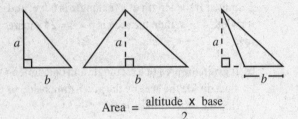

$$\text{Area} = \frac{\text{altitude} \times \text{base}}{2}$$

Example: The area of a triangle having a height of 5 inches and a base of 4 inches is $\frac{1}{2} \times 5 \times 4 = \frac{1}{2} \times 20 = 10$ square inches.

c. In a right triangle, one leg may be considered the height and the other leg the base. Therefore, the area of a right triangle is equal to one-half the product of the legs.

Example: The legs of a right triangle are 3 and 4. Its area is $\frac{1}{2} \times 3 \times 4 = 6$ square units.

33. a. The area of a circle is equal to the radius squared, multiplied by π: $A = \pi r^2$.

Example: If the radius of a circle is 6 inches, then the area $= 36\pi$ square inches.

b. To find the radius of a circle given the area, divide the area by π and find the square root of the quotient.

Example: To find the radius of a circle of area 100π.

$$\frac{100\pi}{\pi} = 100$$

$$\sqrt{100} = 10 = \text{radius}.$$

34. Some figures are composed of several geometric shapes. To find the area of such a figure it is necessary to find the area of each of its parts.

Illustration: Find the area of the figure below:

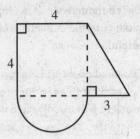

SOLUTION: The figure is composed of three parts: a square of side 4, a semi-circle of diameter 4 (the lower side of the square) and a right triangle with legs 3 and 4 (the right side of the square).

$$\text{Area of square} \ = \ 4^2 = 16$$

$$\text{Area of triangle} \ = \ \frac{1}{2} \times 3 \times 4 = 6$$

Area of semicircle

$$\text{is } \frac{1}{2} \text{ area of circle} = \frac{1}{2} \pi r^2$$

$$\text{Radius} \ = \ \frac{1}{2} \times 4 = 2$$

$$\text{Area} \ = \ \frac{1}{2} \pi r^2$$

$$= \ \frac{1}{2} \times \pi \times 2^2$$

$$= \ 2\pi$$

Answer: Total area $= 16 + 6 + 2\pi = 22 + 2\pi$.

Three-Dimensional Figures

35. a. In a three-dimensional figure, the total space contained within the figure is called the **volume**; it is expressed in **cubic denominations**.

b. The total outside surface is called the **surface area**; it is expressed in **square denominations**.

c. In computing volume and surface area, all dimensions must be expressed in the same denomination.

36. a. A **rectangular solid** is a figure of three dimensions having six rectangular faces meeting each other at right angles. The three dimensions are length, width, and height.

The figure below is a rectangular solid: "*l*" is the length, "*w*" is the width, and "*h*" is the height.

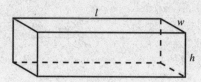

b. The volume of a rectangular solid is the product of the length, width, and height: $V = l \times w \times h$

Example: The volume of a rectangular solid whose length is 6 feet, width 3 feet, and height 4 feet is $6 \times 3 \times 4 = 72$ cubic feet.

37. a. A **cube** is a rectangular solid whose edges are equal. The figure below is a cube; the length, width, and height are all equal to "*e*."

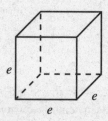

b. The volume of a cube is equal to the edge cubed: $V = e^3$.

Example: The volume of a cube whose height is 6 inches equals $6^3 = 6 \times 6 \times 6 = 216$ cubic inches.

c. The surface area of a cube is equal to the area of any side multiplied by 6.

Example: The surface area of a cube whose length is 5 inches $= 5^2 \times 6 = 25 \times 6 = 150$ square inches.

38. The volume of a circular cylinder is equal to the product of π, the radius squared, and the height.

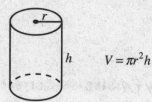

Example: A circular cylinder has a radius of 7 inches and a height of $\frac{1}{2}$ inch. Using $\pi = \frac{22}{7}$, its volume is

$\frac{22}{7} \times 7 \times 7 \times \frac{1}{2} = 77$ cubic inches

39. The volume of a **sphere** is equal to $\frac{4}{3}$ the product of π and the radius cubed.

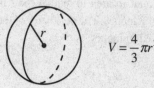

Example: If the radius of a sphere is 3 cm., its volume in terms of π is

$\frac{4}{3} \times \pi \times 3$ cm. $\times 3$ cm. $\times 3$ cm. $= 36 \pi$ cm.^{3}

Practice Problems Involving Geometry

1. If the perimeter of a rectangle is 68 yards and the width is 48 feet, the length is

   (A) 10 yd.
   (B) 18 yd.
   (C) 20 ft.
   (D) 46 ft.
   (E) 56 ft.

2. The total length of fencing needed to enclose a rectangular area 46 feet by 34 feet is

   (A) 26 yd. 1 ft.
   (B) $26\frac{2}{3}$ yd.
   (C) 48 yds.
   (D) 52 yd. 2 ft.
   (E) $53\frac{1}{3}$ yd.

3. An umbrella 50" long can lie on the bottom of a trunk whose length and width are, respectively,

   (A) 26", 30"
   (B) 39", 36"
   (C) 31", 31"
   (D) 40", 21"
   (E) 40", 30"

4. A road runs 1200 ft. from A to B, and then makes a right angle going to C, a distance of 500 ft. A new road is being built directly from A to C. How much shorter will the new road be?

   (A) 400 ft.
   (B) 609 ft.
   (C) 850 ft.
   (D) 1000 ft.
   (E) 1300 ft.

5. A certain triangle has sides that are, respectively, 6 inches, 8 inches, and 10 inches long. A rectangle equal in area to that of the triangle has a width of 3 inches. The perimeter of the rectangle, expressed in inches, is

(A) 11
(B) 16
(C) 22
(D) 24
(E) 30

6. A ladder 65 feet long is leaning against the wall. Its lower end is 25 feet away from the wall. How much farther away will it be if the upper end is moved down 8 feet?

(A) 60 ft.
(B) 52 ft.
(C) 14 ft.
(D) 10 ft.
(E) 8 ft.

7. A rectangular bin 4 feet long, 3 feet wide, and 2 feet high is solidly packed with bricks whose dimensions are 8 inches, 4 inches, and 2 inches. The number of bricks in the bin is

(A) 54
(B) 320
(C) 648
(D) 848
(E) none of these

8. If the cost of digging a trench is $2.12 a cubic yard, what would be the cost of digging a trench 2 yards by 5 yards by 4 yards?

(A) $21.20
(B) $40.00
(C) $64.00
(D) $84.80
(E) $104.80

9. A piece of wire is shaped to enclose a square, whose area is 121 square inches. It is then reshaped to enclose a rectangle whose length is 13 inches. The area of the rectangle, in square inches, is

(A) 64
(B) 96
(C) 117
(D) 144
(E) 234

10. The area of a 2-foot-wide walk around a garden that is 30 feet long and 20 feet wide is

(A) 104 sq. ft.
(B) 216 sq. ft.
(C) 680 sq. ft.
(D) 704 sq. ft.
(E) 1416 sq. ft.

11. The area of a circle is 49π. Find its circumference, in terms of π.

(A) 14π
(B) 28π
(C) 49π
(D) 98π
(E) 147π

12. In two hours, the minute hand of a clock rotates through an angle of

(A) 90°
(B) 180°
(C) 360°
(D) 720°
(E) 1080°

13. A box is 12 inches in width, 16 inches in length, and 6 inches in height. How many square inches of paper would be required to cover it on all sides?

(A) 192
(B) 360
(C) 720
(D) 900
(E) 1440

14. If the volume of a cube is 64 cubic inches, the sum of its edges is

(A) 48 in.
(B) 32 in.
(C) 24 in.
(D) 16 in.
(E) 12 in.

Geometry Problems—Correct Answers

1. **(B)**	6. **(C)**	11. **(A)**
2. **(E)**	7. **(C)**	12. **(D)**
3. **(E)**	8. **(D)**	13. **(C)**
4. **(A)**	9. **(C)**	14. **(A)**
5. **(C)**	10. **(B)**	

Problem Solutions—Geometry

1.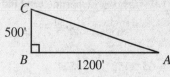

48'   48'

Perimeter = 68 yards
Each width = 48 feet = 16 yards
Both widths = 16 yd. + 16 yd. = 32 yd.
Perimeter = sum of all sides
Remaining two sides must total 68 − 32 = 36 yards.
Since the remaining two sides are equal, they are each 36 ÷ 2 = 18 yards.

Answer: **(B)** 18 yd.

2. Perimeter = 2(46 + 34) feet
   $\quad\quad\quad = 2 \times 80$ feet
   $\quad\quad\quad = 160$ feet
   160 feet $= 160 \div 3$ yards $= 53\frac{1}{3}$ yards

Answer: **(E)** $53\frac{1}{3}$ yd.

3. The umbrella would be the hypotenuse of a right triangle whose legs are the dimensions of the trunk.

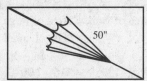

50"

The Pythagorean Theorem states that in a right triangle, the square of the hypotenuse equals the sum of the squares of the legs. Therefore, the sum of the dimensions of the trunk squared must at least equal the length of the umbrella squared, which is 50^2 or 2500.

The only set of dimensions filling this condition is **(E)**:

$$40^2 + 30^2 = 1600 + 900$$
$$= 2500$$

Answer: **(E)** 40", 30"

4. The new road is the hypotenuse of a right triangle, whose legs are the old road.

C
500'
B 1200' *A*

$$AC^2 = AB^2 + BC^2$$
$$AC = \sqrt{500^2 + 1200^2}$$
$$= \sqrt{250,000 + 1,440,000}$$
$$= \sqrt{1,690,000}$$
$$= 1300 \text{ feet}$$
Old road $= 1200 + 500$ feet
$\quad\quad\quad = 1700$ feet
New road $= 1300$ feet
Difference $= 400$ feet

Answer: **(A)** 400 ft.

5. Since $6^2 + 8^2 = 10^2$ (36 + 64 = 100), the triangle is a right triangle. The area of the triangle is $\frac{1}{2} \times 6 \times 8 = 24$ square inches. Therefore, the area of the rectangle is 24 square inches.

If the width of the rectangle is 3 inches, the length is $24 \div 3 = 8$ inches. Then the perimeter of the rectangle is $2(3 + 8) = 2 \times 11 = 22$ inches.

Answer: **(C)** 22

6. The ladder forms a right triangle with the wall and the ground.

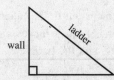

wall   ladder

First, find the height that the ladder reaches when the lower end of the ladder is 25 feet from the wall:

$$65^2 = 4225$$
$$25^2 = 625$$
$$65^2 - 25^2 = 3600$$
$$\sqrt{3600} = 60$$

The ladder reaches 60 feet up the wall when its lower end is 25 feet from the wall.

If the upper end is moved down 8 feet, the ladder will reach a height of 60 − 8 = 52 feet.

The new triangle formed has a hypotenuse of 65 feet and one leg of 52 feet. Find the other leg:

$$65^2 = 4225$$
$$52^2 = 2704$$
$$65^2 - 52^2 = 1521$$
$$\sqrt{1521} = 39$$

The lower end of the ladder is now 39 feet from the wall. This is 39 − 25 = 14 feet farther than it was before.

Answer: (C) 14 ft.

7. Convert the dimensions of the bin to inches:

$$4 \text{ feet} = 48 \text{ inches}$$
$$3 \text{ feet} = 36 \text{ inches}$$
$$2 \text{ feet} = 24 \text{ inches}$$
$$\text{Volume of bin} = 48 \text{ in.} \times 36 \text{ in.} \times 24 \text{ in.}$$
$$= 41,472 \text{ cubic inches}$$
$$\text{Volume of}$$
$$\text{each brick} = 8 \text{ in.} \times 4 \text{ in.} \times 2 \text{ in.}$$
$$= 64 \text{ cubic inches}$$
$$41,472 \div 64 = 648 \text{ bricks}$$

Answer: (C) 648

8. The trench contains

$$2 \text{ yd.} \times 5 \text{ yd.} \times 4 \text{ yd.} = 40 \text{ cubic yards}$$
$$40 \times \$2.12 = \$84.80$$

Answer: (D) $84.80

9. Find the dimensions of the square: If the area of the square is 121 square inches, each side is $\sqrt{121}$ = 11 inches, and the perimeter is 4 × 11 = 44 inches.

Next, find the dimensions of the rectangle: The perimeter of the rectangle is the same as the perimeter of the square, since the same length of wire is used to enclose either figure. Therefore, the perimeter of the rectangle is 44 inches. If the two lengths are each 13 inches, their total is 26 inches, and 44 − 26 inches, or 18 inches, remain for the two widths. Each width is equal to 18 ÷ 2 = 9 inches.

The area of a rectangle with length 13 in. and width 9 in. is 13 × 9 = 117 sq. in.

Answer: (C) 117

10.

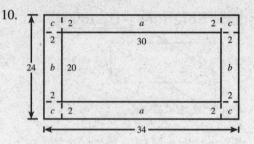

The walk consists of:

a. 2 rectangles of length 30 feet and width 2 feet.

Area of each rectangle = 2 × 30 = 60 sq. ft.
Area of both rectangles = 120 sq. ft.

b. 2 rectangles of length 20 feet and width 2 feet.

Area of each = 2 × 20 = 40 sq. ft.
Area of both = 80 sq. ft.

c. 4 squares, each having sides measuring 2 feet.

Area of each square =   = 4 sq. ft.
Area of 4 squares   = 16 sq. ft.
Total area of walk   = 120 + 80 + 16
= 216 sq. ft.

Alternate solution:

Area of walk = Area of large rectangle–
area of small rectangle
= 34 × 24 − 30 × 20
= 816 − 600
= 216 sq. ft.

Answer: (B) 216 sq. ft.

11. If the area of a circle is 49π, its radius is $\sqrt{49}$ = 7. Then, the circumference is equal to 2 × 7 × π = 14π.

Answer: (A) 14π

12. In one hour, the minute hand rotates through 360°. In two hours, it rotates through 2 × 360° = 720°.

Answer: (D) 720°

13. Find the area of each surface:

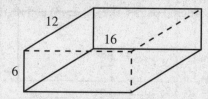

Area of top = 12 × 16 = 192 sq. in.
Area of bottom = 12 × 16 = 192 sq. in.
Area of front = 6 × 16 = 96 sq. in.
Area of back = 6 × 16 = 96 sq. in.
Area of right side = 6 × 12 = 72 sq. in.
Area of left side = 6 × 12 = +72 sq. in.
Total surface area = 720 sq. in.

Answer: (**C**) 720

14. For a cube, $V = e^3$. If the volume is 64 cubic inches, each edge is $\sqrt[3]{64}$ = 4 inches.
A cube has 12 edges. If each edge is 4 inches, the sum of the edges is 4 × 12 = 48 inches.

Answer: (**A**) 48 in.

Coordinate Geometry

Perhaps the easiest way to understand the coordinate axis system is as an analog to the points of the compass. If we take a plot of land, we can divide it into quadrants:

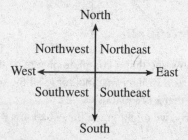

Now, if we add measuring units along each of the directional axes, we can actually describe any location on this piece of land by two numbers. For example, point *P* is located at 4 units East and 5 units North. Point *Q* is located at 4 units West and 5 units North. Point *R* is located at 4 units West and 2 units South. And Point *T* is located at 3 units East and 4 units South.

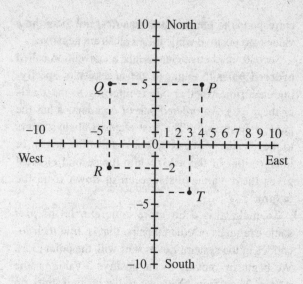

The coordinate system used in coordinate geometry differs from our map of a plot of land in two respects. First, it uses *x* and *y* axes divided into negative and positive regions.

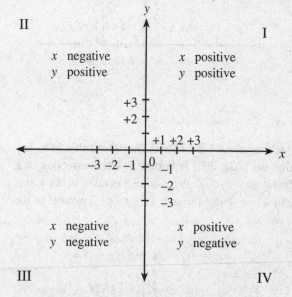

It is easy to see that Quadrant I corresponds to our Northeast quarter, and in it the measurements on both the *x* and *y* axes are positive. Quadrant II corresponds to our Northwest quarter, and in it the measurements on the *x* axis are negative and the measurements on the *y* axis are positive. Quadrant III corresponds to the Southwest quarter, and in it both the *x* axis measurements and the *y* axis measurements are negative. Finally, Quadrant IV corresponds to our Southeast quarter, and there the *x* values are positive while the *y* values are negative.

Second, mathematicians adopt a convention called **ordered pairs** to eliminate the necessity of specifying each time whether one is referring to the *x* axis or the *y* axis. An ordered pair of coordinates has the general form (*a,b*). The first element always refers to the *x* value (distance left or right of the *origin,* or intersection, of the axes) while the second element gives the *y* value (distance up or down from the origin).

To make this a bit more concrete, let us *plot* some examples of ordered pairs, that is, find their locations in the system: Let us start with the point (3,2). We begin by moving to the positive 3 value on the *x* axis. Then from there we move up two units on the *y* axis.

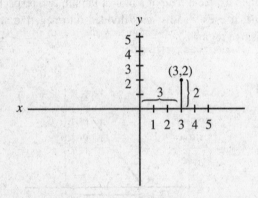

An alternative way of speaking about this is to say that the point (3,2) is located at the intersection of a line drawn through the *x* value 3 parallel to the *y* axis and a line drawn through the *y* value 2 parallel to the *x* axis.

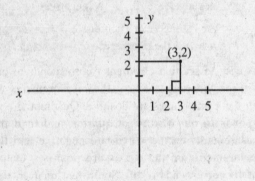

Both methods locate the same point. Let us now use the ordered pairs (–3,2), (–2,–3) and (3,–2):

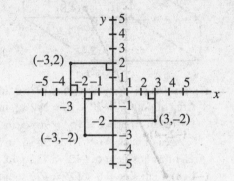

One important use of the coordinate axis system is that it can be used to draw a picture of an equation. For example, we know that the equation $x = y$ has an infinite number of solutions:

x	1	2	3	5	0	–3	–5	etc.
y	1	2	3	5	0	–3	–5	

We can plot these pairs of *x* and *y* on the axis system:

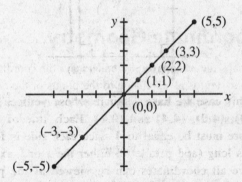

We can now see that a complete picture of the equation $x = y$ is a straight line including all the real numbers such that *x* is equal to *y*.

Similarly, we might graph the equation $y = 2x$:

x	–4	–2	–1	0	1	2	4
y	–8	–4	–2	0	2	4	8

After entering these points on the graph, we can complete the picture:

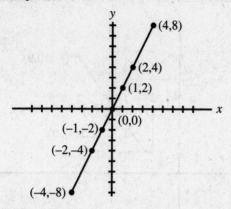

It too is a straight line, but it rises at a more rapid rate than does $x = y$.

A final use one might have for the coordinate system on the GRE is in graphing geometric figures:

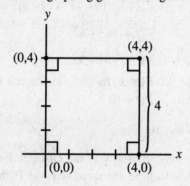

In this case we have a square whose vertices are $(0,0)$, $(4,0)$, $(4,4)$ and $(0,4)$. Each side of the square must be equal to 4 since each side is four units long (and parallel to either the x or y axis). Since all coordinates can be viewed as the perpendicular intersection of two lines, it is possible to measure distances in the system by using some simple theorems.

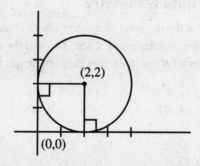

Illustration: What is the area of the circle?

SOLUTION: In order to solve this problem, we need to know the radius of the circle. The center of the circle is located at the intersection of $x = 2$ and $y = 2$, or the point $(2,2)$. So we know the radius is 2 units long and the area is 4π.

Answer: 4π

Illustration: What is the length of PQ?

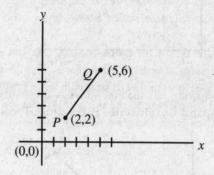

SOLUTION: We can find the length of PQ by constructing a triangle:

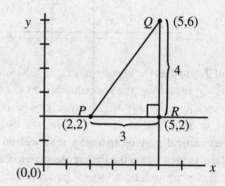

Now, we see that QR runs from $(5,6)$ to $(5,2)$ and so it must be 4 units long. We see that PR runs from $(2,2)$ to $(5,2)$ so it is 3 units long. We then use the Pythagorean Theorem to determine that PQ, which is the hypotenuse of our triangle, is 5 units long.

Answer: 5 units

It is actually possible to generalize on this example. Let us take any two points on the graph (for simplicity's sake we will confine the discussion to the First Quadrant, but the method is generally applicable, that is, will work in all quadrants and even with lines covering two or more quadrants)

P and *Q*. Now let us assign the value (x_1, y_1) to *P* and (x_2, y_2) to *Q*.

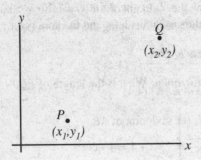

Then, following our method above, we construct a triangle so that we can use the Pythagorean Theorem:

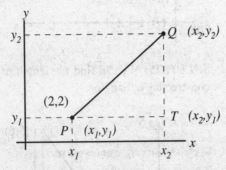

Point *T* now has the coordinates (x_2, y_1). Side *PT* will be $x_2 - x_1$ units long (the *y* coordinate does not change, so the length is only the distance moved on the *x* axis), and *QT* will be $y_2 - y_1$ (again, the distance is purely vertical, moving up from y_1 to y_2, with no change in the *x* value). Using the Pythagorean Theorem:

$$PQ^2 = PT^2 + QT^2$$
$$PQ^2 = (x_2 - x_1)^2 + (y_2 - y_1)^2$$
$$PQ = \sqrt{(x_2 - x_1)^2 + (y_2 - y_1)^2}$$

And we have just derived what is called the **Distance Formula.** We can find the length of any straight line segment drawn in a coordinate axis system (that is, the distance between two points in the system) using this formula.

Illustration: What is the distance between *P* and *Q*?

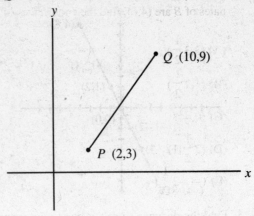

SOLUTION: Point *P* has the coordinates (2, 3) and *Q* the coordinates (10, 9). Using the formula:

$$PQ = \sqrt{(10 - 2)^2 + (9 - 3)^2}$$
$$PQ = \sqrt{8^2 + 6^2}$$
$$PQ = \sqrt{64 + 36}$$
$$PQ = \sqrt{100}$$
$$PQ = 10$$

Answer: 10

For those students who find the Distance Formula a bit too technical, be reassured that the Pythagorean Theorem (which is more familiar) will work just as well on the GRE. In fact, as a general rule, any time one is asked to calculate a distance which does not move parallel to one of the axes, the proper attack is to use the Pythagorean Theorem.

Practice Problems Involving
Coordinate Geometry

1. *AB* is the diameter of a circle whose center is *O*. If the coordinates of *A* are (2,6) and the coordinates of *B* are (6,2), find the coordinates of *O*.

   (A) (4,4)
   (B) (4,–4)
   (C) (2,–2)
   (D) (0,0)
   (E) (2,2)

2. AB is the diameter of a circle whose center is O. If the coordinates of O are (2,1) and the coordinates of B are (4,6), find the coordinates of A.

(A) $(3, 3\frac{1}{2})$

(B) $(1, 2\frac{1}{2})$

(C) $(0, -4)$

(D) $(2\frac{1}{2}, 1)$

(E) $(-1, -2\frac{1}{2})$

3. Find the distance from the point whose coordinates are (4,3) to the point whose coordinates are (8,6).

(A) 5
(B) 25
(C) $\sqrt{7}$
(D) $\sqrt{67}$
(E) 15

4. The vertices of a triangle are (2,1), (2,5), and (5,1). The area of the triangle is

(A) 12
(B) 10
(C) 8
(D) 6
(E) 5

5. The area of a circle whose center is at (0,0) is 16π. The circle passes through each of the following points *except*

(A) (4,4)
(B) (0,4)
(C) (4,0)
(D) (-4,0)
(E) (0,-4)

Coordinate Geometry Problems— Correct Answers

1. **(A)**
2. **(C)**
3. **(A)**
4. **(D)**
5. **(A)**

Problem Solutions—Coordinate Geometry

1. Find the midpoint of AB by averaging the x coordinates and averaging the y coordinates.

$$\left(\frac{6+2}{2}, \frac{2+6}{2}\right) = (4,4)$$

Answer: **(A)** (4,4)

2. O is the midpoint of AB.

$$\frac{x+4}{2} = 2 \quad x+4 = 4 \quad x = 0$$

$$\frac{y+6}{2} = 1 \quad y+6 = 2 \quad y = -4$$

A is the point (0,-4)

Answer: **(C)** (0,-4)

3. $d = \sqrt{(8-4)^2 + (6-3)^2} = \sqrt{4^2 + 3^2} = \sqrt{16+9} = \sqrt{25} = 5$

Answer: **(A)** 5

4. Sketch the triangle and you will see it is a right triangle with legs of 4 and 3.

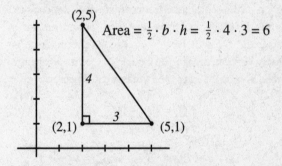

Area $= \frac{1}{2} \cdot b \cdot h = \frac{1}{2} \cdot 4 \cdot 3 = 6$

Answer: **(D)** 6

5. Area of a circle $= \pi r^2$

$\pi r^2 = 16\pi \qquad r = 4$

Points B, C, D, and E are all 4 units from the origin. Point A is not.

Answer: **(A)** (4,4)

EIGHT

Appendices

PREVIEW →

APPENDIX A

GRE Writing Assessment

APPENDIX B

Financing Your Graduate Education

GRE Writing Assessment

You'll Find Answers to These Questions

What is the GRE Writing Assessment?
How do you handle the GRE Writing Assessment?
What do smart test-takers know about the GRE Writing Assessment?

WHAT IS THE GRE WRITING ASSESSMENT?

The GRE Writing Assessment is a test offered by the GRE Board that helps graduate programs evaluate your ability to write.

The Writing Assessment requires you to respond to two essay topics (called "prompts"). One of the prompts will be an "issue" topic and the other an "argument" topic. The time limit for the "issue" topic is 45 minutes, and the time limit for the "argument" topic is 30 minutes. You can produce your responses either by using the word processing function of the computer at the testing center or by writing them out in hand. The essays are then assigned to readers who score them.

The Writing Assessment is not part of the GRE proper (the CAT) and does not affect your GRE scores, nor is it a subject test (like Physics or Psychology). It is an independent test with its own scoring system, and you have to complete a special registration and pay an additional fee to take the Writing Assessment.

TIME MANAGER STUDY PLANS

PLAN A: ACCELERATED
- *Read* the appendix
- *Study* "What Smart Test-takers Know"
- *Complete* Exercises 1 and 2

PLAN B: TOP SPEED
- *Read* "How Do You Handle the Writing Assessment"
- *Study* "What Smart Test-takers Know"
- *Complete* Exercise 1

The Writing Assessment was added to the battery of tests sponsored by the GRE Board because the Board has been concerned about deficiencies in the writing skills evidenced by graduate students. The goal is to help admissions officers and advisors evaluate a student's ability and needs. It can be used as another tool in the admission process (in addition to GRE scores, GPA, and personal statements) and as a guidance tool to direct students who need special help in developing writing skills into appropriate programs.

Anatomy of the Writing Assessment

ISSUE TOPIC
Issue Task: Present Your Views on an Issue
Time: 45 minutes

The task is to express your point of view. So you have a lot of flexibility in deciding what to say.

You have 45 minutes to plan and write an essay that presents your views on an assigned topic.

You must write on the assigned topic. An essay on any other topic is classified as "off topic" and given an automatic zero for a grade. On some versions, you may be permitted to choose from one of two topics.

The topic is summarized in a brief quotation that states or suggests a position. You can accept, reject, or modify the position. Support your views with reasons and examples drawn from your experience, observation, reading, or study.

The "issue" topic is a quote that expresses the speaker's opinion. When you give your own point of view, you can agree or disagree with the speaker or even agree somewhat and disagree somewhat. You don't need any special knowledge to answer; instead, you should draw from your own experience and study.

Trained graders will score your response, taking account of how well you:

- Understand the complexities and ramifications of the issue
- Organize, develop, and express your ideas
- Deploy the elements of standard written English

Your essay is graded "holistically," taking into account many factors. These are discussed in greater detail below.

You may wish to spend a few minutes thinking about your response before you begin writing and leave time to reread what you have written in order to make any revisions you think necessary.

Outline your essay before you begin to write. And make sure that you leave some time for proofreading.

Present your point of view on the following issue: "Despite the occurrence of natural disasters and human tragedies, often on a large scale, the human condition continues to improve materially, spiritually, ethically, and culturally."

This is the speaker's position. You can agree that things are getting better; you can disagree and say that things are getting worse; you can qualify the position by saying that it's a little of both and only time will tell; or you can take any other position that you can defend.

ARGUMENT TOPIC
Argument Task: Analyze an Argument
Time: 30 minutes

You have 30 minutes to plan and write an essay that presents your views on an assigned topic. Consider the logic of the argument and the soundness of its conclusion.

Trained graders will score your response, taking account of how well you:

- Identify and analyze the structure of the argument
- Organize, develop, and express your ideas
- Deploy the elements of standard written English

You may wish to spend a few minutes thinking about your response before you begin writing and leave time to reread what you have written in order to make any revisions you think necessary.

Read the following argument and discuss whether it is well-reasoned. You are *not* being asked to agree or disagree with the conclusion of the argument; you are being asked to analyze the reasoning in the argument. Consider what, if any, assumptions the argument makes and whether they are justified; what evidence is offered for the conclusion and whether it is reliable; as well as any other factors or information that would strengthen or weaken the argument.

Recently, it was reported in the news media that a school bus returning from a field trip overturned on a highway and rolled down an embankment, seriously injuring several students who were tossed from their seats. Common sense says that these children would not have been injured if they had been wearing seat belts. Therefore, the federal government should require all school buses to have seat belts for passengers.

The task is to analyze the argument. Assess the strengths and weaknesses of the reasons given for the conclusion.

Analyze the argument by assessing the conclusion and considering whether the reasons given support the conclusion. You must write on the assigned topic. An essay on any other topic is classified as "off topic" and given an automatic zero for a grade.

Your essay is graded "holistically," taking into account many factors. These are discussed in greater detail below.

Outline your essay before you begin to write. And make sure that you leave some time for proofreading.

The task is not to say what you believe but to comment on how well the speaker's reasons support the conclusion. Good points to make include:

1. *The argument makes assumptions without proof.*
2. *The evidence is not reliable.*
3. *The conclusion does not follow from the evidence.*
4. *The argument fails to consider some important points.*

The conclusion of this argument is: Seat belts should be required on school buses. You should not take a position. But you might raise the following points:

1. *Is this a frequent occurrence?*
2. *Would the children have been injured anyway?*
3. *Can the driver make the children wear the seat belts?*
4. *Was excessive speed or some other controllable factor the cause of the accident?*

HERE'S THE ANSWER

Is the Writing Assessment very important?

The answer to this question varies from school to school and from applicant to applicant. But almost surely it is not nearly so important to schools as your undergraduate GPA (or its international equivalent) and your GRE CAT score. On the other hand, a good performance on the Writing Assessment might just be the thing for an individual to tip the scales. So, in that respect, it has the potential to be very important and you should give it your best shot.

TESTSMARTS

Be specific. The directions given to test-takers emphasize that a good essay uses illustrations or examples.

Both Writing Assessment essays are graded substantially according to the same criteria (setting aside for the moment the fact that the two prompts require somewhat different approaches). So it is a good idea to know what counts and what does not count in the grading system. Essays are graded on content, organization, and mechanics. Contrast the following descriptions of an "Outstanding" essay (a "6" on the scale of 0 to 6) and a "Seriously Flawed" essay (a "2"):

OUTSTANDING (6)

An essay that presents a cogent analysis. An outstanding essay

- states and develops a position with reasons and illustrations
- is focused and clearly well organized
- expresses ideas clearly and effectively
- uses language fluently with a variety of sentence structures and rich vocabulary
- demonstrates superior facility with the conventions of Standard Written English (grammar, usage, mechanics) but may have minor flaws

SERIOUSLY FLAWED (2)

An essay that shows serious weakness in analytical writing. A seriously flawed essay

- is unclear or seriously limited in presenting or developing ideas
- provides few, if any, relevant examples
- is disorganized
- contains numerous errors in grammar, usage, or mechanics which interfere with understanding

The most important elements of these contrasting descriptions can be summarized in a table that will help you better see what's required for a good essay score:

	Outstanding (6 out of a possible 6)	Seriously Flawed (2 out of a possible 6)
Content	Insightful Reasons Persuasive Examples	Unclear Position Few Examples
Organization	Well-Focused Well-Organized	Unfocused Disorganized
Execution	Substantially correct with only minor flaws	Numerous errors in grammar, usage, or mechanics

So writing a good essay means doing three things well: generating interesting content, organizing the ideas, and presenting the ideas effectively. We'll look more closely at each of these three aspects in "What Smart Test-takers Know" later on.

HOW DO YOU HANDLE THE GRE WRITING ASSESSMENT?

Here is a simple, four-step plan to help you succeed on the GRE Writing Assessment.

GRE Writing Assessment: Getting It Right

1. Read the topic and decide what position or positions you'll take.
2. Outline your thinking using the scratch paper that is provided.
3. Produce your essay either by keyboarding or writing.
4. Proofread your essay.

Now let's try out these steps on the "argument" topic given earlier.

1. Read the topic and decide what position or positions you'll take.

You want to generate three or four ideas that critique the *structure* of the argument:

- The proof of the harm is anecdotal.
- There is no evidence that seat belts will be effective.
- The money could be better spent on driver training or other safety equipment such as better brakes.

2. Outline your thinking using the scratch paper that is provided.

  I. There is no real proof of serious problem.

    A. The evidence is anecdotal: one example but no statistics.

    B. "Common sense" may be wrong that seat belts would have prevented all or most of the injuries. More information is needed.

  II. There is no evidence that seat belts will be effective.

    A. Perhaps other equally serious injuries would have occurred.

    B. Is it reasonable to believe that children will wear the belts or that a bus driver has the authority to enforce such a rule?

  III. The proposal may not be cost effective.

    A. It would be necessary to analyze the cost of installing seat belts in all school buses.

    B. Perhaps the money could be spent better elsewhere, for example, on more driver training.

3. Produce your essay either by keyboarding or writing.

You would then write your essay using your outline. Importantly, you can use the main headings in your outline as topic sentences for your paragraphs and your subheads as main sentences within each paragraph. Be sure to add some further detail, e.g., children of school age are notoriously difficult to discipline, particularly in a "free-for-all" situation at the end of the school day.

4. Proofread your essay.

In the next section you will find a checklist of the errors most commonly made by test-takers and tips on how to avoid them.

WHAT SMART TEST-TAKERS KNOW

Smart test-takers know that the grading system for the Writing Assessment emphasizes three elements: content, organization, and execution. Let's look at what you can do to maximize your performance on each of the yardsticks.

What Smart Test-takers Know About Content

YOU SHOULD NEVER WRITE ON A TOPIC OTHER THAN THE ONES YOU ARE GIVEN.

The directions are very clear on this, and the readers are specifically instructed to assign a grade of zero (the lowest possible) to any response that is written on a different topic.

The prompts are specifically designed to provide you with an opportunity to write. To work, then, they must be topics that are accessible to everyone. For this reason, the topics do not presuppose any special knowledge.

YOU SHOULD NOT TRY TO MAKE THE SUBJECT OF THE PROMPT MORE IMPORTANT THAN IT IS.

Many candidates imagine that their essays will be considerably improved if they make clear to the reader that they feel passionately about the topic or that they consider the topic of very grave concern. Unfortunately, extreme passion or grave concern is usually simply out of place—even when the topic is one of great importance.

YOU SHOULD NOT TRY TO DO TOO MUCH.

Half or three-quarters of an hour may seem like a lot of time, but it's not. By the time you read the topic, think about the issue or the argument, formulate some ideas, create an outline, and generate your response, you'll probably be running out of time—wishing that you had more for the proofreading phase. So in this case, more is not necessarily better. It is preferable to write a shorter essay that is complete than to aspire to write a magnum opus only to run out of time with the project only barely started.

YOU SHOULD ILLUSTRATE YOUR IDEAS WITH EXAMPLES.

Another way of generating ideas for your essay is to think about the topic concretely rather than abstractly. In fact, "use of examples" figures prominently in the scoring analysis set out above. An important feature of the "outstanding" essay is the use of "persuasive examples," and a noticeable weakness of the "seriously flawed" essay is the use of "few, if any, relevant examples."

What Smart Test-takers Know About Organization

YOU SHOULD ORGANIZE YOUR ESSAY BY USING THE "THREE MAIN POINTS" APPROACH.

This "three main points" approach results in a five-paragraph essay:

Paragraph 1: Introduction.

Paragraph 2: First point.

Paragraph 3: Second point.

Paragraph 4: Third point.

Paragraph 5: Conclusion.

YOU SHOULD BEGIN BY CLEARLY STATING A POSITION.

One of the features of the "outstanding" essay is that it states a clear position. This is absolutely essential for the "issue" topic where you are expected to voice your own opinion. But it is true of the "argument" topic as well, even though your conclusion may be more formalistic, e.g,. "The reasons given in support of the plan to require seat belts do not support the conclusion that the plan would be beneficial."

YOU SHOULD BEGIN EACH PARAGRAPH WITH A TOPIC SENTENCE.

You know what you want to say; your reader does not. That's why good writers use topic sentences. Let the first sentence of each paragraph announce to the reader what aspect of the topic will be discussed in that paragraph. For example:

First, the limited evidence in the argument doesn't support so broad a conclusion as a law requiring seat belts in all school buses.

YOU SHOULD USE TRANSITIONAL WORDS AND PHRASES.

Even though you announce your paragraph topic in the first sentence, you still need to help the reader follow the details of the development. If you want to make two points of equal importance, then signal the transition from the first to the second with words such as "Additionally," "Furthermore," and "Moreover." Here's an example:

First, the limited evidence in the argument doesn't support so broad a conclusion as a law requiring seat belts in all school buses. The speaker cites a single example of an accident involving a school bus. Without statistical evidence on the number of such accidents each year and the types of injuries sustained, it would be unwise to reach a broad public policy conclusion. Additionally, even the brief description of the accident does not cite the cause. Perhaps it was driver inattention, weather, or a careless motorist in another vehicle, all factors that can and should be addressed in different ways.

What Smart Test-takers Know About Execution

YOU SHOULD MAKE SURE THAT EACH SENTENCE EXPRESSES ONE MAIN THOUGHT.

You've been taught since the first day of school to begin your sentences with a capital letter and to end them with a period (or question mark or exclamation point). Why? These are signals to the reader that a thought begins (the capital letter) and ends (the period). For this convention to be useful, you have to follow it. Make sure that you develop only one main idea in each sentence.

YOU SHOULD PROOFREAD YOUR ESSAY USING A CHECKLIST OF COMMON ERRORS.

The literature that describes the scoring of the Writing Assessment clearly indicates that grammar is an important concern of the graders. The essays that get poor grades are described as having "frequent errors in grammar, usage, and mechanics." So you want to make certain that your essay is as free as possible from mistakes. As you proofread your essay, read each sentence individually and consciously ask the following questions:

Does this sentence have a main verb?

Every sentence must have a main verb. If one doesn't, you need to add one. Here is an example:

> Seat belts in school buses, which are almost always part of the original equipment of passenger cars.

There is no main verb in this sentence. The subject of the sentence seems to be "seat belts in school buses," and there is a dependent clause or thought introduced by "which"; but there is no main verb. So it's not clear what the sentence means to say. However, a way of eliminating the grammatical mistake would be:

> Seat belts, which are almost always part of the original equipment of passenger cars, are not required in school buses.

Does this sentence come to a point?

A real danger with an exercise like the Writing Assessment is writing sentences that seem to go on without stopping. As the name implies, a run-on sentence does just that. Here is an example:

> Initially, industry leaders were skeptical of seat belts, afterwards it occurred to them that saving lives might also save them money.

This sentence contains two independent clauses that are not properly joined. The portion of this sentence before the comma is an independent clause (which means a clause that can act as a sentence all by itself), and the portion of the sentence after the comma is also an independent clause. A comma by itself is not sufficient to separate two independent clauses; rather, a coordinating conjunction like *and, but, yet, for, or,* or *nor* must be used between the comma and the second independent clause. The sentence can be improved in the following way:

> Initially, industry leaders were skeptical of seat belts, but it later occurred to them that saving lives might also save them money.

Does the verb in this sentence agree with its subject?

It is a hard and fast rule of English grammar that verbs have to agree with their subjects. The following sentence violates this rule:

> Often times, injuries sustained in a motor vehicle accident is aggravated by the failure of the passenger in the vehicle to observe simple safety precautions other than wearing a seat belt.

The subject in this sentence is "injuries," a plural noun, so you need the plural verb "are" rather than the singular "is":

> Often times, injuries sustained in a motor vehicle accident are aggravated by the failure of the passenger in the vehicle to observe simple safety precautions other than wearing a seat belt.

The problem of subject-verb agreement is made more difficult anytime that you put modifiers between the subject and the verb. You probably wouldn't miss:

> Injuries is aggravated . . . .

But you could easily miss:

> Injuries that are caused by the failure to install and require the use of seat belts is . . . .

So in your proofreading, point your finger at the subject and at the verb and, in your mind, juxtapose the two to make sure that they agree.

Does each pronoun have a referent (antecedent)?

A pronoun must always substitute for another word. The following sentence is incorrect because the pronoun "which" doesn't have a referent:

> Not equipping large vehicles with seat belts, which is common practice in the manufacture of buses of all types, is not likely to increase the severity of injuries.

The "which" seems to refer to something, but try to find a word that it substitutes for, and you won't be able to. The sentence needs to be rewritten so that "which" has a referent:

> The failure to equip large vehicles with seat belts, which is common practice in the manufacture of buses of all types, is not likely to increase the severity of injuries.

If the sentence uses a series of the elements, are the elements presented in the same form? (Are the elements parallel?)

When you write a series of elements into a sentence, those elements must have the same form, e.g., shooting skeet, playing tennis, and climbing mountains. (All three use the parallel -ing form.) The following sentence fails in this respect:

> Seat belts are the best way to reduce the severity of injuries, save lives, and, in general, minimizing the danger of riding in a bus.

The three elements "reduce," "save," and "minimizing" are a parallel series, so they should have parallel forms:

> Seat belts are the best way to reduce the severity of injuries, save lives, and, in general, minimize the danger of riding in a bus.

Using a series such as this will boost your score on the "variety of sentences" meter, but a mistake in parallelism will just create an offset in the category of mechanics.

Does each sentence say what it means to say? (Have you avoided misplaced modifiers?)

When you were in school, you probably heard a lot about the notorious "dangling modifier." (And maybe the concept was even defined for you.) You don't need to worry about whether or not a modifier is dangling if you just make certain that all of your modifiers are logically placed, and that usually means placed close to what they modify. Here's an example of a sentence with a misplaced modifier:

> Properly installed as original equipment, bus passengers will enjoy an additional safety margin if they are securely belted in during the trip.

The introductory modifier "properly installed" sounds as though it is intended to modify the element of the sentence closest to it, which would be "bus passengers." But the sentence clearly does not mean to say that the passengers should be installed on the bus as original equipment. Here's what the sentence really means to say:

> Properly installed as original equipment, seat belts offer bus passengers an additional safety margin if the passengers are securely belted in during the trip.

Is each sentence properly punctuated?

Punctuation is one of those topics that strikes fear into the hearts of most students—like "factoring" in algebra. But for purposes of writing your response to the GRE WA, this should not be a grave concern for two reasons. First, since you are doing the writing, you control the structure of your sentence and therefore the punctuation that is needed. If you are in doubt as to how to punctuate a sentence, just change the sentence to avoid the problem. Second, you can let your "ear" be your guide. Punctuation marks are like signals on a car. Just as signals like turn indicators and brake lights help other drivers know what you're doing, punctuation marks let your reader know what you're up to. You should be able to read your sentences to yourself, pausing at each comma and coming to a full stop at a period, to determine whether you've punctuated correctly. If your reading sounds correct to your "ear," then it is what you meant to say and is probably correct. Here is an example of a sentence that is not properly punctuated:

> Retrofitting school buses with seat belts, would probably not be a cost effective measure considering the small number of accidents involving schools buses each year.

If you read this to yourself, you should wonder why there ought to be a pause between "belts" and "would." And there should not be, so eliminate the comma there. In general, so long as you maintain tight control of the other elements of writing and don't try to create overly elaborate structures, punctuation should not be a major problem.

Exercise 1

ISSUE TASK

Issue Task: Present Your Views on an Issue
Time: 45 minutes

You have 45 minutes to plan and write an essay that presents your views on an assigned topic.

The topic is summarized in a brief quotation that states or suggests a position. You can accept, reject, or modify the position. Support your views with reasons and examples drawn from your experience, observation, reading, or study.

Trained graders will score your response, taking account of how well you:

- Understand the complexities and ramifications of the issue

- Organize, develop, and express your ideas

- Deploy the elements of standard written English

You may wish to spend a few minutes thinking about your response before you begin writing and to leave time to reread what you have written in order to make any revisions you think necessary.

Present your point of view on the following issue:

> "Hierarchical structures such as corporations and governments are neither moral nor immoral. The decisions made on behalf of such entities are made by individuals who ultimately bear the ethical responsibilities for the effects of the policies of the hierarchies."

GRE: Graduate Record Examination

Exercise 2

Argument Task: Analyze an Argument
Time: 30 minutes

You have 30 minutes to plan and write an essay that presents your views on an assigned topic. Consider the logic of the argument and the soundness of its conclusion.

Trained graders will score your response, taking account of how well you:

- Identify and analyze the structure of the argument
- Organize, develop, and express your ideas
- Deploy the elements of standard written English

You may wish to spend a few minutes thinking about your response before you begin writing and to leave time to reread what you have written in order to make any revisions you think necessary.

Read the following argument and discuss whether it is well-reasoned. You are *not* being asked to agree or disagree with the conclusion of the argument; you are being asked to analyze the reasoning in the argument. Consider what, if any assumptions the argument makes and whether they are justified, what evidence is offered for the conclusion and whether it is reliable, as well as any other factors or information that would strengthen or weaken the argument.

Discuss how well reasoned you find the following argument:

> The government makes available guarantees of loans not only for students attending college but for students enrolled in training schools for trades such as cosmetology and automotive repairs. It was recently found that a school located in a large city encouraged unqualified students to enroll in their training programs and take out government loans for tuition but then did little to ensure that they would learn a trade. Once the government backed tuition loan was paid to the school, its operators didn't care whether the students failed or graduated. This is a waste of taxpayer money and does a disservice to the students themselves. Government guarantees for tuition loans for trade schools should be discontinued.

What You Must Know About the GRE Writing Assessment

Review this page the night before you take the GRE Writing Assessment.

- The Writing Assessment requires essay responses to two topics ("prompts"): an "issue" topic and an "argument" topic.

- Essays are graded on a scale of 0 to 6 for content, organization, and execution.

- These steps can help you handle the Writing Assessment:

   1. Read the topic and decide what position you want to take.

   2. Outline your thinking using the scratch paper that is provided.

   3. Type your essay.

   4. Proofread your essay.

- You should always write on the given topic.

- You should illustrate your ideas with examples.

- You should organize each essay by using the "three main points" approach

Financing Your Graduate Education

Education is expensive, and the higher the level of education, the greater the cost. As you contemplate going on to graduate or professional school, you must face the awesome question, "How am I going to pay for this?"

With the possible exceptions of a winning lottery ticket, a windfall inheritance, or a very wealthy family, no single source of funds will be adequate to cover tuition, other educational costs, and living expenses during your years of graduate study. While the funding task is daunting, it is not impossible. With patience and hard work, you can piece together your own financial package.

CONSIDER DEFERRING YOUR APPLICATION

You might consider putting off applications for a few years while you work at the highest paying job you can find and accumulate some funds. A few years' savings will not cover the entire bill, but they can help. A real effort to earn your own way is a show of sincerity and good faith when you approach funders, too. You are probably better off delaying your applications altogether rather than applying and deferring your entry once you have been accepted. Deferral, if permitted, is generally limited to one year, and one year may not be sufficient to build your tuition fund.

If you cannot find a really high-paying job, you might seek a position or series of positions closely related to your field for the years between undergraduate and graduate or professional school. A year or more of exposure and involvement can help you to focus your interest. Experience in the field shows up as an asset on your graduate admissions applications and on your applications for fellowships. The more crystallized your interests, the better essays and personal statements you can write to support your requests.

Another benefit to deferral is the opportunity to establish residence. As you research the various graduate programs, you are likely to discover that some of the most exciting programs in your field of interest are being offered at state universities. State universities tend to have lower rates than do private universities. Furthermore, the tuition charged to bona fide residents is considerably lower than that charged to out-of-state residents. The requirements for establishing residence vary from state to state; make it a point to inquire about the possibility of in-state tuition at each state university you are considering. The suggestion that you delay application until you are nearly ready to enter graduate school does not hold with regard to delay for purposes of establishing residence. Since you can only establish residence in one state, you want to apply and be accepted before you select your new home state. Most universities will cooperate and will allow you to move to the state, find employment, and defer enrollment until you qualify for in-state tuition.

WORKING PART-TIME

Another possible way to pay is to be a part-time student and a full- or part-time wage earner. Again, there are a number of options. You might find a totally unrelated but high-paying job. You will have to be creative in your search. Sanitation workers, for instance, tend to have hours like 7 am to 3 pm, which leaves afternoon and evening for classes and study. The job of the sanitation worker is physically exhausting but makes no mental demands and in most localities is quite well paid.

Another job which does not take too much thought is working for a courier service like United Parcel. Such delivery services operate twenty-four hours a day. During the night, packages are off-loaded from big interstate trucks and from bulk deliveries from individual shippers and are sorted and loaded onto delivery trucks for route drivers the next day. There is usually plenty of turnover among these night workers, and most parcel service employees are unionized, so the hourly rate is attractive.

An alternative to physical labor might be seeking a job in a field related to your studies. Such a job could reinforce your learning and contribute to the job experience section of your resume. If you are earning a degree in computer science, you might find computer-related employment. If you are entering law school, you might work as a paralegal.

If you both defer application and enter a related field, you may be fortunate enough to find an employer who will pay for a part or even all of your graduate education. This option is most viable if the advanced degree is to be in business or law, but some corporations will finance a master's degree or even a doctorate if the further training will make the employee more valuable to them. Employers cannot require that you continue your employment for any specified number of years after earning your degree. Rather they rely on your gratitude and goodwill.

The programs under which employers help pay for education are as varied as the number of employers and the graduate programs. Many banks, insurance companies, and brokerage houses offer tuition rebates as part of their benefits packages. These companies rebate part or all of the tuition for courses successfully completed by their employees. Sometimes the rate of reimbursement is tied to the grade earned in the course.

Some large law firms will advance part of the law school tuition for promising paralegals after a number of years of service. If these students successfully complete law school and return to the firm for summers and a certain number of years afterwards, the balance of the tuition may be reimbursed. And some industrial corporations will cover the cost of part-time study that enhances the skills of employees, thus making them still more useful to the organization. Such corporations may permit these employees to work a shortened workweek at full-time pay while they study.

Some companies even give the employee a year's leave, without salary but with tuition paid, and with a guarantee that the employee will have a job at the end of the leave. This guaranteed position at the end of the leave is worth a lot. It offers peace of mind and freedom to concentrate on research and writing and assures that you will immediately begin earning money with which to repay supplementary graduate loans and leftover undergraduate loans.

If you have been working for the same employer for a year or more, you might do well to inquire about a tuition rebate program. If you are a valuable employee, your employer may be willing to make an investment in you.

THE MILITARY OPTION

If you are heavily burdened with loans from your undergraduate years and are willing to serve for three years in the armed forces, the government will pay off a large portion of your college loans for you. Without the under-graduate debt, you will be eligible for larger loans for your graduate study, and you will not have so many years of high repayment bills to face.

After your three years of service, you will be eligible for GI Bill benefits so that you will not need to incur such hefty loans for graduate school. While you are actually in the service, you can attend graduate school part time and have 75% of the cost paid for you. Funding for medical school and law school is even more attractive.

From the point of view of footing the bill for graduate studies, the military option sounds too good to be true. Of course there are strings attached. You must serve in the armed forces. You are subject to military rules and military discipline. You may find that a transfer of location totally disrupts your studies if you are trying to attend part-time. And, in case of war or other military emergency, you must serve and quite possibly face physical danger. This is the trade-off. If the advantages of having the government pay your education bills outweigh the drawbacks in your eyes, by all means explore the military option. Check with more than one branch of the services;

programs vary and change frequently. Ask lots of questions. Be certain that you fully understand all of your obligations, and insist that the funding commitment be in writing. You cannot change your mind and just quit the armed forces, so you must be certain that this route is right for you before you sign up.

If full-time military service is out of the question for you, but having the government underwrite your education is still attractive, consider the National Guard or the Reserves. The all-volunteer standing armed forces are not adequate for all national security needs, so efforts are constantly being made to increase the appeal of the Guard and the Reserves. The benefits offered are frequently readjusted, so you must make your own inquiries about loan repayments and funding of ongoing education while you are in service.

Life in the Guard or the Reserves is not nearly so restrictive on a daily basis as life in the regular armed forces, but both Guard members and Reservists are subject to call-up in times of need, and if you are called, you must serve. Circumstances of a call-up may include dangerous assignment, severe economic difficulties, or service that you find morally repugnant (such as strike-breaking if you are a member of a Guard unit called by the governor). If these contingencies do not upset you, this form of long-term, part-time military service can relieve you of much of the cost of your advanced degree.

NEED-BASED FUNDING

The need-based funding picture for graduate studies is quite different from its counterpart at the undergraduate level. Most undergraduate funding is need-based; most graduate funding is not. All universities have a mechanism for distributing graduate need-based funding, in grant/loan/self-help packages similar to undergraduate packages, but the funds are more limited. Your application information packet will tell you how to apply for need-based funding.

Basically you will have to fill out a university financial aid application, a U.S. Department of Education approved multi-data entry form (FFS, the family financial statement of American College Testing service; FAE, the financial aid form of the Educational Testing Service; or GAPSFAS, the graduate and professional school financial aid service of the Educational Testing Service in California), and whatever other forms the university requires. The university will coordinate its need-based package with department sponsored merit funding and with any outside funding you can gather. Plan to look beyond university need-based funding. It will be top-heavy toward loans and will not be adequate for all your needs.

The following information distributed to all graduate school applicants by a leading large state university is specific to that university yet, at the same time, is representative of the need-based funding situation nationwide.

ASSISTANCE THROUGH THE OFFICE OF STUDENT FINANCIAL AID (OSFA)

You may be eligible for financial aid if you are enrolled at least half-time (five semester hours during the academic year, or three semester hours during the summer session) as a graduate student in a program leading to a degree. Students admitted as Special Nondegree Students may also be eligible for some of the programs listed below.

How to Apply

Specific information and application materials may be obtained from OSFA. To determine your eligibility for aid through the OSFA, you must provide information about your financial situation by submitting either the Financial Aid Form (FAF) to the College Scholarship Service (CSS) or the Family Financial Statement (FFS) to American College Testing (ACT). This University does not accept the Graduate and Professional School Financial Aid Service (GAPSFAS) form.

OSFA will process your financial aid application as soon as your file becomes complete. Some financial aid programs are subject to the availability of funds (first-come, first-served) and others are not. To be considered for all limited funds, be sure to submit your materials as soon as possible after January 1 for the upcoming academic year.

Financial need is an eligibility requirement for all of the following sources of assistance except the Supplemental Loans for Students (SLS) program and part-time jobs.

Graduate Tuition Grants are based on exceptional need. These institutional grant funds are very limited. Approximately 200 students are awarded tuition grants early in March prior to the academic year in which they plan to enroll.

Educational Opportunity Program (EOP) Grants are institutional grants for minority students who demonstrate exceptional need.

The College Work-Study Program is an employment program subsidized by the federal government and the state.

Perkins Loans are long-term federal loans based on exceptional need.

Stafford Loans (formerly Guaranteed Student Loans—GSL) are long-term federal loans based on need and arranged with a bank, credit union, or savings and loan.

Supplemental Loans for Students (SLS) are arranged with a bank, credit union, or savings and loan and are available to students with or without need.

In addition, part-time jobs (not to be confused with College Work-Study jobs) available throughout the campus and community are posted daily on bulletin boards outside of the OSFA.

Special Note to Assistantship/Fellowship Recipients

Since most assistantship income is classified as "wages," it will not affect your academic year financial aid award (which is usually based on your

continues

continued

previous year's income, according to the federal formula for determining financial aid eligibility). However, fellowship income classified as "scholarship" rather than "wages" will be treated as "scholarship resources" in your financial aid package, and thus may affect your eligibility for other financial aid programs.

Nonresident financial aid awardees who receive assistantships that allow resident classification for tuition purposes may have their need-based aid decreased due to the decrease in their educational cost.

Outside need-based funding in the form of grants is confined mainly to special populations. Since these grants are limited in number, they too are based on a combination of merit and need, not merely upon demonstrated need. Some of these special population grants are targeted toward bringing minority students into the professions, such as those sponsored by the Black Lawyers' Associations of various states. Others aim to develop academic talent among Native Americans and Hispanics. Others, such as Business and Professional Women's Foundation Scholarships, are earmarked for mature women reentering the academic world in search of advanced degrees.

Grant and fellowship directories tend to index grants by specialty, by region of the country, by point in the studies and time span of funding, and by targeted population. When you consult these directories, you must consider your own identity along every possible dimension in order to locate funding that could apply to you.

Much outside funding comes in the form of loans. Although helpful and often necessary, loans are still a last resort. For this reason, we shall defer our discussion of loans until the end of this chapter.

FELLOWSHIPS AND ASSISTANTSHIPS

By far the greatest source of funding for graduate study is the graduate department or program itself. Most departments dispense a mixed bag of fellowships, teaching assistantships, and research assistantships. Some of these may be allocated to the department by the university; still others are foundation fellowships for which the department nominates its most promising candidates. In most cases, the amount of money attached to the various fellowships and assistantships varies greatly—from tuition abatement alone, to tuition abatement plus stipend (also of varying sums), to stipend alone. Some of the fellowships and assistantships are specifically earmarked for only the first year of graduate study. Others are annually renewable upon application and evidence of satisfactory work in the previous year. Still others are guaranteed for a specified number of years—through three years of course work, for one year of research or fieldwork, or a stipend to pay living costs during the year of writing a dissertation, for example.

The information below describes graduate student funding only at the University of Iowa. It is presented here to open the array of possibilities. The information provided by other universities is similar, but each is unique.

SUPPORT FROM THE GRADUATE COLLEGE AND YOUR DEPARTMENT OR PROGRAM

The following awards and appointments are the primary sources of financial assistance available to graduate students through their department or program.

Teaching and Research Assistantships available in most departments offer stipends typically ranging from $9,000 to $10,000 for half-time appointments. In accordance with general University policy, assistantship holders (quarter-time or more) are classified as residents for fee purposes for the terms during which their appointments are held and any adjacent summer sessions in which they are enrolled. Students on an appointment of half-time or more may have to carry a reduced academic load.

Iowa Fellowships for first-year graduate students entering doctoral programs carry a minimum stipend of $14,500 plus full tuition for four years on a year-round basis (academic year and summer session). For two of the four years and all summers, recipients have no assignments and are free to pursue their own studies, research, and writing.

Graduate College Block Allocation Fellowships carry a stipend of $8,000 for the academic year.

Graduate Opportunity Fellowships for first-year graduate students from underrepresented ethnic minority groups carry a one-year stipend of $8,000 for the academic year.

Scholarships, traineeships, and part-time employment are offered by many graduate departments and programs. Funds are received from both public and private agencies, individuals, corporations, and philanthropic organizations. In general, submission of the *Application for Graduate Awards and Appointments* places eligible applicants in consideration for these awards.

How to Apply

Submit your Application for Graduate Awards and Appointments to your department or program by February if you wish to be considered for the following fall. These non-need-based awards are made on the basis of academic merit. Only students admitted to a graduate department or program are eligible to apply. Fellowship and assistantship recipients are also eligible to apply for tuition scholarships awarded in amounts up to full-time tuition and fees. Contact your program or department for more specific information.

Surprisingly, the overall wealth of the institution is not necessarily reflected in the graduate funding it offers. Some universities choose to devote the bulk of their discretionary funds to undergraduate need-based aid. Others offer a greater share to graduate students. Some graduate departments in some universities have separate endowments apart from the university endowment as a whole. A department with its own source of funds can dispense these funds as it wishes, within the restrictions of the endowment, of course.

The case of Clark University in Worcester, Massachusetts, is illustrative of the ways a particular department funds its students. Clark is a relatively small, financially strapped institution. University-based funding for undergraduates is severely limited. Yet, every doctoral candidate in the geography department is equally funded; each receives tuition abatement and an equal stipend in return for teaching or research assistance. The funding is guaranteed for three years of course work. How can this be? The geography department at Clark has, over the years, developed an extremely high reputation. It is considered one of the premier geography departments in the United States. The university considers investment in its geography department to be one of its priorities because maintaining the reputation of its flagship department enhances the reputation of the university as a whole. Leading professors are eager to be associated with leading departments, so the Clark geography faculty includes some luminaries in its ranks. These faculty members in turn attract research funds. Research funds are used in part to pay for the services of research assistants. Publication of results of the research attracts further grants. These funds cover a number of graduate students. The reputation of the department also leads it to draw the best and the brightest among its doctoral candidates. These highly qualified students often draw outside fellowships on the basis of their own merit. Students who bring in their own funding release department funds for other students. And because of its reputation and the reputed caliber of its students, the department is often offered the opportunity to nominate its students to compete for private fellowships. Money entering the department in this way releases still more of the limited funds for student support. In a good year, there may even be funds to help some students at the beginning of their dissertation research.

The situation at Clark, while it is Clark's alone, indicates that it may be possible to find funding even in a small, struggling school. Graduate aid is not monolithic. You must ask about the special features in each department and in each program. Do not limit your research to the overall university bulletin!

Sometimes a university will offer some departments the opportunity to nominate candidates for outside fellowships open to students of certain specified departments or to students of the university at large. For example, the MacArthur Foundation funds a number of interdisciplinary fellowships in peace studies at a few selected universities. Each participating university is allocated a number of fellowships to dispense at its discretion. The university then opens the competition to appropriate departments, and the departments in turn nominate candidates from among their most promising applicants. The departments choose nominees on the basis of personal statements submitted at the time of application and on the basis of those applicants' credentials and background experiences. They then solicit the nominees to prepare additional application materials and essays and supply additional recommendations to support application for the fellowship. Having MacArthur fellows among its students brings both money and prestige to the department. Each department studies credentials and statements carefully before soliciting applicants. However, the department could overlook someone. If you have not been invited to apply for a fellowship which you think you qualify for, you can suggest to the department— diplomatically, of course—that you consider yourself a likely candidate.

Few individuals are awarded any one fellowship, but each person who does win one is assured a comfortable source of funding. And someone has to win. It might as well be you. Those who win the named fellowships are removed from the competition for other merit-based or need-based funding, thus increasing the chance of other applicants to win any remaining funds.

Most foundation-funded fellowships, especially those for entering graduate students, are channeled through the department or program. To be considered for these fellowships you must be recommended by the department. There are some fellowships out there, however, for which you must apply as an individual. Some of these are regional, and some are targeted at a specific population. Some are tied to a field such as economics or philosophy, and others have a specific purpose in mind such as studies aimed at improving the welfare of the homeless. Of the privately funded fellowships some are for the first year only, some for the full graduate career, some for the last year of course work only, and still others to support the dissertation at a specific stage or throughout research and writing. Some are relatively small awards; others are so generous that they provide total financial security to the student. The sources of these fellowships range from your local Rotary Club to Rotary International, to AAUW (American Association of University Women) fellowships, to the prestigious Rhodes Scholarships.

FUNDING POSSIBILITIES FROM PRIVATE FOUNDATIONS

The names of some of the philanthropic foundations that give grants for graduate study are almost household words—Dana, Mellon, Ford, Sloan, Rockefeller, Guggenheim, MacArthur, Fulbright, Woodrow Wilson are but a few. These foundations, and others like them, offer funding at many levels of study and for a variety of purposes.

The National Science Foundation offers funding for the full graduate program in science and engineering for minority students as well as for the general population. Other National Science Foundation fellowships specifically fund the research and writing of doctoral dissertations. The U.S. Department of Education Jacob K. Javits Fellowships fund full doctoral programs in the arts, humanities, and social sciences. The National Research Council Howard Hughes Medical Institute Doctoral Fellowships offer tuition and a $10,000 per year stipend for three to five years of doctoral work in biology or the health sciences. The Eisenhower Memorial Scholarship Foundation offers a number of $3,000 per year scholarships. The Mellon and Ford Foundations both fund ABD (all but dissertation) fellowships for minority Ph.D. candidates. Under the terms of the ABD fellowships, candidates teach one course per term at a liberal arts college and receive a healthy stipend while writing their dissertations. This program has the double-barreled purpose of assisting minority students while developing teaching talent.

The AAUW (American Association of University Women) is very active in disbursing funds to women for graduate study. Local units give small gifts to undergraduates. Larger grants are made by the AAUW through its Educational Foundation Programs office. In some years the AAUW supports as many as fifty women at the dissertation stage. The Business and Professional Women's Foundation gives scholarships to mature women entering graduate programs. Some of these scholarships are earmarked for women over the age of 35. The American Women in Selected Professions Fellowships fund women in their last year of law or graduate studies in sums ranging from $3,500 to $9,000 apiece.

Other funding for doctoral dissertations comes from the Woodrow Wilson National Fellowship Foundation (in social sciences and humanities), from the Social Science Research Council, and the Guggenheim Foundation. Some foundation funding is reserved for study abroad. Rhodes Scholarships, in particular, support students studying at Oxford. Various Fulbright, Wilsons, Marshalls, and MacArthurs, among others, support research in foreign universities and at field sites.

The above listing is far from exhaustive. In fact, this is only a tiny sampling of the funding possibilities from private foundations. Even so, the number of grants available is far exceeded by the number of graduate students who would like to have them. You must work hard to identify and to earn the grants for which you qualify.

FINDING SOURCES OF FINANCIAL AID

There are a number of directories that list these prizes, scholarships, and fellowships one by one. The directories give the name of the sponsor, who to contact, addresses, phone numbers, and deadlines. They also tell something of the purpose of the grants, the number of grants awarded, specific qualification requirements, and the dollar amounts. If the grants are awarded to support research, the directories may give representative titles of projects funded. One of the most useful features of the directories is their cross-indexing. When you consult a grants directory you can look up sources under ethnic designations, geographic designations, subject of study, purpose of research, duration of funding, etc. These directories are very useful as a starting point in the search for outside funding.

Consult the list of directories in the bibliography at the end of this appendix. With list in hand, go to a college library, large public library, or the financial aid office of your current institution and sit down with a directory and pad of paper. Give yourself many hours to find all the grants for which you qualify and to photocopy or write down the important details of each. Immediately call or write each sponsor requesting application materials. Do not rely on deadlines printed in the directories and put off requesting materials. Deadlines change. Do not discount grants or prizes with low dollar amounts attached. A small grant may not be adequate to see you through even a semester of study, but it will do much to enhance your resume. The fact that you were able to compete successfully for any prize makes you a more attractive candidate for the higher-tagged fellowships you apply for next year. If a grant cannot be combined, you may have to decline it, but the fact of having won is already in your favor. Most often, small grants can be combined with other sources of funding, so even small ones help.

APPLYING FOR A GRANT

The procedure for applying for grants and fellowships for your coursework years is similar for both university-administered and private foundation sources. The best advice is to start early. Everything takes longer than you expect, and deadlines tend to be inviolate. Everyone with money to give away is besieged by applicants. There is no need to extend deadlines.

Once you receive application material, begin immediately to accumulate the specified documentation. Each sponsor has different requirements, so read carefully. You will probably need official transcripts from every college you ever attended, even if you took only one course over the summer. You are likely to be asked for official copies of test scores, too. Letters of recommendation are always required. Think about them carefully. You want to request letters from people who have known you as a scholar—professors with whom you have worked closely or authors for whom you have done research or fact checking. You want your letters to be written by people whom you believe have admired your work and who express themselves well. And, consider the reliability of the people from whom you request letters of recommendation. Your application can be seriously jeopardized or even torpedoed if your recommendations do not come through on time. Choose carefully. Consider asking for one extra recommendation just in case someone lets you down. Having recommendations sent to you and then forwarding them in their sealed envelopes is the best way to keep track of what has come in if this procedure is permitted by the sponsor. Be aware that you may have to make a pest of yourself to get transcripts and letters in on time.

You are more in control of the other documents you are likely to be asked for in support of your application. The first of these is a "personal goals statement." This is a carefully reasoned, clear statement of your interests, the reasons for your choice of program, personal growth goals, and career goals. Ideally you should prepare this statement on a word processor so you can retain the basic exposition but tailor each statement to the needs and interests of the specific sponsor. Try to tie in your statement with the special strengths of the program and with the advantages offered by a particular sponsor. Be sincere and enthusiastic. Adhere to the page limits or word count specified in the application instructions. And remember, neatness counts.

You may also be asked for your resume, samples of scholarly writing, or summaries of research you have done. If the grant you seek is meant to finance research or dissertation, you may have to go into detail about the scope of your research, methodology, purpose, expected final results, and even proposed budget. Give thought before you write. Then follow the sponsor's instructions, providing all the information that is requested, but not so much more as to overwhelm or bore the reader.

One caveat: Read the requirements carefully before you apply. If you do not fully qualify, do not apply. There are ample qualified applicants for every grant. Requirements will not be waived. The application process is an exacting one and requires you to impose upon others. Do not waste their time or your own.

EMPLOYMENT OPPORTUNITIES ON CAMPUS

While your department is clearly the best university-based source for fellowships, teaching assistantships, and research assistantships, do not totally discount the university as a whole. If you have an area of expertise outside of your own graduate department, by all means build upon it. If you are bilingual in a language taught at the university, you may be able to teach in the language department. Your best chance for a teaching assistantship outside of your department is in a university with relatively few graduate programs. Departments must favor their own graduate students, but if a department has no qualified students of its own, it may be delighted to acquire the services of a graduate student from another department. Some universities even have a formalized mechanism for allocating teaching assistants where they are needed.

To return to the example of Clark, where all graduate students must serve as research or teaching assistants, often there are not as many openings for assistants in the undergraduate geography department as there are students. Clark has relatively few graduate programs, and geography students tend to have strong backgrounds in political science, economics, and ecology. The graduate geography department and the undergraduate deans readily cooperate to place geography students where they are most needed. In universities with less defined needs for teaching assistants, you may have to be your own advocate. Regardless of your current department, if you can document your ability to assist in another department, you should pursue opportunities there. Do not be shy; let your area of special competence be well known.

Another possible source of university employment is as a residence advisor or freshman advisor. At some colleges and universities, residence advisors are undergraduates. At other institutions, older students—graduate students or students in one of the professional schools—are preferred. If you took peer-counseling training while in high school, consider yourself a candidate. If you were successful in a counseling function during your own undergraduate years, you should be a natural. In very large universities with big freshmen dormitories, a few graduate students with experience in residence advising may be taken on to coordinate and supervise the senior undergraduates who serve as floor or wing advisors. Obviously there are not many such coordinator positions available, but if you qualify, you may get the job.

There are a number of possible advantages to being appointed to a major university-based position such as teaching assistant or residence advisor. One is that, at a state university, you will become eligible instantly for in-state tuition. The reduced tuition is a valuable, non-taxable benefit. Another possibility is that you will be classified as an employee of the university. Policies vary, of course, but at many institutions employees of the university are eligible for reduced tuition or even for total remission of tuition. In addition, assistants generally receive a stipend, which, even if it does not totally cover living expenses, is certainly a big help. Residence hall advisors may get free room along with tuition abatement, and they generally get choice accommodations.

If you were a member of a fraternity or sorority as an undergraduate, you may fulfill a role similar to that of residence advisor in your fraternity or sorority house. As an employee of the fraternity or sorority rather than of the university, you will not be eligible for employee-of-the-university benefits, but you will have free housing and, quite possibly, a salary or stipend as well. Fraternity employment will count toward self-help in a need-based package, but it should have no adverse effect on your winning a merit-based fellowship as well. Be aware, though, that if you are holding what is in effect two jobs, you may have to carry a lighter course load.

Students who work part time in the library, equipment and facilities departments, or in food service will probably not qualify for the perquisites of employees of the university (though depending on the institution and the number of hours worked they might). Campus-based hourly work tends not to be very well paid, but it does offer certain advantages such as elimination of travel time and costs and exemption from FICA (social security) deductions from your paycheck. Exemption from FICA is at the option of the institution, but is permitted by the federal tax code. The contribution which is not deducted has the effect of adding more than 7% to your salary.

ALL LOANS ARE NOT ALIKE

Finally loans come in to fill the financing gap. If you are already saddled with loans from your undergraduate education, you may cringe at the prospect of accumulating further debt. Don't panic. Not all loans are alike, and not all repayment schedules are equally onerous.

In particular, members of minority groups find creative financing routes available to them. The Consortium on the Financing of Higher Education (C.O.F.H.E.), a group of thirty-one universities and colleges including the Ivies and Sister colleges, is making a concerted effort to encourage minority students to pursue advanced degrees. The Kluge Foundation program at Columbia University is only one response to the funding problem. Because Columbia University is an expensive private university, its undergraduates often find themselves heavily indebted to the university by commencement. Under the terms of the Kluge grant, minority alumni of Columbia who successfully complete doctoral programs at accredited universities will have their undergraduate indebtedness wiped out by the Kluge funds. The Minority Issues Task Force of the Council of Graduate Schools is working on the funding problems of minority students, many of whom have very few resources. The funding picture is in constant flux. Be sure that you have the most current information at the moment you are ready to begin applying.

The loan forgiveness possibilities for members of the armed forces have already been touched upon. If military service is not for you, there are other loan forgiveness programs you may find attractive. With the shortage of highly qualified, highly motivated public school teachers, there has been a concerted effort to attract liberal arts graduates, even without full teaching credentials, into public school teaching. Liberal arts graduates who enter the public school teaching force under certain programs can have their undergraduate loans written off. If you enter public school teaching after receiving a graduate degree, you may still receive considerable help with those undergraduate loans. Paying off your own graduate school loans, then, will not be so overwhelming.

Most student loan forgiveness programs for graduate loans apply to professional studies—medicine, dentistry, law, social work—rather than to straight academic disciplines. If your graduate studies will lead to a professional degree, you should not discount loan forgiveness programs out of hand.

A doctor who forgoes a lucrative suburban practice in favor of practicing for a number of years in an underserved area, be it poverty-ridden inner city or isolated rural community, may have a good portion of his or her loans paid off by the government or by private foundations or forgiven by the medical school itself. The doctor may find that the challenges of this practice and the gratitude of the population served are so satisfying that he or she will choose to make this practice a lifelong career. If not, the experience will certainly have been valuable as the doctor moves in new directions. Similarly a number of prestigious law schools will wipe out the loans of their graduates who enter public service law instead of high-paying corporate law firms. And schools of social work or professional associations of social workers may help to pay off the loans of social workers who utilize their advanced degrees in certain aspects of social work or in highly underserved areas.

If your ideals encourage using your educational opportunities to help others, you may find this assistance with your loan payments to give you the best of all possible worlds. The time commitment tends to only be a few years, after which you can move into the private sector with excellent experience to further your applications. Or, you may find that you really enjoy the work you have taken on and build a satisfying career in public service.

There are a number of other loan programs which, while they entail repayment, offer attractive features. The Hattie M. Strong Foundation, for instance, offers interest-free loans for the final year of graduate school or law school on the assumption that without money worries the student can earn higher grades in the final year and obtain a better position after graduation.

From your undergraduate days, you are probably aware of Stafford loans, formerly known as GSLs or Guaranteed Student Loans. At the graduate level the annual cap is $7,500 per year up to a borrowing limit of $54,750. The Stafford loan carries a lower rate of interest than most other loans. More important, repayment need not begin until six months after receipt of the degree, and the government pays the interest in the interim. There is a means test attached to the Stafford loan. Not every applicant is automatically eligible. However, many graduate students who are no longer dependent on parental income or assets do qualify for Stafford loans even though they did not as undergraduates.

University sponsored loans tend to be heavily need-based and to come as parts of total financial aid packages with grants, assistantships, and jobs. And even need-based loans are often earmarked for specific underrepresented populations. If you think that you qualify, ask for the information and forms.

Everything that has been said about private foundation funding applies equally to loans as to grants and fellowships. The same directories that can lead you to grants and fellowships can lead you to foundation loans. Again, some of these require evidence of need; others are strictly merit-based. Some apply to the early years of graduate study; others are geared to the dissertation years. Some carry no or low rates of interest, and some have forgiveness provisions if certain conditions are met. In general, foundation loans are less painful than commercial loans. Do not limit your search through the grant directories to high-paying grants. Give equal attention to the smaller prizes and to the loan programs.

Most other loan programs are unrestricted as to income or assets but tend to have restrictions related to total debt with which the student is already burdened and to security or cosigners for the loan. The financial aid office of your current institution or the school to which you have been accepted can help you find your way through the maze of acronymic loan programs: SLS, PLUS, ALAS, TERI, Sallie Mae, Nellie Mae, and the Law Access Program administered by the Law School Admission Service. These last four are non-profit loan agencies that allow for greater flexibility than do the first three. In general, the rates are tied to prime + 2 which is better than commercial rates. Repayment schedules, loan consolidation arrangements, cosigning requirements, etc. are all considered on a case-by-case basis.

GETTING INTO GRADUATE SCHOOL

Now that you know it is possible to pay for your graduate education, you must move toward securing admission and funding.

You have already taken a step toward graduate school because you have in hand a preparation book for a graduate school admission exam. Presumably you are about to take or have already taken one or more of these exams. A good score on the exam is an important component of the picture of competence and capability that you present to graduate programs and funding sponsors. If your grades and achievements have been impressive, a high score confirms you as an all-around good candidate. If either grades or achievements are mediocre, then high scores are imperative to bolster your cause. If you have not already taken the exam, study hard; prepare well. If you did not achieve a competitive score on a previous exam, it might be worthwhile to prepare further and try again.

The next thing to do is to begin to investigate which schools have the right programs for you. If you are still in college or out only a year or two, consult with professors who know you well, who are familiar not only with your interests but with your style of working. Professors may suggest programs that suit your needs, universities that offer emphasis in your areas of interest, and faculty members with whom you might work especially well. Your professors may have inside information about contemplated changes in program, focus, or personnel at various institutions. This information can supplement the information in university bulletins and help you decide which schools to apply to. If you have been out of school for several years, you may have to rely more on information bulletins. But do not stop there. Ask for advice and suggestions from people in the field, from present employers if your job is related to your career goals, and from the current faculty and advising staff at your undergraduate school. While the current personnel may not be familiar with you and your learning style, they will have up-to-date information on programs and faculties.

Send for university and departmental literature. Read everything you can about programs offered. Then study the statements on aid, both need-based and merit-based. Be sure that you are completely clear as to the process-criteria, forms required, other supporting documents, and deadlines. If any step of the process seems ambiguous, make phone calls. You can't afford to miss out on possible funding because you misinterpreted the application directions.

It's a good idea to prepare a master calendar dedicated to graduate school. Note the deadlines for each step of the process for every school, for every foundation, for every possible source of funds. Consult the master calendar daily. Anticipate deadlines, record actions taken by you and by others, follow up, keep on top of it. Do not just let events happen. Be proactive every step of the way.

The university, graduate school, and departmental bulletins will inform you about need-based aid and about any merit-based funding—teaching assistantships, research assistantships, no-strings fellowships, and private foundation fellowships—administered by the university or any of its divisions. This information will be complete for the funding to which it applies. It will include all procedures documentation required, and deadlines. None of the literature you receive from the university, however, will tell you about fellowships or other funding for which you must apply directly. You must consult grant directories, foundation directories, and other source books to find the prizes, awards, scholarships, grants, and fellowships for which you might qualify.

The following bibliography is an eclectic list of directories. The directories are listed by title and publisher without dates of publication. Most directories are updated frequently. Whenever you ask for a directory, look at the copyright date. If the directory appears to be more than a year old, ask the librarian if there is a newer edition available. Consult the most recent edition you can find. No matter how frequently a directory is updated, you should never rely on deadline dates given for grants. Write or call the sponsor of each grant that you are considering, and request the most current literature. Make certain that names and addresses have not changed. Verify dates for each step of the process. The information in the directory is a valuable starting point, but it is just that: a starting point.

Most of the directories listed at the end of this section apply to more than one population. Use the index and the list of categories to find which portions of the book apply to you. Disregard any categories into which you do not fit. Concentrate in those areas where you do.

Aside from their copious cross-referencing, most directories also include bibliographies listing other information sources. Do not neglect these lists. One may send you to the perfect source for you.

BIBLIOGRAPHY

General Directories

American Legion Education Program. Need a Lift? To Educational Opportunities, Careers, Loans, Scholarships, Employment. American Legion: Indianapolis, IN.

Annual Register of Grant Support. Marquis: Chicago, IL.

Catalog of Federal Domestic Assistance. U.S. Office of Management and Budget: Washington, D.C.

Chronicle Student Aid Annual. Chronicle Guidance Publication: Moravia, NY.

The College Blue Book, Vol. entitled *Scholarships, Fellowships, Grants & Loans.* Macmillan, NY.

Directory of Financial Aids for Minorities. Reference Service Press: Santa Barbara, CA.

Directory of Financial Aids for Women. Reference Service Press: Santa Barbara, CA.

DRG: Directory of Research Grants. Oryx Press: Scottsdale, AZ.

A Foreign Student's Selected Guide to Financial Assistance for Study and Research in the United States. Adelphi University Press: Garden City, NY.

Foundation Directory. The Foundation Center: New York.

Foundation Grants to individuals. The Foundation Center: New York.

The Graduate Scholarship Book, by Daniel J. Cassidy. Prentice Hall: New York.

Grants for Graduate Students, edited by John J. Wells and Amy J. Goldstein. Petersons: Princeton, NJ.

The Grants Register. St. Martins: New York.

Selected List of Fellowships and Loans, Vols. VI-VIII. Bellman Publishing Co.: Arlington, MA.

Selected List of Fellowship Opportunities and Aids to Advanced Education for United States Citizens and Foreign Nationals. National Science Foundation: Washington, D.C.

Taft Corporate Giving Directory: Comprehensive Profiles & Analyses of Major Corporate Philanthropic Programs. The Taft Group.

Field and Subject Directories

American Art Directory. R.R. Bowker: New York.

American Mathematical Society Notices: "Assistantship and Fellowships in the Mathematical Sciences." December issue, each year.

American Philosophical Association. Proceedings and Addresses: "Grants and Fellowships of Interest to Philosophers." June each year.

Graduate Study in Psychology and Associated Fields. American Psychological Association: Washington, D.C.

Grants for the Arts, by Virginia P. White. Plenum Press: New York.

Grants and Awards Available to American Writers. PEN American Center: New York.

Grants, Fellowships and Prizes of Interest to Historians. American Historical Association: Washington, D.C.

Grants in the Humanities: A Scholar's Guide to Funding Sources. Neal-Schuman: New York.

Journalism Career and Scholarship Guide. The Newspaper Fund: Princeton, NJ.

Money for Artists: A Guide to Grants and Awards for Individual Artists. ACA Books: New York.

Music Industry Directory. Marquis: Chicago.

Scholarships and Loans for Nursing Education. National League for Nursing: New York.

Where to Look

The best bibliography is of no use if you cannot locate the books that you seek. If you are in college, start with your college library and with the library of the office that promotes graduate study. The dean of the college may have a selection of directories on a bookshelf in the Dean's Office. Ask around. Financial aid offices may also have directories of foundation grants on their shelves. If your college is small or if you are no longer affiliated with a college, you might try the libraries of larger colleges and universities in your vicinity. Call before you go. The libraries of some large universities in major cities are restricted to students with ID cards and are closed to the public even for reference purposes. If the library is open to the public, a kind library assistant may tell you which directories are available so that you may make your trip to the most fruitful library.

One of the most helpful organizations in terms of a well-stocked library of directories and general assistance in the search for grants is The Foundation Center. The Foundation Center is the publisher of a number of the directories listed. The Center also operates libraries and cooperating collections throughout the country. The center has four full-scale libraries. These are at:

79 Fifth Ave. (at 16th St.)
New York, NY 10003-3050
212-620-4230

1001 Connecticut Ave., N.W.
Suite 938
Washington, DC 20036
202-331-1400

312 Sutter St.
San Francisco, CA 94108
415-397-0902

1442 Hanna Building
1422 Euclid Ave.
Cleveland, OH 44115
216-861-1934

If any of these is convenient for you, call for current hours. The Center also operates a network of over 180 Cooperating Collections located in host nonprofit organizations in all 50 states, Australia, Canada, Mexico, Puerto Rico, the Virgin Islands, Great Britain, and Japan. All contain a core collection of the Center's reference works and are staffed by professionals trained to direct grant seekers to appropriate funding information resources. Many host organizations also have other books and reports on funders and private foundations within their state.

Call toll-free 1-800-424-9836 for a complete address list.

If you have exhausted all other funding possibilities—need-based aid; university or department administered merit-based grants, fellowships, and assistantships; privately sponsored grants, fellowships, and loans; and government guaranteed loans—you may need to look into non-profit lending organizations. Start by contacting:

The Education Resources Institute (TERI)
330 Stuart St.
Boston, MA 02116
617-426-0681

Student Loan Marketing Association (Sallie Mae)
1050 Jefferson St., NW
Washington, DC 20007
202-333-8000

New England Educational Loan Marketing Corp. (Nellie Mae)
25 Braintree Hill Park
Braintree, MA 01284
617-849-1325

Law School Admission Services (for law school loans, only)
P.O. Box 2000
Newtown, PA I 8940-0998
215-9684001

NOTES

NOTES

NOTES